WISC-V

WISC-V
Clinical Use and Interpretation

Second Edition

Lawrence G. Weiss
Research and Measurement Consultant, San Antonio, TX, United States

Donald H. Saklofske
Department of Psychology, University of Western Ontario, London, ON, Canada

James A. Holdnack
Research and Statistical Consultant, Bear, DE, United States

Aurelio Prifitera
Assessment Consultant, San Antonio, TX, United States

ACADEMIC PRESS
An imprint of Elsevier

Academic Press is an imprint of Elsevier
125 London Wall, London EC2Y 5AS, United Kingdom
525 B Street, Suite 1650, San Diego, CA 92101, United States
50 Hampshire Street, 5th Floor, Cambridge, MA 02139, United States
The Boulevard, Langford Lane, Kidlington, Oxford OX5 1GB, United Kingdom

Notices
Knowledge and best practice in this field are constantly changing. As new research and experience broaden
our understanding, changes in research methods, professional practices, or medical treatment may become
necessary.

Practitioners and researchers must always rely on their own experience and knowledge in evaluating and
using any information, methods, compounds, or experiments described herein. In using such information or
methods they should be mindful of their own safety and the safety of others, including parties for whom
they have a professional responsibility.

To the fullest extent of the law, neither the Publisher nor the authors, contributors, or editors, assume any
liability for any injury and/or damage to persons or property as a matter of products liability, negligence or
otherwise, or from any use or operation of any methods, products, instructions, or ideas contained in the
material herein.

British Library Cataloguing-in-Publication Data
A catalogue record for this book is available from the British Library

Library of Congress Cataloging-in-Publication Data
A catalog record for this book is available from the Library of Congress

ISBN: 978-0-12-815744-2

For Information on all Academic Press publications
visit our website at https://www.elsevier.com/books-and-journals

Working together
to grow libraries in
developing countries

www.elsevier.com • www.bookaid.org

Publisher: Nikki Levy
Acquisition Editor: Nikki Levy
Editorial Project Manager: Barbara Makinster
Production Project Manager: Bharatwaj Varatharajan
Cover Designer: Miles Hitchen

Typeset by MPS Limited, Chennai, India

Dedication

To Judy Ann, my wife of 34 years — L.G.W.

In memory of Micah Aaron Kowalchuk, brilliant young lawyer and humanitarian — D.H.S.

I want to thank my family Tina, Julia, and Adam for all their support — J.A.H.

In memory of Doug Kubach colleague, boss and friend who supported my career which helped to make this book possible — A.P.

Contents

List of Contributors

Abigail Batty Pearson Clinical, United Kingdom

A. Lynne Beal Private Practice, Toronto, ON, Canada

Kristina Breaux Pearson, Clinical Assessment, San Antonio, TX, United States

Lisa Whipple Drozdick Clinical Content Development, Pearson, San Antonio, TX, United States

Jacques Grégoire Université Catholique de Louvain, Psychological Sciences Research Institute, Louvain-la-Neuve, Belgium

Jossette G. Harris Department of Psychiatry, University of Colorado School of Medicine, Denver, CO, United States

Victoria Locke The University of Texas at San Antonio, San Antonio, TX, United States

Daniel C. Miller Woodcock Institute for the Advancement of Neurocognitive Research and Applied Practice, Texas Woman's University, Denton, TX, United States

Jessie L. Miller R&D, Pearson Canada Assessment, Toronto, ON, Canada

María R. Muñoz Pearson, San Antonio, TX, United States

Tianshu Pan Department of Clinical Psychometrics, Pearson Assessment, San Antonio, TX, United States

Susan Engi Raiford Pearson, Clinical Assessment, San Antonio, TX, United States

Bennett A. Shaywitz Yale Center for Dyslexia & Creativity, Yale University School of Medicine, New Haven, CT, United States

Sally E. Shaywitz Yale Center for Dyslexia & Creativity, Yale University School of Medicine, New Haven, CT, United States

Fons J.R. van de Vijver Higher School of Economics, Russia; Tilburg University, the Netherlands; University of Queensland, Australia; North-West University, South Africa

Dustin Wahlstrom Pearson Clinical Assessment, San Antonio, TX, United States

Biography

Lawrence G. Weiss, PhD was vice president of Global Research and Development at Pearson Clinical Assessment where he worked for 27 years before retiring in 2018. He began his career in test development with The Psychological Corporation and rose to oversee Pearson's R&D Department of more than 150 professionals in 13 countries across 4 continents. He was responsible for all research and test development activities related to the company's large suite of clinical assessment instruments including the WISC-III, WISC-IV, and WISC-V. In addition, he has authored more than 100 books, book chapters, technical reports, and research articles in peer-reviewed journals including two special issues devoted to his work. He continues to be active in the profession by serving on the editorial boards of journals, writing, consulting, and appearing as an expert witness in criminal and civil legal cases in which psychological test results are germane to the outcome. He and his wife of 34 years, Judy Ann, divide their time between San Antonio, TX; Angel Fire, NM; and Satellite Beach, FL.

Donald Saklofske, PhD is currently a professor in the Department of Psychology, University of Western Ontario, Canada; adjunct professor at the University of Calgary and University of Saskatchewan, Canada; visiting professor in the Faculty of Psychology at Beijing Normal University, China; and a research member in the Laboratory for Research and Intervention in Positive Psychology and Prevention at the University of Florence, Italy. He has served on the boards of various professional associations and contributed to psychological research and practice through his consultations to organizations such as Pearson Assessment. His research program is focused on individual differences in intelligence and personality with an emphasis on emotional intelligence, resiliency, mental health, and psychological assessment. He is a frequent presenter and invited speaker at conferences and professional meetings and has published more than 35 books and 300 journal articles and book chapters. He is editor of *Personality and Individual Differences* and the *Journal of Psychoeducational Assessment*. He is an elected Fellow of the Association for Psychological Science, Canadian Psychological Association, and Society for Personality and Social Psychology.

James A. Holdnack, PhD is a research and statistics consultant and licensed psychologist in Delaware. As senior/principal scientist at Pearson Clinical Assessment, he collaborated on the development of psychological, neuropsychological, achievement, motor, and speech-language measures used by US and international professionals. As head of the neuropsychology team, he developed numerous test batteries including: D-KEFS, WMS-IV, NEPSY-II, and ACS. He has extensive research experience in designing and implementing large normative, clinical validation, reliability studies, developing novel statistical models to aid test interpretation, and developing digital assessments. He has over 60 publications, is a frequent presenter at professional conferences, serves on several editorial boards, and is an adjunct faculty at University of Delaware, United States.

Aurelio Prifitera, PhD until last year was Managing Director at Pearson, leading the clinical assessment group. He continues to be involved in the psychology and assessment fields though consulting, journal editorial board member, writing, and volunteer work. In addition to his psychology training, he holds an MBA degree. He was trained as a clinical psychologist and worked in clinical and private practice settings and taught graduate-level assessment courses prior to working in the test development field over 25 years ago. He has led several major clinical development projects over the years including several of the Wechsler scales and helped grow the availability of assessments outside of the United States into many international markets. More recently he drove the innovation efforts in digital assessment at Pearson. He has published numerous peer-reviewed research articles, books, and book chapters in the areas of assessment. He, along with Dr. Saklofske, is one of the founding editors and authors of the WISC clinical book series first published in 1998 by Academic Press. He is also a licensed psychologist in the state of Texas and a Fellow of the American Psychological Association.

Preface

In this second edition of our Wechsler Intelligence Scale for Children—Fifth Edition (WISC-V) Assessment and Interpretation book, we have added important new content based on ongoing research and development activities with the Weschler scales, while keeping much of what students and professionals appreciated about the first edition. Several chapters now include case studies or brief case vignettes designed to illustrate clinical interpretation. The chapter on basic administration and scoring was removed as that information is readily available in the manual and multiple other sources. While the second edition continues to be relevant for new students, we wanted our book to go beyond simple a how-to book on the mechanics of testing and dive deeper into the clinical context of assessment. We are especially pleased to be able to add two new chapters by Dan Miller and Fons van de Vijver. In Chapter 3, A School Neuropsychological Approach to Interpretation of the WISC-V Integrated, Dan Miller details the use of Wechsler Intelligence Scale for Children—Fifth Edition Integrated as an adjunct to WISC-V when exploring and unpacking the various component processes required to successfully perform each WISC-V subtest, thus adding clinical nuance to the interpretation of low scores. In Chapter 7, A Cross-Cultural Analysis of the WISC-V, Fons van de Vijver provides a new cross culture tour of WISC-V data from around the world, first evaluating the invariance of the five-factor structure across countries, and then comparing score differences across countries as a function of societal-level variables that differ between them. This chapter is a replication and extension of our book titled, *Culture and Children's Intelligence: Cross-Cultural Analysis of the WISC-III* (Georgas, Weiss, van de Vijver, & Saklofske, 2003). In Chapter 4, Theoretical and Clinical Foundations of the Wechsler Intelligence Scale for Children—Fifth Edition, we added a new section to address a current controversy in the literature about models of intelligence, and discuss the relative merits of hierarchical versus bifactor models. In Chapter 6, Testing Hispanics with WISC-V and WISC-V Spanish, we added an important section on the WISC-V Spanish edition, which was not yet published at the time of the first edition of this book. In Chapter 8, The Flynn Effect and Its Clinical Implications, we add significant new content about flaws in FE research and show empirically that when the methodological flaws are controlled the size of the effect is as predicted by Flynn. Chapter 9, WISC-V and the Evolving Role of

Intelligence Testing in the Assessment of Learning Disabilites, Chapter 10, Translating Scientific Progress in Dyslexia Into 21st Century Diagnosis and Interventions, and Chapter 11, Issues Related to the WISC-V Assessment of Cognitive Functioning in Clinical and Special Groups, address various learning disabilities, dyslexia, and other clinical and special groups. These chapters have been updated to include new studies published on these groups in peer-reviewed literature. In Chapter 12, Digital Assessment With Q-interactive, we add significant new content regarding advances in the assessment capabilities of the digital platform, Q-interactive. Since the first edition of this book, the digital platform has expanded beyond digital replicas of stimulus books to dynamic and interactive versions of new tasks, particularly in the assessment of processing speed. This chapter reviews issues related to the development and clinical validity of 21st century digital tasks. Dr. Holdnack's final chapter completes the book by showing how to personalize an assessment based on the referral question and adjust the tests to give based on confirming or disconfirming initial hypotheses early in the session. Overall, we are very pleased with the balance of scientific and practitioner perspectives in the second edition of our book.

Beginning with the third revision of the WISC in 1990, we have developed an accompanying book with chapters on important clinical and research topics cast within the scientist—practitioner framework. While the evidence for the psychometric integrity and clinical efficacy of the Wechsler intelligence scales is vast, given the number of published articles that have included the scales, bringing the information together in such a way to address some of the key clinical and practice issues has always been the main driver of this Academic Press series on the Wechsler intelligence tests.

We have attempted always to give a balance between the empirical basis established during the extensive standardization studies and subsequent published research studies with clinical practice and utility. The editors of the series, some of whom worked directly on the revisions to the WISC-V and earlier versions, also included editors and chapter authors who were not part of the extensive test development process. We believe this balance of in-depth information of the process of test development as well as the perspective of those from clinical, professional training, and research settings has resulted in a unique perspective and insights into the testing and assessment process using the Wechsler scales. We have been pleased with the positive response received to all of the volumes in this series and thank our readers for their support. We are also most grateful to the numerous authors who have contributed to the chapters over the years, and this book in particular.

Most importantly, we owe so much to David Wechsler for his genius and dedication to the psychological assessment of children, youth, and adults. His original conceptualization of the Wechsler tests was visionary and has allowed the scales to continue to evolve as valuable, leading assessment tools in the field of psychology since the original Wechsler—Bellevue published in 1939. There are only a handful of instruments in the field of psychological and psychoeducational assessment that have lasted that long, and we, the editors of this series, are proud to be able to have participated to a small degree in that long legacy of excellence in cognitive assessment.

One reason the Wechsler tests have endured is because of the openness to change from revision to revision and the significant resources and investment that have gone into those revisions. The amount of investment into the Wechsler scales has been second to none in the testing field. The scales have also benefited from the wisdom of David Wechsler himself through the first revisions and from his family's support on the later revisions after his death in 1981. In addition, others who have worked on various aspects of the tests over the years such as Joseph Matarazzo and Alan Kaufman have paved the road for these later test revisions. The tradition has continued and those of us who have also worked inside the organizations responsible for the revisions have been fortunate to have the unwavering support and freedom to do what we thought was best for the assessment of intelligence and cognitive abilities.

The iconic Wechsler scales, even with all their success and changes, are not immune to a multitude of factors that have shaped and will continue to impact both psychological tests and the assessment of intelligence and cognitive processes. We see already on the horizon a significant shift in the future direction of the scales, how they will be used, and the changes that will be different in the next generation of assessments. One of the main drivers of the change is the move from paper toward digital assessment. Although the WISC-V is available in both paper and digital modes, it is fairly clear that the usage patterns are changing rapidly and clinicians are adopting the digital administration. We are just now seeing some of the benefits of a digital modality through the Q-interactive application and know there are more advantages that will emerge that are not apparent today. In addition to the clear advantages such as portability, ease of use, lower entry costs for tests, faster administration and scoring, and ease of accessibility of tests, a digital format will allow for many more benefits in the near future. One of the main benefits is the flexibility that will let the psychologist choose to give a subset of the tests most relevant to addressing the key clinical questions. It is also very easy to give a set of subtests from across various tests on the Q-interactive system that are custom selected for the assessment needs of particular children. This allows for greater personalization of the test battery and for much more flexibility in the approach to assessment. A digital format will also allow the measurement of variables that could not be measured in a paper and pencil format.

Introducing a digital format brings new challenges and measurement issues into the test development process such as validating task equivalence with paper versions but also the need for understanding and incorporation of design and usability into the development so that the testing experience is valid and optimized. Additions and new information on interpretation, meaning of score patterns, norms, and new tests can be easily added and accessed through a digital format. This, we believe, will give the clinician and researcher unprecedented access to tools, data, and analysis. This overall more "flexible" approach concept (now enabled with technology) was originally proposed by Edith Kaplan and advocated through her many students including Dean Delis who is carrying that model forward. With access to these data, the empirical basis of score patterns and levels will be more readily available and reach users of the test more quickly.

Another major change over the years has been the growth of international editions of the WISC. One of the most powerful aspects of the Wechsler model of intelligence is that it is fairly robust, consistent, and congruent in terms of the constructs measured and factor structures replicated across different cultures. The WISC-IV is now available with country norms in at least a dozen countries, and WISC-V standardization data are being collected in six countries at the time of writing. As the world shrinks due to technology and mass communication, the ability to use these tests consistently and compare results across various cultures brings a new dimension in the understanding of intelligence and various clinical conditions. The usage of the Wechsler scales has grown significantly outside the United States over the past 25 years to the point where usage now is higher outside than inside the United States.

Finally, the ways of interpreting the WISC will see continuing evolution. Much of it due to the impact of digital capabilities mentioned above and the ability to quickly access data from a variety of sources globally. This "big data" capability will have enormous impact and benefit to the research base and clinical understanding and interpretation of these tests. Also, with each revision there has been a steady movement away from simple reliance on summary Intelligence Quotient (IQ) scores (i.e., Verbal IQ, Performance IQ, and Full-Scale IQ) to more sophisticated and nuanced views of the five major domains of cognitive ability now built into WISC-V (i.e., Verbal Comprehension, Visual-Spatial, Fluid Reasoning, Working Memory, and Processing Speed) and their combination. The neuropsychologist and author Muriel Lezak was a major force advocating this approach in her writings. These newer approaches to interpretation have been greatly influenced by approaches such as the "process" approach advocated by Edith Kaplan, Dean Delis, and others and the "processing strengths and weakness" approach advocated by, among others, Hale and Fiorello. Finally longitudinal research by Sally Shaywitz documenting dyslexia as an unexpected difficulty in reading relative to intelligence, as well as research similar to the work done by Virginia Berninger linking patterns of performance to brain imaging and interventions for specific disorders is changing how tests are used and interpreted. These new approaches share a focus of looking at all tests within the context of other tests and not just those in a particular test battery, are driven by hypothesis testing and discover, and are based on solid understanding of the cognitive processes and clinical conditions. We expect this next edition of this book series to follow this dynamic change in interpretative process and benefit from the digital transformation in testing that is just beginning.

We end here by thanking our contributing authors who added a depth of knowledge that has made these chapters much richer in both empirical and practice information. As always, we thank Nikki Levy and Barbara Makinster who have so professionally guided all of our Wechsler books to publication. We also appreciate the professional editing work of Melissa Read and Bharatwaj Varatharajan seen throughout this book. Finally, our hope is that you, the readers of this book, will find it an important and useful resource both in your use of the WISC-V and the assessment of children's intelligence.

Lawrence G. Weiss, Donald H. Saklofske,
James A. Holdnack and Aurelio Prifitera

REFERENCE

Georgas, J., Weiss, L. G., Van de Vijver, F., & Saklofske, D. (2003). *Culture and children's intelligence: Cross-cultural analysis of the WISC-III*. New York: Elsevier.

Chapter 1

WISC-V: Advances in the Assessment of Intelligence

Lawrence G. Weiss[1], Donald H. Saklofske[2], James A. Holdnack[3] and Aurelio Prifitera[4]

[1]Research and Measurement Consultant, San Antonio, TX, United States, [2]Department of Psychology, University of Western Ontario, London, ON, Canada, [3]Research and Statistical Consultant, Bear, DE, United States, [4]Assessment Consultant, San Antonio, TX, United States

INTRODUCTION

The Wechsler scales are the most widely used measures of intelligence, and have been translated, adapted, and standardized in dozens of countries around the world. Since first introduced in the Wechsler—Bellevue Intelligence Scale (WBIS), the Wechsler model has evolved substantially, but remains grounded in Dr. Wechsler's foundational definition of intelligence:

> ...the aggregate or global capacity of the individual to act purposefully, to think rationally, and to deal effectively with his (or her) environment.
>
> (Wechsler, 1939, p. 3).

A BRIEF HISTORICAL RECAP

The Wechsler series of tests consists of the Wechsler Intelligence Scales for Children (WISC) for school-age children, the Wechsler Preschool and Primary Scales of Intelligence (WPPSI) for preschool children, and the Wechsler Adult Intelligence Scales (WAIS) for adults. Each of these tests has undergone multiple revisions over several decades. This book is about the fifth edition of the WISC. As we discuss the evolution of the WISC-V, we must necessarily refer to various editions of the WPPSI and WAIS as the evolution of these assessment tools are interrelated theoretically and conceptually as part of the contemporary Wechsler model of intelligence.

Some readers may recall that the original Wechsler model was based on a two-part structure comprised of the Verbal Intelligence Quotient (VIQ) and Performance IQ (PIQ), which combined formed the Full Scale IQ (FSIQ). In

WISC-V. DOI: https://doi.org/10.1016/B978-0-12-815744-2.00001-X

a series of major theoretical shifts from the original Wechsler model described in 1939, the Wechsler tests have evolved with each version. The WISC-V is based on a five-part structure, and the resulting five factor-based index scores have become the primary level of clinical interpretation. The contemporary Wechsler theoretical model measures the following five domains of cognitive ability: verbal comprehension visual spatial, fluid reasoning (FR), working memory, and processing speed.

The modern expansion of the Wechsler model began in 1991 when the WISC-III became the first of the Wechsler scales to offer four factor-based scores as an optional alternative to the traditional VIQ/PIQ scores; verbal comprehension, perceptual organization, freedom from distractibility, and processing speed. The WAIS-III followed suit in 1997 with the same dual model in which those four index scores were offered but considered supplemental to the main VIQ, PIQ, and FSIQ scores. At that time, working memory was referred to as "freedom from distractibility," an older term that reflected the incomplete understanding of the construct at that time.

Following advances in cognitive psychology, neuropsychology, and clinical psychology, in 2003 the scientific caretakers of the Wechsler Scales at PsychCorp/Pearson broke the proverbial "apron strings" and tied the Wechsler tests to the VIQ and PIQ model proposed by David Wechsler in the original WBIS. The VIQ and PIQ were eliminated completely from the WISC-IV, along with changing the name of the freedom from distractibility index to the working memory index to reflect the improved understanding of that construct, and changing the name of the perceptual organization index to the perceptual reasoning index to reflect the increased focus on FR among the newly created perceptual subtests. The WISC-IV elevated the four index scores to the primary level of clinical interpretation. The WAIS-IV followed this model in 2008. In 2012, the WPPSI-IV (Wechsler, 2012) introduced the first five-factor Wechsler model for children ages 4–7 years. To accomplish this, new subtests were created and combined with selected perceptual reasoning and working memory subtests to create a FR factor.

FROM THE PAST TO THE PRESENT

The 75-year (1939–2014) history of the Wechsler tests has seen major changes from a focus on general mental ability complemented by VIQ and PIQ scores to either a four- (WISC-IV, WAIS-IV) or a five-factor structure (WPPSI-IV). The debate over both the empirical foundations and clinical utility of a four- versus five-factor structure was the focus of an influential set of papers published in a special issue of the *Journal of Psychoeducational Assessment* (Tobin, 2013). This five-factor model was shown to fit the data slightly better than the four-factor model for both WISC-IV and WAIS-IV

(Weiss, Keith, Zhu, & Chen, 2013a; Weiss, Keith, Zhu, & Chen, 2013b). The fifth factor, of course, was FR, and was formed by some subtests previously assigned to the perceptual reasoning and working memory factors.

Another key finding from these papers was that the five-factor solution fit the data well in large samples of mixed clinical subjects for both WISC-IV and WAIS-IV, thus supporting the clinical application of the model. As the two target papers in a special issue of the *Journal of Psychoeducational Assessment*, these papers were subject to invited critiques by eight prominent researchers, and generally positively reviewed (see Kaufman, 2013 for a summary and discussion of the reviews, and see Weiss, Keith, Zhu, & Chen, 2013c for a rejoinder). Thus, these papers served as the catalyst for a five-factor model of WISC-V.

The Wechsler five-factor model overlaps substantially with the Cattell—Horn—Carroll (CHC) theory of intelligence that predates it (Carroll, 1993). As a result, recent literature concerning a fifth Wechsler factor has sometimes been cast as a competition between the Wechsler and CHC models of intelligence (Benson, Hulac, & Kranzler, 2010; Ward, Bergman, & Herbert, 2011). However, adding working memory and processing speed factors to the original two-factor Wechsler model has been a systematic research goal for the Wechsler test development team, which began in 1990 with the third editions and was fully implemented in the fourth editions (Weiss, Saklofske, Coalson, & Raiford, 2010; Weiss, Saklofske, Prifitera, & Holdnack, 2006). Similarly, adding a FR factor to the Wechsler model has also been a systematic research goal since 1997, leading to the development and validation of three FR subtests introduced successively in various subsequent editions: Matrix Reasoning, Picture Concepts, and Figure Weights.

While the psychometric fit of the third and fourth editions of the Wechsler series to a four-factor model has been well established for decades, the continuous evolution of the contemporary Wechsler scales to a five-factor theoretical model has been guided less by CHC-related factor analytic findings and more by ongoing clinical research in neuropsychology and cognitive information processing, as described in Chapter 5. The good news for our science is that independent research labs have derived surprisingly similar models of intelligence based on different lines of research, ultimately confirming the progress the field is making in better understanding the nature of intellectual functioning.

To be fair to Dr. Wechsler's legacy, his model has always included subtests researchers now understand as measures of working memory, processing speed, and FR. These were buried inside the VIQ and PIQ depending on whether the stimuli and response processes were verbal or visual-perceptual, respectively. Still, Dr. Wechsler knew that mental manipulation of numbers was importantly related to intelligence, which is why he included the Arithmetic and Digit Span subtests in the VIQ. Similarly, he knew that quick visual scanning played an important role in cognition and so he included the Coding subtests as part of the PIQ. As we have also seen, with the addition of newer subtests to reflect contemporary models of and research on intelligence, subtests such as Arithmetic have emerged from being initially included in the VIQ to being a key subtest tapping working memory and now to finding a place as an optional subtest in the FR domain.

Present-day researchers have developed well-articulated theories about the underlying neurocognitive processes attached to these tasks and how they are related to intelligence. Much like the well-known aspirin that continues to be found relevant in the treatment of many more health issues than initially considered, Digit Span is now understood as tapping working memory, especially when digits are recalled in reverse or rearranged in an ordered sequence. Coding is now understood as a measure of cognitive processing speed rather than just simple copying or hand-eye coordination. As more has been learned about these areas, the Wechsler tests have changed over time such that these constructs have been disentangled from VIQ and PIQ, and stand alone. Furthermore, new tasks such as Letter—Number Sequencing and Cancellation were added to elaborate on the assessment of working memory and processing speed, respectively. Also, Digit Span was significantly revised in the WAIS-IV and now WISC-V by adding the digit-sequencing items to make it a better measure of working memory based on our current understanding of that construct.

Similarly, although the term FR was not used in Dr. Wechsler's time, some of the original Wechsler subtests were believed related to the ability to solve novel problems (i.e., Similarities, Block Design). It was very much the seminal contributions of Horn and Cattell (1966) that led to describing and distinguishing between fluid (Gf) and crystallized (Gc) intelligence somewhat in comparison to Wechsler's VIQ and PIQ. While most intelligence tests going back to the early Binet measures seem to have amply covered the more crystallized side, further research on FR led to the development of four new Wechsler subtests that measure this construct more directly. Specifically, Matrix Reasoning (which first appeared in WISC-III and was then added to WAIS-III and WISC-IV, and retained in WAIS-IV and WISC-V); Picture Concepts (which first appeared in WISC-IV and was then added to WPPSI-III); and Figure Weights (which appeared for the first time in WAIS-IV, and has now been added to WISC-V).

The key point of this brief 75-year historical backdrop is that the Wechsler scales have changed substantially over the decades, keeping pace with rapid advances in the understanding of intelligence. Yet, without Dr. Wechsler's far reaching clinical insights, the field of intellectual assessment would not be where it is today. The WISC-V is a very different test than the one that Dr. Wechsler gave us—one that builds to multiple modern theories of cognitive neuroscience informed by ongoing clinical and neuropsychological research.

STRUCTURE AND CONTENT OF THE WISC-V

Psychologists have come to recognize that while general mental ability measured by the FSIQ is a powerful metric for more global descriptions of a person's cognitive abilities, the greatest clinical usefulness comes from analysis of the index scores; those "primary" mental abilities that more specifically describe the key or most important components of intellectual and cognitive functioning. As we often state at workshops, 100 children all with FSIQs of 100 can show many different patterns of strengths and weaknesses among the primary cognitive abilities, leading to considerable variability in school achievement and many other facets of behavior in which intelligence plays a major role.

The WISC-V consists of five primary index scores: Verbal Comprehension Index (VCI), Visual Spatial Index (VSI), Fluid Reasoning Index (FRI), Working Memory Index (WMI), and Processing Speed Index (PSI). Each of these five index scores is defined and measured by two primary subtests. Most of these five domains include secondary subtests that are optional, and when administered, may provide additional information regarding performance in the respective domain. In later chapters we will more fully describe the index scores and their relevance in diagnostic assessment and program-intervention planning. The focus here is to provide an overview of the "parts" or subtests that comprise the "whole" as reflected in both the index scores and the FSIQ. As those familiar with the Wechsler tests will note, many of the subtests included in the WISC-V are psychometrically and clinically improved versions from earlier editions of the WISC and WAIS tests, while others were specifically developed to enhance the five-factor model that now defines the newest addition to the Wechsler family. Fig. 1.1 shows the structure of the WISC-V as defined by basic composition of the FSIQ, the five primary index scores, the five ancillary index scores, and the three complementary index scores.

Verbal Comprehension Index

The VCI is formed by the two primary verbal comprehension subtests: Similarities and Vocabulary. There are also two secondary verbal comprehension subtests: Information and Comprehension. All four subtests have demonstrated their largest contribution to this index in earlier versions of the WISC.

Similarities. For Similarities, the child is read two words that represent common objects or concepts and describes how they are similar. The subtest is designed to measure verbal concept formation and abstract reasoning. It also involves crystallized intelligence, word knowledge, cognitive flexibility, auditory comprehension, long-term memory, associative and categorical thinking, distinction between nonessential and essential features, and verbal expression (Flanagan & Kaufman, 2009; Groth-Marnat, 2009; Sattler, 2008; Wechsler, 2014).

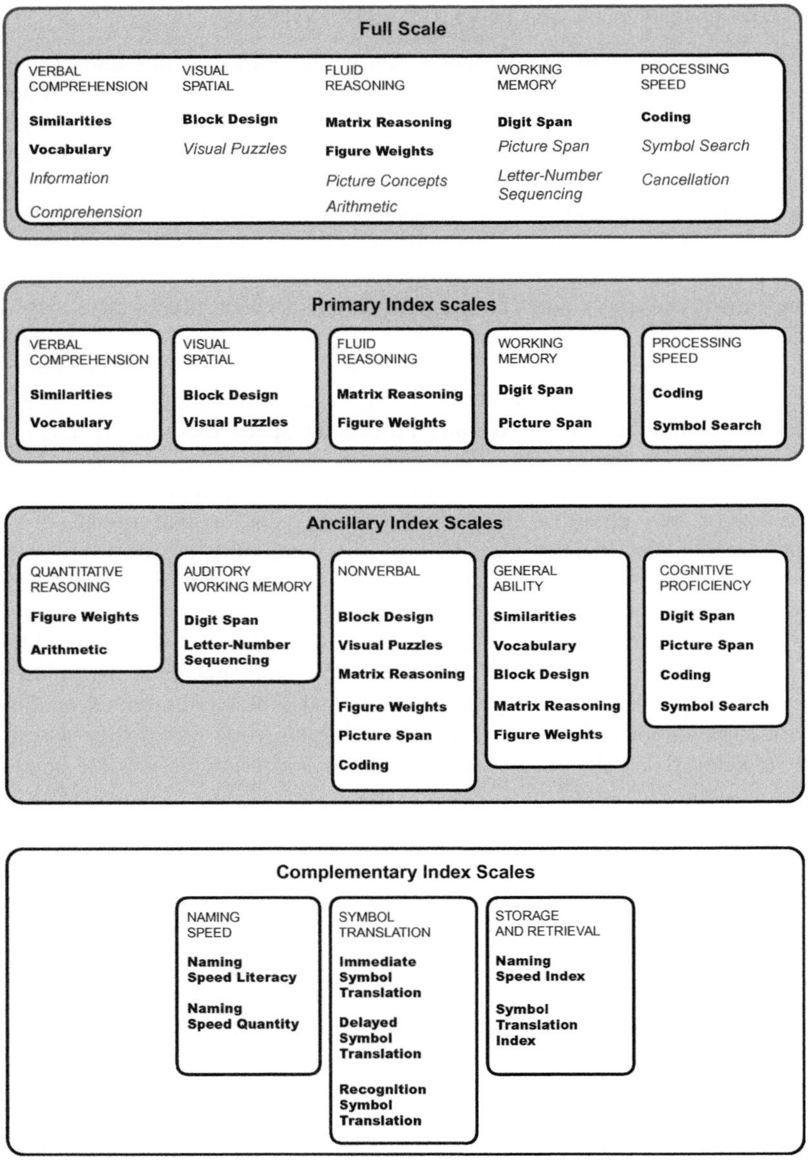

Full Scale

VERBAL COMPREHENSION	VISUAL SPATIAL	FLUID REASONING	WORKING MEMORY	PROCESSING SPEED
Similarities	**Block Design**	**Matrix Reasoning**	**Digit Span**	Coding
Vocabulary	*Visual Puzzles*	**Figure Weights**	*Picture Span*	*Symbol Search*
Information		*Picture Concepts*	*Letter-Number Sequencing*	*Cancellation*
Comprehension		*Arithmetic*		

Primary Index scales

VERBAL COMPREHENSION	VISUAL SPATIAL	FLUID REASONING	WORKING MEMORY	PROCESSING SPEED
Similarities	**Block Design**	**Matrix Reasoning**	**Digit Span**	**Coding**
Vocabulary	**Visual Puzzles**	**Figure Weights**	**Picture Span**	**Symbol Search**

Ancillary Index Scales

QUANTITATIVE REASONING	AUDITORY WORKING MEMORY	NONVERBAL	GENERAL ABILITY	COGNITIVE PROFICIENCY
Figure Weights	**Digit Span**	**Block Design**	**Similarities**	**Digit Span**
Arithmetic	**Letter-Number Sequencing**	**Visual Puzzles**	**Vocabulary**	**Picture Span**
		Matrix Reasoning	**Block Design**	**Coding**
		Figure Weights	**Matrix Reasoning**	**Symbol Search**
		Picture Span	**Figure Weights**	
		Coding		

Complementary Index Scales

NAMING SPEED	SYMBOL TRANSLATION	STORAGE AND RETRIEVAL
Naming Speed Literacy	**Immediate Symbol Translation**	**Naming Speed Index**
Naming Speed Quantity	**Delayed Symbol Translation**	**Symbol Translation Index**
	Recognition Symbol Translation	

FIGURE 1.1   The WISC-V primary indexes and subtests. *Subtest descriptions are reused with permission from the WISC-V Manual (Wechsler, 2014).*

Vocabulary. Vocabulary has both picture and verbal items. For picture items, the child names simple objects. For verbal items, the child defines more difficult words that are read aloud by the examiner. Vocabulary is designed to measure word knowledge and verbal concept formation. It also measures crystallized intelligence, fund of knowledge, learning ability, verbal expression, long-term memory, and degree of vocabulary development. Other abilities that may be used during this task include auditory perception and comprehension and abstract thinking (Flanagan & Kaufman, 2009; Groth-Marnat, 2009; Sattler, 2008; Wechsler, 2014).

Information. For Information, the child answers questions about a broad range of general-knowledge topics. The subtest is designed to measure a child's ability to acquire, retain, and retrieve general factual knowledge. It involves crystallized intelligence, long-term memory, and the ability to retain and retrieve knowledge from the environment and/or school. Other skills used include verbal perception, comprehension, and expression (Flanagan & Kaufman, 2009; Groth-Marnat, 2009; Sattler, 2008; Wechsler, 2014).

Comprehension. For Comprehension, the child answers questions based on his or her understanding of general principles and social situations. Comprehension is designed to measure verbal reasoning and conceptualization, verbal comprehension and expression, the ability to evaluate and use past experience, and the ability to demonstrate practical knowledge and judgment. It also involves crystallized intelligence, knowledge of conventional standards of behavior, social judgment, long-term memory, and common sense (Flanagan & Kaufman, 2009; Groth-Marnat, 2009; Sattler, 2008; Wechsler, 2014).

Visual Spatial Index

The VSI is formed by two primary visual spatial subtests: the long-standing Block Design and newly created Visual Puzzles. There are no secondary visual spatial subtests.

Block Design. Working within a specified time limit, the child views a model and/or a picture and uses two-color blocks to construct the design. The Block Design subtest is designed to measure the ability to analyze and synthesize abstract visual stimuli. It also involves nonverbal concept formation and reasoning, broad visual intelligence, visual perception and organization, simultaneous processing, visual-motor coordination, learning, and the ability to separate figure-ground in visual stimuli (Carroll, 1993; Flanagan & Kaufman, 2009; Groth-Marnat, 2009; Sattler, 2008; Wechsler, 2014).

Visual Puzzles. Visual Puzzles is a new WISC-V subtest adapted for children from the WAIS-IV. Working within a specified time limit, the child views a completed puzzle and selects three response options that, when combined, reconstruct the puzzle. The subtest is designed to measure mental, non-motor, construction ability that requires visual and spatial reasoning, mental rotation, visual working memory, understanding part-whole relationships, and the ability to analyze and synthesize abstract visual stimuli. Similar measures, such as the WPPSI-IV Object Assembly task and the *Revised Minnesota Paper Form Board Test* (Likert & Quasha, 1995), involve visual perception, broad visual intelligence, fluid intelligence, simultaneous processing, spatial visualization and manipulation, and the ability to anticipate relationships among parts (Carroll, 1993; Groth-Marnat, 2009; Kaufman & Lichtenberger, 2006; Likert & Quasha, 1995; Sattler, 2008). It is described as measuring visual processing and acuity, spatial relations, integration and synthesis of part-whole relationships, nonverbal reasoning, and trial-and-error learning (Flanagan & Kaufman, 2009; Flanagan, Alfonso, & Ortiz, 2012; Sattler, 2008; Wechsler, 2014).

The WISC-V Fluid Reasoning Index

The FRI is a major and new addition to the WISC-V. It is formed by two primary FR subtests: Matrix Reasoning and Figure Weights. Matrix Reasoning was an established subtest in both the WISC-IV and WAIS-IV, while Figure Weights first appeared in the WAIS-IV. There are also two secondary FR subtests, Picture Concepts and Arithmetic, both of which will be known to those familiar with the Wechsler tests.

Matrix Reasoning. For Matrix Reasoning, the child views an incomplete matrix or series and selects the response option that completes the matrix or series. The task requires the child to use visual-spatial information to identify the underlying conceptual rule that links all the stimuli and then apply the underlying concept to select the correct response. The subtest is designed to measure fluid intelligence, broad visual intelligence, classification and spatial ability, knowledge of part-whole relationships, and simultaneous processing (Flanagan & Kaufman, 2009; Groth-Marnat, 2009; Sattler, 2008; Wechsler, 2014). Additionally, the test requires attention to visual detail and working memory.

Figure Weights. Figure Weights is a new WISC-V subtest adapted for children from the WAIS-IV. Working within a specified time limit, the child views one or two scales balanced by weights and a scale with missing weight(s) and then selects the weight(s) that keep the scale balanced from the response options. This task requires the child to apply the quantitative concept of equality to understand the relationship among objects and apply the concepts of matching, addition, and/or multiplication to identify the correct response. The subtest measures quantitative FR and induction (Flanagan et al., 2012; Flanagan & Kaufman, 2009; Sattler, 2008; Wechsler, 2014). Quantitative reasoning tasks involve reasoning processes that can be expressed mathematically, emphasizing inductive or deductive logic (Carroll, 1993). Although Figure Weights involves working memory to some extent, it reduces this involvement relative to typical quantitative tasks (e.g., the Arithmetic subtest), by using visual items so that the child can refresh her or his memory as necessary.

Picture Concepts. For Picture Concepts, the child views two or three rows of pictures and selects one picture from each row to form a group with a common characteristic. No image appears more than once within the subtest. This test requires the child to use the semantic representations of nameable objects to identify the underlying conceptual relationship among the objects and to apply that concept to select the correct answer. The subtest is designed to measure fluid and inductive reasoning, visual-perceptual recognition and processing, and conceptual thinking (Flanagan & Kaufman, 2009; Sattler, 2008; Wechsler, 2014). It may also involve crystallized knowledge (Sattler, 2008). Additionally, this task requires visual scanning, working memory, and abstract reasoning.

Arithmetic. For this subtest the child mentally solves arithmetic problems that are presented verbally by the examiner as word problems, within a specified time limit. Arithmetic involves mental manipulation, concentration, brief focused attention, short- and long-term memory, numerical reasoning ability, applied computational ability, and mental alertness. It may also involve sequential processing; fluid, quantitative, and logical reasoning; and quantitative knowledge (Groth-Marnat, 2009; Kaufman & Lichtenberger, 2006; Sattler, 2008; Wechsler, 2014). Additionally, this task requires intact auditory/linguistic processes, including discrimination, and comprehension, and to a lesser degree expression.

Working Memory Index

The WMI is formed by two primary working memory subtests: Digit Span and Picture Span. There is one secondary working memory subtest: Letter–Number Sequencing.

Digit Span. This subtest consists of three parts. The child is read a sequence of numbers and recalls the numbers in the same order (Digit Span Forward), reverse order (Digit Span Backward), and ascending order (Digit Span Sequencing). The latter condition was adapted for children from the WAIS-IV, and is intended to increase the working memory demands of the subtest.

The shift from one Digit Span task to another requires cognitive flexibility and mental alertness. All Digit Span tasks require registration of information, brief focused attention, auditory discrimination, and auditory rehearsal. Digit Span Forward assesses auditory rehearsal and temporary storage capacity in working memory. Digit Span Backward involves working memory, transformation of information, mental manipulation, and may involve visuospatial imaging (Groth-Marnat, 2009; Flanagan & Kaufman, 2009; Reynolds, 1997; Sattler, 2008; Wechsler, 2014).

Digit Span Sequencing, a new task for the WISC-V, is similar to other tasks designed to measure working memory and mental manipulation (MacDonald, Almor, Henderson, Kempler, & Andersen, 2001; Werheid et al., 2002). Digit Span Sequencing is included to increase the cognitive complexity demands of the subtest. Both the backward and sequencing tasks require the resequencing of information. The primary difference between the tasks is how the sequence is determined. In the backward task, the location of the number in the sequence must be maintained in working memory for proper resequencing to occur. In the sequencing task, the quantitative value of the number must be maintained in working memory and compared to numbers before and after its occurrence. In this task, the child does not know where the number will occur in the response until all the numbers are administered.

The total raw score for the Digit Span subtest is based on the Digit Span Forward, Digit Span Backward, and Digit Span Sequencing raw scores. This total score enters the WMI and the FSIQ. Digit Span Forward must be administered, as the omission of this task results in lower Digit Span Backward scores for some children (possibly due to the loss of instructional progression). Retaining Digit Span Forward ensures sufficient floor items for children with intellectual disability or low cognitive ability.

The child's performance on Digit Span Forward, Backward, and Sequencing can also be examined separately using the Digit Span process scores. These process scores provide information about relative variability in performance across the three Digit Span tasks.

Picture Span. For Picture Span, a new Wechsler subtest, the child views a stimulus page with one or more pictures of nameable objects for a specified time and then selects the picture(s) (in sequential order, if possible) from options on a response page. Picture Span measures visual working memory and working memory capacity. Similar tasks are thought also to involve attention, visual processing, visual immediate memory, and response inhibition (Flanagan et al., 2012; Flanagan, Alfonso, Ortiz, & Dynda, 2010; Miller, 2010, 2013). The subtest is constructed similarly to existing visual working memory tasks (Hartshorne, 2008; Makovski & Jiang, 2008; Wechsler, 2009), but it is relatively novel in its use of semantically meaningful stimuli. The use of these stimuli may activate verbal working memory as well. The working memory demands of Picture Span stem from the use of proactive interference as well as sequencing requirements. Proactive interference is introduced by occasionally repeating pictures across items, sometimes alternating whether the repeated picture is the target or a distractor.

Letter–Number Sequencing. For Letter–Number Sequencing, the child is read a sequence of numbers and letters and recalls the numbers in ascending order and then the letters in alphabetical order. Like the Digit Span task, the Letter-Number Sequencing task requires some basic cognitive processes such as auditory discrimination, brief focused attention, concentration, registration, and auditory rehearsal. Additionally, the task involves sequential processing, the ability to compare stimuli based on quantity or alphabetic principles, working memory capacity, and mental manipulation. It may also involve information processing, cognitive flexibility, and fluid intelligence (Crowe, 2000; Flanagan & Kaufman, 2009; Groth-Marnat, 2009; Sattler, 2008; Wechsler, 2014). The latter skills representing executive control and resource allocation functions in working memory. Two qualifying items are given to establish that the child has the prerequisite counting and alphabet skills to perform the task.

Processing Speed Index

The PSI is formed by two well-established primary processing speed subtests: Coding and Symbol Search. There is one secondary processing speed subtest: Cancellation.

Coding. For Coding, the child works within a specified time limit and uses a key to copy symbols that correspond with simple geometric shapes or numbers. In addition to processing speed, the subtest measures short-term visual memory, procedural and incidental learning ability, psychomotor speed, visual perception, visual-motor coordination, visual scanning ability, cognitive flexibility, attention, concentration, and motivation. It may also involve visual sequential processing and fluid intelligence (Flanagan & Kaufman, 2009; Groth-Marnat, 2009; Sattler, 2008; Wechsler, 2014).

Symbol Search. For Symbol Search, the child scans search groups and indicates if target symbols are present, while working within a specified time limit. In addition to visual-perceptual (e.g., visual identification and matching) and decision-making speed, the subtest involves short-term visual memory, visual-motor coordination, inhibitory control, visual discrimination, psychomotor speed, sustained attention, and concentration. It may also measure perceptual organization, fluid intelligence, and planning and learning ability (Flanagan & Kaufman, 2009; Groth-Marnat, 2009; Sattler, 2008; Wechsler, 2014).

Cancellation. For Cancellation, the child scans two arrangements of objects (one random, one structured) and marks target objects while working within a specified time limit. The subtest measures rate of test taking, speed of visual-perceptual processing and decision-making, visual scanning ability, and visual-perceptual recognition and discrimination (Flanagan & Kaufman, 2009; Sattler, 2008; Wechsler, 2014). It may also involve attention, concentration, and visual recall (Sattler, 2008). Cancellation tasks have been used extensively in neuropsychological settings as measures of visual neglect, response inhibition, and motor perseveration (Lezak, Howieson, & Loring, 2004).

THE WISC-V FULL SCALE INTELLIGENCE QUOTIENT

The FSIQ is one of the most established measures in psychology, reflecting general mental ability as described by numerous experts in the study of intelligence spanning the decades from Spearman, Wechsler, and Vernon to

Carroll, Horn, and Cattell. General intelligence has been consistently shown to be associated with many important outcomes in life, and is thus of considerable applied importance in the assessment of children's potential, predicting school achievement, higher educational attainment, job advancement, and career success. (Deary et al., 2004; Gottfredson & Saklofske, 2009; Squalli & Wilson, 2014; Lubinski, 2004; Sternberg & Grigorenko, 2002). As practicing psychologists often voice, intelligence as assessed by the Wechsler scales includes both the breadth and depth of critical information needed to understand a person's overall cognitive capacity to successfully interact with the world around them.

The FSIQ is comprised of 7 of the 10 primary subtests described above: 2 verbal comprehension subtests, 1 visual spatial subtest, 2 FR subtests, 1 working memory subtest, and 1 processing speed subtest. Extensive empirical analyses revealed that this weighting of the five factors yields the optimal balance of predicting school achievement and key clinical criteria while maintaining high reliability and other psychometric standards.

As shown in Fig. 1.1, the FSIQ is comprised of the following seven primary subtests: Similarities, Vocabulary, Block Design, Matrix Reasoning, Figure Weights, Digit Span, and Coding. Best practice is to administer all 10 primary subtests in order to obtain the FSIQ and the 5 primary index scores: VCI, VSI, FRI, WMI, and PSI.

THE WISC-V ANCILLARY INDEXES AND SUBTESTS

In this section we review the five ancillary indexes: the General Ability, Cognitive Proficiency, Nonverbal, Quantitative Reasoning, and Auditory Working Memory Indexes (AWMI). The ancillary indexes are optional. They allow the clinician to explore specific cognitive hypotheses related to children's WISC-V scores in the context of their performance in the real world of the classroom, in daily interactions, and among everyday demands. Some, but not all, of these composites require administration of selected secondary subtests beyond the 10 primary subtests required to obtain the 5 primary index scores. Fig. 1.1 shows the subtest composition of each of the five ancillary index scores.

The General Ability Index

The GAI is a composite score that summarizes the performance of all FSIQ subtests except Digit Span and Coding into a single number. The WISC-V GAI differs from FSIQ in that it excludes the contributions of working memory and processing speed. Thus, GAI and FSIQ can lead to different impressions of a child's overall ability when there is variability across the five primary indexes. The GAI is comprised of five of the seven primary subtest scores that enter the FSIQ: Similarities, Vocabulary, Block Design, Matrix

Reasoning, and Figure Weights. No secondary subtests are necessary to calculate the GAI.

We originally developed GAI with WISC-III, specifically for use in ability-achievement discrepancy analyses because many learning-disabled and ADHD students exhibit cognitive processing deficits in working memory and processing speed concomitant with their learning disabilities (Prifitera, Weiss, & Saklofske, 1998). Lowered performance on WM and PS subtests in turn lowers the FSIQ for many learning-disabled students, which decreases the magnitude of the discrepancy between ability and achievement weaknesses, and may result in denial of needed special education services when that model is used for special education eligibility determinations. In those situations, the GAI may be used in the ability-achievement discrepancy analysis in order to better identify eligible students. Other uses for the GAI have since been identified. For similar reasons to those described above, it also may be appropriate to use GAI when evaluating the extent to which general memory functions are commensurate with overall intelligence for children with LD or ADHD. Further, GAI may be an appropriate estimate of overall ability when physical or sensory disorders invalidate performance on the working memory or processing speed tasks, or both.

For these reasons, we previously suggested that some practitioners may prefer the GAI as an alternative way of summarizing overall ability (Saklofske, Prifitera, Weiss, Rolfhus, & Zhu, 2005). However, this suggestion has led to an increasing number of psychological evaluations in which the GAI is described as a better estimate of overall ability than FSIQ whenever the child scores significantly lower on the working memory and/or processing speed subtests. We subsequently clarified that this is not what we intended, and can be a very problematic practice (Weiss, Beal, Saklofske, Alloway, & Prifitera, 2008). Ultimately, we believe that working memory and processing speed are essential components of intelligence, and excluding them from the estimate of overall intelligence simply because the child scored low on those subtests is poor practice. Such practice will result in unrealistically high estimates of intelligence for those students and possibly create expectations they cannot live up to without accommodations. To be clear, it is sometimes appropriate to report GAI and compare it to other scores such as achievement and memory. It is not good practice to describe GAI as a better estimate of overall intelligence than FSIQ solely because the child scored poorly on Digit Span or Coding.

The Cognitive Proficiency Index

The CPI summarizes performance on the primary working memory and processing speed subtests of the WISC-V into a single score. The CPI is comprised of 4 of the 10 primary subtests. No secondary subtests are required to calculate the CPI. Creating a new composite by combining the WMI and PSI was first suggested in relation to WISC-III by Dumont and Willis (2001), and subsequently extended to WISC-IV by Weiss et al. (2006), and WAIS-IV by Weiss, Saklofske, Coalson, and Raiford (2010). In WISC-V, the CPI is included as part of the test's manual (Wechsler, 2014).

The CPI represents a set of functions whose common element is the proficiency with which one processes certain types of cognitive information. As we explain more fully in Chapter 5, the abilities represented in the CPI are central to the FR process. Proficient processing—through quick visual speed and good mental control—facilitates FR and the acquisition of new material by reducing the cognitive demands of novel or higher-order tasks. More simply, efficient cognitive processing facilitates learning and problem-solving by "freeing up" cognitive resources for more advanced, higher-level skills.

The WISC-V CPI excludes the contributions of verbal comprehension, visual spatial organization, and FR. Thus, the CPI and GAI can provide different views into a child's cognitive abilities when there is significant variability across the relevant index scores. Both views are sometimes necessary to form a complete picture of an individual's strengths and weaknesses that is not distorted by combining a set of diverse abilities into a single overall FSIQ score. Rather than reporting GAI as the best estimate of overall ability when the profile of subtest scores is diverse, it is sometimes better practice to describe both the GAI and CPI in the psychological evaluation and discuss how deficits in proficient cognitive processing interfere with the expression of the child's general ability.

Nonverbal Index

The Nonverbal index (NVI) is formed by six subtests: Block Design, Visual Puzzles, Matrix Reasoning, Figure Weights, Picture Span, and Coding. All of these are primary subtests, but Visual Puzzles is not an FSIQ subtest. Thus, calculating the NVI does not require administration of secondary subtests.

This index substantially minimizes, but does not eliminate, verbal comprehension because the subtests still require the child to understand the directions, which are spoken verbally. Of course, such tasks can be mediated by oral language or private and internal silent speech.

In a sample of English language learners in which the WISC-V FSIQ was 8.3 points lower than matched controls, the WISC-V NVI was only 1.8 points lower (Wechsler, 2014). Thus, the NVI can be useful in a variety of situations in which English language skills are either under-developed or impaired.

Quantitative Reasoning Index

The Quantitative Reasoning Index (QRI) is formed by combining the Arithmetic and Figure Weights subtests. Thus, calculation of the QRI requires administration of one secondary subtest (Arithmetic) beyond the 10 primary subtests. The Arithmetic subtest involves mentally solving arithmetic problems presented verbally as word problems. The Figure Weights subtest involves estimation of relative quantities of abstract symbols based on learning and applying their quantitative relationships to each other.

Quantitative Reasoning is a type of FR. That is, quantitative reasoning is FR using quantitative concepts. Further research is needed on the relationship of quantitative reasoning to achievement in higher-order mathematics.

Auditory Working Memory Index

The primary WMI is comprised of Digit Span and Picture Span, which are auditory and visual working memory tasks, respectively. The WMI allows full construct coverage of working memory across both sensory modalities (visual and auditory). The AWMI removes the contribution of visual working memory by replacing Picture Span with Letter-Number Sequencing. Thus, the AWMI consists of Digit Span and Letter-Number Sequencing, which are both auditory working memory tasks. Calculation of the AWMI requires administration of one secondary subtest (Letter-Number Sequencing). In clinical situations in which the visual modality is impaired, the AWMI allows better evaluation of working memory functions than the WMI.

THE WISC-V COMPLEMENTARY INDEXES AND SUBTESTS

Complementary indexes and subtests are new to WISC-V. They are different from the primary and ancillary indexes because they are not part of any of the broad cognitive abilities measured by the WISC-V. Rather, they are designed to provide examiners with more detailed information relevant to psychoeducational evaluations of children referred for specific learning disorders such as in reading and mathematics.

Naming Speed Index

The Naming Speed Index is comprised of two optional subtests: Naming Speed Literacy and Naming Speed Quantity.

Naming Speed Literacy. In the Naming Speed Literacy subtest the child names elements of various stimuli as quickly as possible. The tasks utilize stimuli and elements that are traditional within rapid naming task paradigms (e.g., colors, objects, letters, and numbers) and that have shown sensitivity to reading and written expression skills and to specific learning disorders in reading and written expression. Similar tasks are closely associated with reading and spelling skill development, with reading achievement, and with a number of variables related to reading and spelling, and have shown sensitivity to a specific learning disorder in reading (Crews & D'Amato, 2009; Korkman, Barron-Linnankoski, & Lahti-Nuuttila, 1999; Korkman, Kirk, & Kemp, 2007; Powell,

Stainthorp, Stuart, Garwood, & Quinlan, 2007; Willburger, Fussenegger, Moll, Wood, & Landerl, 2008). Some studies suggest they are also related to mathematics skills, specific learning disorder—mathematics, and a number of other clinical conditions (McGrew & Wendling, 2010; Pauly et al., 2011; Willburger et al., 2008; Wise et al., 2008). In order to ensure sensitivity beyond very early grades, the tasks involve naming multiple dimensions simultaneously and alternating stimuli. Such tasks are also sensitive to a wide variety of other neurodevelopmental conditions such as ADHD (Korkman et al., 2007), language disorders in both monolingual and bilingual children (Korkman et al., 2012), and autism spectrum disorder (Korkman et al., 2007). Children at risk for neurodevelopmental issues have been reported to score lower on similar measures (Lind et al., 2011), which are described as measuring storage and retrieval fluency and naming facility (Flanagan et al., 2012). These subtests specifically measure the automaticity of visual-verbal associations, which should be well developed in school-aged children.

Naming Speed Quantity. In the Naming Speed Quantity subtest the child names the quantity of squares inside a series of boxes as quickly as possible. The subtest is similar to tasks in the experimental literature that show greater sensitivity to mathematics skills and specific learning disorders in mathematics than do the traditional rapid automatized naming tasks that are more closely associated with reading- and writing-related variables (Pauly et al., 2011; van der Sluis, de Jong, & van der Leij, 2004; Willburger et al., 2008). Tasks that involve rapid naming of stimuli are described as measuring naming facility and storage and retrieval fluency (Flanagan et al., 2012).

Symbol Translation Index

The Symbol Translation Index (STI) measures learning associations between unfamiliar symbols and their meanings, and applies them in novel ways. The subtest consists of three conditions: immediate, delayed, and recognition.

Immediate Symbol Translation. In the Immediate Symbol Translation subtests the child learns visual-verbal pairs and then translates symbol strings into phrases or sentences. Tasks similar to Immediate Symbol Translation are described as measuring verbal-visual associative memory or paired associates learning, storage and retrieval fluency and accuracy, and immediate recall (Flanagan et al., 2012). This is a cued memory paradigm, that is, the child recalls information related to a specific visual cue.

Visual-verbal associative memory tasks similar to the Symbol Translation subtests are closely associated with reading decoding skills, word-reading accuracy and fluency, text reading, and reading comprehension (Elliott, Hale, Fiorello, Dorvil, & Moldovan, 2010; Evans, Floyd, McGrew, & Leforgee, 2001; Floyd, Keith, Taub, & McGrew, 2007; Hulme, Goetz, Gooch, Adams, & Snowling, 2007; Lervåg, Bråten, & Hulme, 2009; Litt, de Jong, van Bergen, & Nation, 2013). Furthermore, they are sensitive to dyslexia when they require verbal output (Gang & Siegel, 2002; Li, Shu, McBride-Chang, Liu, & Xue, 2009; Litt & Nation, 2014). Visual-verbal associative memory tasks are also related to math calculation skills and math reasoning (Floyd, Evans, & McGrew, 2003; McGrew & Wendling, 2010).

Delayed Symbol Translation. In the Delayed Symbol Translation condition the child translates symbol strings into sentences using visual-verbal pairs previously learned during the Immediate Symbol Translation condition. Tasks similar to Delayed Symbol Translation are described as measuring verbal-visual associative memory or paired associates learning, storage and retrieval fluency and accuracy, and delayed recall (Flanagan et al., 2012). This task is a cued memory paradigm.

Recognition Symbol Translation. In the Recognition Symbol Translation subtest the child views a symbol and selects the correct translation from response options the examiner reads aloud, using visual-verbal pairs recalled from the Immediate Symbol Translation condition. Tasks similar to Recognition Symbol Translation are described as measuring verbal-visual associative memory or paired associates learning, storage and retrieval fluency and accuracy, and delayed recognition (Flanagan et al., 2012). This task constrains the child's responses to words that have been presented in the task and therefore eliminates the possibility of an erroneous word being recalled. This task allows the examiner to identify the strength of the associate learning and not the learning of content (e.g., correct words). The examiner may compare performance on this task to the delayed condition to determine the impact of constraining recall on memory performance.

Storage and Retrieval Index

The Storage and Retrieval Index is formed by combining the scores from the Naming Speed Index and the STI. This provides an overall measure of the child's ability to store and retrieve learned information quickly and efficiently.

SUMMARY

In this chapter we have shown how the contemporary Wechsler model has evolved and expanded from two to five factors based on a careful research program spanning decades and multiple editions of the various Wechsler tests (WPPSI, WISC, and WAIS). We have described the WISC-V subtests related to each of the five primary and five ancillary cognitive indexes as well as the three complementary indexes designed to assist psychologists with psychoeducational evaluations of specific learning disabilities. As with all tests, including the WISC-V, they are based on theory and empirical findings from research as well as clinical practice, and are intended to provide the clinician with a standardized measure to aid in the assessment process including diagnosis, planning, and prescription of the child or adolescent. The very nature of the WISC-V should contribute to guiding, informing, and confirming clinical hypotheses in the very complex process of clinical and psychoeducational assessment when the definition of problem areas and solutions are not readily apparent. Yet, the WISC-V, as sophisticated and important as it may be in the psychological assessment of children and adolescents, does not make decisions. . .psychologists do!

REFERENCES

Benson, N., Hulac, D. M., & Kranzler, J. H. (2010). Independent examination of Wechsler Adult Intelligence Scale-Fourth Edition (WAIS-IV): What does the WAIS-IV measure? *Psychological Assessment*, 22(1), 121−130.

Carroll, J. B. (1993). *Human cognitive abilities: A survey of factor-analytic studies*. New York, NY: Cambridge University Press.

Crews, K. J., & D'Amato, R. C. (2009). Subtyping children's reading disabilities using a comprehensive neuropsychological measure. *International Journal of Neuroscience*, *119*, 1615−1639. Available from https://doi.org/10.1080/00207450802319960.

Crowe, S. F. (2000). Does the letter number sequencing task measure anything more than digit span? *Assessment*, 7(2), 113−117.

Deary, I. J., Whiteman, M. C., Starr, J. M., Whalley, L. J., & Fox, H. C. (2004). The impact of childhood intelligence on later life: Following up the Scottish mental surveys of 1932 and 1947. *Journal of Personality and Social Psychology*, 86(1), 130−147. Available from https://doi.org/10.1037/0022-3514.86,1.130.

Dumont, R., & Willis, J. (2001). Use of the Tellegen & Briggs formula to determine the Dumont-Willis Indexes (DWI-1 & DWI-2) for the WISC-III. http://alpha.fdu.edu/psychology/

Elliott, C. D., Hale, J. B., Fiorello, C. A., Dorvil, C., & Moldovan, J. (2010). Differential Ability Scales−II prediction of reading performance: Global scores are not enough. *Psychology in the Schools*, 47(7), 698−720. Available from https://doi.org/10.1002/pits.20499.

Evans, J. J., Floyd, R. G., McGrew, K. S., & Leforgee, M. H. (2001). The relations between measures of Cattell-Horn-Carroll (CHC) cognitive abilities and reading achievement during childhood and adolescence. *School Psychology Review*, 31(2), 246−262.

Flanagan, D. P., Alfonso, V. C., & Ortiz, S. O. (2012). The cross-battery assessment approach: An overview, historical perspective, and current directions. In D. P. Flanagan, & P. L. Harrison (Eds.), *Contemporary intellectual assessment: Theories, tests, and issues* (3rd ed., pp. 459−483). New York, NY: The Guilford Press.

Flanagan, D. P., Alfonso, V. C., Ortiz, S. O., & Dynda, A. M. (2010). Integrating cognitive assessment in school neuropsychological evaluations. In D. C. Miller (Ed.), *Best practices in school neuropsychology: Guidelines for effective practice, assessment, and evidence-based intervention* (pp. 101−140). Hoboken, NJ: John Wiley & Sons.

Flanagan, D. P., & Kaufman, A. S. (2009). *Essentials of WISC−IV assessment* (2nd ed.). Hoboken, NJ: John Wiley & Sons.

Floyd, R. G., Evans, J. J., & McGrew, K. S. (2003). Relations between measures of Cattell-Horn-Carroll (CHC) cognitive abilities and mathematics achievement across the school-age years. *Psychology in the Schools*, 40(2), 155−171. Available from https://doi.org/10.1002/pits.10083.

Floyd, R. G., Keith, T. Z., Taub, G. E., & McGrew, K. S. (2007). Cattell-Horn-Carroll cognitive abilities and their effects on reading decoding skills: *g* has indirect effects, more specific abilities have direct effects. *School Psychology Quarterly*, *22*(2), 200–233. Available from https://doi.org/10.1037/1045-3830.22.2.200.

Gang, M., & Siegel, L. S. (2002). Sound-symbol learning in children with dyslexia. *Journal of Learning Disabilities*, *35*(2), 137–157.

Gottfredson, L. S., & Saklofske, D. H. (2009). Intelligence: Foundations and issues in assessment. *Canadian Psychology/Psychologie Canadienne*, *50*(3), 183–195. Available from https://doi.org/10.1037/a0016641.

Groth-Marnat, G. (2009). *Handbook of psychological assessment* (5th ed.). New York, NY: John Wiley & Sons.

Hartshorne, J. K. (2008). Visual working memory capacity and proactive interference. *PLoS One*, *3*(7), e2716. Available from https://doi.org/10.1371/journal.pone.0002716.

Horn, J. L., & Cattell, R. B. (1966). Refinement and test of the theory of fluid and crystallized general intelligences. *Journal of Educational Psychology*, *57*, 253–270.

Hulme, C., Goetz, K., Gooch, D., Adams, J., & Snowling, M. J. (2007). Paired-associate learning, phoneme awareness, and learning to read. *Journal of Experimental Child Psychology*, *96*, 150–166. Available from https://doi.org/10.1016/j.jecp.2006.09.002.

Kaufman, A. S. (2013). Intelligent testing with Wechsler's fourth editions: Perspectives on the Weiss et al. studies and the eight commentaries. *Journal of Psychoeducational Assessment*, *31*(2), 224–234.

Kaufman, A. S., & Lichtenberger, E. O. (2006). *Assessing adolescent and adult intelligence* (3rd ed.). Hoboken, NJ: John Wiley & Sons.

Korkman, M., Barron-Linnankoski, S., & Lahti-Nuuttila, P. (1999). Effects of age and duration of reading instruction on the development of phonological awareness, rapid naming, and verbal memory span. *Developmental Neuropsychology*, *16*(3), 415–431.

Korkman, M., Kirk, U., & Kemp, S. (2007). *NEPSY–II*. Bloomington, MN: Pearson.

Korkman, M., Stenroos, M., Mickos, A., Westman, M., Ekholm, P., & Byring, R. (2012). Does simultaneous bilingualism aggravate children's specific language problems? *Acta Pædiatrica*, *101*, 946–952.

Lervåg, A., Bråten, I., & Hulme, C. (2009). The cognitive and linguistic foundations of early reading development: A Norwegian latent variable longitudinal study. *Developmental Psychology*, *45*(3), 764–781. Available from https://doi.org/10.1037/a0014132.

Lezak, M. D., Howieson, D. B., & Loring, D. W. (2004). In H. J. Hannay, & J. S. Fischer (Eds.), *Neuropsychological assessment* (4th ed.). New York, NY: Oxford University Press.

Li, H., Shu, H., McBride-Chang, C., Liu, H. Y., & Xue, J. (2009). Paired associate learning in Chinese children with dyslexia. *Journal of Experimental Child Psychology*, *103*, 135–151. Available from https://doi.org/10.1016/j.jecp.2009.02.001.

Likert, R., & Quasha, W. H. (1995). *Revised Minnesota paper form board test manual* (2nd ed.). San Antonio, TX: The Psychological Corporation.

Lind, A., Korkman, M., Lehtonen, L., Lapinleimu, H., Parkkola, R., Matomäki, J., ... The Pripari Study Group. (2011). Cognitive and neuropsychological outcomes at 5 years of age in preterm children born in the 2000s. *Developmental Medicine & Child Neurology*, *53*(3), 256–262. Available from https://doi.org/10.1111/j.1469-8749.2010.03828.x.

Litt, R. A., de Jong, P. F., van Bergen, E., & Nation, K. (2013). Dissociating crossmodal and verbal demands in paired associate learning (PAL): What drives the PAL–reading relationship? *Journal of Experimental Child Psychology*, *115*, 137–149. Available from https://doi.org/10.1016/j.jecp.2012.11.012.

Litt, R. A., & Nation, K. (2014). The nature and specificity of paired associate learning deficits in children with dyslexia. *Journal of Memory and Language, 71*, 71−88. Available from https://doi.org/10.1016/j.jml.2013.10.005.

Cognitive abilities: 100 years after Spearman's (1904) "General Intelligence. Objectively Determined and Measured" (Special section). In D. Lubinski *Journal of Personality and Social Psychology* (86, pp. 96−199).

MacDonald, M. C., Almor, A., Henderson, V. W., Kempler, D., & Andersen, E. S. (2001). Assessing working memory and language comprehension in Alzheimer's disease. *Brain and Language, 78*, 17−42.

Makovski, T., & Jiang, Y. V. (2008). Proactive interference from items previously stored in visual working memory. *Memory & Cognition, 36*(1), 43−52.

McGrew, K. S., & Wendling, B. J. (2010). Cattell−Horn−Carroll cognitive-achievement relations: What we have learned from the past 20 years of research. *Psychology in the Schools, 47*(7), 651−675. Available from https://doi.org/10.1002/pits.20497.

Miller, D. C. (2010). *Best practices in school neuropsychology: Guidelines for effective practice, assessment, and evidence-based intervention.* Hoboken, NJ: John Wiley & Sons.

Miller, D. C. (2013). *Essentials of school neuropsychological assessment* (2nd ed.). Hoboken, NJ: John Wiley & Sons.

Pauly, H., Linkersdörfer, J., Lindberg, S., Woerner, W., Hasselhorn, M., & Lonnemann, J. (2011). Domain-specific rapid automatized naming deficits in children at risk for learning disabilities. *Journal of Neurolinguistics, 24*, 602−610. Available from https://doi.org/10.1016/j.jneuroling.2011.02.002.

Powell, D., Stainthorp, R., Stuart, M., Garwood, H., & Quinlan, P. (2007). An experimental comparison between rival theories of rapid automatized naming performance and its relationship to reading. *Journal of Experimental Child Psychology, 98*(1), 46−68.

Prifitera, A., Weiss, L. G., & Saklofske, D. H. (1998). The WISC-III in context. In A. Prifitera, & D. H. Saklofske (Eds.), *WISC-III clinical use and interpretation: Scientist − practitioner perspectives* (pp. 1−38). San Diego, CA: Academic Press.

Reynolds, C. R. (1997). Forward and backward memory span should not be combined for clinical analysis. *Archives of Clinical Neuropsychology, 12*, 29−40.

Saklofske, D. H., Prifitera, A., Weiss, L. G., Rolfhus, E., & Zhu, J. (2005). Clinical interpretation of the WISC-IV FSIQ and GAI. In A. Prifitera, D. H. Saklofske, & L. G. Weiss (Eds.), *WISC-IV clinical use and interpretation: Scientist − practitioner perspectives.* San Diego, CA: Academic Press.

Sattler, J. M. (2008b). *Resource guide to accompany assessment of children: Cognitive foundations* (5th ed.). San Diego, CA: Author.

Squalli, J., & Wilson, K. (2014). Intelligence, creativity, and innovation. *Intelligence, 46*, 250−257.

Sternberg, R. J., & Grigorenko, E. L. (Eds.), (2002). *The general intelligence factor: How general is it?* Mahwah, NJ: Erlbaum.

Tobin, R. M. (2013). The Wechsler intelligence tests: Revisiting theory and practice. *Journal of Psychoeducational Assessment, 31*(2), 91−94.

van der Sluis, S., de Jong, P. F., & van der Leij, A. (2004). Inhibition and shifting in children with learning deficits in arithmetic and reading. *Journal of Experimental Child Psychology, 87*(3), 239−266. Available from https://doi.org/10.1016/j.jecp.2003.12.002.

Ward, L. C., Bergman, M. A., & Herbert, K. R. (2011). WAIS-IV subtest covariance structure: Conceptual and statistical considerations. *Psychological Assessment, Advance online publication.* Available from https://doi.org/10.1037/a0025614.

Wechsler, D. (1939). *The measurement of adult intelligence*. Baltimore, MD: Williams & Wilkins.

Wechsler, D. (2009). *Wechsler memory scale* (4th ed.). Bloomington, MN: Pearson.

Wechsler, D. (2012). *)* Manual for the Wechsler preschool and primary scales of intelligence — *Fourth Edition*. San Antonio, TX: Pearson.

Wechsler, D. (2014). *Technical manual for the Wechsler intelligence scale for children —Fifth Edition*. San Antonio, TX: Pearson.

Weiss, L. G., Beal, A. L., Saklofske, D. H., Alloway, T. P., & Prifitera, A. (2008). Interpretation and intervention with WISC-IV in the clinical assessment context. In A. Prifitera, D. H. Saklofske, & L. G. Weiss (Eds.), *WISC-IV clinical assessment and intervention*. San Diego, CA: Academic Press.

Weiss, L. G., Keith, T. Z., Zhu, J., & Chen, H. (2013a). WAIS-IV Clinical validation of the four- and five-factor interpretive approaches. *Journal of Psychoeducational Assessment, 31* (2), 114—131.

Weiss, L. G., Keith, T. Z., Zhu, J., & Chen, H. (2013b). WISC-IV Clinical validation of the four- and five-factor interpretive approaches. *Journal of Psychoeducational Assessment, 31* (2), 94—113.

Weiss, L. G., Keith, T. Z., Zhu, J., & Chen, H. (2013c). Technical and practical issues in the structure and clinical invariance of the Wechsler scales: A rejoinder to commentaries. *Journal of Psychoeducational Assessment, 31*(2), 235—243.

Weiss, L. G., Saklofske, D. H., Coalson, D., & Raiford, S. E. (2010). *WAIS-IV clinical use and interpretation*. San Diego, CA: Academic Press.

Weiss, L. G., Saklofske, D. H., Prifitera, A., & Holdnack, J. A. (2006). *WISC-IV: advanced clinical interpretation*. San Diego, CA: Academic Press.

Werheid, K., Hoppe, C., Thöne, A., Müller, U., Müngersdorf, M., & von Cramon, D. Y. (2002). The adaptive digit ordering test: Clinical application, reliability, and validity of a verbal working memory test. *Archives of Clinical Neuropsychology, 17*, 547—565.

Willburger, E., Fussenegger, B., Moll, K., Wood, G., & Landerl, K. (2008). Naming speed in dyslexia and dyscalculia. *Learning and Individual Differences, 18*, 224—236.

Wise, J. C., Pae, H. K., Wolfe, C. B., Sevcik, R. A., Morris, R. D., Lovett, M., & Wolf, M. (2008). Phonological awareness and rapid naming skills of children with reading disabilities and children with reading disabilities who are at risk for mathematics difficulties. *Learning Disabilities Research & Practice, 23*(3), 125—136.

Chapter 2

Practical Considerations in WISC-V Interpretation and Intervention

A. Lynne Beal[1], James A. Holdnack[2], Donald H. Saklofske[3] and Lawrence G. Weiss[4]

[1]*Private Practice, Toronto, ON, Canada,* [2]*Research and Statistical Consultant, Bear, DE, United States,* [3]*Department of Psychology, University of Western Ontario, London, ON, Canada,* [4]*Research and Measurement Consultant, San Antonio, TX, United States*

INTRODUCTION

Interpretation of the WISC-V scores is typically done in the context of making recommendations for educational interventions for children and adolescents. This chapter provides a guide for interpretation of the WISC-V as a measure of g, or overall ability, as well as a set of measures of specific abilities. To aid practitioners with developing intervention strategies, the chapter continues by linking interventions to the specific cognitive abilities that the WISC-V measures.

In this chapter, we first discuss common challenges to interpreting WISC-V scores for students where there is broad variance among the scores. Next, we present an analogy designed to promote a more intuitive understanding of the abilities measured by each index. Finally, we consider some fundamental suggestions for teachers and parents who have children with weaknesses in one of the primary cognitive abilities. These suggestions, guidelines, and heuristics are drawn from both research and clinical practice to provide further insights into the applications of the WISC-V as an important part of the clinical assessment process. Suggestions are not presented as a clinical "cookbook" of either diagnostic hypotheses or clinical interpretations of the abilities.

WISC-V. DOI: https://doi.org/10.1016/B978-0-12-815744-2.00002-1
23

LEVELS OF INTERPRETATION: WHEN THE OVERALL ABILITY SCORE DOES NOT TELL THE WHOLE STORY

Tracey's WISC-V scores show that her abilities are not evenly developed. There were significant differences between 3 of the index scores that call into question the meaningfulness of the FSIQ. But our Director says that this score is needed in order to secure additional funding for special education support for this student.

Wally's teachers have commented on his variable performance across school subjects since entering school 3 years ago. While some earlier test results reporting a summary IQ score indicated that he may have the overall cognitive ability to cope with a regular program, the results of the current assessment suggest that the more relevant focus of his school learning and achievement difficulties may be found in the significant and rarely occurring score differences between his high average Verbal Comprehension, low average Working Memory and Processing Speed, with borderline Visual Spatial and Fluid Reasoning abilities.

Analysis of the discrepancies among the index score is routinely accepted as good clinical practice, especially when such interpretation occurs in the context of general ability (Flanagan & Kaufman, 2004; Kaufman, 2013; Sattler, 2008). Significant discrepancies among a student's index scores should be interpreted as indications of strengths or weaknesses in the cognitive constructs they measure. As most practitioners have observed, an identified strength or weakness in one of these major cognitive abilities will often manifest in classroom behavior. For example, teachers will likely find that a student who has a significant weakness on the Working Memory Index (WMI) tends to forget assignments; or one has who has a weakness on the Processing Speed Index (PSI) takes longer than their classmates to process instructions. Such information is beneficial to educational planning.

However, profile analysis of the WISC-V index scores is not by itself diagnostic of any particular psychoeducational or clinical disorder. The index scores represent major cognitive abilities. Therefore, a cognitive deficit in one of these areas may be associated with any of several disorders related to that ability. A significant weakness on WMI, for example, may be a common finding in groups with Attention-Deficit/Hyperactivity Disorder (ADHD) but also occurs with some frequency in groups with Learning Disabilities (LD) and Traumatic Brain Injury (TBI). It is for this reason that index score patterns should be considered consistent with, but not confirmatory of, a diagnosis, and must be combined with other information to rule out alternative diagnostic hypotheses. The cognitive deficits related to such disorders will be discussed further in the final two chapters of this text.

Two examples of a student with a deficit as measured by the WMI demonstrate this concept: For a student referred for possible ADHD, a low

WMI, combined with high scores on a parent rating scale for ADHD behaviors, low scores on a continuous performance task of sustained attention, and a developmental and educational history of deficits in attention, impulsivity or hyperactivity, the practitioner may feel confident in making a diagnosis of ADHD. The preponderance of supporting information along with the low WMI leads to this conclusion. However, a low WMI score found in a student athlete referred for reading comprehension problems following an on-field concussion would instead warrant further evaluation to investigate a possible TBI.

Investigation of Wechsler scores, at all levels, should be conducted within an ecological context (Prifitera, Saklofske, & Weiss, 2005, 2008; Weiss, Saklofske, Prifitera, & Holdnack, 2006). Interpretation of score patterns may vary depending on the sociocultural background (Georgas, Weiss, van de Vijver, & Saklofske, 2003; Harris & Llorente, 2005), family values, pattern of academic strengths and weaknesses, motivation, and psychiatric and medical history. Interpretation also needs to consider behaviors observed during the test session (Oakland, Glutting, & Watkins, 2005; Sattler & Dumont, 2004). A common mistake is to offer stock interpretations of index score patterns while ignoring the effects of these mediating influences (see Kamphaus, 1998). Consider, for example, two children each having a Full Scale IQ (FSIQ) score of 112, which, by itself, suggests high average ability. The child with a superior Verbal Comprehension Index (VCI) and low average WMI will certainly present differently in the classroom than a typically developing child with statistically consistent subtest and index scores yielding a FSIQ of 112. The first child may appear much brighter and much less attentive than the second children even though they have the same FSIQ score. Remember that children may perform contrary to expectations on testing. For all of these reasons, the interpretations of WISC-V test scores will differ in relation to the examinee's personal context and history. In addition, the examiner's expectations of the likelihood of finding certain patterns will be influenced by the referral questions and hypotheses.

How Important Is g, the Measure of Overall Ability?

Curiously, one camp of psychometric researchers argues that the modest portions of variance attributed to the first-order factors (the index scores) may be too small to be of clinical importance, should not be used diagnostically, and that FSIQ is thus the only score worth interpreting (Canivez & Kush, 2013; Canivez & Watkins, 2010). However, careful review of these studies indicates that the researchers statistically removed g, the general intelligence factor from the index scores and examined only their residual validity. This approach is problematic because an individual's investment of g resources in particular directions will, over time, result in greater development of some abilities over others (Reynolds & Keith, 2013). Thus, removing the influence of g from the index scores effectively cripples their power and creates a rather artificial situation. We critique this line of research more thoroughly in Chapter 4 (see section Hierarchical vs Bifactor Models of Intelligence).

Another camp of neuropsychological researchers and clinicians argues that FSIQ is a meaningless composite of various disparate abilities and should not be interpreted at all (Hale, Fiorello, Kavanagh, Holdnack, & Aloe, 2007; Kaplan, 1988; Lezak, 1988; Lezak, Howieson, & Loring, 2004). This demonstrates the diversity of opinion that exists in the field. One camp argues that interpretation of index scores is invalid and recommends interpreting only FSIQ while the other camp argues that interpretation of FSIQ is invalid and recommends interpreting only the index scores.

We do not agree with either camp. Both views have merit, but both views are too one-sided to be workable. We believe that both g and the specific broad abilities are important and that each construct has a place in the practice of assessment.

What is a practitioner to do? We suggest that it depends on the referral question. When the purpose of the evaluation is to efficiently predict a broad range of cognitively driven behaviors, then g—as defined by the FSIQ—is always the best score to use. Further, we think that heterogeneous tasks that require integration of multiple abilities for successful performance will enhance the ecological validity of predicting a broader range of cognitively driven, real-world behaviors. On the other hand, examining particular broad and narrow abilities is necessary when evaluating clients for specific cognitive impairments, neurological conditions, learning and attentional disorders. Thus, it is not one approach or the other. Strength and weakness interpretations vary in the context of the child's overall level of g as evidenced by differing frequencies of discrepant indexes by ability level (Wechsler, 2014).

There is evidence that having one or more low cognitive ability scores is common among healthy individuals; therefore, practitioners should be cautious when interpreting low scores as conclusive evidence of brain injury or disease in forensic evaluations (Brooks, Holdnack, & Iverson, 2011). The common finding of one or more low index scores in normal subjects, however, suggests that for individuals, g does not manifest itself equally across the broad cognitive abilities. Whether for reasons of environmental opportunity or personal and vocational interest, individuals appear to invest g resources selectively. They thereby develop some broad abilities at the expense of others over time (cf. Cattell, 1987; Kvist & Gustafsson, 2008; Reynolds & Keith, 2013). This is one reason clinicians find it difficult to conceptualize the broad abilities independent of g, although it is possible to accomplish statistically. As Claeys (2013) observes, "No one is more aware that test factors don't always 'hang together' than those assessing children and adults on a daily basis." How true!

One issue remains: Should the FSIQ be reported when there is significant variability among the index scores? In other words, is there a statistical or clinical point where the FSIQ "fractures" into more meaningful parts, and is no longer a valid measure of general mental ability nor clinically useful for differential diagnosis or program planning?

The child's overall level of cognitive ability provides a critical backdrop to interpretation of individual differences among the various domains of ability as assessed by the index scores. The calculation of a FSIQ continues to be important for this and several other reasons. From a purely psychometric perspective, a general factor clearly emerges in all studies of intelligence (Carroll, 1993). This fact, combined with the integrity of the five-factor structure and the magnitude of the correlations between the index scores, makes a psychometrically compelling case for the interpretation of the FSIQ.

Further, WISC-IV studies suggest that the FSIQ may be an equally valid measure of general ability for individuals or groups with highly variable index scores as for those having consistent index scores (Daniel, 2007). WISC-III and WISC-IV studies further suggest that there may be no difference in the predictive validity of FSIQ for low-scatter and high-scatter groups (Watkins, Glutting, & Lei, 2007).

The FSIQ is an especially strong predictor of school achievement, occupational success, and memory functioning. In fact, the FSIQ and achievement correlate more strongly than any two variables known to the behavioral sciences, typically around 0.70. For example, Deary, Strand, Smith, and Fernandes (2007) reported that general mental ability measured at age 11 years is highly correlated $(r = 0.81)$ with general educational achievement and further with different subject areas at age 16 years. This means the FSIQ explains about half the variance in achievement. Additional relevant factors likely include the student's perseverance, drive to task mastery, self-regulation toward a goal, and other constructs related to emotional intelligence. Beyond the relationship with achievement, there is considerable ecological and criterion validity for the use of an overall estimate of general intelligence in a variety of areas related to success in life including college readiness, predicting job performance, creativity, and innovation (Gottfredson, 1997, 1998; Kuncel, Hezlett, & Ones, 2004; Squalli & Wilson, 2014).

The Importance of Interpreting the Component Abilities

Although the FSIQ has strong psychometric integrity and predictive power, large discrepancies among the component abilities of the FSIQ are often observed in clinical practice. We believe that it is these large discrepancies that may provide the most clinically interesting and useful information of relevance to the assessment protocol. In cases of intellectual giftedness or moderate-to-severe developmental disability, we can expect a relatively flat profile and a summary, or the FSIQ score can certainly be used to describe the cognitive component of this finding. Similar subtest and index scores of a child with an FSIQ of 107 also allows the psychologist to describe this child as having average ability and further manifesting average Verbal Comprehension (VC), Visual Spatial (VS), Fluid Reasoning (FR), Working Memory (WM), and Processing Speed (PS) abilities. This would then shift the hypotheses related to poor school performance to other cognitive factors, such as auditory phonemic awareness or long-term memory retrieval; or to noncognitive factors such as work and study skills, personality, motivation, learning style, and the teaching—learning—social environment of the classroom. However, in other cases such as recent lateralized brain trauma, the presence of a large discrepancy between, for example, VC and VS abilities may be very meaningful and should be the focus for interpreting cognitive abilities.

Thus, it is prudent to take the position that the presence of large discrepancies among index scores, reflecting unevenly developed cognitive abilities, makes interpretation of the child's overall intellectual functioning more difficult and complex. Such variability then points to the need to shift test interpretation to the index scores where the most clinically relevant information is more likely to be found. Having five cognitive factors to interpret a child's abilities is strength of the WISC-V theoretical structure.

Similarly though, any factor-based score such as the PSI becomes more difficult to interpret when the subtest scores within the index are too variable. Significant score differences between the subtests on the same index are clear indicators that the composite does not provide a reliable indication of the child's ability in that domain. Rather than focus on a less meaningful summary score, determine the clinical relevance of the subtest findings. Assumptions to cover are that the test was properly administered and scored, the testing conditions were adequate, and the examinee was both motivated and seemed to understand the task demands. An example for PS would show scaled scores of 13 for Symbol Search versus 4 for Coding. These scores might result from differences in the task and the greater requirement for fine-motor coordination on Coding. Consider also noncognitive factors, such as interest and motivation or even scoring errors! While careful administration and scoring are essential to providing valid data, one should always have enough clinical commonsense to be able to say: "that score can't be right, because the child answered almost all of the items on the Similarities subtest."

Once the analysis of test scores is accomplished in this detailed, bottom-up manner, the interpretation may be made in the traditional top-down manner, whether it begins with the FSIQ or index scores. Top-down and bottom-up approaches can be used in an integrative way to explore various clinical interpretations. Thus, while the FSIQ can be a clinically meaningful summary of a child's overall cognitive functioning, the subtest scores and index scores can also provide insight into the child's abilities. Targeting the examination to specific abilities can also be informed by information from referral sources. Kamphaus (2001) states that a hypothesized pattern of strengths and weaknesses based on such factors subsequently observed in the test data leads to a more meaningful interpretation than the same pattern identified by comparing all possible test scores. Looking for significant differences between all subtest scores is bound to lead to a statistically significant finding simply because of the number of comparisons being made. This possibility is further confounded comparing score differences based on the statistical analyses of a large standardization sample to the single case (nomethetic or generalized vs idiographic or more personalized comparisons).

There has clearly been a change in emphasis in the evolution of the Wechsler tests from primarily measuring IQ only, to focusing on the five major cognitive abilities assessed by the VC, VS, FR, WM, and PS indexes. This change brings the WISC-V more in line with the psychologist's current need for a test that has implications for description, diagnosis, and prescription.

While the standard procedure for investigating and reporting a child's WISC-V profile may begin at the Full Scale level and then proceed with an analysis of the index and subtest scores, invariably there are times when this is not the best practice to follow. In fact, extreme discrepancies between scores are the more common finding.

In summary, a general intelligence factor is one of the most robust findings in the history of psychology. A century of evidence shows that *g* is substantially related to school achievement as well as a wide variety of real-world outcomes. Some psychometric researchers have suggested that *g* is so robust that it fully accounts for all of the broad cognitive abilities and argue that interpretation should be restricted to the FSIQ alone. Nonetheless, *g* needs to be interpreted within the context of its component abilities. Since each of the WISC-V subtests is predicated on a broader interpretation of the ability being assessed, it is impossible to separate the overall ability from its components. One can't remove WM from FR or verbal comprehension. A second order *g* factor also emerges in all other major intelligence tests including but not limited to the Stanford-Binet, Woodcock-Johnson − IV, Differential Abilities Scales − II, Kaufman Assessment Battery for Children − II, and the Das-Naglieri Cognitive Assessment System.

Arguing the opposite, other researchers state that the FSIQ should never be interpreted because it is simply a mathematical averaging of diverse cognitive functions with different neuropsychological underpinnings.

Our view is that test results showing significant variance among the index scores or subtest scores are not psychometric or clinical problems at all. Rather, the variance in scores within the ability test provides clinical opportunities to gain insight into a child's unique pattern of strengths and weaknesses. When large discrepancies among index scores are present, we recommend reporting the FSIQ, but focusing interpretation solidly on the index scores. Many children have relatively stronger and weaker abilities. For example;

> *The pattern of Aalyah's scores suggests uneven development across various areas of cognitive ability, even though the combination of her abilities gives an Average FSIQ score of 97. In particular, her verbal conceptualization abilities (VCI 109) are much better developed than her visual spatial abilities (VSI 89). Given her strengths, Aalya will likely perform well on tasks involving verbal skills, but find it hard to keep up on visual spatial tasks.*

PERSONIFYING THE PRIMARY ABILITIES: A SIMPLE ANALOGY

In most workplaces, people are hired for specific skills or abilities, and they work together on teams in important ways. Thus, a school team may include a teacher, school psychologist, speech pathologist, nurse, and assistant principal. Each member of the team contributes unique knowledge, skills and abilities to develop the best intervention plan for a struggling learner.

At the risk of oversimplifying, the work of the brain is to learn facts and relationships among them, remember them when needed, and use them to quickly and efficiently solve problems in life. In our analogy the brain has at least five primary team members that correspond, more or less, to the five broad abilities measured by the WISC-V. These team members are the Librarian, Architect, General Manager, Clerk, and Detective.

Verbal Comprehension Index: The Librarian

The library shelves contain all of the verbal knowledge that has been crystallized in the brain. When someone comes into the library looking for information, an expert librarian can help to solve their problem by recommending certain books, so the person can retrieve them and access knowledge relevant to the problem at hand. The knowledgebase of the librarian can be broad and deep, reflecting all of the information that has been acquired through reading, studying, and listening during her or his life. The librarian knows what information may aid in solving a problem.

If the librarian is not effective, the customer will receive information that does not help solve the problem at hand, is only marginally relevant, or maybe misleading. An effective librarian will not only provide the best information relevant to the question but will do so with the minimum amount of information required to complete the job, thus not wasting the customer's valuable time and limited resources.

The VCI mainly measures crystalized knowledge and some verbal reasoning. But the librarian must also know where the information is stored and how to retrieve it. Thus, verbal comprehension assumes adequate long-term retrieval functions as well.

Visual Spatial Index: The Architect

The Architect prepares blueprints to build things by constructing geometric designs based on spatial relationships. Architects have the ability to see how things fit together to form a whole, and how those things can be rearranged to form something different. In some cases they do this by simply matching pieces and parts together, but for other jobs they may need to see these relationships in their mind's eye and imagine how they might fit together differently. This is why it is necessary to hire a trained architect for these jobs rather than a construction site manager who simply matches the job to a blueprint.

An ineffective architect creates blueprints that do not meet building codes, creates structures that are not structurally sound (e.g., does not balance structural load), have limited structural lifespan (e.g., selects wrong materials), are not functional for the stated purpose of the space, or may be esthetically displeasing (e.g., uses wrong combination of visual details). An effective architect efficiently designs structures using the most appropriate structurally sound materials, that are efficient for the required usage and are visually appealing. Visual Spatial Index (VSI) measures visual-spatial reasoning and requires mental rotation and visual WM.

Working Memory Index: The General Manager

The brain is a very busy workplace. It is barraged minute by minute with requests for previous information, new information that needs to be processed, and decisions that must be made. All of these demands can be loosely thought of as "orders from customers" received at a factory. The General Manager controls which customer orders the factory workers pay attention to, based on importance, what work is assigned to which departments within the brain, and in what priority the orders get processed. Once the work is completed, the General Manager makes sure the remaining clutter is cleared from the shop floor so the next job can be processed efficiently.

An ineffective manager can slow order processing by not allocating sufficient resources or misallocating resources, not assigning work to the proper groups, not reserving sufficient space for new orders, or not maintaining an organized workflow and work environment. An effective manager creates strategies to handle low and high work volumes, is organized, allows systems for multitasking, and provides the correct amount of resources to get the job completed.

The WMI measures the ability to sustain focus on incoming stimuli it assigns to the phonological loop or the visual-spatial sketchpad until completely processed, and to clear out facts that are no longer relevant to the next issue processed in order to avoid proactive interference.

Processing Speed Index: The Clerk

The clerk is an often an entry-level employee who is expected only to complete the assigned work as quickly and accurately as possible. The clerk does not decide what to work on. He or she is not expected to make any really important decisions. The job of the clerk is to do what they are told to do, get it done fast, and not make any mistakes. They then move to the next task assigned by the general manager.

An ineffective clerk can incorrectly fill out forms, fail to notice important missing information, or complete work too slowly for organizational efficiency. An efficient clerk completes tasks quickly and efficiently, identifies incomplete, erroneous, or missing information, and quickly learns and adapts to novel procedures. The PSI measures speed of information processing with visual stimuli.

Fluid Reasoning Index: The Detective

The Detective figures things out by considering all the facts, deducing underlying relationships among them, making inductive inferences, and putting relevant facts together to solve the crime (i.e., the problem). Some facts come from the immediate environment (i.e., the crime scene) while other facts are stored in the library (e.g., knowledge of forensics). The Detective relies on the Librarian for relevant facts stored in the library. He or she relies on the Architect to imagine how the items in the room were arranged before the crime. The Detective tells the General Manager which leads to pursue first, and relies on the General Manager to maintain focus on them and selectively ignore facts the Detective deems irrelevant. The Detective relies on the Clerk to process all these facts quickly to solve the problem before the criminal gets away.

A good Detective knows where to look for clues, quickly integrates complex and sometime disparate information into a cohesive understanding of the events of the crime. With this information he or she is able to narrow down a list of possible suspects to the one that committed the crime. A hapless Detective fails to draw upon relevant knowledge, does not visualize relevant scenarios, cannot prioritize or maintain focus on the most relevant facts, does not process the information in the correct priority while it is still current and relevant, and ultimately draws incorrect conclusions from the various facts at hand—perhaps even arresting an innocent person.

The Fluid Reasoning Index (FRI) measures the ability to solve novel problems. It is most closely related to general intelligence, or "g," in that it requires successful integration of multiple cognitive abilities working in concert. For the Detective to be successful, the Librarian, Architect, General Manager, and Clerk must work together as one team with a common goal of solving the problem.

We hope the reader has appreciated our lighthearted attempt at explaining the primary abilities using personifications that are, of course, somewhat unrealistic. To be sure we are taken seriously, however, in Chapter 4, Theoretical and Clinical Foundations of the WISC-V, we discuss in greater depth the abilities measured by each WISC-V primary index in terms of neuropsychological functions, clinical research, models of cognitive information processing, and theories of intelligence.

ISSUES RELATED TO INTERVENTION

Understanding what ability is measured by an index Score is the first step toward planning accommodations for a student who is weak in that ability. Knowing how this weakness would be manifested in daily activities in the classroom is the next step to validating the hypothesized weak ability indicated by the test score.

A first line of intervention is to draw upon the student's strong abilities, be they personal strengths or normative strengths, to compensate for weaker abilities. Now we suggest classroom modifications and teacher-oriented accommodations for children with weaknesses in each of the five major cognitive abilities measured by the WISC-V (VC, VS, FR, WM, and PS). In this regard, weaknesses can either be defined normatively or ipsatively, but it is not necessary that the student be achieving below his or her potential in the context of a discrepancy approach to be considered for one or more of these modifications or accommodations.

Modifications are changes made in the age-appropriate grade-level expectations for a subject or course in order to meet a student's learning needs. These changes might involve developing expectations that reflect the knowledge and skills required in the curriculum for a different grade level, or increasing or decreasing the number or complexity of the regular grade-level curriculum expectations, or both. Thus, we may hear a teacher say that, "Given Bill's limited cognitive ability and that he is functioning three grades below his placement in math, he will require a modified arithmetic program over the next year so he can achieve some proficiency with fundamental math operations."

Accommodations are the special teaching and classroom assessment strategies, human supports or individualized equipment, required to enable a student to learn and to demonstrate learning. Accommodations do not alter the curriculum expectations for the grade. The accommodations that the student requires in connection with instruction, assessment, and functioning in the physical environment may be conceptualized as instructional, environmental, or assessment.

Instructional accommodations are adjustments in teaching strategies required to enable the student to learn and to progress through the curriculum (e.g., Mary will require the use of voice-to-text software to enable her to dictate her assignments to a computer due to her learning disability in written language.).

Environmental accommodations are changes or supports in the physical environment of the classroom or the school, or both (e.g., Greg requires modified seating arrangements in the classroom. Provide him with an alternative quiet area or study carrel where distractions from windows, noise, vents, and disruptive students are minimized.).

Assessment accommodations are adjustments in assessment activities and methods required to enable the student to demonstrate learning (e.g., Crystal will require extra time, up to 150% of the time required to take tests and exams.).

The use of program modifications and accommodations is rooted in a belief that deficits in specific cognitive processes restrict the student's access to the curriculum, and that the cognitive deficit likely cannot be remediated directly. Therefore, the teacher must find ways to teach around the deficit. Empirical support for some of the intervention ideas made in this section is evident (see Gathercole & Alloway, 2008; Gathercole, Lamont, & Alloway, 2006). Yet, many of these intervention ideas are simply suggested teaching tips intended to be tried and used only if they can be demonstrated to work for an individual student. Thus, single case studies are recommended as one method of providing empirical support for the strategies suggested below on a student-by-student basis. Methodologies for single case designs exist and are well accepted. In this case, the methodology would include tracking the student's progress on a series of brief academic probes before and after implementation of one or more of the accommodations or modifications. This can be an effective and powerful methodology for demonstrating empirical support at the student level, and collections of these studies will begin to build a body of evidence. If implemented on a school-wide scale, a data management system that charts progress on frequent academic probes as a function of a series of attempted interventions can be a very powerful administrative and scientific tool. One such software system is AIMSweb (Pearson, 2012).

Selection from among the tips offered here can be made based on the pattern of classroom behaviors observed (see below) for learners who have not responded to standard group-level educational interventions (i.e., Tier II of a three-tier Response to Intervention (RTI) model), or based on patterns of WISC-V test scores for students in, or being considered for special education (i.e., Tier III of a three-tier RTI model).

The hardest part of the job of assessment for the purposes of intervention is to translate test results into appropriate modifications and accommodations to the student's work in the classroom. Yet, this is the function that teachers rely on the most when they refer students for psychological assessment. If there is one major criticism that teachers and other educational personnel make about psychological assessment and the reports that follow, it is that they lack sufficient information to guide the teacher on "what to do next or what to do differently" that will have a positive impact on the child (Mastoras, Climie, McCrimmon, & Schwean, 2011; Schwean et al., 2006).

The interventions tips provided here follow directly from the cognitive abilities that are measured by the WISC-V index Scores. For many children, these strategies will not be sufficient if applied in isolation. Targeted academic interventions are also necessary for specific learning disabilities. Examples are interventions to address weaknesses found in the academic skills of reading, written language, and mathematics. Excellent sources for such interventions are Mather and Jaffe (2002), Naglieri and Pickering (2003), Wendling and Mather (2008), and Mather and Wendling (2012). Further examples are interventions to address executive skills, such as organization, time management, self-regulation, and others. Excellent resources for interventions on executive functions are Hale and Fiorello (2004) and Dawson and Guare (2004).

Evidence on the effectiveness of specific educational and academic interventions is assessed and rated by the US Department of Education through panels of experts organized by the Institute of Educational Services. These reviews and ratings can be found on a website called the What Works Clearinghouse: ies.ed.gov/ncee/wwc/.

The intervention suggestions in this chapter are not intended to replace more targeted educational interventions for specific academic conditions such as dyslexia or written language disorders. Rather, these general strategies are intended to supplement specific academic instructional interventions by providing simple, practical suggestions for teachers whose students may have a weakness in one of the broader cognitive domains measured by the WISC-V.

While the intervention suggestions in this chapter focus on academics, we remind the reader to always consider the whole child. Modifications and accommodations may also be needed in the area of social-emotional and interpersonal functioning. While the cognitive factors do not speak as directly to this, it is important to note that children with cognitive weaknesses may also need accommodation in this emotional area to make them successful in school as well. So a child with low verbal skills may have more difficulty communicating effectively with teachers, parents, and peers. Low FRI scores may mean a child needs more time in understanding and getting comfortable with new social situations, etc. Other factors like inhibitory control, persistence, self-efficacy, grit, and executive functions may also play a role in emotions.

The bulleted lists of classroom indicators, modifications, accommodations, and assessment strategies are reprinted with permission from *The Special Education Handbook: A Practical Guide for All Teachers, Updated,* (Elementary Teachers Federation of Ontario, 2015).

INTERVENTION SUGGESTIONS RELATED TO VERBAL COMPREHENSION

The VCI measures crystallized knowledge and verbal FR. Crystallized intelligence, as measured by the VCI, shows a strong and consistent relationship with the development of reading and math achievement. Contributions of crystallized intelligence to writing achievement are important primarily after age 7. Its contributions to reading, math, and writing achievement become increasingly important for reading and math achievement with age (Berninger & Abbott, 2003; Berninger &Wagner, 2008; Flanagan, Alfonso, Mascolo, & Sotelo-Dynega, 2012; Flanagan & Mascolo, 2005).

A student with needs in these areas has difficulty in understanding oral language, or in expressing himself or herself through oral language, or in both. Classroom indicators of this need in the student's daily performance related to verbal comprehension include:

- Having a limited receptive vocabulary needed to understand words and their meaning, or having a limited expressive vocabulary to express thoughts and ideas using language in terms of correct word meanings, or both;
- having difficulty in listening and comprehending oral language, including gleaning the meanings of phrases, sentences, idiom and colloquialisms, despite adequate attention and auditory processing skills;
- having difficulty in speaking in "real-life" situations in an age-appropriate manner;
- having difficulty with language comprehension and usage, evident in their native language and impacting their learning of a second language in similar ways; and
- having a limited range of general knowledge and subject-specific knowledge, despite indicators of adequate memory functioning. This limitation is evidenced by limited expression of the ideas and knowledge through oral language.

Possible instructional accommodations for children with low verbal comprehension abilities include:

- Keep the language of instruction as simple as possible.
- Provide definitions for all new terms and concepts before teaching the lesson. Be alert for subject-specific terms that the student does not know. Teach the student to keep a separate page at the back of each subject's notebook to write the new terms and their definitions. Advise the student to study the list regularly.
- Teach new vocabulary in the context of information that the student already knows about the topic. Make explicit links to known vocabulary, information, and concepts.

- Provide models for more elaborate language usage when conversing with the student. Respond to their statements by repeating their utterances with revised vocabulary and sentence structure that is more age-appropriate.
- Teach the student how to use the dictionary to look up words to find their meanings. Use grade-appropriate resources, both in book form and electronic format.
- Teach the student how to use a thesaurus to look up words to find synonyms and related words. Use grade-appropriate resources, both in book form and electronic format.
- Ask the student whether he or she understood instructions that were given orally. If he or she did not understand, then
  - paraphrase the instruction using more simple language;
  - explain the terms used in the instruction; and
  - reduce the complexity of the instruction by breaking it down into parts.
- Teach the student to recognize when he or she has not understood an oral instruction or lesson, and to ask for clarification to build understanding.
- Use instructional strategies that are not reliant on language, or that include other formats, such as:
  - Demonstrations and modeling to teach concepts and procedures
  - Hand over hand guidance for young students, coupled with verbal explanations
  - Pictures, graphs, charts
  - Maps, diagrams, flow charts, logic models
  - Semantic webbing maps
- Teach the student to create a visual image of what he or she hears to supplement the language with visual and procedural representations.
- Communicate with parents in writing through notes, the student's agenda book, postings on the class website or chat group, or by email.
- Check for knowledge gaps when teaching new information and concepts that rely on prior knowledge. Where gaps occur, teach the material as though it were new.
- Permit the student to make an audio recording of explanations given to clarify assignments and projects so he or she can replay it while working and getting assistance from a parent or tutor.

Environmental accommodations for children with low verbal comprehension abilities include the following considerations:

- Seat the student near the teacher and away from noise sources.
- Reduce the background noise against which oral language is heard in order to reduce the possibility of distortions of the speech stream.

Classroom assessment strategies for children with low verbal comprehension abilities include:

- Confirm that the student understand the instructions and directions before beginning a test or project.
- Use assessment methods with reduced demands on verbal output, such as true/false, multiple choice, or short answer.
- Reduce the demands for language comprehension when assessing competencies in mathematics and sciences. Use language and structures that scores low in reading level.
- Minimize the requirement for oral presentations.
- Assign projects whose products are visual representations, models, charts and other constructions.

Further intervention strategies related to oral language are available in Dehn (2013).

INTERVENTION SUGGESTIONS RELATED TO VISUAL SPATIAL PROCESSING

The VSI measures visual processing that may be important for doing higher-level or advanced mathematics, such as geometry and calculus (Flanagan & Mascolo, 2005). A student with educational needs related to visual processing has difficulty in organizing visual information into meaningful patterns and understanding how they might change as they rotate and move through space.

Indicators of a need in the student's daily performance related to visual processing may include the following behaviors:

- Having difficulty making visual images to "see something in the mind's eye";
- Having difficulty remembering and differentiating left and right;
- Having difficulty manipulating simple visual patterns or maintaining their orientation to see things in space;
- Having difficulty mentally manipulating objects or visual patterns to see how they would appear if altered or rotated in space;
- Having difficulty in combining disconnected, vague or partially hidden visual information patterns into meaningful wholes;
- Having difficulty finding a path through a spatial field or pattern
- Having difficulty in estimating or comparing visual lengths and distances without measuring them;
- Having difficulty understanding math concepts in geometry, calculus and other higher math;
- Having difficulty in remembering letter formations and letter patterns;
- Having difficulty in reading charts, maps and blueprints and extracting the needed information;

- Having difficulty arranging materials in space, such as in their desks or lockers or rooms at home;
- Missing visual details; and
- Having difficulty copying information from far point, like the blackboard or from near point, like texts.

Possible instructional accommodations for a weakness in visual processing abilities include:

- Reduce the number of visual displays involving manipulative materials, drawings, diagrams and charts that could overwhelm the student, and replace them with clear verbal instructions.
- Explain in words all new skills and concepts, and all graphics and visually-based concepts and tasks.
- Provide the support of clear verbal instructions for tasks requiring spatial organization.
- Encourage student to use verbal mediation to talk themselves through visual or spatial work.
- Teach the student to write from left to right. Use a green for "go" margin on the left side of paper where the student begins to write. Use a red for "stop" line at the right edge of the paper.
- Do not require the student to use any visual strategies that he or she finds confusing, such as webs, diagrams, charts and schemas for math operations.
- Provide activities with manipulative materials, particularly in the primary grades.
- Replace copying from the blackboard with providing copies of the notes or assignments.
- When copying is required, do not require speed. Allow extra time for the student to proofread for accuracy.
- Provide math exercises on worksheets with only a few questions and plenty of white space. Do not require the student to copy problems from the blackboard or textbook.
- Teach the student to use verbal mediation, by saying each word or number or detail when copying from far point to paper.
- Provide extra visual structure on worksheets and assignments. Use organizers like numbered boxes, or color codes where instructions and similar questions have the same color.
- Provide graph paper and lined paper to use for completing math exercises while the student learns how to line up numbers by place value.
- Teach the student how to interpret the organization of a page of text having an unusual format by using numbers to identify the sequence, or colors to link related information.
- Provide Direct Instruction in reading and interpreting maps, graphs, charts, and diagrams.

Environmental Strategies that may be considered when working with children who have visual processing deficits include:

- Keep work space free from extraneous distractions, by removing all visual clutter that is not necessary to the task.
- Ensure that the student clears his or her desk completely before beginning a task. Remove all visual clutter from the work space before assembling the materials needed for the current task.
- Ensure that presentations using colors have enough contrast to be distinguishable in all light conditions.
- Modify color usage in visual presentations to avoid reliance on color coding for students with deficits in color vision.

Classroom assessment strategies for children with weaknesses in visual processing abilities include the following suggestions:

- Put few math questions on each page, with a lot of white space for calculations on math tests.
- Provide manipulative materials when testing concepts involving spatial relationships.
- Emphasize verbal and written answers, rather than charts, diagrams and maps, where possible.
- Permit students to explain spatial information from their perspective without the requirement to rotate it to the examiner's point of regard.
- Reduce the emphasis on charts and mapping, unless that is the skill being taught and evaluated.
- Relax standards of production for art assignments and accept approximations of accepted criteria.
- Do not penalize the student for placing information incorrectly on a page.

Further intervention strategies related to visual-spatial thinkingare available in Dehn (2013).

INTERVENTION SUGGESTIONS RELATED TO FLUID REASONING

The FRI measures FR. FR shows a strong relationship with the development of math achievement, and contributes moderately to the development of reading skills. In the elementary grades it contributes moderately to basic writing skills, and at all ages it relates to written expression (Flanagan & Mascolo, 2005). A student with needs related to FR has difficulty when faced with relatively novel tasks that require reasoning, recognizing and forming concepts, and drawing inferences (Elementary Teachers' Federation of Ontario, 2015).

Indicators of this need in the student's daily performance related to FR may include:

- Having difficulty recognizing, forming and understanding concepts;
- Having difficulty perceiving relationships among patterns;
- Having difficulty drawing inferences from information that is presented;
- Having difficulty understanding the implications of an issue or an action;
- Having difficulty with complex problem solving and concept formation;
- Having difficulty understanding and using "and logic";
- Having difficulty understanding and using "or logic";
- Having difficulty with extrapolating, or following a logical pattern through to another conclusion;
- Having difficulty with quantitative reasoning needed for understanding and computing mathematics;
- Relying heavily on the use of language to aid in their comprehension of concepts and to solve problems that are new to them and cannot be solved automatically;
- Having difficulty understanding the Piagetian concepts of conservation and classification; and
- Having difficulty transferring and generalizing information to new situations.

Consider the following instructional strategies when working with children who demonstrate a weakness in FR in the perceptual domain:

- Provide verbal instructions to all tasks (assuming verbal skills are adequate).
- Use teaching approaches that promote the development of self-talk to mediate all tasks.
- Rely on the student's verbal memory skills to teach problem-solving through repetition and rote recall.
- Present concepts and procedures verbally, in a straightforward fashion to ensure comprehension.
- Teach strategies for solving problems, paying close attention to the proper sequence of events that can be memorized as verbal instructions.
- Provide repetition and review of concepts to ensure over-learning. Check that a student's memory for material includes comprehension.
- Teach mechanical arithmetic in a systematic, verbal, step-by-step fashion.
- Use real objects and manipulative materials, along with verbal descriptions to teach concepts.
- Teach strategies to increase understanding and retention of concepts, including:
  - self-talk, so the student guides himself or herself through the problem verbally; and
  - lists of procedures or steps to follow.
- Teach problem-solving techniques in the contexts in which they are most likely to be applied.

- Teach and emphasize reading comprehension skills as early as possible so the student may rely on reading and rereading to ensure comprehension of concepts.
- Teach verbal strategies that will help them to organize their written work into sequential steps.
- Structure and adjust the difficulty level of the task, where possible.
- Explain homework and assignments in a sequential, step by step, fashion.
- When teaching concepts or providing instructions, avoid:
  - complicated and lengthy instructions and directions
  - figurative language, since the student is likely to interpret language literally
  - complex instructions.
- Watch for associated problems with organizational skills and follow instructional strategies for organization, if needed.
- Watch for associated problems with social skills, and provide interventions, if needed.

For children with deficits in FR there are no obvious environmental strategies. However, the following classroom assessment strategies may be considered:

- Initially, rely more on verbal instructions and less on charts, maps and diagrams.
- Pair verbal explanations with visual material to make use of the child's relative strength in verbal reasoning to help them learn how to interpret and organize visual information.
- Ask clear, specific questions, rather than asking open-ended questions or asking students to make inferences.
- Rely more on verbal responses and less on the production of charts, maps and diagrams.
- Test for knowledge of the material, where possible.
- Ask student to show all of their work (e.g., complete math calculations, or the outline for a long answer). Give partial marks for the process they followed.
- Provide a scoring rubric to the student so he or she knows how many marks they got for their knowledge, and how many they got for applications and problem solving using the knowledge.

Further intervention strategies related to FR are available in Dehn (2013).

INTERVENTION SUGGESTIONS RELATED TO WORKING MEMORY

How do marked WM deficits affect classroom activities? Two observational studies are informative. The first study involved a group of children with low WM but typical scores in general ability measures (Gathercole, Alloway, Willis, & Adams, 2006). Compared with classmates with typical WM skills, the low WM children frequently forgot instructions, struggled to cope with tasks involving simultaneous processing and storage, and they lost track of their place in complex tasks. The most common consequence of these failures was that the children abandoned the activity without completing it. A detailed description of common characteristics of low WM children in the classroom can be found in Gathercole and Alloway (2008) and Gathercole et al. (2006). The second observational study by these authors drew a selection of children from the screening study described above. They were observed in mainstream primary classrooms in demographically diverse areas that included children with either low or average WM skills. Examples of frequently observed behaviors that corresponded to WM deficits included: "The child raised his hand but when called upon, he had forgotten his response"; "She lost her place in a task with multiple steps"; and "The child had difficulty remaining on task." Children with poor WM struggled in many classroom activities, simply because they were unable to hold in mind sufficient information to allow them to complete the task. Losing crucial information from WM caused them to forget many things: instructions they were attempting to follow, the details of what they were doing, and the next step in a complicated task.

In the observational study described above (Gathercole et al., 2006), children with poor WM function often gravitated toward lower-level strategies with lower processing requirements resulting in reduced general efficiency. For example, instead of using number aids such as blocks and number lines to reduce processing demands, these children relied on more error-prone strategies like simple counting instead.

Frequent failures of children with low memory to meet the WM demands of classroom activities may be at least one cause of the poor academic progress that is typical for them. If the children cannot store and manipulate information in WM, their progress in acquiring complex knowledge and skills in areas such as literacy and mathematics will be slow and difficult.

For a review of WM, from theories to assessment approaches and measures, to its impact on various academic skills to intervention strategies for WM, see Dehn (2008) and Dehn (2015). A further resource is Alloway (2011). Further intervention strategies related to WM are available in Dehn (2013).

Indicators of difficulties with WM may include the following behaviors:

- Having difficulty following directions beyond the first steps;
- Forgetting what they have to do next;
- Difficulty with sentence writing;
- Losing his or her place in complex activities;
- Having difficulty with writing sentences or paragraphs;

- Having difficulty with mathematics computations that involve more than one step, such as long division; and
- Having difficulty attending to and immediately recalling information they have just seen or heard.

There are several possible interventions and instructional accommodations for children with WM difficulties. The ideal solution to ameliorate the learning difficulties resulting from impairments in WM would be to remediate the memory impairment directly. There is increasing evidence that directly training WM with digital WM training programs such as CogMed can lead to improvement on nontrained WM tasks (Holmes, Gathercole, & Place, 2009; Klingberg, Fernell, Olesen, Johnson, & Gustafsson, 2005; Klingberg, Forsberg, & Westerberg, 2002) and perhaps in academic attainment as well (Dahlin, Holmes, Gathercole, & Dunning, 2009; Holmes, Gathercole, & Dunning, 2009). These programs capitalize on the well-accepted principle of neuroplasticity, which postulates that the brain can grow new connections based on experience. WM training programs are indirectly supported by basic neuroimaging research that relates increases in cognitive ability to the development of cortical thickness in healthy children and adolescents (Burgaleta, Johnson, Waber, Colom, & Karama, 2014), Nonetheless some researchers remain unconvinced (Melby-Lervåg & Hulme, 2012), and the debate continues (Schinaver, Entwistle, & Soderqvist, 2014).

The active ingredients of WM training programs are carefully constructed tasks that directly stress the WM structures, algorithms that constantly adjust item difficulty to the upper limit of the student's ability, and effective coaching to keep students motivated during the training. When implemented with fidelity, the CogMed program can be an effective adjunct to a comprehensive psychoeducational intervention program. However, it is unreasonable to expect achievement to improve immediately when WM abilities remediate. Rather, once the students WM capacities increase, he or she may be better able to access the curriculum through effective instruction over the following semester.

Thus, in addition to direct training, we recommend a number of classroom management techniques to minimize memory-related failures in classroom-based learning activities frequently experienced by children with WM impairments.

- First, ensure that the child can remember what he or she is doing, to avoid failure to complete all steps of a learning activity. Strategies include:
  - Use instructions that are as brief and simple as possible. Break instructions down into individual steps where possible.
  - Repeat the instructions frequently.
  - For tasks that take place over an extended period of time, remind the child of crucial information for that phase of the task instead of repeating the original instruction.

- Ask the child to repeat critical instructions back to you.
- Since children often have good insight into their WM failures, check with the child to make sure he or she remembers what to do.
- To help students to follow instructions:
  - Give brief and simple instructions with limited extraneous verbalization.
  - Break down instructions into simple steps when possible. Use numbered points for any sequence.
  - Reduce the number of steps given at one time.
  - Repeat instructions frequently.
  - Ask the child to repeat the instructions to ensure that they are remembered.
  - Give specific reminders targeted to the current step of a multistep task.
- To prevent a child from losing his or her place in a complex task:
  - Decompose tasks into discrete steps.
  - Encourage older students to practice and actively use memory aids
  - Provide support for use of external memory aids.
  - Encourage student to ask for forgotten information.
- To improve the learning successes of individuals with poor WM skills teach them self-help strategies to promote their development as independent learners who can identify and support their own learning needs. Teach them to develop effective strategies to cope with WM failures, including:
  - Encourage the child to ask for forgotten information where necessary
  - Train the child in the use of memory aids.
  - Encourage the child to continue with a complex task rather than abandon it, even if some of the steps are not completed due to memory failure.
- Provide supports for spelling frequently occurring words. This will prevent children from losing their place in the complex task of writing activities.
  - Reducing the processing load and opportunity for error in spelling individual words will increase the child's success in completing the sentence as a whole.
  - Making available spellings of key words on the child's own desk rather than on a distant board may reduce these errors by making the task of locating key information easier and reducing opportunities for distraction.
  - Develop ways of marking the child's place in word spellings as a means of reducing place-keeping errors during copying.
- For writing tasks:
  - Reduce the linguistic complexity of sentences to be written.
  - Simplify the vocabulary of sentences to be written.

- Reduce length of sentences to be written.
- For older students, introduce the use of outlines and techniques to keep place in the outline when writing.
- Teach memory aids, such as verbal mediation or rehearsal, and mnemonic strategies, such as:
  - Dracula's Mother Sucks Blood, to cue the order of operations in long division (Divide, Multiply, Subtract, and Bring down)
  - Every Good Boy Deserves Fudge, for the names of the lines in the treble clef music staff
  - The method of loci to match items with landmarks on the route to school
- Teach student to use lists, advance organizers, and personal planners as aids to memory.
- Communicate frequently with parents about school activities, equipment needed, homework and assignments through a communication book, a class website or chat group, or regular email.
- Provide notes to the student from presentations and lectures.

Environmental accommodations for children with WM problems:

- Reduce opportunities for distraction and reduce the number of distractions in the vicinity.
- Provide visual reminders and other memory supports for multistep tasks
- Attach the student's daily schedule or timetable to the notebook cover that the child takes home every day.
- Post the student's daily schedule or timetable on the student's desk or classroom wall. Send a copy of the schedule or timetable home for posting in the student's room or on the fridge.

Assessment accommodations:

- Allow the student to use appropriate memory supports during testing. Supports typically provide information about procedures to use, rather than providing content that the student should know.
- Use open-ended questions with more than one correct answer to allow for marks for anything the student remembers.
- Reduce the demands on WM on tests by providing a structure and outline for responding.

INTERVENTION SUGGESTIONS RELATED TO PROCESSING SPEED

PS shows a strong relationship with the development of reading and math achievement, especially during the elementary school years when children are learning the skills in reading and math, and developing speed and automaticity in their use (Flanagan & Mascolo, 2005). Older school children use these basic academic skills with automaticity, and integrate them with more complex tasks such as problem-solving, subject-focused writing, and complex reading. When mental efficiency in focusing concentration is required, students with slower PS have difficulty performing simple cognitive tasks fluently and automatically. Indicators of this need in the student's daily performance related to the speed with which he or she processes information and completes tasks include:

- being slow to perform basic arithmetic operations, not learning the times tables, and not attaining automaticity in calculations and so uses fingers or counters;
- taking longer to complete assignments in class;
- not finishing tests and exams within the time allotted;
- not finishing a copying exercise within the time allotted;
- reading slowly;
- taking even more time to complete tasks under pressure; and
- coming to the right answer, but taking longer to do it.

Consider the following possible instructional accommodations when PS is a weakness:

- Allow the student longer response times:
  - to respond orally to questions asked in class;
  - to make decisions when offered a choice of activities; and
  - to complete assignments in class.
- Do not require the student to work under time pressure.
- Reduce the quantity of work assigned in favor of quality.
- When copying is required, do not require speed. Allow extra time for the student to proofread for accuracy.
- Provide the student with ample time to complete his or her work, or shorten the assignment so it can be accomplished within the time allotted.
- Provide extra time for the student to complete in-class assignments in a way that does not bring negative attention to him or her.
- Shorten drill and practice assignments that have a written component by requiring fewer repetitions of each concept.
- Provide copies of notes rather than requiring the student to copy from the board in a limited timeframe.
- Provide instruction to increase the student's reading speed by training reading fluency and ability to recognize common letter sequences automatically that are used in print and sight vocabulary.
- Teach the student how to monitor time spent on each task. The student could use a stopwatch or timer. He or she could record the start and end times on paper. Set a goal for the student to gradually reduce the time needed to do each task.

- Provide timed activities to build speed and automaticity with basic skills, such as:
  - reading a list of high-frequency words as fast as possible;
  - calculating simple math facts as fast as possible;
  - learning simple math calculations through flash cards and educational software exercises;
  - charting daily performance for speed and accuracy.

In the classroom and other settings where the student does tasks such as homework provide environmental accommodations:

- Reduce environmental distractions to improve performance.

When taking tests in the classroom consider the following strategies for assessment accommodations to obtain maximum performance:

- Emphasize accuracy rather than speed in evaluating the student in all subject areas.
- Do not use timed tests for evaluation. Instead, use assessment procedures that do not rely on speed.
- Allow a specified amount of extra time for tests and exams (usually time and a half).
- Provide supervised breaks during tests and exams.
- Break long tests into more sittings of shorter duration across a few days.
- Provide a reader or text-to-voice app to read test and exam questions to a student to accommodate for slow reading fluency.
- Provide a voice-to-text app to record the student's answers on tests to accommodate for slow writing fluency.
- Use test and exam formats with reduced written output formats to accommodate for slow writing fluency.
  - Examples include: multiple choice formats, true/false formats, and short answer formats where a student fills in the blank.

Further intervention strategies related to PS are available in Dehn (2013).

COMMENTS ON INTERVENTION SUGGESTIONS

Younger children have a lot of support available in the classroom in the form of various aids, such as visual displays of number lines, letters, and rhymes. Once children get older, learning becomes more autonomous and there are fewer opportunities to rely on external supports. For instance, while memory aids such as dictionaries and spelling charts are still available, there is less repetition of instructions, fewer visual cues such as number lines or multiplication tables, and more individual rather than group or supervised activities. At the same time, instructions get lengthier, classroom lessons get more complex, and specific cognitive demands become greater. The combination of these factors can serve to widen the gap in performance between children with average abilities and those with specific impairments as they grow into adolescence and enter middle and high school settings.

The strategies described above for modifying the environment and classroom assessment demands and differentiating the style of instruction are appropriate for children of all ages. For some children with cognitive processing deficits these modifications and accommodations are necessary to ensure that they have equal access to the curriculum. As these children age, however, they need to be directly taught compensatory strategies that they can employ on their own across environments. Thus, general recommendations for improving the learning successes of children with a weakness in one or the domains of cognitive ability are to encourage them to develop their own learning strategies and to take advantage of available classroom resources. Strategies may include encouraging the child to ask for forgotten information where necessary, training the child in the use of memory aids, and encouraging the child to continue with complex tasks rather than abandon them, even if some of the steps are not completed due to memory failure. Providing the child with such self-help strategies will promote development as independent learners able to identify and support their own learning needs. The following case example provides a clear demonstration.

Case Example

Mariana is a 10-year old girl with an impairment of WM. Her teacher requested a psychoeducational assessment when she observed that Mariana's achievement and progress in class were somewhat variable. She showed difficulty when required to use both new and previously acquired information to address new questions and especially to then continue to build on these themes by revisiting and modifying previous solutions. These difficulties were observed in subjects ranging from social studies to mathematics, and seemed to occur mainly when the task involved more "mental" than "paper and pencil" work.

The psychologist reported that Mariana's earned average scores on the WISC-V were VCI (104), VSI (110), FRI (98), and PSI (99). However, her WMI (82) was significantly lower compared to her average scores on the other index scores. The base rate tables showed that very few children in the average ability range demonstrated such a large discrepancy between the WMI and VCI and VSI. Of particular interest was that Digit Span Backwards (DSB) and Digit Span Sequencing (DSS) were both relatively weak scores for Mariana in contrast to average Digit Span Forward (DSF). Thus, her classroom achievement, under particular learning conditions, was being compromised by her verbal WM difficulties. Mariana's classroom learning will require support with visual prompts and cues as well as the pacing of material. She will also require support to develop strategies for managing tasks that require greater demands on verbal WM.

(Continued)

(Continued)

Mariana was observed in a numeracy lesson in which there were 10 pupils of relatively similar ability who were split into 2 groups. The lesson began with the children sitting at their tables for the "mental math" session in which the class played "What number am I?" The teacher reminded the children how to play the game as she encouraged them to ask focused questions about the number she was thinking of. She modeled examples of questions that could be asked to help the children work out her number, for example, "Is the number less than 20?" and emphasized the use of specific mathematical vocabulary before giving volunteers the opportunity to lead the game.

Mariana participated well when asking questions about other pupils' numbers, though she did ask the same type of question each time. Her questions were all based on an example that had been modeled by the teacher, for example, "If I partition it, will it be 30 and 3? Does it partition into 20 and 4? Does it partition into 70 and 2?" She was also keen to take the leading role partway through the game. However, as soon as the other pupils began to ask questions about her number, she quickly lost her enthusiasm to participate. When asked, "Does the number have 8 tens?" Mariana did not respond. The teacher repeated the question and reminded her to think of the place value of her number, giving the prompts "Does your number have tens? Do you know how many tens there are?" Mariana was evidently struggling to hold the number in mind while attempting to answer questions about it. She eventually told the teacher that she had forgotten it. At this point, the teacher spent a few minutes revising the concept of place value. She referred the children to the 100 square and the place value chart as she asked key questions such as "How many tens does a number in the eighties have?" and "If a number has six tens, which row do we to point to on the 100 square?" Mariana successfully answered this question, making good use of the visual aids available.

As this took place, the teacher constantly repeated crucial information such as the key vocabulary (more than, less than) and asked target questions to help the children gain greater understanding of the concepts being taught. For example, "If we are working out ten more or ten less than a number, which part of the number changes?" She often directed such questions toward Mariana to support her thinking processes. For instance, "When thinking about 10 less than 307, Mariana, which part of the number will stay the same?"

Mariana correctly stated, "7."

"Which part of the number will change?"

Mariana replied, "The 30. It gives 29."

As this main part of the lesson developed, Mariana became increasingly more distracted and appeared to lose total concentration. She began to swing on her chair, talk to her neighbor, and shout out random comments unrelated to the task. The teacher reminded Mariana on several occasions to follow the usual classroom routines and actually stopped the class at one point to reinforce her expectations of behavior: "Stop talking. Put your pens down. Listen to me when I'm talking and put your hand up if you have something to say."

(Continued)

(Continued)

These instructions were clearly delineated by the teacher as she simultaneously pointed to the classroom rules displayed on the wall, thus allowing the children time to store and process the information.

During the lesson, students were challenged to perform simple calculations using some of the mental strategies taught in previous lessons. They were encouraged to use the tables' charts, number lines, and 100 square and to note key information on their whiteboards to help them in their calculations. Mariana responded well and made excellent use of these visual strategies to support her WM. For example, she regularly referred to the poster to help her remember multiplication facts, used her fingers to count on from a given number when performing additions, and used diagrams to calculate divisions.

Here, we see that the teacher regularly repeated key questions to Mariana to support working memory, so that she would not fall behind in understanding the mathematical concepts. This is also a good example of how to encourage children to develop and use strategies to support their learning as Mariana was able to complete the activity on her own.

REFERENCES

Alloway, T. P. (2011). *Supporting improving working memory: Supporting students; learning.* London: Sage Publications Ltd.

Berninger, V., & Abbott, S. (2003). *PAL research supported reading and writing lessons.* San Antonio: Pearson.

Berninger, V., & Wagner, R. (2008). *Best practices for school psychology assessment and intervention in reading and writing, . Best Practices in School Psychology V* (Vol. 4, pp. 1205–1219). Bethesda, WA: National Association of School Psychologists, Chapter 74.

Brooks, B. L., Holdnack, J. A., & Iverson, G. L. (2011). Advanced clinical interpretation of the WAIS-IV and WMS-IV: Prevalence of low scores varies by intelligence and years of education. *Assessment, 18*(2), 156–167.

Burgaleta, M., Johnson, W., Waber, D., Colom, R., & Karama, S. (2014). Cognitive ability changes and dynamics of cortical thickness development in healthy children and adolescents. *Neuroimage, 84,* 810–819.

Canivez, G. L., & Kush, J. C. (2013). WISC-IV and WAIS-IV structural validity: Alternate methods, alternate results. Commentary on Weiss et al. (2013a) and Weiss et al. (2013b). *Journal of Psychoeducational Assessment, 31*(2), 157–169.

Canivez, G. L., & Watkins, M. W. (2010). Investigation of the factor structure of the Wechsler Adult Intelligence Scale–Fourth Edition (WISC-IV): Adolescent subsample. *School Psychology Quarterly, 25,* 223–235.

Carroll, J. B. (1993). *Human cognitive abilities: A survey of factor-analytic studies.* New York, NY: Cambridge University Press.

Cattell, R. B. (1987). *Intelligence: Its structure, growth, and action.* New York, NY: North-Holland.

Claeys, J. (2013). Theory and research: The nexus of clinical inference. *Journal of Psychoeducational Assessment, 31*(2), 170–174.

Dahlin, K. I. E., Holmes, J., Gathercole, S., & Dunning, D. (2009). Adaptive training leads to sustained enhancement of poor working memory in children. Developmental Science. *Reading and Writing*. Available from https://doi.org/10.1007/s11145-010-9238-y.

Daniel, M. H. (2007). "Scatter" and the construct validity of FSIQ: Comment on Fiorello et. al. (2007). *Applied Neuopsychology*, *14*(4), 291−295.

Dawson, P., & Guare, R. (2004). *Executive skills in children and adolescents: A practical guide to assessment and intervention*. New York, NY: The Guilford Press.

Deary, I. J., Strand, S., Smith, P., & Fernandes, C. (2007). Intelligence and educational achievement. *Intelligence*, *35*, 13−21.

Dehn, M. J. (2008). *Working memory and academic learning: Assessment and intervention strategies*. New York, NY: John Wiley and Sons, Inc.

Dehn, M. J. (2013). *Essentials of processing assessment (2nd ed.)*. New York, NY: John Wiley and Sons, Inc.

Dehn, M. J. (2015). *Essentials of working memory assessment and intervention*. New York, NY: John Wiley and Sons, Inc.

Elementary Teachers' Federation of Ontario. (2015). *Special education handbook: A practical guide for all teachers, Updated*. Toronto, ON: Elementary Teachers' Federation of Ontario (ETFO).

Flanagan, D. P., & Kaufman, A. S. (2004). *Essentials of WISC-IV assessment*. New York, NY: Wiley.

Flanagan, D. P., & Mascolo, J. T. (2005). Psychoeducational assessment and learning disability diagnosis. In D. P. Flanagan, & P. Harrison (Eds.), *Contemporary intellectual assessment: Theories, tests, and issues, second edition* (pp. 521−544). New York, NY: The Guilford Press.

Flanagan, D. P., Alfonso, V. C., Mascolo, J. T., & Sotelo-Dynega, M. (2012). Use of ability tests in the identification of specific learning disability within the context of an operational definition. In D. P. Flanagan, & P. L. Harrison (Eds.), *Contemporary intellectual assessment* (third ed.). New York, NY: The Guilford Press.

Gathercole, S. E., & Alloway, T. P. (2008). *Working memory & learning: A practical guide*. London: Sage Press.

Gathercole, S. E., Alloway, T. P., Willis, C., & Adams, A. M. (2006). Working memory in children with reading disabilities. *Journal of Experimental Child Psychology*, *93*, 265−281.

Gathercole, S. E., Lamont, E., & Alloway, T. P. (2006). Working memory in the classroom. In S. Pickering (Ed.), *Working memory and education* (pp. 219−240). Elsevier Press.

Georgas, J., Weiss, L. G., van de Vijver, F. J. R., & Saklofske, D. H. (2003). *Culture and children's intelligence: Cross-cultural analyses of the WISC-III*. San Diego, CA: Academic Press.

Gottfredson, L. S. (1997). Why g matters: The complexity of everyday life. *Intelligence*, *24*, 79−132.

Gottfredson, L. S. (1998). The general intelligence factor. *Scientific American Presents*, *9*, 24−29.

Hale, J. B., Fiorello, C. A., Kavanagh, J. A., Holdnack, J. A., & Aloe, A. M. (2007). Is the demise of IQ interpretation justified? A response to special issue authors. *Applied Neuropsychology*, *14*(1), 37−51.

Hale, J. B., & Fiorello, C. A. (2004). *School neuropsychology: A practitioners' handbook*. New York, NY: The Guilford Press.

Harris, J. G., & Llorente, A. M. (2005). Cultural considerations in the use of the WISC-IV. In A. Prifitera, D. H. Saklofske, & L. G. Weiss (Eds.), *WISC-IV clinical use and interpretation: Scientist-practitioner perspectives* (pp. 381−413).

Holmes, J., Gathercole, S., Place, M., et al. (2009). Working memory deficits can be overcome: Impacts of training and medication on working memory in children with ADHD. *Applied Cognitive Psychology*. Available from https://doi.org/10.1002/acp.1589. (www.interscience.wiley.com).

Holmes, J., Gathercole, S. E., & Dunning, D. L. (2009). Adaptive training leads to sustained enhancement of poor working memory in children. *Developmental Science*, *12*(4), F9−F15.

Kamphaus, R. W. (1998). Intelligence test interpretation: Acting in the absence of evidence. In A. Prifitera, & D. H. Saklofske (Eds.), *WISC-III clinical use and interpretation: Scientist-practitioner perspectives* (pp. 39−57). San Diego, CA: Academic Press.

Kamphaus, R. W. (2001). *Clinical assessment of child and adolescent intelligence* (2nd ed). Needham Heights, MA: Allyn & Bacon.

Kaplan, E. (1988). A process approach to neuropsychological assessment. In T. Boll, & B. K. Bryant (Eds.), *Clinical neuropsychology and brain function: Research, measurement, and practice* (pp. 129−231). Washington, DC: American Psychological Association.

Kaufman, A. S. (2013). Intelligent testing with Wechsler's fourth editions: Perspectives on the Weiss et al. studies and the eight commentaries. *Journal of Psychoeducational Assessment*, *31*(2), 224−234.

Klingberg, T., Fernell, E., Olesen, P. J., Johnson, M., Gustafsson, P., et al. (2005). Computerized training of working memory in children with ADHD—A randomized, controlled trial. *Journal of the American Academy of Child and Adolescent Psychiatry*, *44*, 177−186.

Klingberg, T., Forsberg, H., & Westerberg, H. (2002). Training working memory in children with ADHD. *Journal of Clinical and Experimental Neuropsychology*, *24*, 781−791.

Kuncel, N. R., Hezlett, S. A., & Ones, D. S. (2004). Academic performance, career potential, creativity, and job performance: Can one construct predict them all? *Journal of Personality and Social Psychology*, *86*, 148−161.

Kvist, A. V., & Gustafsson, J. E. (2008). The relation between fluid intelligence and the general factor as a function of cultural background: A test of Cattell's investment theory. *Intelligence*, *36*, 422−436.

Lezak, M. D. (1988). IQ: RIP. *Journal of Clinical and Experimental Neuropsychology*, *10*, 351−361.

Lezak, M. D., Howieson, D. B., & Loring, D. W. (2004). In H. J. Hannay, & J. S. Fischer (Eds.), *Neuropsychological assessment* (4th ed.). New York, NY: Oxford University Press.

Mastoras, S. M., Climie, E. A., McCrimmon, A. W., & Schwean, V. L. (2011). A C.L.E.A.R. approach to report writing: A framework for improving the efficacy of psychoeducational reports. *Canadian Journal of School Psychology*, *26*, 127−147.

Mather, N., & Jaffe, L. E. (2002). *Woodcock-Johnson III reports, recommendations and strategies*. New York, NY: John Wiley & Sons.

Mather, N., & Wendling, B. J. (2012). *Linking cognitive abilities to academic interventions. In contemporary intellectual assessment* (3rd ed.). New York, NY: The Guilford Press.

Melby-Lervåg, M., & Hulme, C. (2012). Is working memory training effective? A meta-analytic review. *Developmental Psychology*, *49*(2), 270−291.

Naglieri, J. A., & Pickering, E. B. (2003). *Helping children learn: Intervention handouts for use in school and at home*. Baltimore, MD: Paul H. Brookes Publishing Co.

Oakland, T., Glutting, J., & Watkins, M. W. (2005). Assessment of test behaviors with the WISC-IV. In A. Prifitera, D. H. Saklofske, & L. G. Weiss (Eds.), *WISC-IV clinical use and interpretation: Scientist-practitioner perspectives* (pp. 435−463). San Diego, CA: Academic Press.

Pearson. (2012). *Aimsweb technical manual*. Available at <http://www.aimsweb.com/resources/research-articles-and-information>.

Prifitera, A., Saklofske, D. H., & Weiss, L. G. (2005). *WISC-IV clinical use and interpretation: Scientist-practitioner perspectives*. San Diego, CA: Academic Press.

Prifitera, A., Saklofske, D. H., & Weiss, L. G. (2008). *WISC-IV clinical assessment and intervention 2e*. San Diego, CA: Academic Press.

Reynolds, M. R., & Keith, T. Z. (2013). Measurement and statistical issues in child assessment research. In C. R. Reynolds (Ed.), *Oxford handbook of child and adolescent assessment*. New York, NY: Oxford University Press.

Sattler, J. M., & Dumont, R. (2004). *Assessment of children: WISC-IV and WPPSI-III supplement*. San Diego, CA: Author.

Sattler, J. M. (2008). *Assessment of children: Cognitive foundations* (5th ed.). San Diego, CA: Author.

Schinaver, C. S., Entwistle, P. C., & Soderqvist, S. (2014). CogMed WM training: Reviewing the reviewers. *Applied Neuropsychology: Child, 3*(3), 163–172.

Schwean, V. L., Oakland, T., Weiss, L. G., Saklofske, D. H., Holdnack, J., & Prifitera, A. (2006). Report writing: A child-centered approach. In L. G. Weiss, D. H. Saklofske, A. Prifitera, & J. Holdnack (Eds.), *WISC-IV advanced clinical interpretation*. San Diego, CA: Elsevier.

Squalli, J., & Wilson, K. (2014). Intelligence, creativity, and innovation. *Intelligence, 46*, 250–257.

Watkins, M. W., Glutting, J. J., & Lei, P. W. (2007). Validity of the full-scale IQ when there is significant variability among WISC-III and WISC-IV factor scores. *Applied Neuropsychology, 14*, 13–20.

Wechsler, D. (2014). *Manual for the Wechsler intelligence scale for children − Fifth edition*. San Antonio, TX: Pearson.

Weiss, L. G., Saklofske, D. H., Prifitera, A., & Holdnack, J. A. (2006). *WISC-IV: Advanced clinical interpretation*. San Diego, CA: Academic Press.

Wendling, B. J., & Mather, N. (2008). *Essentials of evidence based interventions*. New York, NY: Wiley.

Chapter 3

A School Neuropsychological Approach to Interpretation of the WISC-V Integrated

Daniel C. Miller

Woodcock Institute for the Advancement of Neurocognitive Research and Applied Practice, Texas Woman's University, Denton, TX, United States

ADVANCED CLINICAL INTERPRETATION OF THE WECHSLER INTELLIGENCE SCALE FOR CHILDREN—FIFTH EDITION INTEGRATED

The purpose of this chapter is to review neuropsychological and process-oriented interpretative approaches for the Wechsler Intelligence Scale for Children—Fifth Edition Integrated (WISC-V Integrated: Wechsler & Kaplan, 2015) test scores. A case study is also presented at the end of the chapter to illustrate how the two tests can be used in clinical practice. The WISC-V (Wechsler, 2014) is a compilation of tests designed to measure various aspects of cognitive or intellectual functioning. "Administration of the WISC-V often serves as baseline assessment for a broader test battery" (Miller & Jones, 2016, p. 459). Hypotheses may be generated about strengths and weaknesses from the initial WISC-V results and then additional measures administered to support or nullify those hypotheses. If clinicians want to use the WISC-V as part of a comprehensive neuropsychological assessment, they should ideally be familiar with the WISC-V Integrated. "The WISC-V Integrated is designed to systematically test the limits for various tests from the WISC-V and provide clinicians with more clinically relevant qualitative information about the examinee's performance" (Miller & Jones, 2016, p. 459).

The WISC-V Integrated (Wechsler & Kaplan, 2015) reflects the revision of the WISC-IV Integrated (Wechsler, 2004) and the updated process assessment approach tasks and procedures originally used in the WISC-III as a Processing Instrument (WISC-PI: Kaplan, Fein, Kramer, Delis, & Morris, 1999). Werner (1937) proposed that understanding the problem-solving

55

strategies employed by an examinee on a task may be more useful than the obtained quantitative test score. Edith Kaplan and her colleagues at the Boston Veterans Administration Medical Center expanded and refined Werner's work. Their approach was termed the Boston Process Approach (Milberg & Hebben, 2013), and is now referred to as the process approach in general. The goal of the process approach is to evaluate the underlying cognitive processes and test taking behaviors that can help explain poor test performance, by systematically altering task demands. The process approach has been used in clinical neuropsychology to identify strengths and weaknesses and to develop evidence-based interventions.

THE WECHSLER INTELLIGENCE SCALE FOR CHILDREN—FIFTH EDITION INTEGRATED TEST

The WISC-V Integrated is suitable for children between the ages of 6:0 and 16:11 years. The test is designed to be an extension of the WISC-V and not designed to be a standalone battery. As standard practice, any time a WISC-V subtest score is below average compared to other WISC-V subtest scores, and a related WISC-V Integrated subtest is available, that additional WISC-V Integrated test should be administered. The WISC-V Integrated is comprised of 14 subtests. Eight of the subtests are adaptations of WISC-V subtests. These adapted subtests contain the same items found on the WISC-V, but the presentation or response modes are changed, and/or the administration of the items is modified. The eight WISC-V adapted subtests on the WISC-V Integrated include: Similarities Multiple Choice, Vocabulary Multiple Choice, Picture Vocabulary Multiple Choice, Figure Weights Process Approach, Arithmetic Process Approach, and Written Arithmetic. The WISC-V Integrated Block Design Multiple Choice and Cancellation Abstract subtests are variations of the original WISC-V subtests. These variations make the WISC-V Integrated version of the task similar to the WISC-V version, but item content is different, and presentation or response mode and/or the test procedures are modified. Coding Recall and Coding Copy are unique to the WISC-V Integrated and are designed to "test the limits" of the WISC-V Coding test performance. Spatial Span and Sentence Recall are unique to the WISC-V Integrated and are designed to strengthen the coverage of the working memory construct when used in combination with the WISC-V (Raiford, 2017). The relationship between the WISC-V and WISC-V Integrated tests is illustrated in Table 3.1.

Integrated School Neuropsychology/Cattell Horn Carroll Interpretative Model

The Integrated School Neuropsychology (SNP)/Cattell Horn Carroll (CHC) framework was introduced by Miller (2013) as a way to conceptually group cross-battery assessment data into specific cognitive functions and to link

TABLE 3.1 WISC-V Integrated Framework

Domain	WISC-V Subtest	WISC-V Integrated Subtest	Derived Index Score
Verbal Comprehension	Similarities	Similarities Multiple Choice -- >	Multiple Choice Verbal Comprehension Index
	Vocabulary	Vocabulary Multiple Choice -- >	
		Picture Vocabulary Multiple Choice -- >	
	Information	Information Multiple Choice	
	Comprehension	Comprehension Multiple Choice	
Visual Spatial	Block Design	Block Design Multiple Choice	
Fluid Reasoning	Figure Weights Arithmetic	Figure Weights Process Approach	
		Arithmetic Process Approach	
		Written Arithmetic	
Working Memory	Picture Span ----- >	Spatial Span -------------------- >	Visual Working Memory Index
		Sentence Recall	
Processing Speed	Coding	Coding Recall	
	Cancellation	Coding Copy	
		Cancellation Abstract	

Source: Adapted from Raiford, 2017.

these constructs to regional brain functions. The purposes of the Integrated SNP/CHC Model are to: (1) facilitate clinical interpretation by providing an organizational framework for the assessment data, (2) strengthen the linkage between assessment and evidence-based interventions, and (3) provide a common frame of reference for evaluating the effects of neurodevelopmental disorders on neurocognitive processes (Miller, 2013). The Integrated SNP/CHC model encompasses four major classifications: (1) basic sensorimotor functions, (2) facilitators and inhibitors for cognitive processes and acquired knowledge skills, (3) basic cognitive processes, and (4) acquired knowledge (Miller, 2013). In addition to these four major classifications, the test results must be interpreted within the social—emotional, environmental, and cultural backgrounds of the individual child.

Within each of these major classifications, the neuropsychological constructs are classified into broad areas, and then further classified into second-order and third-order classifications, as appropriate. As an example, tests within the broad classification of sensorimotor functions can be further classified into the second-order classifications of lateral preference, sensory functions, fine motor functions, visual—motor integration skills, visual scanning, gross motor functions, and qualitative behaviors. Some of these second-order classifications can be further subdivided into third-order classification such as the sensory functions domain, and then can be subdivided into auditory and visual acuity; tactile sensation and perception; kinesthetic sensation and perception; and olfactory sensation and perception. For the purposes of this chapter only the broad classifications that relate to cognitive processing (sensorimotor functions, visuospatial processes, auditory/phonological process, learning and memory, executive functions, facilitators/inhibitors of allocating and maintaining attention, working memory, and/or speed, fluency, and efficiency of cognitive processing, and acquired knowledge: language) are utilized in Tables 3.2—3.4 to illustrate the relationship of the WISC-V and WISC-V Integrated subtests to these broad neuropsychological constructs. Additional qualitative behaviors often observed in the performance of these tasks are included in Tables 3.2—3.4 as they relate to the WISC-V/WISC-V Integrated tests. See Miller (2015) for a review of how the WISC-V, WISC-V Integrated, and Wechsler Individual Achievement Test-Third edition (WIAT; Wechsler, 2009) test scores can be classified according to the complete Integrated SNP/CHC Model.

Task-Specific Cognitive Construct Level of Interpretation

Tests developed to assess a broad range of intellectual functioning abilities are by design cognitively complex to capture very low to very high abilities. In order to assess higher ability levels of any construct, it is necessary to tap multiple cognitive processes simultaneously. To the degree possible, tests are designed to evaluate specific elements of cognitive functioning, but they are not designed to assess basic cognitive functions that have a nonnormal distribution and a restricted-range in healthy populations. Therefore, measures developed for the assessment of intellectual impairment through giftedness will all have some element of cognitive complexity, regardless of the measurement models (i.e., number of factors) employed. Additionally, some cognitive processes cannot be assessed in isolation (i.e., working memory) as they provide supportive/facilitative functions for cognitive integration and problem-solving. Therefore, discerning lower level cognitive difficulties using complex cognitive measures can only be inferred and should be validated by using more direct assessment of these suspected problems. The

TABLE 3.2 Primary and Secondary Cognitive Constructs and Executive Functions of WISC-V/WISC-V Integrated Verbal Comprehension Subtests Related to the Integrated SNP/CHC Model

Integrated SNP/CHC Model	Cognitive Construct/Related Executive Functions	Verbal Comprehension Subtests								
		SIM	SIM-MC	VOC	VOC-MC	VOC-PV	INF	INF-MC	COM	COM-MC
Sensorimotor functions		*Primary Cognitive Constructs*								
	Auditory acuity	C	C	C	C	C	C	C	C	C
	Initial registration of auditory stimuli	C	C	C	C	C	C	C	C	C
	Visual acuity		S		C	C		S		S
	Initial registration of visual stimuli							C		C
Visuospatial processes		*Primary Cognitive Constructs*								
	Visual perception/representation		S		S	S		S		S
	Visual discrimination (representation)				C	S				
Auditory/phonological processes		*Primary Cognitive Constructs*								
	Auditory discrimination	S	S	S	S	C			S	S
	Auditory comprehension	C	C	C	C	C	S	S	S	S
		Related Executive Processes								
	Directing auditory perception, discrimination, and comprehension	S	S	S	S	S	S	S	S	S

(Continued)

TABLE 3.2 (Continued)

Integrated SNP/ CHC Model	Cognitive Construct/ Related Executive Functions	Verbal Comprehension Subtests								
		SIM	SIM-MC	VOC	VOC-MC	VOC-PV	INF	INF-MC	COM	COM-MC
Learning and memory processes	*Primary Cognitive Constructs*									
	Retrieval of verbal knowledge	S	S	P	P	P	P	P	C	C
	Related Executive Processes									
	Directing retrieval	C	C	S			C	C	C	C
	Directing the retrieval of information from recent/remote long-term storage						P	P		
Executive functions	*Primary Cognitive Constructs*									
	Reasoning with verbal content	P	P						P	P
	Related Executive Processes									
	Cueing appropriate consideration of the cognitive capacities and mental effort required to perform a task	S	S	S	S	S	S	S	S	S
	Directing reasoning	S	S							
	Directing flexible shifting of reasoning mindset	P	P						S	S
	Coordinating the use of multiple capacities simultaneously	S	S	S	S	S	S	S	S	S
	Cueing and directing the inhibition of impulsive responding	C	C	C	C	C	C	C	C	C

		Primary Cognitive Constructs							
Facilitators/ inhibitors: allocating and maintaining attention	Auditory attention	C	C	C	C	C	C	C	C
	Attention to visual stimuli	C	C	S	C	C	C	S	C
	Related Executive Processes								
	Cueing the focusing and sustaining of attention to auditory details	C	C	C	C	C	C	C	C
	Cueing and directing the focusing of attention to visual details and task demands			S				S	
	Directing attention to details of stimuli being presented			S				S	
Facilitators/ inhibitors: working memory	*Primary Cognitive Constructs*								
	Working memory	C	↓	C	↓	C	↓	C	↓
	Related Executive Processes								
	Directing working memory	C	↓	C	↓	C	↓	C	↓
Acquired knowledge: language	*Primary Cognitive Constructs*								
	Expressive language ability/ production	S	S	P	S	C	S	S	S
	Related Executive Processes								
	Recognizing and responding to prompts for more information	C	C	C	C	C	C	C	C
	Directing language expression	S	S	S	S	C	S	S	S

P, Primary cognitive constructs targeted for assessment with the task; *S*, Secondary cognitive construct highly likely to affect task performance; *C*, Secondary cognitive construct possibly affecting task performance.

Note: The left-hand column classifies the cognitive constructs and executive function facilitators/inhibitors into the Integrated School Neuropsychological/Cattell–Horn–Carroll Model (Miller, 2013).

Where *SIM*, Similarities; *SIM-MC*, Similarities Multiple Choice; *VOC*, Vocabulary; *VOC-MC*, Vocabulary Multiple Choice; *INF*, Information; *INF-MC*, Information Multiple Choice; *COM*, Comprehension; *COM-MC*, Comprehension Multiple Choice.

Source: This table was adapted from McCloskey, Slonim, Whitaker, Kaufman, and Nagoshi's chapter in Flanagan and Alfonso (2017).

TABLE 3.3 Primary and Secondary Cognitive Constructs and Executive Functions of WISC-V/WISC-V Integrated Visual Spatial and Fluid Reasoning Subtests Related to the Integrated SNP/CHC Model

Integrated SNP/CHC Model	Cognitive Construct/Related Executive Functions	Visual Spatial Subtests			Fluid Reasoning Subtests			
		BD	BD-MC	FW	FW-PA	AR	AR-PA	AR-WA
Sensorimotor functions	Primary Cognitive Constructs							
	Visual acuity	S	S	S	S	S	S	S
	Graphomotor functioning							S
	Motor dexterity	S						
	Related Executive Processes							
	Direct perception and registration of stimuli					S	S	S
	Cueing and directing the execution of motor routines	S						C
Visuospatial processes	Primary Cognitive Constructs							
	Visual perception/representation	P	P↑	S	S		S	
	Visual discrimination (representation)	S	S	S	S			
	Visualization	C	S↑	C	C			
	Related Executive Processes							
	Cueing and directing efficient perception of visual stimuli	P	P	S	S		S	
	Cueing and directing the balance between pattern (global) and detail (local) processing	S	S	C	C			S

	Primary Cognitive Constructs					Related Executive Processes			
Auditory/ phonological processes									
Auditory discrimination				C	C	C	C	C	C
Auditory comprehension				S	C	C	S	C	S
Language representation of visual stimuli		C	C						
Learning and memory processes									
Directing the retrieval of information from recent/remote long-term storage				S	S	S	S	S	
Executive functions									
Reasoning with nonverbal visual materials	P	P	P	P	S	S	S	S	S
Reasoning with quantity		P	P	P					
Sequencing ability				S	S	S	S	S	S
Cueing appropriate consideration of the cognitive capacities and mental effort required to perform a task	S	S	S	S	S	S	S	S	S
Cueing and directing the coordination of the use of multiple mental capacities simultaneously	S	S	S	S	S	S	S	S	S
Cueing and directing the inhibition of impulsive responding	S	S	S						
Cueing the modulation of effort				S	S	S	S	S	S

(Continued)

TABLE 3.3 (Continued)

Integrated SNP/CHC Model	Cognitive Construct/Related Executive Functions	Visual Spatial Subtests		Fluid Reasoning Subtests				
		BD	BD-MC	FW	FW-PA	AR	AR-PA	AR-WA
	Cueing and directing the use of reasoning abilities (generating novel solutions or making associations with prior knowledge that lead to problem solutions)	C	C	P	P	S	S	S
	Cueing the shift to an imbalanced emphasis on processing details over patterns						S	S
	Cueing and directing the flexible shifting of cognitive mindset to consider and respond to the specific demands of the test	C	C	S	S			
	Cueing and directing the monitoring of work and the correcting of errors	S	S	S	S			
	Cueing the organization of information					S	S	S
	Cueing the execution of sequencing routines					C	C	C
Facilitators/inhibitors: allocating and maintaining attention				Primary Cognitive Constructs				
	Attention to visual stimuli	S	S	S	S	S	S	S
				Related Executive Processes				
	Cueing the focusing and sustaining of attention to auditory details			S	S		S	
	Cueing and directing the focusing of attention to visual details and task demands	S	S	S	S	S	S	S
	Directing attention to details of stimuli being presented					S	S	S
	Cueing and directing sustained attention to task	S	S	S	S	S	S	S

Facilitators/inhibitors: working memory		Primary Cognitive Constructs						
	Working memory					P	P	P
	Mental manipulation of auditory stimuli					S	S	S
	Mental manipulation of visual stimuli						S	S
	Use of working memory with visually presented material	C	C	S	S			
	Related Executive Processes							
	Directing mental manipulation	C	C			C	C	C
	Cueing and directing the use of working memory resources	C	C	S	S	P	P	P
Facilitators/inhibitors: speed, fluency, and efficiency of cognitive processing		Primary Cognitive Constructs						
	Mental processing speed	S	C	S	S	C	C	C
	Auditory processing speed					S	S	S
	Visual processing speed	S	S	S	S↑			
	Motor processing speed	S						
	Motor and/or graphomotor processing speed						S	S
	Visual-motor processing speed	S						

(Continued)

TABLE 3.3 (Continued)

Integrated SNP/CHC Model	Cognitive Construct/Related Executive Functions	Visual Spatial Subtests			Fluid Reasoning Subtests			
		BD	BD-MC	FW	FW-PA	AR	AR-PA	AR-WA
	Related Executive Processes							
	Cueing and directing of processing speed					S	S	S
	Cueing and directing mental, visual, motor, and visual-motor processing speed	S	S	S	S		S	S
	Primary Cognitive Constructs							
Acquired knowledge: language	Expressive language ability/production					C		

P, Primary cognitive constructs targeted for assessment with the task; S, Secondary cognitive construct highly likely to affect task performance; C, Secondary cognitive construct possibly affecting task performance.

Note: The left-hand column classifies the cognitive constructs and executive function facilitators/inhibitors into the Integrated School Neuropsychological/Cattell–Horn–Carroll Model (Miller, 2013).

Where *BD*, Block Design; *BD-MC*, Block Design Multiple Choice; *FW*, Figure Weights; *FW-PA*, Figure Weights Process Approach; *AR*, Arithmetic; *AR-PA*, Arithmetic Process Approach; *AR-WA*, Written Arithmetic.

Source: This table was adapted from McCloskey, Slonim, Whitaker, Kaufman, and Nagoshi's chapter in Flanagan and Alfonso (2017).

TABLE 3.4 Primary and Secondary Cognitive Constructs and Executive Functions of WISC-V/WISC-V Integrated Working Memory and Processing Speed Subtests Related to the Integrated SNP/CHC Model

Integrated SNP/CHC Model	Cognitive Construct/Related Executive Functions	Working Memory Subtests				Processing Speed Subtests			
		PS	SS-B	SR	CD	CD-R	CD-C	CA	CA-A
Sensorimotor functions	Primary Cognitive Constructs								
	Initial registration of auditory stimuli			S					
	Visual acuity	S							
	Initial registration of visual stimuli	S	S						
	Graphomotor functioning				S	C↓	S	C	C
	Motor dexterity		S			C	C		
	Related Executive Processes								
	Direct perception and registration of stimuli	S							
	Cueing and directing the execution of motor routines	C	S		S	C↓		C	C
Visuospatial processes	Primary Cognitive Constructs								
	Visual perception/representation	S			S	S	C	S	S
	Visual discrimination (representation)	S			S	S	C	S	C
	Visualization		S						
	Related Executive Processes								
	Cueing and directing efficient perception of visual stimuli	S	S		C	C	C	C	C

(Continued)

TABLE 3.4 (Continued)

Integrated SNP/CHC Model	Cognitive Construct/Related Executive Functions	Working Memory Subtests				Processing Speed Subtests			
		PS	SS-B	SR	CD	CD-R	CD-C	CA	CA-A
Auditory/phonological processes		Primary Cognitive Constructs							
	Auditory discrimination			S					
	Auditory comprehension			S					
		Related Executive Processes							
	Directing auditory perception, discrimination, and comprehension			S					
Learning and memory		Primary Cognitive Constructs							
	Retrieval of visual paired associations from recent long-term memory					P			
		Related Executive Processes							
	Directing retrieval					P			
Executive functions		Primary Cognitive Constructs							
	Sequencing ability	S	S	C					
	Multitasking				P			C	
	Organization skills				C				C

Related Executive Processes

Related Executive Process									
Cueing appropriate consideration of the cognitive capacities and mental effort required to perform a task	S	S	S	S	S	S	S	S	S
Cueing and directing the coordination of the use of multiple mental capacities simultaneously	S	S	S						
Cueing and directing the inhibition of impulsive responding	S	S	S						
Cueing the modulation of effort	S	S	S						
Cueing and directing the generating of novel solutions or retrieving associations to improve performance			C					S	S
Cueing the shift to an imbalanced emphasis on processing details over patterns	S	S	S		S				S
Coordinating the use of multiple capacities simultaneously			S						S
Cueing and directing the inhibition of impulsive responding			S		S			S	S
Cueing and directing the monitoring of work and the correcting of errors	C	C	C	S	S	S	S	S	S
Cueing the organization of information			C		C				
Cueing and directing the organization of work strategies					C				
Cueing the execution of sequencing routines	S	S	S						S

(Continued)

TABLE 3.4 (Continued)

Integrated SNP/CHC Model	Cognitive Construct/Related Executive Functions	Working Memory Subtests				Processing Speed Subtests			
		PS	SS-B	SR	CD	CD-R	CD-C	CA	CA-A
Facilitators/inhibitors: allocating and maintaining attention		Primary Cognitive Constructs							
	Auditory attention			S					S
	Attention to visual stimuli	S	S		S	S	S	S	S
		Related Executive Processes							
	Cueing the focusing and sustaining of attention to auditory details			S					
	Cueing and directing the focusing of attention to visual details and task demands	S	S	S	S	S	S		S
	Directing attention to details of stimuli being presented	S	S	S	S	S			
	Cueing and directing sustained attention to task	S	S	S	S	S	S		S
Facilitators/inhibitors: working memory		Related Executive Processes							
	Working memory				C	C			
	Mental manipulation of auditory stimuli			P					
	Use of working memory with visually presented material	P	P						
		Related Executive Processes							
	Directing mental manipulation	C							
	Cueing and directing the use of working memory resources	P	P	P	C	C			

Facilitators/inhibitors: speed, fluency, and efficiency of cognitive processing	Primary Cognitive Constructs							
Mental processing speed	S							
Visual processing speed	S					P		P
Motor processing speed								
Motor and/or graphomotor processing speed				P	C	C	S	S
Visual-motor processing speed	C				P			
Related Executive Processes								
Cueing and directing a work pace that can achieve a balance between speed and accuracy				P	C	P	S	S
Cueing and directing mental, visual, motor, and visual-motor processing speed	S			S	S	S	P	P

P, Primary cognitive constructs targeted for assessment with the task; *S*, Secondary cognitive construct highly likely to affect task performance; *C*, Secondary cognitive construct possibly affecting task performance.
Note: The left-hand column classifies the cognitive constructs and executive function facilitators/inhibitors into the Integrated School Neuropsychological/Cattell–Horn–Carroll Model (Miller, 2013).
Where *PS*, Picture Span; *SS-B*, Spatial Span (Backward); *SR*, Sentence Recall; *CD*, Coding; *CD-R*, Coding Recall; *CD-C*, Coding Copy; *CA*, Cancellation; *CA-A*, Cancellation Abstract.
Source: This table was adapted from McCloskey, Slonim, Whitaker, Kaufman, and Nagoshi's chapter in Flanagan and Alfonso (2017).

WISC-V/WISC-V Integrated may help clinicians identify possible subprocesses that may be contributing to low scores on more complex measures. A child's performance on a particular measure can be affected by many of the multiple skills required to perform the task, observe if the task itself is a complex process (i.e., making it a good estimator of global cognitive ability) and if the test is a reflection of that complexity. For example, the development and use of vocabulary requires the integration of language, memory, executive search and filtering of information, and some form of motor expression (e.g., pointing, talking). Given that the cognitive constructs of interest are complex, the WISC-V and Integrated measures will also require complex cognitive functions and these skills have been articulated by many authors.

Every test of higher order cognitive abilities can be affected by impairments in basic sensorimotor, attention regulation, task engagement, and effort. Test results affected by significant deficits in these domains are likely invalid assessments of intellectual functions. Those with mild or moderate deficits in specific areas may yield inconsistent results on measures of intellectual ability. Clinicians must be aware of any visual, auditory, or motor deficits before administering and interpreting performance on the WISC-V or WISC-V Integrated. These tests also assume a sufficient level of cooperation and effort on the part of the examinee. Deficits in sustained attention or brief focused attention can impact performance, but these can occur at any time in testing and may contribute to inconsistent performance across measures. Basic processes that can impact performance on the WISC-V/WISC-V Integrated will not be discussed further in this chapter but are detailed in Table 3.3.

Verbal Comprehension Subtests

In the verbal domain, poor test performance may occur for a number of reasons. The key hypotheses that should be explored when low verbal index scores are obtained include delayed language development; language disorder; reading disorder; difficulties retrieving knowledge (i.e., low ability versus access to knowledge); impaired auditory attention, acuity, and/or discrimination; auditory working memory deficits; or impaired executive functioning. At the subtest level, the demands for specific language skills vary. The subtest content and task demands affect the impact that language skills have on performance. Interpretation of subtest variability should consider the degree to which knowledge deficits are present versus active cognitive supports (e.g., language working memory, and executive functioning) that are affecting performance.

The WISC-V Integrated versions of the verbal subtests reduce some of the cognitive demands required by the standard free-recall format; however, several nonlinguistic cognitive processes also contribute to a child's performance on the multiple-choice adaptations. The presentation of multiple response options requires the child to engage in a comparative evaluation to determine the "best" response. This evaluation of options may not have been present during the free-recall condition. The child is presented with highly salient alternative responses that they had not considered previously. Some of the distracter response options (i.e., response options with lower point values) were designed purposely to be phonetically similar to the target word or key phrases to pull "stimulus-bound" responses. This type of distracter is typically more difficult to reject for those children who have difficulty disassociating acoustic or visual features from semantic or abstract characteristics of the stimuli. Impulsive children may also select phonetically, orthographically, or morphologically similar items due to a failure to consider all available options. In some children, there will be a "pull" to respond to that item as it "looks" the most correct based on its stimulus feature. In this case, other evidence of stimulus-bound behavior would likely be present in other contexts as well. The executive functioning behaviors most relevant to the standard and integrated verbal subtest are directed semantic search of long-term memory, initiation of verbal responses, verbal productivity, self-monitoring of response accuracy, cognitive flexibility, and ability to inhibit responding to highly salient alternative responses.

Wechsler Intelligence Scale for Children—Fifth Edition Similarities and Wechsler Intelligence Scale for Children—Fifth Edition Integrated Similarities Multiple Choice

Within the Integrated SNP/CHC Model (Miller, 2013), the Similarities subtests are classified as measures of executive functions, specifically measures of abstraction and concept formation, or the ability to generate multiple ways of classifying or categorizing objects. These tests require flexibility in thinking as multiple meanings of words must be considered to correctly identify the abstract relationship between two seemingly disparate words. The WISC-V Similarities subtest primarily measures reasoning with verbal content (see the "P" denotation in Table 3.2). Secondary cognitive constructs *highly likely to affect* task performance (see the "S" denotations in Table 3.2) include retrieval of verbal knowledge and expressive language ability/production. From a brain—behavior perspective, the Similarities subtest requires long-term retrieval of verbal concepts (crystallized and memory processes of the left hemisphere) and verbal reasoning skills (left hemisphere frontal executive functions) to engage in concordant (recognizing how the two words are similar) and convergent (the word that best represents both stimulus words) thought (Miller & Hale, 2008).

The expressive and receptive demands of the task are minimal, since the examinee only needs to recognize the presented words and respond with a simple categorical response; however, retrieval deficits may be suggested if the examinee produces a simple categorical response. For example, the examinee produces a concrete similarity (e.g., "they are both green"), resulting in a one-point response, compared to a more abstract similarity (e.g., "they are both vegetables"), resulting in a desired two-point response. An explanation for this type of concrete versus abstract response is an indication of a less intellectually advanced examinee. However, sometimes the response pattern across items is inconsistent between concrete and abstract responses, which may reflect difficulty with efficient long-term memory retrieval and would suggest further hypothesis testing (Miller & Hale, 2008). The WISC-V Integrated Similarities test reduces the impact of expressive language, working memory, and memory search and retrieval demands compared to the WISC-V Similarities version.

Wechsler Intelligence Scale for Children—Fifth Edition Vocabulary and Wechsler Intelligence Scale for Children—Fifth Edition Integrated Vocabulary Multiple Choice and Picture Vocabulary

Within the Integrated SNP/CHC Model (Miller, 2013), the Vocabulary subtests are classified as measures of acquired knowledge: language skills, specifically measures of vocabulary knowledge and oral expression. The WISC-V Vocabulary subtest primarily measures expressive language ability/production (acquired knowledge: language skills) and retrieval of verbal knowledge (learning and memory) (see the "P" denotations in Table 3.2). The WISC-V Integrated Vocabulary Multiple Choice subtest is designed to measure word knowledge, verbal concept formation, and semantic memory (Raiford, 2017). The WISC-V Integrated Picture Vocabulary Multiple Choice subtest is designed to measure word knowledge, verbal concept formation, and receptive vocabulary (Raiford, 2017). Compared to the WISC-V Vocabulary and the WISC-V Integrated Vocabulary Multiple Choice formats of the test, the Picture Vocabulary Multiple Choice reduces the expressive language ability/production demands (acquired knowledge: language). This subtest requires the ability for examinees to translate visual images into verbal concepts. Visual-perceptual integration/abstraction deficits may impact performance on this test.

The Vocabulary tests do not require the degree of executive functioning as reported for Similarities as examinees only need to identify and/or state one correct meaning for each word. Verbal productivity, self-monitoring of responses, and directed retrieval from long-term memory are executive functions related to Vocabulary performance. Observationally, examinees making very long circumlocutive responses or achieving many one-point responses may have retrieval difficulties warranting further assessment with multiple-choice versions.

Wechsler Intelligence Scale for Children—Fifth Edition Information and Wechsler Intelligence Scale for Children—Fifth Edition Integrated Information Multiple Choice

Within the Integrated SNP/CHC Model (Miller, 2013), the Information subtests are classified as measures of acquired knowledge: acculturation knowledge, specifically measures of semantic memory or the ability to retrieve from memory knowledge of basic information. The WISC-V Information subtest primarily measures retrieval and expression of verbal knowledge (see the "P" denotation in Table 3.2). The WISC-V Integrated Information test is a multiple-choice adaptation of the WISC-V Information test. The multiple-choice format reduces the memory search and working memory demands compared to the standard version.

Wechsler Intelligence Scale for Children—Fifth Edition Comprehension and Wechsler Intelligence Scale for Children—Fifth Edition Integrated Comprehension Multiple Choice

Within the Integrated SNP/CHC Model (Miller, 2013), the Comprehension subtests are classified as measures of executive functions: specifically measures of verbal reasoning. The WISC-V Comprehension test requires the examinee to answer questions based on one's understanding of general principles and social situations. The WISC-V Integrated Comprehension test is a multiple-choice adaptation of the WISC-V Comprehension test.

The WISC-V Comprehension subtest requires the most expressive/receptive language functioning of all the verbal measures. In addition to the greater verbal productivity required to answer the questions, the examinee is required to provide multiple different response on some items. This increases the demands on cognitive flexibility. It has been postulated that individuals with autism perform more poorly on Comprehension due to the content of the subtest, but the high demand on language functions and cognitive flexibility likely contribute to their difficulties on this subtest. The WISC-V Integrated version reduces the expressive language demands and response flexibility; however, there is a bigger demand on auditory attention and receptive language skills compared to the standard version.

Visual-Spatial and Fluid Reasoning Subtests

Poor test performance on tests in the visual-spatial and fluid reasoning domain may occur for a number of reasons. The main hypotheses to consider when low Visual-Spatial Reasoning or Fluid Reasoning Index scores are obtained include visual-spatial development, visual discrimination, visual scanning (visual fields)/attention, visual working memory, global versus local processing, executive functioning, procedural learning, processing speed, and motor skills. The impact of these skills at the subtest level varies. The subtest content and task demands will affect the degree to which intact visual-perceptual skills are required. Interpretation of subtest variability should consider the degree to which the visual-perceptual demands of the task affect performance. Working memory skills are particularly important on tasks with a high degree of reasoning, particularly fluid reasoning measures. Clinicians should consider more detailed evaluation of visual working memory skills when low Fluid Reasoning Index scores are observed.

Wechsler Intelligence Scale for Children—Fifth Edition Block Design and Wechsler Intelligence Scale for Children—Fifth Edition Integrated Block Design Multiple Choice

Within the Integrated SNP/CHC Model (Miller, 2013), the Block Design subtests are classified as measures of visuospatial processes, specifically visual-motor constructions. Global (e.g., configural) abilities are observed as maintenance of the exterior shape of the design (e.g., 3×3 square) and local processes in the completion of the correct visual design. Motor planning, procedural learning, and visuomotor integration impact the speed and efficiency of performance on this test. In the executive functioning domain, planning and strategy facilitate test performance. Compared to the WISC-V version, the WISC-V Integrated Block Design subtest decreases the motor dexterity or motor-output requirements, increases the demands on visual-spatial reasoning and integration of local detail, and maintains the processing speed demands. Inhibitory control and attention to detail are heightened on the multiple-choice edition.

Wechsler Intelligence Scale for Children—Fifth Edition Figure Weights and Wechsler Intelligence Scale for Children—Fifth Edition Integrated Figure Weights Process Approach

Within the Integrated SNP/CHC Model (Miller, 2013), the Figure Weights subtests are classified as measures of executive functions, specifically quantitative reasoning skills.

The WISC-V Integrated Figure Weights Process Approach subtest uses only the items from the WISC-V version for which a score of 0 points was obtained by the examinee and extra completion time is allotted for each of the previously failed items.

Both versions of the Figure Weights subtest primarily measure reasoning with nonverbal visual materials coupled with reasoning with quantity. When the clinician believes the examinee's performance was affected by subtest time limits and slowed processing speed, the use of the Integrated version can confirm or disconfirm that hypothesis.

Wechsler Intelligence Scale for Children—Fifth Edition Arithmetic and Wechsler Intelligence Scale for Children—Fifth Edition Integrated Arithmetic Process Approach and Written Arithmetic

Within the Integrated SNP/CHC Model (Miller, 2013), the Arithmetic subtests are classified as measures of facilitators/inhibitors: working memory, specifically verbal working memory. Quantitative reasoning skills are required in the form of identification and implementation of mathematic operations and proper computational sequences. The WISC-V Arithmetic subtest requires the examinee to mentally solve a series of arithmetic problems read by the examiner. This is a timed test. The WISC-V Integrated has two adapted versions of the WISC-V Arithmetic test: Arithmetic Process Approach and Written Arithmetic. On the WISC-V Arithmetic Process Approach subtest, Items 6-34 are presented in multiple modalities to be solved in a defined time period. The test has two parts: A and B. For Part A of the test, only the WISC-V Arithmetic items on which the examinee scored 0 points are readministered visually and while read aloud by the examiner. The added visual presentation of the numerical operations to be solved is what makes this task unique from the original version. For Part B of the test, the examinee is only administered those items on which 0 points were scored on the Part A administration. For Part B, the examinee is presented with paper and pencil to help facilitate solving the missed arithmetic problems. Both Part A and B are timed tests. For some examinees, the added paper and pencil for writing down the arithmetic problems helps achieve correct solutions to the problems. The WISC-V Integrated offers a third measure to determine if the examinee has sufficient basic math skills to complete the test. The Written Arithmetic subtest presents the math problems on paper without the requirement of the examinee needing to determine the correct math operations and correct sequence of operations to obtain the correct result. The written version eliminates the working memory and math reasoning elements to evaluate if poor math skills have impacted performance on the test.

The WISC-V Arithmetic subtest is a very complex measure. In nearly every edition of the Wechsler scales, this test has multiple factor loadings including working memory, fluid reasoning, and verbal domains. The WISC-V version reduced the language demands significantly from predecessor versions. While working memory, phonological loop, and central executive functions are the primary skill assessed, quantitative reasoning is an important core ability on this test. The use of the additional integrated versions helps determine if low scores are related to working memory or quantitative reasoning. The verbal impact is reduced when the written arithmetic version is used.

Working Memory Tests

Low scores in the Working Memory domain can occur for a number of reasons. The primary factors that affect performance are auditory or visual discrimination, attention, mental sequencing, basic automaticity of letter and digit processing, and executive control. There is a reciprocal relationship between working memory skills and other cognitive domains such as language and visual-perceptual processing. Therefore, there will be instances in which significant impairments in one of these domains will limit or reduce the level of performance on the specific working memory tasks. For instance, significant impairments in visual-spatial ability will affect performance on the Spatial Span task. In some cases, it may be difficult to ascertain if working memory skills are impairing language or visual-perceptual processes, or vice versa. Performance on working memory measures may be affected by a number of basic cognitive processes such as sensorimotor functions, visuo-spatial processes, executive functions, allocating and maintaining attention, working memory, and speed, fluency, and efficiency of cognitive processing.

Wechsler Intelligence Scale for Children—Fifth Edition Picture Span and Wechsler Intelligence Scale for Children—Fifth Edition Integrated Spatial Span (Backward) and Sentence Recall

Within the Integrated SNP/CHC Model (Miller, 2013), the Picture Span, Spatial Span (Backward), and the Sentence Recall subtests are classified as measures of working memory.

The WISC-V Picture Span subtest requires the examinee to view a stimulus page for a brief period, then select from a response page one or more target pictures in proper order. This is a timed test. The test measures visual working memory, visual sequential processing, and rote learning, and requires attention and concentration (Flanagan & Alfonso, 2017). The WISC-V Integrated Spatial Span subtest has two parts: Spatial Span (Forward) and Spatial Span (Backward). On the Forward condition, the examinee is asked to reproduce a series of tapped blocks in the same order that were demonstrated by the examiner. On the Backward condition, the examinee is asked to reproduce a series of tapped blocks in reverse order that were demonstrated by the examiner. Spatial Span (Forward) measures immediate visual memory; whereas Spatial Span (Backward) measures visual working memory. Compared to the Picture Span subtest, the Spatial Span (Backward) subtests has an added motor output demand.

The WISC-V Integrated Sentence Recall subtest is comprised of two tasks: answering a question task and recalling of target word task. For the question task, the examinee is read a question statement and asked to respond "yes" or "no." The responses to the questions are not scores as part of the test. For the recall portion of the test, the examinee is asked to recall the last word of each question in the order presented. The examinee must process significant linguistic information and recall a portion of the information.

The primary measure for the WISC-V Picture Span is the use of working memory with visually presented semantically meaningful material. The primary measure for the Spatial Span (Backward) is mental manipulation of visual-spatial stimuli. Both of these measures use a sequencing paradigm to engage multiple elements of working memory including the central executive, visual-spatial sketchpad and for linguistically related material, the phonological loop. These tasks are designed to require mental manipulation of information such that information must be both held in conscious awareness and altered to get a correct answer. The Sentence Recall subtest requires the examinee to answer a question about the presented stimuli that produces cognitive interference with the maintenance of the phonological loop. Therefore, the examinee must dual-task by holding onto the content of the sentence while responding to a question before recalling the needed information. On this test, managing resource allocation and interference from competing information requires executive control of verbal working memory.

Processing Speed Tests

Low scores on processing speed measures can occur for a number of reasons. The primary hypotheses that need to be explored when low Processing Speed Index scores are obtained include visual-perceptual skills such as visual discrimination, visual scanning, visuomotor skills (i.e., drawing), working memory, procedural and incidental learning, and executive control of visual-perceptual processes. The subtest content and task demands will affect the degree to which intact visual discrimination and motor skills impact performance. Also consider that poor performance on processing speed tasks can include psychological as well as cognitive reasons, such as anxiety, depression, and/or poor motivation.

Wechsler Intelligence Scale for Children—Fifth Edition Coding, Wechsler Intelligence Scale for Children—Fifth Edition Integrated Coding Copy, and Coding Recall

Within the Integrated SNP/CHC Model (Miller, 2013), the WISC-V Coding and the WISC-V Integrated Coding Copy subtests are classified as measures of speed, fluency, and efficiency of cognitive processing, specifically measures of perceptual fluency. The WISC-V Coding subtest requires the examinee to copy symbols as quickly as possible that are paired with geometric shapes or numbers using a key. The WISC-V Integrated Copying Recall subtest is administered immediately after the administration of the WISC-V Coding subtest, because it is measuring immediate incidental visual memory. Incidental learning is thought to facilitate performance on the standard version of the Coding test and therefore the Coding Recall subtest c identifies if poor memory function accounts for slow performance on the standard version of the test. The WISC-V Integrated Coding Copy test requires the examinee to copy symbols as quickly as possible within 90 seconds. The Coding Copy subtest increases the processing speed demands of the task as well as visual-motor integration while reducing the visual scanning and incidental recall demands.

The primary cognitive measure for the WISC-V Coding subtest is visual processing speed and motor and/or graphomotor speed (speed, fluency, and efficiency of cognitive processing). The primary cognitive measure for the WISC-V Integrated Coding Recall subtest is incidental recall from immediate memory. In comparison, the primary measure for the WISC-V Integrated Coding Copy subtest is visual-motor processing speed (speed, fluency, and efficiency of cognitive processing). Comparison between versions identifies the degree to which slow visual scanning may have impacted performance on the WISC-V coding subtest.

Wechsler Intelligence Scale for Children—Fifth Edition Cancellation and Wechsler Intelligence Scale for Children—Fifth Edition Integrated Cancellation Abstract

Within the Integrated SNP/CHC Model (Miller, 2013), the WISC-V Cancellation and the WISC-V Integrated Cancellation Abstract subtests are classified as measures of speed, fluency, and efficiency of cognitive processing, specifically measures of perceptual fluency. The WISC-V Cancellation subtest requires the examinee to visually scan a random and structured set of pictures and as quickly as possible mark designated target pictures. The WISC-V Integrated Cancellation Abstract reduces the semantic loading by using shapes (colored triangles or squares) compared to pictures of animals or objects used as stimuli on the Coding subtest. The primary cognitive measures for the WISC-V Cancellation and the WISC-V Integrated subtests are visual processing and scanning speed (speed, fluency, and efficiency of cognitive processing).

Case Study Example

The following case study example is from a comprehensive school neuropsychological evaluation conducted as part of a requirement for the KIDS, Inc. School Neuropsychology Post-Graduate Certification Program. The WISC-V and WISC-V Integrated were administered as part of a larger battery of tests. The test scores from these to tests have been extracted from the larger report along with other basic sections of the report, such as reason for referral, background information, summary, and recommendations. Please note that some of the diagnostic impressions could not be formed on the basis of the WISC-V/WISC-V Integrated alone, but these tests were very helpful in formulating hypotheses about the child's levels of functioning.

Case Study

Student's name: Bethany	Age: 11	Gender: Female
Grade: 5th	Ethnicity: Hispanic	Primary language spoken at home: Spanish

Reason for Referral

Bethany is a bilingual 11-year old female, referred by her mother, for an initial baseline neuropsychological evaluation due to persistent decline in performance in major academic areas.

Bethany has a medical history that includes neurofibromatosis type-1 (NF-1) treated by two neurosurgical treatments, at ages 8 and 9 years, resection a low-grade cerebellar glioma, then juvenile pilocytic astrocytoma (JPA). Following her return to school, an accommodation plan under section 504 was provided at school. Bethany's academic difficulties were not adequately served under the 504 plan and a psychoeducational evaluation was recommended, resulting in provision of special education services under the handicapping condition of Other Health Impairments.

Background Information

Developmental and Medical History

Bethany was full term and weighed 9 pounds, 13 ounces. No complications were noted during pregnancy and delivery. Bethany's mother reported that developmental milestones were met within the following timeframe: sitting 3 months, crawling 6 months, walking 11 months, toilet training 2 years, using single words 18 months, and saying short phrases 2 years. At 8 years old and following persistent episodes of headaches and vomiting, she was diagnosed with a cerebellar tumor consistent with a history of type 1 neurofibromatosis (NF-1). The tumor was surgically removed. The final pathological results suggested, "cerebellar cortex with focal low-grade glioma." A year later, Bethany was diagnosed with JPA, a common low-grade astrocytoma/glioma, with lesions in the posterior cranial fossa. Subsequent neurosurgery was performed for posterior fossa craniotomy. Bethany tolerated the surgery well and without complication. She also has café au lait spots spreading over *Lisch nodules* on both eyes and has had difficulty in her peripheral vision. Currently there is no evidence of residual tumor and her exam was normal. She has been symptom-free since her second neurosurgery. Bethany wears glasses and her teachers report that Bethany complains of headaches if she does not wear her glasses. Currently, she is being monitored with regular visits to an ophthalmologist to monitor vision and by a neurologist with MRIs every 4 months to rule out return of lesions.

Educational History

Bethany has attended one school since kindergarten. She was enrolled in a bilingual "English/Spanish" program until 3rd grade. She is currently in the 5th grade with continued academic instruction in English. Bethany's teachers, who have known her for several years, report that since her second brain surgery she appears very forgetful, more distracted, and takes longer to complete tasks.

(Continued)

(Continued)

Bethany's special education services include Specialized Academic Instruction, and 1,920 min/month served in the special education setting outside of the general education setting. Goals are in the areas of reading comprehension and math fluency.

Current Assessment Instruments and Procedures

A comprehensive battery of tests was administered to Bethany as part of a neuropsychological evaluation. In addition to standardized tests, a thorough record review was conducted along with clinical interviews of the parents, teachers, and student. Classroom observations were conducted in a structured academic setting and in an unstructured activity. For purposes of this chapter, only the results from the WISC-V and the WISC-V Integrated are reviewed (see Table 3.5).

TABLE 3.5 Case Study Example WISC-V and WISC-V Integrated Test Results

Domain	WISC-V Subtest	WISC-V Integrated Subtest	Derived Index Score
Verbal Comprehension	Similarities (3)	Similarities Multiple Choice (8) ----- >	Multiple Choice Verbal Comprehension Index
	Vocabulary (4)	Vocabulary Multiple Choice (7) ----- >	
		Picture Vocabulary Multiple Choice (7)	
	Information (4)	Information Multiple Choice (2)	
	Comprehension (5)	Comprehension Multiple Choice (8)	
Visual Spatial	Block Design (6)	Block Design Multiple Choice (7)	

(Continued)

(Continued)

Domain	WISC-V Subtest	WISC-V Integrated Subtest	Derived Index Score
Fluid Reasoning	Figure Weights (5) Arithmetic (8)	Figure Weights Process Approach (4)	
		Arithmetic Process Approach—A (10)	
		Arithmetic Process Approach—B (10)	
		Written Arithmetic (9)	
Immediate Memory[a]	Digit Span (5)	Spatial Span Forward (7)	
Working Memory	Picture Span (7)-- > Digit Span	Spatial Span Backward (5) ---------- >	Visual Working Memory Index (21%)
	Backward (6)	Sentence Recall (6)	
Processing Speed	Coding (8)	Coding Recall (11)	
	Cancellation (3)	Coding Copy (15)	
		Cancellation Abstract (4)	
		Cancellation Abstract Random (4)	
		Cancellation Abstract Structured (4)	

[a]Not part of the WISC-V domain structure.

(Continued)

(Continued)

Verbal Comprehension Domain

Executive functioning difficulties were an area of significant concern for Bethany's mother and teacher. Concerns were noted regarding Bethany's struggles to steer her away from a desired activity and towards academics. Her teacher explained that Bethany loves drawing and seeks any opportunity during instructional time to leave academic tasks for drawing; this has been a significant distractor and has been interfering with her attending to tasks. It was also noted that Bethany has difficulty prioritizing her time. As a fifth grader, she is expected to use a planner and independently plan a study/work completion schedule, but she lacks abilities to prioritize what is more important at a given period. The teacher and mother expressed Bethany's struggles with initiation and completion of complex tasks. Mother mentioned that, at home, she cries and avoids approaching her math and reading assignments because she perceives them as difficult. She often makes similar computation errors even after reviewing the materials multiple times. At school, the teacher noted that Bethany is not concerned about the quality of her work and mainly wants to complete her assignments as quickly as possible. Bethany's mother complained about her lack of common sense and immature judgment in social settings and says she sometimes behaves like her 5-year-old twin sisters.

Bethany's performance was significantly poor when asked to verbally describe how two items were similar, using knowledge of semantic categories, abstract thinking, and concept generation skills (WISC-V Similarities). The ceiling rule was met within the first few items on this task. Bethany's responses did not demand any querying and lacked concept recognition, associative thinking, and knowledge of semantic categories (e.g., when asked, "how are a brother and sister alike?" Bethany responded, "They have hair—they walk"). When Bethany was administered a multiple-choice version of the same task (WISC-V Integrated Similarities Multiple Choice) her performance improved to the average range of functioning. This suggests that Bethany has adequate semantic knowledge but struggles with word retrieval and perhaps with verbally initiating broad associations; her performance improved with recognition versus free recall. In addition, her performance may be hindered by the excessive language demand embedded in the Similarities task and her word retrieval abilities. Bethany's evident disengagement from tasks in the classroom can be suggestive of an excessive verbal demand, beyond her comprehension skills, and in contrast with her best information retrieval style (recognition).

Bethany's performance on tasks that measured her vocabulary knowledge and ability to find meaning for words was very poor, which was consistent with the teacher's concerns. She struggled when asked to find the correct label/name for pictures of common objects (hanger, doorknob) or define word meanings (soap, coat). The picture-naming task was administered in both English and Spanish (Woodcock Johnson Fourth Edition Tests of Oral Language: Picture Vocabulary and Vocabulario sobre dibujos), in order to detect whether a dominant-language-effect was impacting Bethany's performance. Test results

(Continued)

(Continued)

indicated that Bethany's ability to recognize and label common objects is equally impaired in both languages. The vocabulary test that required defining word meaning was administered in differed modalities such as verbal multiple choice and pictorial multiple choice to minimize the language and free-recall effect. Bethany's performance slightly increased when items were presented in a multiple-choice format.

Bethany had difficulty answering questions about a wide range of general knowledge topics (e.g., "why do people use a calendar?") (WISC-V Information). She responded "I don't know" to most of the testing items resulting in early discontinuation. In an effort to decrease the verbal demand and minimize the effect of possible receptive language and long-term memory deficit, the "Information" test was also administered in a multiple-choice format (WISC-V Integrated Information). Bethany's performance was consistent with her abilities on the free-recall version. Therefore, the possibility of an expressive language and recognition recall deficit may be ruled out. In general, Bethany's knowledge of basic information retrieved from memory in either English or Spanish is poor. Her retrieval is facilitated by using recognition rather than free recall. The instructional implication for this is that Bethany will perform better on multiple-choice tests in content areas rather than fill-in-the blank or essay questions.

Bethany demonstrated poor abilities to answer questions based on understanding of general principles and social situations (WISC-V Comprehension). The questions measured verbal reasoning skills and abstract thinking abilities (e.g., "why do people brush their teeth?" or "why do the teachers ask students to turn off their cellphones in the classroom?") with increased complexity. In order to decrease the influence of verbal demands, this task was administered in a multiple-choice format (WISC-V Integrated Comprehension Multiple Choice), which resulted in improved average performance for her age. This suggests, as noted previously, that Bethany performs better when given multiple-choice formats.

Visual-Spatial Domain

Bethany scored slightly below the expected level when she was required to analyze and synthesize abstract visual information and use fine motor manipulation of blocks to match visual patterns (WISC-V Block Design). She performed somewhat poorly when she was asked to recreate a constructed design using block pieces in a specific timeframe. This task required organization, visual perception, visual-motor integration, problem-solving, and intact motor abilities. During this task, Bethany easily gave up trying when she encountered more complex designs (e.g., "I don't know how to do it"), did not notice small details, and made rotational mistakes. Bethany was given a multiple-choice version of the same test (WISC-V Integrated Block Design Multiple Choice) that required matching the correct block configuration to recreate a design. Similar to her previous performance on this task, she performed somewhat poorly and did not carefully consider rotations, location of the pieces, and grid lines. Signs of inattention,

(Continued)

(Continued)

neglecting visual details, and low stamina appeared during her performance on this task.

Bethany's mother and teacher did not express any concerns in the area of visuospatial processes. Her performance on visuospatial perception and reasoning tasks ranged from "at expected level" to "slightly below expected level." Some struggle was identified with tasks that were timed and required motor planning and visual-motor construction. Overall, Bethany presented adequate skills for mental rotation, visuospatial analysis, and visuospatial perception. Qualitative observation of her performance on the test items suggested neglecting small details especially with increased complexity, slow task completion, and lack of judgment as to when additional steps were required to complete the task. Such challenges could be linked to her history of left suboccipital craniotomy, which can cause eye movement difficulties. Difficulties with visuospatial skills can contribute to poor performance in math, which is an area of concern for Bethany.

Fluid Reasoning Domain

Bethany's ability to mentally solve orally presented arithmetic problems within time limits (WISC-V Arithmetic) was within the average range compared to her same-aged peers. Bethany's responses were fast and accurate, inconsistent with her previous performance on auditory tasks and her mother and teacher's concerns. The WISC-V Integrated Arithmetic Process Approach test presents the missed items from the WISC-V Arithmetic test in different formats, visual presentation while read aloud by the examiner, and allowing the examinee to use of paper and pencil to possibly aid in solving the missed arithmetic problems. These additional modality options did not significantly improve Bethany's performance on the arithmetic test items.

Bethany was administered the Figure Weights test from the WISC-V, which measures quantitative reasoning or the ability to determine what weight is needed to balance a scale. Bethany achieved a below-average score on this test. Bethany often overlooked small details in visual stimuli, did not persist to complete testing items, did not carefully examine visual stimuli as a whole rather than small bits, and demonstrated slow task completion. Bethany's performance did not improve when administered the Figure Weights Process Approach test from the WISC-V Integrated. Modifying the processing speed demands of the task did not change the quality of performance on these two tests. Bethany's performance on these fluid reasoning tests suggests that she will exhibit the following behaviors in the classroom: careless mistakes, inattention, and lack of problem-solving skills.

Immediate Memory Tests

Immediate Memory is not a domain that is formally recognized as being measured by the WISC-V/WISC-V Integrated, but from a neuropsychological perspective there are several tests that measure immediate memory. Bethany presented with difficulties on immediate verbal memory tests. On the WISC-V Digit Span test, Forward numbers condition, Bethany had difficulty recalling strings of digits

(Continued)

(Continued)

of increasing length when spoken to her by the examiner. She performed slightly better on the WISC-V Integrated Spatial Span, Forward numbers condition. On the Spatial Span (Forward) test, Bethany was asked to watch the examiner tap a sequence of blocks then reproduce the tapping sequence herself. By removing the auditory demands of the Digits Span-like task, she performed slightly better when tasks were paired with visual cues. She demonstrated poor abilities to immediately and correctly remember a string of words or numbers in isolation as they progressed in complexity and length.

Working Memory Domain

Bethany's mother and teacher expressed mild-to-severe concerns regarding her working memory at home and in the school setting. Mother's concerns were mostly regarding math and writing tasks. She noted that Bethany has trouble remembering multiplication tables and order of operations in division and multi-digit subtraction and heavily relies on her help. The teacher noted that Bethany struggles with working independently and loses her place in the middle of solving math and writing assignments. He noted that Bethany specifically forgets steps for division, multidigits computation, and any operation with decimals. Although they have been reviewing sequential math operations throughout the school year, she still can't pull the information from memory. Summarizing anything is difficult for Bethany, and she often doesn't remember what was read/discussed earlier. The teacher appeared very concerned when he explained that Bethany does not remember the classroom routines and order of group rotations after having the same schedule for the past 8 months. He reported that Bethany asks daily about the order of classroom rotations, which alternates between computer (for reading), math, and writing groups.

Bethany demonstrated poor abilities to perform dual-tasks of mental manipulations verbally and visually (WISC-V Digit Span Backward & WISC-V Integrated Spatial Span Backward). On these tasks Bethany was asked to repeat number strings in reverse order after spoken by the examiner. Bethany's performance indicated the impact of primacy effect; she successfully remembered a few initial items and her recalling abilities declined with increasing length. Bethany's visual working memory was slightly better based on her performance on the WISC-V Picture Span test, which measured her ability to recall the order of visual stimuli. On the WISC-V Integrated Sentence Recall, the complexity of the auditorally presented stimuli increased as compared to memory for digits, and her performance on this test was still below average. Sometimes the added contextual cues help performance improve but not in Bethany's case.

Processing Speed Domain

Bethany's performance was average compared to her peers when she was required to copy symbols paired with numbers (WISC-V Coding). During this task, she referred back and forth to the target stimuli without sacrificing speed. It should be noted that this task is presented in a more visually structured format with visual items more spaced out on the worksheet. On the WISC-V Integrated Coding Recall test, visual memory was emphasized, and she obtained a score in

(Continued)

(Continued)

the average range. Likewise, on the WISC-V Integrated Coding Copy test, fine motor skills were emphasized, and she obtained a score in the above-average range. Bethany's processing speed was not adversely affected by her immediate visual memory or fine motor skills.

In contrast to Bethany's average to above-average performance on the Coding tests, Bethany demonstrated difficulties when she was asked to mark target pictures within a set of visual pictures on the stimulus page, in a random and structured order (WISC-V Cancellation and WISC-V Integrated Cancellation Abstract, Random or Structured). The Coding tasks required solid visual tracking, perceptual skills, visual-motor coordination, speed, and attention; whereas, cancellation, in addition to solid visual scanning abilities and perceptual fluency, requires additional skills such as visual discrimination, selective attention, decision-making, and response inhibition. In other neuropsychological findings, Bethany demonstrated difficulties with selective attention, response inhibition, problem-solving/decision-making, and visual discrimination. The deficits in these areas interfered with Bethany's performance on the visual cancellation test. In addition, the cluttered visual background, amount of space between items on the page, and the fonts should be taken into consideration regarding her performance on this task. Bethany has shown that she requires more times to get through visual information when it is presented densely.

Diagnostic Impressions

It is important to consider that children who have been treated for brain tumors are at risk for physical, cognitive, academic, and social challenges. It is important to note the risks associated with neurosurgical treatment options when evaluating neurocognitive functioning. With this treatment option, healthy brain tissue may also be removed in order to resect as much of the tumor as possible. Children who undergo this treatment may experience decline in certain functions based on the area of the brain involved. In particular, surgical resection for posterior fossa tumor (Bethany's case) may likely result in short-term memory impairment, attention (sustained and selected) deficits, slower processing speed, semantic memory deficits, and visual-constructive difficulties. Neurosurgical treatments also increase the risk of mild-to-moderate deficits in nonverbal reasoning, motor output, verbal memory, visuospatial processes, and memory (Begyn & Castillo, 2010).

Sensorimotor Deficits

With respect to Bethany's medical history of cerebellar tumor, neurosurgical treatments on posterior fossa, and suboccipital craniotomy, evaluations of sensorimotor functions were conducted (as part of the comprehensive neuropsychological evaluation). Throughout the evaluation, Bethany exhibited intact sensory motor abilities. She possesses strong abilities with balance, fine and gross motor coordination, gait and station, and tactile sensation/perception. Some deficits were observed with visual scanning and tracking and slow eye movement across busy visual backgrounds.

(Continued)

(Continued)

Learning and Memory Deficits

According to the evaluation results, Bethany's academic performance appears significantly impacted by weak memory skills. Her performance on direct measures of various memory functioning suggests an impairment and deficit in learning and memory. The memory deficits characterized by lower than same-age peers rate of learning, difficulty with learning new information, recalling recently learned information from short-term memory, retrieving information from long-term memory, delayed recall, and recalling information with increasing complexity and length appear to significantly impact her ability to keep up with increasing academic demands. Bethany exhibits a persistent pattern of challenges with learning, storing, and recalling new information.

Executive Function Deficits

Although Bethany presented with difficulties in various measures of executive functioning, her overall functioning may also be impacted by deficits in language, memory, and visual scanning skills. The executive function skills that appeared to be impacted by other underlying deficits include verbal deductive/inductive reasoning, difficulties using verbal skills to explain (generate) concepts, performing simultaneous verbal/visual tasks, and verbal cognitive flexibility in the presence of language and memory demands. However, inconsistency across Bethany's performance on executive functioning tasks (difficulties shifting between different tasks) leaves an open assumption of possible true deficits with executive functions. Thus, Bethany's executive functioning skills should be supported in the classroom. Relevant accommodation should be added to the Individualized Education Plan (IEP) to support this area and assist with behaviors related to executive function difficulties.

Attentional Processing Deficits

According to standardized testing and behavior observations, Bethany exhibits patterns of performance consistent with inattentiveness. She demonstrated difficulties with selective and sustained attention visually and auditory and attentional capacities. In addition, qualitative observations indicated an inability to stay on task for a long period of time, making carless errors, requiring extra time to complete tasks, and feeling overwhelmed with excess details. It is important to consider memory skills when determining attention deficits. Attention and memory deficits may present as comorbid difficulties. While Bethany may possess an attentional deficit, her significant challenges with memory and visual tracking skills must be taken to consideration since most given tasks for evaluation of attention and concentration require intact memory skills and solid visual scanning/tracking. At this time, challenges with attention and focus may be linked to deficits in memory and visual tracking skills. However, Bethany should be monitored closely for true symptoms of attention deficit disorder after given strategies to enhance her memory functioning and accommodated for visual tracking difficulties.

(Continued)

(Continued)

Language Deficits

According to the DSM-5, a communication disorder includes difficulties with acquisition and use of language across modalities (spoken, written, sign, or others) due to deficits in comprehension or production that includes reduced vocabulary, limited sentence structure, and an inability to use vocabulary and connect sentences to explain or describe a topic or series of events. Bethany's difficulties were consistent with this criteria of a communication disorder. Bethany displayed oral expression deficits in both expressive and receptive language, in English and Spanish. She presented with limited vocabulary, difficulty following verbal multistep directions, listening comprehension, and difficulty with using words and forming sentences in order to explain an idea or explore a topic. This was confirmed by her better performance on multiple-choice format when the language demand required to explain a concept is reduced. Further clinical evaluation of Bethany's language function and communication skills is important to determine specific deficits with language functioning. It is important to consult with a speech and language pathologist for further evaluation.

Difficulties With Mathematics

Bethany presents with significant math weakness characterized by deficits in number sense, computation skills, retrieval of math facts, understanding concepts, following procedure, and special relation alignments. Her deficits are consistent with verbal, procedural, and semantic dyscalculia, in which challenges with retrieval of number facts (impairment in multiplication), comprehending sequencing and counting numeric information (e.g., difficulty recalling sequence of steps when performing longer math problems), and nonsymbolic skills (e.g., alignment of numbers in columns, pattern recognition) were displayed. Bethany should continue to receive support via IEP math goals.

Difficulties With Written Expression

According to limited standardized measures and extensive review of classroom performance, a deficit in writing skills consistent with executive dysgraphia was observed. Executive dysgraphia is characterized by inability to master grammar rules, difficulties with verbal retrieval skills, and planning cohesive and sequential writing, consistent with her difficulties with complex sentence structures, grammar, organization, planning, and sequencing events. Bethany's writing should be supported through IEP goals for writing—she currently does not have any writing goals.

Difficulties With Reading

A serious reading comprehension deficit characterized by difficulty deriving meaning from text was obtained through curriculum-based assessments. The results from limited standardized assessments indicated mild difficulties with reading comprehension skills. Bethany's deficits may also be linked to challenges with language functioning and memory skills. Reading comprehension deficits may coexist with language and memory deficits and/or may be impacted by such deficits. Bethany's performance should be closely monitored for a true

(Continued)

(Continued)

deficit in reading comprehension after implementing interventions for language disorders and memory deficits. Reading comprehension should be supported through IEP goals for comprehension.

Recommendations for School Instructions
Strategies to Improve Memory Skills

- Present new materials in more than one format (visual, verbal, tactile)—Bethany has strengths and weaknesses within each modality. Using multi-modality to teach information will best utilize her skills.

- Use visual representations of verbal instructions and daily routines—for example, Bethany has difficulty remembering the order of classroom daily group rotation; use a chart with visual representation of the routines paired with their sequential orders (e.g., 1st = /picture of a computer/representing rotation to the computer center).

- Confirm encoding—to ensure learning of the initial materials, at the end of each section ask her to briefly repeat what she had learned and then move on to the next part. If she is not able to demonstrate learning, review the information as many times as needed.

- Pair new information with cues (contextual cues) that represent something relevant—link new information with what she already knows. She can use her existing knowledge as a reminder to recall new information over time. For example, when teaching about sea animals, make reference and connections to Disney movies that she likes (e.g., Finding Nemo).

- Review new information multiple times throughout the day and week—she learns better after multiple exposures. An opportunity for rehearsal and practice should be provided at different times of the day multiple times per day; multiple times per week, previously learned information needs to be reviewed.

- Provide brief verbal information—she has difficulty with verbal information increasing language content. It is beneficial to eliminate excess language from the instructions.

- Give one verbal direction at a time and wait for response; allow doing one task at a time—she requires more time to think about what was asked before following the directions. Give verbal directions one at a time and allow for processing time before adding more directions. Similarly, allow her to do one task at a time—especially with writing that requires performing multiple tasks at the same time. For example, first think of an idea, then say it, then write it down, and last edit it.

Strategies to Improve Communication Skills

- Teach how to group objects, pictures, words into categories—categorization will help with vocabulary, conceptual, and semantic development. Give her pictures to put into categories and give her word choices to identify why they are similar (e.g., eatable, you can use them to build things, furniture)—similar to the multiple-choice format.

(Continued)

(Continued)

- Play word games or object-naming games. For example, look around the room and name different objects present in the room—this will help in building vocabulary.
- Continue support with the English Language Learner program at school to continue developing English language knowledge.

Strategies to Improve Attention Skills
- Break down new information into smaller chunks and ensure understanding of small pieces—this will relieve her anxiety, reduce overwhelming feelings toward tasks, and reduce task-avoidance behavior such as going back to drawing as a possible coping skill.
- Provide multiple breaks between a given task—Bethany usually disengages when instructions are one upon another. Taking short breaks and chunking work into smaller increments will help with disengaging behavior.
- Use a different color, font, or size for computation signs (e.g., $+$, $\times$, $-$), which may draw more attention to small details and increase accuracy.

Strategies to Improve Executive Function Skills
- Teach priorities and model planning—it is beneficial to sequentially explain priorities before expecting planning. Bethany has difficulties with sequential thinking and prioritizing may not come naturally for her. She will benefit when she is given priorities rather than having to figure it out on her own (e.g., we should practice the multiplication table today because we have a multiplication test tomorrow morning). After priorities are spelled out for her, with an assistance of an adult, she may fill out a sequential planner to guide her as to what to study first.
- Use premade checklists when completing assignments—this is especially crucial during writing. Help her take the necessary steps required for task completion.
- Ask her to set goals for herself. It is important to attach a goal or meaning to an assignment so she can understand why she is learning the presented information and how she is going to use it in the near future—for example, learning monetary values will allow her to correctly count and use her allowance.

Strategies to Improve Math Skills
- Break up word problems into smaller sections and allow work on each section separately.
- Use a large font for simple math computations—difficulties with visual scanning may appear during math computations. It is important to adjust the arrangement, font, color, and presentation of the material to a level that she can easily scan and access.
- Use manipulatives and teach hands-on versus mentally. She will benefit from a visual representation when learning values and quantities.
- Use graph paper to line up equations to provide visual structure.

(Continued)

(Continued)

- Attach number-line to desk—this will provide an immediate visual aid and eliminates the struggles associated with visuospatial memory in regards to number-sense.

Strategies to Improve Writing Skills

- Give graphic organizer for writing—organization is a significantly difficult task. It is very important for Bethany to use a visual guide to help her organize her ideas, paragraphs, and essays.
- Allow the use of a word-bank when writing—this will assist with not using the same words over and over and expand her limited vocabulary.
- Provide a template for writing—instead of using a blank sheet to formulate a writing assignment, provide writing worksheets that are divided into different sections for the purpose of organization, direction, and planning. For example, a box to write the title of the essay on the top, a separate box to write an opening sentence, and so on.
- Use mnemonic strategies or rubric for self-monitoring and editing. Self-monitoring strategies are helpful to check off each step, one at a time, to complete a writing assignment with higher accuracy—COPS = Capitalize, Organize, Punctuation, Spelling.

Strategies to Improve Reading Skills

- Frontload prior to reading—when reading a new book or text, briefly talk about what the text is about, then ask for prior knowledge or questions about the topic. If she demonstrates no prior knowledge about the topic (e.g., using service dogs to help blind people), then discuss some facts and show some pictures to make the text more relevant. If the task is meaningful and interesting, Bethany will be more engaged and can follow along more efficiently. This will decrease irrelevant responses to comprehension questions.
- Ask comprehension questions prior to reading. This is similar to the above strategy with the additional opportunity to know what questions may be asked and what to attend to while reading.
- Outline important information with different color highlighters—this strategy helps her to identify what needs attention within the text and provides additional emphasis on the most important information (e.g., information highlighted in pink is highly important, the yellow ones are not as important).

Recommendations for Home

- Do daily homework at the same time and in the same location.
- Break up homework into smaller increments and take short breaks in between.
- Practice math facts before bed and shortly before going to school everyday in the morning.
- Give a visual to-do list for daily chores and morning routines.
- In order to expand vocabulary, use apps—Word of the Week, Words with Friends—to introduce new words regularly.

(Continued)

(Continued)

- Watch documentary movies, motion picture biographies, National Geographic/History channels for kids to increase general knowledge.
- Use math apps—Math Crunch, Cool Math, Math is Fun, Illuminations—to practice math skills through exciting games.
- Discuss concerns regarding language skills with a speech language pathologist at school and within a medical facility.
- Discuss possible benefits of vision therapy to enhance visual scanning/tracking with her ophthalmologist or optometrist.

SUMMARY

The WISC-V Integrated used in conjunction with the WISC-V can be useful in generating hypotheses about the underlying cognitive processes and executive functions used by examinees during task performances. These tests can be useful in providing an understanding of a child's level and pattern of intellectual performance, which in turn can be used to develop meaningful academic and behavioral interventions that have ecological and treatment validity (Miller & Hale, 2008). The WISC-V/WISC-V Integrated tests can serve as a foundation for a school neuropsychological assessment; however, if used in isolation, these tests will not address many of the areas typically addressed in a comprehensive school neuropsychological assessment. The WISC-V Integrated is a useful supplement to the WISC-V, as a means of clarifying the causal factors of low scores on WISC-V subtests. Any time a low score, relative to overall performance on the WISC-V is obtained, the alternative WISC-V Integrated test should be administered. For a comprehensive school neuropsychological evaluation, the WISC-V and WISC-V Integrated must be supplemented with other neuropsychological measures based on the referral question(s) and the pattern of performance on the baseline measures. Supplemental measures of sensorimotor functions, attentional processing, and memory and learning processes should be considered as warranted. The case study presented in this chapter illustrated how the WISC-V Integrated and WISC-V subtests can fit within a school neuropsychological conceptual model (Miller, 2013). The case study also illustrates the fact that if the WISC-V/WISC-V Integrated were the only tests administered, the underlying reasons for Bethany's academic difficulties would have not been fully discovered.

An important point to reiterate is that the classification of the WISC-V Integrated and WISC-V subtests based on their underlying neurocognitive task demands is intended to serve as a tentative interpretative guide only. A child's performance on a particular test may be a result of multiple factors that relate to the manifestation of the child's neurocognitive strengths and weaknesses, the reliability and validity of the test measure itself, or noncognitive factors (e.g., motivational, cultural, social, or environmental). The "art" of psychology, and the specialized areas of school psychology and school neuropsychology, lies in generating hypotheses about the causal factors of samples of behavior; testing and verifying those hypotheses with multiple sources of data (e.g., observations, direct samples of behavior, behavioral rating scales); and ultimately linking empirically based interventions to help remediate identified areas of weakness (Miller & Hale, 2008).

REFERENCES

Begyn, E. L., & Castillo, C. L. (2010). Assessing and intervening with children with brain tumors. In D. C. Miller (Ed.), *Best practices in school neuropsychology: Guidelines for effective practice, assessment, and evidence-based intervention* (pp. 737–765). Hoboken, NJ: John Wiley & Sons.

Flanagan, D. P., & Alfonso, V. C. (2017). *Essentials of WISC-V assessment*. Hoboken, NJ: John Wiley & Sons.

Kaplan, E., Fein, D., Kramer, J., Delis, D., & Morris, R. (1999). *WISC-III PI manual*. San Antonio, TX: The Psychological Corporation.

McCloskey, G., Slonim, J., Whitaker, R., Kaufman, S., & Nagoshi, N. (2017). A neuropsychological approach to interpretation of the WISC-V. In D. P. Flanagan, & V. C. Alfonso (Eds.), *Essentials of WISC-V assessment* (pp. 287–333). Hoboken, NJ: Wiley.

Milberg, W., & Hebben, N. (2013). Historical foundations of the Boston process approach. In L. Ashendorf, D. J. Libon, & R. Swenson (Eds.), *The Boston process approach to neuropsychological assessment*. New York: Oxford.

Miller, D. C., & Jones, A. M. (2016). Interpreting the WISC-V from Dan Miller's integrated school neuropsychological/Cattell-Horn-Carroll model. In A. S. Kaufman, S. E. Raiford, & D. L. Coalson (Eds.), *Intelligence testing with the WISC-V* (pp. 459–470). Hoboken, NJ: John Wiley & Sons.

Miller, D. C. (2013). Essentials of school neuropsychological *assessment* (2nd ed.). Hoboken, NJ: John Wiley & Sons.

Miller, D. C. (2015). Integration of the WJ IV, WISC-V, WISC-V integrated, and WIAT-III into a school neuropsychological assessment model. *School Psychology Forum: Research in Practice, 9*(3), 251–268.

Miller, D. C., & Hale, J. B. (2008). The neuropsychological applications of the Wechsler Intelligence Scale for Children-Fourth edition. In A. Prifitera, D. H. Saklofske, & L. G. Weiss (Eds.), *WISC-IV advanced clinical interpretation* (2nd ed., pp. 445–495). San Diego, CA: Academic Press.

Raiford, S. E. (2017). *Essentials of WISC-V integrated assessment*. Hoboken, NJ: John Wiley & Sons.

Wechsler, D. (2004). *Wechsler intelligences scale for children integrated* (4th ed.). San Antonio, TX: Harcourt Assessment, Inc.

Wechsler, D. (2009). *Wechsler individual achievement test* (3rd ed.). Bloomington, MN: PsychCorp.

Wechsler, D. (2014). *Wechsler intelligence scale for children* (5th ed.). Bloomington, MN: PsychCorp.

Wechsler, D., & Kaplan, E. (2015). *Wechsler intelligence scale for children integrated* (5th ed.). Bloomington, MN: Pearson.

Werner, H. (1937). Process and achievement: A basic problem or education and developmental psychology. *Harvard Educational Review, 7,* 353−368.

Chapter 4

Theoretical and Clinical Foundations of the Wechsler Intelligence Scale for Children— Fifth Edition

Lawrence G. Weiss[1], James A. Holdnack[2], Donald H. Saklofske[3] and Aurelio Prifitera[4]

[1]Research and Measurement Consultant, San Antonio, TX, United States, [2]Research and Statistical Consultant, Bear, DE, United States, [3]Department of Psychology, University of Western Ontario, London, ON, Canada, [4]Assessment Consultant, San Antonio, TX, United States

INTRODUCTION

In this chapter we cover advanced topics related to interpretation of the five primary Index scores. We conduct a detailed analysis of the cognitive constructs assessed by each of the indexes, how each is related to intelligence through models of cognitive information processing and neuroscience, and how the various cognitive abilities interact with one another and the executive functions (EFs) in the service of solving problems in real life.

We remind psychologists that while an understanding of the abilities being tapped by the Index and subtest scores are fundamental to using this test, these scores must also be placed in the larger context of each child and their "world." There are a huge number of endogenous factors such as genetics and a host of external factors such as culture and education that impact not only the growth and expression of intelligence, but also performance on intelligence tests. This topic is elaborated on in the chapter on Societal Context in this book.

WISC-V. DOI: https://doi.org/10.1016/B978-0-12-815744-2.00004-5

THE WECHSLER INTELLIGENCE SCALE FOR CHILDREN—FIFTH EDITION INDEX SCORES

Confirmatory Factor Analysis

The original Wechsler model contained only two factors labeled Verbal IQ and Performance IQ, together with a composite Full Scale IQ (FSIQ). The modern Wechsler model is based on a five-factor theoretical model of intelligence consisting of the Verbal Comprehension Index (VCI), Visual-Spatial Index (VSI), Fluid Reasoning Index (FRI), Working Memory Index (WMI), and Processing Speed Index (PSI), and retains the composite FSIQ. The contemporary five-factor Wechsler model has been shown to fit the data very well for all current and recent editions of the Wechsler tests including the Wechsler Preschool and Primary Scales of Intelligence—Fourth Edition (Wechsler, 2012), Wechsler Adult Intelligence Scale—Fourth Edition (WAIS-IV; Weiss, Keith, Zhu, & Chen, 2013a; Niileksela, Reynolds, & Kaufman, 2013), WISC-IV (Weiss, Keith, Zhu, & Chen, 2013b), and Wechsler Intelligence Scale for Children—Fifth Edition (WISC-V; Wechsler, 2014). Fig. 4.1 shows the fit of this five-factor model to the WISC-V standardization data ($n = 2200$). For more information about the evolution of the contemporary Wechsler five-factor model, the reader is referred to Chapter 1 of this book.

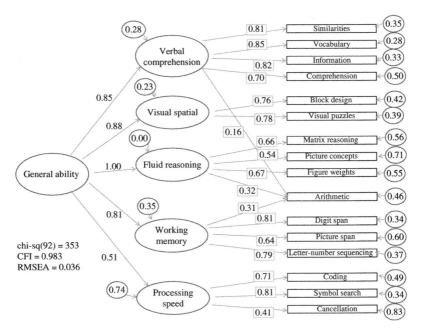

FIGURE 4.1 WISC-V Five-factor hierarchical model for all subtests, ages 6–16. *Data and table copyright Pearson (2014). Reproduced with permission. All rights reserved.*

Hierarchical Versus Bifactor Models of Intelligence

Although well supported by empirical data, the WISC-V factor structure is not without criticism. Alternative theoretical models of intelligence and the tests that are based on them have been hotly debated for more than a century. The major current controversy pits hierarchical or higher-order models of intelligence, as reflected in the WISC-V and all other major tests of intelligence, against a bifactor model of intelligence. In this alternative model, the subtests are directly influenced by general mental ability, or g, as operationalized by the FSIQ rather than via the five broad abilities (e.g., the first-order factors). Employing bifactor analysis, these first-order factors in some cases are shown to account for very little unique variance beyond g. The five broad ability indexes are dismissed as an unnecessary middle layer between g and the subtests. Proponents of this approach state that eliminating this middle layer would result in a more parsimonious or streamlined model of intelligence. They insist that clinical interpretation should rest with FSIQ, and perhaps the subtests. Moreover, bifactorists argue that continued clinical interpretation of the broad abilities is malpractice because they do not measure anything different than g (Canivez, Watkins, & Dombrowski, 2016; Canivez, Watkins, & Dombrowski, 2017; Dombrowski, Canivez, Watkins, & Beaujean, 2015).

There are three major problems with this line of reasoning: statistical, theoretical, and clinical! First, a brief statistical riposte: When comparing competing hierarchical and bifactor models, researchers compare statistical tests or indices of model fit (e.g., Chi-square test of model differences, Bayesian information criterion) to identify which model more accurately fits the data. While the above researchers point to marginally improved statistical test/fit statistics as justification for the superiority of the bifactor model, recent simulation work has shown that these statistical tests/fit statistics often favor bifactor over higher-order models in general. This bias tends to increase as the number of unmodeled complexities, such as cross-loadings, increases (Gignac, 2016; Gignac & Watkins, 2013; Mansolf & Reise, 2017; Morgan, Hodge, Wells, & Watkins, 2015; Murray & Johnson, 2013; Yang, Spirtes, Scheines, Reise, & Mansoff, 2017). Thus, it appears that advocates of the bifactor model likely have employed a statistical test that is inherently biased in favor of their preferred model.

Reynolds and Keith (2017) also compared results of higher-order and bifactor models but came to different conclusions. They reported that both g and the five distinct broad abilities are necessary to explain the covariance among the WISC-V subtests, and that this finding was the same whether a bifactor or higher-order model was used. They note that their findings are inconsistent with studies reported by Canivez et al. (2016, 2017) and Dombrowski et al. (2015).

We would suggest that perhaps a somewhat more balanced summary of the current state of this contentious and still evolving line of research would be that "while both the bifactor and higher-order models fit the data very well, the bifactor model appears to provide a small but significant improvement in fit — although the possibility remains that this improved fit is partially influenced by an inherent statistical bias in the method, which tends to favor bifactor over the higher-order models."

We now consider some of the theoretical issues related to the bifactor model. The key concept for practitioners to understand is that bifactor analysis statistically removes all g-related variance from the Index scores, and considers only the residual variation that remains after g is removed from them as valid. This is a very different approach than all traditional theoretical models of intelligence, which posit a hierarchy of abilities in which similar narrow abilities, represented by the subtests (e.g., Vocabulary (VC) and Similarities (SI)), are grouped into conceptually related broad abilities represented by the indexes (e.g., Verbal Comprehension), with g (represented by FSIQ) sitting at the apex of a typical three-stratum hierarchical model. Bifactor researchers refer to the hierarchical model as an indirect model because it requires the subtests to pass through a first-order or group factor (i.e., an index) on the way to g. They test this indirect (i.e., hierarchical) model against a direct (bifactor) model in which the subtests load directly on g.

Researchers employing bifactor analysis and related techniques that remove g from the first-order factors typically find, not surprisingly, that there is insufficient broad ability variance remaining in some of the Index scores after g is removed from them and declare—somewhat sophistically—that the Index scores have no value apart from g. This finding is not specific to the WISC-V as it also has been reported in analyses of the Woodcock–Johnson test of intelligence (Dombrowski, McGill, & Canivez, 2017a; Dombrowski, McGill, & Canivez, 2017b; McFarland, 2016). Rather than representing a criticism unique to the WISC-V factor structure, this line of research represents a substantial challenge to the various hierarchical models of intelligence that have dominated the field for more than a century, including the Cattell, Horn, Carroll (CHC) model, as well as an attempted rebuke of all clinicians who have been interpreting Index scores in their practices for decades.

Ultimately, the bifactorists are attempting to reinterpret Wechsler's scales (and the Woodcock–Johnson scales) from the perspective of Spearman's (1904) original two-factor theory of intelligence in which the two factors are g and the specific reliable variance from each of the subtests. But that is not the theory that underlies new versions of Wechsler's scales. Rather, five group-level factors—whether derived from CHC or neuroscience research—underlie the new Wechsler scales. Since confirmatory factor analysis techniques are supposed to test the fit of the data to the theoretical structure that underlies the battery, the appropriate theory to serve as the guide for the underlying model should be the theory that the test authors and developers chose for the test. It should not be a different theory (Spearman's two-factor theory) that someone else, such as the bifactor researchers, impose on Wechsler's scales. (Alan Kaufman, personal communication, November 30, 2017.) While it is always important to compare competing theories, it must be noted that when the theory the WISC-V was built to measure is evaluated, that model fits the data very well (Reynolds & Keith, 2017). Even Spearman, a strong believer in the overriding power of g, was eventually forced to admit the existence of group factors akin to the current Index scores (Spearman, 1923, 1927).

Current versions of Wechsler's scales are much more closely aligned with the Carroll three-strata (narrow, broad, and general cognitive ability) and the CHC (Carroll, 1993) than Spearman theory, and have strong historical roots in the theories of Burt and Vernon (see Vernon, 1950) who proposed a hierarchical structure with group factors between g and the specific subtests. The original Burt and Vernon group factors (verbal-educational and practical-spatial-mechanical) have evolved and been enumerated with ongoing clinical research, but the three-stratum model is essentially the same hierarchical structure as the current Wechsler and Woodcock—Johnson scales. Finally, the larger number of fluid and crystallized subtests in the FSIQ reflects the alignment of WISC-V with R.B. Cattell's fluid—crystallized model of intelligence (Cattell, 1963, 1987), which is also a three-stratum model that includes narrow, broad, and general abilities in hierarchical sequence. Later in this chapter we expand on how the five group factors work together to support the accumulation of crystalized knowledge, and in particular, the execution of fluid reasoning.

Thus, apart from the desire for parsimony, there is no sound theoretical reason to remove g variance from the Index scores, and every reason not to do so! We note that all of the current data suggest that the fluid reasoning factor is virtually isomorphic with psychometric g in WISC-V. This observation has led to rather silly arguments about deleting either fluid reasoning or g from the model—in the name of parsimony. But Cattell (1987) viewed fluid reasoning as a source trait; a substantive underlying causal variable— much like g itself. In his *investment theory*, Cattell attributed a casual role to fluid intelligence in the development of other cognitive abilities. Learning requires perceiving relations, and fluid intelligence is the capacity to do this. Cattell's investment theory states that people "invest" their fluid intelligence to acquire specific skills, strategies, and knowledge in all kinds of fields (Cattell, 1963, 1987, pp. 138—147). Moreover, people do not necessarily invest their g resources evenly across other domains of knowledge and abilities, but rather, direct these resources toward the development of specific areas depending on personal interest and environmental demands or opportunities. The extent to which specific narrow skills and associated broad abilities develop or not as the brain matures and the individual gains experience in her environment depends in part on where she focuses the g resources. This is why it makes little theoretical sense to remove g from the broad abilities and then claim they measure nothing important. A sports-related analogy offered by Schneider (2013) makes this point:

> *We care about a sprinter's ability to run quickly, not residual sprinting speed after accounting for general athleticism. So it is with [the broad abilities]: g is part of the mix. (p. 6)*

We have discussed a few of the statistical and theoretical issues we consider most related to the debate over hierarchical versus bifactor models of intelligence. Now we briefly consider issues related to the clinical utility of the test scores in practice. Our main point is that evidence for the validity of a theoretical construct should not be limited to factor analyses of tests purported to measure that construct. Although one important piece of psychometric evidence, factor analysis, is limited to an examination of the internal structural relations between the various subtest scores and their hypothesized latent factors. Factor analysis provides no information about the relationship of the test scores to any criteria external to the test itself. For a statistician, the internal structure of a battery of subtests can be a thing of pure beauty. For a clinician, however, that is wholly insufficient. What matters in practice is how the test scores relate to meaningful clinical criteria, and how the test performs in the real world. Does the model well represent the development of cognitive abilities from childhood through older adulthood? Does the model help to explain children's difficulties with reading, math, or attentional control? How do patients diagnosed with traumatic brain injury (TBI) or dyslexia or Attention-Deficit/Hyperactivity Disorder (ADHD) perform on the test? This is what our book is about—the clinical utility of the WISC-V five-factor model in psychological practice.

Certainly, neuropsychologists have long argued that FSIQ is too multidimensional to be neuropsychologically informative and favor interpretation of scores that are more construct specific (Lezak, Howieson, Bigler, & Tranel, 2012), including the Index scores. How do models of intelligence relate to what we know about neuropsychological functioning? How do the broad cognitive abilities relate to measures of memory or EF? Researchers are increasingly demonstrating important relations between neural systems and intraindividual differences within and between broad cognitive abilities measured by the Wechsler scales using fMRI and CT imaging techniques (e.g., Margolis et al., 2013; Barbey, Colom, & Grafman, 2013; Colom, Martinez-Molina, Shih, & Santacreu, 2011; Langeslag et al., 2012; Martinez et al., 2011; Tang et al., 2010). We expand on this topic later in the chapter. For now, we simply ask what is wrong with our statistical techniques that they contradict what medical procedures show is happening in the brain when people are administered specific cognitive tasks? All forms of factor analysis are mathematical techniques designed to reduce the matrix of subtest correlations to the smallest number of unobservable latent factors and produce the simplest internal structure. But evidence suggests that the brain is not necessarily organized according to the rules of statistics, and neurocognitive functioning may not be subject to the law of parsimony.

Those who advocate for bifactor models hold very strong beliefs in the power and value of the IQ score. So do we! While we differ about the value of Index scores, we all agree that IQ is likely the most powerful and ecologically important variable in the field of psychology. At various times in history, IQ tests have come under unfair attack in the popular literature for limiting people's potential or lacking cultural fairness. Whenever these issues flare up in the mainstream press, our *g* theorist colleagues raise up in support of IQ—and make a formidable, empirically and clinically, grounded defense indeed.

We now turn our attention to an in-depth discussion of the theoretical, clinical, and neuropsychological foundations of the WISC-V five factors, individually and in combination.

Verbal Comprehension

Tim appears to have a sizeable vocabulary and can recite learned facts but does not appear to reason effectively using words and language. This is also quite obvious in more authentic and everyday tasks that require, for example, comprehending the meaning of stories read in class and in analogical thinking. This is further corroborated by his WISC-V subtest scores for Vocabulary (12) and Information (11) in contrast to Similarities (6) and Comprehension (8).

The VCI reflects an individual's ability to comprehend verbal stimuli, reason with semantic material, and communicate thoughts and ideas with words. Such abilities are imperative for intelligent functioning in modern society.

Although the VCI includes tasks that require prior knowledge of certain words and information, it would be a mistake to consider this index only as a measure of words and facts taught in school. Clearly, some base knowledge of words must be assumed in order to measure verbal reasoning—after all, one could not measure verbal reasoning without using words. Barring a particularly limiting linguistic environment, however, performance on these tasks reflects a person's ability to grasp verbally presented facts typically available in the world around them, reason with semantic constructs, and to express their reasoning with words. Crystallized knowledge is the background within which these abilities are assessed. It is defined as the breadth and depth of a person's acquired knowledge of a culture and the effective application of this knowledge. This store of primarily verbal or language-based knowledge may represent those abilities that have been developed largely through the investment of other abilities during educational and general life experience (McGrew & Flanagan, 1998, p. 20).

The VC and Information (IN) subtests require that a fact or the meaning of a word was learned, can be recalled, and expressed coherently. There is no apparent demand to reason in the VC subtest; it is essentially the case that one "knows" the word or in the case of IN, the person has been exposed to, knows, and can recall the "fact." However, VC is one of the highest "*g*" loaded subtests, and one of the best predictors of overall intelligence. We believe this is due to two reasons. First, higher-order thinking requires analysis of increasingly differentiated verbal constructs and second, larger pieces of related information can be chunked into a coherent whole for quicker processing. Individuals with larger vocabularies have words to describe increasingly differentiated views of the world. Second, they can chunk larger concepts into a single word for more efficient reasoning. While they may have enjoyed a more enriched learning environment, they must also be able to apply their knowledge appropriately. Knowledge of advanced vocabulary words requires the individual to accurately comprehend nuances of situations—which requires a higher level of intelligence. For example, do we say that the AIDS vaccine was "discovered" or "invented" —what is the difference? As another example, consider that to use the word "obviate" appropriately in conversation, one must first perceive that some action will make another action unnecessary. Finally, consider how intelligent one must be to tell the difference between "placating" and "appeasing" another person? Thus, crystallized knowledge is not a simple matter of reciting learned facts or definitions of words. The ability to acquire higher levels of crystallized knowledge reflects the intelligence necessary to comprehend that knowledge. Furthermore, appropriate application of the stored information requires advanced comprehension of the situation. Finally, adequate vocabulary is necessary for reading comprehension, and reading educational materials can improve crystallized knowledge and facilitate higher-order learning. This is how vocabulary development is related to intelligence and higher-order reasoning.

The SI and Comprehension (CO) subtests also require a base knowledge of information; however, they are considered to require some reasoning because they involve thinking with crystallized words and facts in ways that may not have been considered previously. For example, CO items typically assume certain facts are known (e.g., cars must have license plates), but the reasons for these facts are typically not taught directly in school. The child must engage in both recall of stored information relevant to the presenting problem but also reasoning to answer the question, "Why must cars have license plates?"

The SI subtest asks how two words representing objects or concepts are alike. The two words are expected to be known, but their relationship is not usually taught directly in most educational settings and must be reasoned. Consider, for example, the child's response process when the examiner asks how "war" and "peace" are alike. A correct response requires that both concepts have been acquired and stored in long-term memory and the child be able to access that knowledge from semantic memory upon demand. Once these words are recalled, the child can begin the reasoning process to determine how they are similar. This reasoning process appears to take place within a temporary working memory space. The ability to reason in this way may be related to a certain type of working memory capacity (WMC) and the efficiency with which ideas are worked in this transient memory space before the trace fades or becomes unavailable due to interference—as will be elaborated on further in the Working Memory section of this chapter. Similar issues are in play with CO. Thus, the SI, and CO subtests require a higher level of reasoning for successful performance than the VC and IN subtests. Students with deficits in crystallized knowledge and/or retrieval from long-term memory of previously acquired information may score higher on SI and CO than on VC and IN if they have adequate verbal reasoning ability. Conversely, students with an age-appropriate knowledge base that is readily accessible but who have deficits in higher-order categorization of abstract verbal concepts may show the reverse score pattern. In these cases, it may then also be instructive to compare performance on SI with Picture Concepts (PCn). Both subtests require categorization of abstract verbal concepts, but PCn does not require that the child verbally explain his or her thinking. Thus, children with good abstract reasoning skills but poor verbal expression may perform better on PCn than SI.

Recall that a low score on an intelligence test such as the WISC-V may reflect low ability, a lack of opportunity to develop particular abilities, or some kind of "interference" that compromises the acquisition or expression of particular abilities (e.g., learning disabilities, auditory processing deficits, TBI due to repeated sports-related concussions, etc.), which can also include performance or task demands ranging from speech impediments, motor coordination deficits to test anxiety. Prior to making an interpretation of low verbal ability, the psychologist should also ask: was the knowledge encoded but cannot now be recalled (for several possible reasons), or was it never acquired in the first place? One useful methodology for addressing this issue is the "recognition paradigm." All of the WISC-V VC subtests involve free recall, which is a much more difficult cognitive task than cued recall or recognition. Some students who answered incorrectly because they could not retrieve the information from long-term storage may more readily recall the information if given a clue or recognize the correct information from a set of possible answers. We can see this in our everyday lives when someone tries to recall the name of a colleague by using clues such as what university she is from or the letter-sound her name begins with, but once a possible name is suggested it is instantly recognized as correct or incorrect. The reader is referred to the Chapter 3, A School Neuropsychological Approach to Interpretation of the WISC-V Integrated about WISC-V Integrated for further information on these issues.

Visual-Spatial Organization

Tracey has a history of a somewhat variable pattern of school achievement and fine motor difficulties. A recently administered WISC-V shows that the VCI, FRI, WMI, and PSI Index scores were all in the average range, but that she obtained a much lower score of 82 on the VSI.

The WISC-V VSI is a measure of visual-spatial organization. The Index is comprised of the Block Design (BD) and Visual Puzzles (VP) subtests. One of the most venerable of Wechsler subtests, BD is designed to measure the ability to analyze and synthesize abstract visual stimuli. It also involves nonverbal concept formation, visual perception and organization, simultaneous processing, visual-motor coordination, learning, and the ability to separate figure and ground in visual stimuli. For young children, it may also involve visual observation and matching abilities, as well as the ability to integrate visual and motor processes.

Children are given bonus points for completing BD items quickly. A score can also be calculated without time bonuses, but the Block Design No Time Bonus (BDN) score may not be used to calculate the VSI or FSIQ. This supplemental score may be useful for students whose motor coordination interferes with their ability to manipulate the blocks. In this way, the examiner can evaluate the student's visual-spatial organization abilities somewhat independently of speed of performance. Those who score low only on BD but not BDN may have adequate visual-spatial abilities that require additional time to process. For more severe coordination problems, the WISC-V Integrated includes optional procedures to further parse out these issues (see Chapter 3, A School Neuropsychological Approach to Interpretation of the WISC-V Integrated on WISC-V Integrated).

VP was also designed to measure the ability to analyze and synthesize abstract visual material. Successful performance requires the ability to maintain a visual image in mind temporarily while mentally rotating, inverting, and otherwise manipulating that image and matching the resulting percept to a visual target. Like many tasks on the Wechsler series of tests, VP requires the integration of multiple related cognitive processes including visual perception, simultaneous processing, working memory, spatial visualization, and spatial manipulation.

Visual-spatial stimuli are employed in many fluid reasoning subtests, but the fluid tasks typically place higher demands on reasoning than the pure visual-spatial tasks. As a result, some students with weak visual-spatial abilities may struggle with certain fluid reasoning tasks that employ visual-spatial stimuli. While it would seem ideal to assess reasoning alone without tapping other domains of cognition, this is patently impossible. Reasoning must take place on some subject. Just like verbal reasoning cannot be assessed without invoking verbal stimuli and therefore some base of crystallized knowledge, fluid reasoning cannot occur in a vacuum. Once any type of stimulus is presented, other factors come into play. Some may view matrix analogies tasks as pure measures of fluid reasoning, but even the presentation of an abstract visual image that has no known meaning and cannot be verbally encoded will invoke multiple cognitive domains as described above in this section. Although factor analytic studies show that each task loads primarily on one factor there is often minor loading on other factors. Indeed, it may be the successful integration of multiple cognitive processes to solve a novel problem that is at the essence of fluid reasoning.

Fluid Reasoning

Maria's mother and teacher report that she appears bright and comes up with good solutions to problems conversationally, but struggles to complete simpler assignments from school. WISC-V testing shows superior scores on FRI and VCI but relative weaknesses in VSI and PSI.

Fluid reasoning is generally considered to be the ability to solve novel problems for which there is little prior experience, cultural expectation, or crystallized knowledge to guide the solution. This is why visual-spatial stimuli are often employed because they are relatively free of cultural or linguistic expectation and crystallized knowledge. But fluid reasoning should not be thought of as limited to visual-spatial problems and can take verbal or numerical forms as well.

Importantly, the Fluid Reasoning (FR) factor is virtually synonymous with psychometric "*g*," loading near 1.0 in five-factor solutions of WISC-IV (Weiss et al., 2013b), WISC-V (Wechsler, 2014), and WAIS-IV (Weiss et al., 2013a).

The FRI is comprised of the Matrix Reasoning and Figure Weights subtests. Arithmetic is a supplemental subtest on the FRI. A standard task on most intelligence batteries, Matrix Reasoning consists of visual analogy problems set in a matrix. It was designed to provide a reliable measure of visual information processing and abstract reasoning skills. Matrix Reasoning includes items that tap continuous and discrete pattern completion, classification, analogical reasoning, and serial reasoning.

Figure Weights was designed to measure quantitative and analogical reasoning. Quantitative reasoning tasks involve fluid reasoning processes that can be expressed mathematically, emphasizing either inductive or deductive logic. As such, quantitative reasoning is considered a subtype of fluid reasoning. In a clinical study of adults with focal strokes or cortical excisions, Figure Weights appeared to critically involve the right temporoparietal junction involved in numerical magnitude estimation (McCrea, Simon, & Robinson, 2011). While the solution to each FW item can be expressed with algebraic equations there is no task requirement to do so—thus eliminating demand for acquired knowledge of advanced mathematical equations. Although Figure Weights involves working memory it reduces this involvement relative to typical quantitative tasks (e.g., mental arithmetic) through the visual presentation of items in a stimulus book, which allows the child to continually refresh stimuli held in working memory while solving the problem.

AR is among the highest g loaded subtest in the Wechsler battery, often first or second depending on the analysis, with VC in the other position. As a word problem that must be solved mentally, AR has always been known as a complex task that invokes multiple abilities including verbal conceptualization, working memory, and numerical skills. The task involves performing simple but multiple, sequential mental arithmetic calculations while keeping the word problem in mind and referring back to it for the next step in the problem sequence.

As such, the Arithmetic subtest likely requires examinees to integrate a complex mix of abilities, and this integrative requirement may be responsible for its high "g" loading. This is consistent with previous research with WISC-IV (Chen, Keith, Chen, & Chang, 2009; Keith, Fine, Taub, Reynolds, & Kranzler, 2006). These findings are also consistent with much research into the theoretical structure of intelligence, which documents considerable shared variance between working memory and fluid reasoning (Conway, Cowan, Bunting, Therriault, & Minkoff, 2002; de Jone & Das-Smaal, 1995; Engle, Tuholski, Laughlin, & Conway, 1999; Fry & Hale, 1996, 2000; Kane, Hambrick, & Conway, 2005). Specifically, the cognitive control mechanisms involved in working memory have been identified as the source of the link between working memory and fluid intelligence (Engel de Abreu, Conway, & Gathercole, 2010). This potentially explains the cross-loading of the Arithmetic subtest on the WMI and PRI in four-factor solutions, and the movement of Arithmetic from the WMI to the FRI factor in the five-factor solutions of WISC-IV (Weiss et al., 2013b) and WAIS-IV (Weiss et al., 2013a).

As shown in Fig. 4.1, Arithmetic has moderate loadings on FRI and WMI, and a small loading on VCI due to the use of word problems. This is the so-called "problem" of the Arithmetic subtest as a measure of working memory, perceptual reasoning, fluid reasoning, and verbal comprehension (Flanagan, Alfonso, & Reynolds, 2013). From our perspective, the "messy" multidimensionality of Arithmetic is not a problem at all. In fact, the very high loading of Arithmetic on g is an opportunity to assess the cross-functional integrity of the brain. Kaufman (2013) also makes an impassioned case for retaining Arithmetic in the Wechsler tests, reminding us that Binet believed multidimensional tasks were the key to intelligence and that Wechsler knew full well that Arithmetic tapped more than one ability. David Wechsler knew the value of including subtests that had a somewhat broader bandwidth, not only because there was a kind of "ecological" validity or at least utility to such subtests when assessing intelligence, but they were also more likely to be "correlated" with the very clinical questions of interest to psychologists. Thus, Wechsler, following from Binet, moved away from the much narrower "brass instrument" measures characteristic of the Galton era. We agree completely, and recommend the routine administration of the Arithmetic test. Intriguingly, Schneider (2013) suggests that Arithmetic should contribute to FSIQ directly rather than through any one of the first-order factors. Rather than continue to argue about what factor Arithmetic belongs to, we should seek to understand why the integrative demands of complex multifactorial tasks like Arithmetic are so highly *g* saturated and which brain pathways are activated when performing such tasks.

At the same time, however, the numerical content of the Arithmetic subtest and its high correlation with mathematics achievement (Wechsler, 2014) are difficult to ignore. The numerical stimuli of the Arithmetic task logically invoke interpretations based partly on numerical skill. Yet, the requisite numerical calculations of Arithmetic are relatively simple and the reasoning requirements are equally compelling. Arithmetic is best interpreted as a measure of Quantitative Reasoning (RQ), which is considered a narrow ability under fluid reasoning in the CHC model of intelligence (Carroll, 1993; see Keith & Reynolds, 2012, pp. 793–795 for a test of the RQ-Gf hypothesis). As reasoning must necessarily occur in the context of some stimuli, QR is essentially fluid reasoning with numerical stimuli and as such requires a base numerical skill. Similarly, MR and VP are essentially fluid reasoning with abstract visual stimuli and require a base ability of visual-spatial organization.

Working Memory

Mary's teacher reports has such difficulty remembering things that we have been working on in class. I know she is paying attention and her records show that she has earned average scores on group intelligence tests. However, she just can't seem to keep the information in her mind long enough to use it.

Barry's teacher reports that he seems confused when engaging in more complex mental tasks. For example, he can solve printed problems, especially when using paper and pencil or computer presented questions. But if the same question is orally present to him, he appears to forget parts, asks questions about what he should be doing and generally just 'gets lost'. Of interest is that his score on the WMI was significantly lower than the average of the five WISC-V index scores. Further the psychologist noted that Barry required additional repetition and asked for clarification especially on the VCI subtests that placed increasing cognitive demands on his short and long term memory and required some reasoning (SI and CO).

The WMI measures attention, concentration, and working memory. Working memory is the ability to hold information in mind temporarily while performing some operation or manipulation with that information, or engaging in an interfering task, and then accurately reproducing the information or updated result. Working memory can be thought of as mental control or focused attention (an executive process) involving reasonably higher-order tasks (rather than rote tasks), and it presumes attention and concentration. As described by Jonides, Lacey, and Nee (2005):

"Working memory is a system that can store a small amount of information briefly, keeping that information quickly accessible and available for transformation by rules and strategies, while updating it frequently" (p. 2).

So, what is the key difference between Working Memory (WM) and FR? There is no decision-making involved in WM—only keeping in mind and manipulating whatever stimuli are presented. FR goes further by requiring students to sort out relevant from irrelevant information, determine what order to manipulate the variables (first, second, etc.), and to do this in the service of solving a novel problem with a correct answer. Fluid reasoning always requires working memory, but working memory does not always result in fluid reasoning. The cognitive control mechanisms of the working memory system appear to constitute the active link between working memory and fluid reasoning.

Baddeley's (2003) seminal model of the working memory system proposes a phonological loop and a visual-spatial sketchpad in which verbal and visual stimuli, respectively, are stored and refreshed, and a central executive that controls attention directed toward these sources. A fourth component known as the *episodic buffer* was subsequently included in this model. This buffer is assumed to be attentionally controlled by the central executive and to be accessible to conscious awareness. Baddeley regards the episodic buffer as a crucial feature of the capacity of working memory to act as a global workspace that is accessed by conscious awareness. When working memory requires information from long-term storage, it may be "downloaded" into the episodic buffer rather than simply activated within long-term memory (Baddeley, 2003).

The term WMC concerns the amount that can be held in immediate memory. Updating or refreshing the information is necessary to keep it active in immediate memory, even for short periods of time. The working memory system involves mechanisms for maintaining information in short-term memory. These mechanisms can be as simple as rehearsing, or chunking information, thereby continuously refreshing the contents of the short-term storage buffer. The working memory system involves processes responsible for cognitive control that regulate and coordinate these maintenance operations. The boundary between short-term and working memory is not always clear. For example, although attending to, storing, and repeating a license plate number may appear only to involve short-term memory, the role of working memory may enter the picture when there is interference from other sources—for example, if the observer is asked to describe the driver and then asked to recall the license plate number. Thus, the distinction between short-term and working memory appears to involve the use of active cognitive control mechanisms to maintain focused attention in the face of distractions competing for conscious attention.

The WMI subtests of the WISC-V are Digit Span (DS), Picture Span (PSp), and Letter-Number Sequencing (LN). The DS subtest has changed substantially from WISC-IV in order to reflect advances in the understanding of working memory. In WISC-V, Digit Span Sequencing (DSS) was added to the traditional Digit Span Forward (DSF) and Digit Span Backward (DSB) tasks. This was done to because of concern that DSF was a measure of short-term and not working memory based on research that indicated different cognitive demands for DSF and DFB (Reynolds, 1997). DSF requires initial registration of the verbal stimuli—a prerequisite for mental manipulation of the stimuli. DSF was retained as part of the subtest to reflect the role of registration in short-term memory as a precursor skill to working memory, and to maintain a set of easier items for evaluation of low functioning students. In some cases, DSF also requires auditory rehearsal to maintain the memory trace until the item presentation is concluded. To the extent that longer spans of digits require the application of a method for maintaining the trace, such as rehearsal or chunking, some degree of mental manipulation of the stimuli is also involved. The point in the DSF item set at which this is required will vary as a function of age and ability level, and the response processes utilized by the examinee. In DSS, the child must hold the string of presented numbers in short-term memory while reorganizing and reproducing them in the correct sequence from lowest to highest. In DSB, the child must also hold a string of numbers in short-term memory store, but this time reverse the given sequence, and then correctly reproduce the numbers in the new order. The task demands of these DSB and DSS are clear examples of mental manipulation, which is one of the hallmarks of working memory.

The developmental level and other cognitive factors such as general mental ability and processing speed (see section below) also may vary the role played by working memory in the DSB item set. For example, short spans of digits backward may tax working memory resources only marginally in older or brighter students. Again, the point at which these students substantially invoke executive control in DSB will vary by age and ability. In DSS, the child hears a string of numbers presented out of order and must repeat them in numerical order. The task is more difficult than it sounds because the numbers presented are not continuous, creating gaps in the rearranged number line, and some numbers are repeated. Thus, the working memory demands of DSB and DSS are similar to each other.

The LN task involves listening to a string of random letters and numbers, and repeating the letters in alphabetical order and the numbers in order of increasing magnitude. Again, this is not as easy as it sounds because some numbers must be retained in the short-term storage buffer while ordering the letters, and then the contents of the buffer updated into conscious awareness before ordering the numbers. Interference is built into the task through occasional repetitions of numbers or letters in the same string, and also by proactive interference of letters and numbers heard in previous strings. Overall, the task demands of LN are very similar to those of DSB and DSS.

PSp adds a new dimension to the assessment working memory not previously available in any Wechsler intelligence test. All previous WM subtests relied on verbally presented stimuli pulling for auditory working memory, whereas PSp assesses visual working memory. While the stimuli may be temporarily stored in the visual-spatial sketchpad rather than the phonological loop, the same executive control mechanisms are invoked to maintain focused attention on the task and overcome distractions. Proactive interference is built into the task by repeating target pictures from previous items as distractors in subsequent items. This significantly increases the task demand for controlled attention to determine not only that the image was seen before, but if it was seen on the current item or a previous and now irrelevant item, and not to mistake it as a distractor on the current item when it was the correct target on a previous item.

A serious deficit in working memory may create difficulties at school and in daily life functioning and also may have major implications for the academic lives of young adults in school or vocational training programs. The role of WM has been implicated in learning and attention disorders. Students diagnosed with LD or AD/HD may be more likely to experience problems with working memory as suggested by significantly lower scores on this index. Schwean and Saklofske (2005) summarized the results of several studies of children and adolescents with AD/HD, suggesting that they tended to earn their lowest scores on the WM composite.

As always, caution must always be applied when using group data to make diagnostic inferences about individuals. The WISC-V was never intended to be diagnostic of AD/HD or LD nor can it be, given the complexity of these disorders. Such nomothetic descriptions should rather be used as another "indicator" supporting or not the eventual diagnosis of any condition in which cognition is implicated. Thus, we are clearly advocating that diagnosis is of an individual, and the test score findings from the WISC-V or any other assessment battery be demonstrated to be relevant to each individual rather than being assumed to apply to all students with a particular diagnosis or being used as a diagnostic "marker" (see Kaufman, 1994).

In What Ways Are Working Memory and Fluid Reasoning Alike? How Are They the Same?

The capacity of one's working memory has been found to account for 50%–75% of the variance in general fluid intelligence (Kane et al., 2005; Oberauer, Sub, Wilhelm, & Sanders, 2007). As a result, the link between WM and FR is actively being studied by several research teams. These research programs are exploring WMC with the goal of understanding what causes rapid forgetting of information in short-term storage. Several groups of cognitive experimental psychologists employing well-designed studies are finding that rapid forgetting of stimuli is not caused by simple decay of the memory trace over short periods of time (Oberauer & Lewandowsky, 2013), but rather, due to distractions that interfere with the cognitive control mechanisms (Unsworth & Engle, 2005). Purely temporal views of working memory may no longer be adequate to explain forgetting during fluid reasoning tasks.

Engel de Abreu et al. (2010) showed that cognitive control mechanisms are the source of the link with fluid intelligence through their influence on WMC in children as young as 5–9 years of age. Thus, the strength of the child's cognitive control mechanisms, such as focused attention, allows him or her to overcome interference from distracting stimuli and successfully complete the steps of the reasoning process, monitor performance, backtrack from wrong paths, and adapt the resolution strategy as performance proceeds. Early evidence suggests that systematic working memory training programs might improve performance on fluid reasoning tasks in typically developing 4-year-olds (Nutley et al., 2011), although not in children with limited intellectual capacity (Soderqvist, Nutley, Ottersen, Grill, & Klingberg, 2012), and much research remains to be accomplished in this area.

With young children, interference can be as simple as seeing the same stimulus as before but this time as a distractor and not the target stimulus. Interference can also be irrelevant detail, or distractors that are similar to the memory target. In real life, interference can also come from interruptions such as are likely when a student is attempting to focus on homework in a distracting environment, or multitasking between digital social media apps and homework. Consider also the difficulties an ADHD child may have with interference-induced forgetting when continually shifting attention between compelling but irrelevant stimuli in the environment. Further, distractors are not always external environmental events. Some children can be distracted by their own extraneous thoughts, especially if they are anxious or under stress.

The strength of the association between fluid intelligence and working memory has prompted some, including us, to suggest that they might be the same thing (Kyllonen & Christal, 1990; Weiss, Saklofske, & Prifitera, 2005).

However, Chuderski (2013) finds that the strength of the association depends on the time demands of the task. He found that working memory and fluid intelligence were indistinguishable under conditions of highly speeded FR tasks, but only moderately correlated when unspeeded tasks were used. Thus, individuals with low WMC may be able to compensate for their capacity limitations through sustained effort over time. This is because low WMC individuals must refresh and retrace their steps in the reasoning logic more frequently as interference-induced forgetting occurs, and this simply takes longer. As Chuderski points out, assessing fluid intelligence with highly speeded tests "…will measure the ability to cope with complexity in a dynamic environment, thus having high real-world validity especially as the technological and informational pressures of the world continue to increases rapidly, but it also may underestimate people who regardless of their limited (working memory) capacity could work out good solutions in less dynamic environments" (p. 260). We would offer that adding time alone may not be sufficient and the individual would also need to have a strong drive to task-mastery motivating them to sustain effort as long as necessary to solve the problem. As recognized by David Wechsler, clinicians should also take note of such noncognitive, or conative, factors that may interact with the cognitive factors being assessed by intelligence tests.

Other groups of experimental neurocognitive researchers are using brain imaging technology to study the neural architecture of cognitive flexibility and fluid intelligence. A recently exploding trend in brain imaging research is to explore the strength of neural connectivity between brain regions as they relate to fluid intelligence. Evidence has emerged that one of the largest networks in the brain—the fronto-parietal control network—is central to cognitive control and fluid reasoning (Cole & Schneider, 2007; Jung & Haier, 2007). Although some researchers in this area are finding that fluid intelligence does not require attentional control and can be reduced to simple short-term storage processes of encoding, maintenance, and retrieval (Martinez et al., 2011), this finding may be related to the particular experimental tasks employed (Engel de Abreu, et al., 2010).

More centrally, much of this research highlights the importance of white-matter associative tracts that speed the processing of information along the pathway. Parieto-Frontal Integration Theory suggests that widespread networks of distal brain areas are involved in *g*, which require well-functioning white-matter pathways to allow for fast and orchestrated information transfer between brain areas.

Roberto Colom and his colleagues found that cognitive flexibility shares neural substrates with both working memory and processing speed (Barbey et al., 2013). They posit that individual differences in fluid intelligence may be related to the integrity (speed and sequencing) of the interactions between brain regions. In our view, this finding allows for both the central executive component of the working memory system and processing speed abilities to play a role in fluid intelligence. Executive or cognitive control mechanisms are central to dealing with interference while attending to and sequencing information. Processing speed abilities are central to moving the relevant information quickly between brain regions — before forgetting occurs either due to temporal decay, interference, or both.

Much of this research has been conducted on adults, and until recently, it has been unclear when in the course of child neurodevelopment this functional connectivity between brain regions begins to mature. However, this connectivity has now been demonstrated for children between 6 and 8 years of age (Langeslag et al., 2012).

These lines of research and thought are important because cognitive flexibility and fluid abilities are believed to draw upon the combination of conceptual knowledge and executive processes, and so the sequence and speed of communication between areas associated with these capacities is of critical importance. These mechanisms allow the integration and synthesis of crystallized knowledge with supporting cognitive insights, enabling people to see connections that previously eluded them. Recent research suggests that memory places constraints on hypothesis generation and decision-making (Thomas, Dougherty, & Buttaccio, 2014). In our view, both working memory and processing speed may function as rate-limiting factors on fluid reasoning. That is, when weak or dysfunctional, they conspire to limit the rate of fluid reasoning in individuals by placing constraints on the number of hypotheses that can be generated and evaluated during the decision-making process. But when working memory and processing speed abilities are well developed and work in synchrony, they may help to expand the effectiveness of one's fluid reasoning by allowing multiple hypotheses to be generated, retained, and efficiently evaluated. This is why we have referred to the aggregate of the WM and PSIs as the Cognitive Proficiency Index (CPI; see below) (Saklofske, Zhu, Coalson, Raiford, & Weiss, 2010; Weiss, Saklofske, Prifitera, & Holdnack, 2006; Weiss, Saklofske, Coalson, & Raiford, 2010).

In our view, working memory is largely about cognitive control, while fluid reasoning is largely about cognitive flexibility. Thus, fluid reasoning always requires working memory. But working memory does not always result in fluid reasoning. This is because there is no (or little) decision-making involved in working memory tasks—only keeping in mind and manipulating whatever stimuli are presented. The demands of fluid reasoning tasks go further by requiring one to sort out relevant from irrelevant information, determine what order to manipulate the variables first, second, etc., and to do this in the service of solving a novel problem with a correct answer. Further, we think that individual differences in fluid reasoning may be partly a function of individual differences in the speed and sequencing of information transfer between brain regions.

Processing Speed

Rapid transmission of critical information along neural pathways connecting relevant areas of the brain is important to effective fluid reasoning processes, as elaborated on in the previous section of this chapter. The PSI measures the speed of mental processing, using visual stimuli and graphomotor skills, and is importantly related to the efficient use of other cognitive abilities. A weakness in simple visual scanning and tracking may leave a child less time and mental energy for the complex task of understanding new material. Referring to the WISC-V and WAIS-IV, it was for these reasons that PSI along with the WMI were referred to collectively as the CPI (Saklofske et al., 2010; Weiss et al., 2006; Weiss et al., 2010).

The PSI is comprised of the Coding (CD), Symbol Search (SS), and Cancellation (CA) subtests. These tasks utilize an apparently simple visual scanning and tracking format. A direct test of speed and accuracy, the CD subtest assesses the child's ability to quickly and correctly scan and sequence simple visual information. Performance on this subtest also may be influenced by short-term visual memory, attention, or visual-motor coordination. Thus, while a low score does raise the question of processing speed, it may also be influenced by graphomotor problems so practitioners should be alert to alternative reasons for low scores. Students may complete fewer items on this task if they present with fine motor difficulties, but this does not necessarily imply a problem with processing speed. An obsessive-compulsive child may also earn lower scores on CD, again not due to a processing speed deficit but rather because of a personality disposition.

The SS subtest requires the child to inspect several sets of symbols and indicate if special target symbols appeared in each set. It is also a direct test of speed and accuracy and assesses scanning speed and sequential tracking of simple visual information. Performance on this subtest may be influenced by visual discrimination and visual-motor coordination. Here again we alert psychologists to use their observation skills and also ensure that the findings from the WISC-V corroborate or are supported by other "clinically relevant" findings. For example, an ADHD child who rushes through this task will likely make sufficient errors that will lower the SS score. Again, this is not necessarily due to an underlying processing speed deficit but rather a behavioral correlate (i.e., impulsivity) that impedes performance on the task.

Cancellation is a supplemental processing speed subtest and should in general be used when either of the other two PS subtests cannot be used or are considered invalid. Working within a specified time limit, the examinee scans a structured arrangement of shapes and marks targets shapes. It is similar to previously developed cancellation tasks designed to measure processing speed, visual selective attention, vigilance, perceptual speed, and visual-motor ability (Bate, Mathias, & Crawford, 2001; Geldmacher, Fritsch, & Riedel, 2000; Wojciulik, Husain, Clarke, & Driver, 2001). Cancellation tasks have been used extensively in neuropsychological settings as measures of visual neglect, response inhibition, and motor perseveration (Adair, Na, Schwartz, & Heilman, 1998; Geldmacher et al., 2000; Lezak et al., 2012; Na et al., 1999).

From a neurodevelopmental perspective, there are large and obvious age-related trends in processing speed that are accompanied by age-related changes in the number of transient connections to the central nervous system and increases in myelination. Processing speed has been shown to mediate the development of general intelligence in adolescents (Coyle, Pillow, Snyder, & Kochunov, 2011), and several previous investigators have found that measures of infant processing speed predict later IQ scores (e.g., Dougherty & Haith, 1997).

Thus, speed of mental processing is more than simply doing a task at a faster or slower rate but in itself is a key cognitive and individual differences variable. There is consistent evidence that both simple and choice reaction time correlate about 0.20 or slightly higher with scores from intelligence tests while inspection time (hypothesized by some to be a measure of the rate that information is processed) correlates about 0.40 with intelligence test scores (see Deary, 2001; Deary & Stough, 1996).

The PSI subtests included in tests such as the WISC-V are relatively simple visual scanning tasks for most students. However, it would be a mistake to think of the PSI as a measure of simple clerical functions that are not relevant or related to intellectual functioning. In matched controlled clinical group studies with the WISC-V, the PSI was observed to have an effect size greater than 1.0 in a group of children with Autism Spectrum Disorder and language impairment (Wechsler, 2014). Yet, we once again caution practitioners from considering these profiles as diagnostic markers; they may guide the clinician to forming hypotheses about a child's cognitive abilities in relation to, say, school difficulties, but this should in turn encourage a complete clinical evaluation based on test results combined with observations, history, and background factors.

As operationally defined in WISC-V, the PSI indicates the rapidity with which a child processes simple or routine information without making errors of either omission or commission. Many novel learning tasks involve information processing that is both routine for most students (such as reading at grade level) and complex (such as drawing inferences and predictions based on what was read). When speed of processing information is at least in the average range or a relative strength for a child, this may facilitate both reasoning and the acquisition of new information. Slowness in the speed of processing routine information may make the task of reasoning and integrating novel information more time consuming and consequently more difficult. It may be hypothesized that students with processing speed deficits learn less material in the same amount of time, or take longer to learn the same amount of material compared to students without processing speed deficits. These children mentally tire more easily at school because of the additional cognitive effort required to perform routine tasks at their desks, perhaps leading to more frequent paperwork errors and academic stress. As the months and years pass, these students are likely to spend less time on mentally demanding tasks involving new learning thus leading to smaller stores of crystallized knowledge over time relative to classmates, and possibly less interest in the rigors of further education. Slow processing speed taxes the entire cognitive network and has wide-ranging effects on other cognitive processes that are observable outside the testing room and important consequences in the lives of children.

In some cases, children with serious processing speed deficits may be slower to comprehend conversation and formulate responses, especially in fast-paced conversations that change direction quickly as are characteristic of group interactions in adolescence. Thus, processing speed strengths and weaknesses can have important implications in the lives of children beyond cognitive functioning, and potentially extend to their social and emotional lives as well. In summary, processing speed interacts in a critical way with other higher-order cognitive functions and may impact reasoning, new learning, general academic performance, and everyday performance.

THE ROLE OF EXECUTIVE FUNCTIONS IN INTELLIGENCE

This is an opportune spot to comment on the influence of other cognitive functions on WISC-V scores. Organization, planning, and other executive function (EFs) can impact performance on various WISC-V subtests. But if we move away from the focus on test performance and consider intelligence in the broader ecology of society, we can at least say that EFs are inexorably linked with the expression of intelligent behavior at work and in life. Clearly, we all know bright, well-educated colleagues whose disorganization and poor planning interferes with their ability to achieve otherwise obtainable career goals. Similarly, many of us can think of friends and relatives whose intently focused attention on work activities has begot considerable success even though they seem no smarter than the rest of us. But are EFs really something apart from intelligence—simply mediators of how well one utilizes his or her intelligence in the larger world outside the testing room? To what extent might EFs be an integral part of an integrated, ecological view of intelligence? To what extent might EFs even influence the growth of other intellectual abilities during the developmental years? More to the point, what are the theoretical, clinical, and empirical relationships of intelligence and EF?

Although the term EF was not coined at the time, Dr. Wechsler knew that such abilities were importantly related to intelligence because his original tests included tasks that we would call EF today. The WISC-R and WISC-III included a Mazes subtest that was widely believed to measure planning and organization. It was an optional subtest, however, and rarely used by practitioners because of the long administration time. For this and other reasons, Mazes was dropped from the WISC-III. But the assessment of organization and planning abilities was never replaced by another subtest in the Wechsler model.

EFs as currently conceptualized involve more than planning and organization. Although there is no formally agreed upon definition, EF may be tentatively defined as the effective integration of multiple cognitive processes relevant to goal-directed behavior (Salthouse, 2009). A list of specific cognitive processes included under this umbrella term was offered by Cheung, Mitsis, and Halperin (2004) as planning, decision-making, judgment, working memory, set shifting, and cognitive flexibility that enables one to orient toward the future and self-regulate toward a goal. Chan, Shum, Toulopoulou, and Chen (2008) similarly offered a wide range of cognitive processes and behavioral competencies including verbal reasoning, problem-solving, planning, sequencing, the ability to sustain attention, resistance to interference, utilization of feedback, multitasking, cognitive flexibility, and the ability to deal with novelty.

In reviewing the extent literature on EF, Diamond (2013) groups the core EFs into four categories: inhibition, interference control, working memory, and cognitive flexibility. In this schema, inhibition is more behavioral or emotional and includes response inhibition, self-control, resisting temptations, and resisting acting impulsively. Interference control is more cognitive and includes selective attention and cognitive inhibition. Cognitive flexibility includes the ability to see things from different perspectives and quickly and flexibly adapting to changed circumstances.

Salthouse (2009) directly addressed the theoretically important question of the relationship of EF and IQ by studying the pattern of convergent and divergent validity between fluid reasoning tasks and three key measures of EFs, which were inhibition control, switching, and updating in nonclinical samples. Inhibition control involves the ability to focus attention on relevant information and processes while inhibiting irrelevant ones. Switching is described as scheduling processes in complex tasks that require switching of focused attention between tasks. Updating involves checking the contents of working memory to determine the next step in a sequential task and then updating the contents. Salthouse reported that convergent validity among these measures was not significantly higher than the typical correlations among all cognitive abilities—reflecting a lack of homogeniety of the EF construct. More importantly, he showed evidence of divergent validity for inhibition control and fluid reasoning measures, but not for measures of switching or updating with fluid reasoning. He concluded that the EF construct needs better specification before it finally can be determined if it is a useful construct distinct from fluid reasoning.

It is unknown if evidence of divergent validity between EF and fluid reasoning would emerge in specific clinically disordered samples, or if there is divergent validity between EF and measures of crystallized intelligence. Also, the Salthouse study did not address the emotion regulation aspects of EF. However, his controversial study is important because it raises a key theoretical question about the construct overlap between fluid intelligence and EFs: Are EFs really something different and apart from fluid intelligence?

Diamond (2013) goes further, stating that EFs make possible mentally playing with ideas; taking the time to think before acting; meeting novel, unanticipated challenges; resisting temptations; and staying focused. Rather than asking how EFs influence intelligence, Diamond flips our perspective and argues that what is commonly called fluid intelligence is the reasoning and problem-solving component of EF.

Much work remains to be done in this area. What would a structural model of general cognitive ability look like that included both EF and the five major domains in the contemporary Wechsler model of intelligence as expressed in WISC-V? Perhaps more precisely, which facets of EF have substantial construct overlap with which domains of intelligence, and which EF functions serve as moderators or mediators of these domains of intelligence or the dynamic interactions among them? We discuss specific aspects of EF in more detail in the next section, with a focus on their role in facilitating working memory and fluid reasoning.

AN INTEGRATIVE THEORY OF GENERAL INTELLIGENCE

In this section we discuss how the five primary cognitive abilities are necessarily interdependent upon each other for successful problem-solving. Any discussion of this topic must begin by considering the role of psychometric "g," which is the extent to which all of the subtests in the battery measure a single underlying dimension of general ability. But psychometric g is a mathematically determined definition of general intelligence that is statistically extracted from whatever subtests are included in the battery. We offer a more theoretically appealing definition of general intelligence as follows:

General intelligence is the fluid ability to integrate multiple cognitive abilities in the service of solving a novel problem and thereby accumulating crystalized knowledge that, in turn, facilitates further higher-level reasoning.

As implied in this definition, we view fluid and crystallized intelligence at the epicenter of an integrative model of intelligence, with the remaining broad abilities plus the EFs operating in their service. As Gregoire (2013) reminds us, fluid and crystallized intelligence have special status in the original Cattell–Horn model, and should not be considered just one among a set of five or seven equally important broad abilities. As neuropsychologists have been implying for decades, simply summing scores from a multitude of narrowband abilities certainly is not the same thing as performance on a task that requires real-time integration of those abilities. Perhaps FR, when conceptualized as an integrative ability, is the "ecological *g*" that has eluded researchers for more than a century. Supporting this view is the consistent finding from all factor analytic studies of WISC-V that the fluid reasoning factor loads virtually 1.0 on psychometric *g*.

Fluid reasoning and working memory are integrally related conceptually and neurologically. The role of the central executive is critical to the relationship between working memory and fluid reasoning. The central executive controls attention to the target task in the face of interfering or distracting stimuli (Engle et al., 1999; Kane, Bleckley, Conway, & Engle, 2001). The more efficiently attention is focused the more effectively working memory is utilized, regardless of WMC. Similarly, the ability to inhibit irrelevant information, or the degree to which working memory is "clutter free," also may influence efficient cognitive performance regardless of the size of the working memory space (Lustig, May, & Hasher, 2001). Thus, individual differences in performance on working memory tasks may primarily reflect differences in various EFs such as the ability to sustain focused attention and inhibit competing responses, rather than the size of one's working memory space—particularly in real-life situations outside of the laboratory where interference and distraction are commonplace. The most current research suggests that it may be the cognitive control mechanisms of the central executive that account for the strong relationship between working memory and fluid reasoning tasks through the mechanism of controlled attention (Chuderski, 2013; Engel de Abreu et al., 2010; Oberauer & Lewandowsky, 2013).

Resolution of novel problems typically requires relational learning. More effective relational learning strategies require the induction of some problem-solving schema to pursue, setting, and managing processing goals based on the schema, and strategic control over processing activities to allow backtracking from wrong paths, elimination of irrelevant information, and blocking of competing or distracting stimuli. Failure of the controlled attention mechanisms results in loss of the schema and relevant facts from short-term memory. The individual must then refresh these traces and begin again, which may eventually result in successful resolution of the problem—unless the environmental distractions continue unabated, or if there is a real-life demand to solve the problem quickly.

Together with the central executive, the episodic buffer plays a role in the efficient processing of information in working memory. As the source of controlled attention, the central executive activates long-term memory traces through controlled retrieval and maintains them in buffer storage systems for use by the visual-spatial sketchpad and phonological loop. For any given individual, there are obvious differences in the long-term traces that can be activated in the buffer based on prior knowledge and familiarity with the task at hand. *The more crystallized knowledge the person brings to a problem, the less fluid reasoning is required to respond correctly.*

VC and the other VCI subtests are not simply based on facts taught in school, but rather, reflect one's ability to comprehend information that is readily available in most environments. Crystallized information in long-term storage can then be accessed and used as inputs into higher-order reasoning processes. This *reciprocal relationship between fluid reasoning and crystallized knowledge* is one reason these two factors held a special place in the Cattell–Horn model (Cattell, 1963, p. 16). During childhood, fluid ability supports the development of school and cultural abilities. Following a cumulative process, these abilities allow for the acquisition of new abilities, which are gradually integrated into a larger and more organized cluster. Through this process, crystallized intelligence becomes progressively more independent of fluid intelligence; however, luid intelligence (Gf) and crystalized intelligence (Gc) continue to be correlated, even in adulthood (Horn & Cattell, 1966).

Contemporary Wechsler research supports placement of the fluid and crystallized intelligence factors at the epicenter of our integrative model. Recent studies show that the fluid factor is isomorphic with psychometric "*g*" loading 1.0 and .99 on "*g*" in children and adults, respectively (Weiss et al., 2013a; Weiss et al., 2013b; Wechsler, 2014). The field has yet to come to grips with the finding that Gf and "*g*" are synonymous. Further, the VC subtest, as the marker variable for crystallized knowledge, has the highest "*g*" loading of any subtest in the WISC-V.

Arithmetic, a quantitatively based fluid reasoning task, is often among the highest "*g*"-loaded subtest for both children and adults (Weiss et al., 2013a; Weiss et al., 2013b; Wechsler, 2014). We interpret this as consistent with our hypothesis that intelligence involves the successful integration of various cognitive abilities toward correct resolution of a problem. Arithmetic requires verbal comprehension of the word problem, controlled attention in sequencing the steps, and some crystallized knowledge of math facts. Further, the quicker the resolution of the problem, the less of a burden placed on the cognitive control mechanisms in blocking interference. As such, Arithmetic requires the integration of several broad and executive abilities working in tandem—hence, the high "*g*" loading.

Processing speed is another important cognitive ability that influences the efficiency of working memory functions. Perhaps before their time, Fry and Hale (1996) stated that as students age and mature, the changes that occur in processing speed lead to changes in working memory and "in turn, lead to changes in performance on tests of fluid intelligence" (p. 237). Only moderately correlated with each other, working memory and perceptual processing speed are differentially related to fluid reasoning. Modern neuroimaging research suggests that processing speed is related to white-matter associative tracts involved in transmission of "information" along neural pathways (Barbey, et al., 2013; Colom et al., 2011; Martinez et al., 2011; Tang et al., 2010). Thus, processing speed exerts its effect on fluid reasoning indirectly by increasing the quickness of neural transmissions between areas of the brain required to solve the problem at hand. Controlled attention appears to be the active ingredient required for working memory operations to result in fluid intelligence. Quick neural processing speed mediates the relationship between working memory and fluid reasoning by decreasing the demand on the central executive to control attention and block distractors (i.e., focus) during problem resolution. In this way, WMC is more efficiently utilized for higher-order reasoning tasks. Thus, processing speed, working memory, and the EFs combine to support fluid reasoning. If the problem involves perceptual stimuli then the visual-spatial abilities may be invoked to support problem resolution as well.

In short, fluid reasoning may occur in working memory space but requires the central executive to control the flow of information and dense white matter to increase the pace of information transmission between relevant areas of the brain. The cognitive control mechanisms sort and sequence relevant information while neural processing speed transfers that information rapidly before the cognitive control mechanisms fail and interference sets in causing forgetting and consequent disruption in the reasoning process.

Crystallized knowledge also may effectively increase fluid reasoning ability. As new facts and ideas are integrated with previously learned knowledge structures, increasingly larger chunks of information can be held in working memory and manipulated or combined with other chunks in novel ways. If an advanced vocabulary word can be retrieved from long-term storage through the episodic buffer and held in the phonological loop to represent a broader set of facts, then there is still time and capacity for other material to be integrated into the thinking process before the memory trace is disrupted and no longer accessible. Such interrelationships among the cognitive abilities are based on informed speculation at present, and require further research. But effective integration of these and other specific cognitive functions through the central executive may lie at the heart of any neurologically and ecologically valid theory of intelligence.

There is almost no meaningful activity in life that can be successfully performed by one narrowband cognitive ability in isolation as was clearly demonstrated by the minimal or zero correlations of the Galton-type tests with such complex factors as school achievement. Research in this area is still unfolding. However, practitioners should keep in mind that scores on factor-based indexes are not necessarily orthogonal; multiple reciprocal interactions are expected among the underlying neurological pathways. Understanding the clinical and behavioral correlates of these reciprocally interacting broad cognitive abilities—including the EFs—is critical to any ecologically meaningful theory of intelligence, including its development during childhood and adolescence, and its application to real-world problems in the classroom, preparing for college, and work.

An integrative, neurologically and ecologically valid model of cognitive information processing suggests that impairments—whether developmental or acquired—that interfere with the rapid processing of information may burden the cognitive control mechanisms of working memory and reduce the student's capacity for reasoning, comprehension, and new learning. For example, TBI, perhaps due to repeated sports-related concussions in high school athletes, may reduce processing speed, which reduces effective working memory and thereby makes problem-solving and the acquisition of new learning more effortful and difficult. Even learning-disabled and ADHD students with working memory and processing speed deficits seems to mentally tire more easily than others because of the extra cognitive effort required. Some may begin to spend less time studying, and eventually avoid academic environments. This is where personality factors—such as drive to task mastery, resiliency, and motivation—interact with cognitive abilities and cause other students to work even longer and harder despite these cognitive challenges. But that is a topic for another book!

SUMMARY

In this chapter we addressed the interpretation of each of the five primary factors measured by the WISC-V, with particular attention to their theoretical, empirical, and clinical foundations. We considered not only how these cognitive abilities differ, but more importantly, how they relate and interact with each other in the real-life expression of intelligent behavior outside the testing situation. We further considered the relationship of these cognitive abilities to EFs.

REFERENCES

Adair, J. C., Na, D. L., Schwartz, R. L., & Heilman, K. M. (1998). Analysis of primary and secondary influences on spatial neglect. *Brain and Cognition, 37*, 351–367.

Baddeley, A. (2003). Working memory: Looking back and looking forward. *Nature Reviews/Neuroscience, 4*, 829–839.

Barbey, A. K., Colom, R., & Grafman, J. (2013). Architecture of cognitive flexibility revealed by lesion mapping. *Neuroimage, 82*, 547–554.

Bate, A. J., Mathias, J. L., & Crawford, J. R. (2001). Performance on the test of everyday attention and standard tests of attention following sever traumatic brain injury. *The Clinical Neuropsychologist, 15*, 405–422.

Canivez, G. L., Watkins, M. W., & Dombrowski, S. C. (2016). Factor structure of the Wechsler Intelligence Scale for Children – Fifth Edition: exploratory factor analyses with the 16 primary and secondary subtests. *Psychological Assessment, 28*(8), 975–986.

Canivez, G. L., Watkins, M. W., & Dombrowski, S. C. (2017). Structural validity of the Wechsler Intelligence Scale for Children – Fifth Edition: Confirmatory Factor Analyses With the 16 primary and secondary subtests. *Psychological Assessment, 29*(4), 458–472.

Cattell, R. B. (1963). Theory of fluid and crystallized intelligence: A critical experiment. *Journal of Educational Psychology, v54*, 1–22.

Cattell, R. B. (1987). *Intelligence: It's structure. Growth, and action.* New York: Elsevier.

Carroll, J. B. (1993). *Human cognitive abilities: A survey of factor-analytic studies*. New York: Cambridge University Press.

Chan, R. C. K., Shum, D., Toulopoulou, T., & Chen, E. Y. H. (2008). Assessment of executive functions: Review of instruments and identification of critical issues. *Archives of Clinical Neuropsychology.*, *23*, 201–216.

Chen, H., Keith, T., Chen, Y., & Chang, B. (2009). What does the WISC-IV measure?: Validation of the scoring and CHC-based interpretative approaches. *Journal of Research in Education Sciences*, *54*(3), 85–108.

Cheung, A. M., Mitsis, E. M., & Halperin, J. M. (2004). The relationship of behavioral inhibition to executive functions in young adults. *Journal of Clinical and Experimental Neuropsychology*, *26*, 393–403.

Chuderski, A. (2013). When are fluid intelligence and working memory isomorphic and when are they not? *Intelligence*, *41*, 244–262.

Cole, M. W., & Schneider, W. (2007). The cognitive control network: Integrating cortical regions with dissociable functions. *Neuroimage*, *37*(1), 343–360.

Colom, R., Martinez-Molina, A., Shih, P. C., & Santacreu, J. (2011). Intelligence, working memory, and multitasking performance. *Intelligence*, *38*(6), 543–551.

Conway, A. R. A., Cowan, N., Bunting, M. F., Therriault, D. J., & Minkoff, S. R. B. (2002). A latent variable analysis of working memory capacity, short-term memory capacity, processing speed, and general fluid intelligence. *Intelligence*, *30*, 163–183.

Coyle, T. R., Pillow, D. R., Snyder, A. C., & Kochunov, P. (2011). Processing speed mediates the development of general intelligence in adolescents. *Psychological Science*, *22*(10), 1265–1269.

de Jone, P. F., & Das-Smaal, E. A. (1995). Attention and intelligence: The validity of the star counting test. *Journal of Educational Psychology*, *87*(1), 80–92.

Deary, I. J. (2001). *Intelligence: A very short introduction*. Oxford: Oxford University Press.

Deary, I. J., & Stough, C. (1996). Intelligence and inspection time: Achievements, prospects, and problems. *American Psychologist*, *51*, 599–608.

Diamond, A. (2013). Executive functions. *Annual Review of Psychology*, *64*, 134–168.

Dombrowski, S. C., Canivez, G. L., Watkins, M. W., & Beaujean, A. A. (2015). Exploratory bifactor analysis of the Wechsler Intelligence Scale for Children – Fifth Edition with the 16 primary and secondary subtests. *Intelligence*, *53*, 194–201.

Dombrowski, S. C., McGill, R. J., & Canivez, G. L. (2017a). Exploratory and hierarchical factor analysis of the WJ-IV cognitive at school age. *Psychological Assessment*, *29*(4), 394–407.

Dombrowski, S. C., McGill, R. J., & Canivez, G. L. (2017b). Hierarchical exploratory factor analyses of the Woodcock-Johnson – IV full test battery: Implications for CHC applications in school psychology. *School Psychology Quarterly*. Available from https://doi.org/10.1037/spq0000221.

Dougherty, T. M., & Haith, M. M. (1997). Infant expectations and reaction times as predictors of childhood speed of processing and IQ. *Developmental Psychology*, *33*(1), 146–155.

Engel de Abreu, P. M. J., Conway, A. R. A., & Gathercole, S. E. (2010). Working memory and fluid intelligence in young children. *Intelligence*, *38*, 552–561.

Engle, R. W., Tuholski, S. W., Laughlin, J. E., & Conway, A. R. A. (1999). Working memory, short term memory, and general fluid intelligence: A latent variable approach. *Journal of Experimental Psychology: General*, *128*(3), 309–331.

Flanagan, D. P., Alfonso, V. C., & Reynolds, M. R. (2013). Broad and narrow CHC abilities measured and not measured by the Wechsler Scales: Moving beyond with-in battery factor analysis. *Journal of Psychoeducational Assessment*, *31*(2), 202–223.

Fry, A. F., & Hale, S. (1996). Processing speed, working memory, and fluid intelligence: Evidence for a developmental cascade. *Psychological Science, 7*(4), 237–241.

Fry, A. F., & Hale, S. (2000). Relationships among processing speed, working memory, and fluid intelligence in children. *Biological Psychology, 54*, 1–34.

Geldmacher, D. S., Fritsch, T., & Riedel, T. M. (2000). Effects of stimulus properties and age on random-array letter cancellation tasks. *Aging, Neuropsychology, and Cognition, 7*(3), 194–204.

Gignac, G. E. (2016). The higher-order model imposes a proportionality constraint: That is why the bi-factor model tends to fit better. *Intelligence*, 57–68.

Gignac, G. E., & Watkins, M. W. (2013). Bi-factor modelling and the estimation of model-based reliability in that WAIS-IV. *Multivariate Behavioral Research, 48*, 639–662.

Gregoire, J. (2013). Measuring components of intelligence: Mission impossible? *Journal of Psychoeducational Assessment, 31*(2), 138–147.

Horn, J. L., & Cattell, R. B. (1966). Refinement and test of the theory of fluid and crystallized intelligences. *Journal of Educational Psychology, 57*, 253–270.

Jonides, J., Lacey, S. C., & Nee, D. E. (2005). Process of working memory in mind and brain. *Current Directions in Psychological Science, 14*, 2–5.

Jung, R. E., & Haier, R. J. (2007). The Parieto-Fronto Integration Theory (p_FIT) of intelligence: Converging neuroimaging evidence. *Behavioral & Brain Sciences, 30*(2), 135–154.

Kane, M. J., Hambrick, D. Z., & Conway, A. R. A. (2005). Working memory capacity and fluid intelligence are strongly related constructs: Comment on AcKerman, Beier, and Boyle (2005). *Psychological Bulletin, 131*(1), 66–71.

Kane, M. J., Bleckley, M. K., Conway, A. R. A., & Engle, R. W. (2001). A controlled attention view of working memory capacity. *Journal of Experimental Psychology: General., 130*, 169–183.

Kaufman, A. S. (1994). *Intelligent testing with the WISC − III*. New York: Wiley.

Kaufman, A. S. (2013). Intelligent testing with Wechsler's fourth editions: Perspectives on the Weiss et al. studies and the eight commentaries. *Journal of Psychoeducational Assessment, 31*(2), 224–234.

Keith, T. Z., & Reynolds, M. R. (2012). Using confirmatory factor analysis to aid in understanding the constructs measured by intelligence tests. In D. P. Flanagan, & P. L. Harrison (Eds.), *Contemporary intellectual assessment: Theories, tests, and issues* (3rd ed., pp. 758–799). New York: Guilford.

Keith, T. Z., Fine, J. G., Taub, G., Reynolds, M. R., & Kranzler, J. H. (2006). Higher order, multisample, confirmatory factor analysis of the Wechsler Intelligence Scale for Children −Fourth Edition: What does it measure? *School Psychology Review, 35*(1), 108–127.

Kyllonen, P. C., & Christal, R. E. (1990). Reasoning ability is (little more than) working memory capacity. *Intelligence, 14*, 389–433.

Langeslag, S.J.E., Schmidt, M., Ghassabian, A., Jaddoe, V.W., Hofman, A., Van der Lugt, A... White, T.J.H. (December, 2012). Functional connectivity between parietal and frontal brain regions and intelligence in young children: The generation R study. In *Symposium presented at the thirteenth annual conference of the International Society for Intelligence Research (ISIR)*. San Antonio, TX.

Lezak, M. D., Howieson, D. B., Bigler, E. D., & Tranel, D. (2012). *Neruopsychological assessment* (5th ed.). New York: Oxford University Press.

Lustig, C., May, C. P., & Hasher, L. (2001). Working memory span and the role of proactive interference. *Journal of Experimental Psychology: General., 130*, 199–207.

Mansolf, M., & Reise, S. P. (2017). When and why the second-order and bifactor mdoesl are distinguishable. *Intelligence*. Available from https://doi.org/10.1016/j.intell.2017.01.012.

Margolis, A., Bansal, R., Hao, X., Algermissen, M., Erickson, C., Klahr, K. W., . . . Peterson, B. S. (2013). Using IQ discrepancy7 Scores to examine the neural correlates of specific cognitive abilities. *The Journal of Neuroscience, v 33*(35), 14135−14145.

Martinez, K., Burgaleta, M., Roman, F. J., Escorial, S., Shih, P. C., Quiroga, M. A., & Colom, R. (2011). Can fluid intelligence be reduced to 'simple' short term memory? *Intelligence, 39* (6), 473−480.

McCrea., Simon., & Robinson, T. P. (2011). Visual Puzzles, Figure Weights, and Cancellation: Some preliminary hypotheses on the functional an dneural substrates of these three new WAIS-IV subtests. *Neurology*, 1−19.

McFarland, D. J. (2016). Modeling general and specific abilities. *Assessment, v23*(6), 9.

McGrew, K., & Flanagan, D. P. (1998). *The intelligence test desk reference (ITDR) Gf − Gc cross-battery assessment*. Boston, MA: Allyn and Bacon.

Morgan, G. B., Hodge, K. J., Wells, K. E., & Watkins, M. W. (2015). Are fit indices biased in favour of bi-factor models in cognitive ability research: A comparison of fit in correlated factors, higher-order, and bi-factor models via Monte Carlo simulations. *Journal of Intelligence, 3*, 2−20.

Murray, A. L., & Johnson, W. (2013). The limitations of model fit in comparing the bi-factor versus higher-order models of human cognitive ability structure. *Intelligence, 41*, 407−422.

Na, D. L., Adair, J. C., Kang, Y., Chung, C. S., Lee, K. H., & Heilmand, K. M. (1999). Motor perseverative behavior on a line cancellation task. *Neurology, 52*(8), 1569−1576.

Niileksela, C. R., Reynolds, M. R., & Kaufman, A. S. (2013). An alternative Cattell-Horn-Carroll (CHC) factor structure of the WAIS-IV: Age invariance of an alternative model for ages 70−90. *Psychological Assessment, 25*, 391−404.

Nutley, S. B., Soderqvist, S., Bryde, S., Thorell, L. B., Humphreys, K., & Klingberg, T. (2011). Gains in fluid intelligence after training non-verbal reasoning in 4-year-old children: a controlled, randomized study. *Developmental Science, 14*(3), 591−601.

Oberauer, K., & Lewandowsky, S. (2013). Evidence against decay in verbal working memory. *Journal of Experimental Psychology: General, 142*(2), 380−411.

Oberauer, K., Sub, H. M., Wilhelm, O. L., & Sanders, N. (2007). Individual differences in working memory capacity and reasoning ability. In A. R. A. Conway, C. Jarrold, M. J. Kane, A. Miyake, & J. N. Towse (Eds.), *Variation in working memory* (pp. 49−75). Oxford: Oxford University Press.

Reynolds, C. R. (1997). Forward and backward memory span should not be combined for clinical analysis. *Archives of Clinical Neuropsychology, 12*, 29−40.

Reynolds, M. R., & Keith, T. Z. (2017). Multi-group and hierarchical confirmatory factor analysis of Wechsler Intelligence Scale for Children − Fifth Edition: What does it measure? *Intelligence, 62*, 31−47.

Saklofske, D. H., Zhu, J. J., Coalson, D. L., Raiford, S. E., & Weiss, L. G. (2010). Cognitive proficiency index for the Canadian edition of the Wechsler Intelligence Scale for Children−fourth edition. *Canadian Journal of School Psychology, 25*(3), 277−286.

Salthouse, T.A. (2009). Operationalization and validity of the construct of executive functioning. In *Continuing education workshop presented at the annual meeting of the International Neuropsychological Society*. Athens, GA.

Schneider, W. J. (2013). What if we took our models seriously? Estimating latent scores in individuals. *Journal of Psychoeducational Assessment, 31*(2), 186−201.

Schwean, V. L., & Saklofske, D. H. (2005). Assessment of attention deficit hyperactivity disorder with the WISC-IV. In A. Prifitera, D. H. Saklofske, & L. G. Weiss (Eds.), *WISC-IV clinical use and interpretation: Scientist-practitioner perspectives* (pp. 235–280). San Diego, CA: Elsevier.

Soderqvist, S., Nutley, S. B., Ottersen, J., Grill, K. M., & Klingberg, T. (2012). Computerized training of non-verbal reasoning and working memory in children with intellectual disability. *Frontiers in Human Neuroscience, 6*, 1–8, Article 271.

Spearman, C. E. (1904). General intelligence, objectively determined and measured. *The American Journal of Psychology, 15*(2), 201–292.

Spearman, C. E. (1923). *The nature of "intelligence" and the principles of cognition.* London: Macmillan.

Spearman, C. E. (1927). *The abilities of man: Their nature and measurement.* London: MacMillan.

Tang, C. Y., Eaves, E. L., Ng, J. C., Carpenter, D. M., Mai, X., Schroeder, D. H., ... Haier, R. J. (2010). *Intelligence, 38*(3), 293–303.

Thomas, R., Dougherty, M. R., & Buttaccio, D. R. (2014). Memory constraints on hypothesis generation and decision making. *Current Directions in Psychological Science*, 264–270. Available from https://doi.org/10.1177/0963721414534853.

Unsworth, N., & Engle, R. W. (2005). Working memory capacity and fluid abilities: Examining the correlation between operation span and Raven. *Intelligence, 33*, 67–81.

Vernon, P. E. (1950). *The structure of human abilities.* London: Methuen.

Wechsler, D. (2014). *Technical manual for the Wechsler Intelligence Scales for children—fifth edition (WISC-V).* San Antonio, TX: Pearson.

Wechsler, D. (2012). *Technical manual for the Wechsler preschool and primary scales of intelligence—fourth edition (WISC-IV).* San Antonio, TX: Pearson.

Weiss, L. G., Keith, T. Z., Zhu, J., & Chen, H. (2013a). WAIS-IV Clinical validation of the four- and five-factor interpretive approaches. *Journal of Psychoeducational Assessment, 31* (2), 114–131.

Weiss, L. G., Keith, T. Z., Zhu, J., & Chen, H. (2013b). WISC-IV Clinical validation of the four- and five-factor interpretive approaches. *Journal of Psychoeducational Assessment, 31* (2), 94–113.

Weiss, L. G., Saklofske, D. H., Coalson, D., & Raiford, S. E. (2010). *WAIS-IV clinical use and interpretation.* San Diego, CA: Academic Press.

Weiss, L. G., Saklofske, D. H., & Prifitera, A. (2005). Interpreting the WISC-IV index scores. In A. Prifitera, D. H. Saklofske, & L. G. Weiss (Eds.), *WISC-IV clinical use and interpretation: Scientist-practitioner perspectives* (pp. 71–100). San Diego, CA: Academic Press.

Weiss, L. G., Saklofske, D. H., Prifitera, A., & Holdnack, J. A. (2006). *WISC-IV: Advanced clinical interpretation.* San Diego, CA: Academic Press.

Wojciulik, E., Husain, M., Clarke, K., & Driver, J. (2001). Spatial working memory deficit in unilateral neglect. *Neuropsycholgia, 39*, 390–396.

Yang, R., Spirtes, P., Scheines, R., Reise, S. P., & Mansoff, M. (2017). Finding pure submodels for improved differentiation of bifactor and second-order models. *Structural Equation Modeling: A Multidisciplinary Journal.* Available from https://doi.org/10.1080/10705511.2016.1261351.

Chapter 5

Wechsler Intelligence Scale for Children—Fifth Edition: Use in Societal Context

Lawrence G. Weiss[1], Victoria Locke[2], Tianshu Pan[3], Jossette G. Harris[4], Donald H. Saklofske[5] and Aurelio Prifitera[6]

[1]Research and Measurement Consultant, San Antonio, TX, United States, [2]The University of Texas at San Antonio, San Antonio, TX, United States, [3]Department of Clinical Psychometrics, Pearson Assessment, San Antonio, TX, United States, [4]Department of Psychiatry, University of Colorado School of Medicine, Denver, CO, United States, [5]Department of Psychology, University of Western Ontario, London, ON, Canada, [6]Assessment Consultant, San Antonio, TX, United States

Intelligence has been repeatedly shown to be predictive of a wide variety of important life outcomes and is thus of considerable practical importance in our lives, leading to higher educational attainment, job advancement, and career success. (Deary et al., 2004; Gottfredson, 1998; Gottfredson & Saklofske, 2009; Squalli & Wilson, 2014; Lubinski, 2004; Sternberg & Grigorenko, 2002). At the societal level, regions with higher Intelligence Quotient (IQ) citizens have been shown to contribute differentially to innovative ideas in business (Squalli & Wilson, 2014), and the technological and economic progress of nations (Burhan, Mohamad, Kurniawan, & Sidek, 2014). Thus, the measurement of intelligence is of considerable importance at both individual and societal levels.

An individual's intelligence is traditionally measured relative to a sample of people the same age that is representative of a national population. This helps psychologists answer the question of how a particular person compares to other people across the nation in which that individual lives and competes. However, even though we may live in the United States or Canada or France, no person lives in the country "as a whole." Rather, people live in neighborhoods or communities that can vary along simple dimensions such as size (San Antonio, the Bronx, Ontario), and along more complex dimensions such that communities may reflect unique characteristics that can impact the development and maintenance of cognitive abilities in novel

WISC-V. DOI: https://doi.org/10.1016/B978-0-12-815744-2.00005-7

ways. Those who measure intelligence also want to know how the person being tested compares to other people in the local community or culture. This is the essence of *contextual interpretation*. It is contextually informed interpretation of population-based cognitive ability scores in concert with salient demographic and environmental variables.

Most chapters written on intelligence test interpretation conclude with a statement such as, "The examiner should also take into account other factors such as the client's educational, medical, cultural, and family history—as well as other test scores." This advice has been repeated so frequently that it is often taken for granted, and while most psychologists acknowledge its veracity, not all implement it in practice. With experience, however, many psychologists come to understand that each profile of test scores has a range of meanings depending on the person's history and the context of the evaluation. In fact, one defining characteristic of an expert assessment psychologist may well be the ability to refine standard, cookbook interpretations of test profiles based on environmental, medical, and other relevant contextual issues.

In the *WISC-IV Advanced Clinical Interpretation* book (Weiss, Saklofske, Prifitera, & Holdnack, 2006), we devoted the first chapter to an exploration of the enriching and inhibiting influences of environment on cognitive development of children and adolescents, and some of that ground is revisited in the present chapter. In the *WAIS-IV Clinical Use and Interpretation* book (Weiss, Saklofske, Coalson, & Raiford, 2010) we explored changing environmental issues with respect to various generations of adults. We revisit some of that material because many of these adults are parents who play a major role in shaping the cognitive, physical, social, and emotional development of their children. Just as important, the environmental contexts surrounding adults also may impact cognitive development of their children. For example, changes in parental employment status can affect children's academic performance (Schmitt, Sacco, Ramey, Ramey, & Chan, 1999). Further, the range of physical and psychological stressors on individuals living in war-torn countries, suffering from malnutrition due to famine, or affected by environmental pollutants (e.g., mercury, lead) impacts all humans of all ages, albeit in potentially different ways. On the positive side, and much closer to home, Kaufman and colleagues have recently shown that significant reductions in environmental lead that have occurred in the United States due to increasingly tighter government standards over the past several decades can be associated with as much as a four to five point increase in average IQ scores, even after controlling for urban status and education (Kaufman et al., 2014).

In this chapter, we provide information that may inform the integration of salient cultural and home environmental considerations into clinical assessment practice with children. In doing so, we continue to challenge the belief that the intellectual growth and development of individuals represents the unfolding of a predominantly fixed trait only marginally influenced by the nature and quality of environmental opportunities and experiences. And more so, it is the opportunity to develop and express one's intelligence that is the key issue here. No matter how intellectually gifted a person might potentially be, it is well known from psychological studies over many years (e.g., Hunt & Mcvicker, 1961) that without early environmental stimulation and nurturing that so often comes from parents and caregivers, access to quality education, encouragement for engaging in intellectual and creative activities, etc., children will be restricted in their cognitive growth. Added to this, the effects of poverty, poor nutrition, limited health care, and living in unstable environments will further impact the development and expression of ones "genetic" intelligence!

BIAS ISSUES IN INTELLECTUAL ASSESSMENT

Prior to beginning our discussion of contextually informed interpretation of cognitive test scores, we must devote several pages to the widely held conception that cultural demographic differences in IQ test scores are due to biases built into the test. Our intent in this section of the chapter is to put aside these concerns so that we can focus on contextual mediators of cognitive performance, skill acquisition, and maintenance. Considerable advances have been made since the earlier efforts to produce culture-fair tests (Cattell, 1949; Mercer & Lewis, 1978). We discuss advances in item and method bias research and show that disproportionate representation of individuals in specific categories or groups is not limited to cognitive and achievement test scores but is present in many areas of life. We acknowledge a legacy of controversy in these areas, and must address it so that we can move forward.

Item bias has been studied extensively, and all reputable test developers take special precaution to avoid it. Best practice in test development first entails systematic reviews of all items for potential bias by panels of cultural experts and such methodology is well documented and practiced (see Georgas, Weiss, Van de Vijver, & Saklofske, 2003). Test developers typically determine representation of ethnic minority examinees in acquiring test cases based on census percentages, but purposely exceed the percentages so that advanced statistical techniques may be undertaken to detect and replace items that perform differently across ethnic groups. Conceptually, these techniques seek to identify items on which subjects from different demographic groups score differently despite possessing the same overall ability on the particular construct being assessed.

When items are identified as operating differently by examinee group, the reason for any identified differences cannot be determined by these analyses alone. Expert panels commonly predict that certain items will be biased because some groups have less direct experience with the subject of those items than other groups, but then find that various statistical procedures designed to detect bias do not identify the same items as the panel. Perhaps this is because the cultural expert panel is not typically required to provide an evidenced-based theory to explain how culture, as they conceive it, interacts with item content. At the same time, statistical techniques sometimes point to a particular item as problematic when the expert panel can find no contextual reason. This may be due to the very large number of statistical comparisons undertaken (e.g., every test item is evaluated across multiple racial and ethnic group comparisons, and also by gender, region of the country, and educational level) and so even with a $P < .01$ criteria there may be some items that randomly test positive for differential functioning when more than a thousand comparisons are made.

For these and other reasons this line of research is no longer referred to as item bias research, but as an analysis of differential item functioning (DIF) because the underlying reasons that items perform differently across groups are not always known. In light of the care taken in the development of items for most modern intelligence tests it seems unlikely that item bias accounts for the bulk of the variance in demographic differences in IQ test scores. However, differential item performance statistics are not very suitable to detect factors that influence entire tests as opposed to single items (van de Vijver & Bleichrodt, 2001). This is because most DIF studies match respondents from different racial/ethnic groups by using total test scores as the indication of ability or intelligence. If one presumes that some aspect of the dominant culture is inherent in the construct being evaluated by the test, and not just in isolated items, then by matching on test scores researchers may be matching on adherence to some unknown aspect of the majority culture. This larger issue can be framed as one of possible construct or method bias in which the construct being tested, or the method used to measure the construct, functions differently across groups.

This type of bias is more general than item bias, and more difficult to study empirically. According to this view, the formats and frameworks of most major intelligence tests are literacy dependent and middle-class oriented. Further, the testing paradigm itself is a stimulus response set that could be considered a social-communication style specific to Western European cultures (Kayser, 1989). The testing paradigm assumes that the test takers will perform to the best of their ability, try to provide relevant answers, respond even when the task does not make sense to them, and feel comfortable answering questions from people who are strangers to them. In some cultures, individuals are expected to greet unfamiliar events with silence or to be silent in the presence of a stranger. Guessing is not encouraged in other cultures and learning takes place through practice rather than explanation. Unfortunately, there are methodological difficulties in determining the amount of variance that may be explained by each of these factors. No studies have attempted to parse out the extent to which these influences may be ameliorated by the examinees experiences within the US educational system where western paradigms are pervasive. At the same time, evidence suggests that amount of US educational experience may explain significant variance in IQ test scores of Hispanic children and adolescents (Wechsler, 2005), as well as immigrant adults (Harris, Tulsky, & Schultheis, 2003).

Therefore, an important question is whether a test measures the same constructs across groups. One common way to examine this question is through factor analysis, and more sophisticated approaches include measurement invariance techniques. Basically, if it can be shown that the various facets (i.e., subtests) of a test correlate with each other in similar ways across groups then such findings are typically taken as evidence in support of the hypothesis that the test is measuring the same constructs across those cultures. A series of studies have shown invariance of the four factor WAIS-III measurement model between large and representative samples of subjects in the United States, Australia, and Canada, as well as across education levels and age bands. (Bowden, Lloyd, Weiss, & Holdnack, 2006; Bowden, Lange, Weiss, & Saklofske, 2008; Bowden, Lissner, McCarthy, Weiss, & Holdnack, 2003). While these studies are important, it must be noted that they are limited to comparisons between English-speaking nations that are westernized, industrialized, and share common historical roots.

In a large international study of 16 North American, European, and Asian nations, Georgas et al. (2003) found reasonable consistency of the factor structure of WISC-III, with each nation studied reporting either three or four factors. In all cases the difference between the three- and four-factor solutions were due to a single subtest (Arithmetic) cross-loading on two factors (i.e., verbal and working memory). Importantly, these analyses included not only nations from 3 continents and 16 countries that speak 11 different languages, but also included both westernized and nonwesternized societies (i.e., South Korea, Japan, and Taiwan), albeit all were developed countries. Another important finding from this study is that the mean FSIQ scores for the countries were found to vary systematically with the level of affluence and education of the countries as indicated by key economic indicators such as gross national product (GNP), percent of the GNP spent on education, and percent of the countries workforce in agriculture. As encompassing as this study is, we again note that there were no preindustrialized nations included. The reader is referred to chapter 7 where we continue this line of research and present new data comparing WISC-V scores across multiple countries.

Still, examining differences in mean scores across groups is a relatively simple but flawed procedure for assessing cultural bias in tests (see Gottfredson & Saklofske, 2009). A more sophisticated approach is to examine how the relationship of intelligence test scores to important criterion variables differs across groups. This begs the question, however, of what is an appropriate criterion variable for validating an intelligence test. In many, though not all, cultures educational success is considered an important behavioral outcome of intelligence, and thus the prediction of academic achievement from IQ has been studied extensively. Studies have shown a general absence of differential prediction of standardized achievement test scores from IQ scores across racial/ethnic groups for WISC-R (Poteat, Wuensch, & Gregg, 1988; Reschly & Reschly, 1979; Reschly & Saber, 1979; Reynolds & Gutkin, 1980; Reynolds & Hartlage, 1979), and this finding has been replicated with WISC-III for nationally standardized achievement tests scores in reading, writing, and math (Weiss, Prifitera, & Roid, 1993; Weiss & Prifitera, 1995). Typically, these regression-based studies show differences in the intercept but not the slope, and this lack of difference in the slopes is taken as evidence in support of a lack of differential prediction. In other words, IQ scores predict scores on standardized achievement tests equally well for all demographic groups studied. Yet, the possibility exists that this finding is attributable to bias being equally present in both the predictor (i.e., the standardized intelligence test) and the criterion (i.e., the standardized achievement test). This question was partially addressed by Weiss et al. (1993) who used teacher-assigned classroom grades as the criterion rather than standardized achievement test scores, and again, no differential prediction was observed. A general lack of differential prediction to achievement also was demonstrated more recently with WISC-IV (Konold & Canivez, 2010).

It is unknown if the construct of intelligence as we currently conceptualize it, albeit reliably measured with replicable factor structure across many cultures, predicts behaviors and outcomes that would be uniquely defined as intelligent by each culture and particularly by nonindustrialized cultures. Many researchers weigh as important studies that show a relationship between intelligence and academic achievement because the societies in which they live tend to value education as an important outcome of intelligence. In cultures of preindustrialized nations, or perhaps some subcultures of industrialized nations, were success in school is not necessarily central to success in life, such studies may not be as relevant. Other valued outcomes of intelligence may vary considerably across cultures and might include such behaviors as the ability to resolve conflict among peers, influence one's elders, build useful machines without instructions, survive in a dangerous neighborhood, grow nutritious crops in poor soil, etc. The point is that while tests of intelligence have stable factor structures across groups and predict academic achievement very well, this does not necessarily mean that they predict things that every culture would value as intelligent behavior in real life. Demonstrating the stability of the factor structure across cultures is an important yet insufficient step in demonstrating cross-cultural validity. Further, if we were to design a new test to predict culturally specific outcomes of intelligence we would begin by seeking to understand what constitutes intelligent behaviors as defined by that population and then create tasks designed to predict those behavioral outcomes. If the important outcomes (i.e., the criterion) of intelligence differ across cultures, then we might not end up with the same constructs that comprise most modern tests of intelligence—but, we don't know that.

CONSEQUENCES OF TESTING AND THE FAIRNESS OF TEST USE IN SPECIAL EDUCATION

Some writers have argued that any discussion of test bias is incomplete without commenting on test use, which explicitly involves decisions made about special educational programming based on the test results (Valencia & Suzuki, 2001, p. 145). This view is endorsed in the Standards for Educational and Psychological Testing (American Education Research Association, American Psychological Association, & National Council on Measurement in Education, 2014). This apparently innocuous statement has some inherent dangers. Clearly, studying the consequences of test use is an important area of research. However, we believe that considering the consequences of test use under the heading of test bias runs the risk of confounding the concept of test bias with possible differential need for services across groups. This is because studies have generally found that low socioeconomic status (SES), culturally and linguistically diverse (CLD) youth are at greater risk for learning delays (Hall & Barnett, 1991; Reid & Patterson, 1991; Schaefer, 2004; Walker, Greenwood, Hart, & Carta, 1994). *If two groups are truly at differential risk for a particular set of problems, then a test which results in a higher percentage of subjects from the at-risk group receiving services should be considered valid rather than biased.* This is an extremely important, but frequently ignored issue. Some state education authorities establish proportionate representation criteria by setting acceptable limits around state census targets without regard to risk status. Fair usage is intended to distinguish individuals in need of differential services from those who have been wrongly referred and would not be aided by remedial services. Thus, fair usage should be viewed as a person-level rather than a group-level concept. Much of this chapter concerns taking into account contextual variables in the interpretation of psychological test scores to improve the fairness of individual evaluations. Nonetheless, we continue with a discussion of disproportionate representation of minorities in special educational programs because decisions about entry into these programs lead to claims of unfairness in testing, and because the Individuals with Disabilities Education Act (IDEA) legislation contains important provisions designed to reduce overrepresentation of minorities in special education programs (IDEA, 2004).

Despite the general lack of evidence for both item bias and differential prediction of achievement, differences in average IQ test scores between demographic groups persist, even when differences in SES are taken into account. These differences contribute to disproportionate representation in some special educational programs. First, let's examine programs for learning disabilities (LD). At the national level, the percentage of students in each racial/ethnic group enrolled in LD programs is close to the percentage of each racial/ethnic group enrolled in public school.

According to the National Center for Education Statistics (2012a), in the 2011−12 school year, African Americans (AAs) comprise 20.2% of students in LD programs, as compared to 15.4% of overall school enrollment. When interpreting data related to the AA population, be aware that researchers commonly identify all Black individuals living in the United States as AA, including those who migrated from non-African countries such as Haiti. We use the term AA in the present chapter because it is common practice at the time in which we write, and because Black individuals from different countries of origin were not recorded separately in the majority of the available data. The reader should keep in mind, however, that the AA samples described herein are likely to be more heterogeneous than the label implies.

Twenty-five percent (25.7%) of Hispanics are in LD programs, compared to 23.9% enrolled in school. The percentage of Whites in LD programs is 48.6%, as compared to 51.4% of all students in school. Thus, the national data for the 2011−12 school year do not support the hypothesis that minorities are grossly overrepresented in LD programs. Hispanics and AAs are overrepresented in LD programs by 1.8% and 4.8%, respectively.

The national picture for both intellectual disability (ID) and gifted/talented (GT) programs, however, is not proportionate to the population percentages by racial/ethnic group. At the national level, AAs are substantially overrepresented in ID programs (27.7% as compared to 15.4% enrolled in school), whereas Hispanics (19.6%) and Whites (46.8%) are each slightly underrepresented. There is some variation among the states. For example, AAs comprise about one quarter of the school population in Florida (NCES, 2012b), but nearly 40% of the state's ID enrollment. In Illinois, Hispanics represent 22% of the student population, but 18.4% of the ID enrollment (NCES, 2012c). However, in New York, Hispanics are 22.1% of the school population, but 27.6% of the ID enrollment (NCES, 2012d). Historically, the sparse availability of cognitive ability and adaptive behavior measures in the Spanish language has constrained potential identification of ID in this population. Since these measures are now available, identification of Hispanics in these special education categories may have increased over past numbers.

LD and ID enrollment percentages should be considered in relation to each other because mild ID can sometimes be difficult to differentiate from severe or comorbid learning disorders. Historically, there has been an inverse relationship between the proportion of students identified as LD versus mild (or, educable) ID—perhaps as funding sources shifted emphasis or as social acceptance of LD classifications changed over time. Controversies also have been raised regarding the lack of use of adaptive behavior measures when diagnosing ID, and it has been observed that about one third of mild ID students may be diagnosed with no record of an adaptive behavior measure (Reschly & Ward, 1991). The lack of adaptive behavior measures may call into question the validity of many of the mild ID diagnoses. The relationship of LD and mild ID rates, how they cofluctuate over time and vary across states, deserves the attention of scholars.

In seeking to understand the relationship between rates of LD and ID, it may be instructive to consider mean scores by demographic groups in combination with established rules for determining eligibility for special education services. In some local education agencies, the ability-achievement discrepancy (AAD) criteria were still a component of eligibility determinations for LD services over the past decade. In other education agencies, however, the Individual Education Plan (IEP) committee is permitted considerable discretion in determining eligibility, which can lead to a lack of standard criteria for deciding which students receive special education services. Typically, students must have a large (usually 15 points or greater) discrepancy between intelligence and achievement, with achievement being lower, in order to qualify for placement in an LD program. Strict application of the AAD criteria may have made LD service less accessible for some low SES AA students whose ability test scores are not above the threshold, or whose ability and achievement test scores were both low and thus not discrepant from each other. Although there are no data on the subject, we speculate that IEP committees may have come to view placement in programs for students with mild ID as the best available option to obtain much needed assistance for some struggling students. The rules for determining eligibility for LD services have been changing over the past decade as school districts have implemented the current IDEA legislation, which no longer requires that the AAD method be used in determining eligibility for LD services.

The IDEA encourages local education agencies to consider other methods of eligibility determination such as response to intervention (RtI), or the student's failure to respond to empirically supported instruction. Even when more contemporary RtI or processing strength and weakness methods are used, the student often must have an IQ score above some minimum level, such as 80, in addition to other criteria. Despite promises to the contrary, however, the application of RtI appears to have had no impact on reducing disproportionate representation. Bouman (2010) found that RtI districts in California did not have significantly lower placement rates for CLD students than non-RtI districts. Orosco and Klinger (2010) showed that RtI gives false confidence about removing bias from special education determinations. Hernandez-Finch (2012) concluded that despite recent high-quality studies, insufficient research currently exists to support full implementation of an RtI model with CLD students. Culturally responsive models of RtI have been proposed (Rhodes, 2010; Rhodes, Ochoa, & Ortiz, 2005).

When seeking to understand differential rates of LD it is important to examine the larger process of special education eligibility determination, a process in which test scores play only one role—albeit an important one. While the process varies across schools, it is almost always the teacher who first identifies a student as needing assistance to keep up with work in the classroom. In most schools, the teacher is then required to demonstrate that one or more instructional modifications have been attempted and were not effective. At that point, other options are considered including afterschool tutoring, mentoring programs with community volunteers, retention in the same grade, referral for testing, etc. Researchers and policy advocates are now beginning to examine disproportionate impact in each of the various steps along the way toward placement in LD and ID programs. For example, possible differential rates of teacher referrals for tutoring versus testing by racial/ethnic group.

It is also important to mention that placement in a special education program can be perceived favorably or unfavorably depending on the perspective of the observer. When a student is placed in a special education program, one can either claim that he or she is receiving the help needed, or that the student has been unfairly labeled and segregated. Of students found not eligible for the same special education program, one can argue that they have successfully avoided a stigmatizing label, or that they were unfairly denied access to needed services.

The problem of disproportionate representation is large and complex. The present extent of overrepresentation in some areas is so large that it may not be fully accounted for by the differential rates of risk for cognitive and learning problems between racial/ethnic groups. The extent of overrepresentation that is accounted for by differential risk needs to be better understood. Given that ethnic minority students who are CLD and living in low SES environments are at risk for cognitive and learning problems, we are concerned that enforcing strictly proportionate representation could eventually lead to legal challenges of unfair denial of services. This could occur if CLD children are denied access to special education because the program has exceeded its quota of minorities. We hope that state guidelines will allow local education agencies to take into account differential rates of risk by racial/ethnic group when setting acceptable percentages of minorities in special education. Careful attention to these issues will be important in order to balance both perspectives and ensure that no child is either placed inappropriately or unfairly denied service.

For GT programs, disproportionate representation by racial/ethnic group is evident at the national level. According to the National Center for Education Statistics (2012), in 2006, the last year for which data are available, AAs comprised 9.2% of students in GT programs, as compared to 17.1% of overall school enrollment in Fall 2006. The percent of Hispanics are in GT programs was 12.9, compared to 20.5% enrolled in school in the Fall 2006. The percentage of Whites in GT programs was 68.4%, while they comprised only 56.5% of all students enrolled in school. In addition to Whites, Asian/Pacific Islanders are also overrepresented in GT programs. Approximately 9.4% of students enrolled in GT programs were Asian/Pacific Islanders, while they comprised 4% of all students (Sable & Noel, 2008).

Again, there is great variation across states. Enrollment of Hispanics in New York was 20.6% (Sable & Noel, 2008), but only 13.8% of GT students in NY were Hispanic (NCES, 2012). Similarly, enrollment of AAs in North Carolina (NC) was 29.2% (Sable & Noel, 2008), but only 12.1% of GT students in NC were AA (NCES, 2012), and Hispanics were 9.6% of the student population (Sable & Noel, 2008), but 2.7% of GT students in NC (NCES, 2012).

Whenever any group has a lower mean test score than the national average, that group will be overrepresented in programs that require low test scores for eligibility, and underrepresented in programs that require high test scores for admission. However, neither ID or GT determinations should be made based on the IQ test score alone. As noted above, an ID diagnosis requires that intelligence and adaptive functioning test scores be both significantly below average (by more than two standard deviations); yet there is evidence to suggest that many ID placements are made without any adaptive behavior measure. Similarly, IQ should not be the sole requirement for entrance into GT programs. Starting with Terman (1925), the tendency to equate giftedness solely with high IQ has persisted for several decades, and continues to influence daily practice. Scholars suggest three general characteristics of giftedness (Renzulli, 1986; Winner, 1996). First, there should be evidence of precocious ability in general or in some specific area such as mathematics, guitar, ballet, etc. Second, a strong task commitment to that activity should be obvious, or a "rage to master" the skill. Third, creativity and originality should be evident, or a tendency to "march to one's own drummer" with respect to the gifted skill. It is in the intersection of these three characteristics that true giftedness resides. While IQ testing has an important role to play in GT determinations, it is not an exclusive role and GT assessments should broaden as our understanding of the concept of giftedness expands.

It is somewhat widely believed that there are different types of intelligences that can be associated with analytical, synthetic, or practical giftedness (Sternberg & Davidson, 1986; Sternberg, 1997), and it is possible to consider that giftedness is not a stable trait of the person but an interaction between culturally defined opportunities for action and personal talents that are recognized by the gifted person and acted upon (Csikszentmihalyi & Robinson, 1986). These expansions of the construct of giftedness are more inclusionary, and may provide answers to persistent criticisms of the elitist nature of gifted programs (Margolin, 1994).

As with LD and ID programs, understanding disproportionate representation in GT programs requires examination of the larger process. In most cases, teachers nominate students for GT evaluations, although these nominations can be heavily influenced by parent pressure and community expectations. Teachers rely primarily on academic performance, but may include other idiosyncratic criteria. Structured teacher nomination rating scales of observable classroom behavior based on the newer theories of multiple domains of giftedness have been shown to reduce the unreliability inherent in the nomination process and increase valid identification of gifted and talented students (The Gifted Rating Scales, Pfeiffer & Jarosewich, 2003)

While the literature on test bias acknowledges the role of SES on intelligence test scores, the literature on disproportionate representation in special education programs has paid insufficient attention to the known effects of poverty on learning and cognitive development. This is a serious oversight because poverty, and the associated effects from physical health to psychological well-being, is known to have an impact on learning and cognitive development, is disproportionately represented across racial/ethnic groups, and it may explain much of the disproportional representation in special education. This will be discussed in greater detail later in this chapter.

DEMOGRAPHIC DISPARITIES IN VARIOUS AREAS OF LIFE

Disparities exist when differences in outcomes are observed across different groups within a population (Centers for Disease Control & Prevention, 2013). Disparities by racial/ethnic groups within the United States are not limited to disproportionate representation in special education and differences in test scores. Rather they are well documented for a variety of factors including physical and mental health status, infant mortality, longevity, access to health care, educational attainment and opportunities, income, occupational status and job stability, wealth, equality of schools, and more (Hummer, 1996).

These disparities are becoming more important for children's well-being as there has been a wide shift in the demographic composition of the US population in the last decade, especially in the child population. The US Census Bureau estimates that non-Hispanic Whites (Whites) will be a plurality rather than a majority in the US population between 2040–45 (US Census Bureau, 2013), and this change has already occurred in the young child population (Johnson & Lichter, 2010). These changes are important because the children being assessed with the WISC-V belong to one of the most diverse cohorts of youngsters since David Wechsler published the first edition of this assessment. In 2012, less than 50% of children were born to White non-Hispanic families, and the largest increases are occurring in the Hispanic population (US Census Bureau, 2012). While some of this increase is due to immigration, most of it can be attributed to a higher birth rate among US-born Hispanics, as Hispanics on average have more children than the Asian, AA, or White non-Hispanic populations, who have the lowest birth rates. The percentage of children who are White will continue to drop every year in the near future as family size declines and there are fewer White non-Hispanic women in the childbearing years. While the shifts are widespread, they are not uniform across the country, and they are more pronounced in the west and south than they are in other areas. The southeast in particular has become remarkably more diverse with growing numbers of Hispanics in addition to the historical AA and White non-Hispanic populations (Johnson & Lichter, 2010). For these reasons, this book includes a special chapter on testing Hispanics with WISC-V and WISC-IV Spanish.

While the disparities are present across a wide variety of outcomes, we confine this discussion to areas that are theoretically and conceptually related to children's cognitive development and skill acquisition. Because race/ethnicity and SES are highly correlated (Massey, 2007), it is very difficult to disentangle the two. What may first appear as a racial or ethnic difference may actually be more attributable to poverty and inequality. The premise of this section is that race and ethnicity are socially constructed; yet, they function in society to stratify people across a broad series of outcomes. To illustrate how they are malleable constructs, the US Census has updated the racial/ethnic categories in nearly every decennial census (LaVeist, 2005). In the first census in 1790, it asked for number of White persons, other free persons (typically American Indians), and the number of slaves. In 1850, Mulatto (mixed race) was added, and in 1890, several categories of mixed race were available. However, by 1930, mixed-race categories were no longer an option. Until 2000, people could only indicate one category, making it difficult to calculate how many mixed-race people there were in the country. Currently people are asked their race and whether or not they are of Hispanic origin, and they are allowed to check more than one race (US Census Bureau, 2014). This categorization is likely to change again in the next census, and the Census Bureau is currently undertaking research to determine how race and ethnicity will be collected in 2020.

It is also important to recognize that while the racial ethnic groups are grouped into the five categories of White, AA, Hispanic, Asian, and Other race/ethnicities, these groups are not homogeneous. AAs include those whose ancestors came to North America nearly 400 years ago, as well as those who have recently arrived from the Caribbean and Africa. Hispanics are an especially heterogeneous group, and there are socioeconomic and linguistic differences depending on the place of origin such as Mexico, Puerto Rico, Dominican Republic, Cuba, and Central and South America. Asians include those whose origins are from areas as diverse as China, Japan, Indonesia, Vietnam, Korea, and India. Other race/ethnicities typically include American Indian and Alaska Natives, and people of mixed ancestry. The exception is people who are mixed race and of Hispanic origin; they are included in the Hispanic category. We realize that some of the terminology for the racial/ethnic groups is controversial, and there is a wide variety of opinion regarding which term is best. We have used the terms AA, Hispanic, Asian, Other, and White (i.e., non-Hispanic), as they appear to be the most current in the literature. Although Latino/a is gaining in prominence, it is not as preferred as Hispanic according to research conducted by the Pew Research Center

(Lopez, 2013). This section will explore disparities in four key areas: Education, Income and Occupation, Physical Health Status, and Mental Health Status.

Racial/Ethnic Group Disparities in Education

Group differences in education are important because the education children receive in childhood can have lifelong consequences. Education determines whether or not a person goes to college, and, often, qualifies for a well-paying job with health benefits. That in turn can determine where s/he lives and sends his/her own children to school, the type of education the children receive, and thus the cycle perpetuates.

Racial/ethnic differences in achievement show up at the kindergarten door in reading (Foster & Miller, 2007), social studies and science (Chapin, 2006), and mathematics (Chatterji, 2005). Most of these disparities can be explained by poverty and the mother's education (Padilla, Boardman, & Hummer, 2002), however, the impact of poverty can be mediated by parenting style and cognitive stimulation (Guo & Harris, 2000). We will discuss this in more depth later in this chapter.

After a child enters kindergarten, the type of school he or she attends can make a difference in their cognitive development. In many areas of the country, racial/ethnic or socioeconomic residential segregation is persistent, and concentrating AAs or Hispanics into neighborhoods also concentrates poverty (Massey & Fischer, 2000). This in turn impacts the school children attend and the type of education they receive. Most schools are neighborhood schools, especially in the elementary years (Ong & Rickles, 2004), and schools that are predominately AA and Hispanic also typically serve students who are poor. The National Center for Education Statistics (NCES) considers schools with greater than 75% participation in the free or reduced price lunch program to be high poverty schools, and schools with less than 25% participation are considered to be low poverty schools. Using that criteria, we analyzed data from the NCES Common Core Data File for the school year 2010−11, and we found that high poverty schools are 80.9% AA or Hispanic, while low poverty schools are 75% White. Forty-three percent (43.2%) of AA and 34.9% of Hispanic children attend a high poverty school. While there are instances of high achieving, high poverty schools, it still remains that low poverty schools typically have higher achievement levels (Harris, 2007). Low poverty schools are in areas with a higher tax base, they have more resources, there are more opportunities for cognitive development than in high poverty schools, and they have higher test scores. Higher poverty schools are often characterized by high faculty turnover, lower achievement, and offer fewer higher-level courses, such as AP classes, in high school.

Poor and minority students also have higher dropout rates, and fewer of these students pursue or finish postsecondary education. Accurate dropout rates are difficult to obtain, because often schools do not know if a student has dropped out or transferred, or has opted for homeschooling. What we do know is that some students disappear from the enrollment records. Therefore, we looked at the status dropout rate, which is defined by the NCES as people ages 16−24 who are not enrolled in school, and have not completed a high school diploma or GED. We analyzed data from the US Census Bureau's *American Community Survey* (ACS), *2012 1-year period estimates*, available from integrated public use microdata series (IPUMS) (Ruggles et al., 2010). Hispanics (12.8%) have the highest status dropout rate, followed by AAs (9.0%), Other race/ethnicities (7.1%), Whites (4.7%), and Asians (2.8%). These results are not surprising, as the dropout rate for Hispanics is higher than other groups, and this estimate includes immigrants. When we look at only US-born Hispanics, the rate drops to 8.9%, which is very similar to AAs. The difference between the foreign-born and US-born Hispanics is likely due to either language mastery, socioeconomics, or migration patterns. Often if a student is not proficient in English by high school, he or she will drop out, and some are compelled to leave school early to help support the family. What is notable, however, is how the Hispanic dropout rate has declined in the last decade. In the early 2000s, the percentage of Hispanic children ages 6−16 that had parents with less than a high school diploma was 47%: By 2012 it had dropped to 33.5%. This is a large decrease in the dropout rate, and represents a change for the better in the Hispanic population.

Next, we turn to disparities in undergraduate education. A college degree is becoming increasingly more important as a ticket to the middle class and a well-paying job. In the adult population ages 25−68, Asians have the highest college completion rate at 52.3%, followed by Whites at 34.7%, Others at 26.4%, AAs at 19.5%, and Hispanics at 14.4%. Also worth noting are the differences in the type of degree pursued. Asians (40.4%) are the most likely to complete degrees in the more lucrative STEM fields (Science, Technology, Engineering, and Mathematics), and they are ahead of all other racial/ethnic groups in these fields, including Other race/ethnicities (23.15%), Hispanics (19.9%), and Whites (19.5%). AAs have a lower completion rate in the STEM fields at 16.3%. We will examine these differences again when we discuss variances in occupation and family income.

Table 5.1 shows the percentages of each racial/ethnic group that obtained various levels of education for parents of children in the WISC-V age range, based on data from the ACS. These differences are large. For

TABLE 5.1 Educational Attainment by Racial/Ethnic Group

	High School Drop Out Rate (%)	College Entrance Rate (%)
White	4	78
AA	12	62
Hispanic	31	43
Asian	8	78
Other	7	72

Note: Individuals obtaining a GED are considered to have completed high school.
Source: Data and table Copyright Pearson 2014. All rights reserved.

example, 43% of Hispanics enter college, while 62% of AAs, and 78% of Asians and Whites do so. Among parents of children ages 6−16, 31% of Hispanics drop out of high school while 12% of AAs, 8% of Asians, and 4% of Whites do so.[1]

These differences in educational attainment are important for children's IQ, because there is an increase in FSIQ in every educational category for the WISC-V. Table 5.2 shows the mean FSIQ for children in the WISC-V standardization sample by level of parent education. In this table, we have also added a sixth category for graduate school education, although it was not a stratification variable when the data were collected. While the children's mean WISC-V FSIQ scores below are based on the average parent education, the FSIQ for the graduate level is based on one parent having a graduate degree. The mean FSIQ is similar for both levels of less than high school, but with each increase, there is a jump in the mean FSIQ score. These differences are meaningful, as there is a 22.9-point difference in FSIQ between the lowest and highest education levels, and the difference between the child of a college graduate versus the child of someone with a high school diploma or GED is 14.2 points.

We started with education because it has a profound impact on disparities, starting with income and employability. The US Department of Labor estimates that a college education pays dividends in much higher earnings and lower unemployment (US Department of Labor, 2014). Parent income and occupation often determine whether or not the family has health benefits,

---

1. The ACS includes questions on which language a person speaks, and how well a person speaks English if he or she also speaks another language. Since it is not good clinical practice to administer the WISC-V to children who do not speak English well, when composing the census targets Pearson included those children who speak English well or very well in addition to another language, or speak English only. Therefore, the high school dropout rate for Hispanics reported in this table (31%) is slightly lower than the one quoted above (33.5%).

TABLE 5.2 Mean FSIQ of Children by Parent Education Level

Parent Education Level	Children's Mean FSIQ
8 years or less	87.8
	(10.18)
	n = 67
9–12 years, no diploma	88.6
	(16.24)
	n = 168
High school diploma, or GED	93.8
	(13.43)
	n = 460
Some college or technical school, associate's degree	99.7
	(12.45)
	n = 777
Undergraduate degree or more	108.04
	(13.98)
	n = 726
Graduate degree (at least one parent with a graduate degree)	110.7
	(13.03)
	n = 350

and what kind, thus impacting children's access to treatment for physical and mental health issues.

Racial/Ethnic Group Disparities in Income, Occupation, and Poverty Status

Parents' occupations and family income directly impact the SES of families, which relates to IQ tests scores of children through various social and psychological mechanisms, which are discussed throughout this chapter. Group differences in occupation and income are difficult topics to discuss as there is evidence that despite a transformation in personal attitudes since the Civil Rights era, AA and Hispanic individuals experience more discrimination in hiring, which has an impact on income and opportunities for promotion. In addition, higher-paying jobs typically require more education, and as noted in the previous section, there are strong group differences in educational attainment for parents of young children. For this section, we analyzed data from the 2012 ACS.

First, there are disparities in occupational status, and this discussion flows from the differences we discussed in education. Managerial and STEM-related occupations are higher paying, and Whites and Asians predominate in these fields. For people ages 25−68, the overall population is 65.2% White, 5.5% Asian, 12.0% AA, and 15.1% Hispanic, but the highest represented managerial ranks are 70.2% White and 6.8% Asian. Engineers are also White (68.6%) and Asian (14.6%), as are scientists and social scientists at 64.2% White and 17.0% Asian. Health care workers, who are paid less, are 28.5% AA and 19.6% Hispanic. Food service jobs are also held by Hispanics at 31.0%. One exception for AAs is jobs in legal services, which are better paying. In that profession, AAs are slightly overrepresented at 17.6%. These disparities in occupation stem from educational attainment as the more lucrative managerial and STEM professions require a college education, which may be less accessible to lower income families. In addition, AAs and Hispanics have experienced discrimination in some industries and areas of the country, and may have difficulty gaining promotions into management. With these caveats, we now turn to differences in family income.

From the ACS, we selected households that have children ages 6−16, to better understand the differences for children in the WISC-V age ranges. After accounting for households that had a negative income, Asians have the highest median family income at $80,151, with Whites at $72,702. Families of Other race/ethnicities have an income of $45,998, and AAs have the lowest median family income levels at $34,993. The median for all Hispanics is $38,196, but this differs by country of origin. Based on the origin of the head of the household, Dominicans have the lowest median family income at $29,984, and Mexican or Mexican Americans (MAs) have a median family income of $36,942, which is similar to those whose origin is from Central America, at $36,936, and Puerto Rico at $36,435. South Americans at $45,726 and Cubans at $47,944 have considerably higher incomes. These differences represent different migration patterns over the years. Mexicans, Dominicans, Puerto Ricans, and Central Americans came to the continental United States looking for work and opportunity, and in recent years, people from Mexico and Central America have migrated to escape violence associated with the drug cartels. Political and social issues have historically motivated Cubans and South Americans to come to the United States, and they are better educated with higher college completion rates.

Next, we will demonstrate how disparities in income work across the spectrum, from poverty to prosperity. Poverty is important because the stress of living in a poor household can have a negative impact on cognition, specifically working memory and language. Poor children are more food insecure, move more often, and experience more stress than nonpoor children, which can impact their cognitive development (Guo & Harris, 2000). Stress-related hormones such as cortisol have been found to impact learning and memory (van Ast et al., 2013). The differences in the percentage of children living in poverty by race/ethnicity are striking. While 37% of AA children, 23% of Other race/ethnicities, and 33% of Hispanic children live at or below the poverty line, only 13% of White and 15% of Asian children are in similar circumstances. Poverty status is based on a combination of income and number of people in the household.

Extreme poverty, where the income is at 50% or more below the poverty line, is an especially harsh environment, and here the numbers bring these disparities even more into focus as 13.3% of AA households with children ages 6–16 have incomes that are at or below 50% of poverty. Next, 11.25% of Other race/ethnicity households are in extreme poverty, followed by Hispanics at 9.7%, Whites at 4.6%, and Asians at 5.0%. Equally striking are the differences in wealthier households, as 33.1% of Asians and 27.2% of White children live in households that are 500% or more above the poverty line. In contrast, 16.4% of Other race/ethnicities, 10.7% AAs, and 8.3% of Hispanics live in these prosperous households.

We point out these differences in occupation, income, and poverty because they have an impact on children's home lives, and therefore the opportunities families and children have for cognitive development. They also provide a graphic picture of how disparities are pervasive throughout our economic system, and thus it is not surprising when these disparities show up in special education services.

Racial/Ethnic Group Disparities in Physical Health Status

We now turn to group disparities in the physical health status of both children and adults with the presumption that indirect relationships exist between the physical health of families and the neurocognitive status of children in those families that operate through multiple mechanisms, including prenatal care, visits to the pediatrician, and so on. Physical health may also impact employment and occupational stability, thus limiting parents' ability to provide access to resources if their children are having health- or school-related difficulties. Also, we wish to simply point out that group disparities are not restricted to special education programs.

AAs have more health problems than other racial/ethnic groups, and these disparities have a long legacy in the United States. Many AAs have a distrust of the health system due to mistreatment, exploitation, and discrimination (LaVeist, 2005). The disparities for AAs and physical health begin at birth. Low birth weight and infant mortality often serve as benchmarks for comparing living conditions across groups (LaVeist, 2005). AAs have more babies who are born with low birth weight and they also have higher infant mortality, even after accounting for the mother's education. Put plainly, young AA infants die at twice the rate of Whites, Asians, or Hispanics. Infants are fragile, and while they can die from a variety of causes in the early years of life, their environment heavily influences their overall health and survival. Higher neonatal and infant mortality rates may indicate poor maternal health or lack of access to health care, environmental stress, poverty, or other suboptimal living conditions (Centers for Disease Control & Prevention, 2013).

These disparities continue into adulthood. The following information is from the Centers for Disease Control and Prevention Health Disparities and Inequalities Report—United States, 2013. In comparison to Whites, AAs have higher rates of heart disease (47.1%), hypertension, 49.1% (although they are more likely to be on medication than Whites), colorectal cancer (23.1%), and diabetes (66.2%). For HIV/AIDS, the rate is an astounding 823.1% higher. AAs also have the highest rates of obesity, a recent public health concern, at 37% for men and 53% for women. At the end of life, AAs have the shortest lifespan. Current life tables available from the CDC indicate that an AA child born today can expect to live 3.5 years less than Whites if she is female, and 5.0 years less if he is male.

In contrast, Hispanics often have better health than Whites or AAs despite their SES. This is known in the health and mortality literature as the *Hispanic Paradox*. Explanations for this paradox include the presumption that generally only healthy people are capable of migrating, thus giving US Hispanics a health advantage. Other explanations include strong family and social ties, psychological and physical resilience, and individual behavior (Ruiz, Steffen, & Smith, 2013), and Hispanics live longer. Current life tables show that a Hispanic baby born today is likely to live 2.3 years longer than a White child, and this is the same for both males and females. Despite their overall better health, they have a higher risk of adult-onset diabetes (69.2%). Their obesity rates are just behind AAs at 44% for women and 35% for men. (Note these figures are for MAs only, data for Hispanics was not available.) Of particular importance is that Hispanics have a high uninsured rate at 41%. It is unknown at this time how their rates of health insurance will change after the implementation of the Affordable Care Act of 2010.

In the CDC report, Whites often served as a referent group, and it is worth noting where some of their health issues reside, as they are more on the behavioral side of health care. Whites are more likely than other groups to report binge drinking than any other group at a 21.1% prevalence rate, they binge more frequently at 4.1 times a month, with an intensity (number of drinks on a binge) at 6.8. This is higher than all other groups, except for American Indians/Alaska Natives. Although American Indians/Alaska Natives report a lower prevalence rate, with less frequency, they report drinking greater quantities during a binge, at 8.4 drinks. White (10.2%) and American Indian/Alaska Native (13.6%) teenagers are also more likely to report they smoke cigarettes, but these percentages even out more in the adult population across groups. Asians have fewer health problems than other groups with the exception of tuberculosis, which is 2388% higher than Whites.

Health disparities show up in children's home environments. A parent who is not well, either physically or mentally, often will have more difficulty caring and providing for children. We wanted to know if minority children have a higher risk of living with someone with a disability, and the ACS asks people if they have any physical or cognitive disabilities, or difficulty caring for themselves. For this analysis, we selected households that have children ages 6–16 years, and we ran a series of logistic regression analyses to calculate racial/ethnic disparities. The sample was restricted to working aged adults 18–68 years, and the outcomes were hearing, physical limitations, mobility, cognitive impairments including memory, difficulty caring for oneself, and sight. After controlling for education and gender, across all types of disabilities except for hearing, AAs and American Indians/Alaska Natives have a higher risk for disabilities than Whites. AAs have a 29% higher risk of physical disabilities, a 24% higher risk of mobility problems, a 13% greater risk of cognitive disabilities, a 38% higher risk of having limitations in caring for themselves, and a 64% higher risk of having sight problems. American Indians/Alaska Natives have a 45% higher risk of physical disabilities, 34% higher risk for mobility, 40% cognitive, 54% higher risk of self-care limitations, 88% higher for hearing, and 104% higher for sight problems. In contrast, and in alignment with the Hispanic paradox, Hispanics have 15%–60% lower risk than Whites across all of these categories.

We discuss physical health status to not only demonstrate that disparities exist in other realms beside special education, but also to point out that parents with health difficulties may often have trouble providing care, attention, and financial support for their children as they grow and develop. Physical health also has an impact on employment opportunities and thus family income and available resources to address children's needs.

Racial/Ethnic Group Disparities in Mental Health Status

Disparities in mental health status and services for children are included to further demonstrate that disparities are not restricted to special education services, and to point out that parents with significant mental health concerns may have fewer personal resources available to appropriately attend to the cognitive and academic development of their children.

AAs and Hispanics are less likely to initiate mental health services, and when they do, they receive fewer days of treatment (Cook et al., 2014). The rates of psychological disorders amongst AA, Whites, and Hispanics appear to be similar after controlling for SES. We analyzed data from the 2011−12 National Survey of Children's Health (NSCH). This survey was conducted by the CDC, and they interviewed parents about their child's well-being and physical and mental health status. They asked parents if the child currently had autism, attention-deficit hyperactivity disorder (ADHD), anxiety, depression, developmental delay, or behavioral problems. These data were self-reported by parents, and thus there are some limitations and the rates should not be considered true prevalence rates. Whites (2.1%) and Asians (1.6%) had the highest rates for autism, and Whites also had the highest rates of ADHD (9.4%). While AAs had higher reports of developmental delay (3.7%) and behavior problems (4.4%), their risk was not significantly different from Whites after controlling for SES. Compared to children living at 400% above the poverty line, children living in poverty are at greater risk for ADHD (91%), anxiety (81%), depression (342%), developmental delay (114%), and behavioral problems (453%), indicating that living in poverty has a significant impact on these disorders. These results are consistent with previous research on SES and mental health (Hudson, 2012).

The proportion of individuals with mental illness is much higher among those who are homeless, incarcerated, or in foster care, and AAs are disproportionately represented in these settings. Accurate data on homelessness is difficult to come by given the transient nature of the population. However, the proportion of homeless population who are AAs is estimated at 37%, and 9.7% are Hispanic (SAMHSA, 2011). Families in homeless shelters are 39% AA, and 22% Hispanic (Child Trends, 2013). These numbers do not include the unsheltered homeless families, which are difficult to count. Homeless children are more likely to have been abused or neglected.

Abuse and neglect can also lead to a child being placed in foster care, and this may exacerbate their disadvantage. Older children especially may end up in a series of foster homes before they age out of the system (The Annie E. Casey Foundation, 2008). According to the US Department of Health and Human Services (2013), children in foster care are also predominately AA, although the rates have fallen from 17.4 in 2002 to 9.6 in 2012. AA children are 13.9% of the total child population, yet they represent 25.5% of all children in foster care. American Indians/Alaska Natives are also overrepresented, as they are less than 1% of the population, yet represent 2% of all children in foster care.

Another mental health risk is suicide. According to the CDC, suicide is much more common amongst Whites, especially males, followed by American Indians/Alaska Natives. All other groups have suicide rates that are substantially lower than Whites. For people ages 10−24, the rate of suicide is much higher for American Indians/Alaska Natives for both males and females, with the male rate being 31.27 for every 100,000 people (Centers for Disease Control and Prevention, 2012).

The Surgeon General distributed a report detailing the disparities in mental health status, and the details in this next section are from that report, except where noted (US Department of Health and Human Services, 2001). The availability of mental health services depends on where one lives and the presence or absence of health insurance. A large percentage of AAs live in areas with diminished access to both physical and mental health care services, and nearly 25% of AAs have no health insurance as compared to 10% of Whites. Medicaid, which subsidizes the poor and uninsured, covers nearly 21% of AAs.

With respect to Hispanics, most studies support the lack of differences in rates of mental illness as compared to Whites; however, sample size issues have restricted the generalizability of this finding beyond the MA population. In general, Hispanics underutilize the mental health care system, and they are the most uninsured of all of the racial/ethnic groups, perhaps because many of them are immigrants (García, 2012). The lifetime prevalence for mental disorders is 25% for Mexican immigrants, but 48% for the US-born MAs. Mexican immigrants with less than 13 years of US residence have better mental health than their US-born counterparts and the overall US sample. In general, Hispanics underutilize and in many cases, receive insufficient mental health care services relative to Whites. Approximately 11% of MAs access mental health services as compared to 22% of Whites. The trend appears to be that new Mexican immigrants have relatively good mental health, which is consistent with the healthy migrant theory. However, their problems become more prevalent the longer they stay in the United States. Their immigrant status makes access more difficult, particularly in areas that are not used to receiving new immigrants and may have a shortage of clinicians who speak Spanish or understand the culture. Areas that historically have more Mexican immigrants may be more friendly and provide better care (García, 2012). One strength of Mexican immigrants may be their social cohesion and family ties. Research conducted in Arizona found that Hispanics who lived in a neighborhood where they have friends that they trust has a positive impact on both their mental and physical health. People in poorer, more diverse areas had poorer mental health; however, if the poor area was predominately Hispanic, then the residents had better mental and physical health (Rios, Aiken, & Zautra, 2012), indicating the strength of their social ties.

Another area of strength for Hispanics involves attitudes toward mental health disorders. There appears to be a cultural norm to not hold the person blameworthy, and this may predispose people to take care of one another. At least among Mexicans, there appears to be a cultural norm to care for one's ill within the family, regardless of physical or mental health status, which may be reflected in the underutilization of some mental health services.

Implications of Demographic Differences in Various Areas of Life

Some reviewers will undoubtedly critique our overview of racial/ethnic group disparities in various areas of life as too limited to do the topic justice while other readers may wonder why we spent so much time on the topic and how these issues are relevant to intellectual assessment and specifically assessment using the WISC-V. In many cases the magnitude of the gaps described above are shocking, and have serious political, legal, and economic implications for our country. Our intention in including this discussion in the current chapter is more modest. First, we wish to make the basic point that disparities between racial/ethnic groups have been observed in many important areas of life, and are not limited to IQ test scores, nor special education proportions. We do not imply cause and effect in either direction, but simply note that racial/ethnic group discrepancies are not unique to IQ test scores, nor rates of special education.

Second, and much more importantly for our purposes in this chapter, the differences described above suggest, for the most part, that people of different racial ethnic backgrounds have differing levels of opportunity for cognitive growth and development. The effects of these differences on the development of cognitive abilities are critical during childhood but also continue well into middle adulthood depending on level of education, income, mental and physical health, and the resources available in the communities in which they live.

Americans are fond of saying that all children are born with equal opportunity, and that any child can grow up to be President of the United States. The election of Barack Obama as the first AA US President demonstrates that this is true—although not for immigrant children. Still, while opportunity under the law may be equal, implementation of the law can sometimes vary by jurisdiction for racial/ethnic groups as suggested by differential rates of incarceration. However, this is not the kind of opportunity we are talking about in this chapter. We are talking about opportunity in terms of the development of one's cognitive abilities; the opportunity for a child's mind to grow and expand to its fullest potential through adolescence and into early adulthood.

Even though genetics is a very large factor in determining intelligence (see Neisser, 1998), our central tenant is that IQ is not an immutable trait. Rather, it is a basic ability that can be influenced—to some reasonable extent—positively or negatively during the long course of cognitive development beginning in early childhood (if not prenatally) and continuing through adolescence and into early or middle adulthood. Cognitive development can be influenced by the environment in multiple, interactive and reciprocal ways. When it comes to intellectual development of children, schools and cultures count as integral parts of the environmental mix (Nisbett, 2009). We know that the level of education obtained by the parents is highly correlated with the parent's occupational status and household income. This in turn is related to the quality of schools and libraries available in the neighborhoods that are affordable to the parents, the models for success and advancement present in those neighborhoods, the culturally defined expectations for educational attainment, the expectations for the child's occupational future that surround him or her in the family and community, and the extent to which an adolescent can pursue academic or other cognitively enriching activities free from concerns about economic survival or fears of personal safety that may impede educational progress and career development.

In many ways, education is only a proxy for a host of variables related to the quantity and quality of cognitively enriching activities available to a person, and that parents or care providers can provide for children. Therefore, education is only a gross indicator replete with numerous exceptions. Certainly, there are many individuals with little formal education who are quite successful in business and society, and their success affords critical opportunities to their offspring that belie expectations based on their own education. Similarly, many readers of this chapter will likely know that even advanced academic credentials do not always equate with success in life. What is amazing is that with all of its imperfections, one variable—education—relates so much to cognitive ability.

COGNITIVE DEVELOPMENT, HOME ENVIRONMENT, AND CULTURE

Theoretical Considerations

The family system is the most influential and proximal influence in children's early learning (Bronfenbrenner, 1992). Home environment research findings from developmental psychology have a long history, with roots as far back as Piaget's work in the 1920s. Credited as one of the founders of the Chicago school of family environment research, Bloom (1964) concluded that the preschool years were the most important period for children's intellectual stimulation and that family subenvironments should be identified and researched for unique effects on different aspects of cognitive development. These views were elaborated on by several of his students including Wolf (1964) who reported a multiple correlation of 0.69 between children's measured intelligence and home environment ratings in three subenvironments characterized by the parents "press" for achievement motivation, language development, and general learning. During the 1970s, a set of international studies based on the Chicago school's approach suggested that ethnicity is a significant variable that should be accounted for in examining the relation between home environment variables and children's intelligence and achievement, and that causal relationships established for one group may not hold for other times, social classes, ethnic groups, or countries (Marjoribanks, 1979; Walberg & Marjoribanks, 1976). In the 1980s, Caldwell and coinvestigators developed the Home Observation for Measurement of the Environment (HOME; Caldwell & Bradley, 1984), which is still the most widely used home environment measure in current research. As summarized by Bradley & Caldwell (1978), HOME scores obtained during the first year of life correlated at low but significant magnitudes with the Mental Development Index of the Bayley Scales of Infant Development at both 6 and 12 months and at moderate to strong levels with Stanford Binet IQ scores at 36 and 54 months, and moderate to high correlations were found between 24 months HOME scores and 36 month Stanford Binet IQ scores.

Children with psychological or psychoeducational disorders ranging from ADHD, Autism Spectrum Disorders, Intellectual Disability, and Specific Learning Disorder provide additional stressors for parents. Although it is common to say that these children need more structure than others, researchers are now systematically studying what this means in terms of home environment. The ability of a family to sustain a daily routine has been shown to be an important factor in the outcome of developmentally delayed children (Weisner, Matheson, Coots, & Bernheimer, 2005). Sustaining meaningful daily routines involves juggling ongoing demands while meeting long-term goals, rather than coping with crises and stress. Difficulty sustaining daily routines was more likely to be encountered in single-parent families, expanded families, poor families, and multiply troubled families. When family troubles are high and unpredictable, routines are more difficult to sustain. While increasing family resources was associated with higher sustainability, families with low income are often able to create and sustain reasonable daily routines even while struggling with limited resources. These low-income families with sustainable daily routines were found to be troubled by no more than one additional issue beyond caring for a delayed child. However, these researchers also point out that the ability of a family to sustain a daily routine is unrelated to the level of stimulation provided the child, or family warmth and connectedness. Quality of interaction is as important as the structure.

If home environment is such a powerful predictor of cognitive development, than one must ask how two children from the same family sometimes can be so different from each another in terms of expressed cognitive ability. Writing from another line of research involving behavior genetics, Plomin & Petrill (1997) offered the concept of shared versus nonshared environment to help explain differences between family members. They argued that during childhood cognitive development is largely influenced by aspects of the home environment that are shared by siblings, whereas by the end of adolescence IQ is largely influenced by nonshared aspects of the environment. However, methodological and other issues have been raised regarding this research (Stoolmiller, 1999), and further studies are needed to fully answer this question.

Certainly adolescents are more influenced by peers than children. Thus, even children of the same parents may experience different environments as they enter adolescence a few years apart and come under the influence of different circles of friends. Prior to this period, however, children of the same family may experience different environments as they enter the preschool or preadolescent stages a few years after their older siblings for reasons as varied and normal as changes in job stress, employment status, or marital satisfaction during the intervening years.

Even absent environmentally induced changes in the family, parents often interact differently with each child simply because each is different in personality. Speaking purely as parents we are quite sure that each of our respective children experienced different aspects of ourselves as parents, and thus did not fully share the same developmental environment. We prefer to believe that our changing parental behavior was in response to their unique temperaments (rather than some pathological variability in our own personalities). While much of the discussion in this literature is one directional concerning how parental behavior influences children's development, practitioners evaluating children in troubled families should keep in mind that children's approaches to the world around them vary greatly and influence parental responses. Simply put, some children are easier to rear than others—which is something that most everyone figures out by the time they become grandparents!

Expert clinicians spend time considering the ways in which each child's unique characteristics interact with the family systems in the home environment, and how these dynamics facilitate or impede the child's unique developmental needs. Many examples exist of children with psychoeducational disorders and/or troubled home environments who turn out to be well adapted. We relate these positive outcomes, in part, to the characteristic of resiliency. Resiliency involves the extent to which a child is sensitive to perceived environmental threats and the speed with which they recover when upset. These characteristics are important to the child's sense of optimism, self-efficacy, and adaptability. While the ability to regulate one's own emotions, attention, and behavior may be related to basic temperament, there are also effective strategies for teaching resilience to children at home and in school (Goldstein & Brooks, 2005). Further, resilience is improved with increases in the child's sense of relatedness to others—which is rooted in basic trust, access to support, social comfort, and tolerance of differences—and these drivers are firmly in the family's domain. A measure of resiliency in children and adolescents is available for clinical use (Prince-Embury, 2006; Prince-Embury & Saklofske, 2014).

We have already discussed income inequities by racial ethnic group. Clearly, poverty can have significant consequences on family functioning, thus affecting the home environment. Shah, Mullainathan, and Shafir (2012) suggest that poor individuals often engage in behaviors, such as excessive borrowing, that reinforce the conditions of poverty. Past explanations for these behaviors have focused on personality traits of the poor, or emphasized environmental factors such as housing or financial access. Providing a completely different perspective, Shah and colleagues show in a series of experiments that scarcity necessarily changes how poor people allocate their attention, and suggest that this leads to the poor engaging more deeply in proximal problems while neglecting distal goals. Mani, Mullainathan, Shafir, and Zhao (2013) take this argument one large step further and show that poverty directly impedes cognitive functioning in a set of experiments. These authors suggest that poverty-related concerns consume mental resources, leaving less cognitive capacity for other tasks.

As an added point from a nonresearch point of view, the current authors in their clinical work have observed parents who themselves have limited education and often live in economically impoverished settings not realize the impact of "what they do as parents" on their children in the short and longer term. One parent, when asked if she spoke to her young infant or read to her preschool children, simply said "I didn't know I should do that." Such clinical observations are consistent with research showing that vocabulary development of young children varies as a function of maternal speech frequency (Hoff, 2003), and that language development can be enhanced through active exposure to quality auditory stimuli in infancy (Benasich, Choudhury, Realpe-Bonilla, & Roesler, 2014). Parents living in poverty spend less time talking and reading to young children, which negatively impacts the prelinguistic process of acoustic mapping in infancy, and exposes them to fewer new words during later, critical periods of language development.

These findings are consistent with Ruby Payne's popular book (Payne, 2013) in which she proposes a culture of poverty, and describes how this leads people to think differently, sometimes making choices based on immediate needs, which may not be in their best long-term interest. Because many teachers are not from a culture of poverty, they sometimes have difficulty understanding the behaviors of their students' parents, and Payne's book provides a framework for that understanding that is not based on supposed personality flaws of the poor. As such the book has become very popular in workshops for teachers. Valencia (2010) seems to argue that the notion of a culture of poverty, however, leads to deficit thinking, which is just another form of blaming the victim when the real culprit is the flawed educational system.

In our chapter, we seek to blame no one. Our purpose is only to promote an understanding that children's cognitive abilities do not develop by themselves; rather cognitive abilities develop partly in response to physical and social milieus that support development to varying degrees. The societal and familial issues are far too encompassing for any one experimenter to study in entirety. Further, the interactions between this myriad of influences are both complex and reciprocal, and so assigning causality is arbitrary and mostly a function of which segment of the problem one is examining at what point in time. In any reciprocally interacting system, the origin of causality is unknowable by definition. Put more simply, we will not debate here which came first, "the chicken or the egg."

Home Environment and African American Children

Researchers have examined the role of home environment in specific populations. In this way it is possible to explore the hypothesis that the same proximal processes are differentially employed by individuals in different cultures. Several studies correlated home environment and SES ratings with children's measured intelligence and/or academic achievement (Brooks-Gunn, Klebanov, & Duncan, 1996; Bradley & Caldwell, 1981; Bradley & Caldwell, 1982; Bradley, Caldwell, & Elardo, 1977; Bradley et al., 1989; Johnson et al., 1993; Ramey, Farran, & Campbell, 1979; Trotman, 1977).

Although SES was defined differently across studies, this set of papers generally showed that for AA children the relationship between SES and IQ test scores was not as strong as the relation between home environment and IQ tests scores, nor as strong as the relationship between SES and IQ test scores among White children. This may be because the range of SES within the AA groups was likely both skewed and truncated, regardless of how it was measured (e.g., parent education, income, occupation). This has led some writers to speculate that historical limitations in educational and employment opportunities lead to more variability in parental behavior within the lower SES AA group than within the lower SES White group. In the studies cited above, home environment ratings typically added significant information to the prediction of IQ scores from SES for AA children, and this increment in variance was often larger than that for White children.

What this means is that SES, however it is measured, may not be as powerful of a predictor of IQ test scores for AA children as it is for White children. It also means that home environment factors may play a more powerful role in the prediction of IQ test scores for AA than White children.

Home Environment and Mexican American Children

Several studies examined the relation of home environment and cognitive ability in MA children (Bradley et al., 1989; Henderson, 1972; Henderson, Bergan, & Hurt, 1972; Henderson & Merritt, 1968; Johnson, Breckenridge, & McGowan, 1984; Valencia, Henderson, & Rankin, 1985).

In general, the results of these studies also support the view that parent's in-home behavior is important to cognitive development and academic performance. It has been shown that MA children with purportedly low educational potential are exposed to a more restricted range of developmental experiences than their high potential MA counterparts (Henderson, & Merritt, 1968). MA parents who demonstrate higher degrees of valuing language (e.g., reading to the child), valuing school-related behavior (e.g., reinforcing good work), and providing a supportive environment for school learning (e.g., helping the child recognize words or letters during the preschool stage) have children who tend to score higher on tests of basic concepts and early achievement (Henderson et al., 1972), and neither SES nor family size made a significant unique contribution to predicting cognitive ability scores beyond that accounted for by home environment (Valencia et al., 1985).

We must offer a modest word of caution about generalizing these findings. First, these studies do not address the likely impact of parental language on children's test scores. Perhaps English-speaking parents develop more acculturated children who perform better in American schools and on US-based IQ tests. Further, only MA families were studied and so generalization to Puerto Rican, Cuban, or other Spanish-speaking populations may or may not be valid. As discussed earlier, SES varies systematically with country of origin because of the historical patterns influencing immigration from the various Spanish-speaking nations. The interaction between parent education, home environment and cognitive development has not been fully studied by language status of the parents or country of origin. Yet, there is growing evidence that home environment is an important predictor of cognitive development across cultures.

Home Environment and Academic Achievement

The association of home environment with academic achievement has also been studied. Higher levels of parent involvement in their children's educational experiences at home have been associated with children's higher achievement scores in reading and writing, as well as higher report card grades (Epstein, 1991; Griffith, 1996; Keith et al., 1998; Sui-Chu & Williams, 1996). Research has also shown that parental beliefs and expectations about their children's learning are strongly related to children's beliefs about their own competencies, as well as their achievement (Galper, Wigfield, & Seefeldt, 1997). Improving the home learning environment has been shown to increase children's motivation and self-efficacy (Dickinson & DeTemple, 1998; Mantzicopoulos, 1997; Parker, Boak, Griffin, Ripple, & Peay, 1999).

Fantuzzo, McWayne, Perry, and Childs (2004) extended the above finding in a longitudinal study of very low SES AA children in an urban Head Start program, showing that specific in-home behaviors significantly predicted children's receptive vocabulary skills at the end of the school year, as well as motivation, attention/persistence, and lower levels of classroom behavior problems. Homes with high levels of parent involvement in their children's education were characterized by specific behaviors reflecting active promotion of a learning environment at home. For example, creating space for learning activities at home, providing learning opportunities for the child in the community, supervision and monitoring of class assignments and projects, daily conversations about school, and reading to young children at home.

Home environment influences the learning behaviors demonstrated by children in the classroom, and learning behaviors such as competency motivation, attention, and persistence are important predictors of academic success. The likelihood of specific learning behaviors has been shown to vary with gender, age, ethnicity, urban residence, parent educational level, and special education classification status (Schaefer, 2004). Researchers have provided data suggesting that differential rates of inattention across racial/ethnic groups may explain as much as 50% of the gap in achievement test scores between AA and White students (Rabiner, Murray, Schmid, & Malone, 2004). Screening attentional behaviors related to learning, such response inhibition, in the early grades may be useful additions to school psychology practice.

THE ROLE OF COGNITIVE STIMULATION IN INTELLECTUAL DEVELOPMENT

At this point in the discussion, we elaborate upon our central thesis: *Enriching, cognitively stimulating environments enhance intellectual development, whereas impoverishing environments inhibit that growth.* Further, the factors that inhibit cognitive enrichment interact with each other such that the presence of one factor makes the occurrence of other inhibitory factors more probable. The net result is even worse than the sum of its parts—akin to geometric rather arithmetic increases. Finally, the negative effects of cognitively impoverished environments can accumulate over the course of a child's developmental period and the impact may further worsen with age. The terms enrichment and impoverishment, as used here, are not considered synonymous with the financial status of rich and poor. These terms refer to cognitively enriching versus impoverishing environments, specifically environments that encourage growth, exploration, learning, creativity, self-esteem, etc.

Potter, Mashburn, and Grissmer (2013) state that current explanations of social class gaps in children's early academic skills tend to focus on noncognitive skills that more advantaged children acquire in the family. According to those explanations, social class matters because the cultural resources more abundant in advantaged families cultivate children's repertories and toolkits, which allow them to more easily navigate social institutions, such as schools. Within these accounts, parenting practices matter for children's academic success, but for seemingly arbitrary reasons. Alternatively, Potter and colleagues show that *findings from current neuroscience research indicate that family context matters for children because it cultivates neural networks that assist in learning and the development of academic skills. That is, children's exposure to particular parenting practices and stimulating home environments contribute to the growth in neurocognitive skills that affect later academic performance.* We agree!

Stephen Ceci and Urie Bronfenbrenner have proposed a bioecological model of intellectual development (Bronfenbrenner, 2004; Bronfenbrenner & Ceci, 1994; Ceci, 1996; Ceci & Bronfenbrenner, 2004; Ceci & Williams, 1999). These authors tackle the nature—nurture issue directly, arguing that there is nothing inconsistent about saying a trait is both highly changeable and highly heritable. This is particularly obvious when comparing studies that focus on group averages or means with studies that focus on variances or differences among individuals. They make the point that even when the heritability of a trait is extremely high, such as it is with height, the environment can still exert a powerful influence.

The bioecological model involves (1) the existence of multiple cognitive abilities that develop at different rates from each other; (2) the interactive and synergistic effect of gene-environment developments; (3) the role of specific types of environmental resources (e.g., proximal behavioral processes and distal family resources) that influence how much of a genotype gets actualized in what type of environment; and (4) the role of motivation in determining how much one's environmental resources aid in the actualization of his or her potential. According to this model, certain epochs in development can be thought of as sensitive periods during which a unique disposition exists for a specific cognitive ability to crystallize in response to its interaction with the environment. Not all cognitive abilities are under maturational control, however, as new synaptic structures may be formed in response to learning that may vary widely among people at different developmental periods. Yet, the sensitive period for many abilities appears to be neurologically determined such that the proper type of environmental stimulation must be present during the critical developmental period, and providing that same stimulation at another time may have less impact. In this model, the relative contributions of environment and genetic endowment to intellectual outcome change with developmental stage. For example, general intelligence at age 7 relates to key aspects of home environment at ages 1 and 2, but not at ages 3 or 4 (Rice, Fulker, Defries, & Plomin, 1988). This suggests that it may be difficult to completely compensate for an impoverished early environment by enhancing the child's later environment, although some positive effects from positive environments still may be expected when out of developmental sequence. Where we need more research is in the elucidation of the key paths and the critical developmental timing.

Interestingly, this model does not separate intelligence from achievement because schooling is assumed to elicit certain cognitive potentials that underlie both (see Ceci, 1991). Further, problem-solving as operationalized in most intelligence tests relies on some combination of past knowledge and novel insights. Studies conducted more than 50 years ago have shown structural and biochemical changes in animals after exposure to enriched environments (Diamond et al., 1966; Mollgaard, Diamond, Bennett, Rosenzweig, & Lindner, 1971; Rosenzweig, 1996). We would add that the act of academic learning enhances formation of new synaptic connections and neural networks, and therefore increases intellectual ability directly, in addition to the indirect effect of accumulated knowledge on problem-solving. Thus, schooling and the quality of education play a powerful role in intellectual development. This is part of the reason that achievement and crystallized knowledge exhibit substantial overlap with reasoning ability in psychometric studies of intelligence tests. Although theoretically distinct, these constructs are reciprocally interactive in real life.

Distal resources are background factors such as SES that effect cognitive development indirectly through the opportunities afforded or denied. Proximal processes are behaviors that directly impact cognitive development. Proximal processes occur within the context of distal resources and interact to influence the extent to which cognitive potentials will be actualized. For maximum benefit, the process must be enduring and lead to progressively more complex forms of behavior. Parental monitoring is an example of an important proximal process. This refers to parents who keep track of their children, know if they are doing their homework, who they associate with after school, where they are when they are out with friends, and so forth. Parents who engage in this form of monitoring tend to have children who obtain higher grades in school (Bronfenbrenner & Ceci, 1994). In the bioecological model, proximal processes are referred to as the engines that drive intellectual development, with higher levels of proximal processes associated with increasing levels of intellectual competence.

The distal environment includes the larger context in which the proximal, parent–child behaviors occur. Perhaps the most important distal resource is SES, because it relates to many other distal resources such as neighborhood safety, school quality, library access, as well as the education, knowledge, and experience that the parent brings with him or her into the proximal processes. For example, helping the developing child with homework, an effective proximal process, requires that someone in the home possesses enough background knowledge about the content of the child's lessons, a distal environmental resource, to help the child when he or she studies.

Distal resources can place limits on the efficiency of proximal processes because the distal environment contains the resources that need to be imported into the proximal processes in order for them to work to full advantage, and because an adequate distal environment provides the stability necessary for the developing child to receive maximum benefit from the proximal processes over time. While an educated parent may be able to help a child with algebra homework, a valuable distal resource, a parent with little education can still provide a valuable proximal process of quiet space, a regular time for homework, and ensure that the assigned work is completed. This monitoring and support can be very beneficial.

At the same time, it is unlikely that there is a universal environment whose presence facilitates performance for all children of all cultures, or even for children of all ages. The likelihood of person by environment interactions suggests that there are different developmental pathways to achievement. School and home environments may be benevolent, malevolent, or null with respect to a variety of dimensions. Practitioners conducting clinical assessments with children might include an evaluation of distal environmental resources within the family and community and consider how these factors facilitate or inhibit their parent's expectations for their children, and the chidlren's expectations for themselves.

THE ROLE OF THE CHILD IN ACADEMIC AND INTELLECTUAL DEVELOPMENT

Without detracting from the critical roles that parents and educators play in the cognitive achievement of children, we believe that one also must examine the role of noncognitive individual differences in children's approach to the learning environment. Assuming that proper cognitive stimulation is present at the right time, there are noncognitive characteristics of the developing child that mediate the actualization of cognitive potential. Clearly, cognition plays a role in every aspect of human functioning and thus can never be fully partialled out of the human factor. Yet, the list of possible noncognitive factors is long and encompasses basic temperament. Some children actively engage with the world around them, drawing inspiration and energy from others, and proactively seeking positive reinforcement from their environment. This stance enhances development of cognitive abilities as well as fosters social-emotional development. Others turn inward for energy and insight, passively accommodate to the world around them, and seek only to avoid negative stimulation from the environment. This stance seeks to preserve current status, and if extreme, may inhibit social-emotional growth and even cognitive development through restricting cognitive stimulation. This *enhancing* versus *preserving* trait is one of the three basic dimensions of Millon's theory of normal personology (Weiss, 2002; Weiss, 1997). Children who seek out versus shut off stimulation will have different experiences even in the same environment, and their developmental opportunities for cognitive and social-emotional growth will likewise differ. Some children are receptive to new information, continuously revising and refining concepts based on an open exchange of information with the world around them. This curious, open, perceiving stance may facilitate cognitive growth. Other children prefer to systematize new information into known categories as soon as possible, and shut off further information as soon as an acceptable classification can be made. While a strong organizational framework can be a positive influence on cognitive development, a closed, judging stance can inhibit intellectual growth if extreme.

Also relevant to cognitive development, learning and the expression of intelligent behavior are general conative (i.e., noncognitive) characteristics such as focus, motivation, and volition. Focus involves directionality of goal. Volition involves intensity toward the goal, or will. Motivation can be proximal or distal. A proximal motivation would be a specific near-term goal. A distal motivation might be a desired state (e.g., to be respected by one's peers) or a core trait (e.g., need for achievement). The list of positive characteristics is long, but includes self-efficacy and self-concept. Self-efficacy is driven by positive self-concept in combination with learned skill sets. Self-efficacy is task specific whereas self-concept is general. Children who have high self-efficacy with respect to intellectual tasks may have experienced initial successes with similar tasks. They also are likely to learn more from new intellectual activities than other children of similar intelligence because they are intellectually engaged in the task and have an internal drive to master it. Intellectual engagement and mastery motivation are critical elements of cognitive growth, along with the ability to self-regulate one's actions toward a goal. The presence of these personal characteristics may enhance cognitive development and the likelihood of success at a variety of life endeavors. However, different factors may be related to success versus failure at intellectual endeavors. After controlling for intellectual level, it may not be simply the absence of positive factors but the presence of specific negative personal factors that are associated with failure to thrive intellectually. Negative predictors may include severe procrastination, extreme perfectionism, excessive rumination, distractibility from goals, rigid categorical thinking, cognitive interference due to social-emotional disorders, or diagnosed psychopathology.

Research into these constructs has been criticized as fragmented in the past. In more recent research programs, many of these constructs are coming together under the umbrella heading of achievement motivation, and various groups of researchers in diverse areas of the world are refining the construct of achievement motivation and validating questionnaires to assess it in different cultures. Some of the current work is based on cultural adaptations of Martin's Motivation and Engagement Scale (Martin, 2008), or Pintrich's original Motivated Strategies for Learning Questionnaire (Pintrich, Smith, Garcia, & McKeachie, 1993). The Martin model clusters these sometimes fragmented skills into four areas: adaptive cognitions (i.e, self-efficacy, mastery motivation, valuing learning); maladaptive cognitions (i.e., anxiety, failure avoidance); adaptive behaviors (i.e, planning, task management, persistence or effort); and maladaptive behaviors (i.e., disengagement, self-handicapping). The Pintrich model organizes these constructs into the two domains of motivation (i.e., intrinsic and extrinsic value) and learning styles (i.e., self-regulation and strategy use).

Martin and Hau (2010) found that differences in achievement motivation between students in Australia and Hong Kong are primarily ones of degree rather than kind. This suggests that the achievement motivation construct, as it is currently being organized, has some cross-cultural validity, and may be more universal than originally thought. In addition, these authors found that enjoyment of school, class participation, positive academic intentions, and academic buoyancy also were importantly related to the motivation to achieve in school. Interestingly, academic buoyancy is much like the concept of resiliency discussed above. Although a significant predictor of achievement test scores, the percent of variance accounted for by motivation is small (Sachs, Law, Chan, & Rao, 2001). We think this is possibly due to complex interactions of student motivation with ability, teaching styles, and home environment.

Lee, Yin, and Zhang (2010) reported that peer learning was importantly related to achievement motivation through the construct of learning strategies in a sample of 12- to 17-year-old students in Hong Kong, and proposed adding this construct to the Pintrich model. Peer learning involves working on assignments collaboratively with other classmates, explaining material to them, and asking questions of them. Such collaboration skills are increasingly considered important in US education because the ability to work in teams is one of the pillars of 21st century skills.

The work of Angela Duckworth and her colleagues on "grit" has received considerable attention with regard to student motivation. Alternately known as self-control or self-regulation, grit is perseverance and passion for a goal that is consistently acted upon over a long period of time, usually months or years. It is related to the concept of resilience, which involves bouncing back from failure. Resilience and grit overlap when resilience is applied to the pursuit of a goal in the face of failure or obstacles. Grit also bears a relationship to the conscientiousness factor of general personality. But grit requires neurologically mature executive functioning systems for voluntary self-regulation of emotions, behaviors, and attentional impulses in the face of immediate distractions.

In a longitudinal study of 8th grade students, Duckworth and Seligman (2005) showed that self-control measured in the fall semester predicted final grades, even after controlling for IQ and achievement test scores. The authors concluded that a major reason for students falling short of their intellectual potential is the failure to exercise self-control. In another longitudinal analysis, Duckworth and colleagues found that measures of self-control predicted report card grades better than IQ, but IQ predicted standardized achievement test scores better than self-control (Duckworth, Quinn, & Tsukayama, 2012). The authors reasoned that self-control helps students study, compete homework, and behave positively in the classroom, whereas IQ helps children learn and solve problems independent of formal instruction.

The seminal work of Carol Dweck shows the importance of having a "growth mindset" with regard to intelligence, rather than a "fixed ability mindset." Individuals with fixed ability mindsets believe that one's intelligence is immutable. Individuals with growth mindsets believe that one's intelligence can increase with effort. She demonstrates that this mindset differs by culture, with Asian cultures generally having growth mindsets and western cultures having fixed ability mindsets. Fixed ability mindsets respond to intellectual and academic failures with helplessness, whereas growth mindsets respond with a mastery orientation, which fuels persistence or grit. Importantly for applied psychologists, her research shows that having a growth mindset can be taught to children, and leads to increasing IQ test scores over time. This corpus of work earned her an award for distinguished scientific contributions from the American Psychological Association (Dweck, 2012). Dweck's work on growth mindsets speaks to the malleability of cognitive growth as a function of environment and is germane to the central tenant of our chapter — cognitively enriching environments enhance intellectual development.

PATTERNS OF WECHSLER INTELLIGENCE SCALE FOR CHILDREN—FIFTH EDITION INTELLIGENCE QUOTIENT SCORES ACROSS CULTURALLY AND LINGUISTICALLY DIVERSE GROUPS

With the above discussion on test bias, fairness, and demographic differences in various areas of life as background, we now present mean WISC-V FSIQ and Index scores by racial/ethnic group in Table 5.3. Although we have taken care to elaborate the home environmental and other issues that must be considered when interpreting these data, we are nonetheless concerned that some will take this information out of context and interpret it either as evidence of genetically determined differences in intelligence among the races, or as proof of test bias. We are convinced that such interpretations are scientifically unsound based on the content of this chapter, but also divisive to society and harmful to children.

As we have shown in Tables 5.1 and 5.2, parent education levels vary systematically by racial/ethnic group and are associated with substantial differences in mean FSIQ scores for children. This fact has critical implications for the collection of standardization samples when developing intelligence, achievement, and other cognitive tests. The first step in defining an appropriate standardization sample is to identify the variables that account for substantial variance in the construct of interest and stratify the sample to represent the population on those variables. For intelligence tests, these variables have traditionally been SES, race/ethnicity, age, gender, and region of the country. These variables may act singly, or in complex interactions such

TABLE 5.3 WISC-V Mean Composite Scores by Racial/Ethnic Group

N	White (1228)		African American (312)			Hispanic (458)		Asian (89)		Other (113)	
	Mean	SD	Mean	SD		Mean	SD	Mean	SD	Mean	SD
VCI	103.7	14.4	92.1	13.7	−11.6	94.2	13.5	105.9	15.0	100.3	14.6
VSI	103.0	14.8	90.3	13.2	−12.7	96.8	13.3	109.8	14.9	99.7	13.2
FRI	102.8	14.8	93.7	14.4	−9.1	95.6	13.4	107.0	13.3	99.8	16.2
WMI	102.7	14.8	96.1	13.9	−6.5	94.9	14.5	103.9	13.1	99.5	15.7
PSI	100.9	15.1	96.4	15.5	−4.5	98.3	14.0	106.5	15.5	101.9	14.3
FSIQ	103.5	14.6	91.9	13.3	−11.6	94.4	12.9	108.6	14.4	100.4	14.7

that race/ethnicity may be masking other underlying variables. Most test authors select parent education level as the single indicator of SES when developing tests for children because of its high correlation with direct indicators of SES such as household income and parental occupation, and because it is more reliably reported than income. Given the skewed range of education in the non-White and Hispanic groups resulting from the differential dropout rates and other factors reported above, however, parent education may work as a better indicator of indirect SES effects on test scores for Whites than for children of other groups. This hypothesis will be addressed by analyses presented later in this chapter.

Current practice in test development is to fully cross all stratification variables with each other, and most major intelligence test authors follow this practice. Thus, for example, the percentage of Hispanic or AA children of college-educated parents in the standardization sample will be much less than White children of college-educated parents. While this sampling methodology accurately reflects each population as it exists in society, it exaggerates the difference between the mean IQ scores of these groups because the SES levels of the various racial/ethnic samples are not equal. If test authors were to use the same national SES percentage for all racial/ethnic groups, the IQ score gap between groups would be smaller—although not eliminated for all groups as we will demonstrate later in this chapter. At the same time, however, this alternate sampling procedure would obscure the magnitude of societal differences in the developmental milieu of children across racial/ethnic groups.

As shown in Table 5.3, the highest mean FSIQ score was obtained by the Asian sample (108.6), followed by the White (103.5), Hispanic (94.4), and AA (91.9) samples. The largest difference is observed between the Asian and AA groups—more than a full standard deviation (16.7 points). The White/AA difference is 11.6 FSIQ points, and the Hispanic/White difference is 9.1 points. Recall that these data are based on samples matched to the US Census for parent education and region of the country within racial/ethnic group. Thus, these racial/ethnic samples reflect all the educational and social inequities that exist between these groups in the population, as elaborated above. Also noteworthy is that the Other group—consisting of Native American Indians, Alaskan Natives, and Pacific Islanders—obtained mean WISC-V scores very near the population mean at 100.4.

Several additional points are notable concerning differences in the profile of mean Index scores across groups. Hispanics—traditionally considered among the most linguistically diverse groups—exhibit Verbal Comprehension Index (VCI) scores 2.6 points lower than their mean Visual Spatial Index (VSI) scores, whereas the AA and White groups exhibit VCI scores slightly higher than their VSI scores. This is important in terms of interpreting Index scores in a culturally sensitive manner. For a more complete discussion of this topic, see Chapter 6, Testing Hispanics With WISC-V and WISC-V Spanish.

It is particularly interesting that the AA sample shows slightly higher VCI than VSI scores because clinical folklore assumes that the verbal subtests are the most biased for AA children due to this groups distance from the dominant culture and use of AA dialect. However, the available data do not support this view. AA children obtained their lowest mean Index score on VSI, and highest on Processing Speed Index (PSI). However, no studies to date have examined the linguistic diversity within the group classified as AA, which includes Black immigrants from multiple countries and cultures. While the AA group is traditionally considered monolingual, this assumption may not be valid in all cases. Researchers tend to limit discussion of AA linguistic diversity to dialects. Within the group classified as AA, however, there is the indigenous AA language (Gullah), as well as French, Spanish, Portuguese, many continental African languages (e.g., Amharic), and Caribbean languages (e.g., Haitian Creole). Because researchers traditionally have assumed that the AA group is monolingual, the influence of language on acculturation and cognitive or achievement test performance has not been adequately investigated.

While the White group presents reasonably consistent mean scores across the four Index scores, the Asian group shows lower scores on Working Memory Index (WMI) and VCI, and highest on VSI. This may be due to the linguistic demands of the VCI subtests, as well as secondary verbal demands in the Digit Span and Picture Span subtests which comprise the WMI. If some linguistically diverse children translate letters and numbers from the English presentation of these stimuli to their first language, then these tasks will tax working memory functions more than for those children who do not translate because their first language is English or because they have become sufficiently proficient in English.

For the Hispanic sample, the highest mean score is observed for the PSI. For the AA group, there is a clear pattern of both WMI and PSI scores higher than VCI and VSI. These findings are interesting for a number of reasons. First, clinical folklore assumes that some minority cultures place less value on speed of performance and may be penalized by tasks with time limits or time bonuses—yet the PSI score is the highest of the four Index scores for both the Hispanic and AA groups. These data suggest that common assumptions about the cultural effects of speed and timed performance among AA and Hispanic children may not be supported by the available data. We previously observed the same trend with WISC-IV data (Weiss et al., 2006).

It is also worth pointing out that the AA−White gap in FSIQ scores is about the same in WISC-V as WISC-IV, but much smaller than it was in

WISC-III. The mean FSIQ score for the AA group was 88.6 in WISC-III, but rounds to 92 in both WISC-IV and WISC-V. At the same time, the White mean remained relatively constant at approximately 103. Thus, the AA/White gap reduced from almost a full standard deviation (14.9 points) in WISC-III to 11.5 points in WISC-IV, and remained virtually constant in WISC-V at 11.6 points. The mean FSIQ score for Hispanics declined by one point from 94.1 to 93.1 between WISC-III and WISC-IV, but increased to 94.4 in WISC-V. The Hispanic/White gap increased slightly, between WISC-III and WISC-IV, by 0.7 points to approximately 10.1 points. In WISC-V the Hispanic/White gap decreased to 9.1 points.

In the early part of the last century, Spearman (1927, cited in Vroon, 1980) hypothesized that group differences in IQ test scores could be explained by innate differences in "g" between the races, and this position continues to rear its ugly head 70 years later (Jensen, 1998; Murray, 2005). Some will likely follow this antiquated line of reasoning and argue that the AA FSIQ was increased in WISC-IV and WISC-V by increasing the contribution of cognitively less complex subtests with lower "g" loadings (e.g., Coding and Symbol Search) in the FSIQ, and they could be correct in so far as psychometric studies of "g" are concerned. However, we would point out that many of the subtests which are purported to be stronger measures of "g" are also those that are more readily influenced by environmental opportunity, such as Vocabulary. Further, the more abstract tasks found in the fluid reasoning index have also been shown to be susceptible to the effects of changes in environment over time (Flynn, 1984; Flynn, 1987; Neisser, 1998). In fact, the largest change for AAs was observed between the WISC-III POI (87.5) and WISC-IV PRI (91.4), a difference of approximately four points. Conceptual changes in this Index between versions of the tests included a reduction in visual organization and an increase in fluid reasoning subtests. As fluid reasoning was separated into its own factor in WISC-V, the AA sample exhibited its lowest mean Index score of 90.3 on VSI (comprised of Block Design and Visual Puzzles subtests); and a higher mean score of 93.7 points on FRI (comprised of the Matrix Reasoning and Figure Weights subtests), which is the Index score most closely associated with "g."

At this point in our discussion it may be worth stating the obvious: *studies showing between-group differences in IQ test scores say nothing about the source of those differences.* As Sternberg, Grigorenko, and Kidd (2005) concluded, the statement that racial differences in IQ or academic achievement are of genetic origin is a "leap of imagination." We have repeatedly noted that race/ethnicity are likely to be proxy variables for a set of active mechanisms that have only been partially identified. In fact, the reason between-group differences appear to exist may be because the variables that they are substituting for have not been fully identified. Thus, we are not in agreement with Spearman's hypothesis that differences in IQ scores across racial/ethnic groups reflect differences in genotypic ability. We seek to reframe the question in terms of differential opportunity for development of cognitive abilities. Alternatively, cognitively enriched environments may be a synonym for acculturative experiences. Thus, Spearman's hypothesis for IQ score differences across racial/ethnic groups could be reframed either in terms of differential opportunity for cognitive development, or differential acculturation experiences.

In the next section, we report the results of a series of analyses designed to evaluate the extent to which differences in parent education and income are the source of WISC-V FSIQ score differences between racial and ethnic groups. First, however, we review findings from similar studies with WISC-IV and WAIS-IV.

SOCIOECONOMIC STATUS MEDIATORS OF FULL SCALE INTELLIGENCE QUOTIENT DIFFERENCES BETWEEN CULTURALLY AND LINGUISTICALLY DIVERSE GROUPS

In this section we explore how SES mediates the gap between racial and ethnic groups in intelligence test scores. This discussion is not about nature/nurture, nor is it about race and IQ. It is about helping people understand why test scores may vary based on contextual factors and using that information to help children.

Previous Findings With Wechsler Adult Intelligence Scale— Fourth Edition and Wechsler Adult Intelligence Scale—Fourth Edition

We applied a regression-based methodology recommended by Helms, Jernigan, and Mascher (2005), outspoken critics of bias in testing, to examine how much of the variance in test scores can be attributed to racial/ethnic group, and how much that variance is reduced when relevant mediator variables are introduced. We first reported these analyses with WISC-IV data (Weiss et al., 2006). For the AA/White comparison, we reported that race accounted for 4.7% of the variance in WISC-IV FSIQ scores, and that after controlling for parent education and income, race explained only 1.6% of the variance, leaving six points of the group difference remaining unexplained after mediation. For the Hispanic/White comparison, we reported that ethnicity accounted for 1.4% of the variance in WISC-IV FSIQ scores, and controlling for parent education and income fully explained the difference. We attributed the fact that controlling for SES did not fully explain the remaining difference in the AA/White comparison to historical inequalities in access to quality education and discrimination in job promotions among the parents of these children.

We then combined the groups and examined the role of parents' expectations for their children's academic success. We were surprised to find that parental expectations explained 30.7% of the variance in children's WISC-IV FSIQ scores, far more than parent education and income combined at 21.3%. After controlling for parent education and income, parental expectations still explained 15.9% of the variance in children's WISC-IV FSIQ scores, far more than explained by race (4.7%) or ethnicity (1.4%) alone. We interpreted these findings as consistent with the view that home environment matters, concluding that demographics is not destiny.

We subsequently reported the same analyses with adults based on WAIS-IV (Weiss, Chen, Harris, Holdnack, & Saklofske, 2010). For the Hispanic/White comparison, we reported that ethnicity accounted for 11.2% of the variance in WAIS-IV FSIQ scores for adults ages 20–90. After controlling for the adult's level of education, occupation, income, gender, and region where they live, ethnicity explained 3.8% of the variance, leaving a 6.5-point difference between the groups unexplained after mediation. For the AA/White comparison, we reported that race accounted for 14.9% of the variance in WAIS-IV FSIQ scores for adults ages 20–90, far more than for children and adolescents. After controlling for other demographics, race still accounted for 9.2% of the variance, leaving an 11-point difference unexplained. This is still quite large, and again, we attributed the finding to historical discrimination impacting opportunities for quality education and career advancement.

Across these two studies, we observed that SES variables exhibited much more explanatory power for children and adolescent than adults, possibly suggesting an historical trend across generations. So we examined WAIS-IV FSIQ scores by racial/ethnic group for five birth cohorts from 1917 to 1991. There was a striking trend of increasing FSIQ scores with younger generations. WAIS-IV FSIQ scores increased by more than half a standard deviation for adults born between 1988 and 1991 as compared to those born between 1917 and 1942. During the same period, the gap between AA and White means decreased by 9.3 points, and the gap between Hispanic/White means decreased by 8.6 points. Many historical, legal, and cultural factors have likely contributed to the significant reduction observed in the IQ gap across generations. But the fact that score gaps remain for younger generations, though significantly reduced in magnitude, suggests that historical discrimination in educational access, employment, and career advancement opportunities continues to impede racial/ethnic equity to some degree even today.

TABLE 5.4 Regression Analyses of PED and Income as Mediators of White/AA Differences in Children's FSIQ ($n = 1804$)

	R^2	R^2 Difference	Percentage of White/AA Effect Mediated	Mean Difference Between White/AA After Mediation
Model 1				
Race	0.089			12.838
Model 2				
PED	0.176			
PED, race	0.210	0.034	61.8%	8.349
Model 3				
PED	0.176			
PED, income	0.208			
PED, income, race	0.227	0.019	78.7%	6.651

PED, Parent Education.
Source: Data and table Copyright Pearson 2014. All rights reserved.

Wechsler Adult Intelligence Scale—Fifth Edition Findings

Now, we return our attention to WISC-V. Table 5.4 shows the analyses for the AA/White comparison. In model 1, we regress FSIQ on race. As shown in the table, race accounts for 8.9% of the variance in FSIQ score, or 12.8 points.[2] In model 2, we introduce parent education as a mediator and examine the reduction in variance accounted for by racial group after controlling for parent education.[3] As shown in Table 5.4, parent education alone accounts for 17.6.% of the variance in FSIQ between the AA and W samples, which is substantially larger than the variance accounted for by race alone (8.9%). Controlling for parent education level reduces the amount of variance in FSIQ attributed to race alone by 61.8%, from 8.9% to 3.4%. The remaining mean difference between the AA and White samples is 8.3 FSIQ points. As described earlier, parent education is only a rough indicator of

2. The results in these analyses may differ slightly from the mean FSIQ difference reported above based on use of the standardization oversample, which is slightly larger than the standardization sample. The oversample was used because it includes more Hispanic and AA subjects than the standardization sample.
3. Parent education was blocked into four levels as follows: Less than 12th grade, high school graduate, some college, and college graduate or higher. When both parents were living in the home, the average of the two levels of education was used.

SES. Therefore, in model 3 we introduce household income as an additional mediator together with parent education. Parent income explains an additional 3.2% of the variance in FSIQ between groups after controlling for parent education. Together, these two indicators of SES explain 20.8% of the variance in FSIQ scores. Controlling for both parent education and income reduces the variance attributed to race alone by 78.8%. The remaining variance accounted for by racial status is 1.9%. This translates to a mean difference of 6.6 FISQ points between the AA and White samples after taking into account parent education and income. Future researchers should use more sophisticated measures of SES (e.g., zip code or block or residence), and study the incremental effects of controlling for additional variables such as school quality, neighborhood safety, sickle cell disease, etc.

Table 5.5 applies the same methodology to the Hispanic and White, non-Hispanic samples. Model 1 shows that ethnic status accounts for 3% of the variance in FSIQ scores between groups, which amounts to 6.7 FSIQ points. Model 2 shows that parent education alone accounts for 17.1% of the variance, and controlling for parent education reduces the variance in FSIQ accounted for by ethnic group by 96.7%, leaving a mean difference of slightly more than one FSIQ point between the Hispanic and White, non-Hispanic samples. In model 3, parent income contributed an additional 1.7%

TABLE 5.5 Regression Analyses of PED and Income as Mediators of White/Hispanic Differences in Children's FSIQ ($n = 1882$)

	R^2	R^2 Difference	Percentage of White/Hispanic Effect Mediated	Mean Difference Between White/ Hispanic After Mediation
Model 1				
Ethnicity	0.030			6.702
Model 2				
PED	0.171			
PED, ethnicity	0.172	0.001	96.7%	1.285
Model 3				
PED	0.171			
PED, income	0.188			
PED, income, ethnicity	0.188	0.000	98.6%	0.883

PED, Parent Education.
Source: Data and table Copyright Pearson 2014. All rights reserved.

of variance in FSIQ scores, reducing the variance explained by ethnicity by 98.6%. The remaining mean difference between the White and Hispanic FSIQ mean scores was slightly less than one point after controlling for parent education and household income.

We next explored the impact of the number of parents living in the home on children's cognitive ability test scores. Table 5.6 shows mean WISC-V FSIQ scores for children in single- versus dual-parent families by racial/ethnic group. As anticipated, children of dual- parent families obtain higher mean FSIQ scores than single-parent families of the same race by 4–6 points on average. It may be that single parents simply have less time available to engage in linguistically and cognitively stimulating activities with their children. As noted above, single-parent families also have more difficulty sustaining daily routines, and this has been related to outcome in developmentally delayed children. Alternatively, recent parental separation or divorce may temporarily depress cognitive functioning for some children who are experiencing emotional distress at the time of testing. Further, reduced household income may reduce access to quality schools and other positive environmental influences. Thus, single- versus dual-parent family status may be another variable contributing to test score differences between racial/ethnic groups.

In our previous research with WISC-IV, we found no effect in the Hispanic group for single- versus dual-parent families (Weiss et al., 2006). In the present research, an effect was present for Hispanics, but it was smaller than the effect for either AA or Whites. Having one or two parents in the home makes a smaller difference in the cognitive test scores of Hispanic versus AA or White children. This finding requires further research to explain. The possible differential role of extended families across groups may be an appropriate focus of investigation to explain this finding.

In our previous work with WISC-IV, we found that the number of parents living in the home accounts for 2% of the variance in FSIQ between AA and

TABLE 5.6 WISC-V FSIQ Scores of Children in Single- Versus Dual-Parent Families By Racial/Ethnic Group

	Single-Parent Families	Dual-Parent Families	Difference	t	P	Effect Size
AA	87.2	92.1	4.9	2.97	$<.01$	0.32
Hispanic	92.8	96.7	3.8	2.74	$<.01$	0.26
White	96.9	103.5	6.6	6.20	$<.01$	0.44

Whites, reducing the AA/White FSIQ difference by 30% (Weiss et al., 2006). However, when parent education and income were entered into the model first, the incremental effect of parental status was zero.

Theoretically, if differential exposure to cognitively enriching environments fully explains IQ test score differences between groups then fully controlling for cognitive enrichment should eliminate the observed score differences. Thus, it is interesting that the effect of parent education and household income almost completely explains the FSIQ gap between the Hispanic and White samples, but only partially explains the gap between AA and White FSIQ scores. This suggests that parent education and income may relate to cognitive ability scores in a somewhat different manner for AAs than Hispanics, or that additional indirect variables remain unaccounted for.

Why do some studies still show differences in IQ test scores between the AA and White groups even after matching for critical variables such as parent education, income, and the number of parents living in the home? Part of the answer is that these variables exert their effects indirectly, and are therefore called distal rather them proximal. Alternatively, unmeasured inequities in societal forces may dampen the positive effects of education and income for AAs.

The indirect nature of the effect, as we discussed above, means that the relationship is not perfect. These are "proxy" variables. That is, they serve as convenient indicators of other variables that are difficult to measure directly. The level of education attained by the child's parent or parents is a powerful demographic variable influencing cognitive ability scores. Although not perfectly correlated with the financial situation of the family, this variable serves as a reasonable proxy for overall SES. Parent education is, in turn, related to a host of important variables including the parent's employment opportunities, income level, housing, neighborhood, access to prenatal care, adequacy of nutrition during infancy and early development, and the quality of educational experience available to the child. Much of this may have to do with enriched early stimulation and opportunity to learn and grow in a safe and secure environment. Researchers assume that parents with more education have better access to pediatric care, quality schools, and safe neighborhoods—but this is not always the case. To date, no matched studies have been accomplished that directly control for all medical, societal, legal, environmental, financial, and educational factors known to account for variance in cognitive development. In addition to being limited by the use of proxy variables, the available studies are typically cross-sectional rather than longitudinal.

More generally, results from scholarly studies (such as those reviewed in this chapter) provide invaluable information that informs psychologists, sociologists, political scientists, and others about group characteristics. However, psychology is unique in its commitment to understand an individual's differences. Although research studies may provide helpful insights as to qualities that enhance or attenuate cognitive development for groups, psychologists must not assume that the group data characterize every individual being assessed. When we uncritically apply group-level research findings in our clinical practices we may inadvertently stereotype the very children who were referred to us for help.

It is for all of these reasons that we wish to leave behind the study of racial/ethnic differences in cognitive ability test scores and turn the reader's attention to proximal mediators of children's cognitive development, such as what occurs between parent and child in the home. Our direction is influenced by calls from Helms et al. (2005) to cease the use of race as an independent variable in psychological research. This direction is also consistent with recent advances in the study of the human genome that have led writers from diverse academic disciplines to argue that race is a socially constructed and biologically meaningless concept (Cavalli-Sforza, 2001; Marks, 2002; Schwartz, 2001), while others suggest that the division lines between racial/ethnic groups are highly fluid and that far more variation exists within genetic groups than between them (Foster & Sharp, 2002, p. 848). Further, despite the lightening pace of recent advances in genetics, attempts to establish genes for intelligence have so far found only weak effects, been inconclusive, or failed to replicate (Chorney et al., 1998; Hill, Chorney & Plomin, 2002; Hill et al., 1999; Plomin et al., 1995).

At some point in the future, we expect that researchers will cease using racial/ethnic status groupings because of the fluidity of racial boundaries and the wide variability of culture and language within racial and ethnic groups. Future researchers may wish to study how socially constructed concepts of culture mediate development of the particular cognitive abilities assessed by most major intelligence tests in industrialized countries.

At this point, we leave behind the study of racial/ethnic differences in intelligence, and hope that others will do the same. We now turn the proverbial corner and begin a preliminary discussion of home environment variables that enhance children's cognitive development within and across cultural groups. In the remainder of this chapter, we present initial data regarding home environment and language variables, and impact on cognitive development and cognitive ability test scores.

FURTHER CONSIDERATIONS OF HOME ENVIRONMENT ON INTELLECTUAL AND ACADEMIC DEVELOPMENT OF CHILDREN

Many of the SES-related variables typically studied in intelligence research are assumed to operate on children's development in two ways. First, there are the distal effects of the environment in terms of school quality, neighborhood safety, medical care, etc. Many of these are assumed to be captured indirectly by parent education and income level. Second, there are the proximal effects of how parents interact with children in terms of providing linguistically, intellectually, and academically stimulating and encouraging environments. Parent—child interactions may or may not be related to parent education and income. We treat these variables separately because, unlike SES, parents'ß behaviors and attitudes are more within their immediate control.

Implicit assumptions are often made about the manner in which more educated mothers interact with their children in different ways from mothers with less formal education. More educated mothers are assumed to provide increased language stimulation to infants and toddlers, read more often to preschool-age children, assist elementary school children more with homework, and generally provide more intellectually stimulating activities throughout childhood and adolescence. This is a broadly sweeping assumption that deserves to be examined in more detail. It is quite possible that there is considerable variability in parenting practices within SES groups, and that this variability influences the cognitive development of children.

Research with the WPPSI-III suggests that three home environment variables play an important role in the development of verbal abilities among young children. These variables are the number of hours per week that the parents spend reading to the child, that the child spends on the computer, and viewing television. Mean WPPSI-III Verbal IQ (VIQ) scores increased with number of hours spent reading and on the computer, and decreased with number of hours watching television. There is also a clear relationship between these variables and parent education. Number of hours spent reading and on the computer systematically increased with parent education, while number of hours spent watching television decreased. Thus, relative to parents with little formal education, more educated parents read to their children more often, discourage television watching, and encourage computer use. Further, children ages 2½ to 7 who were read to more often, used computers more often, watched less television, and had higher VIQ scores on average (Sichi, 2003). Perhaps SES plays a role in the availability of computers in the home, and the opportunity to interact with children in cognitively stimulating ways (i.e., reading to them versus allowing excessive television watching) in busy single-parent versus dual-employment families. At the same time, however, there was substantial variability in the frequency of these behaviors within levels of parent education. *Thus, even among young children whose parents have similar levels of education, spending more time reading and using the computer, and less time watching television, is associated with higher verbal ability test scores.*

Next, we explore the proximal effects of parental attitudes on school-age children. We selected four items from a larger questionnaire completed by parents of children in the WISC-V standardization sample ($n = 2419$). Parents were asked four simple questions: how likely is it that your child will achieve good grades in school, graduate from high school, graduate from college, and find better employment than yourself? Each question was rated on a four-point scale ranging from not likely to very likely. These four questions clearly relate to parental expectations regarding the child's academic and occupational success. We assume that parents communicate these expectations to a child in a multitude of ways, both direct and indirect, during the course of their developmental years.

To analyze the effects of parental expectation on cognitive ability test scores, we return to the mediator analysis methodology described above— but with a different focus. The dependent variable is no longer the *gap* in FSIQ scores between groups, but the FSIQ score itself—for the total group of children combined across all racial and ethnic groups. Thus, we are no longer seeking to explain the gap in FSIQ scores between racial/ethnic groups, but to understand the effect of parental expectations across groups.

Table 5.7 shows these analyses. For all children, the combination of parent education and income explains approximately 22% of the variance in FSIQ scores. Parent expectations alone explain approximately 26.5% of the variance in FSIQ scores across all children. *Thus, parental expectations alone explain more variance in children's FSIQ scores than parent education and income combined.* This is interesting because previous researchers have assumed that parent level of education has the most powerful effect on cognitive test scores. When all three variables are considered in combination (i.e., parent education, income, and expectations) the model explains approximately 37% of the variance in children's FSIQ scores.

But are parent expectations simply a function of parent education and income? Do more educated and wealthier parents simply have higher expectations for their children? We examine this hypothesis in models 2 and 3 of Table 5.7. In model 2, we find that parent education and income explains only 10.8% of the variance in children's FSIQ scores after parental expectations are controlled. This is a 51% reduction in explanatory power of parent education and income from 21.9% to 10.8% due to the effect of parental expectations.

Next, we examined the reverse question in model 3; how much do parental expectations matter after accounting for parent education and income? As shown in model 3, parental expectations still account for approximately 15.4% of the variance in children's FSIQ scores after controlling for parent education and income. Although the explanatory power of parental expectations declines by 42% after controlling for parent education and income, the size of the remaining effect for parental expectations is substantial.

We were concerned, however, that these data simply reflect the accumulated feedback parents receive about their children's abilities and future potential from various environmental sources such as teachers, community leaders, and even employers for older teenagers. We hypothesized that parents of older children would have received more environmental feedback and would thus have more accurate expectations based on their children's true

TABLE 5.7 Regression Analyses of PEX as Mediator Among PED and Income on Children's FSIQ

	R^2	R^2	Percentage of Effect Mediated
Overall (n = 2419)			
Model 1			
PED, income	0.219		
Model 2			
PEX	0.265		
PEX, PED, income	0.373	0.108	50.7%
Model 3			
PED, income	0.219		
PED, income, PEX	0.373	0.154	41.9%
6–11 years old (n = 1328)			
Model 1			
PED, income	0.234		
Model 2			
PEX	0.285		
PEX, PED, income	0.391	0.106	54.7%
Model 3			
PED, income	0.234		
PED, income, PEX	0.391	0.157	44.9%
12–16 years old (n = 1091)			
Model 1			
PED, income	0.212		
Model 2			
PEX	0.271		
PEX, PED, income	0.384	0.113	46.7%
Model 3			
PED, income	0.212		
PED, income, PEX	0.384	0.172	36.5%

PEX, Parent Expectations; *PED*, Parent Education.
Source: Data and table Copyright Pearson 2014. All rights reserved.

intellectual abilities. So, we repeated the analyses separately for younger (ages 6−11) and older (ages 12−16) children. While the explanatory power of parental expectations rose slightly for older children, the increase was relatively small (from 15.7% to 17.2%). More to the point, the effect of parental expectations was substantial for children of all ages.

In our previous work with WISC-IV (Weiss et al., 2006), we regressed FSIQ on parent expectations within levels of parent education. We found that parental expectations were significantly related to FSIQ scores at all levels of parent education, but more so among parents with high school educations ($R^2 = 0.28$) and least among parents who did not graduate high school ($R^2 = 0.19$). We interpret these findings in relation to the impact of distal environmental resources on proximal attitudes and behaviors. It may be that real societal and economic factors constrain the power of parent expectations among the lowest SES families. *Still, parent expectations remain a powerful force among all SES groups, just not as powerful among parents who did not graduate high school. Parent expectations appear most influential among middle SES families where parents have graduated high school but not attended college.* Although no data exist to explain this finding, we wonder if children in these families may be most on the brink of moving either up or down the SES continuum in adulthood depending on their personal effort, and thus parental expectations are particularly influential.

We also examined the hypothesis that parent expectations operate differently across cultures by examining the effect of parental expectations on the WISC-IV FSIQ gap between racial/ethnic groups after controlling for parent education and income. The remaining variance attributable to parent expectations was approximately 15% for the AA/White FSIQ gap analysis, and 18% for the Hispanic/White FSIQ gap analysis—suggesting that the effect of parent expectations is substantial across cultural and linguistically diverse groups (Weiss et al., 2006).

To recap, parent education and income combined explain approximately 22% of the variance in children's FSIQ, while parental expectations alone explain approximately 26.5%. In combination, these three variables explain about 37% of the variability in the measurement of cognitive ability across all children. The effect of parent expectations is only partially accounted for by parent education and income, and the remaining variance attributable to parent expectation is meaningful. Further, parent expectations appear to account for similar amounts of variance in children's FSIQ scores in the AA/White and Hispanic/White comparisons. While there may be systematic differences in parental expectations across levels of parent education, parental expectations still predict substantial variance in the measurement of children's cognitive abilities within each level of parent education.

The explanatory power of this simple parent expectation variable is both surprising and encouraging. The possibility that parental expectations, attitudes, and behaviors can positively influence the development of cognitive abilities in children of all demographic backgrounds is very exciting, though perhaps a bit naive as well. Do parents express these expectations differently across SES groups? Are there cultural differences in parent expectations that simply mirror differences in standardized test scores? These are all important questions that do not yet have irrefutable data-based answers. However, the analyses above suggest that this may not be the case. Parents' expectations accounted for substantial variance in FSIQ after controlling for two indicators of SES (parent education and income), and a possible indicator of culture (racial/ethnic group). On the other hand, racial/ethnic group is not synonymous with culture, and perhaps more sophisticated measures of cultural or familial beliefs and values will identify systematic differences in parent expectations. For now, however, the data presented above suggest that whatever cultural differences may be captured by simple racial/ethnic group status do not account for substantial differences in the power of parental expectations in children's academic performance.

The psychosocial mechanisms by which parental expectations are translated into specific behaviors in the home, what those behaviors are, whether they vary by culture, and how they increase cognitive ability test scores is an important frontier for potentially fruitful research into contextual interpretation. As Ceci (1996) suggests, these behaviors may differ at different critical stages of cognitive development. Clearly, reading to a preschool child will be more effective than reading to a preadolescent child. Also, playing rhyming games with early elementary children may facilitate the acquisition of phonological awareness, which is critical to the development of early reading skills, but rhyming games with older children who have reading comprehension difficulties may be less effective. When more is known about the timing and active ingredients of home environment behaviors, and how these may vary across cultures, practitioners will be in a better position to intervene with families of children at risk for cognitive delays or learning disorders.

Jirout and Newcombe (2015) found that when parents engage in interactive play at home with their preschool-age children using blocks, puzzles, boardgames, and drawing materials the children have significantly better developed visual-spatial abilities. This is particularly useful in light of the finding reported above that AA children tend to score lower on the VSI than the other WISC-V indexes. These authors also found that playing word games had a significant effect, and suggested that parents who engage in playful cognitive interactions with preschool children are facilitating their general intellectual growth. Perhaps these parents have what Carole Dweck called a "growth mindset" with regard to cognitive abilities (see above).

As Gregoire observes (see Chapter 8: The Flynn Effect and Its Clinical Implications), the relationship of educational achievement and intelligence is difficult to untangle because it is reciprocal. Intelligence is widely accepted to be the best single predictor of success in school. At the same time, there are positive effects of schooling on the intellectual development of children.

Based on several previous studies, Ceci (1996) showed that education stimulates the development of several skills that play an important role in intelligence tests, especially perceptual skills, concept formation, and memory. In fact, this view forms the basis for early intervention and Head Start programs for young children who are developmentally delayed or socioeconomically disadvantaged. Further, improvements to educational systems and access to education are often considered to be one of the primary causes of increases in IQ test scores across the generations, known as the Flynn effect. In a longitudinal study of 2000 identical twins, Ritchie (2015) found that better than average reading skills from age 7 may positively affect children's intellectual abilities in late adolescence. We believe that the rigorous cognitive demands of academic learning in school stimulate development of key cognitive abilities related to intelligence.

These lines of thinking led us to examine the academic monitoring behaviors of parents in relationship to academic achievement test scores on the Wechsler Individual Achievement Test—Third edition using data from the WISC-V home environment questionnaire, an unpublished research instrument collected with the standardization sample. We examined a set of 11 questions related to homework routines and parents' academic monitoring behaviors, and identified those with moderate correlations between 0.20 and 0.30. How often parents talked to their children about school had a consistently positive effect on achievement test scores for children of all ages. For younger children (ages 6–11), ensuring that they do their homework at the same time each day, and asking to see the completed assignments was important. Surprisingly, having a quiet spot to do homework, and turning off electronics while doing homework, was unrelated to achievement at any age.

However, asking older children to see their completed assignments, checking and helping with their assignments, and checking their backpacks for notes and assignments were all inversely related to achievement. Perhaps parents only employ these more intrusive tactics with older children when they are underachieving in school. For older children, asking if they have homework and talking with them about school were positively correlated with achievement. It seems that the simple act of talking with children of any age about school sends an important message that school is important and their parents care about how they do in school. In addition, we found that the amount of time older children spend doing homework was positively correlated with achievement — suggesting that personal factors such as the student's motivation and conscientiousness come into play at these ages, as discussed above.

Still, it is possible that parents know their children's abilities better than anyone, and adjust their expectations and monitoring behaviors accordingly based on feedback from teachers and other sources. We acknowledge that the effect of parent expectations on children's cognitive abilities is probably not unidirectional, but reciprocally interactive. That is, naturally bright children stimulate their parents toward higher quality interactions with them, which, in turn, motivates the child toward intellectually and academically enriching pursuits that further stimulate cognitive development. At the same time, children with limited intellectual endowment may stimulate their parents to have lower expectations for them, monitor them more closely, and steer the child away from intellectual and academic growth activities. There are many factors that may account for the covariation of parental expectations and FSIQ beyond the parents' education, income, and knowledge of their children's abilities. For example, the parents' motivation for upward mobility, or fear of downward mobility are areas for future researchers to investigate. Thus, while parental expectations are worthy of research studies, at the individual level the reasons for those expectations may be far worthier of clinical exploration.

CONCLUSIONS REGARDING HOME ENVIRONMENT AND COGNITIVE DEVELOPMENT

How parental expectations are translated into parental behaviors and the mechanisms by which these behaviors act on children's cognitive development needs further research including more complex modeling and longitudinal studies. But it seems reasonable to hypothesize that there are both general factors (such as parental monitoring), and specific factors (such as the form of monitoring), that vary by age, developmental level, and familial or cultural context.

In a comprehensive review of intelligence testing and minority students, Valencia and Suzuki (2001) drew several major conclusions and cautions from the literature on home environment (pp. 108–110). First, and most importantly, intellectually stimulating and supportive home environments tend to produce bright children. While it is easy to assume that the direction of the effect is from parent to child, Valencia and Suzuki remind us that it is equally possible that bright children capture the attention of parents who respond to them in stimulating ways, which furthers the child's cognitive growth. Second, measures of home environment are more accurate predictors of children's measured intelligence than SES. While SES is a good global predictor, we are reminded that families within each SES stratum differ considerably in the ways in which intellectual climate is structured in the home and in the amounts of stimulation provided. Third, most of the research on minority families has demonstrated significantly positive correlations between home environment and children's intellectual performance. While there probably are some commonalities in what constitutes a cognitively enriching environment, the specific expression of these characteristics may vary across cultures. Fourth, these studies can be taken together to debunk the view that low SES families cannot raise intelligent children. Clearly, specific in-home behaviors are as important, if not more important, than the parents' income, occupation, or education. Stated succinctly, *what parents do is more important than what they are.* This is critical, because SES can be difficult for families to change. But as shown in a series of field studies more than a quarter century ago, low SES minority parents can be trained effectively to teach specific intellectual skills to their children and to influence their motivation toward academic activities (Henderson & Garcia, 1973; Henderson & Swanson, 1974; Swanson & Henderson, 1976). Such intervention programs, however, must be sensitive to cultural differences in the specific expression of cognitively stimulating behaviors, and the ways in which these are taught and reinforced. The same home environment factors may interact in differing ways in school systems outside the United States or when measured by other methods. We also must be cognizant of Ceci's (1996) caution that distal environmental resources can limit the effectiveness of these proximal processes in the home environment. In other words, severely impoverished environments may constrain the influence of parent expectations but does not eliminate it.

The WISC-V findings reported in this chapter are important and have significant implications for practice. While SES (as estimated by parent education and income) explains considerable variance in IQ test scores at the group level, these findings suggest that children born into low SES families are not predetermined to have lower cognitive ability and that parents can play an important role in enhancing their children's cognitive development, thus improving their educational and occupational opportunities as young adults. Understanding the types of parental behaviors that enrich or stimulate cognitive development as compared to those that inhibit or stifle intellectual growth is a critical activity for scholars and practitioners alike. But identifying these behaviors is only the first step. The timing of these behaviors within critical developmental periods must also be understood. Further, developing culturally sensitive models for communicating these findings to parents of different backgrounds and cultures and for training parents to effectively implement these ideas in their homes is essential.

These are not new ideas. Most elementary school teachers can easily distinguish students whose parents work with them at home from those who do not. And, teachers will readily empathize with the difficulty of changing parental behavior relating to academic monitoring of children. But these findings suggest that the benefits for children can be large enough to warrant sustained effort. We strongly encourage psychologists and teachers to speak directly with parents about these in-home behaviors, the benefits of them for their children, doing so at the earliest possible ages, and regular follow-up. Available research suggests that it can be influential to engage parents in conversations about what they do at home to monitor their children's homework and class projects, encouraging quiet time for reading together or independently, limiting time spent watching TV, encouraging computer use (at the local library if necessary), and positively communicating expectations for academic success.

Overall, this is a very positive message for the fields of psychology and education. Initially, we had been concerned that reporting IQ differences between groups of children based on static demographic characteristics such as parent education or income could inhibit the potential of individual children in these groups by reducing expectations for them. But the variability within these groups combined with the finding that parent's interactions with children in the home can ameliorate the impact of low SES and other relatively fixed demographic characteristics encourages us to give voice to hope. If readers remember only one sentence from this chapter, we would want them to remember this: *Demographics is not destiny*. This is the main contribution of our chapter that began with our previous chapters presented in our books on the WISC-IV and WAIS-IV.

While we have attempted to make a strong case in favor of interpreting cognitive ability scores in concert with home environment variables, we also believe it is possible to take such interpretations too far. Mercer and Lewis (1978) developed adjusted IQ scores for the WISC-R based on a myriad of variables including income, urban versus rural status, family size, parent education, etc. Thus, children from families with different incomes and numbers of children would be given "IQ" scores that were different despite answering the same number of questions correctly. While noble in its intent, this effort served to confuse interpretation of IQ test scores, and researchers did not offer these types of adjustments for subsequent editions of WISC. Our approach with WISC-V is to retain a population-based reference group for the IQ and Index scores, while simultaneously providing supplemental information that encourages culturally sensitive interpretation of IQ scores within the context of the child's unique home environment. We refer the reader to our chapter in this book on testing Hispanics.

SUMMARY

In this chapter we lay the foundation for a model of contextual interpretation. Along with others (Saklofske, van de Vijver, Oakland, Mpofu, & Suszuki, 2015), we argue that an evaluation of sociocultural-economic context should be part of the nuts and bolts of a general practice model of clinical assessment. Practitioners should pay attention to context in order to test cognitive hypotheses for referral problems in relation to the child's family and community and to differentiate effective intervention strategies.

We have made a case that while racial/ethnic differences in cognitive ability tests exist, they are not due to item or test bias, nor are they unique with respect to many other areas of life. Further, racial/ethnic differences are likely a proxy for a multitude of other variables that social psychologists are just beginning to identify and study. Still, these differences have important implications for individual students in need of educational assistance as well as contribute—along with variability in prereferral methods and funding mechanisms across local and state education authorities—to disproportionate representation of CLD students in special education programs. We make the point that disproportionate representation in special education may partially reflect the disproportionate risk experienced by ethnically diverse children living in low SES environments. We present the case that intelligence tests do not measure pure intelligence, but some combination of innate ability and learning based on interactions with the environment and that environments vary on critical dimensions that differentially enhance or impede cognitive development. Perhaps most importantly, we argue that cognitive growth is malleable, within limits, based on environmental opportunities for cognitive development. We have shown that SES, as estimated by parent education and income, accounts for a large portion of the variance in children's intelligence test scores between racial/ethnic groups. More importantly, we have shown that substantial variability in cognitive test scores can be explained by home environment behaviors such as parental expectations of children's academic success, even after controlling for parent education and income. While low SES environments place children at risk for cognitive delay, and many other health factors, the negative cognitive effects of low SES can be mitigated by the expectations that parents have for their children's success, how they interact with children in the home with regard to providing language and cognitive stimulation, reading to children, monitoring schoolwork and learning, and more. It is for these reasons that we offer a voice of hope and encourage practitioners to involve families in the treatment of children at risk for cognitive delays and learning disorders. Similarly, we suggest that researchers systematically study the critical developmental periods in which specific types of cognitive stimulation are most effectively applied, and how such interventions may need to be modified when working with CLD families. Therein lays a meaningful life's work!

REFERENCES

American Education Research Association, American Psychological Association, & National Council on Measurement in Education. (2014). *The standards for educational and psychological testing*. Washington, DC: American Psychological Association.

Benasich, A. A., Choudhury, N. A., Realpe-Bonilla, T., & Roesler, C. P. (2014). Plasticity in developing brains: Active exposure impacts prelinguistic acoustic mapping. *The Journal of Neuroscience, 34*(40), 13349–13363.

Bloom, B. S. (1964). *Stability and change in human characteristics*. New York: John Wiley.

Bouman, S. H. (2010). *Response to intervention in California public schools: Has it helped address disproportional placement rates for students with learning disabilities? (Unpublished doctoral dissertation)*. Claremont, CA: Claremont College.

Bowden, S. C., Lange, R. T., Weiss, L. G., & Saklofske, D. (2008). Equivalence of the measurement model underlying the Wechsler Adult Intelligence Scale-III in the United States and Canada. *Educational and Psychological Measurement, 68*(6), 1024–1040.

Bowden, S. C., Lissner, D., McCarthy, K. A., Weiss, L. G., & Holdnack, J. A. (2003). Equivalence of WAIS-III standardization data collected in Australia when compared to data collected in the US. In *CNN satellite symposium of the Australian Psychological Society Conference*, Perth.

Bowden, S. C., Lloyd, D., Weiss, L. G., & Holdnack, J. A. (2006). Age related invariance of abilities measured with the Wechsler Adult Intelligence Scale − III. *Psychological Assessment, 18*(3).

Bradley, R. H., & Caldwell, B. M. (1978). Screening the environment. *American Journal of Orthopsychiatry, 48*, 114−130.

Bradley, R. H., & Caldwell, B. M. (1981). The HOME inventory: A validation of the preschool for Black children. *Child Development, 53*, 708−710.

Bradley, R. H., & Caldwell, B. M. (1982). The consistency of the home environment and its relation to child development. *International Journal of Behavioral Development, 5*, 445−465.

Bradley, R. H., Caldwell, B. M., & Elardo, R. (1977). Home environment, social status, and mental test performance. *Journal of Educational Psychology, 69*, 697−701.

Bradley, R. H., Caldwell, B. M., Rock, S., Barnard, K., Gray, C., Hammond, M., ... Johnson, D. L. (1989). Home environment and cognitive development in the first three years of life: A collaborative study involving six sites and three ethnic groups in North America. *Developmental Psychology, 28*, 217−235.

Bronfenbrenner, U. (1992). Ecological systems theory. In R. Vasta (Ed.), *Six theories of child development: Revised formulations and current issues* (pp. 187−249). Ithaca, NY: Cornell University Department of Human Development and Family Studies.

Bronfenbrenner, U. (2004). *Making human beings human: Bioecological perspectives on human development*. Thousand Oaks, CA: Sage Publications.

Bronfenbrenner, U., & Ceci, S. J. (1994). Nature−nurture reconceptualized in developmental perspective: A bio-ecological model. *Psychological Review, 101*, 568−586.

Brooks-Gunn, J., Klebanov, P. K., & Duncan, G. J. (1996). Ethnic differences in children's intelligence test scores: Role of economic deprivation, home environment, and maternal characteristics. *Child Development, 67*, 396−408.

Burhan, N. A. S., Mohamad, M. R., Kurniawan, Y., & Sidek, A. H. (2014). The impact of low, average, and high IQ on economic growth and technological progress: Do all individuals contribute equally? *Intelligence, 46*, 1−8.

Caldwell, B. M., & Bradley, R. (1984). *Home observation for the measurement of the environment*. Little Rock, AR: Authors.

Cattell, R. (1949). *Culture free intelligence test, scale 1, handbook*. Champaign, IL: Institute of Personality and Ability.

Cavalli-Sforza, L. L. (2001). *Genes, peoples, and languages*. Berkeley: University of California Press.

Ceci, S. J. (1991). How much does schooling influence general intelligence and its cognitive components? A reassessment of the evidence. *Developmental Psychology, 27*(5), 703−722. Available from https://doi.org/10.1037/0012-1649.27.5.703.

Ceci, S. J. (1996). *On intelligence: A bioecological treatise on intellectual development*. Cambridge, MA: Harvard University Press. (expanded Ed.).

Ceci, S. J., & Bronfenbrenner, U. (2004). Heredity, environment, and the question of "how?". In U. Bronfenbrenner (Ed.), *Making human beings human: Bioecological perspectives on human development* (pp. 150−180). Thousand Oaks, CA: Sage Publications.

Ceci, S. J., & Williams, W. M. (1999). *The nature-nurture debate: The essential readings.* Oxford: Blackwell Publishers Ltd.

Centers for Disease Control and Prevention. (2012). *Suicide rates among persons ages 10–24 years, by race/ethnicity and sex, United States, 2005–2009.* Retrieved June 26, 2014, from http://www.cdc.gov/violenceprevention/suicide/statistics/rates03.html.

Centers for Disease Control and Prevention. (2013). *CDC Health Disparities and Inequalities Report—United States, MMWR 2013,* Vol. 62 (Suppl. 3).

Chapin, J. R. (2006). The achievement gap in social studies and science starts early: Evidence from the early childhood longitudinal study. *Social Studies, 97*(6-), 231–238.

Chatterji, M. (2005). Achievement gaps and correlates of early mathematics achievement: Evidence from the ECLS K-first grade sample. *Education Policy Analysis Archives, 13*(46).

Child Trends. (2013). *Homeless children and youth.* Available at: http://www.childtrends.org/?indicators = homeless-children-and-youth—See more at: http://www.childtrends.org/?indicators = homeless-children-and-youth - sthash.bnFoMqNx.dpuf. Retrieved June 25, 2014.

Chorney, M. J., Chorney, K., Seese, N., Owen, M. J., Daniels, J., McGuffin, P., et al. (1998). A quantitative trait locus associated with cognitive ability in children. *Psychological Science, 9,* 159–166.

Cook, B. L., Zuvekas, S. H., Carson, N., Wayne, G. F., Vesper, A., & McGuire, T. G. (2014). Assessing racial/ethnic disparities in treatment across episodes of mental health care. *Health Services Research, 49*(1), 206–229. Available from https://doi.org/10.1111/1475-6773.12095.

Csikszentmihalyi, M., & Robinson, R.E. (1986). Culture, time, and the development of talent. In *The systems model of creativity,* pp. 27-46, Springer

Deary, I. J., Whiteman, M. C., Starr, J. M., Whalley., Lawrence, J., & Fox, H. C. (2004). The impact of childhood intelligence on later life: Following up the Scottish mental surveys of 1932 and 1947. *Journal of Personality and Social Psychology, 86*(1), 130–147. Available from https://doi.org/10.1037/0022-3514.86.1.130.

Diamond, M. C., Lay, F., Rhodes, H., Lindner, R., Rosenzweig, M. R., Krech, D., & Bennett, E. L. (1966). Increases in cortical depth and glia numbers in rats subjected to enriched environment. *Journal of Comparative Neurology, 128*(1), 117–125.

Dickinson, D. K., & DeTemple, J. (1998). Putting parents in the picture: Maternal reports of preschoolers' literacy as a predictor of early reading. *Early Childhood Research Quarterly, 13,* 241–261.

Duckworth, A. L., Quinn, P. D., & Tsukayama, E. (2012). What no child left behind leaves behind: The roles of IQ and self-control in predicting standardized achievement test scores and report card grades. *Journal of Educational Psychology, 104*(2), 439–457.

Duckworth, A. L., & Seligman, M. E. P. (2005). Self-discipline outdoes IQ in predicting academic performance of adolescents. *Psychological Science, 16*(12), 939–944.

Dweck, C. S. (2012). Mindsets & human nature: Promoting change. *American Psychologist, 67* (8), 614–622.

Epstein, J. L. (1991). Effects on student achievement of teachers' practices of parent involvement. In S. B. Silvern (Ed.), *Advances in reading/language research: Vol. 5. Literacy through family, community, and school interaction* (pp. 61–276). Greenwich, CT: JAI Press.

Fantuzzo, J., McWayne, C., Perry, M. A., & Childs, S. (2004). Multiple dimensions of family involvement and their relations to behavioral and learning competencies for urban, low–income children. *School Psychology Review, 33,* 467–480.

Flynn, J. R. (1984). The mean IQ of Americans: Massive gains 1932 to 1978. *Psychological Bulletin, 95,* 29–51.

Flynn, J. R. (1987). Massive IQ gains in 14 nations. *Psychological Bulletin, 101,* 171–191.

Foster, M. W., & Sharp, R. R. (2002). Race, ethnicity, and genomics: Social classifications as proxies of biological heterogeneity. *Genome Research*, *12*, 844−850.

Foster, W. A., & Miller, M. (2007). Development of the literacy achievement gap: A longitudinal study of kindergarten through third grade. *Language, Speech & Hearing Services in Schools*, *38*(3), 173−181.

Galper, A., Wigfield, A., & Seefeldt, C. (1997). Head start parents' beliefs about their children's abilities, task values, and performances on different activities. *Child Development*, *68*, 897−907.

García, J. I. R. (2012). Mental health care for Latino immigrants in the USA. and the quest for global health equities. *Servicios de Salud Mental para los Inmigrantes Latinos en los Estados Unidos y la Lucha por una Igualdad en Salud Global*, *21*(3), 305−318.

Georgas, J., Weiss, L. G., Van de Vijver, F. J. R., & Saklofske, D. H. (Eds.), (2003).). Culture and children's intelligence: Cross cultural analysis of the WISC−III. San Diego, CA: Academic Press.

Goldstein, S., & Brooks, R. B. (2005). *Handbook of resilience in children*. New York: Kluwer Academic/Plenum Publishers.

Gottfredson, L.S. (1998). *The general intelligence factor*. Scientific American, November 1−10. Retrieved February 5, 2002 from http://www.scientificamerican.com/specialissues/1198intelligence/1198gottfred.html.

Gottfredson, L. S., & Saklofske, D. H. (2009). Intelligence: Foundations and issues in assessment. *Canadian Psychology/Psychologie canadienne*, *50*(3), 183−195. Available from https://doi.org/10.1037/a0016641.

Griffith, J. (1996). Relation of parental involvement, empowerment, and school traits to student academic performance. *Journal of Educational Research*, *90*, 33−41.

Guo, G., & Harris, K. (2000). The mechanisms mediating the effects of poverty on children's intellectual development. *Demography*, *37*(4), 431−447. Available from https://doi.org/10.1353/dem.2000.0005.

Hall, J. D., & Barnett, D. W. (1991). Classification of risk status in preschool screening: A comparison of alternative measures. *Journal of Psychoeducational Assessment*, *9*, 152−159.

Harris, D. N. (2007). High-flying schools, student disadvantage, and the logic of NCLB. *American Journal of Education*, *113*(3), 367−394.

Harris, J. G., Tulsky, D. S., & Schultheis, M. T. (2003). Assessment of the non-native English speaker: Assimilating history and research findings to guide practice. In S. S. Tulsky, D. H. Saklofske, G. J. Chelune, R. K. Keaton, R. J. Ivnik, R. Ornstein, A. Prifitera, & M. Ledbetter (Eds.), *Clinical interpretation of the WAIS-III and WMS-III*. San Diego, CA: Elsevier, Inc.

Helms, J. E., Jernigan, M., & Mascher, J. (2005). The meaning of race in psychology and how to change it: A methodological perspective. *American Psychologist*, *60*, 27−36.

Henderson, R. W. (1972). Environmental predictors of academic performance of disadvantaged Mexican−American children. *Journal of Consulting and Clinical Psychology*, *38*, 297.

Henderson, R. W., Bergan, J. R., & Hurt, M., Jr. (1972). Development and validation of the Henderson Environmental Learning Process Scale. *Journal of Social Psychology*, *88*, 185−196.

Henderson, R. W., & Garcia, A. B. (1973). The effects of a parent training program on the question−asking behavior of Mexican−American children. *American Educational Research Journal*, *10*, 193−201.

Henderson, R. W., & Merritt, C. B. (1968). Environmental background of Mexican−American children with different potentials for school success. *Journal of Social Psychology*, *75*, 101−106.

Henderson, R. W., & Swanson, R. A. (1974). Application of social learning principles in a field study. *Exceptional Children, 40*, 53–55.

Hernandez-Finch, M. E. (2012). Special considerations with response to intervention and instruction for students with diverse backgrounds. *Psychology in the Schools, 49*(3), 285–296.

Hill, L., Chorney, M. C., & Plomin, R. (2002). A quantitative trait locus (not) associated with cognitive ability? *Psychological Science, 13*, 561–562.

Hill, L., Craig, I. W., Asherson, P., Ball, D., Eley, T., Ninomiya, T., et al. (1999). DNA pooling and dense marker maps: A systematic search for genes for cognitive ability. *NeuroReport, 10*, 843–848.

Hoff, E. (2003). The specificity of environmental influence: Socioeconomic status affects early vocabulary development via maternal speech. *Child Development, 74*, 1368–1378.

Hudson, C. G. (2012). Disparities in the geography of mental health: Implications for social work. *Social Work, 57*(2), 107–119.

Hummer, R. A. (1996). Black-white differences in health and mortality: A review and conceptual model. *Sociological Quarterly, 37*(1), 105–125. Available from https://doi.org/10.1111/j.1533-8525.1996.tb02333.x.

Hunt, J., & Mcvicker, M. (1961). *Intelligence and experience*. Oxford: Ronald.

Jensen, A. R. (1998). *The g factor: The science of mental ability*. Westport, CT: Praeger.

Jirout, J., & Newcombe, N. (2015). Building blocks for the development of spatial skills: Evidence from a large representative US sample. *Psychological Science, 26*(3), 302–310.

Johnson, D. L., Breckenridge, J., & McGowan, R. (1984). Home environment and early cognitive development in Mexican–American children. In A. W. Gottfried (Ed.), *Home environment and early cognitive development: Longitudinal research* (pp. 151–195). Orlando, FL: Academic Press.

Johnson, D. L., Swank, P., Howie, V. M., Baldwin, C. D., Owen, M., & Luttman, D. (1993). Does HOME add to the prediction of child intelligence over and above SES? *Journal of Genetic Psychology, 154*, 33–40.

Johnson, K. M., & Lichter, D. T. (2010). Growing diversity among America's children and youth: Spatial and temporal dimensions. *Population and Development Review, 36*(1), 151–176.

Kaufman, A. S., Zhou, X., Reynolds, M. R., Kaufman, N. L., Green, G. P., & Weiss, L. G. (2014). The possible societal impact of the decrease in US blood levels on adult IQ. *Environmental Research, 132*, 413–420.

Kayser, H. (1989). Speech and language assessment of Spanish–English speaking children. *Language, Speech, & Hearing Services in Schools, 20*, 226–244.

Keith, T. Z., Keith, P. B., Quirk, K. J., Sperduto, J., Santillo, S., & Killings, S. (1998). Longitudinal effects of parent involvement on high school grades: Similarities and differences across gender and ethnic groups. *Journal of School Psychology, 36*, 335–363.

Konold, T. R., & Canivez, G. L. (2010). Differential relationships among WISC-IV and WIAT-II scales: An evaluation of potentially moderating child demographics. *Educational and Psychological Measurement, 70*(4), 613–627.

LaVeist, T. A. (2005). *Minority populations and health: An introduction to health disparities in the United States*. San Francisco, CA: Jossey-Bass.

Lee, J. C., Yin, H., & Zhang, Z. (2010). Adaptations and analyses of motivated strategies for learning questionnaire in the Chinese setting. *International Journal of Testing, 10*(3), 149–165.

Lopez, M. H. (2013). *Hispanic or Latino? Many don't care, except in Texas*. Retrieved May 1, 2014, from http://www.pewresearch.org/fact-tank/2013/10/28/in-texas-its-hispanic-por-favor/.

Cognitive abilities: 100 years after Spearman's (1904) "General Intelligence. Objectively Determined and Measured" (Special section). In D. Lubinski *Journal of Personality and Social Psychology* (86, pp. 96−199).

Mani, A., Mullainathan, S., Shafir, E., & Zhao, J. (2013). Poverty impedes cognitive function. *Science*, *341*(6149), 967−980.

Mantzicopoulos, P. Y. (1997). The relationship of family variables to Head Start's children's preacademic competence. *Early Education & Development*, *8*, 357−375.

Margolin, L. (1994). *Goodness Personified: The emergence of gifted children*. New York: Aldine de Gruyter.

Marjoribanks, K. (1979). *Families and their learning environments: An empirical analysis*. London: Routledge & Kegan Paul.

Marks, J. (2002). Folk heredity. In J. M. Fish (Ed.), *Race and intelligence: Separating science from myth* (pp. 95−112). Mahwah, NJ: Erlbaum.

Martin, A. J. (2008). *The motivation and engagement scale*. Sydney: Lifelong Achievement Group. (www.lifelongachievement.com).

Martin, A. J., & Hau, K. T. (2010). Achievement motivation among Chinese and Australian school students: Assessing differences of kind and differences of degree. *International Journal of Testing*, *10*(3), 274−294.

Massey, D. S. (2007). *Categorically unequal: The American stratification system*. New York: Russell Sage Foundation.

Massey, D. S., & Fischer, M. J. (2000). How segregation concentrates poverty. *Ethnic & Racial Studies*, *23*(4), 670−691. Available from https://doi.org/10.1080/01419870050033676.

Mercer, J. R., & Lewis, J. F. (1978). *System of multicultural pluralistic assessment: Technical Manual*. San Antonio, TX: The Psychological Corporation.

Mollgaard, K., Diamond, M. C., Bennett, E. L., Rosenzweig, M. R., & Lindner, B. (1971). Quantitative synaptic changes with differential experience in rat brain. *International Journal of Neuroscience*, *2*(3), 113−127.

Murray, C. (2005). *The inequality taboo*. Commentary, September, pp. 13−22.

National Center for Education Statistics. (2012). *Digest of education statistics*. Retrieved June 30, 2014, from http://nces.ed.gov/programs/digest/d12/tables_2.asp.

National Center for Education Statistics. (2012a). *Identification of children with disabilities*. Retrieved June 30, 2014, from http://ww2.ed.gov/fund/data/report/idea/partb-spap/2013/.

National Center for Education Statistics. (2012b). http://www2.ed.gov/fund/data/report/idea/partbspap/2013/fl-acc-stateprofile-11-12.pdf.

National Center for Education Statistics. (2012c). http://www2.ed.gov/fund/data/report/idea/partbspap/2013/il-acc-stateprofile-11-12.pdf.

National Center for Education Statistics. (2012d). http://www2.ed.gov/fund/data/report/idea/partbspap/2013/ny-acc-stateprofile-11-12.pdf

Neisser, U. (1998). Introduction: Rising test scores and what they mean. In U. Neisser (Ed.), *The rising curve: Long term gains in IQ and related measures* (pp. 3−22). Washington, DC: American Psychological Association.

Nisbett, R. E. (2009). *Intelligence and how to get it: Why schools and cultures count*. New York: W.W. Norton & Co.

Ong, P. M., & Rickles, J. (2004). The continued nexus between school and residential segregation. *Berkeley La Raza Law Journal*, *15*(1), 260−275.

Orosco, M. J., & Klinger, J. (2010). One school's implementation of RtI with English language learners: "Referring into RtI.". *Journal of Learning Disabilities*, *43*(3), 269−288.

Padilla, Y. C., Boardman, J. D., & Hummer, R. A. (2002). Is the Mexican American "epidemiologic paradox" advantage at birth maintained through early childhood? *Social Forces (University of North Carolina Press)*, *80*(3), 1101−1123. Available from https://doi.org/10.1353/sof.2002.0014.

Parker, F. L., Boak, A. Y., Griffin, K. W., Ripple, C., & Peay, L. (1999). Parent−child relationship, home learning environment, and school readiness. *School Psychology Review*, *28*, 413−425.

Payne, R. K. (2013). *A framework for understanding poverty: A cognitive approach* (5th ed.). Highlands, TX: Aha! Processes, Inc.

Pfeiffer, S., & Jarosewich, T. (2003). *Gifted rating scale*. San Antonio, TX: Harcourt Assessment, Inc.

Pintrich, P. R., Smith, D. A. F., Garcia, T., & McKeachie, W. J. (1993). Reliability and predictive validity of the Motivated Strategies for Learning Questionnaire (MSLQ). *Educational and Psychological Measurement*, *53*, 801−813.

Plomin, R., Mclearn, G. E., Smith, D. L., Skuder, P., Vignetti, S., Chorney, M. J., et al. (1995). Allelic associations between 100 DNA markers and high versus low IQ. *Intelligence*, *21*, 31−48.

Plomin, R., & Petrill, S. A. (1997). Genetics and intelligence: What's new? *Intelligence*, *24*, 53−77.

Poteat, G. M., Wuensch, K. L., & Gregg, N. B. (1988). An investigation of differential prediction with the WISC−R. *Journal of School Psychology*, *26*, 59−68.

Potter, D., Mashburn, A., & Grissmer, D. (2013). The family, neuroscience, and academic skills: An interdisciplinary account of social class gaps in children's test scores. *Social Science Research [serial online]*, *42*(2), 446−464. Available from: Academic Search Complete, Ipswich, MA. Accessed October 27, 2013.

Prince-Embury, S. (2006). *Resiliency scales for children & adolescents*. San Antonio, TX: Pearson.

Prince-Embury, S., & Saklofske, D. H. (Eds.), (2014). *Resilience interventions for youth in diverse populations*. New York: Springer.

Rabiner, D. L., Murray, D., Schmid, L., & Malone, P. (2004). An exploration of the relationship between ethnicity, attention problems and academic achievement. *School Psychology Review*, *33*, 498−600.

Ramey, C., Farran, D. C., & Campbell, F. A. (1979). Predicting IQ from mother−child interactions. *Child Development*, *50*, 804−814.

Reid, J. B., & Patterson, G. R. (1991). Early prevention and intervention with conduct problems: A social interactional model for the integration of research and practice. In G. Stoner, M. R. Shinn, & H. M. Walker (Eds.), *Interventions for achievement and behavior problems* (pp. 715−739). Bethesda, MD: National Association of School Psychologists.

Renzulli, J. S. (1986). The three−ring conception of giftedness: A developmental model for creative productivity. In R. J. Sternberg, & J. E. Davidson (Eds.), *Conceptions of giftedness* (pp. 53−92). New York: Cambridge University Press.

Reschly, D. J., & Reschly, J. E. (1979). Validity of WISC−R factor scores in predicting achievement and attention for four sociocultural groups. *Journal of School Psychology*, *17*, 355−361.

Reschly, D. J., & Saber, D. L. (1979). Analysis of test bias in four groups with the regression definition. *Journal of Educational Measurement*, *16*, 1−9.

Reschly, D. J., & Ward, S. M. (1991). Uses of adaptive behavior measures and overrepresentation of Black students in programs for students with mild mental retardation. *American Journal on Mental Retardation*, *96*, 257−268.

Reynolds, C. R., & Gutkin, T. B. (1980). Stability of the WISC–R factor structure across sex at two age levels. *Journal of Clinical Psychology*, *36*, 775–777.

Reynolds, C. R., & Hartlage, L. C. (1979). Comparison of WISC and WISC–R regression lines for academic prediction with black and white referred children. *Journal of Consulting and Clinical Psychology*, *47*, 589–591.

Rhodes, R. L. (2010). Multicultural school neuropsychology. In D. Miller (Ed.), *Best practices in school neuropsychology: Guidelines for effective practice, assessment, and evidence-based intervention* (pp. 61–77). Hoboken, NJ: John Wiley & Sons.

Rhodes, R. L., Ochoa, S. H., & Ortiz, S. O. (2005). *Assessing culturally and linguistically diverse students: A practical guide*. New York: Guilford Press.

Rice, T., Fulker, D. W., Defries, J. C., & Plomin, R. (1988). Path analysis of IQ during infancy and early childhood and the index of the home environment in the Colorado adoption project. *Behavior Genetics*, *16*, 107–125.

Rios, R., Aiken, L., & Zautra, A. (2012). Neighborhood contexts and the mediating role of neighborhood social cohesion on health and psychological distress among Hispanic and non-Hispanic residents. *Annals of Behavioral Medicine*, *43*(1), 50–61. Available from https://doi.org/10.1007/s12160-011-9306-9.

Ritchie, S. (2015). Does learning to read improve intelligence? A longitudinal multivariate analysis in identical twins from age 7 to 16. *Child Development*, *86*(1), 23–36.

Rosenzweig, M. R. (1996). Aspects of the search for neural mechanisms of memory. *Annual Review of Psychology*, *47*, 1–32. Available from https://doi.org/10.1146/annurev.psych.47.1.1.

Ruggles, S. J., Alexander, T., Genadek, K., Goeken, R., Schroeder, M. B., & Sobek, M. (2010). *Integrated public use microdata series: Version 5.0 [Machine-readable database]* (p. 2010) Minneapolis, MN: University of Minnesota.

Ruiz, J. M., Steffen, P., & Smith, T. B. (2013). Hispanic mortality paradox: A systematic review and meta-analysis of the longitudinal literature. *American Journal of Public Health*, *103*(3), e52–e60. Available from https://doi.org/10.2105/ajph.2012.301103.

Sable, J., & Noel, A. (2008). Public elementary and secondary school student enrollment and staff from the common core of data: School year 2006–07 *(NCES 2009-305)*. Washington, DC: National Center for Education Statistics, Institute of Education Sciences, US Department of Education. Retrieved June 29, 2014, from http://nces.ed.gov/pubsearch/pubsinfo.asp?pubid = 2009305.

Sachs, J., Law, Y. K., Chan, C. K. K., & Rao, N. (2001). A non-parametric item analysis of the motivated strategies for learning questionnaire and the learning process questionnaire. *Psychologia*, *45*, 193–203.

Saklofske, D. H., van de Vijver, F. J. R., Oakland, T., Mpofu, E., & Suszuki, L. A. (2015). Intelligence and culture: History and assessment. In S. Goldstein, J. A. Naglieri, & D. Princiotta (Eds.), *Handbook of intelligence: Evolutionary theory, historical perspective, and current concepts*. New York: Springer.

SAMHSA. (2011). Current statistics on the prevalence and characteristics of people experiencing homelessness in the United States.

Schaefer, B. (2004). A demographic survey of learning behaviors among American students. *School Psychology Review*, *33*, 481–497.

Schmitt, N., Sacco, J. M., Ramey, S., Ramey, C., & Chan, D. (1999). Parental employment, school climate, and children's academic and social development. *Journal of Applied Psychology*, *84*(5), 737–753.

Schwartz, R. S. (2001). Racial profiling in medical research. *New England Journal of Medicine*, *344*, 1392–1393.

Shah, A. K., Mullainathan, S., & Shafir, E. (2012). Some consequences of having too little. *Science, 338*(6107), 682–685.

Sichi, M. (2003). Influence of free−time activities on children's verbal IQ: A look at how the hours a child spends reading, using the computer, and watching TV may affect verbal skills. *Poster session presented at the Texas psychological association conference*, San Antonio, TX.

Spearman, C. (1927). *The abilities of man*. New York: Mcmillan.

Squalli, J., & Wilson, K. (2014). Intelligence, creativity, and innovation. *Intelligence, 46*, 250–257.

Sternberg, R. J. (1997). A triarchic view of giftedness: Theory and practice. In N. Colangelo, & G. A. Davis (Eds.), *Handbook of gifted education* (2nd ed., pp. 43–53). Boston, MA: Allyn & Bacon.

Sternberg, R. J., & Davidson, J. E. (Eds.), (1986). *Conceptions of giftedness*. New York: Cambridge University Press.

Sternberg, R. J., & Grigorenko, E. L. (Eds.), (2002). *The general intelligence factor: How general is it?* Mahwah, NJ: Erlbaum.

Sternberg, R. J., Grigorenko, E. L., & Kidd, K. (2005). Intelligence, race, and genetics. *American Psychologist, 60*, 46–57.

Stoolmiller, M. (1999). Implications of the restricted range of family environments for estimates of heritability and nonshared environment in behavioral genetic adoption studies. *Psychological Bulletin, 125*, 392–409.

Sui-Chu, E., & Williams, J. D. (1996). Effects of parental involvement on eighth−grade achievement. *Sociology of Education, 69*, 126–141.

Swanson, R. A., & Henderson, R. W. (1976). Achieving home−school continuities in the socialization of an academic motive. *Journal of Experimental Education, 44*, 38–44.

Terman, L. M. (1925). *Genetic studies of genius: Vol. 1. Mental and physical traits of a thousand gifted children*. Stanford, CA: Stanford University Press.

The Annie E. Casey Foundation. (2008). *Data on children in foster care from the census bureau*. Baltimore, MD: William P. O'Hare.

Trotman, F. K. (1977). Race, IQ, and the middle class. *Journal of Educational Psychology, 69*, 266–273.

US Census Bureau. (2012). 2012 national population projections, NP2012_D2: Projected births by sex, race, and Hispanic origin for the United States: 2012 to 2060 *2012 National Population Projections*.

US Census Bureau. (2013). Population division, Table 18. Projections of the population by net international migration series, race, and Hispanic origin for the United States: 2015 to 2060 (NP2012-T18). Release Date: May 2013.

US Census Bureau. (2014). History: Index of questions. Retrieved June 1, 2014, from https://www.census.gov/history/www/through_the_decades/index_of_questions/.

US Department of Health and Human Services. (2001). *Head Start FACES: Longitudinal findings on program performance. Third progress report*. Washington, DC: Author.

US Department of Health & Human Services. Administration on Children, Youth & Families. (2013). Recent Demographic Trends in Foster Care. Retrieved from https://www.acf.hhs.gov/sites/default/files/cb/data_brief_foster_care_trends1.pdf.

US Department of Labor. (2014). Employment projects: Earnings and unemployment by educational attainment. Retrieved June 25, 2014, from http://www.bls.gov/emp/ep_chart_001.htm.

van Ast, V. A., Cornelisse, S., Marin, M. F., Ackermann, S., Garfinkel, S. N., & Abercrombie, H. C. (2013). Modulatory mechanisms of cortisol effects on emotional learning and memory: Novel perspectives. *Psychoneuroendocrinology, 38*(9), 1874–1882.

Valencia, R. R. (2010). *Dismantling contemporary thinking: Educational thought and practice.* New York: Routledge.

Valencia, R. R., Henderson, R. W., & Rankin, R. J. (1985). Family status, family constellation, and home environmental variables as predictors of cognitive performance of Mexican–American children. *Journal of Educational Psychology, 77,* 323–331.

Valencia, R. R., & Suzuki, L. A. (2001). *Intelligence testing and minority students: Foundations, performance factors, and assessment issues.* Thousand Oaks, CA: Sage Publications, Inc.

van de Vijver, F. J. R., & Bleichrodt, N. (2001). Conclusies [Conclusions]. In N. Bleichrodt, & F. J. R. van de Vijver (Eds.), Diagnosteik bij allochtonen: Mogelijkheden en heperkingen van psychologische tests *[Diagnosing immigrants: Possibilities and limitations of psychological tests]* (pp. 237–243). Lisse, The Netherlands: Swets.

Vroon, P. A. (1980). Intelligence on myths and measurement. In G. E. Stelmach (Ed.), *Advances in psychology* (3, pp. 27–44). New York: North–Holland.

Walberg, H. J., & Marjoribanks, K. (1976). Family environment and cognitive models. *Review of Educational Research, 76,* 527–551.

Walker, D., Greenwood, C., Hart, B., & Carta, J. (1994). Prediction of school outcomes based on early language production and socioeconomic factors. *Child Development, 65,* 606–621.

Wechsler, D. (2005). *Wechsler intelligence scale for children* (4th ed.). San Antonio, TX: Harcourt Assessment, Inc., Spanish.

Weisner, T. S., Matheson, C., Coots, J., & Bernheimer, L. P. (2005). Sustainability of daily routines as a family outcome. In A. E. Maynard, & M. I. Martini (Eds.), *Learning in cultural context: Family, peers, and school.* New York: Kluwer Academic/Plenum Publishers.

Weiss, L. G. (1997). The MIPS: Gauging the dimensions of normality. In T. Millon (Ed.), *The millon inventories: Clinical and personality assessment.* New York: The Guilford Press.

Weiss, L. G., Harris, J. G., Prifitera, A., Courville, T., Rolfhus, E., Saklofske, D. H., & Holdnack, J. A. (2006). WISC-IV interpretation in societal context. In L. G. Weiss, D. H. Saklofske, A. Prifitera, & J. A. Holdncack (Eds.), *WISC-IV advanced clinical interpretation.* San Diego, CA: Elsevier Science.

Weiss, L. G., & Prifitera, A. (1995). An evaluation of differential prediction of WIAT achievement scores from WISC-III FSIQ across ethnic and gender groups. *Journal of School Psychology, 33*(4).

Weiss, L. G., Prifitera, A., & Roid, G. (1993). The WISC-III and the fairness of predicting achievement across ethnic and gender groups. *Journal of Psychoeducational Assessment,* 35–42. (monograph series, Advances in Psychological Assessment, Wechsler Intelligence Scale for Children–Third Edition).

Weiss, L. G. (2002). Essentials of MIPS assessment. In S. Strack (Ed.), *Essentials of millon inventories assessment* (2nd ed.). New York: John Wiley & Sons, Inc.

Weiss, L. G., Saklofske, D. H., Coalson, D. L., & Raiford, S. E. (2010). *WAIS-IV clinical use and interpretation.* San Diego, CA: Academic Press.

Weiss, L. G., Saklofske, D. H., Prifitera, A., & Holdnack, J. A. (2006). *WISC-IV advanced clinical assessment.* San Diego, CA: Elsevier, Inc.

Winner, E. (1996). *Gifted children: Myths and realities.* New York: Basic Books.

Wolf, R.M. (1964). The identification and measurement of environmental variables related to intelligence (Unpublished doctoral dissertation). University of Chicago.

Chapter 6

Testing Hispanics with WISC-V and WISC-V Spanish

María R. Muñoz[1], Lawrence G. Weiss[2] and Aurelio Prifitera[3]
[1]*Pearson, San Antonio, TX, United States,* [2]*Research and Measurement Consultant, San Antonio, TX, United States,* [3]*Assessment Consultant, San Antonio, TX, United States*

Culturally sensitive assessment of general intelligence and specific cognitive abilities with Spanish-speaking clients is increasingly important in clinical practice. The United States ranks second in the world in number of Hispanics (57.5 million; Flores, 2017) after Mexico (127 million), as of 2016. By 2060 the Hispanic population will have doubled and one of every three US residents will be of Hispanic origin.

It is a complex and multifaceted area of study, and there is no single solution capable of covering all situations. Spanish-speaking clients may share a primary language but represent diverse linguistic and cultural backgrounds. Individuals from different Hispanic cultures vary greatly regarding country of origin; sociopolitical, economic, and educational experiences; religion; and language(s) spoken. Length of residency in the United States (from recently immigrated to multiple generations in the United States), parent ethnicity (Hispanic or other), and family use of Spanish also vary widely among Spanish-speaking clients (Elliott, 2012). Many of these variables affect test taking and, ultimately, test scores. Moreover, these variables in combination with sociological factors may selectively influence the developmental trajectory of specific cognitive abilities in children, particularly verbal abilities, as well as the form of expression of intelligent behavior in adolescents. Although there are numerous important issues related to competent psychological assessment of culturally and linguistically diverse clients we restrict our focus in this chapter to the issues that are unique or critical to the intellectual assessment of Hispanics living in the United States. Thus, this chapter should be considered in context with more comprehensive texts on the subject of multicultural assessment (Geisinger, 2014; Rhodes, 2010; Rhodes, Ochoa, & Ortiz, 2005; Suzuki & Ponterotto, 2007).

WISC-V. DOI: https://doi.org/10.1016/B978-0-12-815744-2.00006-9

197

We realize that some of the terminology for ethnic groups is controversial, and there is a wide variety of opinion regarding which term is best. We have used the term Hispanic as it appears to be the most current in the literature. Although Latino/a is gaining in prominence, it is not yet as preferred as Hispanic according to research conducted by the Pew Research Center (Lopez, 2013).

When assessing intelligence with Hispanic clients, it is important to acknowledge the incremental improvement in US school performance observed as acculturation increases (Lopez, Ehly, & Garcia-Vazquez, 2002). Experience in US schools may be associated with variables known to affect cognitive performance, such as exposure to new learning opportunities and novel intellectual stimulation, and positive changes in socioeconomic environment. Formal education conveys cultural information and conventions for thinking and categorization skills, all of which may affect both verbal and nonverbal test performance. Customs concerning verbal communication may evolve through exposure to US culture and educational settings. For some immigrants, prior experiences with formal education and acculturation may have been limited due to geographic constraints, economic barriers, or sociopolitical constraints affecting access to high-quality educational resources. Experience with the testing situation and acquisition of test-taking skills is likely to have a positive influence on the individual's performance on cognitive assessments. Moreover, experience with US educational culture is likely to facilitate the development of bilingual skills in native Spanish speakers, which may influence performance on cognitive tests. For example, some research suggests that bilingual children may exhibit greater inhibitory control and executive functioning skills relative to monolingual children (Carlson & Meltzoff, 2008; Bialystok, 2016). Younger Hispanic children acquiring a second language (in this case, English) may take 5–7 years, on average, to approach grade level in academic areas (Ramirez, 1991). Establishing rapport within formal assessment situations involving clients from different cultures cannot be emphasized enough. As elaborated by Elliott (2012), individuals from diverse backgrounds, especially children who face unfamiliar adults in unfamiliar test situations, may be more reluctant to interact and perform at their best. Under some circumstances, parents may be confused or suspicious about the purpose and use of the testing, and directly or indirectly communicate their discomfort to them. Although no such research exists on the topic, clinicians typically report that these concerns increase during periods when the US government increases enforcement of immigration policies, or creates more restrictive policies. Such anxieties could potentially compromise the child's performance and the validity of the evaluation. Testing may be especially stressful for Hispanic clients residing in the United States without documented residency, who may be fearful of any scrutiny by persons in positions of perceived authority. Examiners must be sensitive to these issues. It may be necessary to meet with children and parents over extended periods of time to build rapport and clarify the nature and purpose of an evaluation, the confidential nature of the evaluations, the purposes for which the results will be utilized, what other agencies may have access to the results, and clarify the separation between government immigration agencies and public schools or clinics where the evaluation may be taking place. Such extended effort is well worthwhile as most parents, regardless of immigration status, are very interested in how well their children are adjusting and learning in school.

As Elliott (2012) observes, the issue of what language to test a child in is a critical question. However, the concept of dominant language may be losing favor as proficiency in two languages occurs on a continuum, with bilingual individuals being able to understand or express some concepts better in one language and other concepts in the other language. Proficiency can shift based on context, with some individuals being able to speak fluently about one topic in one language and other topics in the second language. This is especially true for children learning Spanish first as a home language, then English in school. Practitioners should consider the influence of school experience and secondary language acquisition on test performance, but there is no single best way of taking these issues into account because of the myriad of potential influences. For example, types of bilingual programs vary greatly and differentially impact the trajectory of second language acquisition, as does age of first introduction to bilingual programming, and all of these factors interact in known and unknown ways with parental education and community variables.

In this chapter, we focus first on issues related to appropriate use of the Wechsler Intelligence Scale for Children—Fifth Edition (WISC-V) with Hispanic clients who speak English, or both English and Spanish. Then, we review issues related to testing Spanish-speaking clients in Spanish with the WISC-V US Spanish edition (Wechsler, 2017).

TESTING HISPANICS WITH WISC-V

The WISC-V normative samples included culturally and linguistically diverse individuals who were judged by the examiner to speak English well enough to take the test. Most Wechsler norms include Hispanic subjects who speak some Spanish if their English language skills were considered by the examiner to be better than Spanish and adequate for assessment purposes. Clearly, the decision to assess a Spanish-speaking client in English must be made based on numerous factors including but not limited to language spoken as a child or adolescent, years of school in English language classrooms, languages spoken at home and, for older adolescents, languages spoken at work. Such a decision should carefully consider these factors in each case, and not be made based on the preference of the examiner, nor only due to lack of an available Spanish-speaking examiner. Optimally, this decision would be made by an examiner from the same cultural background or at least very experienced with the client's cultural and linguistic background. Further, results of assessments administered in English should be interpreted with caution when there is concern about the child's English language skills. In this section, we provide some data to encourage a more culturally sensitive interpretation of Wechsler intelligence tests administered in English to Hispanic clients who speak English.

The WISC-V normative sample was stratified to represent the US population by race/ethnicity for most groups of Hispanics. Thus, the same percentage of Hispanics is included in the sample as in the population. Because the percentage of US Hispanics has increased over the generations, and differs by US region, the research team carefully matched the Census data for Hispanics at each age band and within each region. In this way, the regional distribution of Hispanics from different countries of origin was represented. Most importantly, the parents' educational attainment for Hispanic children included in the normative sample was carefully matched to the distribution of educational attainment of Hispanics in the population.

The WISC-V yields a Full-Scale Intelligence Quotient (FSIQ), and five Index scores: Verbal Comprehension (VCI), Visual Spatial (VSI), Working Memory (WMI), Fluid Reasoning (FRI), and Processing Speed (PSI). Mean WISC-V FSIQ and Index scores for Hispanics are shown in Table 6.1. The mean scores ranged from 94.2 to 98.3. The lowest and highest mean scores were for VCI and PSI, respectively, which is the same pattern observed in WISC-IV (Weiss, Prifitera, & Muñoz, 2016). Some might argue that these means should be 100. They may say that it is possible that these means are depressed to the extent that some individuals tested did not, in fact, speak English well enough to take the test. While there is no direct way to test this hypothesis with these data, bilingual research assistants carefully reviewed every verbal item response from each individual child to identify and eliminate those who exhibited a preponderance of responses in Spanish—although occasional responses in Spanish were accepted, and thus may be accepted in practice. One might also think that biased items were a contributing factor. However, due to the use of expert item bias review panels combined with the advanced statistical techniques for detecting differential item functioning by group that is in routine use by most major test developers these days, item bias is unlikely to contribute substantially to the lower scores observed for Hispanics (see Chapter 6: Testing Hispanics with WISC-V and WISC-V Spanish for further discussion).

It is more likely that these differences are due to the overall parent educational level of the Hispanic sample. For example, we know that the correlation of education with the FSIQ is 0.53 for adults (Weiss, Chen, Harris, Holdnack, & Saklofske, 2010). Table 6.2 shows mean FSIQ scores of all children by level of parent education. As expected, children of more educated parents have higher test scores. The differences are dramatic, ranging

TABLE 6.1 WISC-V Index Score Means for Hispanic Sample

Index	Mean
Primary Indices	
VCI	94.2
VSI	96.8
FRI	95.6
WMI	94.9
PSI	98.3
FSIQ	94.4
Ancillary Indices	
GAI	94.5
CPI	95.8
NVI	95.5
QRI	94.9
AWMI	94.5
Complementary Indices	
NSI	96.9
STI	95.3
SRI	95.2

Note: $N = 458$.
Source: Data and table Copyright Pearson 2014.

TABLE 6.2 Mean WISC-V FSIQ Scores by Parent Education Level

	FSIQ
8th grade or less	88.2
9th–11th grade	89.4
High school graduate	91.7
Some college	97.3
College graduate	105.0

Note: $N = 2200$. Individuals with a GED are included as high school graduates. College graduates are considered as 16 or more years of education.
Source: Data and table Copyright Pearson 2014.

TABLE 6.3 Percentage of Adults Who Did Not Complete High School Versus Those Who Obtained at Least 1 Year of College

	High School Not Completed (%)	Obtained At Least 1 Year of College (%)
Hispanic	31	43
African American	12	62
White	4	78
Asian	8	78

Note: Individuals obtaining a GED are considered to have completed high school. Based on data from the US Census Bureau's 2012 *American Community Survey* 1-year period estimates.

from 88 to 105 FSIQ points between children of the least and most educated parents. We also know that the average level of education of Hispanics is substantially less than all other racial/ethnic groups. Table 6.3 shows percentages of educational attainment by group. Hispanic adults who are the parents of WISC-V age children have a much larger high school dropout rate (31%) and smaller rate of college entrance (43%) than any other major ethnic group—by far! It should also be mentioned that the mean educational attainment of Hispanics differs significantly between subgroups (e.g., Cuban, Mexican, Puerto Rican).

What is most notable, however, is how the Hispanic dropout rate has declined in the last decade. In the early 2000s, the percentage of Hispanic children ages 6−16 who had parents with less than a high school diploma was 47%. By 2012 it had dropped to 33.5%. This large decrease in the dropout rate represents positive change in educational attainment for the Hispanic population. Yet, the Hispanic dropout rate remains substantially higher than all other groups.

Given the large educational disparities between racial/ethnic groups, and the robust correlation between education and intelligence test scores, somewhat lower mean FSIQ scores might be expected in the Hispanic samples. The mean WISC-V FSIQ scores for Hispanic Children is 94.4, as shown in Table 6.1. This finding is most likely because samples of Hispanics with generally low educational attainment are being compared to a larger US normative sample with significantly more education on average. If the test performance of Hispanic children was normed relative to a sample of children with the same level of parent educational—regardless of ethnicity—the mean Hispanic FSIQ would be almost identical to 100, as described below and in the Societal Context (Chapter 5 in this book). While some might consider that a fairer approach, we must keep in mind that such an education-adjusted score would tell us nothing about how an individual might be able to succeed in a world made up of largely more educated people. For better or worse, the accepted definition of intelligence involves performance relative to the full population within the country of interest.

To better understand the societal factors underlying these score patterns, Weiss et al. (2006) undertook a systematic investigation of the factors that influence FSIQ scores for Hispanics based on variables available in the WISC-IV standardization data. We showed that ethnicity explained 1.4% of the variance in Hispanic/White FSIQ score differences, whereas 17.5% of the variance was explained by the parents' education level. Parent income added an additional 3.5% above parent education. More to the point, after controlling for both parent education and income, ethnicity explained no further variance and the magnitude of the difference between Hispanic and White WISC-IV FSIQ scores was reduced to 0.5 points.

We subsequently repeated the above investigation using WISC-V data (see Chapter 5: WISC-V Use in Societal Context in this book), and found ethnicity alone explained 3.0% of the variance in Hispanic/White FSIQ score differences, whereas 18.8% of the variance was explained by a combination of the parent education level and income. After controlling for these socio-economic variables, ethnicity alone explained no further variance, and the magnitude of the difference between Hispanic and White WISC-V FSIQ scores was reduced 0.9 points. Additionally, we found that Hispanic children in dual-parent households obtained mean FSIQ scores approximately four points higher than Hispanic children in single-parent families (see Chapter 5: WISC-V Use in Societal Context for details).

These findings are reinforced by a multinational study that demonstrated a strong relationship between economic factors and education on WISC-III test scores across 12 nations (Georgas, Weiss, van de Vijver, & Saklofske, 2003). The reader is referred to Chapter 7 of this book for a discussion of international cross cultural issues with respect to WISC-V.

Given all of the above findings, one might expect to see a trend toward higher Hispanic FSIQ scores across generations as children of Hispanic immigrants assimilate into the new culture, gain access to and achieve more education or better paying jobs, and advance in socioeconomic status. Weiss et al. (2010) examined this hypothesis and found it largely supported. We found that average WAIS-IV FSIQ scores (which are age corrected) for Hispanics have increased by eight points from 85 for those born between 1917 and 1942 to 93 for those born between 1988 and 1991, although the trend did not steadily increase across all birth cohorts.

Thus, we put forth a strong body of research evidence covering three editions of the WISC and multiple generations of children and adults (Georgas, et al., 2003; Weiss et al., 2006; Weiss et al., 2010; Weiss et al., 2014), which supports a consistent conclusion: ethnic status is likely a proxy variable for a host of other environmental variables that are more directly related to FSIQ, and when controlling for those variables, ethnicity directly accounts for very little, if any, of the variance in test scores. We should seek to understand better the underlying societal variables responsible for these differences and cease focus on the surface variable of group membership. To this end, we strongly refer the reader to the Chapter 5, WISC-V Use in Societal Context in this book where we elaborate how racial/ethnic differences in education, occupation, income, and physical and mental health status combine to impact the cognitive development of children.

Yet, test scores are not completely determined by societal variables. As mentioned above, individual differences in ability likely account for the largest share of the variance, and noncognitive factors such as achievement motivation are important to cognitive development as well. For children and adolescents, home environment and parental behavior toward children are particularly important in terms of enhancing or impeding children's cognitive development (see Chapter 5: WISC-V Use in Societal Context). *This is because even naturally endowed cognitive abilities must grow and develop over time and require proper doses of nurturance and cognitive stimulation at the right time in the developmental sequence.* To begin to test this idea, Weiss, et al. (2014) asked parents some very basic questions related to the role of education in the family including how likely they believed it was that their child would get good grades, graduate high school, attend college, etc. Surprisingly, we found that these questions explained 26% of the variance in WISC-V FSIQ scores—more than parent education and income combined at 22%. We then controlled for parent education and income and found that parent expectations still explained 11% of the variance in FSIQ scores (see Chapter 5: WISC-V Use in Societal Context for full discussion). These results are consistent with our prior research on WISC-IV (Weiss, et al., 2006). Thus, although the explanatory power of parent expectations reduces by more than half after controlling for parent education and income, the size of the remaining effect is still meaningful. Parents with high expectations for the educational attainment of their children may engage in a wide range of parenting behaviors broadly related to academic and cognitive development such as monitoring and assisting with homework, encouraging exploration, providing meaningful verbal stimulation that improves language development, reading to children and encouraging reading, etc. This finding is supported by the work of Dweck (2012), who has shown that individuals who believe that intelligence can increase based on effort tend to score higher on measures of IQ.

Parent expectations were significantly related to children's FSIQ scores at all levels of parent education, but more so among parents with high school educations, and least among parents who did not graduate from high school. We interpret these findings in the context of distal environmental constraints on proximal attitudes and behaviors in the home environment. It may be that real societal and economic factors constrain the power of parent expectations among the lowest SES families. Still, parent expectations as expressed through parenting behaviors in the home environment remain a powerful force on the cognitive development of children in all families.

HISPANIC BASE RATES FOR WISC-V

With this background firmly in mind, we believe that it is also useful in clinical practice to have a sense of how a client compares to others of the same ethnicity and with similar educational backgrounds. For this reason, we provide new Hispanic percentile norms for WISC-V, stratified by the educational distribution of Hispanics living in the United States in this chapter. *The Hispanic base rates supplement information derived from the FSIQ, but do not replace the FSIQ. Thus, whenever the Hispanic percentile norms are reported they should be clearly identified as such, and the standard FSIQ and percentile should also be reported.*

Hispanic percentile norms for the WISC-V primary, ancillary, and complementary Index scores are provided in Tables 6.4A and 6.4B, respectively. These tables can be used to determine how a child's score compares to other Hispanic children. For example, a WISC-V VCI score of 85 would be at the 26th percentile compared to other Hispanics, whereas the WISC-V norms tables in the Administration and Scoring Manual show that a score of 85 is at the 16th percentile compared to the general population. Both pieces of information are useful. The Hispanic percentile norms provide more culturally specific information to supplement interpretation of test scores.

Tables 6.5A and 6.5B show base rates of WISC-V Index score discrepancies for primary, ancillary, and complementary Index scores, respectively. Inspection of the mean differences by direction reveals that most Hispanic children and adolescents show a pattern of lower VCI, FRI, and WMI scores, with higher VSI and PSI scores compared to the mean of their own Index scores. At the same time, some Hispanic children show the opposite pattern. For example, 22% of the Hispanic sample obtained VCI scores five or more points *higher* than their mean Index score. The pattern of slightly higher PSI scores is somewhat surprising given common clinical lore that speed of performance is a characteristic of US culture not completely shared by all other cultures. While this might be true as a cultural value, the present data suggest no differences in the speed of neurocognitive information processing abilities. This finding is the same pattern as that observed for Hispanic adults on the Wechsler Adult Intelligence Scale—Fourth Edition (WAIS-IV) (Weiss et al., 2010), and for Hispanic children on the WISC-III (Georgas et al., 2003), and WISC-IV (Weiss et al., 2006).

These data are important because they may help prevent overinterpretation of low VCI scores when such scores are in fact relatively common among Hispanics. At the same time, however, some psychologists may tend to overlook even very low verbal scores in Hispanic children on the assumption that such patterns are common due to language variations. The

TABLE 6.4A Percentile Norms From WISC-V Hispanic Sample for the Primary Index Scores

Obtained Score	FSIQ	VCI	VSI	FRI	WMI	PSI
≤ 70	1.1	1.6	1.2	1.2	1.6	1.3
71	2.5	3.8	2.9	2.7	3.5	2.8
72	3.1	4.7	3.9	3.4	3.9	3.3
73	3.5	5.6	4.7	4.0	4.6	3.7
74	4.0	6.8	5.4	4.5	5.6	4.2
75	5.0	8.2	6.0	5.6	6.9	4.6
76	6.2	9.6	6.7	7.1	8.6	5.7
77	7.3	11.2	7.5	8.6	10.2	7.4
78	9.0	13.1	8.3	10.0	11.9	9.0
79	10.9	14.6	9.1	11.5	13.6	10.3
80	12.3	15.9	9.9	13.0	15.5	11.6
81	13.8	17.3	10.7	14.6	17.8	12.8
82	15.2	19.0	11.9	16.2	20.1	13.9
83	17.3	21.2	13.3	18.3	22.7	15.0
84	20.0	23.4	14.8	20.7	25.7	16.5
85	22.5	26.4	17.2	23.2	28.6	18.6
86	26.0	30.4	20.6	25.8	31.6	20.6
87	29.7	33.6	23.5	28.4	34.5	22.4
88	33.3	36.2	26.1	31.0	37.4	23.9
89	37.1	38.9	28.6	33.9	40.3	25.4
90	39.4	41.9	31.5	37.0	43.1	27.6
91	40.5	45.4	34.6	40.1	46.0	30.2
92	43.3	48.9	37.7	43.2	48.8	32.9
93	47.3	52.0	41.8	46.2	51.5	35.6
94	50.6	54.7	46.8	49.2	54.3	38.2
95	53.8	57.4	50.8	52.5	56.9	40.8
96	57.3	60.1	53.7	56.1	59.4	44.0
97	60.8	62.9	56.6	59.8	61.9	47.7
98	63.5	65.7	59.3	62.7	64.2	51.4

(Continued)

TABLE 6.4A (Continued)

Obtained Score	FSIQ	VCI	VSI	FRI	WMI	PSI
99	65.4	68.8	61.7	65.1	66.3	54.9
100	67.3	72.4	64.1	67.4	68.4	58.0
101	69.9	75.0	66.8	69.7	70.6	60.9
102	72.7	76.6	69.9	71.9	73.0	63.4
103	75.7	78.2	72.5	74.2	75.4	66.0
104	78.2	79.9	74.7	76.1	77.3	69.1
105	80.0	81.6	76.9	77.7	78.7	72.8
106	82.1	83.2	79.0	79.3	80.1	75.8
107	84.2	84.9	81.1	81.2	81.4	78.2
108	86.5	86.7	83.2	83.2	82.8	80.5
109	88.7	87.9	84.9	85.2	84.2	82.5
110	90.0	88.7	86.2	86.8	85.6	84.1
111	91.1	89.4	87.6	87.9	87.0	85.7
112	92.1	90.2	88.9	89.0	88.5	87.1
113	93.1	91.1	90.3	90.2	89.7	88.2
114	94.0	91.9	91.7	91.5	90.5	89.4
115	94.7	92.8	92.8	92.8	91.3	90.8
116	95.1	93.7	93.6	93.9	92.3	92.4
117	95.5	94.6	94.4	94.7	93.5	93.6
118	96.0	95.6	95.1	95.5	95.1	94.3
119	96.2	97.0	95.7	96.9	97.0	95.1
≥ 120	98.1	98.9	98.0	98.9	98.9	97.7

Source: Data and table Copyright Pearson 2014.

tables presented here provide culturally specific data to aid in these interpretations. As shown in the Table 6.5a, a VCI score that is 11 or more points below the child's own mean could be considered unusual because it was obtained by about 15% of the Hispanic sample who were tested with the WISC-V in English. VCI scores may even be more depressed in children with lower English proficiency. In clinical practice, such findings should be interpreted in the context of the child's overall ability, years of education in English-speaking schools, language dominance, and parents' level of education.

TABLE 6.4B Percentile Norms from WISC-V Hispanic Sample for the Ancillary Index Scores

Obtained Score	GAI	CPI	NVI	QRI	AWMI	NSI	STI	SRI
≤ 70	0.9	1.5	1.0	1.4	2.5	3.5	2.7	3.6
71	2.0	3.3	2.3	3.4	5.3	7.0	5.9	7.3
72	2.6	3.7	2.8	4.5	5.8	7.2	6.6	7.8
73	3.8	4.0	3.2	5.5	6.3	7.4	7.4	8.6
74	5.4	4.5	3.4	6.3	7.0	7.9	8.7	9.7
75	6.9	4.9	3.8	7.2	7.9	8.3	9.6	11.5
76	8.1	6.4	4.4	8.4	8.7	9.2	10.2	13.1
77	9.3	8.2	5.1	9.8	9.5	10.2	11.6	13.7
78	10.6	8.8	6.1	11.1	10.3	11.0	13.2	14.4
79	12.1	10.4	7.4	12.5	11.7	12.7	14.4	16.2
80	13.7	12.2	9.6	13.8	13.8	14.5	15.5	17.8
81	14.7	13.5	11.6	15.5	15.8	15.5	16.6	18.8
82	16.8	15.8	12.5	17.5	18.0	17.1	18.3	20.2
83	19.4	18.5	13.5	20.0	20.3	19.3	20.3	22.5
84	21.8	20.6	15.0	22.8	22.6	20.9	22.4	24.1
85	24.5	23.5	18.2	25.7	25.3	23.0	24.8	26.3
86	27.0	26.3	22.7	28.7	28.4	25.4	27.1	28.5
87	30.1	28.3	26.0	31.9	31.4	27.3	29.6	30.7
88	33.3	30.5	28.7	35.1	35.4	28.8	32.0	33.4
89	35.7	33.0	31.4	37.7	40.2	31.8	35.9	36.0
90	37.8	35.4	33.9	39.7	43.7	35.6	40.1	38.4
91	39.7	37.7	37.0	41.8	45.9	37.7	42.5	41.4
92	43.5	41.1	41.6	44.4	48.0	39.5	44.5	45.0
93	47.3	44.6	45.4	47.5	51.0	42.3	46.8	47.8
94	49.2	47.3	47.4	50.6	54.9	44.4	49.3	51.3
95	52.5	50.2	49.8	53.4	58.2	47.4	51.8	53.9
96	55.7	53.1	52.7	55.9	60.9	50.2	53.5	55.8
97	57.6	56.1	56.4	58.4	63.7	51.3	54.9	58.4

(Continued)

TABLE 6.4B (Continued)

Obtained Score	GAI	CPI	NVI	QRI	AWMI	NSI	STI	SRI
98	60.5	59.2	61.0	61.1	66.1	53.0	57.6	60.9
99	64.3	62.1	64.6	64.1	68.2	56.1	61.1	63.1
100	67.4	65.0	66.8	67.1	70.3	59.9	63.7	64.6
101	69.9	68.0	70.0	69.9	72.3	63.4	65.5	67.4
102	72.5	71.1	73.5	72.7	74.2	66.5	67.6	70.9
103	75.3	73.8	76.2	75.5	76.1	68.6	69.3	72.5
104	78.4	76.0	78.1	77.8	78.0	70.7	71.3	74.1
105	82.1	77.9	79.2	79.6	79.7	73.1	73.6	76.1
106	84.6	79.5	80.9	81.4	81.4	75.8	75.4	77.4
107	85.5	81.1	82.6	83.2	83.4	78.0	77.2	78.7
108	87.0	82.5	83.7	85.0	85.4	79.0	79.2	80.2
109	88.5	84.5	85.7	86.9	86.9	79.8	80.8	82.1
110	89.3	86.3	87.6	88.5	87.8	80.9	83.1	83.7
111	89.7	87.3	88.9	90.0	88.7	82.2	85.2	85.6
112	90.6	88.2	90.1	91.4	89.7	83.7	85.9	87.3
113	92.0	88.9	90.9	92.9	90.9	85.4	86.9	88.2
114	92.9	89.9	91.7	94.4	91.8	86.7	88.4	89.1
115	93.1	90.8	92.7	95.3	92.4	88.2	89.5	90.0
116	93.7	91.7	93.3	95.6	92.9	89.5	90.5	90.8
117	94.4	92.9	94.1	95.9	93.6	90.9	91.8	91.4
118	95.9	94.1	95.0	96.5	94.4	92.5	92.6	92.0
119	97.7	94.8	95.6	97.2	95.2	93.6	93.2	93.0
≥120	99.2	97.6	97.9	98.8	97.8	96.9	96.8	96.7

Source: Data and table Copyright Pearson 2014.

TESTING SPANISH-SPEAKING CLIENTS

The WISC-V Spanish (Wechsler, 2014) is a translation and adaptation of WISC-V for use with Spanish-speaking Hispanic children ages 6—16 living in the United States. The transadaptation of each item and all subtest directions were reviewed by a panel of expert bilingual psychologists and researchers representing most Hispanic countries of origin included in the

TABLE 6.5A Base Rates of WISC-V Hispanic Sample Obtaining Various Index–Mean Index Score (MIS) Discrepancies

Amount of Discrepancy	VCI–MIS		VSI–MIS		FRI–MIS		WMI–MIS		PSI–MIS	
	VCI > MIS	VCI < MIS	VSI > MIS	VSI < MIS	FRI > MIS	FRI < MIS	WMI > MIS	WMI < MIS	PSI > MIS	PSI < MIS
≥20	0.9	2.4	1.5	1.1	1.5	1.3	1.8	1.1	6.6	1.5
19	1.7	2.8	2.0	1.1	1.5	2.0	2.2	1.3	8.1	2.4
18	2.6	4.1	3.3	1.3	2.6	2.4	2.6	2.2	9.6	3.7
17	3.1	5.5	4.1	2.0	3.5	3.1	2.8	3.7	11.1	5.2
16	3.7	7.0	4.1	2.8	4.1	4.1	4.2	4.6	12.9	5.9
15	3.7	8.3	4.6	3.9	4.4	5.9	5.3	6.1	14.6	7.6
14	5.5	9.8	5.9	4.8	5.9	7.2	7.2	8.8	17.5	8.7
13	6.1	11.1	9.0	5.9	6.8	8.5	7.9	11.2	19.7	9.4
12	6.6	12.9	11.1	6.6	7.4	10.9	10.1	12.9	21.2	11.6
11	8.1	15.5	12.7	8.5	9.4	13.1	11.8	15.3	23.1	13.1
10	10.5	17.7	15.1	10.9	12.0	16.4	12.7	19.0	25.5	14.6
9	11.8	21.0	17.5	15.1	14.2	18.6	13.6	22.5	27.5	17.9
8	14.8	25.1	20.5	16.4	16.8	21.2	16.4	26.0	31.4	20.1
7	16.4	28.8	24.2	18.3	22.3	24.0	19.5	30.4	33.6	22.1

6	20.3	32.8	28.2	22.1	25.1	26.0	22.8	33.9	37.3	25.3
5	21.6	35.6	32.5	25.5	29.9	31.0	25.6	37.0	42.6	29.0
4	25.5	41.0	37.1	29.7	33.0	34.3	30.4	41.4	45.0	31.7
3	28.8	45.4	43.2	34.3	36.5	38.4	33.3	45.1	48.5	34.9
2	33.8	51.5	46.5	37.1	40.6	41.9	37.0	49.5	52.2	38.6
1	37.3	57.0	52.0	43.7	48.5	47.4	42.0	54.3	55.0	41.7
Mean	7.1	7.7	7.3	6.7	6.7	7.6	7.5	7.9	10.6	8.4
SD	5.5	5.7	5.2	5.1	5.1	5.4	5.9	5.1	7.9	5.8
Median	6.0	7.0	6.0	6.0	6.0	7.0	6.0	7.0	8.5	7.0

Source: Data and table Copyright Pearson 2014.

TABLE 6.5B Base Rates of WISC-V Hispanic Sample Obtaining Various Discrepancies Between Ancillary Composites

Amount of Discrepancy	GAI–CPI		WMI–AWMI		NSI–STI	
	GAI > CPI	GAI < CPI	WMI > AWMI	WMI < AWMI	NSI > STI	NSI < STI
≥20	4.6	7.9	1.1	0.7	12.1	8.9
19	5.3	9.0	1.1	0.7	13.6	10.5
18	6.1	9.4	2.0	1.5	15.0	11.4
17	8.3	11.8	2.2	1.8	17.0	13.4
16	9.2	12.9	3.5	2.2	19.4	14.7
15	10.5	14.7	3.7	3.3	20.1	15.2
14	12.3	16.6	3.9	3.7	21.4	17.0
13	14.2	18.8	6.1	4.4	23.4	19.6
12	16.6	21.2	7.7	7.2	26.1	22.1
11	18.4	23.4	8.5	7.9	28.1	23.7
10	21.0	26.7	11.4	9.6	31.5	25.0
9	23.2	29.8	13.8	13.1	34.2	27.5
8	24.1	31.1	15.8	16.8	35.7	29.7
7	28.9	34.4	20.4	19.9	37.3	31.0
6	30.2	37.4	25.2	23.0	40.0	34.6

5	34.1	41.4	27.4	25.8	43.1	36.6
4	37.2	42.7	34.1	29.8	46.9	37.9
3	40.5	44.9	37.2	35.0	50.0	39.3
2	42.2	47.7	43.3	39.6	52.2	41.5
1	45.5	51.4	50.5	43.3	53.8	42.6
Mean	10.0	11.3	6.4	6.7	14.0	14.0
SD	7.0	8.2	5.1	4.6	11.6	10.7
Median	9.0	10.0	5.0	6.0	11.0	12.0

Source: Data and table Copyright Pearson 2014.

sample. To assess further the quality of the items across Hispanic cultures, each item was submitted to multiple procedures for identifying differential item functioning (i.e., item bias) among Hispanic children from different countries of origin, and in comparison to children in the WISC-V (English) sample. Children were excluded from the sample if they reported speaking or understanding English better than Spanish, if Spanish wasn't the primary language of the household, or if they had been in US schools more than five consecutive years. Children with intellectual disability were excluded if they had been in US schools more than seven consecutive years.

As part of the standardization research project, 220 US Hispanic Spanish-speaking children were tested in Spanish and this sample was used together with the WISC-V English normative sample ($N = 2200$) to equate scores on the Spanish version to the full US sample. The Spanish-speaking sample included children from Mexico (58.6%), the Caribbean (21.4%), and other countries in Central and South America (20%). All children were residing in the United States including Puerto Rico[1] ($\sim 20\%$) when tested. Care was taken to ensure the US/Mexican population was undersampled relative to census percentages to ensure that a sufficient number of participants from other Hispanic countries of origin were represented in the sample.

The WISC-V Spanish was designed to produce scores equivalent to the WISC-V. Thus, children can take the test in Spanish and obtain scores that directly compare them to a representative sample of all children in the US population. Because subtest adaptations for the VSI, FRI, and PSI were restricted to translation of instructions to the child, the norms for these subtests were adopted directly from the WISC-V. However, the WISC-V US norms could not be applied directly to the VCI and WMI subtests because these tasks required greater modifications from the original. Adaptation of verbal subtests obviously required changes to item content, item order, and scoring rules—all of which impact item difficulty. Perhaps less obviously, adaptations to the WMI subtests were required because the phonological representation of numbers in Spanish is different than English in length, which impacts working memory demands and thus item difficulty. Aligning the verbal and working memory subtests distributions to the US norms was accomplished through Item Response Theory (IRT) and conventional equi-percentile equating methods (Elliott, 2012; Kolen & Brennan, 2004: Mardell & Goldenber, 2011; Woodcock, 2011).

To verify the precision and accuracy of the norms obtained by these methods, the norms were applied to independent samples of participants with Mild Intellectual Disability (IDMI) and High Cognitive Ability (HCA), as well as demographically matched nonclinical English-speaking and

---

1. Testing in Puerto Rico concluded well before the unfortunate devastation caused by hurricane Maria in 2017; thus, children tested were not experiencing the traumatic stress that may have resulted from this event.

WISC-IV Spanish samples. The 220 participants in the WISC-V Spanish sample were matched to participants who took WISC-V on parent education level. The mean FSIQ was 91.4 and 92.7 for the WISC-V Spanish and WISC-V samples, respectively, and the effect size of the difference was small (0.10). A limitation of this study is that it was not possible to match the US sample to the Spanish sample on years of US education as all of the education of the US sample was in the United States.

A subsample of 83 participants took the WISC-V Spanish and WISC-IV Spanish in counterbalanced order. The correlation between FSIQs was high at $r = 0.89$, with the means being 94 and 95.8, respectively, and a small effect size (-0.13). The lower mean on the newer test is expected due to the Flynn effect (see Chapter 8: The Flynn Effect and its Clinical Implications in this book) and the construct differences contributing to FSIQ by the various broad abilities.

When the equated norms were applied to the IDMI and HCA samples, results were as expected. All composite scores showed significant differences with moderate to large effect sizes. For instance, the mean FSIQ for the IDMI sample was 58, whereas the matched sample obtained a mean FSIQ of 85.9, and a large effect size (2.32). The mean FSIQ of the HCA sample was 115.6, while the mean for the matched sample was 95.3, and also had a large effect size (-1.63). The fact that these samples obtained scores in the expected ranges and with appropriate effect sizes strongly supports the validity of the norms.

The Spanish versions of the WISC in the United States have always attempted to help the user answer two clinical questions: (1) how the child compares to all his or her age peers in the United States, and (2) how the child compares to only those age peers who share a Hispanic cultural and linguistic background. The first question is answered via equated-to-US norms. This is necessary because children in the US school system are held to the same standards, regardless of the language they speak or where they come from. The second question is necessary from an applied point of view to assess at least indirectly the impact of noncognitive factors (such as culture and language) on the WISC Spanish scores. This question is answered using the adjusted verbal scores on the WISC-V Spanish.

During the research phases of the WISC-V Spanish, additional information was gathered regarding distal, intermediate, and proximal variables related to a bilingual child's use of L1 and L2. Distal variables included questions about country of origin and community support for one language or the other, intermediate variables included education factors such as number of years attending school inside versus outside the United States, and proximal variables include factors related to the language used at home and school, by neighbors and close friends, etc. Taken together, these variables indicate the degree of support of Spanish language development in the child's environment. The answers to these questions were analyzed and those factors identified as significant predictors of performance on the verbal subtests were added to a final regression equation used to provide adjusted verbal comprehension scores at the subtest and index levels.

While the equated norms allow the clinician to make statements such as, *the child scored at the Nth percentile compared to all other children of the same age in the United States*, the adjusted scores allow the clinician to make statements such as, *the child's performance on verbal comprehension tasks in Spanish is above/below what's expected given the amount of support for Spanish language in the child's environment.*

Case Vignette

Consider for example, the case of Óscar, a 7-year 11-month student being evaluated for a potential learning disability due to teacher reports of Óscar's apparent difficulty to understand what he reads and to comprehend directions. Óscar was born in the United States into a Spanish-speaking household. He is currently enrolled in second grade, and has completed kindergarten and first grade in a bilingual program. While Óscar's primary caregiver indicates that Óscar would prefer speaking more English than Spanish, he also indicates that Óscar does not understand English well enough to hold a conversation in that language and therefore ends up speaking more Spanish than English. The fact that Óscar would prefer to speak English is not surprising given that English is the language spoken the most at his school. Spanish has been Óscar's and his primary caregiver's first language. Óscar attained developmental milestones as expected, and has intact hearing and vision.

Because Óscar's first language is Spanish, and he speaks it more often than English, the school psychologist included the WISC-V Spanish as part of her assessment. Due to Óscar's mixed language background, she is also interested in determining how his performance compares to other students who are more similar linguistically and culturally. As seen in Table 6.6, when adjusted for the

TABLE 6.6 Adjusted Score Summary

Subtest/ Composite		Scaled/ Composite Score	Adjusted Scaled/ Composite Score
Similarities	SI	8	9
Vocabulary	VC	12	15
Information	IN	10	13
Comprehension	CO	6	7
Verbal Comprehension Index	VCI	100	111
Verbal (expanded crystallized)	VECI	95	106

(Continued)

(Continued)

amount of support for developing and using the Spanish language that Óscar has received, all of his verbal scores increase between 1 and 3 points for subtests, and 11 points for composites. This means that given the somewhat limited support for Spanish in his overall environment outside of the home, Óscar is performing verbal comprehension tasks in Spanish better than might be expected. Let's recall that Óscar's school supports primarily the use of English. Thus, it's not surprising that he is performing above expectations in a language that is not supported academically (i.e., Spanish). Other factors that the practitioner should consider in interpreting Óscar's profile, include the type of bilingual program(s) that he has attended, the age/grade at which he started bilingual education, and current proficiency levels, among others (Olvera & Gomez-Cerrillo, 2011; Rhodes et al., 2005). While the school psychologist should continue her evaluation, these results appear to indicate that Óscar may not have a language disorder (at least not in his primary language), and because research has shown that full development of a bilingual individual's first language facilitates the acquisition of a second language, she may recommend continued support for further growth of Oscar's primary language (Cummins, 1984; Collier, 1989; Rhodes et al., 2005).

It is important to remind the reader that the Spanish Adjusted Scores have not been validated for use in special education decisions and that only the traditional scores should be used for these purposes. Additionally, due to the complexity of the calculations involved, it is not possible to derive the adjusted scores by hand, and they are available only on Pearson's Q-global and Q-interactive platforms.

Obvious limitations of this method include the inability to control for variables related to the language of instruction in the child's US classes (e.g., dual-language programs, English-immersion programs, etc.), or whether the child is a sequential or a simultaneous bilingual. Practitioners should consider these issues as they interpret the adjusted scores. Still, this is a useful beginning on the path to more culturally sensitive interpretation of intelligence test scores.

Culturally sensitive interpretation of test scores is important because patterns of immigration vary by country of origin and across generations, and these patterns have strong effects on mean test scores. Individuals from some countries come to the United States in search of basic skilled or entry level jobs, while others have the financial and educational resources to escape oppressive situations (e.g., political repression, economic turmoil, armed conflict). These patterns are different by country of origin, and they can also differ across generations of immigrants from the same country. *The average socioeconomic status of the immigrant populations from each country of origin has a profound impact on the mean intelligence test scores for that group. These patterns of immigration are different for different countries and can change over time for the same country.* For example, all of the authors of this chapter live in San Antonio, TX, where the pattern of immigration from nearby Mexico is changing in part due to the presence of violent conditions widely associated with drug cartels in several regions of that country. Whereas adults with few years of education have historically emigrated from Mexico to Texas in search of basic skilled jobs, the immigration pattern today includes an increasing number of successful Mexican professionals and wealthy business persons moving their families to a safer environment. As foreshadowed by the data presented in Table 6.2 regarding mean FSIQ scores by level of education, this shift in the pattern of immigration is beginning to have an observable impact on the housing market, local retail businesses, and school systems in upper middle class neighborhoods of the city. Different types of generational shifts have also occurred within Cuban and Puerto Rican immigrant populations. Thus, the adjusted percentile norms could be very informative in these situations.

All of these issues must be considered when evaluating Hispanic children who have recently arrived in the United States. The methods described herein can assist the practitioner in thinking through these issues, but they should be considered as guideposts only. Clinical judgment by culturally similar or trained psychologists knowledgeable of changing conditions in the local community is also necessary for competent, culturally sensitive interpretation.

USE OF INTERPRETERS

Best practice is for Spanish-speaking clients to be assessed by a Spanish-speaking examiner administering a validated Spanish edition of the test. Ideally, the examiner would not only speak Spanish but be from the same cultural and linguistic background as the client. However, this procedure is not always feasible. For non-Spanish-speaking examiners, an interpreter may be necessary to administer a *validated Spanish edition* such as WISC-V Spanish. When using interpreters, it is important to be familiar with the ethical guidelines for the use of interpreters, and follow general guidelines for selection, training, and use of interpreters. For example, relatives of the child should not be used as interpreters. Training is required for the interpreter prior to test administration to ensure valid results. Interpreters should receive specific instruction in the importance of following standard procedures and not offering subtle hints to the person being tested. Psychologists should observe practice administrations to ensure the interpreter achieves proficiency prior to the actual testing. It is recommended that the examiner manage the stimulus book, timer, and manipulatives, and record responses to nonverbal items, while the interpreter reads the verbal instructions to the child and translates the child's verbal responses without embellishment. Even so, some children may notice that the translation and transcription process is cumbersome and voluntarily restrict their responses to "help" the examiners—which may lower their items scores—and these children should be encouraged to say more if it appears they are more capable than their initial response suggests, but of course without asking leading questions. The interpreter should also record verbatim responses in Spanish in addition to translating them for the psychologist during the assessment so that, after the evaluation, the psychologist and interpreter can discuss nuances of scoring based on the written record. If an interpreter is used, the psychologist should note this fact in the psychological report, along with the level of training provided. While a comprehensive discussion of the use of interpreters is beyond the scope of this chapter, the DAS-II Spanish manual (Elliott, 2012) provides further guidance on this complex topic.

Using interpreters to translate English test questions to Spanish during the evaluation is poor practice. But the methods described here, and in the DAS-II Spanish manual, can yield acceptable—though not optimal—results when carefully applied with validated Spanish editions of cognitive ability tests. Because the use of interpreters is not best practice, however, these methods generally should not be used in high stakes evaluations such as may result in restrictive placement, or influence child custody decisions.

SUMMARY AND CONCLUSIONS

The complexity of questions relating to language, bilingualism, culture, and educational experience that impact the development of cognitive abilities in children and their performance on intelligence tests preclude simple, singular answers. Flexible assessment tools that allow professionals supplemental, alternative perspectives based on the client's unique cultural and linguistic background are a part of best practices in the assessment of culturally and linguistically diverse children. Toward this goal, this chapter provides Hispanic percentile norms for WISC-V composites, and base rates of Index score discrepancies between composites not previously available for Hispanics. The Hispanic percentile norms complement information derived from the FSIQ, but do not replace the FSIQ. Both pieces of information are often valuable in psychological evaluations of Spanish-speaking and bilingual children. The WISC-V Spanish edition allows children to be tested in Spanish and their performance compared to the general population of US English-speaking children of the same age through equating. For a discussion on using the WPPSI-IV and WAIS-IV with Spanish-speaking clients, refer to Weiss et al. (2016).

REFERENCES

Bialystok, E. (2016). Bilingual education for young children: Review of the effect and consequences. *International Journal of Bilingual Education and Bilingualism.* Available from https://doi.org/10.1080/13670050.2016.1203859.

Carlson, S. M., & Meltzoff, A. N. (2008). Bilingual experience and executive functioning in young children. *Developmental Science, 11,* 282–298.

Collier, V. (1989). How long? A synthesis of research on academic achievement in a second language. *TESOL Quarterly, 23,* 509–531.

Cummins, J. (1984). *Bilingualism and special education: Issues in assessment and pedagogy.* San Diego, CA: College-Hill.

Dweck, C. S. (2012). Mindsets & human nature: Promoting change. *American Psychologist, 67* (8), 614–622.

Elliott, C. (2012). Differential abilities scale—second edition, Early years Spanish supplement. San Antonio, TX: Pearson.

Flores, A. (2017). *How the U.S. Hispanic population is changing.* Retrieved from <http://www.pewresearch.org/fact-tank/2017/09/18/how-the-u-s-hispanic-population-is-changing/> Accessed 19.10.17.

Geisinger, K. F. (2014). *Psychological testing of Hispanics, second edition.* Washington, DC: APA Press.

Georgas, J., Weiss, L. G., van de Vijver, F. J. R., & Saklofske, D. H. (2003). *Culture and children's intelligence: Cross-cultural analysis of the WISC-III.* San Diego, CA: Academic Press.

Kolen, M. J., & Brennan, R. L. (2004). *Test equating, scaling, and linking: Methods and practices.* New York, NY: Springer.

Lopez, E. J., Ehly, S., & Garcia-Vazquez, E. (2002). Acculturation, social support and academic achievement of Mexican and Mexican American high school students: An exploratory study. *Psychology in the Schools, 39*(3), 245–257.

Lopez, M. H. (2013). *Hispanic or Latino? Many don't care, except in Texas.* Retrieved from <http://www.pewresearch.org/fact-tank/2013/10/28/in-texas-its-hispanic-por-favor/> Accessed 01.05.14.

Mardell, C., & Goldenberg, D. S. (2011). *Developmental indicators for the assessment of learning* (4th ed). Bloomington, MN: NCS Pearson.

Olvera, P., & Gomez-Cerrillo, L. (2011). A bilingual (English & Spanish) psychoeducational assessment MODEL grounded in Cattell-Horn Carroll (CHC) theory: A cross battery approach. *Contemporary School Psychology, 15*(1), 117–127.

Ramirez, J. D. (1991). Executive summary of volumes I and II of the final report: Longitudinal study of structured English immersion strategy, early-exit and late-exit transitional bilingual education programs for language-minority children. *Bilingual Research Journal, 16*(1 & 2), 1–62.

Rhodes, R. L. (2010). Multicultural school neuropsychology. In D. Miller (Ed.), *Best practices in school neuropsychology: Guidelines for effective practice, assessment, and evidence-based intervention* (pp. 61–77). Hoboken, NJ: John Wiley & Sons.

Rhodes, R. L., Ochoa, S. H., & Ortiz, S. O. (2005). *Assessing culturally and linguistically diverse students: A practical guide.* New York, NY: Guilford Press.

Suzuki, L. A., & Ponterotto, J. G. (2007). *Handbook of multicultural assessment: Clinical, psychological, and educational applications.* New York, NY: John Wiley & Sons.

Wechsler, D. (2014). *Wechsler intelligence scale for children—fifth edition: Administration and Scoring manual.* San Antonio, TX: Pearson.

Wechsler, D. (2017). *Wechsler intelligence scale for children: Administration and scoring manual* (5th ed). Bloomington, MN: Pearson, Spanish.

Weiss, L. G., Chen, H., Harris, J. G., Holdnack, J. A., & Saklofske, D. H. (2010). *WAIS-IV use in societal context.* In L. G. Weiss, D. H. Saklofske, D. Coalson, & S. E. Raiford (Eds.), *WAIS-IV clinical use and interpretation* (pp. 97−139). San Diego, CA: Academic Press.

Weiss, L. G., Harris, J. G., Prifitera, A., Courville, T., Rolfhus, E., Saklofske, D. H., & Holdnack, J. A. (2006). *WISC-IV interpretation in societal context.* In L. G. Weiss, D. H. Saklofske, A. Prifitera, & J. A. Holdnack (Eds.), *WISC-IV advanced clinical interpretation* (pp. 1−57). San Diego, CA: Academic Press.

Weiss, L. G., Locke, V., Pan, T., Harris, J. G., Saklofske, D. H., & Prifitera, A. (2014). WISC−V use in societal context. In L. G. Weiss, D. H. Saklofske, & A. Prifitera (Eds.), *WISC−V assessment & interpretation* (pp. 123−185). San Diego, CA: Academic Press.

Weiss, L. G., Prifitera, A., & Muñoz, M. (2016). Issues related to intelligence testing with Spanish-speaking clients. In K. F. Geisinger (Ed.), *Psychological testing of Hispanics, second edition.* Washington, DC. Woodcock, R. W. (2011). Woodcock reading mastery tests (3rd ed.). Bloomington, MN: Pearson.: APA Books.

Woodcock, R. W. (2011). *Woodcock reading mastery tests* (3rd ed). Bloomington, MN: Pearson.

Chapter 7

A Cross-Cultural Analysis of the WISC-V

Fons J.R. van de Vijver[1,2,3,4,*], Lawrence G. Weiss[5],
Donald H. Saklofske[6], Abigail Batty[7] and Aurelio Prifitera[8]

[1]Higher School of Economics, Russia, [2]Tilburg University, the Netherlands, [3]University of Queensland, Australia, [4]North-West University, South Africa, [5]Research and Measurement Consultant, San Antonio, TX, United States, [6]Department of Psychology, University of Western Ontario, London, ON, Canada, [7]Pearson Clinical, United Kingdom, [8]Assessment Consultant, San Antonio, TX, United States

INTRODUCTION

The Wechsler Intelligence Scale for Children (WISC) is the most widely used scale of intelligence worldwide and in previous editions has been adapted in over 20 countries. Three years since the US release of WISC-Fifth Edition (WISC-V), regions across North America, Europe, and Australia/New Zealand have transadapted the tool for use in their countries. As transadaptations of the WISC-V continue to expand globally, it is important to reflect on evidence for the generalizability of the structure of intelligence as operationalized by the WISC constructs.

Models of intelligence have developed over the 20th and 21st centuries and theories mostly agree on a hierarchical model of cognitive abilities. Although there is continuing evolution and debate on the number of factors that make up intelligence, it is agreed that when several cognitive variables are measured and analyzed a factor of general intelligence emerges, which is commonly termed "g" (Prifitera, Weiss, Saklofske, & Rolfhus, 2005).

Across cultures the manifestations of the cognitive abilities that contribute to intelligence can differ, and this is largely determined by the contextual variables that are important for that culture. However, by studying an array of complex cognitive processes across different cultures, researchers have

*The work of Fons van de Vijver was done within the framework of the Basic Research Program at the National Research University Higher School of Economics (HSE) and was supported within the framework of a subsidy by the Russian Academic Excellence Project '5–100'.

WISC-V. DOI: https://doi.org/10.1016/B978-0-12-815744-2.00007-0

demonstrated that a universal factor construct of intelligence emerges, even with cross-national studies showing smaller differences than within-national cross-ethnic studies (e.g., Irvine, 1979; Van de Vijver, 1997).

This universality of the construct of intelligence has been studied with the WISC scales, using methods to assess structural invariance of the WISC factor model across regions. Georgas, van de Vijver, Weiss, and Saklofske (2003) reviewed 16 versions of the WISC-III worldwide, across North America, Europe, and Asia. When comparing the factor structure of the tool they found good equivalence for the WISC-III four-factor structure across regions. Mean score differences were shown to be more related to national indicators of education and economic variables. It should be noted that all countries studied by Georgas et al. (2003) were industrialized, but there was a mix of Westernized and non-Western countries (i.e., South Korea, Japan, and Taiwan), and a range of socioeconomic status across countries.

The four-factor structure of the WISC-IV has been supported by international adaptations across Australia/New Zealand, Europe, the United Kingdom, and in Asian regions. Within each region, confirmatory factor analyses supported the four-factor structure (e.g., Chen, Keith, Weiss, Zhu, & Li, 2010; Wechsler, 2004). Factor invariance has also been shown with the *Wechsler Adult Intelligence Scale: Third Edition* (WAIS-III) between the United States, American, and Canadian studies (Bowden, Lange, Weiss, & Saklofske, 2008).

Most recently, eight adaptations of the tool have taken place on the WISC-V across North America, Europe, and Australia/New Zealand. In each region the WISC-V factor structure has been replicated and supported through separate confirmatory factor analyses within each of the countries (e.g., Wechsler, 2015, 2016, 2017). Additional studies have also found the model to be invariant for gender, age, and clinical groups (Pezzuti & Orsini, 2016).

In this chapter, we take the next step in this research program and examine the five-factor structure of the WISC-V jointly across countries, and the role of national indicators of education and economy in explaining mean score differences between countries if observed. We acknowledge that our WISC-V research program to date covers only industrialized western countries and does not address eastern or nonindustrialized countries. Before examining the evidence for the generalizability of the structure of intelligence across the regions we studied, we briefly review the test development processes and best practices that were used to inform these WISC-V transadaptation in culturally and linguistically diverse countries.

Processes and Best Practices to Support Wechsler Intelligence Scale for Children—Fifth Edition Cross-Cultural Development Projects

Cross-cultural adaptation has occurred since Alfred Binet first published his seminal intelligence measure. However, the practice of good adaptation has been inconsistent (Hambleton & Patsula, 1999). In more recent times a number of key practitioners and academics in the field of cross-cultural assessment have come together to collaborate on the practices that contribute to best development of cross-cultural tools. The work has concentrated not only on good translations, but also on the importance of adaptation in a cultural and theoretical context and sound psychometric evaluation. This has culminated in guidelines for international practice.

The most influential recommendations for cross-cultural adaptation have been proposed by *The International Test Commission Guidelines (ITC) for Translating and Adapting Tests: Second Edition* (International Testing Commission, 2016). This updated edition of the ITC guidelines reflects ongoing advances in the area of cross-cultural research between 2005 and 2015. Important work in the field has been conducted by leading names such as Hambleton, Spielberger, and Grégoire, to name a few. The work has been necessitated by the increasing globalization of our societies and the need to understand performance in a fair way across cultures. Advances have been helped by technical advances in psychometrics, new test translation and adaptation processes, and examples of best practices (OECD/PISA and TIMSS projects) (International Testing Commission, 2016).

The second edition of the ITC guidelines now includes 18 recommendations for cross-cultural research. These are formed around six topics: Precondition, Test Development, Confirmation (Empirical Analyses), Administration, Score Scales and Interpretation, and Documentation. Precondition covers the tasks that should be decided before the project begins (e.g., permissions from a publishing company). The second set of guidelines cover the translation/adaptation process and recommends approaches for best practices. The use of content experts in language translation is strongly advised to ensure the concept being assessed is not subtly changed by the translation. The next topic concentrates on the empirical equivalence that should be collected to support an adaptation and includes comments on normative samples, reliability, and validity measures. The next two topics cover the administration, score scales, and interpretation guidelines. These emphasize the importance of culturally relevant administration guidelines and interpreting scores in reference to the empirical findings. Finally the guidelines cover the recommendation that all adaptors should provide good documentation around the methodology and empirical results of an adaptation to enable informed use by other practitioners (International Testing Commission, 2016).

The publishers of the WISC-V have completed cross-cultural adaptations with the WISC-V. Teams of researchers and test developers based in countries outside of the United States are responsible for the clinical and psychometric standards of each adaptation in their local populations. Best practice is of course informed by guidelines like those published by ITC, as well as research from leading practitioners in cross-cultural assessment, expert local consultations, and considerable experience gained from the adaptation of many previous versions.

From the outset of development of the original US edition of WISC-V, the developers of the tool implemented many steps to minimize the influence of cultural bias when adapted internationally. All items and content in development were reviewed by researchers and clinicians in 10 countries to enable an item set that would be as universally applicable as possible. For example, pictures and other patterns associated with some nonverbal items which were judged to be commonly known symbols in other countries were replaced early in the creation of the US item set. Additionally, some vocabulary words and verbal questions were judged by local reviewers to be much more or less commonly known in certain countries—which would change the difficulty level of the item—and these items were replaced by the US team early in the process. All test adaptation standards note the importance of back translations of verbal items, which involves translation from source language (L1) to target language (L2) and then translation from L2 back to L1 by a different person to ensure the item means the same thing in both languages. While important, our research teams have learned that this process is less applicable to cognitive than personality test items and the more important criteria for cognitive items is the item difficulty level. This is because it is not important that an examinee knows the definition of a particular word, but that he or she has a vocabulary and general verbal conceptualization skills at a certain level of ability. The international teams also reviewed the subtests for practice relevance in their regions. Accordingly decisions were made to only include the primary and secondary subtests in Europe and Australia/New Zealand.

Once the final item set had been decided in the United States, the international teams began their process of translation and adaptation. External local experts in language and intellectual assessment were recruited to provide consultation on the translation and adaptation of the items from the US test. When a set of comparable items had been developed it was subjected to pilot review with small numbers of relevant populations, to check feasibility of test content in each local population.

Following this pilot phase, the content developed (administration instructions, items, artwork, scoring rules) was then evaluated empirically on a larger set of individuals in each region to "test the test" before the tool was standardized on larger, regionally representative samples. Decisions at this stage were taken to change items or instructions as appropriate.

Standardization versions of the tool were then developed in each country for normative data collection. A demographically representative sample of the country was defined and sample sizes set to enable sufficient statistical power for the required psychometric evaluations. In each country the standardization sample was stratified based on the sociodemographic variables most relevant in that culture, and according to local population percentages.

All samples were stratified by age, sex, region of country, and an indicator of socioeconomic status. In some cases, we examined the percentage of variance in Intelligence Quotient (IQ) scores accounting for by each sociodemographic variable to determine its inclusion in the stratification plan, although some variables were stratified simply for completeness. For example, while most countries stratify by parent's level of education as an indicator of socioeconomic status, the German educational system tracks children to different school types based on ability after the fifth grade. Our research showed that school type accounted for more variance in children's IQ scores than parent's level of education after that grade, and so the German team stratified by school type after that grade and by parent education before that grade. Reliability and validity studies, similar to those completed in the United States, were also designed and conducted to enable evaluation of convergent and divergent validity in each region. Separate confirmatory factor analyses of the WISC-V factor structure were conducted within each country, as discussed earlier, and showed support for the five-factor model.

Following data collection and analysis, the final version of the tool was developed. The WISC-V technical manual in each region documented the methodology for development and results for that region. Some countries were also open to more formal review by local testing authorities (e.g., COTAN in The Netherlands). In these regions additional analyses were conducted to complete appropriate requisite evidence where required by local authorities.

We examined data from the following samples: Australia and New Zealand, English-speaking Canada, French-speaking Canada, France, Germany, Dutch-speaking regions (Netherlands and Flanders), Spain, Scandinavia (Sweden, Norway, and Denmark), United Kingdom, and the United States. For convenience, we refer to all samples as countries, which implies that the term country is used here in a loose sense. Furthermore, it may be noted that various samples combine data from children living in different countries (in the case of Scandinavia even with different languages). Descriptive statistics of the samples are provided in Table 7.1. As can be confirmed there, the samples were similar in terms of gender composition and age distribution.

In this chapter, we examine the invariance of the Wechsler five-factor measurement model jointly across the countries where it has been adapted to date. The invariance analysis involves standardized subtest scores (i.e., scores that are based on all items and standardized in each country). The factorial structure of the subtest scores is compared across the countries. Finally, we examine how educational and economic factors account for any observed differences in mean IQ scores across countries.

TABLE 7.1 Sample Descriptives per Country

Country	N	Percentage Girls	Age M (years)	SD
Australia, New Zealand	528	51.3	11.24	3.12
Canada English	1081	50.5	11.49	3.15
Canada French	768	49.8	11.35	3.12
France	1049	49.3	10.81	3.14
Germany	1065	49.8	11.39	3.11
Netherlands, Flanders	1433	49.8	11.41	3.29
Spain	1008	50.4	11.26	3.16
Sweden, Norway, Denmark	660	49.5	11.50	3.15
United Kingdom	415	49.9	11.13	3.19
United States	2201	50.0	11.50	3.18

Source: Data and Table copyright Pearson 2014.

Statistical Analyses

The statistical analyses were different for the first research question (invariance of the factor structure) and second research question (comparison of mean scores per country and relationships between country-level scores on the subtests and country indicators). A main distinction between the two sets of analyses refers to the scores used in both. The first set of analyses uses *standardized* scores per subtest (standardization refers here to the score transformations in which each subtest gets the same mean and standard deviation across countries). These scores allow us to compare the structure of intelligence, as measured by the WISC-V across countries as these scores reflect the standing of the children on the underlying skills. However, not all items are identical across countries. As a consequence, scores cannot be directly compared across countries. These characteristics (partly dissimilar items and standardization per country) have implications for their comparability, as discussed in more detail below. The invariance of the structure of intelligence was tested using these standardized scores.

Invariance Analyses

In the literature three levels of invariance are commonly distinguished in confirmatory factor analysis which is used in the present study, namely configural, metric, and scalar invariance. Configural invariance means that there is identity (invariance) of the global pattern of loadings across countries: the same subtests load on the same underlying latent construct(s). Metric invariance means that the factor loadings are identical across countries. Scalar invariance refers to the identity of item intercepts that link the latent trait to the observed scores. The latter type of invariance means that there is no item bias or differential item functioning.

We tested the WISC-V factorial structure as a hierarchical structure with five factors at the lowest level and one general intelligence factor at the highest level, in line with the Cattell-Horn-Carroll (CHC) model (Carroll, 1993). Different statistical procedures have been used to explore the factorial structure of the WISC-V, including exploratory and confirmatory factor analysis (Canivez, Watkins, & Dombrowski, 2016; Canivez, Watkins, & Dombrowski, 2017; Wechsler, 2017). The statistical analyses did not provide consistent support for the expected five-factor structure. The test manual indicates support for a five-factor Confirmatory Factor Analysis (CFA) model whereas Canivez and colleagues could not entirely replicate the five-factor structure in the original US standardization sample using somewhat modified estimation procedures in the confirmatory factor analysis. Canivez et al.'s (2016) choice of statistical procedures was based on these mixed results as well as on previous factor analyses of large-scale projects. Given the strong theoretical structure of the WISC-V, the choice for an exploratory factor analysis is not obvious. Yet, the choice of confirmatory factor analysis could be problematic for other reasons. It has been repeatedly found that fit statistics of confirmatory models in large-scale assessments are difficult to interpret due to the highly restrictive assumptions of confirmatory factor analyses and that minor, inconsequential and major model misspecifications are difficult to distinguish (Rutkowski & Svetina, 2014, 2017; Van de Vijver, 2011). We used confirmatory factor analysis to test the invariance of the structure of intelligence, taking into account that the fit indices may not be easy to interpret. Our preference of confirmatory factor analysis was mainly conceptually based. The test battery has a clearly defined theoretical structure. The 10 subtests are supposed to be related to 5 first-order factors, which in turn are supposed to be related to a global, overall factor. This expected structure can be more easily implemented in a confirmatory factor analysis than in an exploratory factor analysis.

The pattern of expected loadings is specified in Table 7.2. There is currently no software available that can test the hierarchical factor model in a single analysis. The software package Mplus that was used for model estimation involves two steps and tests the invariance for each level separately (Rudnev, Lytkina, Davidov, Schmidt, & Zick, 2018). In the first step, the invariance of the first-order factors is tested, as specified in the upper part of Table 7.2. Each of the five factors (i.e., Fluid Reasoning, Verbal Comprehension, Perceptual Reasoning, Working Memory, and Processing Speed) is supposed to have two subtests with high loadings; no cross-loadings are allowed. The second step examines the invariance of the links

TABLE 7.2 Target Loadings of the Factor Model of the First- and Second-Order Models: (A) First-Order Factors in Upper Part; (B) Second-Order Factor in Lower Part

(A) First-Order Factors

Subtest	Fluid Reasoning	Verbal Comprehension	Perceptual Reasoning	Working Memory	Processing Speed
Matrix Reasoning	*				
Figure Weights	*				
Similarities		*			
Vocabulary		*			
Block Design			*		
Visual Puzzles			*		
Digit Span				*	
Picture Span				*	
Coding					*
Symbol Search					*

(B) Second-Order Factor

First-Order Factors	General Intelligence
Fluid Reasoning	*
Verbal Comprehension	*
Perceptual Reasoning	*
Working Memory	*
Processing Speed	*

Note: Asterisks denote loadings that were estimated in the Confirmatory Structural Equation Model. Empty cells (only present in the upper panel) were defined to be equal to zero.
Source: Data and Table copyright Pearson 2014.

between the five first-order factors and the general intelligence factor at the second level. At this second level, all first-order factors should have a substantial loading on the general intelligence factor.

The use of standardized subtest scores in each country has implications for the invariance analyses. A disadvantage of standardized scores is that information about country differences in means cannot be meaningfully interpreted as differences in country means are eliminated in the standardization process. As a consequence, scalar invariance is not meaningful in the first analysis (testing the invariance of the link between the 5 factors and the 10 subtests). Another issue refers to the consequences of having dissimilar items across countries. The question is whether the subtest scores can be expected to show the same loadings across countries (which would suggest that scores are metrically invariant across countries). Although it is an empirical question whether the loadings are really identical, we reasoned that there are reasons to expect such invariance. First of all, the number of identical items is much larger than the number of different items. Also, items that are different are always chosen to be tightly linked to their underlying construct. So, items were always adapted with a view of representing the same underlying construct. As a consequence, total subtest scores can be expected to adequately reflect their underlying construct in all countries.

In tests of the invariance of the first-order structure (i.e., subtests have the same loadings in all countries on the five factors), parameters of the second order were left free as much as possible. This means in practice that all parameters of the second order were left free. So, we tested the first-order factors while assuming configural invariance at the second level. Therefore, we tested configural and metric invariance, assuming that both levels of invariance would be confirmed. When testing the invariance of the second-order factor (i.e., factor loadings and intercepts of the link between general intelligence, the second-order factor, and the five first-order factors), the metric invariance model of the first order was used. Clearly, an identical second order requires that the first-order factors are comparable, which is ensured by their metric invariance at the first level. So, the invariance test of the second-order model assumes that metric invariance is supported at the first level. In the analysis of second-order invariance factor loadings of the first-order model are kept the same across countries. Invariance at the second level is more straightforward as all levels of invariance can be reached there. So, in the second analysis all levels of invariance could be tested. In practice, the combination of metric invariance of first-order factors and configural invariance at the second level is addressed in the test of the invariance of first-order factors (as we postulated configural invariance in the tests of the invariance of the first-order factors). It is assumed that metric invariance can be confirmed. There are no theoretical reasons to doubt the confirmation of scalar invariance; however, as argued above, many applications of cross-cultural invariance that involve multiple cultures fail to find support for scalar invariance, due to the presence of biased items.

Comparison of Mean Subtest Scores Per Country and Correlations of Country Means With Social Indicators

A direct comparison of subtest scores (or scores on the first-order factor or second-order factor) is problematic as not all subtests employed identical stimuli for all subtests. More specifically, Block Design, Digit Span, Matrix Reasoning, Visual Puzzles, Picture Span, Figure Weights, Arithmetic, and Picture Concepts were identical across all participating countries, whereas

Similarities, Information, Comprehension, and Vocabulary had one or more country-specific items or had items that had moved from the original position (as they were easier or more difficult in a specific country). These jumps in ordinal position tended to be modest, with the exception of the Vocabulary subtest. These test adaptations make it impossible to directly compare mean scores on the subtests with adapted items.

Item response theory allows for comparisons of test scores even if not all items are identical in all countries (van der Linden & Hambleton, 2013). The analysis assumes, though, that the same latent trait is measured in all countries and that items have the same link with the latent trait in each country. A two-parameter (discrimination and difficulty) model was used to analyze the dichotomous items. The model postulated a logistic curve to link the responses to the latent trait (each subtest was taken to have one latent trait). Computations were done in Mplus (Muthén & Muthén, 1998–2012). Estimated latent trait scores were saved and used in country comparisons of mean scores.

The analysis of Vocabulary scores could not follow the same pattern. Many countries have adapted the subtest items considerably either by replacing words from the English original or by moving words that are shared with the English original to different positions. For example, item 23 in the US version is the same as item 13 in the German version. This means that the approach to use identical stimuli is probably not valid for all country comparisons. Therefore, the approach was complemented by another. We compared the raw scores (all countries have the same number of items). This comparison is based on the strong assumption that Vocabulary subtest scores can be compared across countries although the stimuli are not identical. Items in the subtests are chosen to provide adequate maps of individual differences in a language, but are not chosen to reflect global similarities or differences of scores across countries. Therefore, this approach may not be valid either. In conclusion, our approach to comparing vocabulary scores across countries is pragmatic and is not based on a solid theoretical or statistical reasoning.

The mean scores (latent trait scores for all subtests, with the exception of the Vocabulary subtest where two alternative scores are used) are compared in a multivariate analysis of variance, with country and gender as independent variables (gender is used as a control variable, as gender differences in subtest scores have been documented).

RESULTS

Invariance Analyses

The fit tests of the invariance analyses are presented in Table 7.3. The first-order factor model showed a good fit for the configural and metric model.

TABLE 7.3 Fit Tests of the Invariance Tests of the First-Order and Second-Order Factor Structures

Model	χ^2 (df)	$\Delta\chi^2$ (Δdf)	CFI	ΔCFI	TLI	RMSEA	AIC	BIC
First Order (With Configural Invariance at Second Order)								
Configural invariance	2349.196 (301)***		0.972		0.958	0.082	634,740.277	637,263.836
Metric invariance	2646.971 (346)***	297.775 (45)***	0.969	0.003	0.959	0.081	634,955.339	637,153.511
Second Order (With Metric Invariance at First Order)								
Metric invariance	3296.335 (382)***	649.364 (36)***	0.960	0.009	0.953	0.086	635,525.463	637,463.326
Scalar invariance	4197.993 (453)***	901.658 (71)***	0.949	0.011	0.949	0.090	636,300.883	637,725.356

Note: ***$P < .001$. Scalar invariance is not tested at the subtest level (first order) because the analyses use standardized scores in which country differences in scores have been eliminated. In tests of the first-order invariance, the parameters of the second order are free to vary (with the exception of some constants to set the length of the latent factors). In tests of the second-order invariance, the metric invariance of the parameters of the first-order model is used. All four models tested are hierarchically nested.
Source: Data and Table copyright Pearson 2014.

The χ^2 value was highly significant suggesting a poor fit, but the CFI value of 0.972 and the TLI value of 0.958 yielded favorable results while the RMSEA of 0.082 suggested a moderate fit. Given the dependence of the χ^2 statistic on sample size, we interpreted these fit statistics as supporting the configural invariance model. The $\Delta\chi^2$ gauging the change from the configural to the metric model was highly significant, whereas the CFI, TLI, and RMSEA values (as well as their increments) suggested supported for the metric invariance model. Furthermore, the BIC value also supported the metric invariance model as its value was lower than the value of the configural invariance model. It can be concluded that, in line with expectation, the five-factor model at the first level, comprising Fluid Reasoning, Verbal Comprehension, Perceptual Reasoning, Working Memory, and Processing Speed, was confirmed and that the factor loadings of all countries were identical. Psychologically speaking, this means that the 10 subtests can be viewed as coming from the same 5 factors in all countries and that the link between the subtests and the 5 factors is the same across countries. The loadings in Table 7.4 are not standardized. The standardized loadings of all subtests in all countries were very high, all were above 0.70 and many loadings were above 0.85. It can be concluded that the subtests are very strong markers of their factors.

In the second step the invariance of the second-order factors was tested. As noted above, the metric invariance of the first-order factors was tested while configural invariance was specified at the second level. So, we already know that configural invariance is confirmed at the second level (as this was part of the text of the first-order factors), which means that a general intelligence factor is found at the second level in each country. The analysis in the second step went beyond this finding as we were interested whether metric and scalar invariance could be confirmed at the second level. As can be seen in Table 7.3, the confirmation of metric invariance was strong. With the exception of the $\Delta\chi^2$ and $\Delta\chi^2$ statistics, the fit statistics tended to support the metric invariance model. The transition to the scalar invariance model was more ambiguous. The drop in CFI was just above 0.01 (often viewed as the critical value above which the more restrictive model should be rejected and the less restrictive model is supported) while the drop in TLI was 0.06; the increment in RMSEA was 0.005 while the information measures (AIC and BIC) did not fully support the scalar invariance model. All in all, the support for the scalar invariance model was modest. A closer inspection of the country differences in item intercepts did not suggest major differences across countries, although many intercept differences were statistically significant. Given that the differences were rather small and did not favor any specific country and that the evaluation of fit statistics in large-scale studies is known to be problematic, we concluded that scalar invariance was close to being supported.

TABLE 7.4 Factor Loadings of the Factor Model of the First- and Second-Order Models: (A) First-Order Factors in Upper Part; (B) Second-Order Factor in Lower Part

(A) First-Order Factors

Subtest	Fluid Reasoning	Verbal Comprehension	Perceptual Reasoning	Working Memory	Processing Speed
Matrix Reasoning	1.00[a]				
Figure Weights	1.20***				
Similarities		1.00[a]			
Vocabulary		1.14***			
Block Design			1.00[a]		
Visual Puzzles			0.46***		
Digit Span				1.000[a]	
Picture Span				1.12***	
Coding					1.000[a]
Symbol Search					0.39***

(B) Second-Order Factor

	General Intelligence	
First-Order Factors	**Factor Loading**	**Intercept**
Fluid Reasoning	0.55***	4.85***
Verbal Comprehension	1.000[a]	0.00[b]
Perceptual Reasoning	1.23***	−0.23
Working Memory	0.759***	5.98***
Processing Speed	1.90	1.21***

Note: ***$P < .001$. The factor loadings of the first-order factors are the metric invariant solution, while the second-order factor parameter estimates represent the scalar invariance solution.
[a]Loading fixed at a value of 1.
[b]Intercept fixed at a value of 0.
Source: Data and Table copyright Pearson 2014.

The findings, combining rather strong support for metric invariance at both levels with weaker support for scalar invariance at the second level, provide strong support for the shared psychological meaning of the subtests across the countries. Our study provides evidence for the presumed global applicability of the hierarchical factor structure of the WISC-V throughout the set of Western countries included in our study. This applicability has also been reported for the CHC model, that is in line with the hierarchical factor structure of the WISC-V.

Comparison of Country Means and Correlations With Social Indicators

Country differences in scale, index, and intelligence (IQ) scores were tested in a MANOVA, with country as independent variable and these index, scale, and intelligence scores as dependent variables. Proportion of variance accounted for by country (partial η^2) was used as effect size measure. Threshold values of small, medium, and large effect sizes are 0.01, 0.06, and 0.12 (Cohen, 1992). All scores were standardized prior to the analysis, which means that the global mean and standard deviation across all countries were set at a value of 0 and 1. The purpose of the z score standardization was to make scores comparable across all tests and to ease interpretation. Means, standard deviations, and effect sizes of country differences in standardized scale scores are presented in Table 7.5 and the Index and Global Intelligence Scores in Table 7.6. It can be seen at the bottom of Tables 7.5 and 7.6 that all effect sizes, as measured by the proportion of variance accounted for by countries, are significant, as could be expected given the huge sample size; however, the most salient findings is their very limited effect size. Some of the effect sizes do not even reach the threshold level of 0.01, the marker of a small effect size. No medium or large effect sizes were found. The largest effect sizes were found for the vocabulary subtest and corresponding index. However, as indicated before, country differences in vocabulary scores should be interpreted with caution as these scores are not fully comparable in either of the two comparisons made (comparing all, partly nonidentical items versus comparing identical items, yet allowing for language differences in difficulty level of the identical items). The main global conclusion from our analysis is that country differences in cognitive test scores in these Western samples are small and in many cases negligible from a practical perspective; for example, global IQ differences account for less than 1% of the variance. Individual differences within countries are much larger than country differences. The global pattern in intelligence differences can be best seen in the IQ index (far right column of Table 7.6). The only country with a somewhat lower score than the other countries is France. The lower score is due to a systematic pattern of somewhat lower scores on most scales and all indexes. It is unclear where these differences come from. It is not very likely that translations could play an important role as the scores of the other group in which a rather similar French version was administered, the French Canadian group, were slightly above the global average. Sampling issues such as relatively many immigrants with a rather poor knowledge of the French language and likely an inconsistent or disrupted educational experience, could play a role and deserves further investigation.

The intelligence literature is replete with examples of large ethnic and country differences in scores (e.g., Jensen, 1980; Lynn & Mikk, 2007). These findings fit in a long and controversial tradition about the background

TABLE 7.5 Means (and Standard Deviations) of Standardized Item Response Ability Estimates per Subtest and Country

Country	Matrix Reasoning	Figure Weights	Similarities	Vocabulary[a]	Vocabulary[b]	Block Design	Visual Puzzles	Digit Span	Picture Span	Coding	Symbol Search
					Subtest						
Australia, New Zealand	0.13 (0.96)	0.03 (1.04)	0.06 (1.12)	0.01 (1.00)	−0.01 (0.94)	0.07 (0.98)	0.14 (1.02)	0.22 (1.08)	0.18 (1.02)	−0.05 (1.01)	0.07 (.97)
Canada English	0.00 (1.04)	−0.03 (1.08)	0.13 (1.06)	0.09 (1.01)	0.02 (1.00)	0.04 (1.09)	0.05 (1.07)	0.06 (1.05)	0.03 (1.09)	0.02 (1.05)	−0.04 (1.03)
Canada French	0.03 (0.93)	−0.01 (1.02)	0.13 (1.10)	−0.01 (1.19)	0.07 (1.20)	0.09 (0.95)	0.09 (0.96)	−0.12 (1.00)	−0.05 (0.96)	0.05 (1.00)	0.15 (1.00)
France	−0.16 (1.09)	−0.14 (0.97)	−0.44 (0.88)	−0.30 (0.91)	0.04 (0.90)	−0.05 (1.01)	−0.13 (1.05)	−0.18 (1.04)	−0.10 (1.05)	−0.16 (0.90)	−0.19 (.96)
Germany	−0.07 (1.02)	−0.05 (0.94)	0.19 (1.08)	0.28 (0.93)	0.48 (1.22)	0.13 (1.03)	0.07 (0.97)	−0.03 (0.96)	−0.14 (1.00)	−0.03 (0.92)	0.07 (1.01)
Netherlands, Flanders	0.12 (0.99)	0.24 (0.95)	−0.11 (0.93)	−0.17 (0.96)	−0.32 (0.93)	0.09 (0.95)	0.22 (0.92)	−0.03 (1.00)	0.06 (0.96)	0.04 (1.03)	0.17 (1.00)
Spain	0.11 (0.94)	0.27 (0.96)	−0.11 (1.00)	−0.10 (1.06)	−0.24 (1.07)	0.03 (0.96)	0.22 (0.87)	0.14 (0.99)	0.30 (0.96)	0.08 (0.96)	0.20 (0.98)
Sweden, Norway, Denmark	−0.01 (1.00)	−0.09 (0.91)	0.06 (0.83)	0.19 (0.90)	0.31 (0.65)	−0.10 (0.91)	−0.16 (0.93)	0.11 (0.96)	−0.01 (0.87)	0.11 (1.02)	−0.10 (0.98)
United Kingdom	0.08 (0.94)	0.12 (0.92)	−0.08 (1.00)	−0.13 (1.03)	−0.57 (0.56)	0.13 (0.92)	0.19 (0.88)	−0.08 (0.90)	0.00 (0.98)	−0.17 (0.94)	−0.04 (0.93)
United States	0.01 (0.92)	−0.02 (1.00)	0.00 (0.94)	0.05 (0.95)	0.03 (0.89)	−0.17 (1.00)	0.02 (0.93)	0.18 (0.94)	0.04 (0.92)	0.01 (0.98)	0.00 (0.97)
Effect size	0.007***	0.013***	0.031***	0.026***	0.069***	0.000	0.022***	0.011***	0.009***	0.007***	0.012***

[a]Vocabulary scores based on number of correctly solved items (item set partly dissimilar across countries).
[b]Vocabulary scores based on the number of correctly solved items shared across countries. *P < .05. ***P < .001.
Source: Data and Table copyright Pearson 2014.

TABLE 7.6 Means (and Standard Deviations) of Standardized Item Response Index and Global Intelligence Estimates per Country

Country	Index					
	Fluid Reasoning	Verbal Comprehension	Perceptual Reasoning	Working Memory	Processing Speed	Global Intelligence
Australia, New Zealand	0.09 (1.00)	0.03 (1.06)	0.11 (1.00)	0.22 (1.06)	0.02 (0.99)	0.11 (1.04)
Canada English	−0.02 (1.07)	0.08 (1.05)	0.05 (1.09)	0.05 (1.09)	0.00 (1.05)	0.06 (1.06)
Canada French	0.01 (0.96)	0.11 (1.17)	0.10 (0.95)	−0.09 (0.98)	0.11 (1.00)	0.05 (1.02)
France	−0.17 (1.03)	−0.22 (0.90)	−0.10 (1.03)	−0.16 (1.04)	−0.19 (0.93)	−0.20 (1.00)
Germany	−0.07 (0.98)	0.36 (1.16)	0.10 (0.99)	−0.10 (0.97)	0.02 (0.97)	0.08 (1.01)
Netherlands, Flanders	0.00 (0.98)	−0.23 (0.94)	0.16 (0.94)	0.01 (0.99)	0.11 (1.02)	0.05 (1.00)
Spain	0.21 (0.96)	−0.18 (1.04)	0.13 (0.9)	0.25 (0.97)	0.14 (0.97)	0.09 (0.99)
Sweden, Norway, Denmark	−0.06 (0.95)	0.20 (0.72)	−0.14 (0.92)	0.05 (0.91)	0.00 (0.98)	0.01 (0.88)
United Kingdom	0.11 (0.92)	−0.34 (0.74)	0.17 (0.88)	−0.05 (0.92)	−0.11 (0.94)	−0.06 (0.88)
United States	0.00 (0.94)	0.02 (0.93)	−0.08 (0.97)	0.12 (0.91)	0.00 (0.98)	0.00 (0.95)
Effect size	0.011***	0.038***	0.016***	0.010***	0.007***	0.007***

***$p < .001$.
Source: Data and Table copyright Pearson 2014.

of such differences. The controversy focuses on the question whether these country differences are more genetically or environmentally rooted. There is also a third position in this discussion according to which most instruments to test country differences in intelligence show methodological problems such as item bias which reduces score comparability (Lubke, Dolan, & Kelderman, 2001). Our study also provides evidence for the importance of adequate instruments, in addition to adequate sampling frames. We found that within the group of Western countries that were studied here the country differences in intelligence are very small and not important from a practical perspective. The main reasons for the discrepancy with much other research could be threefold. First, all instruments were carefully adapted and the original US instruments were developed from the perspective that these would be translated in a later stage, which reduces the likelihood of bias in these instruments (Hambleton, Merenda, & Spielberger, 2005; Harkness, 2003). Particulars to cultures were avoided in the early test development stage. This approach deviated from much extant research that is often based on the export of Western instruments to other contexts without much consideration for the applicability of the instrument in the new cultural context. Psychometric procedures, such as differential item functioning techniques, are then used to identify potentially problematic items; however, an approach that starts from items that were developed from the perspective that these would be translated is conceptually more advanced and is less likely to encounter problems of differential fit of items. Second, our samples were not convenience samples but probability samples. Notably research that compares mainstream and immigrant students is susceptible to comparing groups that differ in background characteristics. For example, comparisons of educational performance of Turkish immigrants with their mainstream peers in Western–European countries show that a substantial part of the performance gap of immigrant students is due to the lower socioeconomic status of immigrant students as compared to mainstream students (Arikan, Van de Vijver, & Yagmur, 2017). So, when working with convenience samples, cultural and socioeconomic differences are often confounded. Third, many cross-cultural differences in cognitive test scores compare countries with large cultural distances, such as Western and non-Western countries. The cultural variation in our study was limited; for example, no Low-and-Middle-Income Countries were included in the present study.

The final analysis involved the correlations of the cognitive test scores (scales, indexes, global intelligence) with country-level social indicators. We used three indicators that that been identified before as being related to cognitive test performance (Brouwers, Van de Vijver, & Van Hemert, 2009; Van de Vijver, 1997) and various other psychological characteristics such as well-being (e.g., Diener, Oishi, & Tay, 2018; Georgas, Van de Vijver, & Berry, 2004; King, Renó, & Novo, 2014). The first is the Human Development Index, which is a composite of the level of economic development, life expectancy, and years of schooling (all at country level). The second is the Gross Domestic Product (per capita). The third is educational expenditure (per capita), which refers to the number of dollars spent on education (per capita) in a country. These social indicators are mutually exclusive (they can indeed be expected to be positively associated), as all are related to level of economic development.

The correlations were not strong for any indicator, as can be confirmed in Table 7.7. On average, the Human Development Index showed the strongest correlations, which were positive as could be expected (a higher Human Development Index can be taken to be related to educational indicators such as availability of high-quality schooling). The correlations were closer to zero for the other two indicators. However, the main conclusion is that no systematic relationships were found and that correlations were very weak. Of the 51 correlations computed, two correlations were significant (a positive correlation of 0.60 was found between the Human Development Index and Block design, $P < .05$; the same was true for the Perceptual Reasoning Index). All in all, the main conclusion is that social indicators are more or less unrelated to intelligence scores in the present sample. It should be noted that this finding pertains to country-level data and does not refer to the role of within-country indicators, such as socioeconomic status, which have been shown to be related to intelligence. The combination of test translation, sampling frame, and limited cultural variability that was described before could probably account for the absence of any systematic correlations.

In a previous project involving the WISC-III (Georgas et al., 2003), data were analyzed in the same way as done in the present study. More countries were involved in that study (countries also present in the WISC-V study are italicized): *Australia*; *Canada (English-speaking part)*; the Netherlands and Flanders (Dutch language area); *France* and Francophone Belgium; *Germany*, Austria, and Switzerland (German language area); Greece; Japan; South Korea; Lithuania; Slovenia; *Sweden*; Taiwan; *United Kingdom*; *United States of America*. So, the WISC-III study involved more countries and represented more cultural variation than the present WISC-V study. Still, the similarities in findings of the WISC-III and WISV-V studies are striking. First, the evidence for similarity of factor structure was strong in both studies. Note that the WISC-III and WISC-V were published with four and five factors, respectively. The WISC-III data were analyzed using exploratory factor analysis. Solutions of one up to four factors were extracted and with the exception of the fourth factor in some countries. The invariance of the factor structure was strongly supported. The WISC-V data set of the current project was analyzed with a hierarchical factor analysis, analyzed with structural equation modeling. The structural equation procedure is more sensitive than the procedure employed in the WISC-III project. Yet, the conclusions drawn in both studies were identical: the factor structure of intelligence, as identified by the WISC test, is invariant across the samples of the studies.

TABLE 7.7 Correlations of Scale, Index and IQ Scores With Social Indicators

Subtest	Social Indicators		
	Human Development Index	Gross Domestic Product (per Capita)	Educational Expenditure (per Capita)
Scales			
Matrix Reasoning	0.38	0.38	0.02
Figure Weights	0.19	0.32	−0.03
Similarities	0.39	0.14	0.24
Vocabulary (same items)	−0.25	−0.55	−0.29
Vocabulary (all items)	0.05	−0.23	−0.06
Block Design	0.60*	0.38	−0.24
Visual Puzzles	0.38	0.34	−0.11
Digit Span	−0.04	−0.08	−0.05
Picture Span	−0.02	0.18	−0.06
Coding	0.53	0.36	0.01
Symbol Search	0.33	0.22	0.01
Indexes			
Fluid Reasoning	0.35	0.40	0.03
Verbal Comprehension	0.03	−0.32	−0.08
Perceptual Reasoning	0.60*	0.40	−0.15
Working Memory	0.00	0.07	−0.03
Processing Speed	0.08	0.00	0.04
Global intelligence			
IQ	0.34	0.08	−0.09

*$P < .05$.
Source: Data and Table copyright Pearson 2014.

The second identical conclusion that was drawn in both studies involved the size of the cross-cultural differences in test scores. Contrary to much of the extant literature, no evidence was found in either project for large cross-cultural differences in scores. As explained above, careful test design, probability sampling, and small cultural differences between the countries are among the major factors presumably responsible for the small effects.

There was a slight difference in the conclusions in both studies regarding the link between cognitive test scores and social indicators. Affluence was used in the WISC-III, which was a combination of various economic indicators, including Gross Domestic Product. The Affluence indicator was positively associated with various subtests. These correlations were interpreted as indicating that economic indicators are a proxy for educational quality, which can be expected to be positively associated with cognitive test scores. In the present study no significant correlations between cognitive test scores and social indicators were found. The discrepancy may be due to the limited cultural variation in the present study which mainly involved what are known today as WEIRD countries: Western, Educated, Industrialized, Rich, and Democratic (Henrich, Heine, & Norenzayan, 2010), whereas the WISC-III study showed a larger cultural variation. It should be noted that such analyses were not conducted with the WISC-IV.

MAIN CONCLUSIONS AND IMPLICATIONS

The main conclusions of the present study are threefold: (1) there is strong support for the identical structure of intelligence in the Western countries of the study; (2) the country differences in mean scores are small; (3) these differences are unrelated to social indicators that are derived from educational and economic level of a country. With the exception of the last conclusion, similar results were obtained in a cross-cultural study involving the WISC-III. The present study implies that careful instrument design and adequate sampling frames can go a long way to debunk myths about cross-cultural intelligence differences. Obviously, our study cannot speak to the controversial issue of the relative contributions of genes and cultural factors to group differences in intelligence. However, our study implies that many studies that employed the combination of Western tests administered to convenience samples may erroneously lead to an overestimation of group differences due to confounding factors.

REFERENCES

Arikan, S., Van de Vijver, F. J. R., & Yagmur, K. (2017). PISA mathematics and reading performance differences of mainstream European and Turkish immigrant students. *Educational Assessment, Evaluation and Accountability, 29*, 229–246. Available from https://doi.org/10.1007/s11092-017-9260-6.

Bowden, S. C., Lange, R. T., Weiss, L. G., & Saklofske, D. H. (2008). Invariance of the measurement model underlying the Wechsler Adult Intelligence Scale—III in the United States and Canada. *Educational and Psychological Measurement, 68*, 1024–1040. Available from https://doi.org/10.1177/0013164408318769.

Brouwers, S. A., Van de Vijver, F. J. R., & Van Hemert, D. A. (2009). Variation in Raven's Progressive Matrices scores across time and place. *Learning and Individual Differences, 19*, 330–338. Available from https://doi.org/10.1016/j.lindif.2008.10.006.

Canivez, G. L., Watkins, M. W., & Dombrowski, S. C. (2016). Factor structure of the Wechsler Intelligence Scale for Children—Fifth Edition: Exploratory factor analyses with the 16 primary and secondary subtests. *Psychological Assessment, 28*, 975–986. Available from https://doi.org/10.1037/pas0000238.

Canivez, G. L., Watkins, M. W., & Dombrowski, S. C. (2017). Structural validity of the Wechsler Intelligence Scale for Children—Fifth Edition: Confirmatory factor analyses with the 16 primary and secondary subtests. *Psychological Assessment, 29*, 458–472. Available from https://doi.org/10.1037/pas0000358.

Carroll, J. B. (1993). *Human cognitive abilities*. Cambridge: Cambridge University Press. Available from https://doi.org:10.1017/CBO9780511957130.

Chen, H., Keith, T. Z., Weiss, L., Zhu, J., & Li, Y. (2010). Testing for multigroup invariance of second-order WISC-IV structure across China, Hong Kong, Macau, and Taiwan. *Personality and Individual Differences, 49*, 677–682. Available from https://doi.org/10.1016/j.paid.2010.06.004.

Cohen, J. (1992). A power primer. *Psychological Bulletin, 112*, 155–159. Available from https://doi.org/10.1037/0033-2909.112.1.155.

Diener, E., Oishi, S., & Tay, L. (2018). Advances in subjective well-being research. *Nature Human Behaviour, 2*, 253–260. Available from https://doi.org/10.1038/s41562-018-0307-6.

Georgas, J., Van de Vijver, F. J. R., & Berry, J. W. (2004). The ecocultural framework, ecosocial indices and psychological variables in cross-cultural research. *Journal of Cross-Cultural Psychology, 35*, 74–96. Available from https://doi.org/10.1177/0022022103260459.

Georgas, J., van de Vijver, F. J. R., Weiss, L. G., & Saklofske, D. H. (2003). A cross-cultural analysis of the WISC-III. In J. Georgas, L. G. Weiss, F. J. R. van de Vijver, & D. H. Saklofske (Eds.), *Culture and children's intelligence: Cross-cultural analysis of the WISC-III* (pp. 23–37). New York: Elsevier Science. Available from https://doi.org:10.1016/B978-012280055-9/50004-7.

Hambleton, R. K., Merenda, P. F., & Spielberger, C. D. (Eds.), (2005). *Adapting educational tests and psychological tests for cross-cultural assessment*. Mawhaw, NJ: Erlbaum.

Hambleton, R. K., & Patsula, L. (1999). Increasing the validity of adapted tests: Myths to be avoided and guidelines for improving test adaptation practices. *Journal of Applied Testing Technology, 1*, 1–16.

Harkness, J. A. (2003). Questionnaire translation. In J. A. Harkness, F. J. R. van de Vijver, & P. P. Mohler (Eds.), *Cross-cultural survey methods* (pp. 19–34). New York: Wiley.

Henrich, J., Heine, S. J., & Norenzayan, A. (2010). The weirdest people in the world? *Behavioral and Brain Sciences, 33*, 61–83. Available from https://doi.org/10.1017/S0140525X0999152X.

International Test Commission. (2016). *The ITC guidelines for translating and adapting tests* (2nd ed.). www.InTestCom.org.

Irvine, S. H. (1979). The place of factor analysis in cross-cultural methodology and its contribution to cognitive theory. In L. H. Eckensberger, W. J. Lonner, & Y. H. Poortinga (Eds.), *Cross-cultural contributions to psychology* (pp. 300–341). Lisse: Swets and Zeitlinger.

Jensen, A. R. (1980). *Bias in mental tests*. New York: Free Press.

King, M. F., Renó, V. F., & Novo, E. M. (2014). The concept, dimensions and methods of assessment of human well-being within a socioecological context: A literature review. *Social Indicators Research, 116*, 681–698. Available from https://doi.org/10.1007/s11205-013-0320-0.

Lubke, G. H., Dolan, C. V., & Kelderman, H. (2001). Investigating group differences on cognitive tests using Spearman's hypothesis: An evaluation of Jensen's method. *Multivariate Behavioral Research, 36*, 299–324. Available from https://doi.org/10.1207/S15327906299-324.

Lynn, R., & Mikk, J. (2007). National differences in intelligence and educational attainment. *Intelligence, 35*, 115–121. Available from https://doi.org/10.1016/j.intell.2006.06.001.

Muthén, L. K., & Muthén, B. O. (1998). *Mplus user's guide (7th ed.)*. Los Angeles, CA: Muthén & Muthén.

Pezzuti, L., & Orsini, A. (2016). Are there sex differences in the Wechsler Intelligence Scale for Children – Fourth Edition. *Learning and Individual Differences, 45*, 307–312. Available from https://doi.org/10.1016/j.lindif.2015.12.024.

Prifitera, A., Weiss, L. G., Saklofske, D. H., & Rolfhus, E. (2005). The WISC-IV in the clinical assessment context. In A. Prifitera, D. H. Saklofske, & L. G. Weiss (Eds.), *WISC-IV: Clinical use and interpretation, scientist-practitioner perspectives* (pp. 3–32). San Diego, CA: Elsevier. Available from https://doi.org:10.1016/B978-012564931-5/50002-5.

Rudnev, M., Lytkina, E., Davidov, E., Schmidt, P., & Zick, A. (2018). Testing measurement invariance for a second-order factor: A cross-national test of the Alienation Scale. *Methods, Data, Analyses: A Journal for Quantitative Methods and Survey Methodology (MDA), 12*, 47–76.

Rutkowski, L., & Svetina, D. (2014). Assessing the hypothesis of measurement invariance in the context of large-scale international surveys. *Educational and Psychological Measurement, 74*, 31–57. Available from https://doi.org/10.1177/0013164413498257.

Rutkowski, L., & Svetina, D. (2017). Measurement invariance in international surveys: Categorical indicators and fit measure performance. *Applied Measurement in Education, 30*, 39–51. Available from https://doi.org/10.1080/08957347.2016.1243540.

Van de Vijver, F. J. R. (1997). Meta-analysis of cross-cultural comparisons of cognitive test performance. *Journal of Cross-Cultural Psychology, 28*, 678–709. Available from https://doi.org/10.1177/0022022197286003.

Van de Vijver, F. J. R. (2011). Capturing bias in structural equation modeling. In E. Davidov, P. Schmidt, & J. Billiet (Eds.), *Cross-cultural analysis. Methods and applications* (pp. 3–34). New York: Routledge.

van der Linden, W. J., & Hambleton, R. K. (Eds.), (2013). *Handbook of modern item response theory*. New York: Springer Science & Business Media.

Wechsler, D. (2004). *Wechsler Intelligence Scale for Children: Fourth Edition (WISC-IV UK)*. London: Pearson.

Wechsler, D. (2015). *WISC-V, Escala de inteligencia de Wechsler para niños-V*. Madrid: Pearson.

Wechsler, D. (2016). *Wechsler Intelligence Scale for Children: Fifth Edition (WISC-V UK)*. London: Pearson.

Wechsler, D. (2017). *Wechsler Intelligence Scale for Children – Fifth Edition (WISC-V). Durchführungs- und Auswertungsmanual. German adaptation: F. Petermann*. Frankfurt: Pearson.

Chapter 8

The Flynn Effect and Its Clinical Implications

Jacques Grégoire[1] and Lawrence G. Weiss[2]

[1]Université Catholique de Louvain, Psychological Sciences Research Institute, Louvain-la-Neuve, Belgium, [2]Research and Measurement Consultant, San Antonio, TX, United States

WHAT DO WE KNOW ABOUT THE FLYNN EFFECT?

Definition

The Flynn effect (FE) is a generational phenomenon in which average Intelligence Quotient (IQ) scores have been found to increase across time in developed countries at a startlingly consistent rate of approximately 0.33 points per year, or 3.3 points per decade (Flynn, 1984, 1987).

This occurs because cohorts from more recent generations answer more questions correctly on average than the previous generation. The average number of questions answered correctly for each age group in the standardization sample is set to the mean subtest scaled score of 10, and then to the mean Full-Scale IQ (FSIQ) or Index score of 100 when the test is normed. If subsequent generations answer more questions correctly on average, they will obtain higher mean FSIQ scores using the original norms. Thus, average FSIQ scores tend to inflate as the norms age, that is, the longer it has been since the test was normed.

Eventually, the test is revised and renormed on a contemporary standardization sample and this higher average number of correct items is reanchored to the standard score means of 10 for subtests and 100 for the FSIQ and Index scores. Thus, the newly normed test will produce lower IQ and Index scores than the previous edition of the test given the same number of items answered correctly by the examinee.

The FE is undoubtedly one of the most puzzling observations made during the last 30 years in the domain of human intelligence. In 1984, Flynn

WISC-V. DOI: https://doi.org/10.1016/B978-0-12-815744-2.00008-2

published an article in which he analyzed 73 US studies (N total $= 7431$) comparing the scores on several intelligence tests across a 46-year period of time (Stanford−Binet Intelligence scales and Wechsler scales). All these studies compared the IQs obtained by a sample of individuals on each test and on the previous version of the same test, that is, using norms collected in the US population at two different points of time. These studies used 10 different norms, collected from 1932 to 1978. Analyzing the data of the comparative studies, Flynn observed a steady evolution of the intellectual level of the US population over 46 years. With one exception, he noted that the individuals get a higher IQ on the tests having the older norms, and vice versa. The performances of the individuals who participated in each study being the same from one test to another, the IQ differences came from a difference of the mean IQ score of the population to which the performances were compared. Flynn's observation corresponded therefore to an increase of the average intellectual level of the population across the time. During a period of 46 years, the average intellectual level of the US population increased by 13.8 IQ points, which represented a difference of nearly one standard deviation between the mean intellectual level of the US population in 1932 and in 1978. Flynn concluded that the average annual gain in the US population was 0.33 IQ points.

Flynn's first observation was only made on the US population, based on data from tests whose content was often modified from one standardization to another. To better appraise the phenomenon he had revealed, Flynn (1987) extended his first analysis to data sets from 14 countries where exactly the same test was used across the time. The most interesting data came from military conscripts, since virtually all 18-year-old men took the same test, often the Ravens Progressive Matrices Test, which remained unchanged since their creation in 1938. The cohorts being almost identical to the male population of the age group, the problem of potential sampling bias was eliminated. Table 8.1 shows the IQ gain of military examinees on the Ravens Progressive Matrices Test in four European countries: the Netherlands, Belgium (Dutch-speaking region), France, and Norway. In three of these countries, the examinees also completed a vocabulary test and an arithmetic test, also unchanged. To facilitate the comparisons, all the results are expressed on a scale with a mean of 100 and a standard deviation of 15.

In all four countries, the increase of the average IQ measured by the Ravens Progressive Matrices was significant and exceeded, by far, the 0.33 points observed by Flynn in the United States with the Stanford−Binet and the Wechsler scales. This is particularly interesting because the Ravens Progressive Matrices are considered a good measure of fluid intelligence (Gf) and a culturally reduced test. However, during the 1950s and 1960s, the average scores on the Ravens Progressive Matrices grew more rapidly than on tests measuring crystalized intelligence (Gc), which is more influenced by education and culture. During a rather short period (20 years), such an

TABLE 8.1 Evolution of Average IQ Scores on Ravens Progressive Matrices and of the Scores on Vocabulary and Arithmetic Tests in Four European Countries

Country	Period	Total and Annual Gains		
		Ravens	Vocabulary	Arithmetic
Holland	1952−72	12.43 (0.62)	−	−
Belgium	1958−67	7.82 (0.87)	4.50 (0.50)	4.36 (0.48)
France	1949−74	25.12 (1.01)	9.06 (0.36)	9.64 (0.39)
Norway	1954−68	8.80 (0.63)	8.40 (0.60)	7.90 (0.56)
Norway	1968−80	2.60 (0.22)	1.50 (0.13)	− 3.10 (−0.26)

Note: the average annual gain is in brackets.
Source: From Flynn (1987).

increase of scores on a Gf measure cannot be a consequence of genetic modifications in the population. Only environmental factors could explain the fast growth of scores on the Ravens Progressive Matrices.

Another interesting observation, as can be seen in Table 8.1, is the smaller gain on achievement tests observed in France and Belgium. In these countries, school-related knowledge shows less improvement than performances on a measure of Gf. However, in Norway, the evolution of the scores on the achievement tests was more correlated to the evolution of the scores on the Ravens Progressive Matrices. Norwegians also showed a second feature. The evolution curve of their performances on the Ravens Progressive Matrices changed between the period 1954−68 and the 1968−80. During the first period, a strong growth of the scores was observed (0.63 on average each year), but the growth slowed down during the second period (0.22 on average each year). Such an observation was important because it indicated that the evolution of the average IQ is perhaps not a steady nor an endless process.

Herrnstein and Murray (1994) suggested that the observation made by Flynn be called the FE, even if he was not the very first person to report an increase of the IQ scores over time in developed countries (Lynn, 2013). But Flynn was the first researcher to systematically analyze this phenomenon. In his publications, Flynn discussed several paradoxes related to IQ gains. Among them, he emphasized the intellectual disability paradox (Flynn, 2007, p. 9): "How can our recent ancestors have been so unintelligent compared to ourselves?" He also questioned the persistence of the IQ gains into the 21st century, at least for developed nations. Several of Flynn's questions are discussed in this chapter, bringing into focus the consequences of the FE on the clinical use of intelligence tests, especially the WISC-V.

Variability According to Intellectual Tasks

As mentioned in the previous section, the FE is not uniform across domains of cognitive ability. Much of the research on the FE among children and adolescents has focused on the overall composite scores from multiability batteries (such as the Wechsler scales' FSIQ), and when lower-level measures have been examined, they often have been the dimensions of fluid reasoning and crystallized ability. The research base is smaller regarding domains such as working memory, spatial ability, and processing speed. Thus, evidence from revisions of the more recent editions of the Wechsler scales, which differentiate these domains in addition to fluid and crystallized intelligence, makes an important contribution to the research base.

To put the findings from the most recent revision (WISC-IV to WISC-V) into context, it helps to review what is known about the patterns of FE by cognitive domain. In a recent metaanalysis of 241 studies from 1909 to 2010, Pietschnig and Voracek (2013) estimated average annual standard-score gains by domain to be 0.29 for overall composites such as FSIQ, 0.42 for fluid reasoning, 0.30 for spatial ability, and 0.26 for crystallized intelligence. Table 8.2 provides more specific information by showing the average annual change for the composite and subtest scores of the WISC and WPPSI in their two most recent revisions (from the second to the third editions, and from the third to the fourth editions). Modifications occurred from one edition to the other, with some subtests and subscales being introduced or withdrawn. Therefore, several comparisons cannot be done.

The higher level of FE for fluid/perceptual than crystallized intelligence has been a pervasive and stable finding (Kaufman & Lichtenberger, 2006). In particular, Raven's Progressive Matrices, a highly g-loaded perceptual measure of fluid reasoning, has shown large increases over time, averaging better than 0.50 standard-score points per year, in studies conducted in numerous countries (Flynn, 1987). Consistent with this phenomenon, fairly large FEs have been found for matrices subtests included in cognitive batteries for children, such as the WPPSI (0.40, WPPSI-III to WPPSI-IV) and the Differential Ability Scales (0.31, DAS to DAS−II; Elliott, 2007). However, not all perceptual ability tasks have demonstrated the same high level of FE, as seen in Table 8.2. For example, the Block Design subtest of the Wechsler scales and the similar Block Construction subtests of the DAS and the Kaufman Ability Battery for Children (Kaufman & Kaufman, 2004), which are thought to measure a combination of fluid reasoning and spatial ability, show lower FEs: an average of 0.34 on the WISC (second to third, and third to fourth editions), an average of −0.04 on the WPPSI (second to third, and third to fourth editions), and 0.19 and 0.14 on the DAS and K-ABC (first to second editions). Nonverbal-reasoning task types other than Matrices and Block Design (e.g., Picture Concepts or Picture Arrangement) are not sufficiently prevalent on cognitive batteries to support generalizations about their levels of FE.

TABLE 8.2 Average Annual Standard-Score Change on Composites and Subtests in Recent Revisions of the WISC and WPPSI

Subtests/Composites	WISC		WPPSI	
Editions:	R to III	III to IV	R to III	III to IV
Publication year:	1991	2003	2002	2012
Full-scale IQ	0.31	0.21	0.09	0.33
Verbal	0.14	0.26	0.03	0.25
Performance/Perceptual	0.44	0.25	0.24	0.28
Working Memory	–	0.13	–	–
Processing Speed	–	0.46	–	0.59
Similarities	0.38	0.29	– 0.08	0.55
Comprehension	0.18	0.17	– 0.04	0.25
Vocabulary	0.12	0.04	0.08	0.30
Information	– 0.09	0.13	– 0.04	0.20
Arithmetic	0.09	– 0.08	–	–
Matrix Reasoning				0.40
Block Design	0.26	0.42	– 0.23	0.15
Picture Concepts				0.20
Picture Completion	0.26	0.29	0.58	–
Picture Arrangement	0.56	–	–	–
Object Assembly	0.35	–	0.42	0.15
Digit Span	0.03	0.04	–	–
Symbol Search/Bug Search	–	0.50	–	0.75
Coding/Animal Coding	0.21	0.29	–	0.20
N	206	244	176	246

Notes: For the WISC-R to WISC-III comparisons, WISC-R VIQ and PIQ were compared to WISC-III VIQ and PIQ, respectively.
For the WISC-III to WISC-IV comparisons, WISC-III VCI was compared to WISC-IV VCI, and WISC-III POI was compared to WISC-IV PRI. For the Working Memory comparison, WISC-III Freedom from Distractibility Index (FDI) was compared to WISC-IV WMI. For the Processing Speed comparison, WISC-III PSI and WISC-IV PSI were used.
For the WPPSI-R to WPPSI-III comparisons, WPPSI-R VIQ and PIQ were compared to WPPSI-III VIQ and PIQ, respectively.
For the WPPSI-III to WPPSI-IV comparisons, WPPSI-III VIQ was compared to WPPSI-IV VCI. For the Performance/Perceptual comparison, the average of the WPPSI-III PIQ / WPPSI-IV VSI and the WPPSI-III PIQ/WPPSI-IV FRI was used. For the Processing Speed comparison, the WPPSI-III Processing Speed Quotient (PSQ) and WPPSI-IV PSI was used. The WPPSI-III PSQ is based on the Symbol Search and Coding subtests. The WPPSI-IV Processing Speed Index (PSI) is based on the Bug Search and Animal Coding subtests.
All values are in the standard-score metric where $SD = 15$.
Source: Test manuals of the WISC-IV (Wechsler, D. (2003). WISC-IV technical and interpretive manual. Bloomington, MN: Pearson) and WPPSI-IV (Wechsler, D. (2012). WPPSI-IV technical and interpretive manual. Bloomington, MN: Pearson). Data and copyright Pearson 2014.

As noted above, measures of crystallized ability typically have somewhat lower levels of FE than measures of fluid reasoning. As shown in Table 8.2, the FE for the WISC verbal composite (VIQ or VCI) averaged 0.20 in the two most recent revisions, compared with an average of 0.34 for the performance/perceptual composite (PIQ or PRI) of that instrument. A similar pattern was observed on the WPPSI, with average FEs of 0.14 and 0.26 for the verbal and performance/perceptual composites, respectively. Measures of working memory or short-term retrieval have shown varying levels of FE among children and adolescents, with the average level being low to moderate. From WISC-III to WISC-IV the Working Memory Index showed a FE of only 0.13, and the K-ABC revision yielded FE values for the Sequential Processing scale of 0.09 (preschool) and 0.31 (child). The Digit Span subtest of the WISC had FEs of 0.03 and 0.04 in the two most recent revisions. On the other hand, high levels of FE have been found for measures of processing speed. In the most recent WISC and WPPSI revisions, the Processing Speed Index had FE values of 0.46 and 0.59, respectively. For WISC, these were due mainly to the Symbol Search subtest (0.50) rather than Coding (0.29, as well as 0.21 in the previous WISC revision). Note that the WPPSI-IV PSI is based on two new subtests named Bug Search and Animal Coding which measure the same constructs as Symbol Search and Coding in WPPSI-III, but contain important content differences. In the most recent WPPSI revision, the FE for Processing Speed (0.59) is driven more by Symbol Search/Bug Search (0.75) than Coding/Animal Coding (0.20), which may be partly due to content differences in addition to generational shifting.

In summary, among children and adolescents the FE on Wechsler scales mirrors the pattern generally found across ages and instruments, with higher levels for the performance/perceptual scales that measure fluid reasoning and spatial ability, and lower levels for the verbal scales that measure primarily crystallized ability. Short-term or working memory shows a modest FE, whereas there has been rapid change in processing speed.

Variability According to Gender and Intelligence Quotient Level

Does the FE vary as a function of gender or ability level? A differential FE by gender would imply that the female population has changed over time to a different degree than the male population, which is another way of saying that the size of the gender difference in ability would have changed over that time period. Although this would be of theoretical and scientific interest, it would not have practical implications for score interpretation because intelligence tests use combined-gender rather than gender-specific norms. Although the overall FE might be due more to the change in one half of the population than the other, that would have no impact on how one would interpret a particular individual's performance or even how one would adjust an individual's score for the FE, if one chose to do so. Whether the examinee is male or female, their performance is still compared with that of the overall population.

Perhaps counterintuitively, the demographic characteristics (other than age and ability level) of the sample used to study the FE are not helpful in investigating whether there are differential FEs for different population subgroups, nor do they have any influence on the estimate of the size of the FE. This is because the sole function of the individuals in the sample is to equate the two tests being compared using common persons. The logic of the analysis rests on the assumptions that each person's true ability is the same during both administrations (setting aside practice effects), and that the two instruments measure the same construct equally accurately. If these assumptions hold, then we can see how a constant level of ability translates to scores based on norms constructed at different time points. If different sizes of FE were observed for the male and female participants in the typical one-point-in-time study—that is, if males and females who obtained equal scores on the more recent test scored differently on the older test—this would be evidence of an interaction between gender and the difference in content between the two tests. It would not have implications regarding the relative amounts of change over time in the latent ability distributions of the male and female populations.

Because the FE has to do with population changes, not individuals, addressing questions about differential FEs for subgroups requires studying subgroup population data from different points in time. However, intelligence instruments typically do not provide subgroup norms, making this line of research challenging. Instead, researchers must identify or collect subpopulation-representative samples from different time periods and compare their rates of change. With respect to gender differences in the FE, the limited amount of research that does exist tends to indicate no sex-related differences in the rate of population change in cognitive abilities. A study conducted by Flynn (1998a) on young Israelis addressed this issue. In Israel, both men and women must perform military service. Between 1976 and 1984, all conscripts completed the Raven Progressive Matrices test and a verbal intelligence test. Flynn observed that during this period, the average Raven's IQ of men increased by 0.61 points per year and women by 0.64 points per year. During the same period, the average score on the verbal intelligence test increased, respectively, by 0.37 and 0.35 points. Wai and Putallaz (2011) reported equivalent male and female FEs over three decades among high-ability students taking the SAT, ACT, and EXPLORE. Ang, Rodgers, and Wanstrom (2010) measured the FE as the increase in children's normative scores on a test of mathematical problem solving as the norms got increasingly out of date, and found no sex difference. All these studies showed that the FE seems independent of gender.

Ability level is not subject to the methodological limitation that applies to studying differential FEs by gender or other subgroups. The question being addressed is whether, as the ability distribution shifts over time, its shape changes. Analyzing differential FEs by level of ability is straightforward, as long as regression artifacts are avoided by using something other than the score being analyzed to form the ability groups. For example, this topic may be addressed by using naturally occurring groups that vary in ability level, or by forming ability subgroups according to an independent test score.

Considerable attention has been given to the question of whether the increase in ability over time has been consistent at different levels of ability. One reason for this interest is that a differential FE by ability level would have practical consequences for test interpretation, because it would mean that the best estimate of the impact of the FE on an individual's score would be a function of that person's level of ability. Another reason is that a non-uniform shift in the ability distribution over time (i.e., greater change at some ability levels than others) would be informative regarding causal hypotheses for the FE. For example, a finding that the lower end of the ability distribution had risen quite a bit more than the upper end would lend support to explanations focusing on increasing amelioration of factors that cause low intelligence.

Results of these investigations have been mixed. Some have found greater FEs at lower ability levels. For example, using combined data from four recent Wechsler revisions (involving WPPSI, WISC, and WAIS), Zhou, Zhu, and Weiss (2010) found a significantly larger FE on the Performance IQ/Perceptual Reasoning Index for examinees in the average to low range of verbal ability than for those with above-average verbal ability. Other studies finding greater increase in the low range of the ability distribution include those by Colom, Lluis-Font, and Andrés-Pueyo (2005) and Teasdale and Owen (1989). However, a number of other investigations have found different patterns of effect (e.g., Sanborn, Truscott, Phelps, & McDougal, 2003; Spitz, 1989). Summarizing the existing data through their metaanalysis, Trahan, Stuebing, Fletcher, and Hiscock (2014) found no relationship between ability level and the FE when all studies were considered. When only studies involving modern tests (those normed since 1972) were included, a statistically significant relationship emerged, with a greater average FE at low ability levels. However, because this result was driven by a few atypical results from studies with nonstandard procedures such as lack of counterbalancing or different floors (lowest possible scores) on the two instruments, the authors consider the finding unreliable.

The hypothesis that the FE is driven to a substantial degree by improvement at the lower end of the ability distribution would predict that the variability of ability scores would decrease over time as scores for the low functioning group move closer to the middle of the distribution (Rowe & Rodgers, 2002). Although this analytical approach has also yielded inconsistent results, the majority of studies have reported decreasing variability (Pietschnig & Voracek, 2013).

Overall, there does not seem to be strong evidence from the presently available studies that the FE varies by ability level; thus, there is currently not a good basis for rejecting the assumption that the FE is a uniform upward shift in the ability distribution.

Variation of the Flynn Effect Over Time

The FE does not occur abruptly when new norms are published. It appears gradually, beginning upon publication of new norms. As the characteristics of the population change inexorably, while norms remain fixed, the gap between the two continues to widen between each standardization and the next one. Norms become more and more lenient across time, until the day new norms are set up. Such an evolution of norm validity is a problem for clinical practice, since the value of the cut scores lessens over time and the number of misidentified individuals increases. To solve this problem, Flynn (1998b) suggested correcting the old norms on the basis of an annual change of the average IQ level of the population of 0.25 points. This adjustment value is a rough estimate based on past observations of the FE, postulating a linear evolution of the population average IQ across time and into the future.

But several recent observations suggested that the shape of the FE could no longer be linear. The FE could have reached a ceiling with the consequence that the future evolution of the population average IQ would be flat. In Table 8.1, reporting Flynn's data collected in Norway, we have already seen that the rate of the FE was slower from 1968 to 1980, compared to the trend from 1954 to 1968. Sundet, Barlaug, and Torjussen (2004) reported more recent data from Norwegian conscripts. They observed that the mean scores of the conscripts on a Raven-like test stopped increasing in the mid 1990s, and even slightly decreased. Similar observations were made in Denmark (Teasdale & Owen, 2007), Sweden (Rönnlund, Carlstedt, Blomstedt, Nilsson, & Weinehall, 2013) and Finland (Dutton & Lynn, 2013). Two explanations were proposed for the slowdown of the FE in the Nordic countries of Europe. It could be partly attributable to the non-European immigrants with lower education who settled in the north of Europe from the end of the 1960s (te Nijenhuis, de Jong, Evers, & van der Flier, 2004). It could also be the consequence of dysgenic fertility (Nyborg, 2012), that is, the negative association between fertility and IQ, the families with low IQ having more children than the families with high IQ. The first explanation does not apply to Finland (Dutton & Lynn, 2013) and, consequently, cannot be generalized. The second one is more speculative and needs more empirical data to be supported. Another approach to explaining the FE curve is to consider it as a consequence of several interlinked factors (see below "Causes of the Flynn Effect"). These factors stimulate the development of individual intellectual potential, but their positive influence is likely not infinite and is, therefore, gradually coming to an end. Just as the traditional proverb related to the stock market says, "trees don't grow to the sky," the shape of the FE is likely to be curvilinear.

Causes of the Flynn Effect

The causes of the FE have been much debated in the scientific literature. There is no single cause of the FE, and it should be considered as the consequence of a combination of several factors. The main potential causes are briefly reviewed below, and then concluded with the presentation of a general model proposed by Dickens and Flynn (2001), which explain the FE as the interaction between environmental and genetic factors.

Familiarity with intelligence tests has been suggested as a possible cause of the FE (Jensen, 1998). The FE would be an artifact due to the practice tests. It is true that familiarity with test contents can be a source of bias in testing. Such a risk justifies the confidentiality of test contents and the need to avoid their public release. The mere completion of a test as a source of learning and short-term memory effects is well documented. For example, the test−retest of the WISC-IV ($N = 247$), with a mean interval of 32 days (Wechsler, 2003) led to an increase of 2.1 points for the VCI, 5.9 points for the PRI, 2.6 points for the WMI, 7.1 points for the PSI, and 5.6 points for the FSIQ. This phenomenon is particularly important in tasks where individuals have to learn associations (e.g., Coding) or strategies (e.g., Block Design). However, the learning effect fades over time and tends to disappear after a year (Canivez & Watkins, 1998). We cannot therefore assume that the familiarity with intelligence tests has a significant impact on the FE, especially in countries where the testing of intelligence is not systematic and where a large number of individuals never completed an intelligence test.

Education is a good candidate to explain the FE. Ceci and Williams (1997) collected a large set of data showing the effect of schooling on intelligence. The statistics published by UNESCO highlighted important changes in education around the world during the 20th century. Illiteracy has decreased and the rate of attendance at preschool, primary, secondary, and higher education has sharply increased, especially in industrial countries where the FE was observed. A Spanish study conducted in 1978−79 (cited by Fernandez-Ballesteros & Juan-Espinosa, 2001) showed that after controlling for socioeconomic status, a significant advantage ($P < .001$) in intellectual performances for children who attended kindergarten was seen. Based on several previous studies, Ceci (1990) showed that education stimulates the development of several skills that play important roles in intelligence tests, especially perceptual skills, concept formation, and memory. Rönnlund and Nilsson (2008) analyzed a Swedish data set collected from 1989 to 2004. They noted that years of education, height (used as an index of health and nutrition), and number of siblings[1] accounted for more than 94% of FE observed between 1989 and 2004, education being the strongest predictor among the three. They concluded (p. 204) that "education may exert influence on time−related patterns on (broad) fluid (visuospatial ability, episodic memory) as well as crystallized/semantic aspect of cognition."

Changes in family characteristics also play a role in the FE. During the 20th century, the increase of the average household income, the average level of education, and the professional qualifications of individuals strongly changed the conditions of education within families. Parents have more time and resources to educate their children. They are also better informed about normal child development and the conditions that can foster it. Because of the decrease in family size, more resources can be devoted to the education of fewer children. The quality of the home environment has clearly had an impact on child cognitive development. Espy, Molfese, and DiLalla (2001) conducted a longitudinal study following 105 children between the ages of 3 and 6 years. Each year, these children were tested with the Stanford−Binet−IV Intelligence Scale. The researchers also evaluated the quality of the environment using two measures. The first one was a questionnaire completed by the parents, which assessed the characteristics of the home environment: learning materials, communication skills, physical environment, academic stimulation, behavioral models, variety of experiences, warmth, tolerance, and acceptance of the child. The second measure assessed the socioeconomic status (educational level, occupation of parents, and family income) as an indirect index of the quality of the home environment. The researchers observed that the two measures of the family environment had a moderate but significant relationship with children's intellectual performance. Characteristics measured by the first questionnaire had an equal relationship with all aspects of intellectual activity measured by the Stanford−Binet. The socioeconomic status measure had a significant effect only on nonverbal intelligence tasks. For a detailed analysis of socioeconomic and home environment variables impacting children's WISC-V test performance, we refer the reader to Chapter 5 ("WISC-V Use in Societal Context").

Changes in the family are also related to the increase of technology in everyday life. During the 20th century, we moved from direct interactions with reality to interactions mediated by symbolic representations (Fernandez-Ballesteros & Juan-Espinosa, 2001). For example, in the past, doing washing involved direct interaction with clothes using psychomotor skills. Today, the same task is done through symbolic representations: the instructions to the washing machine. The symbolic mediation reduces the role of psychomotor skills and increases the role of cognitive skills. The growing interactions

---

1. The FE is related to a smaller number of siblings.

with symbolic representations of the world very likely help explain the importance of the FE in fluid reasoning tasks in the Raven's Progressive Matrices. Technology stimulates learning and cognitive development and due to its rapid development requires continuous learning throughout life.

Changes in bioenvironmental conditions seem to play a significant role in the FE, but the importance of their impact is controversial. Bioenvironmental conditions represent the interactions between the environment and the bio-physical characteristics of individuals. Several authors have noted, in parallel with the FE, an increase in life expectancy, a reduction in infant mortality, and an increase in average height in the industrialized countries during the 20th century. Schmidt, Jorgensen, and Michaelsen (1995) analyzed the evolution of the conscript heights between 1960 and 1990 in 11 European countries. In all these countries, a steady increase of the average height of conscripts was observed. For example, in 1960, the average height of the Dutch conscripts was 1.76 m. In 1990, the average height of the conscripts was 1.81 m. However, in Holland and the Scandinavian countries, this growth of height has now peaked for several years. The average height of Norwegian and Swedish conscripts has not increased since 1975, but continued its previous rate of growth in the countries of southern Europe, such as Spain and Italy. Schmidt et al. (1995) showed a close relationship between the increase of height and the decrease of postneonatal mortality (death between 28 days and 1 year). This reduction in postneonatal mortality is linked to improved nutrition and a reduction of the incidence of infectious diseases. Postneonatal mortality reached a floor in the Netherlands and the Nordic countries around the 1970s, while in Spain and Italy, this floor was only reached in the 1980s. The authors concluded that the factors that determine the fall of postneonatal mortality are the same as those responsible for the increase in height, namely the improvement of nutrition and the reduction of infectious diseases during early childhood. Many clues suggest that the factors responsible for the increase in height also have an impact on intellectual development. A study of 32,887 Swedish conscripts at age 18 (Tuvemo, Jonsson, & Persson, 1999) showed a significant relationship between the height of the conscripts and their intellectual performances. The intellectual level of the conscripts actually increased in parallel with their height. A longitudinal study of 3733 Americans of Japanese origin (Abbott et al., 1998) came to the same conclusion. Furthermore, many studies on child malnutrition have clearly demonstrated a negative impact of malnutrition on physical and cognitive development (Pollitt, 2000). It is therefore very likely that during the 20th century, the improvement of child nutrition and the prevention of infectious diseases contributed to the increases in both height and intellectual performances in industrialized countries.

How can the environmental factors discussed above explain an important IQ gain in a rather short period of time, while many studies show the important role of genes in determining individual differences in intellectual performances? Dickens and Flynn (2001) proposed an explanation to this apparent paradox. This explanation is close to the bioecological model of Bronfenbrenner and Ceci (1994). Dickens and Flynn postulated that genes and environment do not act independently of each other, but instead are correlated. This correlation is a consequence of reciprocal causal relationships between the intellectual abilities of an individual and the environment. Innate intellectual abilities allow taking advantage of the environment, which stimulates their own growth. Individuals may then look for new environmental conditions suitable for the development of their abilities, and so on. Through this process, small environmental influences can have large effects on the IQ. Dickens and Flynn (2001, p. 347) called this process "the social multiplier." If the genetic potential of the individual finds adequate environmental conditions, it can get into a cycle of positive relationships with this environment. In the industrialized countries, more favorable environmental conditions emerged during the 20th century, stimulating the development of the intellectual potential of the population. The multiplier effect, which followed, was significant and can easily explain the FE, without denying the role of genetic differences in human intellectual abilities.

It is likely that the stimulating effect of the quality of the environment has some limitations. Even if the conditions for growth are optimal, human intelligence probably has intrinsic limitations that, one day or another, will be achieved. At that moment, the FE will reach a ceiling. Such a phenomenon has already been observed for height (Schmidt et al., 1995). We have seen above that the height of the conscripts peaked around 1975 in Norway and Sweden, but continued to grow in other European countries. It is likely that in the first two countries, the improvement of the bioenvironmental conditions allowed the genetic potential for physical growth to fully express itself. Therefore, the current environmental improvements no longer produce an increase of height comparable to the increase observed in the previous generations. In the case of intelligence, even if an increase of intelligence test scores is no longer observed in some developing countries (see above "Variation of the Flynn Effect Over Time"), we do not have enough data to say that a ceiling is reached and no future increase could be expected. As Bronfenbrenner and Ceci (1994) emphasized, the amount of the genetic potential that has yet to be revealed is unknown and, perhaps, unknowable.

IMPLICATIONS OF THE FLYNN EFFECT FOR PRACTITIONERS

The FE has significant and important repercussions in high-stakes, applied academic and legal settings (Hiscock, 2007). Especially, as intellectual measures are closely related to the determination of intellectual and learning disabilities (e.g., developmental dyslexia, dyscalculia) the FE could potentially impact access to important constitutional and/or educational rights and resources only available to individuals with these disorders. In the next several sections, this impact is analyzed and possible ways to deal with it are discussed.

Implications for the Identification of Learning and Intellectual Disabilities

In 2004, with the Individuals with Disabilities Education Improvement Act (IDEA), federal regulations adopted a new definition of learning disorders (LDs). Currently, the most prevalent diagnosis of LDs in special education programs is under the Code of Federal Regulations (CFR; 34 CFR § 300.8 (c)(10)) and is based on clinical findings and specified clinical criteria. Therefore, some schools no longer use the discrepancy between academic achievement and intellectual level as a criterion for a LD. However, such a discrepancy is still recommended by many school districts and jurisdictions (Bradley, Danielson, & Hallahan, 2002; Fletcher & Vaughn, 2009) for placement in special educational services. In this case, one standard deviation (i.e., 15 points in the WISC-V) is often considered as a large discrepancy and the criterion of LDs. For example, using the discrepancy definition for a reading disorder, if a child's intellectual score on the WISC-V is 100, he will be considered as having a LD if he obtains an overall reading ability score of 84 or lower on a comprehensive test assessing several aspects of reading (decoding, fluency, and comprehension). This example shows the critical role of the global intellectual score as a criterion for specific learning disorder (SLD), ultimately leading to the provision of special educational services. In this approach, the intellectual score is considered as an *"absolute criterion"* (Kaufman & Kaufman, 2001). However, the FE may impact this criterion. The older the norms used as reference, the higher the global intellectual score could be and the larger the gap between the intellectual level and the current academic achievement. Rejecting the discrepancy criterion is not the solution to avoid the impact of the FE on the LD diagnosis. The FE also affects school districts and jurisdictions that have adopted more contemporary qualifying standards for placement in special education programs and learning disability determinations, such as the processing strengths and weaknesses approach, since intellectual tasks are differentially impacted by FE (see above "Variability According to the Intellectual Tasks"). For example, visual spatial tasks often show larger FE than verbal tasks. So, using an older test to compare strength in visual spatial abilities to weakness in verbal abilities could yield a larger difference due to FE. This difference will be smaller if using a recently restandardized test.

Kanaya and Ceci (2012) recently investigated the potential effects of the FE on the diagnosis of SLDs. This research, similar to previous studies (Gaskill & Brantley, 1996; Truscott & Frank, 2001), used logistic regression analyses for examining the changes in diagnoses of learning disability across the time after a new assessment. This study showed a significant decrease in the number of children eligible for special education programs, partially due to the FE. Children who had originally been determined as learning disabled using the discrepancy between IQ and academic achievement were tested using an older version of Wechsler Intelligence Scale for Children (WISC-R; Wechsler, 1974). When they were retested with a more recent version of the same scale (WISC-III; Wechsler, 1991), they showed a decline of their intellectual level, and therefore no longer met the criteria for a LD. In other words, the use of the new test led to a decrease of the number of children determined eligible for special education services as learning disabled. Kanaya and Ceci (2012) also observed that, as a consequence of a lower score on the more recent version of the test, some children were no longer determined as learning disabled, but were labeled as "mentally disabled." As a consequence, they failed to qualify for special educational services under a SLD category, but some may have qualified for services as intellectually disabled. Based on this study, it should be pointed out that it would be easier to qualify for services using older IQ tests. When adopting a newly renormed test, districts may therefore find a slightly lower proportion of the student population eligible for services as learning disabled compared to when using the previous edition of the test during its last few years. However, the magnitude of the impact depends on the size of the FE observed when the test is renormed. The FE between the WISC-IV and WISC-V is somewhat smaller than between some previous editions, so the impact on the percentage of students eligible, while still present, will be correspondingly smaller with this revision. It is also important to mention that the criteria used by school districts to determine eligibility for special education services are administrative criteria only, and not the same as clinical criteria to diagnose developmental dyslexia. For further discussion on that point we refer the reader to Chapter 9 on LD assessment.

Similar observations were made with regard to the diagnosis of intellectual disabilities according to the criteria of intellectual disability specified by the American Association on Intellectual and Developmental Disabilities (AAIDD) (Schalock et al., 2010) and/or the Diagnostic and Statistical Manual of Mental Disorders, Fifth Edition (DSM-5) (American Psychiatric Association, 2013). Under AAIDD and DSM-5 criteria, a deficit or impairment in intellectual functioning is formally defined as a score on an individually administered test of intelligence that is two standard deviations or less below the test mean, that is, a score of 70 or below for tests with a mean of 100 and a standard deviation of 15 points. As a consequence of the FE, we could expect that the number of people diagnosed as mental retarded on the basis of an IQ equal or below 70 IQ should gradually decrease as a function of the aging test norms. On the other hand, this number should increase with the publication of new norms. Based on data from the US Department of Education, Ceci (2000) showed that this scenario was going only partly as expected. He recorded the number of children diagnosed as intellectually disabled between 1977 and 1995. Until 1990, these children were usually diagnosed with the WISC-R. As anticipated, the number of children diagnosed as intellectually disabled declined gradually between 1977 and 1990, from 960,000 to 570,000. In 1991, the introduction of the WISC-III should have stimulated a sharp increase of the number of children diagnosed as mentally disabled, but Ceci did not observe this trend. Instead, the number of children diagnosed as intellectually disabled continued to decline until 1993, and only then rose gradually. Several explanations could be proposed to explain this phenomenon. The most plausible is that practitioners take a while to adopt the new version of a test. A second explanation, not incompatible with the first one, is that practitioners tend to adjust the new norms upward, considering they are harder than the ones previously used. This may be, in part, because this diagnosis also requires that both adaptive and intellectual functioning be two or more standard deviations below the mean. Practitioners seem to be more flexible with the procedures and the scoring criteria of the new test when making such diagnoses.

The available evidence strongly suggests that the shape of the FE curve varies by construct measured, test battery, and country, and may not be as stable across generations as Flynn argued (Kaufman & Weiss, 2010). Thus, FE adjustments for routine evaluations for LDs and intellectual disabilities (IDs) are not recommended (Weiss, 2010). The best course is to use the most current norms available, and take the standard error of the test into account when making special education eligibility determinations. As the Wechsler intelligence scales are revised about every 10 years, a maximum FE of 3–4 points could be expected before the publication of the next revision. This FE is smaller than the 90% confidence interval that every clinician should report around the observed scores. Consequently, always using the most recent version of the Wechsler scales and mentioning the confidence interval around the observed scores seem to be the best recommendation to avoid adverse consequences of the FE on routine special education evaluations.

Implications for High-Stakes Legal Evaluations

Another impact of the FE on the diagnosis of ID is related to the death penalty. Although the majority of jurisdictions in the United States preclude the imposition of capital punishment on children [juveniles or minors prior to the age of 18; c., Roper v. Simmons, 543 US 551 (2005)], as it is viewed as "disproportional punishment," adolescents have faced capital punishment and have been executed in the past, and they have been or are currently on Death Row in a select number of states in the United States. Similarly, with regard to adults, it is common in criminal cases to introduce into evidence archival test scores from the childhood or developmental period of an adult offender who faces capital punishment before a court of law. Therefore, the

WISC-V and its predecessors may be relevant in both child and adult criminal cases to prove the presence of ID or borderline intellectual impairments. This information can be crucial because an impaired intellect is allowable as a mitigating or exculpatory factor, especially in cases associated with capital punishment in the United States during the course of an Atkins claim. An Atkins claim is raised when a defendant or petitioner, through his or her attorney or legal representative, petitions a court to avoid the imposition of capital punishment on constitutional grounds as a result of ID. Such claims emerged from the Atkins *v.* Virginia Supreme Court decision, which deemed unconstitutional to execute individuals with ID (Atkins *v.* Virginia, 2002). In this landmark case, US Supreme Court opined that it was inconsistent with "modern standards of decency" and with the Eight Amendment of the US Constitution addressing "cruel and unusual punishment" to execute persons with ID. An Atkins claim requires a valid and reliable assessment of the individual's intelligence, as it is crucial information used by the defense attorney to require the suspension of capital punishment. However, in actual practice, many defendants who appear before a court of law with a petition on the grounds of ID already may have had their intellect measured many years or even decades before, often with some prior version of WISC. In addition, the individual may have been administered a test of intellect that was published a long time after its original publication. For example, the WISC-III (Wechsler, 1991) may have been administered in 2001, a decade after its publication, but before the WISC-IV was available. In such an event, the defendant's IQ score may not meet the criteria for ID simply because the older norms inflated the obtained score due to the FE.

Interestingly, older norms produce higher scores that favor state prosecutors whose role in the judicial system is to argue that the convicted felon is not mentally retarded and therefore may be legally executed (in those states that allow capital punishment). Current norms produce relatively lower scores that favor defense attorneys whose role it is to argue that the convicted felon is mentally retarded and therefore cannot be legally executed under the Atkins ruling. Further, taking into account the standard error of the test favors the defense attorney's position because scores in the low 70s may still be considered within the mentally retarded range based on the confidence interval. In 2014, however, the US Supreme Court ruled that states must take into account the standard error of measurement of the test when making these determinations (see Hall *v.* State of Florida). Thus, the IQ scores that school psychologists place into record for children may have far-reaching future consequences for children who later commit murder as adults in those states where capital punishment is legal.

Therefore, the question arises whether to adjust the scores obtained using old norms. Some authors remain neutral on this issue (Frumpkin, 2006), but several others advocate a systematic correction of the observed test scores because of its life and death implications (e.g., Reynolds, Niland, Wright, &

Rosenn, 2010). According to Young (2012), not correcting for the FE across jurisdictions in the United States has led to the inconsistent application of the Atkins *v*. Virginia's Supreme Court opinion in American courtrooms in capital punishment cases. Based on Flynn's observations, Fletcher, Stuebing, and Hughues (2010) supported an adjustment of three points per decade. However, such a correction is only a rough estimate from a trend observed in the past on the basis of a selection of intelligence tests. The shape of the FE curve seems not to be linear, but instead curvilinear (see above). Moreover, the impact of the FE varies from test to test. It is much more important with tests measuring mainly Gf intelligence (e.g., Ravens Progressive Matrices) than with tests measuring several facets of intelligence (e.g., Wechsler intelligence scales). Therefore, using a correction of 0.30 point per year could be misleading. Sometimes it will be too large of a correction, but sometimes not enough. In high-stakes cases such as the death penalty, using such a generalized estimate has been debated extensively (Kaufman & Weiss, 2010). In our opinion, when using an older test before the new version is available, a generalized estimate of FE based on 0.30 points per year is reasonable practice in high-stakes legal cases. Once the updated norms are available, however, archival scores previously obtained with the older version of the test should be adjusted based on the known FE empirically obtained from studies comparing the two relevant editions of the test. This will more accurately take into account the changing nature of the FE curve over time with different construct and in different cultures.

THE FLYNN EFFECT IN THE WISC-IV AND WISC-V

Flynn and Weiss (2007) studied the FE on the WISC from its first edition to the WISC-IV. The date of reference for the standardization of the first WISC was 1947.5 and 2001.75 for the WISC-IV. Therefore, the authors had the opportunity to track the gains of intelligence scores across the different editions of the WISC during a period of 54.25 years. During this period, the FSIQ gain grew from 100.00 to 116.83, that is, an increase of more than one standard deviation ($SD = 15$). This global gain corresponds to a gain of roughly 0.30 points per year. Small variations of the pace of FSIQ gain were observed across the time: 0.311 from WISC to WISC-R, 0.322 from WISC-R to WISC-III, and 0.300 from WISC-III to WISC-IV. This last gain was calculated using an estimated gain for Object Assembly and Picture Arrangement,[2] which were no longer core subtests of the WISC-IV. Among the subtests remaining in the mainstream from the WISC to the WISC-IV, small gains (less than one third SD) were observed in 50 years for Information (0.43), Arithmetic (0.46), and Vocabulary (0.88). Moderate gains (more than two thirds SD) were observed for Comprehension (2.20),

---

2. The estimates were the mean gains observed on the other subtests.

Picture Completion (2.20), and Block Design (2.34). Large gains (more than 1 SD) were observed for Coding (3.60) and Similarities (4.77). At the subtest level, gains were more erratic across the time than at the Full-Scale level.

The standardization of the WISC-V was an opportunity to check if the trend observed between the previous versions of the WISC is continuing at the same pace. However, the comparisons are now more complex to interpret than in the past because several modifications were introduced in the WISC-V at the subtest and the subscale levels. Some subtests were withdrawn (Word Reasoning and Picture Completion), while new subtests were introduced (Figure Weight, Visual Puzzles, and Picture Span). The Perceptual Reasoning Index was split into a Visual Spatial Index and a Fluid Reasoning Index. The core subtests for each composite were modified, with the exception of the Processing Speed Index, which was the only index to remain unchanged. Therefore, comparing individual performances between the WISC-IV and the WISC-V should be cautiously done, keeping in mind that the composite scores are calculated from different sets of subtests in the two tests. We should never forget that "a major assumption in comparing manifest scores is that they are measuring the same construct, the same way, across groups" (Beaujean & Sheng, 2014, p. 64).

As we reported in the first edition of this book, the average annualized rate of gain in the FSIQ between WISC-IV and WISC-V was 0.14 during the period from 2001 to 2013, which is well below that observed between other editions of WISC and similarly below the theoretically expected rate of gain of 0.33 points per year. We also reported a surprising reversal of the FE for the PSI of—0.11, which we attributed to subtle but important changes in the task demands between editions (i.e., increased complexity of symbols to be drawn, number of search symbols, number of shapes per row, and of rows per page), which may have increased extraneous sources of variance (e.g., fine motor skills involved in drawing, visual acuity, and visual tracking between lines). This contributed to the lower than expected FSIQ gain, but was not solely responsible for it. The FE for VCI and WMI was reported as 0.13 and 0.11, respectively. No FE was calculated for FRI or VSI as these indexes did not exist in WISC-IV. These data were based on our analyses of the WISC-IV/WISC-V counterbalanced study reported in the WISC-V technical manual (Wechsler, 2014).

We hypothesized that this apparent slowing of the FE was likely due to construct changes made between editions. While some construct changes were made with all prior editions, the changes between WISC-IV and WISC-V were much more substantial than between any two previous editions. In particular, the FSIQ for the WISC-V is comprised of a different mix of the broad cognitive abilities than for the WISC-IV. This is important because the FE is not consistent across domains of cognitive ability. In meta-analysis of FE studies, the rate of increase in verbal comprehension tasks was .26 standard-score points per year as compared to 0.42 for fluid reasoning tasks (Pietschnig & Voracek, 2013). Thus, changes in the relative weighting of the various broad cognitive abilities included in the FSIQ from one edition to the next could change the observed rate of gain.

Subsequently, we reasoned that the best way to examine this question would be to calculate the rate of gain observed when holding test edition constant over the same time period. If the rate of gain holding test edition constant was small, the finding would support a slowing of the FE. If the rate of gain was higher, as theoretically expected, it would support the hypothesis that the smaller FE observed in the WISC-IV/WISC-V counterbalanced study was largely due to content changes between editions.

Using data from the same WISC-IV/WISC-V counterbalanced study cited above, subjects who were administered the WISC-IV first, before the WISC-V, were identified and used in this analysis in order to avoid practice effects. Their WISC-IV scores were then compared to matched controls from the original WISC-IV standardization data set, thus obtaining an estimate of FE over the same time period (2001 to 2013) unconfounded by construct or task changes between test editions. We published that study in a journal (Weiss, Gregoire, & Zhu, 2016), and now summarize the findings in this second edition of the book.

One hundred twenty six subjects were identified who were administered the WISC-IV first, and compared to subjects from the WISC-IV standardization sample carefully matched on age, sex, race/ethnicity, parent education level, and region of the country. Rates of gain in the WISC-IV FSIQ were then calculated, and importantly, these gain scores are unconfounded by the known construct changes in the composition of FSIQ between the WISC-IV and WISC-V. The average annualized rate of gain for the WISC-IV FSIQ was .31 points per year. This is almost precisely as predicted by the FE theory. The reverse FE for PSI was not observed in this study. The rates of gain for the four broad cognitive abilities measured by the WISC-IV were 0.13 for VCI, 0.39 for PRI, 0.16 for WMI, and 0.27 for PSI. This variability in rates of gain by type of cognitive ability is consistent with many prior studies showing smaller rates of gain for crystallized tasks and larger rates of gain for fluid tasks. The Matrix Reasoning and Symbol Search subtests showed the largest rates of gain. Interestingly, the Matrix Reasoning subtest is a marker for the fluid reasoning factor in five-factor solutions of the WISC-IV (Weiss, Keith, Zhu, & Chen, 2013), and highly similar to the Ravens test upon which much previous FE research was based.

The current findings strongly support our hypothesis that the previously reported 0.14 FSIQ gain between the WISC-IV and WISC-V was a restricted estimate due to changes in test content between editions, and that the FE is not slowing down, but rather, continues at much the same pace as predicted by Flynn in well-controlled studies that hold test content constant.

This also means that it is not possible to know the FE for the WISC-V at this time. We must wait for a decade or so to pass, and then compare the performance of subjects tested at that time to the WISC-V standardization sample collected in 2013. In the meantime, use of the theoretically predicted FE appears justified in situations where it is necessary and appropriate to adjust WISC-V scores for FE. In the next section we discuss recommendations for adjusting or not adjusting scores for FE.

RECOMMENDATIONS

To conclude this chapter, some methodological recommendations are presented for researchers studying generational shifts in intelligence and for practitioners to take into account the FE in clinical practice.

Recommendations for Researchers

Comparing different versions of tests in FE research creates potential confounds due to changes in test content that are difficult to untangle from changes due to generational shifts in ability. As noted above, Beaujean and Sheng (2014) clarify that a major assumption of FE research is that the test is measuring the same construct in the same way across groups, and we would add, across versions of the test. Zhu and Tulsky (1999) enumerated the myriad of ways that changes in test content between versions can confuse the results of FE studies. Kaufman (2010) gave a specific example of how Flynn's interpretation of large increases on the Similarities subtest scores over 50 years was flawed and more likely due to changes in subtest instructions, administration, and scoring rules. For all of these reasons, we strongly recommend that future researchers studying generational increases in ability consider using the same version of a test at two points in time, or empirically demonstrate construct equivalence if different versions of the test are compared (Weiss et al., 2016).

Recommendations for Clinical Practice

The most important recommendation for clinical practitioners is to use the most recent version of intelligence tests. Each new version provides new norms offsetting the FE. The new norms are an updated photograph of the intellectual abilities of the population, to which an individual's test performance is compared. However, as photos, norms only provide a static representation of reality at a specific point in time. As soon as they are published, they start aging. During the period between their publication and the next standardization of the same test, the gap between the norms and the true intellectual level of the population is widening. For the Wechsler scales this period is usually around 10 years. During this period, based on previous observations, a difference around three points between the norms and the population true scores could be expected for the FSIQ.

During the aging period of the norms, correcting for the FE is not recommended for most routine evaluations. This is partly because the exact shape of the FE curve is unknown. Several studies showed that the FE does not follow a straight line across the years. Therefore, using a standard correction of 0.33 points per year could be misleading. Sometimes it could be an undercorrection, sometimes an overcorrection. To avoid missing the identification of children with a LD or ID because of the FE, with important adverse consequences for the children and their families, best practice is to always use the most recent version of each test and to report the confidence interval around the observed scores. When a 90% confidence interval is used, it is usually larger than the potential impact of the FE.

However, for certain types of high-stake evaluations with potential life-changing consequences, such as criminal cases involving the death penalty, an FE correction could be applied. In such situations, the correction should be based on empirical data about the FE of the specific test used. If no such data is available, such as is currently the case for theWISC-V, then the correction can be based on the theoretically predicted standard correction of 0.33 points per year. For very high-stakes decisions, such a correction is often a better solution than conducting new testing with an updated version of the test. For example, a teenager was tested in 2008 with the WISC-IV when he was 16. At that time, his FSIQ was 71. In 2011, at the age of 19, he was convicted of murder. In the punishment phase of the trial, the prosecuting attorney used the previous test results to advocate for the death penalty because his client scored above the intellectually deficient range. Note that some states, called "bright line" states, will not consider the confidence interval—even though it is widely viewed as best practice by most psychologists. As the WISC-IV was published in 2003 and the testing was done in 2008, a period of 5 years could be taken into account to correct the observed FSIQ for the FE. A psychologist testifying as an expert witness for the defense applied the empirically determined FE adjustment for WISC-IV of 0.31 reported above and in Weiss et al. (2016). After the correction, the FSIQ was 69.45 ($=71-(5 \times 0.31)$), which is below the cut score for ID, thus potentially avoiding the death penalty. A further option could have been to conduct new testing with a more recent intelligence test, for example, the WAIS-IV, which was published in 2008. However, even with the WAIS-IV, a correction should apply for the 3-year period between the standardization and the test administration. Moreover, testing intelligence in such a high-stakes context is not neutral and the risk of faking is high and difficult to control.

Summary

The FE refers to a consistent upward drift in intelligence test scores across generations of about three points per decade. This occurs when a contemporary examinee's test performance is compared to norms derived from a previous generational cohort when the average performance was lower than it is today. The effect is widely accepted as real, and typically thought to be due to various societal improvements that enhance development of the brain and nervous system such as nutrition, healthcare, and education. The effect is corrected when the test is revised and the norms reanchored to reflect the performance of the current generation.

The size of the FE varies for different broad cognitive abilities and is lowest for crystallized knowledge and highest for fluid reasoning tasks. This makes it difficult to measure the true size of FE when comparing the FSIQ scores from different editions of a test, such as the WISC-IV and WISC-V, because the FSIQ is comprised of different blends of the broad cognitive abilities across editions of the test. When comparing WISC-IV and WISC-V scores, the FE is much smaller than the three points per decade predicted by the FE theory, which is believed to be due to changes made in the composition of the FSIQ between these two editions of the test. When holding test edition constant by comparing WISC-IV scores of a contemporary sample to matched controls from the original standardization sample, the FE is again found to be about three points per decade. For these reasons, it is not yet possible to measure the FE for WISC-V unconfounded by content changes between test editions, until enough time has passed since the standardization of the WISC-V.

We recommend that FE adjustments be reserved for high-stakes legal evaluations with potential life-changing consequences. In these situations, the empirically determined FE for the specific test administered should be applied. If empirical data is not yet available, such as is currently the case for the WISC-V, then the theoretical estimate of three points per decade can be applied until such time as empirical data are available.

FE adjustments are not recommended for most routine clinical evaluations. Rather, it is recommended that practitioners always use the most recent version of a test, and report the confidence interval surrounding the obtained test score. Routine use of confidence intervals when reporting test scores is widely viewed as best practice. In most situations, the 90% confidence interval will be wider than the FE adjustment, making an FE adjustment unnecessary.

REFERENCES

Abbott, R. D., White, L. R., Ross, G. W., Masaki, K. H., Snowdon, D. A., & Curb, J. D. (1998). Height as a marker of childhood development and late–life cognitive function: The Honolulu–Asia aging study. *Pediatrics, 102*, 602–609.

American Psychiatric Association. (2013). *Diagnostic and statistical manual of mental disorders* (5th ed.). Arlington, VA: APA.

Ang, S., Rodgers, J. L., & Wanstrom, L. (2010). The Flynn effect within subgroups in the U.S.: Gender, race, income, education, and urbanization differences in the NLSY–children data. *Intelligence, 38*, 367–384.

Beaujean, A., & Sheng, Y. (2014). Assessing the Flynn effect in the Wechsler scales. *Journal of Individual Differences, 35*, 63–78.

Bradley, R., Danielson, L., & Hallahan, D. P. (Eds.), (2002). *Identification of learning disabilities: Research to practice.* Hillsdale, NJ: Lawrence Erlbaurn.

Bronfenbrenner, U., & Ceci, S. J. (1994). Nature—nurture reconceptualized in developmental perspective: A bioecological model. *Psychological Review, 101,* 568—586.

Canivez, G. L., & Watkins, M. W. (1998). Long—term stability of the Wechsler Intelligence Scale for children—Third edition. *Psychological Assessment, 10,* 285—291.

Ceci, S. J. (1990). *On intelligence... more or less.* Englewood Cliffs, NJ: Prentice Hall.

Ceci, S. J. (2000). So near and yet so far: lingering questions about the use of measures of general intelligence for college admission and employment screening. *Psychology, Public Policy and Law, 6,* 233—252.

Ceci, S. J., & Williams, W. M. (1997). Schooling, intelligence, and income. *American Psychologist, 52,* 1051—1058.

Colom, R., Lluis—Font, J. M., & Andrés—Pueyo, A. (2005). The generational intelligence gains are caused by decreasing variance in the lower half of the distribution: Supporting evidence for the nutrition hypothesis. *Intelligence, 33,* 83—91.

Dickens, W. T., & Flynn, J. R. (2001). Heritability estimates versus large environmental effects: The IQ paradox resolved. *Psychological Review, 108,* 346—369.

Dutton, E., & Lynn, R. (2013). A negative Flynn effect in Findland, 1997—2009. *Intelligence, 41,* 817—820.

Elliott, C. (2007). *Differential ability scales* (2nd ed.). Bloomington, MN: Pearson.

Espy, K. A., Molfese, V. J., & DiLalla, L. F. (2001). Effects of environmental measures on intelligence of young children: Growth curve modeling of longitudinal data. *Merrill—Palmer Quarterly, 47,* 42—73.

Fernandez—Ballesteros, R., & Juan—Espinosa, M. (2001). Sociohistorical changes and intelligence gains. In R. J. Sternberg, & E. L. Grigorenko (Eds.), *Environmental effects on cognitive abilities.* Mahwah, NJ: Lawrence Erlbaum.

Fletcher, J. M., & Vaughn, S. (2009). Response to intervention: Preventing and remediating academic difficulties. *Child Development Perspectives, 3,* 30—37.

Fletcher, J. M., Stuebing, K. K., & Hughues, L. C. (2010). IQ scores should be corrected for the Flynn effect in high—stakes decisions. *Journal of Psychoeducational Assessment, 28,* 469—473.

Flynn, J. R., & Weiss, L. G. (2007). American IQ gains from 1932 to 2002: The WISC subtests and educational progress. *International Journal of Testing, 7,* 209—224.

Flynn, J. R. (1984). The mean IQ of Americans: massive gains 1932 to 1978. *Psychological Bulletin, 95,* 29—51.

Flynn, J. R. (1987). Massive IQ gains in 14 nations: What IQ tests really measure. *Psychological Bulletin, 101,* 171—191.

Flynn, J. R. (1998a). Israeli military IQ tests: Gender differences small; IQ gains large. *Journal of Biosocial Science, 30,* 541—553.

Flynn, J. R. (1998b). WAIS-III and WISC-III gains in the United States from 1972 to 1995: How to compensate for obsolete norms. *Perceptual and Motor Skills, 86,* 1231—1239.

Flynn, J. R. (2007). *What is intelligence?* New York: Cambridge University Press.

Frumpkin, I. B. (2006). Challenging expert testimony on intelligence and mental retardation. *The Journal of Psychiatry and Law, 34,* 51—71.

Gaskill, F. W., III, & Brantley, J. C. (1996). Changes in ability and achievement scores over time: Implications for children classified as learning disabled. *Journal of Psychoeducational Assessment, 14,* 220—228.

Herrnstein, R. J., & Murray, C. (1994). *The bell curve. Intelligence, and class structure in American life.* New York: Free Press.

Hiscock, M. (2007). The Flynn Effect and its relevance to neuropsychology. *Journal of Clinical and Experimental Neuropsychology, 29,* 514–529.

Jensen, A. R. (1998). *The g factor.* New York: Praeger.

Kanaya, T., & Ceci, S. (2012). The impact of the Flynn effect on LD diagnoses in special education. *Journal of Learning Disabilities, 45,* 319–326.

Kaufman, A. S., & Kaufman, N. L. (2001). Assessment of specific learning disabilities in the new millennium: Issues, conflicts, and controversies. In A. S. Kaufman, & N. L. Kaufman (Eds.), *Specific learning disabilities and difficulties in children. and adolescents: Psychological assessment and evaluation* (pp. 433–455). New York: Cambridge University Press.

Kaufman, A. S. (2010). "In what way are apples and oranges alike?" A critique of Flynn's interpretation of the Flynn effect. *Journal of Psychoeducational Assessment, 28*(5), 383–398.

Kaufman, A. S., & Kaufman, N. L. (2004). *Kaufman assessment battery for children* (2nd ed.). Bloomington, MN: Pearson.

Kaufman, A. S., & Lichtenberger, E. O. (2006). *Assessing adolescent and adult intelligence* (3rd ed.). Hoboken, NJ: Wiley.

Kaufman, A. S., & Weiss, L. G. (2010). Special issue on the Flynn effect. *Journal of Psychoeducational Assessment, 28*(5), 379–510.

Lynn, R. (2013). Who discovered the Flynn effect? A review of early studies of the secular increase of intelligence. *Intelligence, 41,* 765–769.

Nyborg, H. (2012). The decay of Western civilization: Double relaxed Darwinian selection. *Personality and Individual Differences, 53,* 118–125.

Pietschnig, J., & Voracek, M. (2013). One century of global IQ gains: A formal meta-analysis of the Flynn effect (1909–2010). Available at SSRN: http://ssrn.com/abstract = 2404239 or https://doi.org/10.2139/ssrn.2404239.

Pollitt, E. (2000). Developmental sequel from early nutritional deficiencies: Conclusion and probability judgments. *Journal of Nutrition, 130,* 350–353.

Reynolds, C. R., Niland, J., Wright, J. E., & Rosenn, M. (2010). Failure to apply the Flynn correction in death penalty litigation: Standard practice of today maybe, but certainly malpractice of tomorrow. *Journal of Psychoeducational Assessment, 28,* 477–481.

Rönnlund, M., & Nilsson, L. −G. (2008). The magnitude, generality, and determinants of Flynn effects on forms of declarative memory and visuospatial ability: Time−sequential analyses of data from Swedish cohort study. *Intelligence, 36,* 192–209.

Rönnlund, M., Carlstedt, B., Blomstedt, Y., Nilsson, L. −G., & Weinehall, L. (2013). Secular trends in cognitive test performance: Swedish conscript data 1970−1993. *Intelligence, 41,* 19–24.

Rowe, D. C., & Rodgers, J. L. (2002). Expanding variance and the case of historical changes in IQ means: A critique of Dickens and Flynn (2001). *Psychological Review, 109,* 759–763.

Sanborn, K. J., Truscott, S. D., Phelps, L., & McDougal, J. L. (2003). Does the Flynn effect differs by IQ level in samples of students classified as learning disabled? *Journal of Psychoeducational Assessment, 21,* 145–159.

Schalock, R. L., et al. (2010). *Intellectual disability: Definition, classification, and systems of support* (11th ed.). Annapolis, MD: American Association on Intellectual and Developmental Disabilities.

Schmidt, I. M., Jorgensen, H. M., & Michaelsen, K. F. (1995). Height of conscripts in Europe: Is post−neonatal mortality a predictor? *Annals of Human Biology, 22,* 57–67.

Sundet, J. M., Barlaug, D. G., & Torjussen, T. M. (2004). The end of the Flynn effect? A study of secular trends in mean intelligence test scores of Norwegian conscripts during half a century. *Intelligence, 32,* 349–362.

Spitz, H. H. (1989). Variations in Wechsler interscale IQ disparities at different level of IQ. *Intelligence, 13*, 157−167.

te Nijenhuis, J., de Jong, M. −J., Evers, A., & van der Flier, H. (2004). Are cognitive differences between immigrants and majority groups diminishing? *European Journal of Personality, 18*, 405−434.

Teasdale, T. W., & Owen, D. R. (2007). Secular declines in cognitive test scores: A reversal of the Flynn effect. *Intelligence, 36*, 121−126.

Teasdale, T. W., & Owen, D. R. (1989). Continuing secular increases in intelligence and a stable prevalence of high intelligence levels. *Intelligence, 13*, 255−262.

Trahan, L. H., Stuebing, K. K., Fletcher, J. M., & Hiscock, M. (2014). The Flynn effect: A meta-analysis. *Psychological Bulletin. Advance online publication.* Available from https://doi.org/10.1037/a0037173.

Truscott, S. D., & Frank, A. J. (2001). Does the Flynn effect affect IQ scores of students classified as LD? *Journal of School Psychology, 39*, 319−334.

Tuvemo, T., Jonsson, B., & Persson, I. (1999). Intellectual and physical performance and morbidity in relation to height in a cohort of 18−year−old Swedish conscripts. *Hormone Research, 52*, 186−191.

Wai, J., & Putallaz, M. (2011). The Flynn effect puzzle: A 30−year examination from the right tail of the ability distribution provides some missing pieces. *Intelligence, 39*, 443−455.

Wechsler, D. (1974). *Wechsler intelligence scale for children—Revised.* San Antonio, TX: The Psychological Corporation.

Wechsler, D. (1991). *Wechsler intelligence scale for children* (3rd ed.). San Antonio, TX: The Psychological Corporation.

Wechsler, D. (2003). *WISC-IV technical and interpretive manual.* Bloomington, MN: Pearson.

Wechsler, D. (2012). *WPPSI-IV technical and interpretive manual.* Bloomington, MN: Pearson.

Wechsler, D. (2014). *Wechsler intelligence scale for children (5th ed.).* Bloomington, MN: Pearson.

Weiss, L. G., Keith, T. Z., Zhu, J., & Chen, H. (2013). WISC-IV and clinical validation of the four- and five-factor interpretative approaches. *Special Issue of Journal of Psychoeducational Assessment, 31*(2), 114−131.

Weiss, L. G. (2010). Considerations on the Flynn effect. In A.S. Kaufman & L.G. Weiss (Eds.) Special issue of JPA on the Flynn effect. *Journal of Psychoeducational Assessment, 28*(5), 482−493.

Weiss, L. G., Gregoire, J., & Zhu, J. (2016). Flaws in Flynn effect research with the Wechsler scales. *Journal of Psychoeducational Assessment, 34*, 411−420.

Young, G. W. (2012). A more intelligent and just Atkins: Adjusting for the Flynn Effect in capital determination of mental retardation or intellectual disability. *Vanderbilt Law Review, 65*, 616−675.

Zhou, X., Zhu, J., & Weiss, L. G. (2010). Peeking inside the "black box" of the Flynn effect: Evidence from three Wechsler instruments. *Journal of Psychoeducational Assessment, 28*, 399−411.

Zhu, J., & Tulsky, D. (1999). Can IQ gain be accurately quantified by a simple difference formula? *Perceptual and Motor Skill, 88*, 1255−1260.

Chapter 9

WISC−V and the Evolving Role of Intelligence Testing in the Assessment of Learning Disabilities

Donald H. Saklofske[1], Kristina Breaux[2], A. Lynne Beal[3], Susan Engi Raiford[2] and Lawrence G. Weiss[4]

[1]*Department of Psychology, University of Western Ontario, London, ON, Canada,* [2]*Pearson, Clinical Assessment, San Antonio, TX, United States,* [3]*Private Practice, Toronto, ON, Canada,* [4]*Research and Measurement Consultant, San Antonio, TX, United States*

INTRODUCTION

One of the most studied groups of exceptional children and adults falls within the broad category of learning disabilities (LDs). Over the past 100 years and particularly in more recent times, considerable progress has been made in defining and diagnosing LDs with most emphasis on dyslexia or specific reading disability. Advances in cognitive psychology, neuropsychology, and brain sciences have also contributed to a greater understanding of the etiology of LDs, which, in turn, has led to the development of educational programs that can enable people with LDs to develop and use strategies so they may fully function without restriction due to their disability. The incidence and significance of LDs has also been addressed in national and state or provincial legislation in countries such as the United States and Canada, which ensures opportunity without restriction in the schools of today.

These advances in our understanding of LDs have engendered widely different views on how to operationalize definitions of LDs for diagnosis or identification. These differing views are further evident across disciplines within psychology (i.e., neuropsychology, school psychology), as well as across school districts and legislative jurisdictions.

This chapter reviews how WISC−V fits into the assessment, diagnosis, and intervention planning for children with LDs. The overview of this

WISC-V. DOI: https://doi.org/10.1016/B978-0-12-815744-2.00009-4

history, up to contemporary perspectives on LDs, is followed by current descriptions of LDs, as reflected in definitions derived from research and legislation. From roots in dyslexia and LD research we trace the current cognitive characteristics and subtypes of LDs. Links between subtypes of LDs and measures of cognitive ability that are logically linked to achievement follow. We acknowledge a legacy of controversy about the role of IQ tests in LD evaluations, and overview these diverse opinions with a focus on an appropriate role for cognitive assessment.

Within this context, we trace the contributions that WISC−V makes to understanding cognitive processes underlying academic achievement and LDs. Data from the clinical studies presented in the WISC−V technical manual as well as current case studies illustrate the relevance of this test in a description of specific LDs.

LEARNING DISABILITIES: CURRENT DEFINITIONS AND SUBTYPES

Definitions of LDs have evolved over time based on research, and operationalized in different jurisdictions. Legislation that provides a functional definition in the United States is from the Individuals with Disabilities Education Act (IDEA, 2004). This legislation links children's impairments in academic, cognitive, and other functions to entitlement to special education services. IDEA mandates that states evaluate all children suspected of having a disability by conducting multidisciplinary comprehensive assessments when determining eligibility for special education services under IDEA. "Specific learning disability," according to IDEA (2004), is defined as:

> ...a disorder in one or more of the basic psychological processes involved in understanding or in using language, spoken or written, that may manifest itself in the imperfect ability to listen, think, speak, read, write, spell, or to do mathematical calculations, including conditions such as perceptual disabilities, brain injury, minimal brain dysfunction, dyslexia, and developmental aphasia.

Although US federal regulations provide general guidelines in regards to identification and classification, states have considerable flexibility in how they interpret and institute policies and practices in definitions, classification criteria, assessment processes, and other considerations (Bergeron, Floyd, & Shands, 2008; Reschly & Hosp, 2004). Since 1990 the Office of Special Education Programs (OSEP) has held that the US federal law and regulations do not require documentation of a processing disorder to identify a LD. Nonetheless, states are allowed to impose their own understanding of these terms based on the congressional definition and to require adherence to those guidelines as an additional burden on eligibility groups. Although each school psychologist practices under the definitions operationalized by their local department or ministry of education, the creation of these local administrative guidelines are often influenced by those in other states and countries. Further, clinical and neuropsychologists who are not employed by a governmental school system often have more flexibility to pursue LD assessments guided by multiple models. Thus, a wider understanding of what constitutes good practice in other geographies and subdisciplines of psychology is useful for practitioners and administrators alike.

The definition of the Learning Disabilities Association of Canada (LDAC) (2002) refers to "average abilities essential for thinking and reasoning," as distinct from "global intellectual deficiency." It goes on to include "impairments in one or more processes related to perceiving, thinking, remembering or learning. These include, but are not limited to, language processing, phonological processing; visual-spatial processing, processing speed; memory and attention; and executive functions (e.g., planning and decision-making)."

Building on the LDAC definition, the Ontario Ministry of Education has adopted the opinion of the Expert Panel on Literacy and Numeracy Instruction for the identification of students with special needs. Their definition notes that, "knowledge about a student's strengths and weaknesses in cognitive processing helps teachers provide appropriate instruction and accommodations for children in their classrooms" (Ontario Ministry of Education, 2005). Specific intervention suggestions arising from the work of the Ontario Ministry are presented in detail in Chapter 2 of this book.

However, in Canada, provincial and territorial ministries of education and advocacy groups promote their own consensus-based definitions within each province (Kozey & Siegel, 2008). For example, in 2014, the Ontario Ministry of Education updated its definition of LDs that entitles students to a special education program. It defines a LD as a neurodevelopmental disorder that persistently and significantly has an impact on the ability to learn and use academic and other skills resulting in academic underachievement that is inconsistent with at least average intellectual ability. Significantly, the definition typically associates the academic underachievement with difficulties in one or more cognitive processes, such as phonological processing (Ontario Ministry of Education, 2014).

More recently, a group of psychologists in Ontario prepared a consensus statement on diagnosis and assessment of children, adolescents, and adults with LDs (A.L. Beal, personal communication, April 21, 2018). The impetus for the project was to achieve consistency among practitioners across sectors in the diagnosis of LDs and in assessment processes. Highlights of their definition includes:

- History of academic functioning below the level typically expected.
- Below average academic achievement, at least one standard deviation below the mean, in reading or writing or mathematics.

- Difficulties in reading, written language, or mathematics are logically related to deficits in psychological processing.
- At least average abilities essential for thinking and reasoning.
- Other factors that cannot account primarily for the difficulties in reading, written language, or mathematics.

Dyslexia is a language-based disorder that affects up to 20% of the population. In 2016, the US Senate voted unanimously as part of the Cassidy Senate Resolution 576 to establish the following definition of dyslexia:

1. an unexpected difficulty in reading for an individual who has the intelligence to be a much better reader; and
2. most commonly due to a difficulty in phonological processing (the appreciation of the individual sounds of spoken language), which affects the ability of an individual to speak, read, spell, and often, learn a second language.

This definition references the unexpected nature of dyslexia, which is revealed by an uneven cognitive profile in which basic academic skill deficits are surrounded by a "sea of strengths" in higher-level processing areas such as reasoning, problem solving, vocabulary, and listening comprehension (Shaywitz, 2005).

Identification and Diagnosis of a Learning Disability

A clinical approach to diagnosis that conceptualizes dyslexia as neurobiological in origin is well supported by research (see Chapter 10 on dyslexia). In school psychology settings, the purpose of LD evaluations is to identify disabilities that would determine eligibility for special education services. These eligibility determinations in the United States are typically based on administrative criteria set by the school district in compliance with more general legal criteria set by the state boards of education consistent with federal regulations. Although informed by research, the administrative eligibility criteria employed by school districts can diverge from diagnostic criteria set forth in the DSM−V (American Psychiatric Association, 2013) and other research-based diagnostic criteria, which are followed more closely by neuropsychologists and clinical psychologists. Differences between diagnostic criteria and criteria for identifying eligibility for LD services can be an area of disagreement between psychologists and school districts in determining appropriate services for students.

The two primary approaches currently used to identify a LD and to provide services in many school settings are problem-solving (instructional) and intraindividual (cognitive).

A problem-solving approach identifies students with low achievement and provides intervention accordingly, relying on tools such as curriculum-based assessment, progress monitoring, and a response to an intervention service delivery model (Fletcher, Morris, & Lyon, 2003). The goal is to intervene with appropriate services early to help as many struggling learners as possible. This approach is not concerned with classification or subtypes. Challenges associated with this approach involve determining the cut point for defining low achievement (Fletcher, 2012), instability in group membership over time (Francis et al., 2005), and determining the predictors and causes of failure to respond to instruction. Further in-depth critique is found in Reynolds and Shaywitz (2009). If a student fails to respond to instruction, then the assumption is that either the student has a disabling condition, such as a LD, attention-deficit hyperactivity disorder (ADHD), or intellectual disability, or the instructional program is inadequate in some way (Vaughn & Fuchs, 2003). At that point, a comprehensive evaluation that includes cognitive and neuropsychological assessment is typically recommended in order to determine the nature of the disabling condition and to make an appropriate diagnosis (Hale et al., 2010).

An intraindividual approach to identification is more closely related to diagnosis. It focuses primarily on cognitive explanations for learning difficulties (e.g., phonological processing, rapid automatic naming, and working memory) and the identification of intraindividual differences as the marker for unexpected underachievement (Fletcher et al., 2003). Limitations of this approach may arise from failing to consider important neurological and environmental factors (Hagen, Kamberelis, & Segal, 1991) and focusing on processing skills that are not directly related to intervention (Torgesen, 2002). Central to the intraindividual approach is the belief that understanding the specific cognitive explanations in each case will lead to more targeted and effective intervention approaches—a view that is the source of much of the current controversy surrounding LD assessment.

Central to the intraindividual approach is the notion that unexpected underachievement, the defining hallmark of a LD, is evidenced by a contrast or discrepancy between intact and deficient abilities (Kaufman, 2008). According to the specificity hypothesis (Broca, 1865, as cited in Fletcher, Lyon, Fuchs, & Barnes, 2007), individuals diagnosed with a LD exhibit specific, as opposed to general, learning difficulties, whereas normally achieving students exhibit more evenly developed cognitive abilities (Compton, Fuchs, Fuchs, Lambert, & Hamlett, 2011; Fuchs, Fuchs, Stuebing, Fletcher, & Hamlett, 2008; Fuchs, Compton, Fuchs, Hollenbeck, & Craddock, 2008). According to Shaywitz (2005), the distinctive learning profile associated with dyslexia may resemble an isolated weakness within a "sea of strengths."

This conceptualization of a LD differentiates students with overall low cognitive and achievement abilities (slow learners or students with intellectual disability) from those who struggle to learn despite average or better cognitive abilities. For this reason, traditional definitions of a LD have excluded individuals with below average intellectual functioning. In addition to intellectual disability, the exclusionary criteria provided in the IDEA regulations and other diagnostic and eligibility criteria include sensory or motor impairments, emotional disturbance, cultural factors, environmental or economic disadvantage, limited English proficiency, and lack of appropriate instruction in reading [34 CFR 300.307].

However, defining LDs on the basis of such exclusionary criteria has been challenged by many researchers primarily because such criteria do not meaningfully differentiate struggling learners in terms of information processing skills, neurobiological factors, or instructional requirements (e.g., Elliott & Gibbs, 2008; Fletcher et al., 2002; Lyon & Weiser, 2013). For example, attempts to differentiate between reading disabilities that are environmental as opposed to neurobiological in origin have been criticized because the factors contributing to reading problems are interrelated and complex, and the resulting distinctions may not be worthwhile for education planning (Elliott & Grigorenko, 2014). In addition, differentiating between poor readers whose IQ is below average and poor readers whose IQ is average or better has been challenged by showing that the two groups do not differ in the cognitive processes that underlie academic performance (Fletcher, 2005; Fletcher et al., 1994; González & Espinel, 2002; Maehler & Schuchardt, 2011; Siegel, 1988, 1992).

Subtypes of Learning Disabilities

An enormous body of research has accumulated with various approaches for identifying subtypes of LDs. Inquiry into possible subtypes of LDs began with Johnson and Myklebust (1967) and colleagues (e.g., Boshes & Myklebust, 1964; Myklebust & Boshes, 1960). They proposed a nonverbal disability characterized by the absence of serious problems in areas of language, reading, and writing, but with deficiencies in social perception, visual-spatial processing, spatial and right—left orientation, temporal perception, handwriting, mathematics, and executive functions such as disinhibition and perseveration. The neuropsychology literature later characterized a nonverbal LD as reflecting a right hemisphere deficit (Pennington, 1991; Rourke, 1989); however, it remains the least well understood.

Subtyping holds widespread appeal because it offers a way to explain the heterogeneity within the category of LDs, to describe the learning profile of students with LDs more specifically, leading to an individualized approach to intervention. Still, there is considerable debate over the existence of LDs subtypes as distinct categories that can be reliably identified, how best to categorize LDs subtypes, and whether instructional implications differ by subtype.

According to Fletcher et al. (2003), there are three main approaches to subtyping LDs: achievement subtypes, clinical inferential (rational) subtypes, and empirically based subtypes.

The first approach, achievement subtypes, relies on achievement testing profiles. For example, subgroups of reading difficulties are differentiated by performance on measures of word recognition, fluency, and comprehension. Subgroups of reading disability, math disability, and persons with a FSIQ score below 80 exhibit different patterns of cognitive attributes (Fletcher et al., 2003; Grigorenko, 2001). Compton et al. (2011) found distinctive patterns of strengths and weaknesses in abilities for several LD subgroups, in contrast to the flat pattern of cognitive and academic performance manifested by the normally achieving group. For example, students with LDs in reading comprehension showed a strength in math calculation alongside weaknesses in language involving listening comprehension, oral vocabulary, and syntax, whereas students with LDs in word reading showed strengths in math problem-solving and reading comprehension alongside weaknesses in working memory and oral language.

The second approach, clinical inferential, involves rationally defining subgroups based on clinical observations, typically by selecting individuals with similar characteristics. One example is students with a core deficit in phonological processing. The double-deficit model of subtypes distinguishes three subtypes: two subtypes with a single deficit in either phonological processing or rapid automatic naming, and a third subtype with a double-deficit in both areas (Wolf & Bowers, 1999; Wolf, Bowers, & Biddle, 2000). Another subtype model classifies two types of poor decoders: those having phonological dyslexia, orthographic/surface dyslexia, and those having mixed dyslexia, meaning weaknesses in both phonological and orthographic processing based on performance on reading nonwords and irregular exception words (Castles & Coltheart, 1993; Feifer & De Fina, 2000).

The third approach, empirically based subtypes of LDs, is based on multivariate empirical classification. It uses techniques such as Q-factor analysis and cluster analysis, and subsequent measures of external validity. Empirical subtyping models have been criticized for being atheoretical and unreliable; however, these models have provided additional support for rational subtyping methods, including the double-deficit model and differentiating garden-variety from specific reading disabilities (Fletcher et al., 2003). For example, a study by Pieters, Roeyers, Rosseel, Van Waelvelde, and Desoete (2013) used data-driven model-based clustering to identify two clusters of math disorder: one with number fact-retrieval weaknesses, and one with procedural calculation problems. When both motor and mathematical variables were included in the analysis, two clusters were identified: one with weaknesses in number fact retrieval, procedural calculation, as well as motor and visual-motor integration skills; a second with weaknesses in procedural calculation and visual-motor skills.

The identification and classification of a LD relies on either a dimensional or a categorical framework. Subtyping efforts are based on evidence that the heterogeneity within LDs is best represented as distinct subtypes. For example, reading and math LDs can be differentiated because students with reading LDs tend to have a relative strength in mathematics, whereas students with mathematics LDs tend to have a relative strength in reading (Compton et al., 2011). However, some researchers contend that the attributes of reading disability and math disability are dimensional, and efforts to categorize these as distinct subtypes are based on cut scores and correlated assessments (Branum—Martin, Fletcher, & Stuebing, 2013). Continued research is needed to advance our understanding of LD subtypes and their instructional implications for providing tailored intervention to a heterogeneous population of individuals with LDs.

INTELLIGENCE: A KEY LINK IN THE ASSESSMENT AND DIAGNOSIS OF LEARNING DISABILITIES

The history of LDs shows an increasingly prominent role of intelligence, or cognitive abilities, as the context for understanding achievement deficits. Cognitive ability tests have been used to estimate academic potential and to predict response to intervention, although the latter is an area of considerable controversy. Currently, all three alternative research-based approaches to LD diagnosis (i.e., third-method approaches) require that general ability or intelligence is average or better in relation to specific academic and cognitive weaknesses (Flanagan, Fiorello, & Ortiz, 2010). Further, Swanson's (2011) review of three meta-analysis studies revealed that IQ accounts for a substantial amount of the explainable variance in reading performance, ranging from .47 to .58, suggesting that there is value in considering IQ as an aptitude measure for identifying LDs in children. Assessment of cognitive ability or cognitive processing has also been defended in order to identify gifted students with LDs (Crepeau-Hobson & Bianco, 2011). As part of a LD evaluation, research indicates the importance of measuring verbal reasoning, which is average or better among individuals with a reading disability (Berninger et al., 2006), and measuring nonverbal reasoning, which is average or better among individuals with oral and written language LDs (OWL—LDs; Berninger, O'Donnell, & Holdnack, 2008).

However, the use of cognitive ability tests for the diagnosis of LDs is not without controversy. Other researchers contend that, although IQ moderately predicts academic achievement, IQ does not assess aptitude for learning that predicts achievement outcomes for students with LDs, and so it should not be used as a benchmark for identifying underachievement (Elliott & Grigorenko, 2014; Fletcher, Coulter, Reschly, & Vaughn, 2004; Sternberg &

Grigorenko, 2002). Some of these same critics do recommend the use of cognitive ability testing to provide information about the level of intellectual challenge that is appropriate for a student with learning difficulties, so that teachers can adjust the curricular demands and activities in the classroom accordingly (Elliott & Grigorenko, 2014). Much of this research ignores the longitudinal findings of Ferrer, Shaywitz, Holahan, Marchione, and Shaywitz (2010), which shows that IQ and reading ability systematically diverge for individuals with dyslexia as they grow older, but not for aging average readers (see Chapter 10).

Similar debate surrounds the use of IQ scores for predicting instructional outcomes. Some studies have shown IQ to be a significant predictor of the response to instruction (e.g., Fuchs, Fuchs, Mathes, & Lipsey, 2000; Fuchs & Young, 2006), whereas many studies assert the opposite finding (e.g., Donovan & Cross, 2002; Gresham & Vellutino, 2010; Stuebing, Barth, Molfese, Weiss, & Fletcher, 2009). Swanson's analysis of treatment outcomes showed that IQ has a moderating role in treatment outcomes; and, further, that approximately 15% of the variance in outcomes is related to instruction (Swanson, 1999; Swanson, 2011; Swanson & Hoskyn, 1998).

Researchers continue to rely on cognitive processing measures to advance scientific understanding as they investigate the specificity hypothesis of LDs, the distinctive cognitive profiles of individuals identified with a LDs, and the possibility of LD subtypes. These cognitive processes constitute the broad abilities assessed by most contemporary cognitive ability tests, including the WISC−V. As we discuss next, intelligence testing in LD evaluations has expanded from an exclusive focus on the composite IQ score to include consideration of each of the broad cognitive processes or abilities that comprise general intelligence. Much of the previous controversy about the relevance of the FSIQ score to LDs is made mute by the current focus on the broad cognitive processes that comprise intelligence.

Beyond the Full-Scale IQ (FSIQ): Advances in Intelligence and its Relevance in LD Assessment

Throughout the above discussion, continuous reference has been made to the critical role of intelligence in the definition and diagnosis of LDs. In turn, advances in cognitive science as well as definitions of LDs have directly influenced the evolution of cognitive ability tests in this century (for descriptions of the evolution from theory to practice, see Greenberg, Lichtenberger, & Kaufman, 2013 and Beal, Willis, & Dumont, 2013). Advances have moved the science beyond an exclusive focus on a global description of intelligence such as an IQ score. The division of the construct of IQ into a set of distinct yet related cognitive abilities, or indexes, has allowed researchers to link achievement in reading, written language, and mathematics to specific cognitive abilities.

The Cattell−Horn−Carroll (CHC) theory (McGrew, 1997; Schneider & McGrew, in press) provides a taxonomy for classifying cognitive abilities that is used to identify the common abilities measured by different intelligence tests, enabling researchers to communicate and extend findings across studies. McGrew and Wendling's (2010) summary of over 20 years of research on CHC classified cognitive- achievement relation has shown that "cognitive abilities contribute to academic achievement in different proportions in different academic domains, and these proportions change over the course of development."

Some argue that the consistent application of this taxonomy to LD research is necessary if LD assessment is to improve and become more reliable and valid (Flanagan, Ortiz, Alfonso, & Mascolo, 2006). An operational definition of LDs that reflects these advances includes the analysis of cognitive ability (Flanagan & Mascolo, 2005). By matching the cognitive processes that underlie success in various academic subjects, practitioners can provide a better understanding of the clear links between deficits in specific cognitive processes and specific academic abilities. Along with the test results, developmental and academic history, tests based on models of cognitive ability provide significant information to draw conclusions about a child's cognitive strengths and deficits, and their implications for education, careers, and other daily activities of the people they assess. A synopsis of the development of specific cognitive ability tests that follow models of cognitive ability is provided by Beal et al. (2013).

A Taxonomy of Cognitive Abilities Related to Learning Disabilities

The LDAC (2002) definition of LD aligns well with the broad abilities identified in the original CHC model (McGrew & Flanagan, 1998), as shown in Table 9.1. As noted by Horn and Blankson (2012), each broad ability involves learning, and is manifested as a consequence of many factors that can affect learning over years of development.

Links between deficits in particular cognitive abilities that are indicative of LDs in specific academic areas have been demonstrated empirically (Flanagan, Alfonso, & Ortiz, 2012). Table 9.2 shows the CHC abilities most related to reading, math, and writing.

PSYCHOEDUCATIONAL RELEVANCE OF THE WISC−V

The Wechsler Intelligence Scale for Children, Fifth Edition (WISC−V; Wechsler, 2014a, 2014b) is the fifth generation of this cognitive ability test. Since its original edition based on Wechsler's view of clinical tasks that are indicative of intelligence, the test has evolved to reflect models of human cognitive functions that measure processes that could enhance or impair learning.

Definitions of LDs that contrast intact cognitive functioning with specific processing deficits are tested well with the WISC—V. The test provides an overall measure of cognitive ability through the FSIQ with an overall reliability of .96 for both the American norms and the Canadian norms. The WISC—V also provides ancillary Index scores that eliminate the impact of processing deficits that are measured through other subtests. The General Ability Index (GAI) is a measure of thinking and reasoning in the auditory-verbal and visual-spatial modalities, with a reliability of .96 for the American norms and .95 for the Canadian norms. Through multidimensional scaling the GAI has been confirmed as a summarization of performance on cognitively complex tasks (Myers & Reynolds, 1997). The GAI is useful for children who have deficits in attention or motor speed.

Alternatively, the Nonverbal Index (NVI) provides a measure of thinking and reasoning separate from language abilities, with a reliability of .95 for both the American and the Canadian norms. It is useful for second-language learners and children with known language impairments. If the WISC—V Integrated (Wechsler & Kaplan, 2015) is available, a Visual Working Memory Index (VWMI) can be derived to provide an estimate of working memory abilities without requiring language production.

In addition, several other nonexpressive scores have been published to accommodate such situations. First, a Nonexpressive Full-Scale Score has been published (Raiford, 2017). This composite draws on the WISC—V and the WISC—V Integrated subtests that includes subtests from all five cognitive domains in the same proportion as the WISC—V Full-Scale IQ.

TABLE 9.1 Alignment of the Cattell—Horn—Carroll (CHC) Model to Areas of Information Processing

Cattell—Horn—Carroll Broad Abilities	Areas of Information Processing
Gf Fluid Reasoning	Thinking
Gc Crystallized Intelligence	Language Processing
Gv Visual-spatial Thinking	Visual-spatial Processing
Glr Long-term Memory Retrieval	Memory
Ga Auditory Processing	Phonological Processing
Gwm Working Memory	Memory
Gs Processing Speed	Processing Speed

Note: Gwm has replaced Gsm (Short-term Memory) used in earlier models.

TABLE 9.2 CHC Abilities Related to Reading, Math, and Writing

CHC Abilities Most Related to Reading

Ability	Relationship to Reading
Gc	Language development, lexical knowledge, and listening abilities become increasingly important with age
Gwm	Memory span especially within the context of working memory
Ga	Phonetic coding or phonological awareness/processing during the elementary school years
Glr	Naming facility or RAN during the elementary school years
Gs	Perceptual speed, particularly the elementary school years

CHC Abilities Most Related to Math

Ability	Relationship to Math
Gf	Induction and general sequential reasoning at all ages
Gc	Language development, lexical knowledge, and listening abilities become increasingly important with age
Gwm	Within the context of working memory
Gv	Primarily for higher-level or advanced math
Gs	Perceptual speed, particularly during the elementary years

CHC Abilities Most Related to Writing

Ability	Relationship to Writing
Gc	Language development, lexical knowledge, and general fund of information primarily after age 7 become increasingly important with age
Gwm	Memory span especially for spelling skills
	Working memory shows relations with advanced writing skills (e.g., written expression)
Gs	Perceptual speed is related to basic writing and written expression at all ages

For this score, multiple choice adaptations of the Verbal Comprehension subtests that contribute to the FSIQ (i.e., Similarities and Vocabulary) are used when deriving the composite norm in lieu of the free-response tasks, and Picture Span rather than Digit Span contributes to the composite. In addition, a host of other nonexpressive composite scores (i.e., Nonexpressive VCI, Nonexpressive Expanded Crystallized Index, Nonexpressive Gf-Gc composite) are available that utilize the WISC−V

Integrated subtests in a similar manner to permit measurement of abilities without requiring expressive responses. The psychometric properties and clinical utility of these composite scores are comparable to their expressive counterparts, and they result in improvements to fairness and accessibility (Raiford, 2017).

Several motor-free composite scores have also been published. The Nonmotor Full-Scale Score (Raiford, 2017) draws on WISC−V complementary subtests and WISC−V Integrated subtests, including subtests from all five cognitive domains in the same proportion as the WISC−V FSIQ. However, instead of Block Design and Coding subtests (i.e., the WISC−V FSIQ subtests that require motor production), subtests from those cognitive domains that do not require motor production were used when deriving the norms. Because the Nonmotor Full-Scale Score has the same representation of the five cognitive domains seen on the WISC−V, it provides a suitable accommodation in the case of motor difficulties. Several other motor-free composite scores were also derived by Raiford (2017). A nonmotor GAI is useful for assessing children with motor difficulties *and* neurodevelopmental disorders that affect working memory and processing speed. A nonmotor NVI is available for children with both expressive problems *and* motor production difficulties. A nonmotor VSI is also available. The psychometric properties and clinical utility of these composite scores are also comparable to their counterparts that require motor production, and as with the nonexpressive scores, result in improvements to fairness and accessibility for children with motor difficulties (Raiford, 2017).

Another motor-free short-form of the WISC−V (MF−SF) (Piovasana, Harrison, & Ducat, 2017) has been published. This short-form is based on six subtests that do not have motor production requirements, and has a reliability index of .97 for American norms. The MF−SF is useful for children with cerebral palsy and other impairments to their motor functioning.

The WISC−V has expanded from an IQ test into a test of multiple cognitive abilities that are easily mapped to six of the seven CHC broad abilities, as follows:

- Verbal Comprehension Index (VCI) (Gc)
- Visual-Spatial Index (VSI) (Gv)
- Fluid Reasoning Index (FRI) (Gf)
- Working Memory Index (WMI) (Gwm)
- Processing Speed Index (PSI) (Gs)
- Symbol Translation Index (STI) (Glr)
- Storage and Retrieval Index (SRI) (Glr)

The five WISC−V primary indexes align with Gc, Gv, Gf, Gwm, and Gs. In addition, Glr is measured by three complementary WISC−V indexes: the Naming Speed Index (NSI), the Symbol Translation Index (STI), and the Storage and Retrieval Index (SRI), which are discussed in detail below.

The Wechsler Individual Achievement Test, Third Edition (WIAT—III) (Pearson, 2009) Oral Expression and Listening Comprehension subtests also measure Gc.

The WIAT—III Pseudoword Decoding and Early Reading Skills subtests measure grapheme-phoneme knowledge, which are auditory processing (Ga) tasks and integral to the reading and writing processes. Thus, when used together, WISC—V and WIAT—III provide coverage of all seven of the CHC broad abilities. Many practitioners routinely administer the empirically linked WIAT—III together with WISC—V in LD assessment for this reason.

Table 9.3 shows the CHC taxonomy in more detail, including both the broad and narrow abilities, and maps the WIAT—III, KTEA—3, and WISC—V subtests to the broad and narrow CHC abilities. Also shown in this table are the new WISC—V complementary subtests. As the table shows, using the WISC—V together with the WIAT—III and/or the KTEA—3 provides measures of the following broad abilities: Ga, Gc, Gf, Gs, Glr (both Gl, Learning Efficiency, and Gr, Retrieval Fluency), Gwm, Gv, Grw—R, Grw—W, and Gq.

The WISC—V complementary indexes and subtests were specifically designed to inform psychoeducational assessment of children being evaluated for specific learning disorders such as in reading and mathematics. Each WISC—V Index score, its component subtests, and their tasks are described next.

Naming Speed Index

The Naming Speed Index (NSI) is comprised of two complementary subtests: Naming Speed Literacy (NSL) and Naming Speed Quantity (NSQ). In the NSL subtest, the child names elements of various stimuli as quickly as possible. The tasks utilize stimuli and elements that are traditional within rapid naming task paradigms (e.g., colors, objects, letters, and numbers) and that have shown sensitivity to reading and written expression skills and to specific LDs in reading and written expression. Similar tasks are closely associated with reading and spelling skill development, with reading achievement, and with a number of variables related to reading and spelling, and have shown sensitivity to specific LDs in reading (Crews & D'Amato, 2009; Korkman, Barron-Linnankoski, & Lahti-Nuuttila, 1999; Korkman, Kirk, & Kemp, 2007; Powell, Stainthorp, Stuart, Garwood, & Quinlan, 2007; Wechsler and Kaplan, 2015; Willburger, Fussenegger, Moll, Wood, & Landerl, 2008). Some studies suggest these tasks are also related to mathematics skills, specific LDs in mathematics, and a number of other clinical conditions (McGrew & Wendling, 2010; Pauly et al., 2011; Willburger et al., 2008; Wise et al., 2008). Such tasks are also sensitive to a wide variety of other neurodevelopmental conditions such as ADHD (Korkman et al., 2007), language disorders in both monolingual and

TABLE 9.3 CHC Taxonomy for WIAT–III, KTEA–3, and WISC–V Subtests

Broad Ability	Narrow Ability	WIAT–III Subtest	KTEA–3 Subtest	WISC–V Subtest
Ga	Phonetic Coding (PC)	Early Reading Skills	Phonological Processing	
Gc	General Verbal Information (K0)			Comprehension
				Information
	Listening Ability (LS)	Oral Discourse Comprehension (LC subtest)	Listening Comprehension	
	Lexical Knowledge (VL)	Receptive Vocabulary (LC subtest)	Reading Vocabulary	Similarities
		Expressive Vocabulary (OE subtest)		Vocabulary
	Language Development (LDs)		Reading Vocabulary	
	Communication Ability (CM)		Oral Expression	
	Grammatical Sensitivity (MY)		Written Expression	
			Oral Expression	
Gf	Quantitative Reasoning (RQ)	Math Problem Solving	Math Concepts & Applications	
	Induction (I)			Matrix Reasoning
				Picture Concepts
	General Sequential Reasoning (RG)			Figure Weights
Gs	Rate of Test-Taking (R9)		Decoding Fluency	Coding
			Word Recognition Fluency	

(Continued)

TABLE 9.3 (Continued)

Broad Ability	Narrow Ability	WIAT–III Subtest	KTEA–3 Subtest	WISC–V Subtest
	Number Facility (N)	Math Fluency—Addition	Math Fluency	Naming Speed Quantity
		Math Fluency—Subtraction		
		Math Fluency Multiplication		
	Perceptual Speed (P)			Cancellation
				Symbol Search
Glr	Meaningful Memory (MM)			Delayed Symbol Translation
	Associative Memory (MA)			
	Ideational Fluency (FI)	Oral Word Fluency (OE subtest)	Associational Fluency	Immediate Symbol Translation
				Recognition Symbol Translation
	Naming Facility (NA)		Object Naming Facility	Naming Speed Literacy
			Letter Naming Facility	Naming Speed Color-Object
				Naming Speed Size-Color-Object
				Naming Speed Letter-Number

Gwm	Memory Span (MS)	Sentence Repetition (OE subtest)	Digit Span Forward
			Picture Span
	Working Memory (MW)		Arithmetic
			Digit Span
			Digit Span Backward
			Digit Span Sequencing
			Letter-Number Sequencing
Gv	Visualization (Vz)		Block Design
			Visual Puzzles
Grw–R	Reading Comprehension (RC)	Reading Comprehension	Reading Comprehension
			Reading Vocabulary
	Reading Decoding (RD)	Early Reading Skills	Letter & Word Recognition
		Word Reading	Word Recognition Fluency
		Pseudoword Decoding	Nonsense Word Decoding
			Decoding Fluency
			Letter Naming Facility
			Silent Reading Fluency
	Reading Speed (RS)	Oral Reading Fluency	Word Recognition Fluency

(Continued)

TABLE 9.3 (Continued)

Broad Ability	Narrow Ability	WIAT–III Subtest	KTEA–3 Subtest	WISC–V Subtest
Grw–W	Writing Ability (WA)	Essay Composition	Written Expression	
	English Usage Knowledge (EU)	Sentence Composition	Written Expression	
	Spelling Ability (SG)	Spelling	Spelling	
	Writing Speed (WS)	Alphabet Writing Fluency	Writing Fluency	
Gq	Mathematical Achievement (A3)	Math Problem Solving	Math Concepts and Applications	
		Numerical Operations	Math Computation	
		Math Fluency—Addition	Math Fluency	
		Math Fluency—Subtraction		
		Math Fluency Multiplication		

bilingual children (Korkman et al., 2012), and autism spectrum disorder (Korkman et al., 2007). Children at risk for neurodevelopmental issues have been reported to score lower on similar measures (Lind et al., 2011), which are described as measuring storage and retrieval fluency and naming facility (Flanagan et al., 2012). These subtests specifically measure the automaticity of visual-verbal associations, which should be well developed in school-aged children.

In the NSQ subtest the child names the quantity of squares inside a series of boxes as quickly as possible. The subtest is similar to tasks in the experimental literature that show greater sensitivity to mathematics skills and specific LDs in mathematics than do the traditional rapid automatized naming tasks that are more closely associated with reading- and writing-related variables (Pauly et al., 2011; van der Sluis, de Jong, & van der Leij, 2004; Willburger et al., 2008). Tasks that involve rapid naming of stimuli are described as measuring naming facility and storage and retrieval fluency (Flanagan et al., 2012).

Symbol Translation Index

The Symbol Translation Index (STI) measures learning associations between unfamiliar symbols and their meanings and applies them in novel ways.

The subtest consists of three conditions: immediate, delayed, and recognition. In the Immediate Symbol Translation (IST) subtest the child learns visual-verbal pairs and then translates symbol strings into phrases or sentences. Tasks similar to IST are described as measuring verbal-visual associative memory or paired associates learning, storage and retrieval fluency and accuracy, and immediate recall (Flanagan et al., 2012, Flanagan & Alfonso, 2017). This is a cued memory paradigm; i.e., the child recalls information related to a specific visual cue.

Visual-verbal associative memory tasks are closely associated with reading decoding skills, word reading accuracy and fluency, text reading, and reading comprehension (Elliott, Hale, Fiorello, Dorvil, & Moldovan, 2010; Evans, Floyd, McGrew, & Leforgee, 2001; Floyd, Keith, Taub, & McGrew, 2007; Hulme, Goetz, Gooch, Adams, & Snowling, 2007; Lervåg, Bråten, & Hulme, 2009; Litt, de Jong, van Bergen, & Nation, 2013; Wechsler and Kaplan, 2015) in addition to math calculation and math reasoning skills (Floyd, Evans, & McGrew, 2003; McGrew & Wendling, 2010). Furthermore, visual-verbal associate memory tasks are sensitive to dyslexia when they require verbal output (Gang & Siegel, 2002; Li, Shu, McBride-Chang, Liu, & Xue, 2009; Litt & Nation, 2014).

In the Delayed Symbol Translation (DST) condition the child translates symbol strings into sentences using visual-verbal pairs previously learned during the IST condition. DST measures verbal-visual associative memory or paired associates learning, storage and retrieval fluency and accuracy, and delayed recall (Flanagan & Alfonso, 2017). This task is a cued memory paradigm.

In the Recognition Symbol Translation (RST) subtest the child views a symbol and selects the correct translation from response options the examiner reads aloud, using visual-verbal pairs recalled from the IST condition. RST is described as measuring verbal-visual associative memory or paired associates learning, storage and retrieval fluency and accuracy, and delayed recognition (Flanagan & Alfonso, 2017). This task constrains the child's responses to words that have been presented in the task and therefore eliminates the possibility of an erroneous word being recalled. This task measures the strength of the associate learning and not the learning of content (e.g., correct words). The examiner may compare performance on this task to the delayed condition to determine the impact of constraining recall on memory performance.

Storage and Retrieval Index

The Storage and Retrieval Index (SRI) is formed by combining the the NSI and the STI. This provides an overall measure of the child's ability to store and retrieve learned information accurately and quickly.

WISC−V Studies of Children With SLDs

The WISC−V Technical and Interpretive Manual reports results from three studies of specific learning disabilities (SLD): SLDs in reading (SLD−R), SLDs in reading and writing (SLD−RW), and SLD in mathematics (SLD−M) (Wechsler, 2014b). The study samples included 30 children diagnosed with SLD−R between the ages of 7 and 16, 22 children diagnosed with SLD−RW between the ages of 6 and 14, and 28 children with SLD−M between the ages of 9 and 16. The sample of SLD−RW were predominantly male (15 males, 7 females), which is expected given that males are at greater risk for writing difficulties than females (Reynolds, Scheiber, Hajovsky, Schwartz, & Kaufman, in submission). The SLD−R and SLD−M groups showed a roughly equal gender split. Control groups of children without a clinical diagnosis were randomly selected from the normative sample and then matched to the clinical groups according to age, sex, race/ethnicity, and parent education level.

Children included in these studies were initially diagnosed or identified with SLDs using various criteria, including DSM−5 (2013) criteria, documentation of an ability-achievement discrepancy, a pattern of strengths and weaknesses approach, or eligibility for receiving LD services. Then all cases included in these clinical studies were reviewed to ensure that the children met DSM−5 criteria for SLDs. These criteria include impairment in reading, reading and writing, or math, as appropriate, which are substantially and quantifiably below those expected for the child's chronological age, causing significant interference with school functioning. Comorbid SLD diagnoses were not permitted except in the SLD—RW group.

The performance of children with SLD—R as compared to matched controls is shown in Table 9.4. The SLD—R group scored significantly lower ($P < .05$) on all the indexes with score differences producing moderate to large effect sizes. All of the global indexes (FSIQ, NVI, and GAI) as well a CPI showed large effects. The lower index scores obtained by the SLD—R group indicate significant difficulties with working memory, long-term storage and retrieval, verbal comprehension, rapid verbal naming, immediate paired associate learning, and quantitative reasoning. At the subtest level, the largest effect sizes were observed for Picture Span, Digit Span, Similarities, and Arithmetic.

The performance of children with SLD—RW as compared to matched controls is shown in Table 9.5. Children with SLD—RW scored significantly lower ($P < .05$) on all indexes with the exception of the VSI and PSI. Similar to the SLD—R group, the SLD—RW group demonstrated significant difficulties with long-term storage and retrieval, working memory, rapid verbal naming, quantitative reasoning, immediate paired associate learning, and (to a lesser extent) verbal comprehension. At the subtest level, the largest effect sizes were observed for Naming Speed Literacy, Letter-Number Sequencing, Digit Span, Similarities, Arithmetic, and Immediate Symbol Translation.

The performance of children with SLDs in mathematics (SLD—M) compared to matched controls is shown in Table 9.6. Children with SLD—M scored significantly lower ($P < .05$) on all indexes with the exception of the WMI and NSI. Among the global indexes, large effect sizes were observed for the NVI, FSIQ, and GAI and moderate for the CPI. Consistent with the nature of math disorders, the SLD—M group demonstrated significant difficulties with quantitative, conceptual, and spatial reasoning abilities. At the subtest level, the largest effect sizes were observed for Visual Puzzles, Arithmetic, Block Design, Figure Weights, and Comprehension. The low effect size for the NSQ subtest is unexpected and inconsistent with results from a later study (Raiford, Drozdick, & Zhang, 2016) showing a large effect size (1.13) for the SLD—M sample. The inconsistent results across studies may be attributed to sampling differences. One possibility is that NSQ is low primarily among younger children with SLD—M. Unlike the SLD—R and SLD—RW studies, the original SLD—M study reported in the manual did not include any children aged 6—8 in the sample, which may represent the grades at which NSQ is most related to the development of math skills. This view is supported by additional data available in the online supplement to the WISC—V Technical and Interpretive Manual (Wechsler, 2014b) in which correlations of NSQ with various WIAT—III math subtests are shown to be substantially higher in the younger than older

TABLE 9.4 WISC–V Mean Performance of Children with SLD–R

Subtest	SLD–R		Matched Control			Group Mean Comparison			
	Mean	SD	Mean	SD	n	Difference	P Value	Standard Difference
SI	8.2	2.2	10.3	2.4	30	2.07	<.01	.90
VC	7.7	2.6	10.0	3.0	30	2.23	<.01	.79
IN	8.5	1.9	10.1	2.4	30	1.60	<.01	.74
CO	8.6	3.2	10.2	2.9	30	1.60	.03	.52
BD	9.1	2.6	10.3	3.0	30	1.13	.11	.40
VP	8.5	3.1	10.3	2.2	30	1.87	<.01	.70
MR	8.6	2.1	10.4	2.6	30	1.83	<.01	.77
FW	8.9	2.3	10.3	3.0	30	1.37	.08	.51
PC	8.8	3.0	9.5	2.4	30	.70	.35	.26
AR	8.4	2.1	10.7	3.2	30	2.30	<.01	.85
DS	8.2	1.6	10.5	2.3	30	2.33	<.01	1.18
PS	7.7	2.6	10.8	2.1	30	3.10	<.01	1.31
LN	8.2	2.3	9.9	2.1	30	1.73	<.01	.79
CD	8.7	3.1	10.1	3.0	30	1.40	.02	.46
SS	8.8	2.7	10.0	2.9	30	1.23	.07	.44
CA	9.5	3.1	9.5	3.3	29	.03	.97	.01
NSL	88.9	16.3	100.4	12.5	29	11.55	<.01	.80

NSQ	89.7	14.6	102.6	14.1	29	12.83	<.01	.89
IST	91.9	12.6	102.5	12.1	30	10.53	<.01	.85
DST	93.6	11.5	101.5	13.7	30	7.93	.02	.63
RST	93.6	9.9	101.5	11.6	30	7.87	.02	.73
Composite								
VCI	89.1	11.2	100.7	12.6	30	11.63	<.01	.98
VSI	93.3	14.1	101.6	12.4	30	8.27	<.01	.62
FRI	92.5	10.8	101.9	13.5	30	9.40	<.01	.77
WMI	87.8	10.1	104.1	11.2	30	16.23	<.01	1.52
PSI	93.0	15.3	100.3	14.4	30	7.37	.02	.50
FSIQ	88.9	10.5	102.0	13.9	30	13.07	<.01	1.06
NVI	89.6	11.8	102.6	13.2	30	13.03	<.01	1.04
GAI	90.0	11.0	101.6	13.1	30	11.63	<.01	.96
CPI	88.6	12.6	102.7	13.3	30	14.17	<.01	1.09
QRI	92.2	9.5	102.7	16.1	30	10.57	<.01	.80
AWMI	90.1	9.1	101.2	10.3	30	11.07	<.01	1.14
NSI	88.4	14.0	101.6	13.7	29	13.14	<.01	.95
STI	91.8	11.3	101.5	12.8	30	9.63	<.01	.80
SRI	87.4	11.4	101.9	12.2	29	14.55	<.01	1.23

TABLE 9.5 WISC–V Mean Performance of Children with SLDs–RW

Subtest	SLD–RW		Matched Control			Group Mean Comparison		
	Mean	SD	Mean	SD	n	Difference	P Value	Standard Difference
SI	7.2	2.0	9.1	2.1	22	1.91	<.01	.93
VC	7.8	2.4	8.9	2.9	22	1.09	.23	.41
IN	8.0	1.8	9.3	1.9	22	1.23	.05	.66
CO	7.5	2.1	8.5	2.6	22	.91	.17	.39
BD	9.1	2.8	10.1	2.5	22	1.00	.13	.38
VP	9.6	2.6	9.2	2.8	22	−.45	.49	−.17
MR	8.2	2.2	9.4	2.8	22	1.14	.21	.45
FW	7.8	3.2	9.9	2.8	22	2.14	.03	.71
PC	9.5	3.0	10.6	2.4	22	1.14	.22	.42
AR	7.4	2.0	9.6	2.8	22	2.27	<.01	.93
DS	7.2	2.6	10.2	3.1	22	3.05	<.01	1.07
PS	8.0	2.0	9.4	3.0	22	1.36	.01	.53
LN	7.4	2.2	9.8	2.0	22	2.45	<.01	1.17
CD	7.8	3.3	9.0	2.8	22	1.14	.20	.37
SS	9.6	2.9	9.7	2.5	22	.09	.91	.03
CA	9.8	3.3	9.7	3.1	22	−.09	.91	−.03

NSL	85.6	16.2	101.9	8.4	21	16.33	<.01	1.27
NSQ	88.8	14.0	99.7	13.4	21	10.95	.02	.80
IST	88.2	15.1	102.0	14.3	22	13.73	<.01	.93
DST	90.1	16.7	101.1	15.7	22	11.00	.03	.68
RST	87.1	13.0	98.8	12.5	21	11.67	.01	.92
Composite								
VCI	86.5	10.1	94.6	11.7	22	8.09	.02	.74
VSI	96.2	13.3	98.0	12.5	22	1.73	.53	.13
FRI	88.4	12.2	97.8	13.3	22	9.45	.02	.74
WMI	85.8	9.7	98.7	13.9	22	12.95	<.01	1.08
PSI	93.0	15.8	96.3	11.3	22	3.36	.42	.24
FSIQ	84.8	11.1	96.2	10.5	22	11.41	<.01	1.06
NVI	88.6	12.7	95.9	11.5	22	7.27	.02	.60
GAI	87.0	10.9	96.4	12.2	22	9.45	.01	.82
CPI	87.2	12.0	96.8	10.0	22	9.64	<.01	.87
QRI	85.9	12.8	98.5	13.0	22	12.64	<.01	.98
AWMI	85.0	11.1	100.2	12.4	22	15.14	<.01	1.29
NSI	86.2	12.6	100.1	9.0	21	13.86	<.01	1.27
STI	87.1	14.2	100.4	14.3	21	13.29	<.01	.93
SRI	83.9	14.1	100.1	10.2	20	16.15	<.01	1.31

TABLE 9.6 WISC–V Mean Performance of Children with SLD–M

Subtest	SLD–M		Matched Control			Group Mean Comparison			
	Mean	SD	Mean	SD	n	Difference	P Value	Standard Difference
SI	8.1	2.3	10.3	3.3	27	2.11	<.01	.74
VC	8.1	3.1	9.4	3.1	28	1.32	.04	.43
IN	7.5	2.3	10.3	3.7	27	2.78	<.01	.90
CO	8.0	2.7	10.4	3.0	28	2.43	<.01	.85
BD	7.1	2.3	9.8	3.3	28	2.64	<.01	.93
VP	7.6	2.6	10.3	2.6	28	2.64	<.01	1.02
MR	7.2	3.4	9.6	3.3	28	2.36	.01	.70
FW	6.5	3.2	9.4	2.9	28	2.82	<.01	.92
PC	8.7	2.9	11.0	3.9	28	2.32	.02	.68
AR	6.4	2.4	9.3	3.2	28	2.86	<.01	1.01
DS	7.9	2.7	9.9	3.5	28	1.93	.04	.62
PS	8.2	2.7	9.4	4.1	28	1.18	.21	.34
LN	7.9	2.1	9.7	3.7	27	1.81	.04	.60
CD	7.6	2.6	9.8	3.7	28	2.14	.01	.67
SS	8.8	2.9	9.4	2.9	28	.57	.39	.20
CA	10.3	2.9	10.6	3.2	28	.32	.66	.10

NSL	95.6	15.8	96.6	18.6	28	1.00	.84	.06
NSQ	91.1	15.4	96.0	19.0	28	4.93	.19	.29
IST	88.6	17.0	101.3	16.8	28	12.75	<.01	.75
DST	92.5	16.0	101.3	14.3	28	8.86	.04	.58
RST	90.4	17.0	98.2	15.0	28	7.79	.09	.49
Composite								
VCI	90.3	13.7	99.5	16.4	27	9.19	<.01	.61
VSI	85.4	12.6	100.0	15.3	28	14.61	<.01	1.04
FRI	82.2	15.4	96.7	16.2	28	14.46	<.01	.91
WMI	88.7	13.5	97.7	20.4	28	9.00	.07	.52
PSI	90.2	14.2	97.7	15.6	28	7.46	.03	.50
FSIQ	83.6	11.9	98.4	16.4	27	14.85	<.01	1.04
NVI	81.5	13.7	97.6	15.9	28	16.11	<.01	1.09
GAI	84.2	12.0	98.6	16.5	27	14.44	<.01	1.00
CPI	87.3	13.9	97.0	16.6	28	9.71	.02	.63
QRI	79.9	13.7	96.2	16.2	28	16.29	<.01	1.09
AWMI	88.3	11.2	99.1	19.2	27	10.78	.02	.69
NSI	92.6	14.2	96.4	18.8	28	3.79	.36	.23
STI	90.1	16.1	100.2	16.0	28	10.07	.02	.63
SRI	89.7	15.7	98.0	14.1	28	8.25	.03	.55

age groups. Another possibility is that NSQ is low only among certain types of math disorders. Further research is needed to investigate possible age or subtype effects among children with SLD−M on the NSQ subtest.

In these studies, across all three SLD groups, low scores with relatively large effect sizes were observed for the FSIQ, GAI, and QRI and, among the subtests, Arithmetic, Similarities, and Immediate Symbol Translation. The results from these studies reveal generally expected trends in performance among each SLD sample, which supports the validity of the WISC−V among children with SLDs.

These studies show emerging performance patterns at the group level, while individual score patterns vary. As such, children with various reading difficulties may show a varying, or even contrasting, pattern of strengths and weaknesses that cancel out in group data. The value of these clinical studies is in identifying trends in abilities of groups of children with LDs that either confirm expectations or raise important questions. As always, diagnostic decisions are a matter of professional judgment by qualified practitioners. They are based not on any single test score, but on a preponderance of evidence including medical and family histories, cognitive, academic, and neuropsychological test scores, as well as the student's academic progress in response to empirically supported educational interventions.

REVISITING SLD IDENTIFICATION WITH THE WISC−V

The federal definition of SLDs in the United States has remained the same for over three decades; however, the 2006 federal regulations introduced changes to the methods of SLD identification that are being implemented differently across school districts. For example, although the ability-achievement discrepancy (AAD) method continues to be permitted under these regulations, it can no longer be mandated as the sole criteria and some schools have eliminated its use, while others continue it as one part of the process. Further, response to intervention (RTI) methods are encouraged by the federal guidelines associated with these regulations and are now used in many states. At the same time, the regulations allow a so-called "third method," which is an alternative research-based approach to SLD identification that has now been adopted by more than 20 of the 50 states (Sotelo-Dynega, Flanagan, & Alfonso, 2011).

According to IDEA 2004 [Sec.602(30)], SLD means a disorder in "one or more of the basic psychological processes..." These processes are not defined by the law nor does the law require evidence of a processing weakness; however, third-method approaches require the assessment of cognitive processing areas in order to determine if the child's pattern of strengths and weaknesses is consistent with an operational definition of SLD. Research-based methods of SLD identification that are consistent with the third-method approach include Berninger's framework of assessment for intervention, Flanagan and colleagues' operational definition of SLDs, Naglieri's Discrepancy/Consistency Model, and Hale and Fiorello's Concordance−Discordance Model (see Flanagan & Alfonso, 2011 for an overview of each method). These approaches share similar features. Each model expects a logical consistency between the achievement weakness and a cognitive processing weakness that is associated with that achievement area (such as performance on a word recognition measure and the NSI or STI). In addition, the models expect statistical discrepancy between the achievement weakness and a cognitive processing strength that is *not* associated with that achievement area (such as performance on a word recognition measure and the VSI). Finally, the models expect statistical discrepancy between the cognitive processing strengths and weaknesses.

According to Berninger's (2011) framework, cognitive assessment is essential for differential diagnosis, especially measures of overall cognitive ability, verbal reasoning, and nonverbal reasoning. Using the WISC−V, these measures would include the FSIQ, VCI, and NVI. As a general estimate of intellectual functioning, the FSIQ is important for ruling out a developmental disability. In addition, measures of verbal and nonverbal intelligence are important for differentiating dyslexia and oral and written language LDs (OWL−LD). In cases of dyslexia, basic reading and spelling are weak in relation to average or better scores on the VCI. The VCI may not be a notable strength in a child with dyslexia, but the score should not be a normative weakness. In cases of OWL−LD, the VCI is often a normative weakness because of the child's language impairments; however, nonverbal reasoning, as measured by the NVI, is at least average. In all three of the WISC−V SLD clinical studies, the VCI was significantly lower than matched controls with mean standard scores of about 89 for SLD−R, 87 for SLD−RW, and 90 for SLD−M. With standard deviations of 10−11 points, the SLD−R and SLD−RW groups included some cases with VCI scores below the average range; a more extensive evaluation would be necessary to confirm whether some of these cases qualified as OWL−LD. Hence, consider the FSIQ, VCI, and NVI scores as one component of an evaluation for determining whether a child may have a developmental disability, a language impairment, or dyslexia.

Pattern of Strengths and Weaknesses

These various "third-method" approaches to SLD identification are generally referred to as the Pattern of Strengths and Weaknesses (PSW) approach. Both of Pearson's digital assessment and interpretation systems, Q-Interactive and Q-global, provide scoring by this model for use with the WISC−V and the Kaufman Test of Educational Achievement, Third Edition (KTEA−3) (Kaufman & Kaufman, 2014) or the WIAT−III. This

PSW approach most closely aligns with Hale and Fiorello's Concordance−Discordance Model (C−DM) (Hale & Fiorello, 2004).

The PSW approach is a statistically sound methodology for identifying the essential operational marker for SLDs: unexpected learning failure, defined as consistency between areas of cognitive processing weakness and academic weakness coupled with a significant discrepancy between areas of cognitive processing strength and cognitive processing weakness (Hale & Fiorello, 2004; Hale, Kaufman, Naglieri, & Kavale, 2006). To use this model, the practitioner selects standardized measures that best represent the student's achievement weakness, cognitive processing strength, and cognitive processing weakness. Index scores with high reliability coefficients are generally preferred, provided that subtest scores within the composites are fairly consistent. Guidelines for selecting measures of strength and weakness include the following: first, the area of achievement weakness should be consistent with the referral concern and cross-validate the low performance with reports from teachers or other measures. Second, the cognitive processing weakness must be clinically or empirically associated with the achievement weakness, so that the student's learning difficulties are reasonably explained, at least in part, by the cognitive processing weakness. Third, the cognitive processing strength should not be strongly associated, clinically or empirically, with the achievement weakness.

Consider an example using the WISC−V and WIAT−III within a PSW approach to evaluate a student referred for reading difficulties. The student demonstrates weaknesses primarily in basic reading skills, as evidenced by a WIAT−III Basic Reading composite score in the below average range, with similarly low scores on both Word Reading and Pseudoword Decoding. Prior research and the validity support for the theoretical constructs measured by the WISC−V indexes identify the following WISC−V Index scores as cognitive processing weaknesses that could be associated with a weakness in basic reading skills: WMI, PSI, AWMI, STI, SRI, and NSI (e.g., Fiorello, Hale, & Snyder, 2006; Hale, Fiorello, Kavanagh, Hoeppner, & Gaither, 2001). Weak phonological processing typically included in diagnostic language and achievement tests is also relevant. The following WISC−V Index scores might be considered as cognitive processing strengths that are not strongly associated with basic reading skills: VCI, VSI, and FRI.

Using the standard error of the difference for statistical comparisons of standard scores, the PSW approach establishes discordance, meaning significant difference, between the cognitive processing weakness and the cognitive processing strength, and between the achievement weakness and the cognitive processing strength. Statistically demonstrating a consistency between the cognitive processing weakness and the achievement weakness is not essential to the PSW approach (see Hale & Fiorello, 2004), but some applications of the CDM model have included this step (e.g., Hale et al., 2013). If the student has not responded to good quality instruction and the criteria of the PSW model are met, the final step for identification is to determine whether IDEA statutory and regulatory requirements are met to qualify the student for special education services.

By incorporating the PSW approach into Tier 3 of an RTI framework, educators benefit from early identification and intervention for at-risk learners as well as a research-supported approach to SLD identification for nonresponders. IDEA 2004 neither suggested nor implied that practitioners must choose either RTI or an intracognitive approach to determine SLDs, and gathering both RTI and cognitive assessment data is ideal for accurate SLD identification as well as for individualized interventions (Hale et al., 2006). Children with LDs require interventions that are tailored to their cognitive and academic strengths and needs. Although controversial, a PSW approach can provide the necessary information for planning differentiated instruction (Fiorello, Hale, & Wycoff, 2012).

The PSW approach may also be appropriate for the identification of students who are gifted with LDs, or "twice exceptional." These students are capable of high intellectual and academic performance, but they also have specific processing weaknesses that make achievement difficult in one or more areas (Brody & Mills, 1997). According to some researchers (e.g., Lovett & Sparks, 2011), a LD requires below average academic achievement. Others contend that, even though academic performance may be in the average range, these students demonstrate intraindividual variability that is the essence of a LD (NJCLDs, 2011; Reynolds & Shaywitz, 2009). Maddocks (2018) found that that a very high proportion of individuals with an IQ of 130 or above, ranging from 2% to 86%, show a discrepancy between their IQ and their academic achievement and would be diagnosed with LDs using this criterion. This high proportion of discrepancies between ability and achievement would be expected based on regression to the mean (Woodcock, 1984).

Using a traditional AAD model of identification, these students are typically not eligible for services because their academic performance is not sufficiently low in an absolute sense. An RTI (or any other) approach to identification that focuses solely on below grade-level performance is similarly problematic for gifted students with LDs. Instead, intraindividual strengths and weaknesses must be considered (see Silverman, 2003). According to Crepeau–Hobson and Bianco (2011, 2013), Tier 2 must include targeted assessment of academic, cognitive processing, and social-emotional areas and, at Tier 3, include a comprehensive psychoeducational evaluation to assess intellectual and academic strengths and weaknesses. For educational settings that recognize intraindividual underachievement, a PSW approach is well suited to the identification of twice exceptional students. Some cautions are warranted, however, regarding use of a PSW model. In particular, Miciak, Fletcher, Vaughn, Stuebing, and Tolar (2013) provide data suggesting there is little agreement in LD classification rates across PSW models, and the models do not adequately identify students who fail to respond to treatment. These authors further argue that there is no evidence that students with unique subtypes respond better to different forms of academic interventions.

When interpreting the PSW analysis results, do not assume that a significant result necessarily indicates SLD or that a nonsignificant result rules out SLD. SLD identification is not a statistical decision; rather, consider the results of this analysis as one component of a comprehensive clinical evaluation. The PSW approach should be used within a balanced practice model that incorporates the benefits of RTI (i.e., early intervention with empirically supported interventions and progress monitoring) while ensuring a research-supported approach to SLD identification (Hale, 2006). For children who do not quickly respond to early intervention, a comprehensive evaluation that incorporates a PSW approach may provide information that is relevant for understanding why a student is struggling, what type or subtype of LDs best describes the student's learning profile, and how to tailor interventions accordingly. For example, struggling readers with phonological weaknesses might be instructed differently than those with fluency weaknesses. Only through careful attention to subtyping based on patterns of strengths and weaknesses will it become possible to meaningfully research subtype by treatment interactions.

CASE STUDY: PSYCHOLOGICAL ASSESSMENT

Case Study: Ann—Mathematics Learning Disorder

Confidential Psychological Evaluation

Name	Ann Bloom	Date of Report	8/21/2017
Date of birth	6/8/2005	Grade	6
Gender	Female	School	A Middle School
Date of testing	8/16/2017	Age at testing	12 years 2 months

Current Symptoms

Mr. and Mrs. Bloom requested an assessment of their daughter, Ann, after the A Middle School admissions assessment indicated her math skills were below grade level. Mrs. Bloom, who has homeschooled Ann for most of her elementary school years, reported the following. Ann is not retaining much of the math she is taught. She tends to learn it, move on, and at a review later she cannot recall what she learned. She has some difficulty memorizing math facts. Math reasoning and word problems were difficult in late elementary school; she drew pictures of everything in order to complete problems. Mental arithmetic remains challenging for her, as do even small changes to a math problem after it is completed. Mr. and Mrs. Bloom stated they hope to document the specific nature of her difficulties in mathematics so accommodations can be made and an intervention plan requested before she enters middle school.

Mr. and Mrs. Bloom additionally reported that in the past Ann was suspected by her kindergarten teacher of having ADHD. They would like to determine if she does and if so, learn what to do to treat it.

They reported on an initial intake symptom checklist that Ann shows many signs of inattention, as follows. She is often off task when she is supposed to do schoolwork, homework, or chores, has trouble completing such tasks, and appears to let her mind wander during them. She loses track of what she is doing due to noises or other things going on, and forgets what she is supposed to do and then acts confused. She avoids tasks that are effortful. She has great trouble concentrating almost all the time. She listens to directions sporadically, and many times seems not to listen carefully when spoken to. She is highly disorganized. She has poor planning skills as well; for example, she has difficulty carrying out responsibilities when given a verbal list of three chores. Ann reported that she has a short attention span and attention problems. Often people (especially her mother) tell her she should pay more attention. She is never a good listener, and she often gets in trouble for not paying attention.

On the intake checklist, Mr. and Mrs. Bloom reported that Ann also displays many behaviors that are consistent with hyperactivity and impulsivity, as follows. She interrupts frequently, acts out of control and without thinking, and is overly active. She acts childish, has poor self-control, and seems unable to slow down. She has trouble keeping her hands or feet to herself and she fiddles with items she holds. She tends to fidget with pencils and chew them, play with her jewelry, and she has great difficulty staying seated. She is almost always in constant motion. Ann is aware of these behaviors and describes them as a problem because it is hard to sit still.

Ann also indicated on the symptom checklist that she often worries. Upon interview, she indicated these worries are sometimes about making mistakes in school, but not always just that. Ann doesn't know why she worries, but she almost always gets worried when things might not or don't go right for her in school, with friends, or at home.

Ann also shows signs of social difficulties. She indicates that other young people sometimes make fun of her. Mrs. Bloom stated Ann complains that she doesn't have any friends, has a hard time understanding certain social cues, and doesn't interact very well with others her age. For example, she doesn't always understand that other young people aren't being "mean" and that they are joking with her. Mrs. Bloom often has to explain to her why her friends may not always want to do what she does. Ann interacts well with children who are younger than her as well as with adults. Mrs. Bloom stated she is unsure as to why Ann has a hard time relating to other young people her age.

Referral Questions

Ann's parents wish to learn the answers to the following questions:

1. Does Ann have a specific LD in mathematics?
2. Does Ann have ADHD?
3. Are there other related issues that may interfere with her academic or social functioning?
4. What intervention and treatment may alleviate these conditions, if yes?
5. What school accommodations may help her to function best academically, if yes?

Responses to Referral Questions

1. Does Ann have a specific LD in mathematics?

   Yes. Ann qualifies for a diagnosis of SLD with impairment in mathematics: number sense, memorization of arithmetic facts, accurate calculation (moderate impairment), and fluent calculation (severe impairment).

2. Does Ann have ADHD?

   Yes. I have diagnosed Ann with ADHD, combined presentation. This means she has significant symptoms of both inattention and hyperactivity/impulsivity. Her parents and Ann herself report these symptoms, which are also observable in objective test results. ADHD is strongly related to (and perhaps inseparable from) executive function difficulties, which Ann also struggles with. Executive functions are abilities that help people to think through short- and long-term consequences of their actions and plan results, evaluate their own actions quickly, and adjust if their actions are ineffective. Success at school and later at work is related to executive skill strength.

3. Are there other issues?

   Yes. I have diagnosed Ann with generalized anxiety disorder and social (pragmatic) communication disorder.

   Follow up is necessary to determine if she has motor coordination disorder. She is referred for an occupational therapy evaluation, and follow up with her physician should focus on ruling out any physical, vestibular, neurological, or vision conditions that can also cause issues with gross motor coordination and balance.

A number of somatic (bodily) complaints accompany Ann's anxiety. Physical conditions related to these symptoms should also be ruled out by a physician.

4. What issues (learning or otherwise) exist that may require school accommodations?

In a public school setting, Ann would be eligible to request accommodations and has grounds to request an individualized education plan. She qualifies as a child with disabilities that interfere with concentration, speech, and academic functioning under the IDEA that governs free public school education. These include:

- SLD category: SLD in mathematics
- Other health impairment category: ADHD: developmental coordination disorder
- Emotional and behavioral disturbance category: generalized anxiety disorder
- Speech or language impairment category: social (pragmatic) communication disorder

Mr. and Mrs. Bloom plan to enroll Ann in a private school. Accommodations for these conditions, if available within the school environment or contracted providers, would be helpful and appropriate. Refer to accommodations in recommendations section at the conclusion of this report.

5. What intervention recommendations can be used in development of a plan to meet her educational needs?

Pharmacotherapy (medication), additional medical and occupational therapy evaluation, executive function coaching, vigorous exercise, martial arts, limiting screen time, content mastery support, and math specialist training are all recommended to assist in improving her school functioning; many of these will need to be carried out at home.

There are various recommendations for interventions that appear in the recommendations section of this report that are tied to the LD in mathematics.

Evaluation Procedures

Intake symptom checklist
Child clinical interview
Parent interview
Behavioral observations

Psychological Testing Procedures

- Wechsler Intelligence Scale for Children, Fifth Edition (WISC−V)
- Wechsler Intelligence Scale for Children, Fifth Edition Integrated (WISC−V Integrated)
- Kaufman Test of Educational Achievement, Third Edition (KTEA−3)
- NEPSY Second Edition (NEPSY−II)
- Clinical Evaluation of Language Fundamentals, Fifth Edition (CELF−5) (selected subtest)
- Behavior Assessment System for Children, Third Edition (BASC−3)
  - Parent Rating Scales: Mr. and Mrs. Bloom
  - Self-Report Form: Ann
- Delis Rating of Executive Functions
  - Parent: Mr. and Mrs. Bloom

History of Presenting Problems

Ann has never been formally evaluated for ADHD, but Mrs. Bloom reports that for as long as she has homeschooled her, Ann daydreams, is easily side-tracked, draws pictures on her work, and is not focused on what she needs to be doing. She observes that Ann tries to divert the conversation to something other than school.

Mrs. Bloom reported that Ann's kindergarten teacher indicated that Ann had difficulties focusing and with attention and concentration and might have ADHD. Ann does not have social difficulties, but her mother reported she seems less mature relative to others her own age. She stated Ann has relatively good academic performance in subjects other than mathematics.

Ann has acquaintances from various activities and a few friends at church. Mrs. Bloom stated that the other young people include her, but do not treat her as a close friend would (e.g., she is not often invited to spend the night at other girls' houses or to go on outings together).

Family and Marital History

Mr. and Mrs. Bloom, Ann's parents, report they have been happily married for 17 years. Ann has one older sister (by 1½ years), Bailey. Ann has a close relationship with both parents (from both Ann and her parents' perspectives). Mrs. Bloom indicated that Mr. Bloom is more patient with Ann than she, and that she has had frustrating times when homeschooling Ann. However, Mrs. Bloom stated she enjoys time with Ann immensely and would continue to homeschool her if Ann hadn't asked to attend school with others. She stated Ann wants to attend school so she can make more friends.

Mr. and Mrs. Bloom report Ann's older sister Bailey becomes annoyed with Ann's impulsive behavior, but that they still spend time together and are very close. Mr. and Mrs. Bloom indicated Bailey is a good student and high achiever with many friends and that she is responsible around the house. They indicated they do not have any concerns about Bailey at this time.

Medical and Developmental History

Mrs. Bloom's pregnancy with Ann was normal. Ann was born three weeks early by C section. When born, she wasn't breathing and had an APGAR of 0. Her airway was cleared, then her second APGAR was normal. Following this rather traumatic birth, her mother reports that Ann screamed continually for almost 2 days. She was a difficult child to parent because she cried frequently and was extremely sensitive to verbal feedback.

Mrs. Bloom reported that Ann's language development was delayed. She received speech therapy from ages 2–3½ and made good progress so was discharged from the early intervention program she attended. Her motor development was slightly delayed (or on the tail end of regular expectations). She did not crawl until 9½ months, and began walking at 17 months. She did not have other health problems.

Ann has had recent vision and hearing screenings. She has worn glasses for 2 years, and reliably wears them for school and when reading.

Current Medications

None

Academic History and Status

Mrs. Bloom began homeschooling Ann shortly after Ann's kindergarten teacher expressed concerns about Ann's concentration and attention. Mrs. Bloom stated she just thought Ann would do better in a one-on-one learning environment and that she has a college degree in education so can teach what is necessary. They stated Ann's spelling, reading skills, and written expression skills are at the expected level and that her grades have been good. However, Mrs. Bloom indicated Ann's numerical operations skills and fluency are low. Review of admissions testing records confirmed that Ann is at or above grade level in these areas and that only math skills were below grade level.

Patient's Strengths, Coping Mechanisms, and Available Support Systems

Mr. and Mrs. Bloom indicated Ann greatly enjoys dancing and music, and is an active person. She is involved in gymnastics, cheer, drama, and church performances. Her parents describe her as warm, friendly, playful, and kind-hearted. She has loving and strong family relationships. When relaxing, she loves to play with Minecraft and Legos and enjoys video games.

Behavioral Observations

Ann arrived on time and was oriented to person, place, time, and purpose of the meeting. She was accompanied by Mrs. Bloom. She presented dressed casually with good grooming and hygiene and appeared her stated age. Her rate of speech was normal. She was well-mannered and respectful. During testing, she answered relatively quickly when confident in an answer. She had fair eye contact; when conversing or listening, Ann looked away from the examiner more frequently than typical of most children her age. Her affect was congruent with her stated mood, which was "fine." She turned away during testing on a number of occasions and quickly apologized when asked to turn back around. Ann's activity level was higher than typical of other young people her age, and eye contact was abnormal. Speech revealed strong vocabulary. Her reported mood was "ok" and her affect was mood congruent.

During testing, Ann was aware that the evaluation was to be used to help her in school and to understand better how she learns. She seemed clear on the purpose of testing and was self-disclosing with me, reporting her problems with math, attention, and anxiety readily. A good rapport was quickly achieved and she appeared to make her best effort on all tasks. She persevered at even challenging tasks. Given this, the testing is likely to be a good estimate of her true cognitive abilities. Three breaks were offered and given to ensure she could give her best effort at all times.

Assessment Results

Overall Intellectual Ability

Ann's FSIQ score suggests that her overall intellectual ability is in the average range compared with other young people her age. Another method of examining general intellectual ability that reduces the influence of working memory and processing speed on the global ability estimate (the GAI) suggests relatively uniform abilities when taken as a group.

In large studies, out of all the scores on cognitive tests, overall intellectual ability does the best job at predicting school success. However, it doesn't always tell you everything you need to know about a child's individual cognitive strengths and needs. An individual's cognitive "story" is usually better and more deeply understood when more narrow areas of ability are also considered.

Language

Speech

Ann responded readily to items that required expressive responses. She was adequately articulate and expressive and elaborated sufficiently.

Verbal Comprehension

Ann's ability to access, apply, and express knowledge she has gained about words and their meanings and to reason with verbal material is in the high average range relative to other young people her age, and is a personal strength relative to her other cognitive abilities. When acquired knowledge and social/practical knowledge is also taken into account, however, Ann's verbal crystallized abilities are in the average range and may reflect reports of inattention in class and low social skills. Providing cues for the social/practical knowledge information so that she is merely required to recognize the correct responses rather than to recall and express them does not result in substantial improvement; she was able to respond slightly more accurately to just two additional questions out of 18 under these conditions.

Listening Comprehension

The kind of listening comprehension that students must do in school involves hearing and understanding relatively formal speech, rather than casual conversation. Ann's listening comprehension abilities are average compared with other young people her age. This suggests Ann grasps the meaning of what is said in the classroom at a level that is typical of her peers.

Visual-Spatial Processing

Visual-spatial processing is the ability to evaluate visual details and to understand relationships of visual parts in space, and to use that information to assemble a geometric design that matches a model (either pictured or real). Sometimes expressing this ability requires the ability to work with and move real objects. Her visual-spatial processing ability is in the low average range compared with that of other young people her age, and is a personal weakness (relative to her other abilities).

Such a weakness is commonly seen in children who have problems learning math, because learning math requires the ability to see objects and lines in your head and use your imagination to understand them and how they are constructed or related. Her difficulty in this area is the same on tasks that involve trial and error problem solving and physical (motor) manipulation of components of a construction or that involve mental imagery. Interestingly, Legos and Minecraft are two of her favorite pastimes. This suggests Ann might not shy away from a challenge.

Fluid Reasoning and Problem Solving

Reasoning is the ability to detect and apply the underlying rules or relationships that define how objects or ideas are understood as a group. Ann's visual reasoning ability is average compared with that of other young people her age. However, her quantitative reasoning ability is in the very low to low average range, which is typically low in children with math difficulties. She is more able to express accurate reasoning and problem solving if it involves analogical relationships rather than quantitative relationships among abstract shapes, or converting word problems into equations (i.e., math reasoning). Providing additional time, the opportunity to use a pencil and paper, or providing the math facts involved in equations did not result in improvement to her performance. This suggests her math difficulties may be limited by low automaticity of basic math facts and perhaps not rooted in math reasoning deficits.

Learning and Memory

Her learning and memory were assessed to examine their role in, and implications for, her future academic success; memory and learning are closely related to each other and are very important to school achievement.

Working Memory

Working memory is the ability to take in, keep, and manipulate information in one's awareness to get some type of output that can be expressed. Her working memory ability is in the average range relative to other young people her age.

Associative Memory

Her visual-verbal associative memory, or the ability to form new associations between symbols and meanings, is average relative to other young people her age. This type of memory is especially relevant to learning to read, write, and do math, because all of these skills involve learning systems of symbols that are assigned meanings.

Her performance suggests uniform memory abilities when she is recalling associations she learned within the past few seconds or minutes or when trying to recall them half an hour later. However, if she can be allowed to choose the meaning among different possibilities rather than having to recall it, she may turn in somewhat stronger performance as her performance on such a task was improved relative to the free recall condition.

Naming Facility

Naming facility (also known as rapid automatic naming) involves recognizing and recalling overlearned information, like letters and numbers or quantities, as efficiently as possible. Her skill at recognizing, recalling, and reciting letters and numbers is in the low average range relative to other young people her age.

Her ability to rapidly recognize and name quantities which is related to math skills is less efficient, and is in the very low range compared with other young people her age. Her math skill weaknesses are partially explained by low efficiency at working with these basic building blocks of overlearned information that are involved in math.

Cognitive Speed

Processing Speed

Processing speed is the ability to make speedy and accurate judgments about visual information and act on those judgments. Slow processing speed can lower academic performance because if information cannot be processed quickly it tends to be lost. Her processing speed is in the low average range relative to other young people her age.

Naming Facility

Naming facility is also sometimes thought of as a part of cognitive speed, and is discussed under the prior heading Learning and Memory.

Math Skills

Her math skills are in the low average range relative to other young people her age. An analysis of errors suggested that she tends to make more errors than others on problems involving even basic mathematical operations such as addition, subtraction, multiplication, and division.

Math computation

Math computation is one's skill with the most basic building blocks of math (like addition and subtraction) all the way through more complicated skills like using fractions, decimals, algebra, roots and exponents, signed numbers, and so on. Her skills in this area are in the low average range relative to other young people her age.

Math fluency

Math fluency involves quickly answering simple math problems using basic operations like addition, subtraction, multiplication, and division that should be mastered by the end of elementary school. Her math fluency is in the very low range relative to others her age.

Math problem solving

Math reasoning involves the application of reasoning and mathematical concepts to solve meaningful problems. Her math reasoning skills are in the average range relative to other young people her age.

Attention and Executive Functioning

Attention and executive functioning were evaluated to provide objective results to examine along with subjective reports (from Ann and her parents) of her issues with inattentive behavior. Ann has clinically significant attention and hyperactive/impulsive symptoms according to consistent subjective informants and objective test findings. Her symptoms and test results are consistent with a diagnosis of ADHD, combined presentation (both inattentive and hyperactive/impulsive symptoms).

In addition to prominent attention difficulties, she has challenges with executive functions, or the central direction of cognitive functions. Executive skill deficits are seen in about 85%−98% of individuals with ADHD. Objective findings show impairment in dividing her attention, low cognitive flexibility and self-monitoring, and slowed responding and increased errors when cognitive flexibility is required. She has difficulty adapting to changing cognitive expectations and situations, and impaired attention when cognitive requirements become complex. These findings are consistent with her parents' observations and responses on symptom checklists and structured instruments.

Emotional and Behavioral Functioning

Ann additionally has a great number of symptoms consistent with generalized anxiety disorder. These further distract her and hinder her functioning at school. She becomes nervous and worried frequently about school as well as friends and family relationships.

Social Functioning

Ann and her parents both indicate that she has few friends, and that she is much less mature than her friends. She has difficulty with the subtle aspects of language involved in conversation and social contact with peers. Ann's parents completed the pragmatics profile checklist and an interview. These data suggested she is overly literal in her interpretation of language. She also does not appear to adjust her verbal approach to be appropriate to context. For example, she may speak similarly at home, out with her friends, and at school to teachers when adjustments are expected for those various settings. She additionally seems to misinterpret others at times and become upset at comments not intended to harm or hurt her.

Clinical Impressions

Ann qualifies for a diagnosis of SLD in math, with impaired skills in number sense, memorization of arithmetic facts, accurate calculation, and fluent calculation. Her math reasoning is somewhat higher than the other areas. It is with great effort and support that she is able to achieve at her present level, which is often seen with SLDs. There are a variety of approaches to diagnosing SLDs. The approach that is becoming most accepted is the pattern of strengths and weaknesses approach to SLD identification. An older methodology, ability-achievement discrepancy, is also still used in some districts. Regardless of the model used, she qualifies for classification as a child with a LD.

Ann also qualifies for a diagnosis of ADHD, combined presentation (both inattentive and hyperactive/impulsive type). She herself reports these symptoms, as do her parents and past teachers from the public school system. She has several symptoms of inattention that are required for this diagnosis, including the following. She has difficulty sustaining attention in tasks. She does not seem to listen when spoken to directly (her mind seems elsewhere, even in the absence of any obvious distraction). She has trouble following through on instructions, needing them repeated by others. She is easily distracted at school. She avoids and dislikes many tasks that require sustained mental effort. She is easily distracted by extraneous stimuli. She also shows several symptoms of hyperactivity and impulsivity. Specifically, she acts out of control and has poor self-control (driven by a motor), blurts out answers, and interrupts others when they are speaking.

Concurrent and perhaps inseparable from ADHD, she shows deficits in a number of executive function skills. Executive function refers to brain functions that activate, organize, integrate and manage other functions. It enables individuals to account for short- and long-term consequences of their actions and to plan for those results. It also allows them to make real-time evaluations of their actions, and make necessary adjustments if those actions are not achieving the desired results. Academic success and subsequent occupational success, are contingent on strong executive skills. When someone experiences deficits in executive skills, they may encounter disorganization, difficulty getting started and finishing work, remembering homework, difficulty memorizing facts, writing essays or reports, working complex math problems, remembering what is read, completing long-term projects, being on time, controlling emotions, and planning for the future.

Ann also qualifies for a diagnosis of social (pragmatic) communication disorder. This involves having difficulties in the social use of verbal and nonverbal communication on a regular basis, such that it impairs social functioning. Individuals with this problem have difficulty using communication for social purposes in a manner that is appropriate for the social context.

They have problems matching communication style to context or the needs of the listener, such as speaking differently in a classroom than with peers. They have difficulty following some conversation rules, including knowing how to use verbal and nonverbal signals to regulate interaction and rephrasing when misunderstood. They also have difficulty understanding what is not explicitly stated (i.e., it is hard to infer meaning unless it is very clear) and with nonliteral or ambiguous meanings of language (e.g., idioms, humor, metaphors).

She also qualifies for a diagnosis of generalized anxiety disorder. She is excessively anxious and worried quite often. She finds it difficult to control the worry and often does not know why she feels worried. She has difficulty concentrating and is restless and irritable. Somatic (bodily) complaints and symptoms are common in children with anxiety disorders. Anxious children may complain of frequent headaches and stomachaches, especially to avoid distressing situations such as school. Generalized anxiety disorder (GAD) is often characterized by somatic complaints, but unlike somatic symptom and related disorders, individuals with GAD also have concerns with areas besides physical functioning. In separation anxiety disorder, children often complain of feeling sick, but these complaints may only occur in an attempt to avoid school (and thus happen in the morning or during the school day, as opposed to somatic symptom and related disorders in which complaints may occur throughout the course of a day). However, Ann does not complain of somatic issues except in relation to missing school.

Ann may qualify for a diagnosis of developmental coordination disorder, a condition in which the acquisition and execution of coordinated motor skills is substantially below that expected given the person's age and opportunity for skill learning and use. Difficulties often involve clumsiness and slowness and inaccuracy of performance of motor skills. This condition should be ruled out or treated if necessary. Medical, physical, neurological, and vision should be assessed to understand her motor development more fully.

Diagnostic Impressions, DSM-5

314.01 ADHD, combined presentation
315.1 Specific learning disorder with impairment in mathematics: number sense, memorization of arithmetic facts, accurate calculation, moderate, and fluent calculation, severe
300.02 Generalized anxiety disorder
315.39 Social (pragmatic) communication disorder

Rule out developmental coordination disorder

Recommendations

Medical and Physical

- **Medication to alleviate her ADHD is strongly recommended**. Medication could make an enormous difference in her school performance. If her physician does not prescribe for children, request that the physician refer Ann to a child psychiatrist (preferably a psychopharmacologist). Be sure to let all doctors know that she has already had a psychological evaluation and provide them with this report; otherwise, they may require additional testing prior to prescribing. Ask them to call me if they have any questions. The most effective treatments for ADHD combine medication with behavior therapy approaches, so more than medication is recommended for maximum benefit.
- **Physical exercise** is critical for health and to reduce ADHD symptoms. The most comprehensive approach is to use both medication and vigorous physical exercise. An hour a day at least five times per week is recommended.
- Supply **methods to cope with the classroom environment** successfully. For example, purchase a seating disk for school use. Consider purchasing fiddle or fidget toys to use in class. Numerous of these are available online and in local stores. They can be helpful for individuals with hyperactivity. Request the ability for her to go to the hallway briefly when she becomes frustrated or seems to need a break.
- Keep **screen time** (smartphone, tablets, computer, TV) to a minimum unless required for school. In particular, smart devices are engaging and exciting to children with ADHD but often make school seem quite boring in contrast and may condition her to be impatient.
- **Address somatic (bodily) complaints.** Keep her physician informed about her somatic complaints, and eliminate any possible explanation for her complaints of pain or feeling sick. Do not permit her to miss school or leave class due to vague somatic complaints. Send her to school unless she has clear and verified reasons to miss (e.g., fever, vomiting, doctor says she is contagious).
- **Address issues with motor coordination and balance.** These can exacerbate and even look like ADHD symptoms. Consult with the physician to check for any neurological condition that might affect movement. Take her to an **ophthalmologist** to ensure there are no issues with vision. Ensure both are aware of the motor coordination and balance issues. Obtain an evaluation from **otology and neurotology** specialists, who assess vestibular/balance issues and are recommended by the national association. Obtain an evaluation from an **occupational therapist** to assess (and potentially treat) her issues with **coordination and balance**.

Therapy/Counseling

I have provided in your takehome folder a list of referrals for providers to address the following:

- Obtain **individual psychotherapy**/counseling to address her behavior, anxiety, and somatic complaints. This report should be shared with her therapist. **Cognitive-behavioral therapy** is the most effective treatment for these conditions, although there are others that are also effective.
- **Group social skills training** may be valuable in developing new social communication behaviors. As middle school begins, consider involving her in controlled group activities (e.g., church youth group) to help her continue to mature socially and practice the social skills she is learning in training.
- Consider obtaining cognitive skill training from an **executive function coach** to improve attention, organization, focus, and concentration. **Neurofeedback training** also can help to alleviate ADHD symptoms in some children.

Home

- **Daily exercise** involving physical exertion has been shown to be as effective as medication at reducing ADHD symptoms. At least 30 minutes a day five times a week is recommended.
- Consider enrolling her in **martial arts**. It could be very beneficial in teaching her to pay attention, focus, and exercise self-control. It also is helpful for balance, coordination, and to provide some of the recommended physical activity. She should continue to take dance class as well if that is feasible.
- **Download the following apps and videos and require use on a regular basis**.
  - Conversation Builder Teen: Gives teenagers with social challenges an opportunity to practice real conversations they encounter. It has a speaker button that lets you hear the *intonation* of each response choice before choosing. The user can preview the content of each conversation before she chooses it. The user has full say over the topics covered within a session.
  - Between the Lines: Teaches figurative speech and idioms.
  - Model Me Friendship: Features teen-aged children demonstrating appropriate social skills at school, playing on sports teams, eating at a restaurant, and in other settings. Each scene lasts between 30 seconds and 3 minutes, depending on the chapter. At the end of each chapter is a storyboard summarizing the rules taught.

- Teach **relaxation techniques** (alternately, a counselor or therapist could teach these)
  - Teach her to recognize when she feels stressed, frustrated, or upset, and to ask if she can go relax.
  - Establish where, when, and how she will initiate and carry out a break to relax. Teach her how she asks to take a relaxation break, how long they are, and how many in an hour or a day.
- Visual spatial development: Teach reading of visual displays, drawings, diagrams, and charts and talk them through. Encourage her to continue using Legos and Minecraft.
- Memory
  - Teach memory aids, such as verbal mediation or rehearsal, and mnemonic strategies (e.g., Never Eat Sour Watermelon for North East South West).
  - Teach use of index cards/drilling/quizzing for studying.
  - Teach use of lists and personal planners.
  - Communicate frequently with teachers about school activities, equipment needed, homework, and assignments.
  - Teach her to take notes during presentations or lectures. Ask the teacher to share his or her notes.

School

Recommended Accommodations

- Allow additional time to complete school tests and standardized tests (50%). While this may be helpful, she requires intervention in the area of mathematics as well because extra time does not appear to help her improve performance on math related tasks.
- Enroll in the content mastery academic support program. They provide extra help and organizational support. If accommodations are approved, they help to enact many of those.
- Check for understanding after instructions. Ask her to verbally repeat what she was instructed to do. Ask her to write down the steps of assignments if she appears confused, and check them/clarify as necessary.
- Discuss daily behavior report cards with the administration. Teach her to read the report cards and reward her for meeting goals.
- Minimize distractions during learning activities, and consider preferential seating arrangements close to the teacher and away from auditory distractions and movement (e.g., doors opening and closing, air conditioning units).
- Provide study guides in advance of math tests to focus her studies.
- Allow her to use a calculator and formula sheet when the ability to perform the computations or knowledge of the formula are not be assessed.

- Use visual materials sparingly, especially if they are abstract. Meaningful visuals (e.g., pictures that can be semantically encoded) will be more helpful than abstract ones.

Outside Help for Math

As math interventions are not available at A Middle School, enroll her in math specialist classes outside of school hours and over the summer. At a minimum, these classes should support the interventions listed in the sections that follow.

Math computation and fluency Encourage Ann to make her own flash cards to practice math facts. Have Ann use a number line to assist with subtraction. A variety of math quiz apps also are available to facilitate memorization and fluency of math facts. Some online resources include https://ca.ixl.com/math/ and www.khanacademy.org.

Math reasoning While her math reasoning is presently at the low end of the average range, her math fluency and math computation skills are low. While working on these more basic skills, she could benefit from becoming accustomed to a streamlined and systematic approach to solving math problems.

- Teach her to analyze math problems, select among known strategies that are appropriate strategies to solve them, then monitor problem solving to ensure they are completed correctly.
- Train her in a three-step coaching process (i.e., say, ask, and check) to work through each of the seven steps below used to approach a word problem.
- Use a seven-step process for attacking a word problem. First, say the purpose of the step. Next, ask what needs to be done for the step. Third, check to make sure the step was completed correctly. The steps include:
  1. Read the problem carefully, and clear up anything that is uncertain, such as words or math terms she doesn't understand.
  2. Restate the problem using her own words.
  3. Draw or create a visual to represent the problem.
  4. Decide how to best solve the problem and create a plan to do it.
  5. Estimate the answer to the problem, using shortcuts such as rounding.
  6. Use the plan to calculate the answer.
  7. Check the calculation of each step and compare the obtained answer to the estimated answer from step 6 to make sure the answer is reasonably accurate.
- As she uses this process, ensure she has the underlying foundation for solving word problems (e.g., can perform calculations involved). Offer feedback on her performance.

Monitor Progress It is important to monitor her developing math skills over time to ensure she is making progress toward expected benchmarks. A private math interventionist will use such monitoring, and A Middle School already engages in formal assessment on a periodic basis. In addition, they provides access to online interventions that also serve to monitor progress over time. Her parents and teachers should discuss short-term goals and progress on a bimonthly basis to ensure an effective plan is in place.

Respectfully Submitted,

Susan Raiford, PhD
Texas Licensed Psychologist

Test Data for Ann

Wechsler Intelligence Scale for Children, Fifth Edition (WISC−V) and Wechsler Intelligence Scale for Children, Fifth Edition Integrated (WISC−V Integrated)

Domain	Subtest Name	Scaled Score
Verbal Comprehension	**Similarities**	15
	Vocabulary	10
	(Information)	8
	(Comprehension)	7
	Comprehension Multiple Choice*	6
Visual Spatial	**Block Design**	7
	Visual Puzzles	7
Fluid Reasoning	**Matrix Reasoning**	11
	Figure Weights	7
	Figure Weights Process Approach *	5
	(Arithmetic)	6
	Arithmetic Process Approach Part A*	6
	Arithmetic Process Approach Part B *	7
	Written Arithmetic *	6
Working Memory	**Digit Span**	10
	Picture Span	11
Processing Speed	**Coding**	9
	Symbol Search	6
		Standard Score
Naming Speed	Naming Speed Literacy	83
	Naming Speed Quantity	77
Symbol Translation	Immediate Symbol Translation	91
	Delayed Symbol Translation	91
	Recognition Symbol Translation	99

Notes. Subtests used to derive the FSIQ are bolded. Secondary subtests are in parentheses.
* = WISC−V Integrated subtest.
The average scaled score is 10. About 68% of scores fall between 7−13 and 95% between 4−16.
The average standard score is 100. About 68% of scores fall between 85−115 and 95% between 70−130.

Composite	Standard Score	Percentile Rank	95% Confidence Interval	Qualitative Descriptor
Verbal Comprehension	113	81	104–120	High average
Verbal (Expanded Crystallized) Index	100	50	96–104	Average
Visual Spatial	84	14	78–93	Low Average
Fluid Reasoning	94	34	87–102	Average
Quantitative Reasoning	80	9	75–87	Average
Working Memory	103	58	95–110	Average
Symbol Translation	92	30	86–99	Average
Storage & Retrieval	80	9	74–88	Low Average
Processing Speed	86	18	79–97	Low Average
Naming Speed	78	7	72–89	Very low
Full Scale IQ	99	47	93–105	Average
General Ability	100	50	94–106	Average
Cognitive Proficiency	92	30	85–100	Average

The average standard score is 100. About 68% of scores fall between 85–115 and 95% between 70–130.

Kaufman Individual Achievement Test, Third Edition

Composite/ Subtest	Standard Score	90% Confidence Interval	Percentile Rank	Descriptive Category
Math Composite	84	80–88	14	Low average
Math Concepts & Applications	90	85–95	25	Average
Math Computation	81	75–87	10	Low average
Math Fluency	78	71–85	7	Very low
Listening Comprehension	108	104–111	70	Average

The average standard score is 100. About 68% of scores fall between 85–115 and 95% between 70–130.

Error Analysis Summary

Error Category	Math Concepts & Applications				Math Computation			
	Last Item Administered: 70				Last Item Administered: 47			
	Items Attempted	Average # of Errors	Student's # of Errors	Skill Status	Items Attempted	Average # of Errors	Student's # of Errors	Skill Status
Number Concepts	22	0—1	1	A				
Addition	3	0	0	A	14	0	1	W
Subtraction	3	0	0	A	12	0	4	W
Multiplication	3	0	2	W	7	0—1	1	A
Division	3	0—1	1	A	4	0—1	2	W
Tables and Graphs	3	0	0	A				
Time and Money	9	0—1	2	W				
Geometry	2	0—1	1	A				
Measurement	7	0—2	2	A				
Fractions	4	0	0	A	1	0	0	A
Decimal					—	—	—	—
Decimals and Percents	2	0—1	1	A				
Data Investigation	2	0—1	1	A				
Multistep Problems	4	0—2	4	W				
Word Problems	11	0—1	3	W				
Exponent or Root					1	0—1	1	A
Algebra	7	0—1	1	A	—	—	—	—
Wrong Operation					38	0—1	0	A
Fact or Computation					38	0—2	0	A
Regrouping: Addition					2	0	0	A
Regrouping: Subtraction					4	0	0	A
Subtract Smaller from Larger					4	0	0	A
Add or Subtract Numerator & Denominator					1	0	0	A
Equivalent Fraction/Common Denominator					—	—	—	—
Multiply/Divide Fraction					—	—	—	—
Mixed Number					—	—	—	—
Incorrect Sign					—	—	—	—
Uncodable					38	0	0	A

Note. A = average; W = weakness.

Ability-Achievement Discrepancy

	Predicted KTEA−3 Score	Actual KTEA−3 Score	Difference	Critical Value (0.05)	Significant Difference Y/N	Base Rate
KTEA−3 Subtests						
Math Concepts & Applications	109	90	19	8	Y	< = 5%
Math Computation	107	81	26	8	Y	< = 2%
Math Fluency	−	78	−	−	−	−
KTEA−3 Composites						
Math	108	84	24	8	Y	< = 2%

Pattern of Strengths & Weaknesses Analysis

Area of Processing Strength: WISC−V Verbal Comprehension Index: 113
Area of Processing Weakness: WISC−V Naming Speed Index: 78
Area of Achievement Weakness: KTEA−3 Math: 84

Comparison	Relative Strength Score	Relative Weakness Score	Difference	Critical Value (0.05)	Significant Difference Y/N	Supports SLDs hypothesis? Yes/No
Processing Strength/ Achievement Weakness	113	84	29	10	Y	Yes
Processing Strength/ Processing Weakness	113	78	35	11	Y	Yes

NEPSY−A developmental neuropsychological instrument-Second Edition

Score Name	Scaled Score	Base Rate
Auditory Attention Total Correct	12	
Response Set Total Correct	4	
Response Set Commission Errors		26−50
Response Set Omission Errors		6−10
Response Set Inhibitory Errors		26−50
Inhibition total errors	8	

(Continued)

(Continued)

Score Name	Scaled Score	Base Rate
Inhibition Naming Completion Time	6	
Inhibition Inhibition Completion Time	3	
Inhibition Switching Completion Time	3	
Inhibition Naming Combined	6	
Inhibition Inhibition Combined	5	
Inhibition Switching Combined	6	
Inhibition Naming total errors		11−25
Inhibition total errors		11−25
Inhibition Switching Total Errors		26−50
Naming Total Uncorrected Errors		51−75
Inhibition Total Uncorrected Errors		26−50
Switching Total Uncorrected Errors		26−50
Naming Total Self-Corrected Errors		11−25
Inhibition Total Self-Corrected Errors		2−5
Switching Total Self-Corrected Errors		26−50

The average scaled score is 10. About 68% of scores fall between 7−13 and 95% between 4−16.

Clinical Evaluation of Language Fundamentals-Fifth Edition (CELF−5)

Pragmatics profile scaled score: 6

Average scaled score is 10. About 68% of scores fall between 7−13. About 95% fall between 4−16.

BASC−3

Respondent: Mr. Bloom, Father

CLINICAL AND ADAPTIVE SCORE TABLE: General Gender-Specific Norm Group

Composite Score Summary

	T Score	Percentile Rank	90% Confidence Interval
Externalizing Problems	51	71	48−54
Internalizing Problems	58	84	54−62
Behavioral Symptoms Index	61	89	58−64
Adaptive Skills	34	8	31−37

Scale Score Summary

	T Score	Percentile Rank	90% Confidence Interval
Hyperactivity	58	83	52−64
Aggression	45	37	40−50
Conduct Problems	49	70	45−53
Anxiety	56	77	51−61
Depression	61	89	56−66
Somatization	55	78	49−61
Atypicality	57	86	53−61
Withdrawal	56	78	50−62
Attention Problems	79	99	73−85
Adaptability	39	15	33−45
Social Skills	38	14	34−42
Leadership	29	2	23−35
Activities of Daily Living	26	1	18−34
Functional Communication	48	37	42−54

CONTENT SCALE SCORE TABLE: General Gender-Specific Norm Group

	T Score	Percentile Rank	90% Confidence Interval
Anger Control	49	60	44−54
Bullying	47	54	43−51
Developmental Social Disorders	56	78	51−61
Emotional Self-Control	56	79	51−61
Executive Functioning	74	99	69−79
Negative Emotionality	55	76	49−61
Resiliency	33	6	28−38

Executive Functioning Index Summary

Overall Executive Functioning Index	Problem Solving Index	Attentional Control Index	Behavioral Control Index	Emotional Control Index
Extremely Elevated	Extremely Elevated	Extremely Elevated	Not Elevated	Not Elevated
Raw Score: 55	Raw Score: 22	Raw Score: 22	Raw Score: 7	Raw Score: 4

Respondent: Mrs. Bloom, Mother

CLINICAL AND ADAPTIVE SCORE TABLE: *General Gender-Specific Norm Group*

Composite Score Summary

	T Score	Percentile Rank	90% Confidence Interval
Externalizing Problems	58	86	55—61
Internalizing Problems	74	97	70—78
Behavioral Symptoms Index	68	94	65—71
Adaptive Skills	30	4	27—33

Scale Score Summary

	T Score	Percentile Rank	90% Confidence Interval
Hyperactivity	75	97	69—81
Aggression	45	37	40—50
Conduct Problems	51	77	47—55
Anxiety	74	97	69—79
Depression	59	87	54—64
Somatization	79	98	73—85
Atypicality	79	97	75—83
Withdrawal	53	72	47—59
Attention Problems	77	99	71—83
Adaptability	35	8	29—41
Social Skills	43	23	39—47
Leadership	29	2	23—35
Activities of Daily Living	26	1	18—34
Functional Communication	28	2	22—34

CONTENT SCALE SCORE TABLE: *General Gender-Specific Norm Group*

	T Score	Percentile Rank	90% Confidence Interval
Anger Control	51	69	46—56
Bullying	44	13	40—48
Developmental Social Disorders	67	93	62—72
Emotional Self-Control	63	90	58—68
Executive Functioning	76	99	71—81
Negative Emotionality	52	69	46—58
Resiliency	29	2	24—34

Executive Functioning Index Summary

Overall Executive Functioning Index	Problem Solving Index	Attentional Control Index	Behavioral Control Index	Emotional Control Index
Extremely Elevated	Extremely Elevated	Extremely Elevated	Elevated	Elevated
Raw Score: 59	Raw Score: 22	Raw Score: 21	Raw Score: 10	Raw Score: 6

Delis Rating of Executive Functions (DREF)
Mother Ratings
Core Index Scores

Index	T Score	Percentile Rank	95% Confidence Interval
Behavioral Functioning	67	96	60–71
Emotional Functioning	53	62	46–59
Executive Functioning	71	98	65–74
Total Composite	64	92	60–67

Clinical Index Scores

Index	T Score	Percentile Rank	95% Confidence Interval
Attention/Working Memory	67	96	61–71
Activity Level/Impulse Control	62	88	53–67
Compliance/Anger Management	57	76	49–62
Abstract Thinking/Problem Solving	69	97	59–72

Top Stressors

Item	Rating
Loses track of what he/she is supposed to do due to noises or other things going on	Daily
Is very messy	Daily
Makes mistakes because he/she is in a hurry to complete a task	Daily
Has trouble completing tasks like homework and chores	Daily
Only puts forth effort on things he/she likes to do	Daily

Father Ratings
Core Index Scores

Index	T Score	Percentile Rank	95% Confidence Interval
Behavioral Functioning	58	79	52−63
Emotional Functioning	42	21	37−49
Executive Functioning	56	73	51−60
Total Composite	53	62	49−57

Clinical Index Scores

Index	T Score	Percentile Rank	95% Confidence Interval
Attention/Working Memory	61	86	55−65
Activity Level/Impulse Control	53	62	46−59
Compliance/Anger Management	49	46	43−56
Abstract Thinking/Problem Solving	39	14	34−48

Top Stressors

Item	Rating
Is off-task when he/she is supposed to do homework or chores	Daily
Is very messy	Weekly
Touches or plays with things that he/she was told not to touch or play with	Weekly
Does not start homework or chores on his/her own	Daily
Loses things easily	Daily

Self Ratings (Ann)
Core Index Scores

Index	T Score	Percentile Rank	95% Confidence Interval
Behavioral Functioning	60	84	52−65
Emotional Functioning	44	27	38−51
Executive Functioning	70	98	61−74
Total Composite	59	82	54−63

Clinical Index Scores

Index	T Score	Percentile Rank	95% Confidence Interval
Attention/Working Memory	70	98	55–70
Activity Level/Impulse Control	63	90	53–67
Compliance/Anger Management	47	38	40–55

Top Stressors

Item	Rating
My teachers complain that my work is sloppy.	Weekly
I find it hard to keep doing a boring task like homework.	Weekly
People tell me that I'm too hyper.	Weekly
Ideas come into my mind so quickly that I can't focus on what is important.	Weekly
I think I need more time than most people to finish my work.	Daily

SUMMARY AND CONCLUDING COMMENTS

The descriptions, conceptualizations, and definitions of dyslexia and other LDs continue to evolve. Lobby groups, researchers, and legislators have defined LDs through operational definitions, diagnostic criteria, and legislation for eligibility criteria, resulting in different model conceptualizations and criteria for identification and diagnosis. Concurrent with these descriptions is the expanding and significant role of cognitive psychology and neuropsychology in understanding and defining LDs. Advances in cognitive science have demonstrated empirical links between achievement deficits and deficits in underlying cognitive processes, which have led to differentiated approaches to teaching students with LDs. Although numerous questions and controversies remain, these data pose considerable challenges to those who dispute that LDs should be considered as cognitive disorders or even disabilities at all (e.g., Penny, 2018).

These scientific advances have become increasingly influential in the development and updating of cognitive ability tests used to identify strengths and deficits in the human cognitive processes underlying academic achievement. WISC−V, the most recent evolution of the Wechsler Intelligence Scale for Children, is designed to measure the cognitive abilities most related to children's academic learning. The WISC−V is well positioned to become an integral component in a battery of tests designed for the assessment of students with academic difficulties.

With these evolutions came considerable diversity in LD assessment practices across settings and disciplines. Researchers and practitioners who identify LDs using a single lens, whether it's neurobiological, instructional, or cognitive, are missing the benefits that a more balanced, hybrid approach might offer. Part of the controversy over methods of evaluating students for LDs may stem from the use of different criteria for LD identification across settings. In particular, a determination of eligibility for dyslexia services in the school setting is not necessarily the same as a diagnosis of developmental dyslexia in a clinical setting. All parties have much to learn from each other. The whole point of diagnosis and assessment is to determine the range of the child's needs and the kinds of evidence-based services required. Much research remains to be accomplished in terms of understanding the subtypes of LDs and associating more targeted interventions to them.

Contemporary LD assessment has expanded to include consideration of the multiple cognitive abilities measured by most modern cognitive ability tests as part of a model of processing strengths and weaknesses. The WISC−V is well suited to this approach to LD assessment. Its five-factor theoretical model and new complementary subtests measuring rapid automatic naming and associative memory are clinically relevant to differential diagnosis and identification of LDs, as well as to psychoeducational planning when interpreted together with a valid measure of achievement such as the WIAT−III or KTEA−III. Use of the processing strengths and weaknesses model in LD assessments holds considerable promise for advancing our understanding of LDs, and systematically researching interventions designed to improve outcomes for children with specific processing weaknesses.

REFERENCES

American Psychiatric Association. (2013). *Diagnostic and Statistical Manual of Mental Disorders*. Washington, D.C: American Psychiatric Publishing.

Beal, A. L., Willis, J. O., & Dumont, R. (2013). Psychological testing by models of cognitive ability. In D. P. Saklofske, C. R. Reynolds, & V. L. Schwean (Eds.), *The oxford handbook of psychological assessment*. New York: Oxford University Press.

Bergeron, R., Floyd, R. G., & Shands, E. I. (2008). States' eligibility guidelines for mental retardation: An update and consideration of part scores and unreliability of IQs. *Education & Training in Developmental Disabilities*, *43*(1), 123−131.

Berninger, V. (2011). Evidence-based differential diagnosis and treatment of reading disabilities with and without comorbidities in oral language, writing, and math: Prevention, problemsolving consultation, and specialized instruction. In D. P. Flanagan, & V. C. Alfonso (Eds.), *Essentials of specific learning disability identification*. Hoboken, NJ: Wiley.

Berninger, V., Abbott, R., Thomson, J., Wagner, R., Swanson, H. L., & Raskind, W. (2006). Modeling developmental phonological core deficits within a working-memory architecture in children and adults with developmental dyslexia. *Scientific Studies in Reading*, *10*, 165−198.

Berninger, V. W., O'Donnell, L., & Holdnack, J. (2008). Research-supported differential diagnosis of specific learning disabilities and implications for instruction and response to instruction. In A. Prifitera, D. H. Saklofske, & L. G. Weiss (Eds.), *WISC−IV clinical assessment and intervention*. San Diego, CA: Elsevier.

Boshes, B., & Myklebust, H. (1964). Neurological behavior study of children with learning disorders. *Neurology, 14*, 7−22.

Branum−Martin, L., Fletcher, J. M., & Stuebing, K. K. (2013). Classification and identification of reading and math disabilities the special case of comorbidity. *Journal of Learning Disabilities, 46*(6), 490−499.

Brody, L. E., & Mills, C. J. (1997). Gifted children with learning disabilities: A review of the issues. *Journal of Learning Disabilities, 30*, 282−296.

Castles, A., & Coltheart, M. (1993). Varieties of developmental dyslexia. *Cognition, 47*(2), 149−180.

Compton, D. L., Fuchs, L. S., Fuchs, D., Lambert, W., & Hamlett, C. (2011). The cognitive and academic profiles of reading and mathematics learning disabilities. *Journal of Learning Disabilities, 45*, 79−95.

Crepeau-Hobson, F., & Bianco, M. (2011). Identification of gifted students with learning disabilities in a response-to−Intervention era. *Psychology in the Schools, 48*, 102−109.

Crepeau-Hobson, F., & Bianco, M. (2013). Response to intervention promises and pitfalls for gifted students with learning disabilities. *Intervention in School and Clinic, 48*(3), 142−151.

Crews, K. J., & D'Amato, R. C. (2009). Subtyping children's reading disabilities using a comprehensive neuropsychological measure. *International Journal of Neuroscience, 119*, 1615−1639.

Donovan, M. S., & Cross, C. T. (Eds.), (2002). Minority students in special and gifted education. Washington, D.C: National Academies Press.

Elliott, C. D., Hale, J. B., Fiorello, C. A., Dorvil, C., & Moldovan, J. (2010). Differential Ability Scales−II prediction of reading performance: Global scores are not enough. *Psychology in the Schools, 47*(7), 698−720.

Elliott, J. G., & Gibbs, S. (2008). Does dyslexia exist? *Journal of Philosophy of Education, 42* (3−4), 475−491.

Elliott, J. G., & Grigorenko, E. L. (2014). *The dyslexia debate*. Cambridge: Cambridge University Press.

Evans, J. J., Floyd, R. G., McGrew, K. S., & Leforgee, M. H. (2001). The relations between measures of Cattell-Horn-Carroll (CHC) cognitive abilities and reading achievement during childhood and adolescence. *School Psychology Review, 31*(2), 246−262.

Feifer, S., & De Fina, P. (2000). *The neuropsychology of reading disorders: Diagnosis and intervention*. Middleton, MD: School Neuropsych Press, LLC.

Ferrer, E., Shaywitz, B. A., Holahan, J. M., Marchione, K., & Shaywitz, S. E. (2010). Uncoupling of reading and IQ over time: Empirical evidence for a definition of dyslexia. *Psychological Science, 21*(1), 93−101.

Fiorello, C. A., Hale, J. B., & Snyder, L. E. (2006). Cognitive hypothesis testing and response to intervention for children with reading problems. *Psychology in the Schools, 43*(8), 835−853.

Fiorello, C. A., Hale, J. B., & Wycoff, K. L. (2012). Cognitive hypothesis testing: Linking test results to the real world. In D. P. Flanagan, & P. L. Harrison (Eds.), *Contemporary intellectual assessment* (3rd ed). New York: Guilford Press.

Flanagan, D. P., & Alfonso, V. C. (2011). *Essentials of specific learning disability identification*. Hoboken, NJ: Wiley.

Flanagan, D. P., & Alfonso, V. C. (2017). *Essentials of WISC−V assessment*. John Wiley & Sons.

Flanagan, D. P., Alfonso, V. C., & Ortiz, S. O. (2012). The cross-battery assessment approach: An overview, historical perspective, and current directions. In D. P. Flanagan, & P. L.

Harrison (Eds.), *Contemporary intellectual assessment: Theories, tests, and issues* (3rd ed, pp. 459—483). New York, NY: The Guilford Press.

Flanagan, D. P., Fiorello, C., & Ortiz, S. O. (2010). Enhancing practice through application of Cattell-Horn-Carroll theory and research: A "third method" approach to specific learning disability identification. *Psychology in the Schools, 47*, 739—760.

Flanagan, D. P., & Mascolo, J. T. (2005). Psychoeducational assessment and learning disability diagnosis. In D. P. Flanagan, & P. L. Harrison (Eds.), *Contemporary intellectual assessment: Theories, tests and issues* (2nd ed, pp. 521—544). New York: Guilford Press.

Flanagan, D. P., Ortiz, S. O., Alfonso, V. C., & Mascolo, J. T. (2006). *The achievement test desk reference (ATDR): A guide to learning disability identification* (2nd ed). Hoboken: Wiley.

Fletcher, J. M. (2005). Predicting math outcomes: Reading predictors and comorbidity. *Journal of Learning Disabilities, 38*, 545—552.

Fletcher, J. M. (2012). Classification and identification of learning disabilities. In B. Wong, & Butler (Eds.), *Learning about learning disabilities* (4th ed, pp. 1—26). New York: Elsevier.

Fletcher, J. M., Coulter, W. A., Reschly, D. J., & Vaughn, S. (2004). Alternative approaches to the definition and identification of learning disabilities: Some questions and answers. *Annals of Dyslexia, 54*(2), 304—331.

Fletcher, J. M., Lyon, G. R., Barnes, M., Stuebing, K. K., Francis, D. J., Olson, R. K., et al. (2002). Classification of learning disabilities: An evidence-based evaluation. *Identification of Learning Disabilities: Research to Practice*, 185—250.

Fletcher, J. M., Lyon, G. R., Fuchs, L. S., & Barnes, M. A. (2007). *Learning disabilities: From identification to intervention*. New York: Guilford.

Fletcher, J. M., Morris, R. D., & Lyon, G. R. (2003). Classification and definition of learning disabilities: An integrative perspective. In H. L. Swanson, K. R. Harris, & S. Graham (Eds.), *Handbook of learning disabilities* (pp. 30—56). New York: Guilford.

Fletcher, J. M., Shaywitz, S. E., Shankweiler, D. P., Katz, L., Liberman, I. Y., Stuebing, K. K., et al. (1994). Cognitive profiles of reading disability: Comparisons of discrepancy and low achievement definitions. *Journal of Educational Psychology, 86*(1), 6.

Floyd, R. G., Evans, J. J., & McGrew, K. S. (2003). Relations between measures of Cattell-HornCarroll (CHC) cognitive abilities and mathematics achievement across the school-age years. *Psychology in the Schools, 40*(2), 155—171.

Floyd, R. G., Keith, T. Z., Taub, G. E., & McGrew, K. S. (2007). Cattell-Horn-Carroll cognitive abilities and their effects on reading decoding skills: *g* has indirect effects, more specific abilities have direct effects. *School Psychology Quarterly, 22*(2), 200—233.

Francis, D. J., Fletcher, J. M., Stuebing, K. K., Lyon, G. R., Shaywitz, B. A., & Shaywitz, S. E. (2005). Psychometric approaches to the identification of LDs IQ and achievement scores are not sufficient. *Journal of Learning Disabilities, 38*(2), 98—108.

Fuchs, D., Fuchs, L. S., Mathes, P. G., & Lipsey, M. W. (2000). Reading differences between lowachieving students with and without learning disabilities: A meta-analysis. *Contemporary special education research: Syntheses of the knowledge base on critical instructional issues*, 81—104.

Fuchs, D., & Young, C. L. (2006). On the irrelevance of intelligence in predicting responsiveness to reading instruction. *Exceptional Children, 73*(1), 8—30.

Fuchs, L. S., Compton, D. L., Fuchs, D., Hollenbeck, K. N., Craddock, C. F., & Hamlett, C. L. (2008). Dynamic assessment of algebraic learning in predicting third graders' development of mathematical problem solving. *Journal of Educational Psychology, 100* (4), 829.

Fuchs, L. S., Fuchs, D., Stuebing, K., Fletcher, J. M., Hamlett, C. L., & Lambert, W. (2008). Problem solving and computational skill: Are they shared or distinct aspects of mathematical cognition? *Journal of Educational Psychology, 100*(1), 30–47.

Gang, M., & Siegel, L. S. (2002). Sound-symbol learning in children with dyslexia. *Journal of Learning Disabilities, 35*(2), 137–157.

González, J. E. J., & Espinel, A. I. G. (2002). Strategy choice in solving arithmetic word problems: Are there differences between students with learning disabilities, GV poor performance and typical achievement students? *Learning Disability Quarterly, 25*(2), 113–122.

Greenberg, D., Lichtenberger, E. O., & Kaufman, A. S. (2013). The role of theory in psychological assessment. In D. H. Saklofske, V. L. Schwean, & C. R. Reynolds (Eds.), *The Oxford handbook of child psychological assessment* (pp. 3–29). New York: Oxford University Press.

Gresham, F. M., & Vellutino, F. R. (2010). What is the role of intelligence in the identification of what is the role of intelligence in the identification of specific learning disabilities?: Issues and clarifications. *Learning Disabilities Research & Practice, 25*(4), 194–206.

Grigorenko, E. L. (2001). Developmental dyslexia: An update on genes, brains, and environments. *Journal of Child Psychology and Psychiatry, 42*(1), 91–125.

Hagen, J. W., Kamberelis, G., & Segal, S. (1991). A dimensional approach to cognition and academic performance in children with medical problems or learning difficulties. In L. V. Feagans, J. Short, & L. Meltzer (Eds.), *Subtypes of learning disabilities: Theoretical perspectives and research* (pp. 53–82). Hillsdale, NJ: Erlbaum.

Hale, J., Alfonso, V., Berninger, V., Bracken, B., Christo, C., Clark, E., et al. (2010). Critical issues in response-to–Intervention, comprehensive evaluation, and specific learning disabilities identification and intervention: An expert white paper consensus. *Learning Disability Quarterly, 33*(3), 223–236.

Hale, J. B. (2006). Implementing IDEA with a three-tier model that includes response to intervention and cognitive assessment methods. *School Psychology Forum: Research and Practice, 1*, 16–27.

Hale, J. B., & Fiorello, C. A. (2004). *School neuropsychology: Apractitioner's handbook.* New York: Guilford Press.

Hale, J. B., Fiorello, C. A., Kavanagh, J. A., Hoeppner, J. B., & Gaither, R. A. (2001). WISC–III predictors of academic achievement for children with learning disabilities: Are global and factor scores comparable? *School Psychology Quarterly, 16*, 31–55.

Hale, J. B., Hain, L. A., Murphy, R., Cancelliere, G., Bindus, D., & Kubas, H. (2013). The enigma of learning disabilities: Examination via a neuropsychological framework. In C. Noggle, & R. S. Dean (Eds.), The neuropsychology of psychopathology. *NewYork.* NY: Springer Publishing.

Hale, J. B., Kaufman, A., Naglieri, J. A., & Kavale, K. A. (2006). Implementation of IDEA: Integrating response to intervention and cognitive assessment methods. *Psychology in Schools, 43*, 753–770.

Horn, J. L., & Blankson, A. N. (2012). Foundations for better understanding of cognitive abilities. In D. P. Flanagan, & P. L. Harrison (Eds.), *Contemporary intellectual assessment. Theories, tests and issues* (3rd ed). New York: The Guilford Press.

Hulme, C., Goetz, K., Gooch, D., Adams, J., & Snowling, M. J. (2007). Paired-associate learning, phoneme awareness, and learning to read. *Journal of Experimental Child Psychology, 96*, 150–166.

International Dyslexia Association (2002). Definition of dyslexia. Available from https://dyslex-iaida.org.

Individuals with Disabilities Education Improvement Act of 2004 (IDEA 2004), Pub. L. No. 108− 446, 118Stat 2647 (2004).

Johnson, D. J., & Myklebust, H. (1967). *Learning disabilities: Educational principles and remedial approaches*. New York, NY: Grune & Stratton.

Kaufman, A. S. (2008). Neuropsychology and specific learning disabilities: Lessons from the past as a guide to present controversies and future clinical practice. In E. Fletcher-Janzen, & C. Reynolds (Eds.), *Neuropsychological perspectives on learning disabilities in an era of RTI: Recommendations for diagnosis and intervention* (pp. 1−13). Hoboken, NJ: Wiley.

Kaufman, A. S., & Kaufman, N. (2014). *Technical manual for the kaufman test of educational achievement* (3rd ed). Minneapolis, MN: Pearson.

Korkman, M., Barron-Linnankoski, S., & Lahti-Nuuttila, P. (1999). Effects of age and duration of reading instruction on the development of phonological awareness, rapid naming, and verbal memory span. *Developmental Neuropsychology, 16*(3), 415−431.

Korkman, M., Kirk, U., & Kemp, S. (2007). *NEPSY−II*. Bloomington, MN: Pearson.

Korkman, M., Stenroos, M., Mickos, A., Westman, M., Ekholm, P., & Byring, R. (2012). Does simultaneous bilingualism aggravate children's specific language problems? *Acta Pædiatrica, 101*, 946−952.

Kozey, M., & Siegel, L. S. (2008). Definitions of learning disabilities in Canadian provinces and territories [Special issue]. *Canadian Psychology/Psychologie Canadienne, 49*, 162−171.

Learning Disabilities Association of Canada (2002). *LDs defined: Official definition of learning disabilities*. Available from http://www.ldac-acta.ca/learn-more/ld-defined/official-definition-of-learning-disabilities.

Lervåg, A., Bråten, I., & Hulme, C. (2009). The cognitive and linguistic foundations of early reading development: A Norwegian latent variable longitudinal study. *Developmental Psychology, 45*(3), 764−781.

Li, H., Shu, H., McBride-Chang, C., Liu, H. Y., & Xue, J. (2009). Paired associate learning in Chinese children with dyslexia. *Journal of Experimental Child Psychology, 103*, 135−151.

Lind, A., Korkman, M., Lehtonen, L., Lapinleimu, H., Parkkola, R., Matomäki, J., et al. (2011). Cognitive and neuropsychological outcomes at 5 years of age in preterm children born in the 2000s. *Developmental Medicine & Child Neurology, 53*(3), 256−262.

Litt, R. A., de Jong, P. F., van Bergen, E., & Nation, K. (2013). Dissociating crossmodal and verbal demands in paired associate learning (PAL): What drives the PAL−reading relationship? *Journal of Experimental Child Psychology, 115*, 137−149.

Litt, R. A., & Nation, K. (2014). The nature and specificity of paired associate learning deficits in children with dyslexia. *Journal of Memory and Language, 71*, 71−88.

Lovett, B. J., & Sparks, R. L. (2011). *The identification and performance of gifted students with learning disability diagnoses: A quantitative synthesis. Journal of Learning Disabilities* (pp. 1−13).

Lyon, G. R., & Weiser, B. (2013). The state of the science in learning disabilities: Research impact on the field from 2001 to 2011. In H. L. Swanson, K. R. Harris, & S. Graham (Eds.), *Handbook of learning disabilities* (2nd ed, pp. 118−144). New York: Guilford Press.

Maddocks, D. L. S. (2018). The identification of students who are gifted and have a learning disability: A comparison of different diagnostic criteria. *Gifted Child Quarterly*, 1−18. Available from https://doi.org/10.177/001698621772096.

Maehler, C., & Schuchardt, K. (2011). Working memory in children with learning disabilities: Rethinking the criterion of discrepancy. *International Journal of Disability, Development and Education*, *58*(1), 5−17.

McGrew, K. S. (1997). Analysis of the major intelligence batteries according to a proposed comprehensive *Gf-Gc* framework. In D. P. Flanagan, J. L. Genshaft, & P. L. Harrison (Eds.), *Contemporary intellectual assessment: Theories, tests, and issues* (pp. 151−180). New York: Guilford.

McGrew, K. S., & Flanagan, D. P. (1998). *The intelligence test desk reference (ITDR): Gf-Gc crossbattery assessment*. Boston, MA: Allyn & Bacon.

McGrew, K. S., & Wendling, B. J. (2010). Cattell−Horn−Carroll cognitive-achievement relations: What we have learned from the past 20 years of research. *Psychology in the Schools*, *47*(7), 651−675.

Miciak, J., Fletcher, J. M., Vaughn, S., Stuebing, K. K., & Tolar, T. D. (2013). Patterns of cognitive strengths and weaknesses: Identification rates, agreement, and validity for learning disabilities identification. *School Psychology Quarterly*, *29*, 21−37.

Myklebust, H., & Boshes, B. (1960). Psycholoneurological learning disorders in children. *Rehabilitation Literature*, *77*, 247−278.

Myers, E. M., & Reynolds, M. R. (1997). Scores in space: multidimensional scaling of the WISCV. *Journal of Psychoeducational Assessment*, 1−14. Available from https://doi.org/10.1177/0734282917696935.

National Joint Committee on Learning Disabilities (NJCLDs) (2011). Learning disabilities: Implications for policy regarding research and practice. Available from www.ldonline.org/njcld.

Ontario Ministry of Education (2005). Education for all, the report of the expert panel on literacy and numeracy instruction for students with special education needs, kindergarten to grade 6. Available from http://www.edu.gov.on.ca.ca/eng/ppm/ppm8.pdf.

Ontario Ministry of Education (2014). Program/Policy Memorandum 8. Available from: http://www.edu.gov.on.ca.ca/eng/ppm/ppm8.pdf.

Pauly, H., Linkersdörfer, J., Lindberg, S., Woerner, W., Hasselhorn, M., & Lonnemann, J. (2011). Domain-specific rapid automatized naming deficits in children at risk for learning disabilities. *Journal of Neurolinguistics*, *24*, 602−610.

Pearson. (2009). *Wechlser individual achievement test−III*. San Antonio, TX: Pearson.

Pennington, B. F. (1991). *Diagnosing learning disorders: A neuropsychological framework*. New York: Guilford Press.

Penny, C. G. (2018). Rethinking the concept of learning disability. *Canadian Psychology*, *59*(2), 197−202.

Pieters, S., Roeyers, H., Rosseel, Y., Van Waelvelde, H., & Desoete, A. (2013). Identifying subtypes among children with developmental coordination disorder and mathematical learning disabilities, using model-based clustering. *Journal of Learning Disabilities*, 0022219413491288.

Piovasana, A. M., Harrison, J. L., & Ducat, J. J. (2017). The development of a motor-free short-form of the Wechsler Intelligence Scale for Children -Fifth Edition. *Assessment*, 1−9. Available from https://doi.org/10.1177/1073191117748741.

Powell, D., Stainthorp, R., Stuart, M., Garwood, H., & Quinlan, P. (2007). An experimental comparison between rival theories of rapid automatized naming performance and its relationship to reading. *Journal of Experimental Child Psychology*, *98*(1), 46−68.

Raiford, S. E., Drozdick, L., W. & Zhang, O. (April 2016). Q-interactive special group studies: The WISC-V and children with specific learning disorders in reading or mathematics. Available from: https://www.helloq.com/content/dam/ped/ani/us/helloq/media/Q-i%20TR13_WISC-V_SLDR_SLDM_FNL.pdf.

Raiford, S. E. (2017). *Essentials of WISC−V Integrated assessment*. Hoboken, NJ: John Wiley & Sons.

Reschly, D. J., & Hosp, J. L. (2004). State SLDs identification policies and practices. *Learning Disabilities Quarterly, 27*(4), 197−213.

Reynolds, C. R., & Shaywitz, S. E. (2009). Response to intervention: Ready or not: Or, from waitto-fail to watch-them-fail. *School Psychology Quarterly, 24*, 130−145.

Reynolds, M.R., Scheiber, C., Hajovsky, D.B., Schwartz, B., & Kaufman, A.S. (In submission). Gender differences in academic achievement: Is writing an exception to the gender similarities hypothesis?

Rourke, B. P. (1989). *Nonverbal learning disabilities the syndrome and the model*. New York: The Guilford Press, S. Res. 576, 114 Cong. (2016).

Schneider, W.J., & McGrew, K.S. (in press). The Cattell-Horn-Carroll theory of cognitive abilities. *Contemporary intellectual assessment: theories, tests, and issues* (4th ed.). New York: Guilford.

Shaywitz, S. E. (2005). *Overcoming dyslexia: A new and complete science-based program for reading problems at any level*. New York: Alfred A. Knopf.

Siegel, L. S. (1988). Evidence that IQ scores are irrelevant to the definition and analysis of reading disability. *Canadian Journal of Psychology é Revue Canadienne De Psychologie, 42*, 201−215.

Siegel, L. S. (1992). An evaluation of the discrepancy definition of dyslexia. *Journal of Learning Disabilties, 25*, 618−629.

Silverman, L. K. (2003). Gifted children with learning disabilities. In N. Colangelo, & G. A. Davis (Eds.), *The handbook of gifted education* (3rd ed, pp. 533−543). Boston, MA: Allyn & Bacon.

Sotelo-Dynega, M., Flanagan, D. P., & Alfonso, V. C. (2011). Overview of specific learning disabilities. In D. P. Flanagan, & V. C. Alfonso (Eds.), *Essentials of specific learning disability identification*. Hoboken, NJ: Wiley.

Sternberg, R. J., & Grigorenko, E. L. (2002). Difference scores in the identification of children with learning disabilities: It's time to use a different method. *Journal of School Psychology, 40*(1), 65−83.

Stuebing, K. K., Barth, A. E., Molfese, P. J., Weiss, B., & Fletcher, J. M. (2009). IQ is not strongly related to response to reading instruction: A meta-analytic interpretation. *Exceptional Children, 76*(1), 31−51.

Swanson, H. L. (1999). Instructional components that predict treatment outcomes for students with learning disabilities: Support for a combined strategy and direct instruction model. *Learning Disabilities Research and Practice, 14*(3), 129−140.

Swanson, H. L. (2011). Learning disabilities: Assessment, identification, and treatment. In M. A. Bray, & T. J. Kehle (Eds.), *The Oxford handbook of school psychology*. New York: Oxford University Press.

Swanson, H. L., & Hoskyn, M. (1998). Experimental intervention research on students with learning disabilities: A meta-analysis of treatment outcomes. *Review of Educational Research, 68*(3), 277−321.

Torgesen, J. K. (2002). Empirical and theoretical support for direct diagnosis of learning disabilities by assessment of intrinsic processing weaknesses. In R. Bradley, L. Danielson, & D. P. Hallahan (Eds.), *Identification of learning disabilities: Research to practice* (pp. 565−613). Mahwah, NJ: Lawrence Erlbaum.

van der Sluis, S., de Jong, P. F., & van der Leij, A. (2004). Inhibition and shifting in children with learning deficits in arithmetic and reading. *Journal of Experimental Child Psychology*, *87*(3), 239−266.

Vaughn, S., & Fuchs, L. S. (2003). Redefining learning disabilities as inadequate response to instruction: The promise and potential problems. *Learning Disabilities Research & Practice*, *18*(3), 137−146.

Wechsler, D. (2014a). *Wechsler intelligence scale for children−V*. San Antonio, TX: Pearson.

Wechsler, D. (2014b). WISC−V technical & interpretive manual supplement: Special group validity studies with other measures, and additional tables. Available from: <http://downloads.pearson-clinical.com/images/Assets/WISC−V/WISC−V-Tech−Manual-Supplement.pdf>.

Wechsler, D., & Kaplan, E. (2015). *Wechsler intelligence scale for children integrated* (5th ed). Bloomington, MN: Pearson.

Willburger, E., Fussenegger, B., Moll, K., Wood, G., & Landerl, K. (2008). Naming speed in dyslexia and dyscalculia. *Learning and Individual Differences*, *18*, 224−236.

Wise, J. C., Pae, H. K., Wolfe, C. B., Sevcik, R. A., Morris, R. D., Lovett, M., et al. (2008). Phonological awareness and rapid naming skills of children with reading disabilities and children with reading disabilities who are at risk for mathematics difficulties. *Learning Disabilities Research & Practice*, *23*(3), 125−136.

Wolf, M., & Bowers, P. G. (1999). The double-deficit hypothesis for the developmental dyslexias. *Journal of Educational Psychology*, *91*, 415−439.

Wolf, M., Bowers, P. G., & Biddle, K. (2000). Naming-speed processes, timing, and reading: A conceptual review. *Journal of Learning Disabilities*, *33*(4), 387−407.

Woodcock, R. (1984). A response to some questions raised about the Woodcock Johnson III: Efficacy of the aptitude clusters. *Schol Psychology Review*, *13*, 355−352.

Chapter 10

Translating Scientific Progress in Dyslexia Into 21st Century Diagnosis and Interventions

Bennett A. Shaywitz[1], Lawrence G. Weiss[2], Donald H. Saklofske[3] and Sally E. Shaywitz[1]
[1]*Yale Center for Dyslexia & Creativity, Yale University School of Medicine, New Haven, CT, United States,* [2]*Pearson Clinical Assessment, San Antonio, TX, United States,* [3]*Department of Psychology, University of Western Ontario, London, ON, Canada*

INTRODUCTION

Dyslexia (or specific reading disability) is the most common and extensively studied of the learning disabilities (LDs), affecting 80% of all individuals identified as learning disabled (Lerner, 1989). Not only is dyslexia the most thoroughly characterized of all LDs, but it is historically the oldest. In fact, the first description of dyslexia in children preceded the first mention of "learning disability" by over 60 years; dyslexia was first described in 1896 while the term "learning disability" was not used until 1962!

EVOLUTION OF DYSLEXIA AS AN UNEXPECTED DIFFICULTY IN RELATION TO INTELLIGENCE

The observation that seemingly otherwise healthy men and women could lose the ability to read had been made as early as the 17th century (see Shaywitz, 2003), and by the 19th century a number of reports described educated adults who suddenly found themselves unable to read, a condition referred to as "acquired alexia." The most prominent of these cases were described in the early 1890s by the French neurologist Jules Dejerine (1891, 1892), who showed that acquired alexia was the result of a stroke involving posterior brain systems in the parieto-temporal and occipito-temporal regions. It was a report by Hinshelwood (1895), an ophthalmologist in Glasgow, Scotland, of an adult with acquired alexia that served as the impetus for the first report of developmental dyslexia by Dr. W. Pringle Morgan

WISC-V. DOI: https://doi.org/10.1016/B978-0-12-815744-2.00010-0

of 14-year-old Percy F. in the *British Medical Journal* on November 7, 1896 (Morgan, 1896): "...He has always been a bright and intelligent boy, quick at games, and in no way inferior to others his age. His great difficulty has been—and is now—his inability to read." Following Hinshelwood's diagnosis of word blindness in adults, Morgan labeled this condition congenital word blindness, emphasizing that the young boy, Percy, had good vision and was intelligent, commenting that "The schoolmaster who has taught him for some years says that he would be the smartest lad in the school if the instruction were entirely oral."

In the years immediately following these early reports, there were many further documented cases of unexpected reading difficulties in children, many from Britain, Europe, and the United States (Shaywitz, 2003). In fact, Hinshelwood (1917) went on to describe a number of other children with dyslexia, noting, for example, that one boy with the "condition" learned very well if the lessons were oral and reporting that his mother believed he was, in many ways, brighter than her other children, except for his inability to learn to read. Hinshelwood also emphasized the unexpected nature of the reading difficulty; it was not due to a generalized deficit in intelligence, but to a "localized" problem affecting reading so that affected children also manifest strengths as well as the weakness in reading. He also observed that the disorder, like most other physiological entities, occurred in gradations rather than as an all-or-none phenomenon, a finding that more recent research has validated (Shaywitz, Escobar, Shaywitz, Fletcher, & Makuch, 1992).

By the early part of the 20th century, clinicians had elaborated descriptions, possible causes, and potential treatments for developmental dyslexia, with perhaps the most cogent described by the physician Samuel Torrey Orton. In his 1937 monograph, *Reading, Writing and Speech Problems in Children*, Orton (1937) noted a number of characteristics of dyslexia that we have come to know 80 years later. These include the observation that though some dyslexic individuals may learn to read, their reading remains slow compared to their peers in age and intelligence, a phenomenon we have come to appreciate as lack of reading fluency. He further knew that although their reading could often appear normal for their age, it was below what was expected for their intelligence. Orton also described characteristic poor spelling as well as how often it was that the smaller function words caused the most trouble in reading. Finally, Orton described how children with difficulty learning to read in the lower grades often had trouble learning a foreign language at adolescence (Orton, 1937, pp. 91–95).

Consistent in the original descriptions by the pioneers who described dyslexia was that they all noted that the reading problem in dyslexic children was *unexpected* in relation to their intelligence. As we review below, the unexpected nature of the reading problem was also the hallmark of what came to be known as LDs.

A decade or two after Orton's prescient descriptions of dyslexia, astute clinicians were beginning to elaborate an entity that came to be known as the brain-injured child (Strauss & Lehtinen, 1947; Strauss & Werner, 1942) and which by 1962 had evolved into what Clements and Peters (1962) described as minimal brain dysfunctions (MBDs). The first finding mentioned was specific learning deficits and the first symptoms noted were failure to read and making dyslexic errors along with poor spelling. In the same year, Kirk and Bateman (1962) first used the term "learning disability," and illustrated the evaluation of a LD with the steps in diagnosing a reading disability. From this very first paper, which used the words LD, the concept of a discrepancy between the child's ability and his achievement was prominent. Thus, Kirk and Bateman (1962) noted the very first step in determining if the child has a LD is to determine the child's reading capacity, a measure reflecting Intelligence Quotient (IQ). Then, actual reading achievement is determined, and the "discrepancy between the capacity for reading and actual achievement in reading is examined."

Myklebust (1968) emphasized the hallmark of a LD as a discrepancy between potential and actual success in learning resulting in significant underachievement. LDs continued to be defined as deficiencies in learning despite adequate intelligence.

By the 1970s parents of thousands of children in the United States knew about LDs, "... even if professional educators and psychologists and pediatricians did not" (Cruickshank, 1972). But this was changing, and within a decade LDs had become one of the most frequently diagnosed conditions in children referred for problems learning in school. Writing in 1985, Kavale and Forness (1985) emphasized that the IQ-achievement discrepancy is essential to the diagnosis of LDs and can be reliably determined. At the same time they reviewed many of the methodological challenges associated with defining LDs on the basis of IQ-achievement discrepancies. More about these problems is discussed in the following.

More than two decades ago Hammill (1990) reviewed the then published proposals for defining a LD, and found that the concept of underachievement was the most consistent element in all the definitions: underachievement within the individual child, that is, underachievement of the child in relation to that child's inherent abilities. But how is underachievement determined? Not surprisingly, many of the definitions suggest that underachievement is indicated by the presence of an ability-achievement discrepancy as discussed above, that is, a significant difference between intellectual ability (usually represented by an IQ) and performance in, for example, reading achievement.

This historical review emphasizes that for over 100 years in the case of dyslexia and over 50 years in the case of LDs, the most consistent and enduring core of the definition is the concept of dyslexia (and LDs) as *unexpected* underachievement. The most up-to-date, scientifically supported definition of dyslexia is US Senate Resolution 680 sponsored by Senator Bill Cassidy and passed unanimously in 2017: "Dyslexia is (1) defined as an unexpected difficulty in reading for an individual who has the intelligence to be a much better reader; and (2) most commonly caused by a difficulty in phonological processing (the appreciation of the individual sounds of spoken language), which affects the ability of an individual to speak, read, spell, and often, learn a second language."

For the first time there is now empirical data confirming the unexpected nature of dyslexia. These data come from the Connecticut Longitudinal Study, a project involving a sample survey of Connecticut schoolchildren representative of those children entering public kindergarten in Connecticut in 1983. All subjects were children whose primary language was English. This cohort, assembled from a two-stage probability-sample survey, has been followed longitudinally beginning in kindergarten, and each was given individualized tests of cognitive abilities and achievement annually up through 12th grade. The racial and ethnic composition of this sample from Connecticut was similar to that of the nation at the time of the study (Statistical Abstract of the United States: 1986, 1985).

Using the Connecticut Longitudinal Study, Ferrer, Shaywitz, Holahan, Marchione, and Shaywitz (2010) demonstrated that in typical readers, reading and IQ are dynamically linked over time. Not only do reading and IQ track together over time, they also influence one another. Such mutual interrelationships are not perceptible in dyslexic readers, suggesting that reading and cognition develop more independently in dyslexia (Fig. 10.1; Ferrer et al., 2010).

Furthermore, these data of an uncoupling between IQ and reading in dyslexia provide evidence to support the conceptual basis of dyslexia as unexpected underachievement. Based on dynamic models, the uncoupling of reading and cognition demonstrate that in dyslexia the reading difficulty is unexpected for an *individual's* level of intelligence, that is, the difficulty is defined as existing *within* the individual. The implication is that for individuals who are dyslexic, the appropriate comparison is between a person's ability and his/her reading. These findings provide the long-sought empirical evidence for the seeming paradox involving cognition and reading in dyslexia. Thus, in dyslexia, a highly intelligent person may read at a level above average but below that expected, based on his/her intelligence, education, or professional status.

Many confuse the impact of dyslexia with an almost total inability to read. While that may occur, most commonly and certainly as defined legally and supported by scientific evidence, there is no reading level below which an individual, student or adult, must score to be diagnosed as dyslexic. Rather, the central point is *how* the individual reads, the effort and work that must go into the reading process for him or her to decipher the word accurately and fluently. Think of a motor disability. The question is not whether

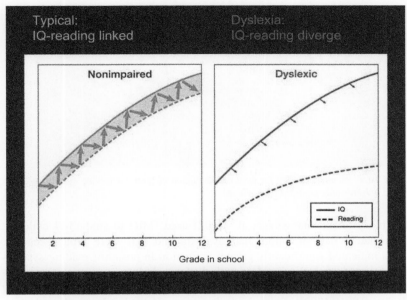

FIGURE 10.1 Mutual interrelationships are not perceptible in dyslexic readers, suggesting that reading and cognition develop more independently in dyslexia. © *Sally Shaywitz, Overcoming Dyslexia, 2nd edition, Based on Ferrer et al. (2010).*

the person can cross a street, but rather what he or she must do to get to the other side, that is, use a cane or a wheelchair.

NEUROBIOLOGICAL EVIDENCE SUPPORTING DYSLEXIA

Making a Hidden Disability Visible

In the early descriptions of dyslexia and LDs, there was serious concern over whether there was evidence of "brain dysfunction." Many of the early reports of dyslexia and LDs attempted to demonstrate nervous system involvement using the methodology available at the time, methodology that is relatively primitive by current standards. The emergence of functional brain imaging using positron emission tomography in the 1980s and then functional magnetic resonance imaging (fMRI) in the 1990s provided the critical evidence the pioneers who described dyslexia and LDs were hoping for. Using these technologies, primarily fMRI, converging evidence from many laboratories around the world demonstrated a "neural signature for dyslexia," that is, an inefficient functioning of posterior reading systems during reading real words and pseudowords (see Fig. 10.2).

This evidence from fMRI has for the first time made visible what previously was a hidden disability. For example, in one of the first studies of

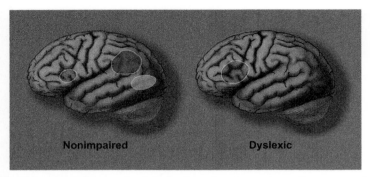

FIGURE 10.2   Neural signature for dyslexia: disruption of posterior reading systems. © *Sally Shaywitz, (Overcoming Dyslexia, 2nd edition).*

fMRI in dyslexia, Shaywitz et al. (2002) used fMRI to study 144 children, approximately half of whom had dyslexia and half were typical readers. Results indicated significantly greater activation in posterior reading systems in typical readers than in readers with dyslexia during a task tapping phonologic analysis. These findings align with the classic 19th century reports by Dejerine (1891, 1892) of acquired alexia caused by left-hemisphere lesions in the parieto-temporal areas as well as areas around the fusiform gyrus.

These data from fMRI studies in groups of children with dyslexia have been replicated in reports from many investigators and show a failure of left-hemisphere posterior brain systems to function properly during reading, particularly the systems in the left-hemisphere occipito-temporal region (see Peterson & Pennington, 2012; Price & Mechelli, 2005; Richlan, Kronbichler, & Wimmer, 2009; Richlan, Kronbichler, & Wimmer, 2011; Shaywitz & Shaywitz, 2005). Similar findings have been reported in German (Kronbichler et al., 2006) and Italian (Brambati et al., 2006) readers with dyslexia. Some studies in Chinese readers with dyslexia show brain abnormalities in left occipito-temporal and anterior frontal regions (Siok, Niu, Jin, Perfetti, & Tan, 2008; Siok, Perfetti, Jin, & Tan, 2004; Siok, Spinks, Jin, & Tan, 2009) similar to those found in dyslexia in alphabetic orthographies. Other studies of Chinese dyslexia have reported reduced activation in *bilateral* occipito-temporal regions and left-middle frontal gyrus (Siok et al., 2004; Siok et al., 2008; Siok et al., 2009), regions not generally found in fMRI studies of dyslexia in alphabetic orthographies. A more recent study demonstrated reduced activation for Chinese dyslexics in right occipital cortex, consonant with a language-specific role of right visual cortex in Chinese reading and suggesting a deficit in holistic visuo-orthographic analysis in Chinese dyslexia (Liu et al., 2012).

Connectivity analyses of fMRI data represent the most recent evolution in characterizing brain networks in dyslexia. Measures of functional connectivity are designed to detect differences in brain regions with similar magnitudes of activation but whose activity is differentially synchronized with other brain systems across subject groups or types of stimuli. Most recently Finn et al. (2014) report that compared to typical readers, dyslexic readers showed reduced connectivity in the visual word-form area, a part of the left-fusiform gyrus specialized for printed words.

Thus, these findings from brain imaging provide still further support for viewing dyslexia as a distinct neurobiological entity, diagnosed by unexpected underachievement and now with a neural signature.

NECESSITY AND CHALLENGE OF BRINGING DIAGNOSIS OF DYSLEXIA INTO THE 21ST CENTURY

As stated by one us (Dr. S. Shaywitz in her testimony before the Congressional Committee on Science, Space and Technology hearing on the Science of Dyslexia in September, 2014), "Education must, and can be, aligned with science. We must ensure that scientific knowledge is translated into policy and practice and that ignorance and injustice do not prevail. We know better, we must act better." Dr. Shaywitz further emphasized that "Dyslexia differs markedly from all other LDs. Dyslexia is very specific and scientifically validated: we know its prevalence, cognitive and neurobiological origins, symptoms, and effective, evidence-based interventions. LD is a general term referring to a range of difficulties that have not yet been delineated or scientifically validated. LDs are comparable to what in medicine are referred to as 'infectious' diseases, whereas dyslexia is akin to being diagnosed with a strep throat—a highly specific disorder in which the causative agent and evidence-based treatment are both known and validated."

A range of scientific studies delineate dyslexia as an unexpected difficulty, that is, there is an uncoupling of reading and intelligence so that one may have average or high intelligence but, at the same time, read at an unexpectedly lower level. Today we know even more that can be used to diagnose dyslexia—the major problem relates to a difficulty in phonological processing, that is, accessing the individual sounds of spoken language. This knowledge, in turn, pinpoints the major symptoms to look for that are caused by this difficulty, as described earlier in this chapter.

Dyslexia is a specific, scientifically supported condition affecting as many as 20% of our student (and adult) population. It is unacceptable to have different groups of professionals ignore the scientific definition of dyslexia and use various administrative criteria to define and diagnose the disorder. Its unexpected nature and its phonological basis must be reflected in any definition used. If particular practitioners or groups of practitioners wish to use additional measures, that is their prerogative. However, we must respect the evidence and base any diagnosis of dyslexia on demonstration of the unexpected nature and of a phonological deficit.

Operationalizing "Unexpected"

More challenging has been the question of how to operationalize the unexpected nature of dyslexia. In fact, the difficulty has been not with the concept of unexpected underachievement, but rather with the real-life practical effect of implementation in a school setting; some have attempted to capture the "unexpected" nature of dyslexia by requiring a discrepancy of a certain degree between a child's measured IQ and his or her reading achievement. In some cases, schools adopted simplified rules; for example, criteria based on a discrepancy, most commonly one or one-and-one-half standard deviations between standard scores on IQ and reading tests, or even more commonly a 20- or 22-point discrepancy between IQ and reading test scores.

Critiques of the methodology were voiced just as soon as the ability achievement discrepancy was codified into PL 94-142 in 1975 and into regulations in 1977 (Kavale & Forness, 1985). One of the first problems that became apparent was that children who were clearly struggling as early as kindergarten or first grade had to wait, often until 3rd grade or later, until their failure in reading was of such a magnitude that they met discrepancy requirements. In other words, in the beginning grades, the use of an ability-achievement discrepancy seemed to reduce the chances of early reading intervention because the child had to fall behind his or her expected reading achievement before he or she would be eligible for services. As a result, identification was often delayed and services were denied until the requisite discrepancy had developed, resulting in what has been described as a "wait-to-fail" approach. By the time a child was identified, he or she might be far behind peers in reading skill. In addition, the size of the required discrepancy varied among states, as well as among school districts within states. Thus, a child might be identified as dyslexic or learning disabled in one school district, but not in another.

More importantly, although these criticisms were directed to *how* the discrepancy was operationalized, they did not negate the construct of *unexpected* underachievement nor did they negate the use of an ability-achievement discrepancy as one component of an overall clinical assessment, one that considers and puts to use the knowledge gained from the scientific study of dyslexia delineating its unexpected nature, its basic difficulty, its impact on, for example, the individual's spoken language, reading, spelling, and even learning a second language.

Identifying Dyslexia at Kindergarten or 1st Grade: Early Screening for Dyslexia

Currently, most children with dyslexia are not diagnosed until they are in 3rd grade or about 9 years old. Recent evidence indicates that a large

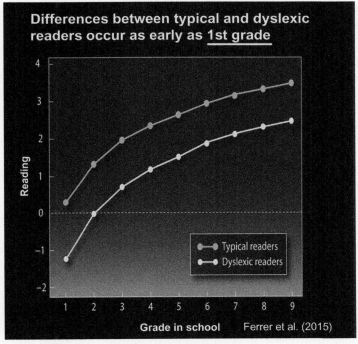

FIGURE 10.3 Reading from grades 1 to 9 in typical and dyslexic readers. The achievement gap between typical and dyslexic readers is evident as early as 1st grade and persists through adolescence. © *Sally Shaywitz, Overcoming Dyslexia 2nd edition, Adapted from Ferrer et al. (2015).*

achievement gap between typical and dyslexic readers is evident as early as 1st grade and persists (Fig. 10.3). These findings provide strong evidence and impetus for early screening, early identification of, and early intervention for young children at risk for dyslexia. We and other researchers have begun to recognize that one source of potentially powerful and highly accessible screening information that has thus far been ignored is the teacher's judgment about the child's reading and readingrelated skills reflecting the hours and hours she or he has devoted to trying to teach this child to read. Remarkably, we found that teachers' response to a small set of questions on the Shaywitz DyslexiaScreen™ (an evidence-based instrument comprising 10 items from kindergarten, 12 items from 1st grade and 10 items from 2nd grade) predict children at high risk for dyslexia with a high degree of accuracy, with excellent sensitivity and specificity. The instrument is completed on a tablet with an algorithm that quickly determines and indicates if the child is "at-risk" or "not at-risk."

Diagnosing Dyslexia: Operationalizing "Unexpected" in Young Children

Difficulties in identifying younger children based solely on a discrepancy score bring into focus that dyslexia is a clinical diagnosis. Although it may not yet be possible to demonstrate a quantitative disparity between ability and achievement in the early grades, it is still possible to demonstrate the fundamental concept of an unexpected difficulty in reading.

In *Overcoming Dyslexia*, Shaywitz (2003) conceptualizes dyslexia as a weakness in phonology (getting to the sounds of spoken words) surrounded by a sea of strengths in higher-order thinking. In younger children there is an encapsulated weakness in decoding surrounded by strengths in, for example, problem solving, critical thinking, concept formation, and reasoning. In older children, adolescents, and adults it may be thought of as an encapsulated weakness in fluent reading surrounded by these strengths in higher-order thinking.

Given that dyslexia is defined on the basis of scientific evidence as an unexpected difficulty in reading in a child or an adult in relation to intelligence, it is not surprising that a measure of intelligence, the Wechsler Intelligence Scale for Children—Fifth Edition (WISC-V) (Wechsler, 2014), is a critical component of a comprehensive assessment of the child (aged 6–16 years) with dyslexia. Very often an intelligence test can reveal areas of strength, particularly in areas of abstract thinking and reasoning, which are very reassuring to parents and especially to the child him/herself. They also indicate that the reading difficulty is isolated and not reflective of a general lack of learning ability or intellectual disability.

The assessment approach we focus on here and elaborated in more detail in Dr. Sally Shaywitz's new edition of *Overcoming Dyslexia* (forthcoming) is an in-depth evaluation of the skills (especially phonologic) known to be related to reading success.

DEVELOPMENT AND ASSESSMENT OF PHONOLOGICAL PROCESSING

Because difficulties in phonological processing are so central to dyslexia, it is imperative that educators and evaluators become more knowledgeable about the developmental progression of children's phonological abilities; these follow a natural progression and so are relatively straightforward to assess across development, beginning at about age 4 (Shaywitz, 2003). In general, what the examiner is looking for is the development of phonological sensitivity that refers to the ability of the child to focus on the sounds, rather than on the meaning, of spoken words. For example, the child can tell what word rhymes with cat rather than simply if a cat is a kind of animal. Phonological skills develop gradually over time and in a predictable, logical

BOX 10.1 Clues to Children at Risk for Dyslexia

- Delayed language
- Trouble learning common nursery rhymes such as "Jack and Jill" and "Humpty-Dumpty"
- A lack of appreciation of rhymes
- Mispronounced words; persistent baby talk
- Difficulty in learning (remembering) names of letters and numbers
- Failure to know the letters in his own name

© *Sally Shaywitz (Overcoming Dyslexia, 2nd edition).*

sequence. Awareness of this sequence and its timing makes it possible to recognize when a child is veering off course. We know that, in general, as children develop phonological skills, they gain the ability to focus on smaller and smaller parts of the word, rather than on the word as a whole, indivisible unit. At the same time, they also work their way from attending to the outside or ends of words to the inside or middle parts of words. And so at first children are able to separate out only the beginning sounds of words, then the end sounds, and, finally, the inside parts of words. Penetrating the inside of a word is much more difficult than noticing either end. And it is the ability to notice and to code each of the parts within a word that marks the maturing reader.

As shown in Box 10.1, from *Overcoming Dyslexia* (Shaywitz, 2003), signs and symptoms of children at risk for dyslexia can be observed even before formal reading begins in school.

In describing a child's phonological skills, two terms are often used: phonological awareness and phonemic awareness. Phonological awareness is a more general and more inclusive term that includes all levels of awareness of the sound structure of words; it is also used to refer to the earliest stages of developing an awareness of the parts of words; for example, sensitivity to rhyme or noticing larger parts of words such as syllables. Phonemic awareness is a much more specific term; it refers to the more advanced ability to notice, to identify, to think about, and to manipulate the smallest particles of language making up a word, phonemes. Phonemic awareness has the strongest relationship to later reading and most tests focus on this level of awareness. The most helpful measures in the young child include: (1) sound comparison, (2) segmentation, and (3) blending. For sound comparison, we would ask a child: "Tell me which word begins with the same first sound as bat: dog, sat, or boy?" For segmentation, we might ask a child to count or pronounce the individual parts of a word; for example, "Can you count the sounds you hear in pan?" (three). Alternatively, we can ask him to blend together the parts of a word that has already been pulled apart: "What word do the sounds /k/ /a/ /t/ make? (cat)." In addition, as he develops increasing phonemic awareness, we can have him add, move around, or delete part of a word by asking, for example, "What word remains if you take the 'r' sound away from frog? (fog)."

In addition to tests of phonemic awareness, there are two other related tests that give valuable information about a young child's readiness for reading.

The first, which measures phonological memory, evaluates a child's ability to temporarily store bits of verbal information; we see how well he can remember a series of numbers or words that were just presented to him orally. (Both spoken numbers and words are stored as phonemes.) In this type of test, a child may be asked, "Can you repeat these numbers to me, five-seven-three-one-six?" This type of memory plays an important role in reading at every level, even for a first grader as he is trying to sound out a word. As a child reads a sentence, he has to hold several bits of information in mind in order to put it all together and make sense of what he has just read. Think of the process: he first decodes the letters into sounds, then holds these sounds in his memory as he tries to decode the remaining letters in the word, and then he takes these stored sounds, blends them together, and forms the word. Words are stored primarily on the basis of their sounds, so the ability to hold words temporarily is really a kind of phonological skill. And the clearer the phonemes, the more efficiently words (or letters or numbers) can be retrieved.

A second kind of test, the rapid automatic naming test, or rapid automatic naming (RAN), examines still another aspect of phonological processing, what is technically referred to as "phonological access." The RAN tries to determine how easily and rapidly a child can retrieve verbal information held in long-term storage. Here, the child is typically shown a card with several rows of pictures of familiar objects and asked to name these, one after another, as quickly as he can. Highly familiar stimuli are used so that this does not turn into a test of the child's vocabulary. Both accuracy and speed are measured. The child's facility in rapid naming is related to just the sorts of processes he must perform as he reads, when he must be able to go into his long-term memory storage and rapidly retrieve the stored phonemes.

Tests Helpful in the Evaluation of Children With Dyslexia

Phonological Processing

Given that phonological processing represents the core weakness in dyslexia, it is fortunate that a robust range of measures are now available for assessment of each of its components. Such tests can be very useful for young children and continuing as the child matures. For example, specific core and primary WISC-V (Wechsler, 2014) subtests and indexes may be useful in dyslexia evaluations. The Digit Span Forward task evaluates phonological memory, the child's ability to temporarily store bits of verbal information—a basic step in the reading process as described above. Further, the Working Memory Index evaluates the child's ability to hold several bits of verbal information in mind and put it all together to make sense of what has just been heard or read.

With its addition of the complementary Naming Speed Index (NSI) and subtests, the new WISC-V can be used to aid in the assessment of a range of a young child's phonological capabilities. More specifically, the WISC-V was designed to provide insights into phonological processing with its measure of phonological access, rapid automatic naming, specifically, the Naming Speed Literacy (NSL) subtest, a component of the NSI. The test requires the child to name colors, objects, letters, and numbers as quickly as possible. For further details about NSL, please see Chapter 1. Clinicians and researchers also use the Comprehensive Test of Phonological Processing, now in its second edition (CTOPP−2) (Wagner, Torgesen, Rashotte, & Pearson, 2013), to test for the full range of phonological skills. Specifically, in children 4−6 years of age, awareness of and access to the phonological structure of oral language may be assessed by three subtests of the CTOPP−2 referred to as phonological awareness composite: Elision, Blending Words, and Sound Matching. In older children and young adults 7 through 24 years of age, phonology is assessed also by the phonological awareness composite but with Sound Matching replaced by Phoneme Isolation. Phoneme Isolation measures the ability to isolate individual sounds within words. For example, "Where does the /t/ sound occur in the word cat—beginning, middle, or end of the word?" Other components of the CTOPP−2 assess phonological memory and rapid automatic naming.

Letter Knowledge

Though not as robust as tests of phonological awareness in predicting whether the young child is at risk for dyslexia, a child's knowledge of letter names and sounds may also serve as a helpful guide to how ready he or she is to read. Testing letter knowledge is straightforward; it can be assessed informally by asking the child to name letters presented one at a time on a card. Similarly, knowledge of letters and sounds is tested by asking the child, "Can you tell me the sound(s) this letter makes in words?" More formal testing can be obtained by using a reading test that contains a letter-identification section; for example, the letter-word subtest on the Wechsler Individual Achievement Test—Third Edition (WIAT-III) (Wechsler, 2009); the Kaufman Test of Educational Achievement—Third Edition (KTEA-III) (Kaufman & Kaufman, 2014); or the Woodcock-Johnson IV Tests of Achievement (WJ-IV Achievement) (Schrank, McGrew, Mather, & Woodcock, 2014).

In addition, it is often helpful to assess a child's familiarity with the conventions of print (i.e., that there are spaces between words and that books are read from top to bottom and from left to right), to ensure that a young child is aware of what books are and how they work.

Academic Achievement

Overall, in the school-age child, reading is assessed by measuring accuracy, fluency, and comprehension. Specifically, in the school-age child, one important element of the evaluation is how accurately the child can decode words (i.e., read single words). This is measured with standardized tests of single real word and pseudoword reading. Because pseudowords are unfamiliar and cannot be memorized, each nonsense word must be sounded out. Tests of nonsense word reading are referred to as "word attack." Reading fluency, the ability to read accurately, rapidly, and with good prosody, an often overlooked component of reading, is of critical importance because it allows for the automatic, attention-free recognition of words.

The WIAT-III, KTEA-III, and WJ-IV are each reliable, valid, and comprehensive measures of academic achievement. Each measure includes multiple tasks designed to evaluate early reading skills such as letter identification, word reading, pseudoword decoding, as well as reading fluency and comprehension tasks. Only the WIAT-III and KTEA-III have been empirically linked to the WISC-V. In addition, fluency also may be assessed by asking the child to read *aloud* using the Gray Oral Reading Test—Fifth Edition (GORT-5) (Wiederholt & Bryant, 2012). This test consists of increasingly difficult passages, each followed by comprehension questions; scores for accuracy, rate, fluency, and comprehension are provided. Such tests of oral reading are particularly helpful in identifying a child who is dyslexic; by its nature oral reading forces a child to pronounce each word. Listening to a struggling reader attempt to pronounce each word leaves no doubt about the child's reading difficulty. In addition to reading passages aloud, single-word reading efficiency may be assessed using; for example, the Test of Word Reading Efficiency—Second Edition (TOWRE-2) (Torgesen, Wagner, & Rashotte, 2013), a test of speeded oral reading of individual real words and pseudowords. Children who struggle with reading often have trouble spelling; spelling may be assessed with the WIAT-III, KTEA-III, or WJ-IV spelling test.

DIAGNOSIS OF DYSLEXIA IN ADOLESCENTS AND YOUNG ADULTS

The developmental course of dyslexia has now been characterized. First, dyslexia is persistent, it does not go away; on a practical level, this means that once a person is diagnosed as dyslexic there is no need for reevaluation following high school to confirm the diagnosis. Second, over the course of development, skilled readers become more accurate and more automatic in decoding; they do not need to rely on context for word identification. Dyslexic readers also become more accurate over time, but they do not become automatic in their reading. Residua of the phonological deficit persist so that reading remains effortful and slow, even for the brightest of individuals with childhood histories of dyslexia. Failure to either recognize or measure the lack of automaticity in reading represents, perhaps, the most common error in the diagnosis of dyslexia in accomplished young adults. It is often not appreciated that tests measuring word accuracy are inadequate for the diagnosis of dyslexia in young adults at the level of college, graduate, or professional school and that, for these individuals, timed measures of reading must be employed in making the diagnosis.

Since they often are able to read words accurately (albeit very slowly) dyslexic adolescents and young adults may mistakenly be assumed to have "outgrown" their dyslexia (Bruck, 1998; Lefly & Pennington, 1991; Shaywitz, 2003). Data from studies of children with dyslexia who have been followed prospectively support the notion that in adolescents, difficulties with reading fluency and, often, poor spelling may be especially useful clinically in diagnosing dyslexia in students in secondary school and college, and even graduate and professional schools. It is important to remember that these older dyslexic students may be similar to their typically reading peers on untimed measures of word recognition yet continue to suffer from the phonological deficit that makes reading less automatic, more effortful, and slow. Thus, the most consistent and telling sign of dyslexia in an accomplished young adult is slow and laborious reading and writing.

Essential Components of Diagnosis in Adolescents and Young Adults

Lack of Automaticity

The failure either to recognize or to measure the lack of automaticity in reading is, along with the failure to assess intelligence, perhaps one of the two most common errors in the diagnosis of dyslexia in older children and in accomplished young adults. Tests relying on the accuracy of word identification alone are inappropriate to use to diagnose dyslexia in accomplished young adults; tests of word identification reveal little to nothing of their *struggles* to read. It is important to recognize that, since they assess reading accuracy but not automaticity, the kinds of reading tests commonly used for school-age children may provide misleading data on bright adolescents and young adults. The most critical tests are those that are timed; they are the most sensitive to a phonological deficit in a bright adult. However, there are very few standardized tests for young adult readers that are administered under timed and untimed conditions; the Nelson–Denny Reading Test (Brown, Fishco, & Hanna, 1993) represents an exception. Any scores obtained on testing should be considered relative to peers with the same degree of education or professional training. Clinicians and researchers have recognized that in bright young adults a history of phonologically based reading difficulties, requirements for extra time on tests, current slow and effortful reading (i.e., signs of a lack of automaticity in reading), and indications of an unexpected difficulty in reading are the sine qua non of a diagnosis of dyslexia.

Measure of Intelligence

The failure to include a test of intelligence such as the WISC-V represents one of the two most common and harmful errors made in the diagnosis of dyslexia. As discussed throughout this chapter, the demonstration of an unexpected difficulty in reading in relation to intelligence is a key hallmark of dyslexia. Dyslexia is an unexpected difficulty in reading that is best and most reliably and clearly demonstrated by performance on a test of intelligence, on the WISC-V, most often observed using the VCI, though the Full-Scale IQ may also be useful.

Use of a reliable test of intelligence such as the WISC-V to diagnose dyslexia is of fundamental importance. It is one of the definitive steps necessary to identifying dyslexia. Once individuals knows their diagnosis, the "world changes." Often following years of frustration, disappointment, and self-doubt, of thinking that they are dumb, there is suddenly an explanation and a name for the difficulties. It is not a problem of "not trying hard enough" or "a lack of intelligence," it is because a phonological deficit, in spite of their average or high intelligence and strong effort, prevents them from reading and achieving at a level and rate according to their intellect.

Here is how celebrated and dyslexic writer John Irving describes the experience of an undiagnosed, bright dyslexic student: "I wasn't diagnosed as dyslexic at Exeter; I was seen as just plain stupid... I wish I'd known, when I was a student at Exeter, that there was a word for what made being a student so hard for me; I wish I could have said to my friends that I was dyslexic. Instead, I kept quiet or—to my close friends—I made bad jokes about how stupid I was" (quoted in Shaywitz, 2003, p. 346).

Self-awareness and self-knowledge, gained by an accurate diagnosis of dyslexia, bring in the light and allow the person to understand himself, to know how he functions and learns, the nature of his difficulties, and how to help himself. One of us (S. Shaywitz) has personally shared the results of a full evaluation for dyslexia, including measures of intelligence, reading, phonological processing, and other components, and witnessed the individual's face light up, sadness slowly transition to at least a half smile, and the outpouring of energy and excitement at being told that she was dyslexic and, indeed, intelligent, often highly intelligent. If, as a result of failure to diagnose dyslexia, everything that is happening in school tells them they are "dumb" or "stupid" because they are not reading well or fluently, we as a society are negligent, if not unethical, in denying such individuals this important information about themselves. Similarly, all educators want their students to learn; it is wrong to deny teachers 21st century, truly evidence-based knowledge of why a particular student is not progressing in reading. Such knowledge is a critical key to providing that student with the evidence-based reading instruction that now exists.

SUMMARY

Awareness of the historical background of dyslexia, now joined together with —21st century scientific advances, provides powerful evidence to address the needs of the large segment of our children who are dyslexic, and who, in turn, represent the overwhelming majority of students labeled as learning disabled. Dyslexia can be reliably identified using 21st century knowledge and assessment tools, including the achievement gap in reading appearing in first grade; its unexpected difficulty in reading; and its phonological basis. It cannot be stressed enough that to ensure timely identification, screening must be implemented early (kindergarten, first and second grade) using an evidence-based screener. Accurate diagnosis, the unexpected nature, the phonological deficit, and the lack of reading fluency in dyslexia must be taken into account, both in making a reliable and timely diagnosis and to ensure that those who require identification and effective interventions are not overlooked.

Currently, we are failing large numbers of our children by failing to screen and then to identify the many who are dyslexic and who can be helped. A dyslexic child who is not identified cannot be counted, will not receive effective interventions, and, perhaps even more importantly, cannot know he or she is not dumb and can have a fulfilling future.

To address the needs of our dyslexic children, early screening, accurate diagnosis, and effective intervention must all be in place. We have focused on scientifically based approaches to screening and to diagnosis; we must do no less when implementing interventions for dyslexia. For education to truly align with 21st century science, we must ensure that modern concepts of evidence-based interventions reflecting randomized clinical trials are the standard in choosing programs, whether professional development, reading programs, or in educating educators about dyslexia. When selecting any of these programs, we must not succumb to received wisdom or tightly held belief systems, but continually insist "show me the evidence!" Putting into practice 21st century advances in the science of dyslexia so that this common condition is reliably screened for and then identified and effectively treated will mark a major positive turning point in meeting the needs of the one in five children who are dyslexic, serving not only the children but their parents, educators, and society as well.

ACKNOWLEDGMENTS

Much of the material in this chapter is based on or appeared in *Overcoming Dyslexia* (Shaywitz, 2003), or will appear in the forthcoming second edition of this book, chapters in *Swaiman's Textbook of Child Neurology*, and pediatric texts.

REFERENCES

Brambati, S., Termine, C., Ruffino, M., Danna, M., Lanzi, G., Stella, G., et al. (2006). Neuropsychological deficits and neral dysfunction in familial dyslexia. *Brain Research*, *1113*(1), 174−185.

Brown, J., Fishco, V., & Hanna, G. (1993). *Nelson Denny reading test—Manual for scoring and interpretation (forms G and H)*. Itaca, IL: Riverside Publishing.

Bruck, M. (1998). Outcomes of adults with childhood histories of dyslexia. In C. Hulme, & R. Joshi (Eds.), *Reading and spelling: Development and disorders* (pp. 179−200). Mahwah, NJ: Lawrence Erlbaum Associates.

Clements, S., & Peters, J. (1962). Minimal brain dysfunctions in the school-age child: Diagnosis and treatment. *Archives of General Psychiatry*, *6*(3), 185−197.

Cruickshank, W. (1972). Some issues facing the field of learning disability. *Journal of Learning Disabilities*, *5*, 380−388.

Dejerine, J. (1891). Sur un cas de cecite verbale avec agraphhie, suivi d'autopsie. *C. R. Societe du Biologie*, *43*, 197−201.

Dejerine, J. (1892). Contribution a l'etude anatomo-pathologique et clinique des differentes varietes de cecite verbale. *Memoires de la Societe de Biologie*, *4*, 61−90.

Ferrer, E., Shaywitz, B., Holahan, J., Marchione, K., & Shaywitz, S. (2010). Uncoupling of reading and IQ over time: Empirical evidence for a definition of dyslexia. *Psychological Science*, *21*(1), 93−101.

Ferrer, E., Shaywitz, B. A., Holahan, J. M., Marchone, K., Michaels, R., & Shaywitz, S. E. (2015). Achievement gap in reading is present as early as first grade and persists through adolescence. *Journal of Pediatrics*, *167*, 1121−1125.

Finn, E., Shen, X., Holahan, J., Scheinost, D., Lacadie, C., Papademetris, X., et al. (2014). Disruption of functional networks in dyslexia: A whole-brain, data-driven approach to fMRI connectivity analysis. *Biological Psychiatry*, *76*(5), 397−404.

Hammill, D. (1990). On defining learning disabilities: An emerging consensus. *Journal of Learning Disabilities*, *23*, 74−84.

Hinshelwood, J. (1895). Word-blindness and visual memory. *The Lancet*, *2*, 1564−1570.

Hinshelwood, J. (1917). *Congenital word blindness*. London: Lewis, HK.

Kaufman, A. S., & Kaufman, N. L. (2014). *Kaufman test of educational achievement* (3rd ed.). Bloomington, MN: NCS Pearson.

Kavale, K., & Forness, S. (1985). Learning disability and the history of science: Paradigm or paradox? *Remedial and Special Education*, *6*, 12−24.

Kirk, S., & Bateman, B. (1962). Diagnosis and remediation of learning disabilities. *Exceptional Children*, *29*(2), 73−78.

Kronbichler, M., Hutzler, F., Staffen, W., Mair, A., Ladurner, G., & Wimmer, H. (2006). Evidence for a dysfunction of left posterior reading areas in German dyslexic readers. [Comparative Study Research Support, Non-U.S. Gov't]. *Neuropsychologia, 44*(10), 1822−1832.

Lefly, D., & Pennington, B. (1991). Spelling errors and reading fluency in compensated adult dyslexics. *Annals of Dyslexia, 41*, 143−162.

Lerner, J. (1989). Educational interventions in learning disabilities. *Journal of the American Academy Child Adolescent Psychiatry, 28*(3), 326−331.

Liu, L., Wang, W., You, W., Li, Y., Awati, N., Zhao, X., et al. (2012). Similar alterations in brain function for phonological and semantic processing to visual characters in Chinese dyslexia. *Neuropsychologia, 50*, 2224−2232.

Morgan, W. (1896). *A case of congenital word blindness. British Medical Journal* (p. 1378) .

Myklebust, H. R. (1968). Learning disabilities: Definition and overview. In H. R. Myklebust (Ed.), *Progress in learning disabilities* (Vol. 1, pp. 1−15). New York: Grune & Stratton, Inc.

Orton, S. T. (1937). *Reading, writing, and speech problems in children.* New York: Norton.

Peterson, R., & Pennington, B. (2012). Developmental dyslexia. *The Lancet, 379*(9830), 1997−2007.

Price, C., & Mechelli, A. (2005). Reading and reading disturbance. *Current Opinion in Neurobiology, 15*, 231−238.

Richlan, F., Kronbichler, M., & Wimmer, H. (2009). Functional abnormalities in the dyslexic brain: A quantitative meta-analysis of neuroimaging studies. *Human Brain Mapping, 30*, 3299−3308.

Richlan, F., Kronbichler, M., & Wimmer, H. (2011). Meta-analyzing brain dysfunctions in dyslexic children and adults. *NeuroImage, 56*, 1735−1742.

Schrank, F., McGrew, K. S., Mather, N., & Woodcock, R. (2014). *Woodcock-Johnson-IV.* Rolling Meadows, IL: Riverside Publishing.

Shaywitz, S., (forthcoming). Overcoming dyslexia: A new and complete science-based program for reading problems at any level (2nd ed.). New York: Alfred A. Knopf.

Shaywitz, B., Shaywitz, S., Pugh, K., Mencl, W., Fulbright, R., Skudlarski, P., et al. (2002). Disruption of posterior brain systems for reading in children with developmental dyslexia. *Biological Psychiatry, 52*(2), 101−110.

Shaywitz, S. (2003). *Overcoming dyslexia: A new and complete science-based program for reading problems at any level.* New York: Alfred A. Knopf.

Shaywitz, S., & Shaywitz, B. (2005). Dyslexia (specific reading disability). *Biological Psychiatry, 57*, 1301−1309.

Shaywitz, S., Escobar, M., Shaywitz, B., Fletcher, J., & Makuch, R. (1992). Evidence that dyslexia may represent the lower tail of a normal distribution of reading ability. *New England Journal of Medicine, 326*(3), 145−150.

Shaywitz, S.E. Shaywitz DyslexiaScreen™ The Shaywitz DyslexiaScreen is an efficient, reliable, and user-friendly dyslexia test for K-1 . . . screening tool that identifies students who are at risk for dyslexia. Available from Pearson Clinical.

Siok, W., Niu, Z., Jin, Z., Perfetti, C., & Tan, L. (2008). A structural-functional basis for dyslexia in the cortex of Chinese readers. *Proceedings of the National Academy of Sciences USA, 105*, 5561−5566.

Siok, W., Perfetti, C., Jin, Z., & Tan, L. (2004). Biological abnormality of impaired reading is constrained by culture. *Nature, 431*, 71−76.

Siok, W., Spinks, J., Jin, Z., & Tan, L. (2009). Developmental dyslexia is characterized by the coexistence of visuospatial and phonological disorders in Chinese children. *Current Biology,* *19,* R890–R892.

Statistical Abstract of the United States: 1986. (1985) (46). Washington, DC: US Government Printing Office.

Strauss, A., & Lehtinen, L. (1947). *Psychopathology and education of the brain-injured child.* New York: Grune and Stratton.

Strauss, A. A., & Werner, H. (1942). Disorders of conceptual thinking in the brain-injured child. *Journal of Nervous and Mental Disease, 96*(2), 153–172.

Torgesen, J., Wagner, R., & Rashotte, C. (2013). *TOWRE-2: Test of word reading efficiency* (2nd ed.). Austin, TX: PRO-ED.

Wagner, R., Torgesen, J., Rashotte, C., & Pearson, N. (2013). *CTOPP-2: Comprehensive test of phonological processing* (2nd ed.). Austin, TX: PRO-ED.

Wechsler, D. (2009). *Wechsler individual achievement test* (3rd ed.). San Antonio, TX: Psych Corp.

Wechsler, D. (2014). Wechsler intelligence scale for children-V. San Antonio, TX: Pearson.

Wiederholt, J., & Bryant, B. (2012). *GORT-5 examiner's manual.* Austin, TX: PRO-ED, Inc.

Chapter 11

Issues Related to the WISC-V Assessment of Cognitive Functioning in Clinical and Special Groups

Jessie L. Miller[1], Lisa Whipple Drozdick[2], Donald H. Saklofske[3] and Lawrence G. Weiss[4]

[1]R&D, Pearson Canada Assessment, Toronto, ON, Canada, [2]Clinical Content Development, Pearson, San Antonio, TX, United States, [3]Department of Psychology, University of Western Ontario, London, ON, Canada, [4]Research and Measurement Consultant, San Antonio, TX, United States

INTRODUCTION

David Wechsler's definition of intelligence has sustained the test of time: "the global capacity of a person to act purposefully, to think rationally, and to deal effectively with his environment" (Wechsler, 1944, p. 3). With the recent publication of the fifth edition of the Wechsler Intelligence Scale for Children (WISC-V; Wechsler, 2014), Dr. Wechsler's legacy remains as integral and important a factor in the description of individual differences as ever. Intelligence was initially viewed and conceptualized as a continuum of the capacity to think, learn, and act in a way that could then be used to describe individual differences in ability along a range of performance from the most intellectually impaired to the most extreme of genius. With time, it was further observed that all individuals fall along this continuum, and regardless of the diagnosed condition, cognitive functioning could be more fully understood by examining the patterns of scores that comprised the tests such as the Wechsler and Binet scales. Contemporary views of intelligence (see Neisser et al., 1996) have expanded the breadth of construct coverage of intelligence tests to include key performance factors that together define general mental ability. While the first intelligence tests were mainly used for classification, selection, and placement, the role of intelligence tests has broadened to include profile analysis that may characterize groups of patients

WISC-V. DOI: https://doi.org/10.1016/B978-0-12-815744-2.00011-2

with specific diagnoses and alternatively to use such information to recognize individual differences that may translate to targeted intervention planning. Intelligence tests play a dominant role in the "strengths-based" models of today.

The study and measurement of intelligence is significantly impacted by current cultural and societal issues (as discussed in Chapter 5), in addition to advances in scientific research (as discussed in Chapter 4). This fact is exemplified by the WISC-V five-factor model. The research and development leading to the WISC-V coincides with a period of tremendous change in cognitive assessment. Less than 18 months after the publication of the widely debated fifth edition of the *Diagnostic and Statistical Manual of Mental Disorders* (DSM-5; American Psychiatric Association [APA], 2013), the WISC-V emerged to a professional landscape marked by uncertainty and opportunity in assessment, measurement, and diagnosis of neurocognitive disorders. The changes to the diagnostic criteria detailed in the DSM-5 have impacted practitioners and research scientists in diverse ways. For some, the question has been the translation of these new diagnostic categories to clinical practice. For instance, how to keep pace with changes to insurance billings and discordance among rules for eligibility of services by region. For others, it has meant a paradigm shift in our understanding of the etiology of mental health disorders, and as such, the theoretical basis of the methodologies employed in psychological research. Perhaps most importantly, it has spurred a wave of new research focused on investigating the reliability and validity of these new definitions in the identification, classification, and treatment of mental disorders. Debate over the classification of mental health disorders is far from new: this debate spans more than a century in the literature, before even the first publication of the DSM in 1952. Yet the momentum with which this latest revision has sparked discussion among professionals working in education and mental health is intriguing. Without question, the push for new research to address the controversial new organization of psychological disorders will serve to advance our understanding in the field.

One of the more significant changes to the DSM-5 was the consolidation of Autism, Asperger's, and Pervasive Developmental disorders. While DSM-IV (APA, 2000) used distinct categories for these classifications, DSM-5 has combined these disorders into one broad category of Autism Spectrum Disorders (ASDs). What were formerly termed Autistic disorder and Asperger's disorder can still be readily distinguished by identifying the level of language impairment in the nosology of the disorder. Still, this change to the categorization of Autism and Asperger's disorders reflects a dynamic shift in the theoretical underpinning of the DSM and in the etiology of mental health disorders. Although the field of psychology has been gradually moving toward a continuum theory of mental health, the integration of Autism and Asperger's disorders is the first time a neurodevelopmental disorder has been reflected by a continuum model similar to the prevailing conceptualization of personality disorders among leading personality theorists. This change is influenced by advanced research in genetic and family studies of children with Autism, along with the need to approach interventions for both Autism and Asperger's from a common core deficit.

A continuum approach to describing neurocognitive disorders is necessary among theorists seeking an explanation for the shared behavioral and cognitive profiles of categorically distinct disorders. It is also necessary for making sense of the substantial comorbidity that occurs among disorders, particularly when comorbid disorders also share common phenotypes. In fact, the lack of specificity among disorders has necessarily relegated Kraeplin's 1913 categorical approach to defining mental health disorders to a small fraction of researchers and practitioners investigating latent class and taxonomic evidence of distinct group membership (Watson & Clark, 2006; Widiger & Samuel, 2005).

With advances in assessment such as with the WISC-V, researchers and clinicians now have the necessary tools to measure atypical profiles across cognitive domains, allowing researchers to map overlapping phenotypes among disorders. Though atypical neurocognitive profiles have been documented in the literature for decades, the empirical studies emerging in more recent literature are bolstered by advances in cognitive neuroscience, brain imaging, epidemiology, and genetic studies. The profiles of cognitive impairment shared within the attention, language, and motor skills disorders as well as the cluster symptoms in executive dysfunction observed in Attention Deficit Hyperactivity Disorder (ADHD), Oppositional Defiant Disorder (ODD), and Conduct Disorder (CD) or the common verbal deficits between ASD and Specific Language Impairment are more recent examples. (Dyck & Piek, 2014; Kjelgaard & Tager-Flusberg, 2001; Lewis, Murdoch, & Woodyatt, 2007; Rapin, Dunn, Allen, Stevens, & Fein, 2009). For some researchers, these cooccurrences in cognitive deficits are indication of a common underlying etiologic factor. Others suggest the lack of neurocognitive specificity is evidence that cognitive dysfunction is not the common denominator among disorders, and that these common weaknesses are superficial correlations (Taylor, Mayberry, Grayndler, & Whitehouse, 2014; Whitehouse, Barry, & Bishop, 2008; Williams, Minshew, & Goldstein, 2008). Evidence that interventions aimed at improving the cognitive weakness in disorders such as ADHD do little to explain or reduce core behavioral symptoms (Coghill, Hayward, Rhodes, Grimmer, & Matthews, 2014; Klingberg et al., 2005; Sonuga-Barke et al., 2013) seems to support this argument. Similarly, findings that the behavioral phenotypes of many mental health problems are also strongly correlated to cognitive deficits in typically developing children, suggest an alternate model of causation (Dyck & Piek, 2014). This is a complex question and current evidence is not conclusive. Whether cognitive deficits contribute to impairment and symptomology or are rooted in the causal mechanism of the disorder, future research using tools such as the WISC-V that can accommodate both comprehensive and targeted assessment of performance along with process analysis are needed to address this issue. Contributions from brain imaging and fMRI studies will also add significantly to an understanding of the phenotypic overlap among neurocognitive disorders.

THE RELEVANCE AND PURPOSE OF COGNITIVE ASSESSMENT

The role of intelligence in understanding individual variations in children's learning and behavior cannot be overstated. Whether from the perspective of diagnostic frameworks such as DSM-5, eligibility criteria from schools determining special education classifications, or the teacher working to identify the unique strengths of a child with ADHD, intelligence tests like the WISC serve an important role in providing information that will guide more effective identification and intervention planning. In the following sections, selected special group studies included in the development of the WISC-V are discussed with respect to the neurocognitive factors associated with each disorder's symptoms and impairment. This is followed by a summary of the results of the special group studies on the WISC-V subtests and composites. The complete data for all special group studies are presented in the *WISC-V Technical and Interpretive Manual* and the *WISC-V Technical and Interpretive Manual Supplement*. The results from the special group studies may serve as guideposts at a group level so that psychologists might use the results of the WISC-V to determine a child's cognitive strengths and weakness both in relation to the normative sample but also for select clinical groups. This is important information because of the variability within and between groups, and while the tables in the manual for the various special group studies are not representative of all clinical populations, they do show average patterns of performance on the various Index and subtests of the WISC-V that can be used to inform and guide the clinician's investigation of diagnostic hypotheses.

Still, while certain WISC-V profiles of cognitive strengths and weaknesses are repeatedly observed in group research relating to specific diagnostic conditions, similar patterns also occur across disorders, especially those that are related neurocognitively. Thus, clinicians must bear in mind that while deficits (or strengths) in specific cognitive abilities can be reliably identified in individual patients using the WISC-V, the presence of such patterns are not conclusive indicators of specific DSM-5 diagnosis, and other disorders with similar cognitive profiles must be systematically ruled out by the clinician. Conclusive diagnoses cannot be made based on the pattern of scores in WISC-V, or any other single test. As always, clinical diagnosis is a matter of professional judgment informed by scores from all relevant tests administered and combined with information from the clinical interview, parents, teachers, medical history, and educational records.

CLINICAL AND SPECIAL GROUPS: GENERAL DESCRIPTION AND INTELLECTUAL FUNCTIONING

Intellectual Disability

The assessment of an intellectual disability (ID) within the context of psychological assessment has a long and, in some instances, controversial history (Sattler, 2008). As noted by Spruill, Oakland, and Harrison (2005), a "diagnosis involving mental retardation" (intellectual disability) "can have a profound impact on a person's life," particularly on a child. Such a diagnosis can have significant impact on the types of services legally afforded to a child or those they fail to receive. A diagnosis of an ID, whether correct or incorrect, can be carried by a child for the rest of his or her life. Clinicians must weigh this burden and exercise caution when diagnosing a child with this condition. In addition, such a diagnosis should only be reached after a careful evaluation has been conducted involving a comprehensive investigation of the child's intellectual and adaptive skills from various sources in which a child is required to function. An extensive review of records associated with the child abilities and functioning also is required.

The most recent and frequently used definitions of IDs are from the American Association on Intellectual and Developmental Disabilities (AAIDD, 2010; Schalock et al., 2010) and the APA under DSM-5. They define an ID as the presence of intellectual impairment that occurs concurrent with the presence of adaptive deficits during the developmental period (APA, 2013; Schalock et al., 2010), defined as before 18 years of age. Currently only one adaptive domain needs to be impaired in the conceptual, social, or practical areas, unlike earlier more restrictive definitions associated with an ID where greater adaptive deficits, or a deficit in overall adaptation, was required. A deficit or impairment in intellectual functioning under AAIDD and DSM-5 criteria is confirmed during a complete clinical assessment, which includes standardized tests of intelligence and adaptive functioning. For tests with a mean of 100 and a standard deviation (SD) of 15 points, identical to the properties of the WISC-V, a score of 70 or below is sufficiently impaired to be considered intellectually disabled when adaptive functioning is also impaired. Scores as high as 75 also may meet criteria as this accounts for error in test measurement, as a result of a set margin of approximately +5 points (AAIDD, 2010; APA, 2013).

An ID is characterized by a failure to achieve developmental milestones in cognitive, language, motor, and other domains including self-care skills, especially when compared to same-age peers. An ID is further defined by academic problems, problems adapting or adjusting to new environments, problems understanding and following social rules, and other more complex problems involving social situations. According to AAIDD (2010), an ID impacts approximately 1%−3% of the US population, and this prevalence rate seems to be supported globally (Maulik, Mascarenhas, Mathers, Dua, & Saxena, 2011). It should be noted that ID is based on a set of criteria that in and of themselves are not a specific disorder or condition. There are many risk factors and causes of an ID including central nervous system (CNS) disorders and other types of infections. An ID can result from many genetic and environmental consequences, but most commonly results from a combination of polygenetic expression coupled with environmental risk factors (e.g., malnutrition; Sattler, 2008). Increases in the number of and exposure severity to risk factors tend to be associated with increased morbidity. Under DSM-5, the level of ID continues to be described as Mild, Moderate, Severe, and Profound using identical criteria as that of DSM-IV (APA, 2000).

Variability in performance across cognitive abilities tends to decrease the further one moves below the mean ability level of the general population (Nunes et al., 2013). That is, cognitive deficits become more global as you move from mild to moderate to severe and profound functioning levels of ID. For instance, Schuchardt, Gebhardt, and Mäehler (2010) found working memory deficits significantly increased with the degree of ID among adolescents with borderline and mild ID, compared to matched controls. Adolescents with mild ID exhibited the most impairment. Similar results have been found in tests of motor performance and perceptual organization among children and adolescents with mild and borderline ID (Di Blasi, Elia, Buono, Ramakers, & Di Nuovo, 2007; Vuijk, Hartman, Scherder, & Visscher, 2010; Wuang, Wang, Huang, & Su, 2008). Moreover, the discrepancies between verbal and nonverbal performance decreases with decreasing ability levels (Gordon, Duff, Davidson, & Whitaker, 2010). Put another way, variability in performance across different domains of cognitive ability is more likely to be observed among individuals with borderline and mild IDs than in individuals with moderate or severe IDs.

While impairment is less severe among borderline and mild forms of ID, performance on measures of cognitive ability are still reliably distinguished from control groups. For instance, Bonifacci and Snowling (2008) compared speed of information processing among typically developing children, children with dyslexia, and children with borderline ID. The children with borderline functioning were slower and more error prone compared to the other two groups and showed greater variability in performance within tasks, even after outliers had been removed. Alloway (2010) found greater verbal and visuo-spatial working memory deficits among individuals with borderline ID compared to typically developing children ages 7−11 years. Within the domain of memory, Van der Molen, Henry, and Van Luit (2014) reported lower auditory working memory performance relative to visual working memory performance among children with mild to borderline ID. Van der Molen, Van Luit, Jongmans, and Van der Molen (2007) also found that adolescents 13−17 years with mild ID exhibited greater impairment in phonological functioning (storage), but not in automatic rehearsal compared to children without ID matched on chronological age. Schuchardt and colleagues (2010) found similar results for adolescents with mild and borderline IDs compared to children without IDs matched on chronological and mental age.

Global deficits in cognitive functioning are the major defining factor in individuals with moderate and severe IDs. This is similar for children with mild ID, but more variability is observed in the cognitive profile of children with mild ID than in moderate or severe IDs, particularly as the child ages. Previous findings in children with mild and moderate IDs using the WISC-IV and WPPSI-IV demonstrate significant discrepancies in performance from typically developing children across all cognitive domains including verbal, perceptual/visuo-spatial and fluid reasoning, working memory, and processing speed. When compared to typically developing children, the largest effect sizes tend to occur across verbal subtests and composites followed by working memory and perceptual/visuo-spatial and fluid reasoning, with the smallest differences appearing in processing speed subtests (Wechsler, 2003, 2004, 2012a, 2012b).

Intellectual Giftedness

Although clearly not a clinical disorder, we include intellectual giftedness (IG) in this discussion as it is the opposite end of the intellectual spectrum from ID, and because it is a common referral question involving WISC-V evaluations.

Sir Francis Galton was one of the first individuals to note the broad and divergent nature of mental abilities. In one of his seminal works, *Classification of Men According to Their Gifts*, Galton (1869) set forth to delineate the tremendous variability that exists in individuals' cognitive abilities and their hereditary factors, after having examined the records ("scale of merit") of over 200 students who obtained "mathematical honors" at Cambridge University in England. In doing so, he started a scholarly and intellectual dialogue and debate that sometimes has verged on argument, controversy, and heated discord that permeates to this day.

This controversy has sometimes overflowed into the gifted and talented (GT) arena, partially because of the difficulty in its definition and actual identification (Pfeiffer, 2002; Stephens & Karnes, 2000). For example, The National Society for the Gifted and Talented (NSGT) uses the definition set forth by the US Department of Education in 1993 noting that "Children and youth with outstanding talent who perform or show the potential for performing at remarkably high levels of accomplishment when compared with others of their age, experience, or environment." In contrast, the National Association for Gifted Children is more precise in its definition of GT, noting that "Gifted individuals are those who demonstrate outstanding levels of aptitude (defined as an exceptional ability to reason and learn) or competence (documented performance or achievement in top 10% or rarer) in one or more domains. Domains include any structured area of activity with its own symbol system (e.g., mathematics, music, language) and/or set of sensorimotor skills (e.g., painting, dance, sports). Finally, Public Law (P.L. 103−382, Title XIV) defines GT as those children and adolescents who "show evidence of high performance capability in areas such as intellectual, creative, artistic, or leadership capacity, or in specific academic fields, and who require services or activities not ordinarily provided by the school in order to fully develop such capabilities."

Conceptual disagreement in the definition of giftedness extends into operational criteria. For example, educational entities and school districts do not agree on the actual cutoff point to use when employing a specific IQ score to define giftedness. One district may use an IQ score representing the top 2% of the population of children, whereas another may use an IQ score representing the top 5% of a population of children, still others may set the cutoff at two SDs above the mean regardless of the population size (Maddocks, 2018; Stephens & Karnes, 2000). This debate notwithstanding, most operationalized definitions of GT use high intelligence as a primordial characteristic and as a result the Wechsler scales have historically and continually played a major role (see Cao, Jung, & Lee, 2017).

The intellectual profile of children identified as IG typically manifests in greater than average performance on measures of intellectual ability compared to the general population (Wechsler, 2002, 2003, 2004, 2012a, 2012b). However, many gifted children do not display uniformly superior cognitive abilities across all domains (Lohman, Gambrell, & Lakin, 2008; Sweetland, Reina, & Tatti, 2006). While some gifted children obtain higher scores across all cognitive areas compared to same-aged peers, others demonstrate lower relative scores on measures of processing speed and working memory (Rimm, Gilman, & Silverman, 2008; Rowe, Kingsley, & Thompson, 2010). These lower scores are still higher than the population average but are typically weaker relative to their verbal and perceptual reasoning abilities (Raiford, Weiss, Rolfhus, & Coalson, 2005).

Conversely there is evidence for a group of GT spatial learners with weak verbal skills that are worth noting. Individuals with high spatial ability often have relative weaknesses in verbal ability and because of verbally loaded FSIQ measures, may obtain FSIQ scores below cutoff requirements for gifted programs (Andersen, 2014; Mann, 2005, 2006; Silverman, 2002).

Children who are gifted and learning disabled have been described as twice exceptional learners. These children have a disability or dysfunction in at least one cognitive domain despite superior cognitive abilities across all other domains (Foley Nicpon, Allmon, Sieck, & Stinson, 2011). According to Maddocks (2018), summary scores from intellectual assessments may not be a valid representation of the cognitive abilities of twice exceptional students, who have diverse cognitive strengths and weaknesses, and recommends using a different composite score such as the General Ability Index (GAI) or Verbal Comprehension Index (VCI) for identification purposes, as they are less influenced by processing speed or working memory. In circumstances of twice exceptional learners, a multiple criteria identification strategy might be useful and has been strongly advocated in the literature on gifted assessment (Cao et al., 2017). This approach uses combined assessment measures to gain a more complete understanding of the gifted student. Acar, Sen, and Cayirdag (2016) recommend *concurrent* assessments from all instruments providing quantitative data, and McBee, Peters, and Waterman (2014) recommend that the instruments used have both at least moderate levels of reliability and correlations with one another. McBee and colleagues also suggest how the criteria from multiple assessments might be combined for identification purposes. Specifically, they noted that requiring students to reach a minimum score on each assessment instrument may lead to the most specificity in identified students, while requiring students to only reach a minimum score on *one* assessment instrument may yield the highest sensitivity in the identification of students with a wide range of abilities. Alternatively, McBee et al. (2014) recommend that the best compromise may be to use the mean of the instruments.

Autism Spectrum Disorder

The cardinal characteristics of ASD are pervasive and protracted deficits in social communication and social interaction across multiple environments, accompanied by repetitive and extremely restrictive profiles of activities, behavioral repertoire, and personal interests (APA, 2013). Children with ASD either fail to reach or regress in their social and communicative abilities when compared to typically developing children. For example, children with ASD frequently exhibit difficulties responding to their own name, fail to develop the ability to make gestures and use imitative play (e.g., makebelieve play), may develop echolalia (exact repetition or echoing), or refer to themselves using the third pronoun ("he" or "she" third pronoun reversal). Also common are pragmatic language difficulties or idiosyncratic usage of words for things that only make sense to them or those close to them (APA, 2013; Naigles, 2013). On the other hand, children with high-functioning autism are characterized by mostly adequate linguistic skills with some pragmatic difficulties particularly around reacting to social and more abstract linguistic cues. Perseverations about topics that represent favorite subjects only to them, or deficits with prosody, are also common.

Children with ASD exhibit deficits interacting with others and reciprocally engaging others in social "give-and-take" exchanges. For example, children with ASD tend to exhibit little or no eye contact, and research has indicated that they tend to pay attention to different visual cues relative to healthy children (APA, 2013). Children with ASD frequently exhibit incongruent nonverbal social cues as they interact with others, such as inappropriate facial expressions, grimaces, and/or gestures and their linguistic prosody does not match the feelings expressed or the content of their speech. As a result, it is difficult for other individuals to understand their social cues and body language. Many children with ASD also exhibit problems understanding other individuals' point of view (APA, 2013; Baron-Cohen, 1989).

Children with ASD also exhibit unusual behaviors such as hand flapping, unique sounds (e.g., "diggy, diggy, diggy"), walking patterns (e.g., tiptoe walking without suffering from hypertonia), or other idiosyncratic behaviors (APA, 2013). Children with ASD often exhibit overly focused interests in specific features of objects or persons while ignoring other important parts or the rest of the object or person. Similarly, they tend to align objects in a row rather than playing or using the objects for their intended play or function. Perseverations, sometimes misconstrued as obsessions, with specific objects or parts of objects such as road signs, toys, or specific aspects of the weather, are often exhibited.

ASD is perhaps one of the most heterogeneous and complex neurocognitive disorders in the DSM. While a substantial percentage of individuals with ASD fall into the intellectually disabled IQ range (i.e., 2−3 SDs below the mean; Baird et al., 2000; Kielinen, Linna, & Moilanen, 2000), there is substantial support for average, above average, and even superior "peaks" of ability in areas of fluid reasoning, visuo-spatial performance, working memory, verbal reasoning, and processing speed (Dawson, Soulières, Gernsbacher, & Mottron, 2007; Muth, Hönekopp, & Falter, 2014; Scheuffgen, Happeé, Anderson, & Frith, 2000; Shah & Frith, 1983, 1993). Indeed, the specifiers in the new DSM-5 include "with or without accompanying intellectual impairment" (p. 51; APA, 2013) and an understanding of the uneven intellectual profile of a child or adult with ASD. Cognitive functioning in ASD is inversely related to symptom severity (Matson & Shoemaker, 2009). Thus, as symptom severity increases, IQ decreases (Matson, Mahan, Hess, & Fodstad, 2010; Szatmari, White, & Merikangas, 2007). Mayes and Calhoun (2011) found IQ to be the most highly correlated variable to symptom severity among those with ASD.

Across cognitive domains, ability levels are best described as atypical among individuals with ASD. For example, visuo-spatial ability has been shown to be a relative strength for children with ASD in some studies (Mayes & Calhoun, 2008; Osmon, Smerz, Braun, & Plambeck, 2006; Wechsler 2003, 2008, 2012a), but not in others (Bölte, Holtmann, Poustka, Scheurich, & Schmidt, 2007; White & Saldaña, 2011). Typical visuo-spatial tasks used in research on ASD include Figure Disembedding (Witkin, Oltman, Raskin, & Karp, 1971), Block Design (Wechsler, 1974), Mental Rotation (Shepard & Metzler, 1971), and Navon Figures (Navon, 1977). Several decades ago Shah and Frith (1983) postulated an explanation for the variable performance observed across visuo-spatial tasks in ASD by deconstructing the two components involved in visuo-spatial processing: orientation and visualization. Orientation refers to the comprehension of the arrangement of elements within a stimulus pattern and is necessary for tasks such as Block Design, Figure Disembedding, and Object Assembly. Visualization involves the ability to mentally manipulate a pictured stimulus through some form of rotation or inversion. Visualization is also necessary for tasks such as Block Design, Object Assembly, Mental Rotation, and Visual Puzzles. Shah and Frith (1983) suggested that among children with ASD, orientation abilities are good but visualization abilities are weak. Evidence cited to support this hypothesis was the speed and accuracy with which children with ASD could find embedded figures in their 1983 experiment. Other research seemed to support this notion of greater visuo-spatial weaknesses for the ability to hold or form mental images (Hammes & Langdell, 1981; Hermelin, 1978; O'Connor & Hermelin, 1975). Over the decades since Shah and Frith published their research, other studies have found performance peaks on tasks involving both orientation and visualization, but less evidence of superior performance on tasks involving strict mental rotation. A recent meta-analysis of visuo-spatial performance among individuals with ASD found support for superior performance on both Block Design and Figure Disembedding, but less clear support for Mental Rotation and Navon Figures (Muth et al., 2014).

Like visuo-spatial performance, working memory abilities show substantial variability among children with ASD. Discrepancies in the literature seem to indicate this variability is the result of the task choice used to measure working memory (Vogan et al., 2014) and the complexity of the material to be remembered (Williams, Goldstein, & Minshew, 2006a). While basic working memory abilities seem to be intact for materials with low levels of structure, working memory is impaired for materials with more complex levels of organization (Williams et al., 2006a). For verbal working memory, Fein et al. (1996) found young children with autism had the least difficulty recalling digits, some difficulty recalling sentences, and the most difficulty for recall of information from stories. Other studies report intact verbal working memory among individuals with ASD, but deficits in visuo-spatial working memory (Ozonoff & Strayer, 2001; Russell, Jarrold, & Henry, 1996; Steele, Minshew, Luna, & Sweeney, 2007). This is noteworthy insofar as verbal working memory has been described as a core cognitive deficit in ASD (Pennington et al., 1997), yet performance on some measures of visuo-spatial ability are relatively superior in ASD (Muth et al., 2014). Again, the conflicting evidence seems to be modulated by the complexity of the visual stimuli, with basic visual discrimination a relative strength among ASD, whereas sequencing and visual discrimination tasks with greater cognitive loads are a relative weakness in ASD (Williams et al., 2006a). For example, Williams, Goldstein, and Minshew (2006b) compared 38 children with high-functioning autism to a matched control sample on the WRAML

(Wide range assessment of memory and learning; Sheslow & Adams, 1990) and found significant differences between measures of visual and verbal memory involving syntactic and discourse elements. However, there were no differences between the high-functioning autism and control groups on measures of associative memory or immediate memory span tasks. Of the WRAML subtests compared across these two groups, the Finger Windows test, a measure of spatial working memory, was the most powerful discriminator between the comparison groups. Most of these studies used DSM-IV criteria to define study groups. Studies of visuo-spatial ability under the new DSM-5 categorization of ASD are needed to address the role of language deficits and ID in the outcome of visuo-spatial task performance among children with ASD.

Language impairment is another cognitive domain where performance can vary significantly among individuals with ASD. In fact, deficits in social communication are one of the hallmark characteristics of ASD. However, impairment in language is not universal across ASD and can be somewhat normal among individuals with high-functioning autism. For this reason, the DSM-5 requires a specifier of "with or without language impairment" in the diagnosis of ASD. In general, ASD with language impairment is associated with poor performance on most measures of verbal ability and lower global IQ scores. Conversely, ASD without language impairment is associated with higher global IQ (Lindgren, Folstein, Tomblin, & Tager-Flusberg, 2009; Mayes & Calhoun, 2007; Rice, Warren, & Betz, 2005). However, even among nonlanguage-impaired ASD groups, the development of structural language is frequently atypical and there are subtle yet persistent anomalies among even the highest performers (Boucher, 2012). For instance, individuals classified as language normal ASD, high-functioning autism, and former classifications of Asperger's show poor performance on tests of comprehension, have difficulty applying commonalties among category members, and show deficits in morphology, pragmatics, and semantics in some studies (Boucher, 2012; Howlin, 2003; Mayes & Calhoun, 2007; McGregor et al., 2012; Rice et al., 2005). Conversely, these same groups demonstrate normal understanding of basic word meaning, have intact performance across letter-cued word fluency tasks, and overall good expressive language abilities (articulation and syntax) (Howlin, 2003; Kjelgaard & Tager-Flusberg, 2001; Koning & Magill-Evans, 2001; Minshew, Goldstein, & Siegel, 1997; Rice et al., 2005; Saalasti et al., 2008; Seung, 2007; Williams et al., 2006b).

One area of cognitive weakness that tends to be a more consistent deficit among children diagnosed with ASD is in motor processing speed. Children with ASD tend to perform poorly on graphomotor and processing speed subtests (Calhoun & Mayes, 2005; Green et al., 2002; Mayes & Calhoun, 2003a, 2003b, 2007; Nydén, Billstedt, Hjelmquist, & Gillberg, 2001). A recent study of handwriting abilities showed lower performance in children with ASD than control group participants (Ramnauth, 2018). This is not surprising given the comorbidity of motor incoordination disorders and dysgraphia observed among children with ASD (Green et al., 2002; Mayes & Calhoun, 2003a, 2003b, 2007; Szatmari, Archer, Fisman, Streiner, & Wilson, 1995; Wechsler, 2003).

Given the degree of heterogeneity in performance on intelligence tests among children with ASD, a comprehensive examination of all domains measured by the WISC-V may be necessary. The subtests necessary for obtaining the FSIQ will be important for identifying the presence of an ID; however, administration of all primary and secondary subtests is recommended as they will be important for analysis of strengths and weaknesses. For instance, in cases where language impairment is suspected, administration of Picture Span and Visual Puzzles is recommended as this will allow for interpretation of the Nonverbal Index (NVI), which may provide a better strength-based estimate than the traditional Full-Scale IQ or General Ability Index. Even for cases where language impairment is not a primary feature, subtle deficits in pragmatics and comprehension tend to occur. Thus, targeted intervention planning will require administration of secondary verbal subtests (Information and Comprehension) for identifying verbal weaknesses even among high-functioning ASD.

Attention Deficit Hyperactivity Disorder

ADHD is categorized using an epidemiological perspective, as a "high prevalence, low morbidity" condition. Its high prevalence emerges out of the fact that ADHD is one of the most commonly occurring childhood disorders, with varying degrees of severity and developmental expression into adolescence and adulthood. ADHD includes difficulty maintaining sustained focus, disinhibition, or the diminished ability to control one's own behavior or impulsivity, coupled in certain cases, with heightened levels of activity labeled as hyperactivity (APA, 2013). In addition, to reach a diagnostic threshold, the presenting symptoms of ADHD must have negative repercussions for the child such as an impact at school socialization with other children, adolescents or adults, or at home (APA, 2013). It is also imperative to note that the conceptualization of ADHD as a low morbidity condition may be greater than once thought, with detrimental effects on a child's overall level of functioning and future outcomes (e.g., driving accidents, marriage outcome, vocational achievement; APA, 2013).

Given its high prevalence, ADHD has been one of the most researched conditions worldwide (Barkley, 2007). Relatively recent studies from several lines of research are better informing investigators about the broad functional effects of ADHD and its psychopathophysiological effects on CNS functions. For example, recent neuroimaging studies have indicated that children with ADHD exhibit normal CNS maturation, but with delays in development by approximately 3 years (Shaw et al., 2007). These studies suggest that the delay is most pronounced in CNS regions involved in attention and regulatory skills, planning, and higher-order functions. Recent studies additionally have noted delays in overall cortical maturation (Shaw et al., 2012), particularly in a brain area important for functional interhemispheric communication (Gilliam et al., 2011). From a neurochemical standpoint, studies of the association between neurotransmitter levels and tasks of executive functioning have emerged. One study found performance on a reaction time task of visual sustained attention-discrimination was positively associated with levels of norepinephrine (NE) but not dopamine (DA) in children with ADHD, with poorer reaction time scores associated with lower levels of NE (Llorente et al., 2006). Similarly, a visual sustained attention-discrimination task that included alternating attention with exploratory behavior (goal-directed search) was also associated with levels of NE as well as DA among children with ADHD (Llorente et al., 2012). Again, poorer scores on this procedure were correlated with lower levels of these metabolites. These neurochemical abnormalities may be useful in understanding underlying functional deficits and symptoms observed in ADHD and help to explain how the disorder may come to develop and impact CNS maturation and subsequent functional problems.

From DSM-IV to DSM-5, the specific diagnostic criteria of ADHD did not change. Thus, the same 18 symptoms under DSM-IV exist in DSM-5, and they continue to be organized across two subdomains termed inattention and hyperactivity–impulsivity. Like DSM-IV, a diagnosis of ADHD in DSM-5 requires at least six symptoms to be met in each applicable subdomain. Substantial clinical heterogeneity can emerge within ADHD because of the possible permutations that result from a diagnostic requirement of 12 from 18 symptoms. This issue remains problematic from a nosological standpoint and needs to be addressed in future DSM revisions.

While clinical symptoms did not change with the revision to the DSM, several other aspects of the diagnostic criteria did, and these changes have an impact on the neurocognitive profile of ADHD under DSM-5 criteria. First, ADHD was placed in the neurodevelopmental disorders chapter of the DSM-5 to reflect a CNS disorder. Second, the cross-situational or cross-environmental requirement has been given greater focus under the new system in order to underscore the importance of several symptoms occurring in each setting. Additionally, age of onset of the disorder changed. DSM-IV required "symptoms that caused impairment" before 7 years of age" whereas DSM-5 uses "several inattentive or hyperactive-impulsive symptoms that have to be present prior to 12 years of age." This change is in many respects a positive one as many children are not referred for evaluation until school-age, particularly those with primarily inattentive symptoms. Another major change that took place under DSM-5 is that the various clinical "subtypes" (e.g., Predominantly Inattentive Type) were changed and replaced with "presentation specifiers" to delineate the prior subtypes. This was a welcome change as the neuropsychological literature suggests that there may be many more "subtypes" than those previously noted under DSM-IV. In addition, unlike DSM-IV, a comorbid diagnosis with ASD is now permitted under DSM-5.

Concerning cognitive performance, intellectual ability is often observed among children with ADHD to be lower than children without ADHD (Carte, Nigg, & Hinshaw, 1996; Clark, Prior, & Kinsella, 2000; Kuntsi et al., 2004; Mariani & Barkley, 1997; Melnick & Hinshaw, 1996; Rucklidge & Tannock, 2001; Schachar & Logan, 1990). One large population-based twin study of 5-year-olds found a difference of nine IQ points between children with ADHD and those without. This study used Vocabulary and Block Design subtests of the Wechsler Preschool and Primary Scales of Intelligence (WPPSI-R) as measures of IQ, and although it sampled children below the WISC age range, the results were consistent with previous literature using older children and adolescents (Fergusson, Horwood, & Lynskey, 1993; Goodman, Simonoff, & Stevenson, 1995; Rapport, Scanlan, & Denney, 1999; Rucklidge & Tannock, 2001). Cognitive impairment in ADHD is frequently implicated through its relation to deficits in executive functioning skills, specifically the inability to plan and execute a strategy (Willcutt, Doyle, Nigg, Faraone, & Pennington, 2005). Children with both inattentive and hyperactive specifiers of ADHD consistently perform poorly on measures of attention, executive function, and processing speed (Calhoun & Mayes, 2005; Clark et al. 2000; Clark, Prior, & Kinsella, 2002; Naglieri, Goldstein, Iseman, & Schwebach, 2003; Nydén et al., 2001; Saklofske, Schwean, Yackulic, & Quinn, 1994; Seidman, 2006; Willcutt et al., 2005; Wodka et al., 2008). Many also have dysgraphia and/or problems with motor coordination (Gillberg & Kadesjo, 2000; Karatekin, Markiewicz, & Siegel, 2003; Pitcher, Piek, & Hay, 2003; Tannock, 2000; Tseng, Henderson, Chow, & Yao, 2004). Relevant WISC-V subtests that tap these domains include Digit Span, a measure of auditory working memory, and Coding and Symbol Search, measures of processing speed.

Poor performance on tests of verbal fluency or rapid naming are also frequently reported in studies comparing typically developing children to children with ADHD, with similar deficits occurring across both combined and inattentive specifiers (Chhabildas, Pennington, & Willcutt, 2001; Geurts, Verté, Oosterlaan, Roeyers, & Sergeant, 2005; Hinshaw, Carte, Sami, Treuting, & Zupan, 2002; Lockwood, Marcotte, & Stern, 2001; Nigg, Blaskey, Huang-Pollock, & Rappley, 2002; Pasini, Paloscia, Alessandrelli, Porfirio, & Curatolo, 2007; Riccio, Homack, Jarratt, & Wolfe, 2006). Paired-Associate Learning, which combines both verbal fluency and working memory, has been similarly shown to be weaker in ADHD samples compared to control groups (Chang et al., 1999; Douglas & Benezra, 1990).

Pragmatic language difficulties are frequently found among children with ADHD, at levels commensurate with those reported for the former

Asperger's syndrome (Bishop & Baird, 2001; Geurts, Verté, Oosterlaan, Roeyers, & Sergeant, 2004). Mulligan et al. (2009) found that ADHD was most strongly associated with neurocognitive difficulties, including language disorders, among children with more autism symptoms, highlighting the phenotypic overlap between the two disorders. Similarly, Geurts and Embrechts (2008) found pragmatic deficits among ADHD children 7—14 years of age that were indistinguishable from children with ASD. The added complexity of comorbid ASD with ADHD makes it difficult to identify these deficits as belonging to one disorder or the other; however, phenotypic overlap is a common theme among neurocognitive disorders and an accurate reflection of the current state of research in both these disorders.

Disruptive Behavior Disorders

ODD and CD form the Disruptive Behavior Disorders (DBD) category of DSM-5. ODD is characterized by age-inappropriate and persistent displays of angry, defiant, irritable, and oppositional behaviors while CD includes far more aggressive and antisocial behaviors such as inflicting pain, denial of the rights of others, and status offenses (Hinshaw & Lee, 2003). Both ODD and CD are highly comorbid with ADHD, and this comorbidity is an important factor in the neurocognitive profile of DBD. Low intelligence is often considered a precursor to DBD given the correlation between behavior disorders and poor academic achievement (Farrington, 1995; Frick et al., 1991). In addition, some research has found persistent low intelligence and deficits in executive functioning among delinquent children compared to the general population (Frick & Viding, 2009; Lynam & Henry, 2001; Moffitt, 2006). However, some experts have argued that studies showing a significant relation between deficits in executive functioning or low IQ and behavior disorders have failed to control for comorbid ADHD (Burke, Loeber, & Birmaher, 2002; Hogan, 1999). Indeed, when studies control for ADHD, the relation between ODD and CD to weak neuropsychological functioning tends to either disappear or become nonsignificant (Clark et al., 2000; Klorman et al., 1999; Kuhne, Schachar, & Tannock, 1997; Mayes & Calhoun, 2007; Van Goozen et al., 2004).

Still, a consistent deficit in receptive vocabulary has been observed among children with antisocial behaviors (Kaufman & Kaufman, 1990; Lansing et al., 2014; Lynam, Moffitt, & Stouthamer—Loeber, 1993; Moffitt & Caspi, 2001; Rosso, Falasco, & Koller, 1984). Additionally, there seems to be evidence that spatial and perceptual forms of cognitive processing may be related to early-onset of antisocial behaviors (Lansing et al., 2014; Raine, Yaralian, Reynolds, Venables, & Mednick, 2002). However, in all other domains, the evidence supports average cognitive functioning for individuals with DBD. For instance, DBD groups do not differ significantly from control children on measures of graphomotor or processing speed tasks (Mayes & Calhoun, 2007). In fact, some studies have shown the opposite trend, with higher intelligence associated with increased conduct problems in children with persistent antisocial behavior, and at a minimum, commensurate intelligence levels with control groups (Christian, Frick, Hill, Tyler, & Frazer, 1997; Lahey et al., 1995). Thus, incorporating more recent evidence on neurocognitive functioning and DBD, significant difficulties with attention, executive function, learning, or memory would not be expected among children with DBD, assuming no comorbid ADHD was present (Mayes & Calhoun, 2007; Oosterlaan, Scheres, & Sergeant, 2005; Pennington & Ozonoff, 1996; Pickering & Gathercole, 2004).

Traumatic Brain Injury

Traumatic brain injury (TBI) is an acquired injury resulting from sudden trauma causing damage to the brain (Hayden, Jandial, Duenas, Mahajan, & Levy, 2007; McCrea, 2007). Although several nosological systems exist (e.g., ICD-10; American Academy of Neurology), the US Department of Defense, Department of Veterans Affairs (2008) provides one of the most comprehensive and updated criteria for classification purposes associated with such injuries. Using this nosological system TBIs are classified as "mild," "moderate," or severe" depending on the Glasgow Coma Scale (GCS) score, presence and length of loss or alteration of consciousness (LOC), and presence and length of posttraumatic amnesia (PTA). TBIs can also be classified as open (penetrating) or closed (nonpenetrating, blunt). In general and basic terms, a closed TBI results when the head violently hits an object or when an object violently and suddenly hits the head, without piercing the skull. In contrast, an open TBI results when perforation of the skull takes place and a projectile enters (or the head violently hits an object) impacting brain tissue (brain parenchyma). TBIs can range from mild concussion to severe TBIs and the resulting symptoms depend on the extent of the damage to the brain and other parameters as noted above (Hayden et al., 2007). A child with a mild TBI may remain conscious or may experience a brief loss of consciousness for a few seconds or minutes. Sports-related concussion is a common form of mild TBI that has been widely overlooked historically but is now receiving focused attention in schools at all levels. The effects of even mild TBI can be exacerbated if the student athlete is allowed to return to play the sport before fully recovering, or if he or she suffers multiple mild concussions. Diagnosis of more severe TBIs requires greater alterations in conscious states as well as the presence of other indicators (lower score on the GCS, greater PTA, etc., McCrea, 2007).

TBI is associated with a broad array of neuropsychological deficits in language skills (verbal reasoning, verbal fluency), visual-perceptual and constructional skills, attention and memory, executive functions, and speeded tasks (Yeates, 2000; Yeates et al., 2002). Although there is variability associated with the age at the time of insult, as well as the location and the severity of the insult, longitudinal and prospective studies support the notion that these deficits are persistent for moderate-to-severe TBIs, with only minor or partial recovery occurring in the first year postinjury for some children (Anderson, Catroppa, Morse, Haritou, & Rosenfeld, 2000; Catroppa, Anderson, Morse, Haritou, & Rosenfeld, 2007; Chadwick, Rutter, Brown, Shaffer, & Traub, 1981; Chadwick, Rutter, Shaffer, & Shrout, 1981; Jaffe, Polisar, Fay, & Liao, 1995; Knights et al., 1991; Yeates et al., 2002). Age of the child at injury is an important predictor of postinjury ability according to Catroppa et al. (2007) because the interruption on an emerging cognitive ability during critical developmental periods may prevent normal development of this ability following injury. The level of impairment as well as the long-term outcome of cognitive functioning following childhood TBI is worse for younger children with severe injury compared to both older children with severe injury and all children with mild or moderate injuries (Anderson, Brown, Newitt, & Hoile, 2009; Anderson, Brown, Newitt, & Hoile, 2011).

INTELLECTUAL ASSESSMENT WITH THE WECHSLER INTELLIGENCE SCALE FOR CHILDREN—FIFTH EDITION IN DIAGNOSTIC AND TREATMENT PLANNING

The general structure of the WISC-V expands upon the WISC-IV Index and subtest score offering. While it retains the FSIQ and factor-based Index scores, it also provides multiple theoretically driven composite scores that are not included in the FSIQ assessment. These ancillary Index scores expand the domains measured by the WISC-V and include the Quantitative Reasoning Index (QRI), Auditory Working Memory Index (AWMI), NVI, GAI, and Cognitive Processing Index (CPI). The theoretical foundations of these indexes are described in greater detail in Chapter 4. The AWMI is comprised of the same subtests as the WISC-IV WMI, allowing a direct comparison of working memory ability across the two editions. The NVI, GAI, and CPI provide comprehensive measures of abilities which can be interpreted independently or compared to the FSIQ for various clinical purposes.

A further enhancement in the WISC-V is the development and inclusion of complementary subtests and indexes. These are not part of the main battery and are not directly related to the primary indexes or FSIQ. Instead, they measure skills and abilities related to the development of reading, writing, and mathematics and are included to enhance the evaluation of children with learning disabilities and other clinical conditions. Because they were not designed to measure intellectual ability, performance on these tasks may differ from performance on traditional intellectual measures. The development of the WISC-V primary, ancillary, and complementary Index scores allows greater flexibility and content coverage to practitioners utilizing the

WISC-V. It enhances the ability of the practitioner to focus the assessment on the cognitive abilities related to the needs of the child while retaining the global ability and Index scores required for a comprehensive intellectual assessment.

In addition to the inclusion of ancillary and complementary subtests and indexes, the digitally administered version of WISC-V on Q-interactive® has provided new data among both clinical and nonclinical groups for exploration. The first studies to report on the subtest and Index scores of the digitally administered WISC-V are presented in conjunction with the results from the traditional paper format. See the Q-interactive technical reports available on Pearson's WISC-V homepage (pearsonclinical.com) for more details on the methods and procedures used to evaluate the utility and clinical validity of the digital administration of WISC-V with special groups.

The WISC-V subtest and composite data for selected special groups with matched control comparisons are presented in Tables 11.1–11.9. These tables represent the scores obtained in the standardization clinical samples from the paper administration of WISC-V. Also included is an overview of the pattern of Index and subtest scores observed for five of the selected special groups using the digital format of the WISC-V (Q-interactive).

Note that the inclusion criteria for participants in the special groups described below are identical across paper and digital formats of the WISC-V, but the samples do not overlap.

Wechsler Intelligence Scale for Children—Fifth Edition Performance in Special Groups

Intellectual Giftedness

Children in the IG group were selected for inclusion if they had previously obtained global scores of intelligence at least two SDs above the mean on any standard measure of cognitive ability. In addition, all children in the IG sample were currently receiving services in school for IG. Data for the GT group who were administered the traditional paper format of WISC-V are shown in Table 11.1.

On the WISC-V paper test, children from the IG group obtained a mean FSIQ score of 127.5. Consistent with previous research using the WISC-IV among gifted children, the highest scores were observed on the VCI and the lowest scores on the Processing Speed Index (PSI). All primary Index scores were greater than 1 SD above the mean, except for the PSI. A similar pattern is observed among subtest scores, with the highest subtest scores observed in the Verbal Comprehension and Working Memory domains, and the lowest scores in the Processing Speed domain. All primary subtest scores, except for Picture Concepts, Picture Span, and the Processing Speed subtests, were greater than 1 SD above the mean.

TABLE 11.1 Mean Performance of Intellectually Gifted and Matched Comparison Groups

Subtest/Process/ Composite Score	Intellectually Gifted		Matched Control		Group Mean Comparison				Standard Difference[a]
	Mean	SD	Mean	SD	n	Difference	t Value	P Value	
SI	15.1	2.4	10.9	2.7	95	−4.16	−10.53	<.01	−1.63
VC	14.9	2.3	11.2	2.8	95	−3.77	−9.62	<.01	−1.47
IN	14.6	2.5	11.0	2.8	95	−3.53	−9.93	<.01	−1.33
CO	14.1	2.5	10.9	2.9	95	−3.19	−7.64	<.01	−1.18
BD	13.9	2.4	10.9	2.6	95	−3.03	−9.50	<.01	−1.21
VP	13.5	2.1	11.0	2.4	95	−2.47	−6.97	<.01	−1.10
MR	13.3	2.8	10.9	2.6	95	−2.38	−6.19	<.01	−0.88
FW	13.8	2.5	10.8	2.4	95	−2.95	−8.55	<.01	−1.20
PC	12.3	2.9	10.5	2.9	95	−1.76	−3.81	<.01	−0.61
AR	13.9	2.5	10.6	2.4	95	−3.24	−8.67	<.01	−1.32
DS	14.0	2.5	11.0	2.6	95	−3.00	−7.69	<.01	−1.18
PS	12.3	2.9	10.4	2.5	95	−1.93	−4.52	<.01	−0.71
LN	14.3	2.5	11.1	2.8	93	−3.20	−7.91	<.01	−1.21
CD	12.1	2.7	9.9	2.6	94	−2.19	−5.78	<.01	−0.83
SS	12.5	2.7	10.2	2.9	91	−2.27	−5.23	<.01	−0.81
CA	11.8	3.2	9.8	2.9	95	−2.01	−4.68	<.01	−0.66
VCI	127.7	12.3	105.8	12.9	95	−21.97	−11.09	<.01	−1.74

VSI	121.2	11.5	105.2	12.2	95	−15.98	−9.55	<.01	−1.35
FRI	120.3	12.0	105.1	12.3	95	−15.26	−8.80	<.01	−1.26
WMI	117.9	11.7	104.0	12.1	95	−13.86	−7.33	<.01	−1.16
PSI	112.9	13.5	100.4	13.5	90	−12.44	−6.05	<.01	−0.92
FSIQ	127.5	8.8	105.7	12.2	94	−21.85	−13.19	<.01	−2.05
QRI	122.1	11.8	104.1	11.4	95	−18.04	−10.41	<.01	−1.55
AWMI	123.0	12.9	105.9	13.0	93	−17.13	−8.49	<.01	−1.32
NVI	122.9	10.5	104.6	11.8	94	−18.28	−10.80	<.01	−1.64
GAI	127.1	9.6	106.3	12.4	95	−20.83	−12.54	<.01	−1.88
CPI	118.8	11.0	102.1	12.4	90	−16.73	−8.71	<.01	−1.43

[a]The Standard Difference is the difference of the two test means divided by the square root of the pooled variance, computed using Cohen's (1996) Formula 10.4.

Source: © Pearson NCS 2014. Reprinted with permission.

TABLE 11.2 Mean Performance of Intellectual Disability—Mild Severity and Matched Control Groups

Subtest/Process/Composite Score	Intellectual Disability—Mild Severity		Matched Control		Group Mean Comparison					
	Mean	SD	Mean	SD	n	Difference	t Value	P Value	Standard Difference[a]
SI	3.8	2.1	9.5	3.2	74	5.74	13.92	<.01	2.12
VC	3.9	1.9	9.0	3.2	74	5.07	12.40	<.01	1.93
IN	3.8	1.9	9.6	3.1	74	5.76	15.00	<.01	2.24
CO	4.0	1.9	8.7	2.9	74	4.69	12.37	<.01	1.91
BD	3.9	2.2	10.1	2.9	74	6.22	14.18	<.01	2.42
VP	4.1	1.6	10.3	2.9	74	6.22	16.03	<.01	2.66
MR	4.1	2.6	10.0	3.4	74	5.89	11.62	<.01	1.95
FW	4.3	2.1	9.8	3.3	74	5.46	11.96	<.01	1.97
PC	4.7	2.5	9.7	3.4	74	5.03	10.16	<.01	1.69
AR	3.2	1.8	9.6	3.2	74	6.34	13.39	<.01	2.44
DS	3.4	1.9	9.9	2.8	73	6.51	15.55	<.01	2.72
PS	4.3	2.3	9.7	2.9	74	5.42	11.49	<.01	2.07
LN	3.5	2.1	9.7	2.7	73	6.18	14.23	<.01	2.56
CD	4.6	2.9	9.6	2.8	70	5.00	11.06	<.01	1.75

SS	5.3	3.3	9.5	2.2	67	4.15	8.51	<.01	1.48
CA	6.1	3.4	10.8	2.5	73	4.67	8.61	<.01	1.56
VCI	66.0	10.9	96.1	16.4	74	30.14	14.21	<.01	2.16
VSI	66.0	9.9	101.1	14.6	74	35.14	16.72	<.01	2.82
FRI	67.0	11.0	99.3	16.1	74	32.34	13.49	<.01	2.35
WMI	65.1	10.5	98.7	14.6	73	33.60	14.93	<.01	2.64
PSI	71.6	16.2	97.3	10.9	67	25.78	11.45	<.01	1.87
FSIQ	60.9	8.9	98.0	15.6	69	37.07	16.22	<.01	2.92
QRI	64.2	9.7	98.1	15.1	74	33.86	15.16	<.01	2.67
AWMI	62.2	11.5	99.2	13.8	72	36.96	15.96	<.01	2.91
NVI	62.1	8.7	99.5	15.2	70	37.40	16.46	<.01	3.02
GAI	63.5	8.8	97.9	15.7	74	34.46	15.95	<.01	2.71
CPI	63.4	12.3	97.6	13.4	67	34.19	14.75	<.01	2.66

[a]The Standard Difference is the difference of the two test means divided by the square root of the pooled variance, computed using Cohen's (1996) Formula 10.4.

Source: © Pearson NCS 2014. Reprinted with permission.

TABLE 11.3 Mean Performance of Intellectual Disability–Moderate Severity and Matched Control Groups

Subtest/ Process/ Composite Score	Intellectual Disability–Moderate Severity		Matched Control		Group Mean Comparison					
	Mean	SD	Mean	SD	n	Difference	t Value	P Value	Standard Difference[a]	
SI	2.2	1.9	10.1	3.5	37	7.89	11.65	<.01	2.80	
VC	2.4	1.7	9.6	3.1	37	7.22	11.75	<.01	2.89	
IN	2.3	1.8	9.6	2.7	37	7.30	13.42	<.01	3.18	
CO	2.6	2.4	9.5	2.9	37	6.89	11.37	<.01	2.59	
BD	2.4	1.5	9.5	2.9	37	7.14	13.18	<.01	3.09	
VP	2.8	1.9	9.3	3.0	37	6.51	12.72	<.01	2.59	
MR	2.4	2.1	9.7	3.3	37	7.30	11.16	<.01	2.64	
FW	3.2	2.1	9.4	3.6	36	6.17	9.24	<.01	2.09	
PC	3.1	2.5	9.9	3.0	37	6.81	10.76	<.01	2.47	
AR	2.2	1.5	10.0	2.9	37	7.81	14.87	<.01	3.38	
DS	2.0	1.4	9.7	3.0	34	7.74	13.32	<.01	3.31	
PS	3.5	2.3	10.2	3.4	36	6.69	9.94	<.01	2.30	
LN	2.6	1.7	9.9	3.0	33	7.27	11.72	<.01	2.98	
CD	3.1	2.6	10.4	2.7	37	7.32	10.86	<.01	2.76	

SS	3.2	2.7	9.9	2.8	37	6.73	10.05	<.01	2.45
CA	4.6	3.5	10.2	2.8	37	5.68	8.56	<.01	1.79
VCI	55.2	11.3	99.4	15.2	37	44.19	13.37	<.01	3.30
VSI	56.8	9.6	96.6	14.6	37	39.86	14.71	<.01	3.23
FRI	58.6	12.0	97.1	17.3	36	38.44	11.36	<.01	2.58
WMI	58.3	10.6	99.4	17.0	33	41.09	11.48	<.01	2.90
PSI	59.3	15.8	101.1	12.6	37	41.76	11.31	<.01	2.92
FSIQ	49.7	8.9	98.5	16.8	33	48.79	13.72	<.01	3.63
QRI	57.1	10.6	98.2	15.2	36	41.08	13.15	<.01	3.14
AWMI	54.1	9.4	99.0	15.2	32	44.94	14.12	<.01	3.56
NVI	53.4	10.1	98.0	17.2	35	44.54	13.27	<.01	3.16
GAI	54.3	9.4	97.8	16.4	36	43.50	13.40	<.01	3.25
CPI	52.5	12.7	99.9	15.8	33	47.45	12.26	<.01	3.31

[a]The Standard Difference is the difference of the two test means divided by the square root of the pooled variance, computed using Cohen's (1996) Formula 10.4.

Source: © Pearson NCS 2014. Reprinted with permission.

TABLE 11.4 Mean Performance of Borderline Intellectual Functioning and Matched Control Groups

Subtest/Process/ Composite Score	Borderline Intellectual Functioning		Matched Control		Group Mean Comparison					Standard Difference[a]
	Mean	SD	Mean	SD	n	Difference	t Value	P Value		
SI	7.0	1.4	9.0	2.9	20	2.00	2.59	.02		0.88
VC	6.2	2.0	8.7	2.9	19	2.53	3.33	<.01		1.02
IN	6.8	2.2	9.1	2.7	20	2.30	2.86	.01		0.93
CO	6.6	2.3	9.2	3.1	20	2.60	3.25	<.01		0.95
BD	6.8	2.1	9.6	2.5	20	2.85	4.53	<.01		1.23
VP	7.1	1.7	9.4	2.4	20	2.30	3.15	<.01		1.11
MR	8.5	3.3	9.8	2.2	20	1.30	1.44	.17		0.46
FW	7.1	1.9	9.3	1.8	20	2.25	3.39	<.01		1.22
PC	7.3	2.7	10.6	3.1	20	3.30	3.94	<.01		1.14
AR	6.5	2.2	9.7	2.7	20	3.20	4.38	<.01		1.30
DS	5.9	2.6	9.6	2.8	20	3.75	5.10	<.01		1.39
PS	6.5	2.3	9.4	2.9	19	2.84	3.57	<.01		1.09
LN	5.7	2.0	9.7	3.3	20	4.05	5.00	<.01		1.48
CD	9.4	2.2	9.3	2.7	20	−0.10	−0.13	.90		−0.04

SS	8.9	3.0	9.5	3.0	19	0.53	0.63	.54	0.18
CA	10.4	2.5	11.1	3.2	20	0.70	0.70	.49	0.24
VCI	81.7	7.6	93.1	13.8	19	11.42	3.08	<.01	1.03
VSI	83.1	8.3	97.2	11.6	20	14.10	5.06	<.01	1.40
FRI	87.1	11.7	97.3	9.0	20	10.25	2.88	<.01	0.98
WMI	78.2	11.9	97.1	14.2	19	18.95	5.10	<.01	1.45
PSI	95.1	11.9	96.4	13.1	19	1.37	0.33	.75	0.11
FSIQ	80.4	5.7	94.5	9.2	19	14.16	5.53	<.01	1.85
QRI	81.3	7.8	97.1	10.4	20	15.75	4.97	<.01	1.71
AWMI	76.6	11.1	98.0	14.9	20	21.35	6.07	<.01	1.63
NVI	82.1	7.9	95.0	8.6	19	12.89	4.18	<.01	1.56
GAI	80.8	7.5	94.6	11.8	19	13.79	4.26	<.01	1.39
CPI	84.0	10.4	95.7	11.5	19	11.74	3.33	<.01	1.07

[a]The Standard Difference is the difference of the two test means divided by the square root of the pooled variance, computed using Cohen's (1996) Formula 10.4.

Source: © Pearson NCS 2014. Reprinted with permission.

TABLE 11.5 Mean Performance of Attention Deficit Hyperactivity Disorder and Matched Control Groups

Subtest/Process/ Composite Score	Attention Deficit Hyperactivity Disorder		Matched Control		Group Mean Comparison				
	Mean	SD	Mean	SD	n	Difference	t Value	P Value	Standard Difference[a]
SI	9.6	2.2	10.3	3.0	48	0.67	1.27	.21	0.25
VC	9.6	2.4	10.7	2.4	48	1.17	2.41	.02	0.49
IN	9.6	2.7	10.3	2.7	48	0.71	1.34	.19	0.26
CO	9.5	2.8	10.3	2.7	48	0.79	1.61	.11	0.29
BD	9.4	3.1	9.8	2.4	48	0.35	0.70	.49	0.13
VP	9.6	3.3	10.8	2.7	48	1.13	1.94	.06	0.37
MR	9.4	2.5	10.4	2.4	48	1.02	2.14	.04	0.42
FW	9.8	3.0	10.5	3.0	48	0.73	1.18	.24	0.24
PC	8.9	2.8	10.4	2.9	48	1.42	2.38	.02	0.50
AR	8.5	2.6	10.6	2.4	48	2.19	4.31	<.01	0.88
DS	9.2	2.6	10.5	2.3	47	1.23	2.99	<.01	0.50
PS	8.9	2.8	10.1	2.8	48	1.23	2.08	.04	0.44
LN	9.0	3.0	10.0	2.7	47	1.02	1.64	.11	0.36

CD	8.4	2.7	10.0	2.5	48	1.69	3.48	<.01	0.65
SS	9.5	3.0	9.9	2.7	47	.36	.57	.57	0.13
CA	9.5	2.6	10.0	2.8	48	.52	.99	.33	0.19
VCI	97.8	11.4	102.7	13.2	48	4.90	1.98	.05	0.40
VSI	97.3	16.7	101.5	12.4	48	4.17	1.51	.14	0.28
FRI	97.6	13.4	102.6	13.1	48	5.04	1.94	.06	0.38
WMI	94.8	13.3	101.7	12.3	47	6.91	2.98	<.01	0.54
PSI	94.2	13.9	99.9	12.5	47	5.70	2.19	.03	0.43
FSIQ	95.6	11.7	102.2	10.2	47	6.66	3.20	<.01	0.61
QRI	94.8	14.2	103.1	12.7	48	8.33	3.13	<.01	0.62
AWMI	95.2	13.3	101.4	11.5	47	6.23	2.73	<.01	0.50
NVI	94.4	13.1	101.7	12.3	48	7.29	3.01	<.01	0.57
GAI	97.1	13.3	102.3	11.1	48	5.21	2.23	.03	0.43
CPI	92.8	12.6	100.8	12.2	46	8.00	3.18	<.01	0.65

[a]The Standard Difference is the difference of the two test means divided by the square root of the pooled variance, computed using Cohen's (1996) Formula 10.4.

Source: © Pearson NCS 2014. Reprinted with permission.

TABLE 11.6 Mean Performance of Disruptive Behavior Disorder and Matched Control Groups

Subtest/Process/Composite Score	Disruptive Behavior		Matched Control		Group Mean Comparison					Standard Difference[a]
	Mean	SD	Mean	SD	n	Difference	t Value	p Value		
SI	9.4	2.6	10.4	3.5	21	1.00	1.10	.28		0.32
VC	8.4	2.3	8.9	2.8	21	0.52	0.89	.38		0.20
IN	9.0	3.0	9.9	2.5	21	0.90	1.17	.25		0.33
CO	9.3	3.3	9.5	3.1	21	0.19	0.18	.86		0.06
BD	9.5	2.7	8.2	2.9	21	−1.24	−1.34	.20		−0.44
VP	9.5	2.7	9.1	2.6	21	−0.43	−0.57	.58		−0.16
MR	9.2	3.1	9.4	2.7	21	0.19	0.26	.80		0.07
FW	8.8	2.8	9.2	2.8	21	0.38	.50	.62		0.14
PC	9.4	2.6	9.3	2.1	21	−0.14	−.20	.84		−0.06
AR	9.0	3.1	9.3	3.3	21	0.29	0.31	.76		0.09
DS	9.3	3.4	9.4	3.1	21	0.10	0.09	.93		0.03
PS	9.0	3.0	8.8	2.6	21	−0.24	−0.24	.81		−0.09
LN	8.7	3.8	9.3	2.2	21	0.62	0.55	.59		0.20
CD	8.7	3.2	8.2	3.4	21	−0.52	−0.55	.59		−0.16
SS	8.8	3.2	9.0	3.1	21	0.24	0.24	.81		0.08

CA	9.6	2.4	9.4	2.4	21	− 0.19	− 0.24	.82	− 0.08
VCI	94.1	11.8	98.2	13.3	21	4.14	1.27	.22	0.33
VSI	97.1	13.9	92.6	13.3	21	− 4.52	− 1.10	.29	− 0.33
FRI	94.4	15.2	95.9	13.3	21	1.52	0.44	.66	0.11
WMI	95.3	13.7	95.0	13.2	21	− 0.29	− 0.06	.95	− 0.02
PSI	92.8	17.1	92.1	16.5	21	− 0.62	− 0.12	.91	− 0.04
FSIQ	93.3	12.4	93.5	12.8	21	0.19	0.06	.96	0.02
QRI	93.8	13.7	95.5	13.7	21	1.71	0.47	.64	0.12
AWMI	94.5	18.0	96.6	13.1	21	2.10	0.39	.70	0.13
NVI	93.6	12.5	91.3	12.7	21	− 2.29	− 0.73	.48	− 0.18
GAI	94.1	12.0	95.1	13.2	21	0.95	0.31	.76	0.08
CPI	92.8	14.3	92.6	14.7	21	− 0.24	− 0.05	.96	− 0.02

[a] The Standard Difference is the difference of the two test means divided by the square root of the pooled variance, computed using Cohen's (1996) Formula 10.4.

Source: © Pearson NCS 2014. Reprinted with permission.

TABLE 11.7 Mean Performance of Traumatic Brain Injury and Matched Control Groups

Subtest/Process/ Composite Score	Traumatic Brain Injury		Matched Control		Group Mean Comparison				Standard Difference[a]
	Mean	SD	Mean	SD	n	Difference	t Value	P Value	
SI	8.5	2.6	9.6	2.0	17	1.18	1.47	.16	0.51
VC	8.1	3.1	10.1	2.7	19	2.00	2.76	.01	0.69
IN	7.9	2.8	10.2	2.6	20	2.25	3.10	<.01	0.83
CO	8.1	2.4	9.5	3.1	20	1.40	1.71	.10	0.51
BD	7.7	3.1	11.1	3.6	19	3.37	3.00	<.01	1.00
VP	7.6	3.4	10.5	2.6	20	2.85	2.72	.01	0.94
MR	8.2	3.4	11.5	2.7	20	3.35	3.19	<.01	1.09
FW	7.8	3.6	10.9	3.1	20	3.10	2.98	<.01	0.92
PC	7.9	3.8	11.3	2.5	20	3.45	3.13	<.01	1.07
AR	7.3	3.0	9.8	1.8	20	2.50	2.86	.01	1.01
DS	7.7	3.1	10.4	3.0	20	2.65	2.74	.01	0.87
PS	7.6	2.6	9.8	2.6	20	2.25	2.64	.02	0.87
LN	7.9	3.1	9.8	2.0	20	1.90	2.93	<.01	0.73
CD	7.2	4.0	9.8	2.0	19	2.58	2.71	.01	0.82
SS	7.4	3.9	9.1	2.4	19	1.74	1.67	.11	0.54

CA	8.5	3.8	10.1	3.0	19	1.53	1.08	.29	0.45
VCI	88.9	12.9	98.3	11.7	17	9.41	2.51	.02	0.76
VSI	87.5	15.9	104.2	14.6	19	16.68	2.99	<.01	1.09
FRI	88.4	18.0	106.9	13.6	20	18.45	3.56	<.01	1.16
WMI	86.2	15.5	100.2	12.8	20	14.00	2.94	<.01	0.98
PSI	84.1	22.2	97.2	8.2	19	13.05	2.55	.02	0.78
FSIQ	83.3	14.1	103.3	13.0	17	20.00	4.10	<.01	1.47
QRI	85.6	17.5	101.7	11.7	20	16.05	3.31	<.01	1.08
AWMI	87.7	16.3	100.3	11.9	20	12.65	3.07	<.01	0.89
NVI	85.0	17.3	104.3	11.8	19	19.32	3.57	<.01	1.30
GAI	85.4	13.5	103.9	12.1	17	18.53	4.15	<.01	1.45
CPI	83.5	18.1	98.2	10.0	19	14.68	3.13	<.01	1.00

[a]The Standard Difference is the difference of the two test means divided by the square root of the pooled variance, computed using Cohen's (1996) Formula 10.4.

TABLE 11.8 Mean Performance of Autism Spectrum Disorder With Language Impairment and Matched Control Groups

Subtest/ Process/ Composite Score	Autism Spectrum Disorder With Language Impairment		Matched Control		Group Mean Comparison				
	Mean	SD	Mean	SD	n	Difference	t Value	P Value	Standard Difference[a]
SI	6.5	3.3	10.9	2.8	29	4.38	5.22	<.01	1.43
VC	6.1	3.6	10.6	2.6	29	4.48	5.64	<.01	1.43
IN	5.8	3.5	11.2	2.9	29	5.34	6.39	<.01	1.66
CO	4.8	3.0	11.1	3.0	30	6.23	8.56	<.01	2.08
BD	7.2	4.1	10.5	2.8	30	3.30	3.67	<.01	0.94
VP	6.7	4.3	11.1	2.4	29	4.45	4.86	<.01	1.28
MR	7.1	4.2	10.3	2.2	30	3.13	3.77	<.01	0.93
FW	7.4	3.6	10.3	3.5	30	2.93	3.07	<.01	0.83
PC	6.3	4.4	11.6	2.2	29	5.21	6.60	<.01	1.50
AR	5.4	3.5	10.6	2.5	30	5.23	6.68	<.01	1.72
DS	5.4	3.9	10.8	2.8	30	5.43	6.37	<.01	1.60
PS	6.9	3.8	10.7	3.0	30	3.77	4.07	<.01	1.10

LN	5.0	3.6	10.3	2.3	29	5.24	7.40	<.01	1.73
CD	5.2	3.5	9.3	3.2	29	4.07	4.94	<.01	1.21
SS	6.2	3.7	9.9	2.7	26	3.69	5.30	<.01	1.14
CA	5.8	3.4	9.7	3.0	29	3.93	4.92	<.01	1.23
VCI	80.4	18.2	104.1	13.6	28	23.68	5.51	<.01	1.47
VSI	82.8	22.3	104.4	13.4	29	21.62	4.49	<.01	1.18
FRI	84.3	20.6	101.6	13.9	30	17.30	3.75	<.01	0.98
WMI	77.6	19.4	104.1	13.9	30	26.47	6.05	<.01	1.57
PSI	75.8	19.0	96.9	14.8	26	21.12	5.41	<.01	1.24
FSIQ	76.3	19.1	102.1	14.5	28	25.82	5.75	<.01	1.52
QRI	78.9	19.2	102.5	15.8	30	23.67	5.07	<.01	1.35
AWMI	72.3	21.6	102.4	12.6	29	30.14	7.14	<.01	1.70
NVI	79.9	20.1	102.8	13.8	28	22.86	4.78	<.01	1.33
GAI	81.8	18.6	102.9	14.2	28	21.18	4.82	<.01	1.28
CPI	74.4	18.4	100.0	13.5	26	25.62	6.24	<.01	1.59

[a]The Standard Difference is the difference of the two test means divided by the square root of the pooled variance, computed using Cohen's (1996) Formula 10.4.

Source: ©Pearson NCS 2014. Reprinted with permission.

TABLE 11.9 Mean Performance of Autism Spectrum Disorder Without Language Impairment and Matched Control Groups

Subtest/ Process/ Composite Score	Autism Spectrum Disorder Without Language Impairment		Matched Control		Group Mean Comparison				
	Mean	SD	Mean	SD	n	Difference	t Value	P Value	Standard Difference[a]
SI	10.8	3.2	10.3	2.4	31	−0.55	−0.98	.34	−0.19
VC	9.9	3.0	11.5	2.6	32	1.56	2.13	.04	0.56
IN	10.5	3.7	10.8	2.5	32	0.31	0.47	.64	0.10
CO	8.9	2.9	10.1	3.2	32	1.19	1.48	.15	0.39
BD	9.4	3.6	11.2	2.9	32	1.78	2.34	.03	0.54
VP	10.8	2.9	10.0	3.2	32	−0.84	−1.22	.23	−0.28
MR	10.2	3.2	10.6	2.2	32	0.47	0.63	.53	0.17
FW	10.2	3.5	10.5	2.9	32	0.38	0.49	.62	0.12
PC	9.9	3.2	10.9	2.6	32	0.97	1.28	.21	0.33
AR	10.4	3.8	10.8	2.8	32	0.31	0.38	.71	0.09
DS	9.2	3.2	10.4	2.3	32	1.22	1.69	.10	0.44
PS	9.3	3.4	11.0	2.7	32	1.75	2.74	.01	0.57

LN	8.7	3.7	10.9	3.0	32	2.22	2.61	.01	0.66
CD	7.8	3.4	10.0	3.0	31	2.23	2.39	.02	0.70
SS	8.4	3.4	9.3	3.0	32	0.91	1.02	.32	0.28
CA	9.8	3.4	9.7	2.8	32	-0.09	-0.11	.91	-0.03
VCI	102.5	14.4	104.8	11.6	31	2.26	0.77	.45	0.17
VSI	100.7	17.1	103.4	14.5	32	2.72	0.77	.44	0.17
FRI	100.9	17.5	103.5	12.7	32	2.53	0.65	.52	0.17
WMI	95.4	16.8	104.3	12.1	32	8.81	2.52	.02	0.60
PSI	89.4	18.4	98.0	14.7	31	8.58	1.79	.08	0.52
FSIQ	98.3	17.4	105.0	11.9	30	6.63	1.75	.09	0.44
QRI	101.7	19.1	103.5	12.4	32	1.78	0.47	.64	0.11
AWMI	94.1	17.2	103.8	12.2	32	9.78	2.59	.01	0.66
NVI	97.5	17.7	104.4	13.9	31	6.87	1.72	.10	0.43
GAI	101.1	17.0	105.5	11.9	31	4.45	1.31	.20	0.30
CPI	91.0	17.9	101.4	13.0	31	10.32	2.35	.03	0.66

Using a distinct sample of children identified as IG ($n = 24$), Raiford, Holdnack, Drozdick, and Zhang (2014) found the WISC-V digital subtests and their related composites to be consistent with the results of the paper format and previous research using digital subtests among the IG. The highest subtest and composite scores among gifted children occurred in the Verbal domain and produced the highest effect sizes in comparison to controls. All primary Index and subtest scores were greater than 1 SD above the mean, similar to the paper format results. In a later study examining the digitally administered processing speed subtests, Raiford et al. (2016) found similar results in a sample of 49 individuals identified as GT. It is important to note that Coding and Symbol Search produced the smallest effect sizes in comparison to controls and produced the lowest scores for the IG group across both the paper study and digital study samples. Effect sizes were large for the digital primary Index scores, with the VCI producing the largest effect (Raiford et al., 2014, 2016) and the PSI producing the smallest effect (Raiford et al., 2016).

Examining the ancillary Index scores derived using the WISC-V paper version, a significant difference is observed between the GAI and CPI with the mean score on the GAI approximately eight points higher than the mean score on the CPI. As discussed in previous chapters, GAI includes the Verbal Conceptualization, Visual-spatial, and Fluid Reasoning subtests, while CPI includes the Working Memory and Processing Speed subtests. For this reason, some practitioners prefer using GAI rather than FSIQ to identify GT in students who perform relatively low on the processing speed tasks (which are excluded in the GAI). This may be appropriate when PSI is low due only to the student's meticulous behavioral approach to the Coding subtest, and there is other evidence that cognitive processing speed is strong. Using GAI rather than FSIQ may qualify more students as GT, but could also result in selecting some students for GT programs who have clinically significant weaknesses in processing speed and/or working memory. As discussed in Chapter 4, each of the primary cognitive abilities is an important facet of intelligence and no area should be ignored in an overall evaluation of intellectual capacity. Issues related to interpretation of GAI are discussed in more detail in Chapter 1.

Among the ancillary Index scores reported using the digital format of WISC-V, the same discrepancy between GAI and CPI is observed (Raiford et al., 2016). The mean GAI derived using the digital subtests of WISC-V was seven points higher than the mean score on the CPI using digital WISC-V subtests (Raiford et al., 2016). In a previous digital study ($n = 24$) examining all but the processing speed subtests of the WISC-V, Raiford et al. (2014) reported a higher Auditory Working Memory Index score than Working Memory Index score, due to higher subtest scores on the Auditory Working Memory tasks than on Picture Span. This pattern holds true across both paper and digital test formats (see Table 10.1 and Raiford et al., 2014). Scores on the complementary subtests and indexes of the paper version were above average for the Symbol Translation subtests and Index and in the average range on the Naming Speed subtests and Index (tables not shown). Likewise, the scores on the complementary subtests and indexes of the digital WISC-V were in the 1 SD above the mean range except for Recognition Symbol Translation with a mean Index score of 109.0. The Storage and Retrieval Index had the highest mean Index score of the complementary scores at 121.2 (Raiford et al., 2014). These results suggest more basic than advanced cognitive processes measured by these tasks, or lower performance on speeded tasks.

Intellectual Disability—Mild and Moderate

Children in the ID groups (ID-Mild, ID-Moderate) were included in the sample if they met the DSM-5 criteria for ID or obtained full-scale scores on a standard measure of cognitive ability that were at least two SDs below the mean for the ID-Mild group and three SDs below the mean for the ID-Moderate group. Data for the ID-Mild and ID-Moderate groups using the paper administration of WISC-V are shown in Tables 11.2 and 11.3.

On the WISC-V paper version, the ID-Mild group obtained a mean FSIQ of 60.9 and the ID-Moderate group obtained a mean FSIQ score of 49.7. Among the primary Index scores, performance across cognitive domains was low with the highest relative scores occurring on the PSI composite and associated Processing Speed subtests, including Cancellation and Symbol Search. Additionally, relatively high scores were also observed in the Fluid Reasoning domain and on Picture Span, compared to the low performance occurring across all other domains. Scores among the ancillary Index scores were relatively similar to the primary Index scores with scores in the low 60s for the ID-Mild group and in the low to mid-50s for the ID-Moderate group. Performance on the AWMI was lower than the WMI for both ID groups. Scores on the complementary subtests and indexes, while still low in comparison to matched controls, were relatively higher than those observed for the primary Index scores and FSIQ, with mean scores 10 to 15 points higher than the mean FSIQ. Overall the ID groups obtained scores roughly two to three SDs below the mean with the exception of the PSI and complementary Index scores, which were relatively higher. Both the Mild-ID and Moderate-ID groups were significantly different from the matched control groups on all subtests and composites and all effect sizes were large.

On the WISC-V digital version, the ID-Mild group reported by Raiford et al. (2016) obtained a mean FSIQ of 60.1 ($n = 63$); no moderate ID group was included in the Raiford, Zhang et al. special group studies. Among the primary Index scores, performance across cognitive domains was generally low, with the highest relative scores in comparison to controls occurring on the PSI composite. The highest subtest-level scores were observed on Block Design, Picture Span, Figure Weights, and Coding. Scores on the ancillary indexes were relatively similar to the primary Index scores with scores in the low 60s, with the highest score observed on the GAI at 64.2 points and the lowest on CPI at 61.7. Looking at the results from Raiford et al. (2014; $n = 24$), performance on the AWMI was lower than the WMI in the sample of intellectually disabled participants who took the digital version of WISC-V. Scores on the complementary subtests and indexes, while still low in comparison to matched controls, were relatively higher than the means observed for the primary and ancillary Index scores, with average standard scores between 10 to 12 points higher. Overall, the ID groups reported by Raiford et al. (2014, 2016) obtained scores roughly two to three SDs below the mean with the exception of the PSI and complementary Index scores, which were relatively higher. This is consistent with the pattern of scores observed in the paper format of WISC-V. Both Mild-ID groups taking the digital version of WISC-V had scores that were significantly different from their matched control groups on all subtests and composites and all effect sizes were large.

Borderline Intellectual Functioning

Children in the Borderline Intellectual Functioning (BIF) group were included if they had prior full-scale IQ scores between 71 and 84 on a standardized measure of ability or met DSM-5 criteria for a diagnosis of BIF. Data for the BIF group is shown in Table 11.4.

On the WISC-V, the BIF group obtained a mean FSIQ of 80.4 which was significantly lower than the matched control group. The pattern of scores on the primary indexes was similar to those observed in the mild and moderate ID groups, although the means were higher. The highest score was obtained on the PSI, followed by the FRI, with lower scores across the other three domains. The ancillary Index scores were similar to the primary Index scores with mean scores in the 75−85 range. Unlike the Mild and Moderate ID groups, scores on the AWMI were not lower than scores on the WMI. In general, complementary subtest and Index scores were similar to those observed on the primary and ancillary subtest and Index scores. In addition, as noted earlier in the chapter and consistent with prior research, variability in group performance across subtests decreased as severity of disability moved from borderline to mild to moderate levels of intellectual functioning. The range of mean scores across subtests for the BIF group was 5.7−10.4, whereas it was 3.2−6.1 for mild-ID and 2.0−4.6 for moderate-ID.

Attention Deficit/Hyperactivity Disorder

Children were included in the WISC-V ADHD paper and digital samples if they met the DSM-5 criteria for a current diagnosis of ADHD (any subtype), had obtained clinically significant parent ratings on the *Brown Attention-Deficit Disorder Scales for Children and Adolescents* (Brown, 2001), and had an estimate of general cognitive ability at least in the average range (FSIQ $\geq$ 80). Any children prescribed psycho-stimulant medication were required to be off medications for at least 24 hours prior to testing. Data for the ADHD group taking the paper format of WISC-V is shown in Table 11.5.

The ADHD group obtained primary Index and subtest scores that while in the average range were still significantly lower than the matched control group on the WMI, PSI, and FSIQ. The VCI, VSI, and FRI were not significantly different between groups, although Vocabulary and Matrix Reasoning were significantly lower for the ADHD group. The lowest scores were obtained on the Arithmetic and Coding subtests. All ancillary Index scores were significantly lower than the matched control group. The CPI was lower than the GAI, as expected, given the PSI and WMI domains contribute to the CPI. The AWMI was similar to the WMI; lower than other Index scores but within the average range. The lowest Index score across all primary, ancillary, and complementary indexes was on the Naming Speed Index. Performance on the Naming Speed Index was eight points lower than on the Symbol Translation Index. Overall the lowest scores were observed on measures involving processing speed and working memory. This is consistent with the extant literature on ADHD, which demonstrates greatest weaknesses in domains tapping executive functioning.

Two separate groups of participants with ADHD took the digital version of WISC-V (Raiford, Drozdick, & Zhang, 2015; Raiford et al., 2016). The participants in the first study (Raiford et al., 2015; $n = 21$) obtained primary Index and subtest scores that were in the average range but significantly lower than the matched control group on FRI, WMI, PSI, and FSIQ. The VCI and VSI were not significantly different between groups. The lowest scores were obtained on the Symbol Search and Coding subtests, as expected given known difficulties in processing speed for this group. The CPI and NVI ancillary Index scores were significantly lower than the matched control group. Finally, the CPI was lower than the GAI, as expected, given that the PSI domain contributes to the CPI.

The participants completing the digital form of WISC-V in the second study by Raiford et al. (2016; $n = 25$) obtained primary Index and subtest scores in the general range of the other digital study, along with the paper study results. However, in this study only Matrix Reasoning and Letter–Number Sequencing were significantly different from the matched control groups. Arithmetic was the lowest subtest score at 8.3; however, this did not reach statistical significance against the matched control group. Among the ancillary Index scores, the AWMI and QRI were lower than other Index scores but were within the average range. The lowest Index score across all primary, ancillary, and complementary indexes was obtained on the Delayed Symbol Translation subtest. Overall, the lowest scores were observed on measures involving quantitative and Fluid Reasoning along with

Working Memory, consistent with the extant literature on ADHD, which demonstrates the greatest weaknesses in domains tapping executive functioning.

Disruptive Behavior Disorder

Children included in the DBD group were diagnosed with ODD or CD, or identified as having a high degree of parent-rated conduct problems (e.g., *T* score > 70) on the BASC-2. Children with a comorbid ADHD diagnosis or ADHD symptoms were excluded. Data for the DBD group taking the paper format of the WISC-V is shown in Table 11.6. Mean scores across the primary, secondary, and ancillary Index and subtest scores are in the average range of intellectual functioning and were relatively similar. Results show no significant differences between DBD and matched control groups on any WISC-V subtest or composite measure. As indicated previously, the neurocognitive profile of DBD is unremarkable once ADHD has been controlled for.

Traumatic Brain Injury

TBI is one of the leading causes of cognitive disability in children. However, unlike other clinical groups, the cognitive sequelae of TBI are expected to vary across individuals due to injury-specific factors, such as location and severity of the injury, type of injury, functioning and age at injury, and length of time since the injury. Children in the TBI group were diagnosed with a moderate-to-severe TBI in the 6–18 months prior to the WISC-V assessment. A premorbid intelligence estimate above the range for ID (i.e., FSIQ > 70) was also required. Comorbid diagnoses of ADHD, CD, anxiety, or mood disorders were allowed as were speech services for language difficulties related to the TBI. Data on the TBI group taking the paper format of the WISC-V is shown in Table 11.7.

Mean scores across the primary, secondary, and ancillary Index and subtest scores are in the low average range of intellectual functioning and were relatively similar. Consistent with previous research and results on the WISC-IV, the PSI was the lowest Index score on the WISC-V. The lowest subtest scores were obtained on Arithmetic, Coding, and Symbol Search. On the complementary scores, naming speed subtests were not significantly different compared to performance by the matched control group whereas performance on the Symbol Translation subtests was significantly lower. Overall, this group demonstrated relatively weaker processing speed abilities, resulting in a lower CPI than GAI.

Autism Spectrum Disorder

Children in the two ASD groups, those *with* accompanying language impairment and those *without* accompanying language impairment, were included in the WISC-V clinical sample if they met the DSM-5 criteria for

ASD. Those *with* accompanying language impairment (ASD-L) were excluded if they had existing general cognitive ability scores more than 2.67 SDs below the mean (e.g., FSIQ < 60) or if they did not have adequate communication skills to complete testing. Those *without* accompanying language impairment (ASD-NL) were excluded if they had existing general cognitive ability scores more than 2 SDs below the mean (e.g., FSIQ < 70).

Data for the ASD-L group taking the paper version of WISC-V is shown in Table 11.8, and the ASD-NL group also taking the paper form of WISC-V is shown in Table 11.9. In the ASD-L group all primary and ancillary Index scores were below 85 and all were significantly lower than the matched control group. The lowest primary Index scores were observed on PSI and WMI, although the largest effect sizes when compared to matched controls were observed on VCI and WMI. Comparatively, FRI and VSI scores were higher, supporting the literature that has indicated visuo-spatial ability is a relative strength for some children with autism. Deficits in auditory working memory were greater than visual working memory, with a relatively high score on Picture Span in comparison to Digit Span and Letter—Number Sequencing. The highest subtest score was obtained on Figure Weights and the lowest on Comprehension. Scores on the NVI and GAI were higher than the FSIQ, reflecting the language difficulties in this group. All complementary indexes were significantly lower than matched controls and naming facility resulted in lower scores than Symbol Translation subtests. Effect sizes for the complimentary subtests were large.

In a separate sample of participants with ASD-L ($n = 30$), the digital version of WISC-V yielded similar patterns of results as the paper version. Note that the processing speed subtests are not included in this digital study by Raiford et al. (2015). All primary and ancillary Index scores were below 86, except for VSI and FRI, which were above 90, and all were significantly lower than the matched control group. The lowest primary Index score was observed on WMI, and the lowest ancillary Index score was AWMI. Comparatively, FRI and VSI scores were higher, which is consistent with the paper study results described above, and with the literature on visual-spatial strengths in ASD-L. Deficits in auditory working memory were greater than visual working memory at the Index level. At the subtest level, there were relatively higher scores on Picture Span and Digit Span compared to Letter—Number Sequencing. The highest subtest score was obtained on Block Design and the lowest on Comprehension. All complementary indexes were significantly lower than matched controls and naming facility resulted in lower scores than Symbol Translation subtests. Effect sizes for the complimentary subtests were large.

In a comparable sample of participants ($n = 26$) with ASD-L taking the digital WISC-V, Raiford et al. (2016) reported primary and ancillary Index scores below 87.5 and significantly lower than the matched control group, except for VSI and FRI, which were both over 90 (VSI 95.5, FRI 91.0). The lowest primary Index scores were observed on PSI and WMI, and these Index scores also showed the largest effect sizes when compared to matched controls. Comparatively, FRI and VSI scores were higher, although VSI scores were not significantly different from the matched control group. The direction of the results generally supports the literature that has indicated visuo-spatial ability is a relative strength for some children with ASD. Again, deficits in auditory working memory were greater than visual working memory, with a relatively high score on Picture Span in comparison to Digit Span. The highest subtest score was obtained on Visual Puzzles and the lowest on Digit Span and Coding. Scores on the NVI and GAI were higher than the FSIQ, reflecting the language difficulties in this group.

In the ASD-NL group, scores on the primary indexes were not significantly different from the matched control group except for the WMI. The PSI was lower than the other Index scores but not significantly different from the control group. The lowest subtest scores were observed on Coding, Symbol Search, Letter–Number Sequencing, and Comprehension. Among the ancillary Index scores, AWMI and CPI were the lowest scores. The CPI was nearly 10 points lower than the GAI. On the complementary subtests, the NSI was 16 points lower than the STI, likely due to the processing speed deficits observed on PSI. Consistent with findings reported by Williams et al. (2006b), impairment in associative memory tasks were not found for the group with high-functioning autism (ASD-NL) compared to matched controls.

THE WECHSLER INTELLIGENCE SCALE FOR CHILDREN—FIFTH EDITION IN CONTEXT

Results from standardized intelligence tests like the WISC-V are used to inform clinical evaluations, identify appropriate placement options, target appropriate resource and funding opportunities, and guide intervention planning. However, the manner with which the results of standardized intelligence tests are used is changing. Increased recognition of the neurocognitive heterogeneity of many clinical profiles has spurred a movement to modify the process for identification of cognitive impairment and determination of service eligibility. Procedures for identifying children needing intervention rely less often on global estimates of intellectual functioning exclusively. Rather, greater weight is placed on contrasting strengths and weaknesses within and across domains of ability. Expanded construct coverage in the WISC-V facilitates this form of assessment and is particularly relevant for children presenting with atypical profiles. Although the focus of clinical interpretation now rests on the five factor–based primary cognitive abilities, a global assessment of functioning (i.e., FSIQ score) continues to be useful for evaluation and comparison with other scores. Most practitioners utilize FSIQ alongside other scores and schools frequently use FSIQ for determining eligibility in gifted identification (McClain & Pfeiffer, 2012). Despite varying criteria for determining service-need, the WISC-V has evolved to accommodate most definitions of eligibility whether it is based on multimethod assessment, single score cutoffs, cross-battery profile analysis, ability-achievement discrepancy, or intraindividual patterns of strengths and weaknesses.

Comparing and contrasting performance across a wider array of broad and narrow cognitive abilities is increasingly seen as a diagnostically relevant method for capturing the complexity of atypical clinical profiles during an evaluation (McGrew & Flanagan, 1998). Examining pairwise comparisons across and within all cognitive domains that are diagnostically relevant to the case at hand provides both breadth in construct coverage and depth in the interpretation of task-specific weaknesses. For instance, an examination of discrepancies within a domain such as between Similarities and Vocabulary will inform appropriateness of using the VCI for Index-level comparisons as well as identify specific verbal weaknesses, such as whether verbal ability is stronger for tasks relying on abstract reasoning or lexical knowledge. Where significant discrepancies exist between Similarities and Vocabulary, use of the VCI in Index-level pairwise comparisons may be difficult to interpret, leading the clinician to limit the number of comparisons with VCI in their scoring and reporting. However, additional pairwise comparisons are available for clinicians to evaluate both relative and absolute weaknesses. Index and subtest pairwise comparisons promote more targeted diagnosis and intervention planning. When comparing scores, practitioners should consider the base rates, confidence intervals, and tests of statistically significant differences found in the test manual to facilitate interpretation of the frequency of these discrepancies in the normal population.

However, subtest-level discrepancies at the primary Index or FSIQ level may not tell the whole story, and clinicians may need to administer secondary or complimentary subtests in addition to primary subtests in order to obtain a comprehensive assessment. Each WISC-V Index score is comprised of two primary subtests, but additional subtests are available to substantiate a hypothesized weakness that is based either on clinical observation or on the extant literature. For example, when language impairment is observed in children with ASD, the greatest weakness often appears in Comprehension, rather than Similarities or Vocabulary, as Comprehension requires social reasoning and tasks involving theory of mind are relative weaknesses for this group (Mayes & Calhoun, 2008; Zayat, Kalb, & Wodka, 2011). However, since the VCI is comprised of the Similarities and Vocabulary subtests, interpretation of the VCI will denote the child's relative strengths but not their relative weakness. Given the importance of understanding both ability and disability for intervention planning, the optional administration of the Comprehension subtest in ASD is one example of the utility of including secondary subtests in the WISC-V battery.

Neurocognitive disorders typically result in mixed cognitive profiles that cannot be easily explained using a measure of full-scale intelligence. Thus, a

GAI and a CPI were developed and published post-WISC-IV to assist with describing less homogeneous clinical populations (Weiss, Saklofske, Prifitera, & Holdnack, 2006). The GAI and CPI are now included in the array of Index scores available with the WISC-V. The GAI does not incorporate Working Memory or Processing Speed subtests and thus represents a cognitive ability score that may provide increased clarity in evaluations of, for example, gifted children who show superior intellect in conceptual thinking and problem solving but who perform poorly on processing speed and working memory tasks (Assouline & Whiteman, 2011; Baum & Owen, 2004; Brody & Mills, 1997). The GAI may be particularly appropriate for the identification of children who are gifted and learning disabled, that is, twice exceptional, as weaknesses in working memory and processing speed tasks are characteristic of some learning and attention disorders (Saklofske, Prifitera, Weiss, Rolfhus, & Zhu, 2005). In these scenarios, the resulting GAI would be higher than the FSIQ (Rowe et al., 2010) with the interpretation being that the GAI is capturing maximum potential of the child being assessed. Maximum potential might be observed in environments where the task demands emphasize the child's strengths, but practitioners should keep in mind that maximum potential is not typical performance. The GAI can also be used with the FSIQ or the CPI in an Index-level pairwise comparison for assessing intelligence among children with TBI who tend to have weaknesses on processing speed and working memory. The CPI estimates cognitive ability without factoring in language-laden subtests or fluid reasoning measures. Therefore, it provides a good option for contrasting and explaining the strengths and weaknesses of individuals with ASD or borderline ID.

The NVI is a composite measure of general ability that eliminates the need for productive language in order to respond to the test item. As described in Chapter 1, the NVI is formed by six subtests: Block Design, Visual Puzzles, Matrix Reasoning, Figure Weights, Picture Span, and Coding. Five of these are primary subtests. Thus, calculating the NVI requires administration of one secondary subtest (Visual Puzzles). The NVI is useful for evaluating cognitive functioning among children with reduced language abilities such as children with ASD or children with IDs. The opportunity to assess cognitive ability by minimizing productive language is important given the reorganization of the neurodevelopmental disorders. The ASD category in the DSM-5 requires clinicians to specify "with or without language impairment" as well as "with or without intellectual impairment." The complex assessment of intelligence in ASD can be informed by interpretation of the NVI in comparison to FSIQ and VCI.

The QRI and AWMI may be useful in assessing gifted or ADHD children with comorbid learning disorders. QRI is formed by Figure Weights and Arithmetic, and thus requires administration of one secondary subtest (i.e., Arithmetic). This Index may be useful when evaluating possible comorbid Specific Learning Disorder—Math in gifted children, along with the complementary Naming Speed Quantity subtest. The AWMI consists of Digit Span and Letter–Number Sequencing, and thus requires administration of one secondary subtest (i.e., Letter–Number Sequencing). Comparing WMI to AWMI allows clinicians to determine domain-specific working memory impairment in various clinical disorders where the sensitivity to detect discrepancies between complex visual-spatial working memory versus verbal working memory may be clinically meaningful.

When significant discrepancies exist within a factor, for example—verbal comprehension—the clinician may choose one of the ancillary Index scores that reduce the demand on language abilities from the estimate of overall ability, such as the NVI or the CPI, in order to estimate the maximum potential of cognitive ability for an individual child. Thus, secondary indexes may be clinically useful because they focus on specific abilities. While informative, however, estimates of maximum potential based on secondary indexes should generally not be considered as better estimates of general intelligence than the FSIQ because all five primary abilities are essential components of general intelligence (see Chapter 4), and are necessary to represent typical performance across a wider range of environmental demands. The obvious exception is when speech, vision, or motor skills interfere with performance, or if the child was clearly not attentive or engaged for some subtests.

Analysis of patterns of strengths and weaknesses among the Index scores is important and widely accepted as part of modern clinical assessment practice. Yet, some cautions are warranted when implementing Index-level profile analysis with individual students or patients. Despite the fact that common profiles tend to emerge in diagnostic group research, the presence of a particular WISC-V profile in an individual should not be considered diagnostic of that disorder, and the absence of that profile should not rule out the disorder. This is because there is considerable heterogeneity within diagnostic groups such that not all individuals with the same diagnosis show the same pattern. Furthermore, similar profiles may be observed in other diagnostic groups that are related neurocognitively. For example, profiles with low WMI are often found in groups of patients diagnosed with ADHD, ASD, and some forms of LD (see chapter 9 on learning disabilities). So, while a significantly low score on WMI clearly indicates that the child has a weakness in working memory, which needs to be described in the report and addressed in the treatment plan, it does not by itself indicate a specific diagnosis. Rather, it suggests a range of possible diagnoses that are related to deficits in that ability. The final diagnosis is a matter of clinical judgment on the part of a trained and experienced practitioner after careful consideration of all DSM-5 criteria based on a comprehensive evaluation including other appropriate tests, clinical interview, behavioral observations, family and medical histories, and other relevant information. The WISC-V is a five-factor model of cognitive ability that aligns more closely to existing theory and other measures of neurocognitive assessment including the WPPSI-IV and recent factor analyses of the WAIS-IV (Benson, Hulac, & Kranzler, 2010; Keith, Fine, Taub, Reynolds, & Kranzler, 2006; Weiss, Keith, Zhu, & Chen, 2013a; Weiss, Keith, Zhu, & Chen, 2013b). Comparisons of subtests and composites within Wechsler tests will be more clinically useful with this alignment of factor models across preschool, school-aged, and adult measures of intelligence. One particular population where this utility will be most valued is in those with TBI. Repeat assessments following a TBI are necessary given that many short-term cognitive deficits will abate in the years following the TBI. Mutable cognitive impairment necessitates repeated assessments for children with a TBI to ensure ongoing eligibility of services, which is tied to funding and intervention planning.

From a scientist—practitioner perspective, continuity of measurement with the new five-factor model of the WISC-V is an important advancement in the field as it ensures the integrity of data collected across time during research. Again, the TBI population serves as a key example of where research will benefit the most from the improved continuity of measurement of the WISC-V. Longitudinal studies are the most robust methodological design for studying the postinjury outcomes of children who sustain TBI (Fletcher, Ewing-Cobbs, Francis, & Levin, 1995; Yeates et al., 2002). The need for continuity of measurement in these multiyear research studies is clear. The overlap in factor structure across the WPPSI-IV and the WISC-V will permit clinicians and researchers to ensure continuity of measurement as developing children require ongoing assessment through adolescence and beyond.

SUMMARY

This chapter provided an overview of general issues related to identification of specific clinical disorders and special groups according to the DSM-5 with an emphasis on variability in cognitive functioning. WISC-V data for select groups including IG, mild and moderate ID, BIF, ADHD, disruptive behavior disorder, ASD with and without language impairment, and TBI have been presented to aid clinicians in understanding the profiles of various clinical and special groups.

The WISC-V is a tool for clinicians to use when evaluating a given child's strengths and weaknesses as it relates to the overall clinical profile and presenting concerns. A test such as the WISC-V should be used by experienced professionals who understand the properties of the measure, including its limitations. Any measure a clinician uses to diagnose or interpret must be applied within the boundaries of best practice recommendations that stipulate multiple sources of information and clinical judgement are necessary for interpretations of ability or disability (see Miller et al., 2015). With the WISC-V there is a larger offering of subtests, more comparison options, and more Index scores available for assisting with interpretation of ability. The addition of process scores, contrast scores, and error scores to the WISC-V further assists clinicians with understanding the contextual details of task performance. The information that can be obtained by administering the WISC-V constitutes much more than a single IQ score, but as always, must be framed within the full family, medical, behavioral, and academic record of the child. Clinical context is a critical component of the diagnostic process because patterns of deficits in the broad cognitive abilities assessed by the WISC-V are not isomorphic with specific disorders, but often can be found in neurocognitively related disorders.

REFERENCES

Acar, S., Sen, S., & Cayirdag, N. (2016). Consistency of the performance and non-performance methods in gifted identification: A multilevel meta-analytic review. *Gifted Child Quarterly*, *60*, 81−101.

Alloway, T. P. (2010). Working memory and executive function profiles of individuals with borderline intellectual functioning. *Journal of Intellectual Disability Research*, *54*, 448−456.

American Association on Intellectual and Developmental Disabilities. (2010). *Intellectual disability: Definition, classification, and systems of supports* (11th ed.). Washington, DC: Author.

American Psychiatric Association. (2000). *Diagnostic and statistical manual of mental disorders* (4th ed., text revision). Washington, DC: Author.

American Psychiatric Association. (2013). *Diagnostic and statistical manual of mental disorders* (5th ed.). Arlington, VA: Author.

Andersen, L. (2014). Visual−spatial ability: Important in STEM, ignored in gifted education. *Roeper Review*, *36*, 114−121.

Anderson, V., Brown, S., Newitt, H., & Hoile, H. (2009). Educational, vocational, psychosocial, and quality-of-life outcomes for adult survivors of childhood traumatic brain injury. *The Journal of Head Trauma Rehabilitation*, *24*, 303−312.

Anderson, V., Brown, S., Newitt, H., & Hoile, H. (2011). Long-term outcome from childhood traumatic brain injury: Intellectual ability, personality, and quality of life. *Neuropsychology*, *25*, 176.

Anderson, V., Catroppa, C., Morse, S., Haritou, F., & Rosenfeld, J. (2000). Recovery of intellectual ability following traumatic brain injury in childhood: Impact of injury severity and age at injury. *Pediatric Neurosurgery*, *32*, 282−290.

Assouline, S. G., & Whiteman, C. S. (2011). Twice-exceptionality: Implications for school psychologists in the post−IDEA 2004 era. *Journal of Applied School Psychology*, *27*, 380−402.

Baird, G., Charman, T., Baron-Cohen, S., Cox, A., Swettenham, J., Wheelwright, S., & Drew, A. (2000). A screening instrument for autism at 18 months of age: A 6-year follow-up study. Journal of the American Academy of Child & Adolescent Psychiatry, *39*, 694-702.Barkley, R. A. (1997). Behavioral inhibition, sustained attention, and executive functions: Constructing a unifying theory of ADHD. *Psychological Bulletin*, *121*, 65−94.

Barkley, R. A. (2007). *Attention-deficit hyperactivity disorder: A handbook for diagnosis and treatment* (3rd ed.). New York, NY: The Guilford Press.

Baron-Cohen, S. (1989). The autistic child's theory of mind: A case of specific developmental delay. *Journal of Child Psychology and Psychiatry*, *30*, 285−297.

Baum, S., & Owen, S. (2004). *To be gifted and learning disabled: Strategies for helping bright students with LD, ADHD, and more.* Mansfield, CT: Creative Learning Press.

Benson, N., Hulac, D. M., & Kranzler, J. H. (2010). Independent examination of the Wechsler Adult Intelligence Scale—Fourth Edition (WAIS-IV): What does the WAIS-IV measure? *Psychological Assessment, 22,* 121.

Bishop, D. V., & Baird, G. (2001). Parent and teacher report of pragmatic aspects of communication: use of the Children's Communication Checklist in a clinical setting. *Developmental Medicine & Child Neurology, 43,* 809–818.

Bölte, S., Holtmann, M., Poustka, F., Scheurich, A., & Schmidt, L. (2007). Gestalt perception and local-global processing in high-functioning autism. *Journal of Autism and Developmental Disorders, 37,* 1493–1504.

Bonifacci, P., & Snowling, M. J. (2008). Speed of processing and reading disability: A cross-linguistic investigation of dyslexia and borderline intellectual functioning. *Cognition, 107,* 999–1017.

Boucher, J. (2012). Research review: structural language in autistic spectrum disorder–characteristics and causes. *Journal of Child Psychology and Psychiatry, 53,* 219–233.

Brody, L. E., & Mills, C. J. (1997). Gifted children with learning disabilities: A review of the issues. *Journal of Learning Disabilities, 30,* 282–296.

Brown, T. E. (2001). *The brown attention-deficit disorder scales.* San Antonio, TX: Psychological Corporation.

Burke, J. D., Loeber, R., & Birmaher, B. (2002). Oppositional defiant disorder and conduct disorder: A review of the past 10 years, part II. *Journal of the American Academy of Child & Adolescent Psychiatry, 41,* 1275–1293.

Calhoun, S. L., & Mayes, S. D. (2005). Processing speed in children with clinical disorders. *Psychology in the Schools, 42,* 333–343.

Cao, T. H., Jung, J. Y., & Lee, J. (2017). Assessment in gifted education: A review of the literature from 2005 to 2016. *Journal of Advanced Academics, 28,* 163–203.

Carte, E. T., Nigg, J. T., & Hinshaw, S. P. (1996). Neuropsychological functioning, motor speed, and language processing in boys with and without ADHD. *Journal of Abnormal Child Psychology, 24,* 481–498.

Catroppa, C., Anderson, V. A., Morse, S. A., Haritou, F., & Rosenfeld, J. V. (2007). Children's attentional skills 5 years post-TBI. *Journal of Pediatric Psychology, 32,* 354–369.

Chadwick, O., Rutter, M., Brown, G., Shaffer, D., & Traub, M. (1981). A prospective study of children with head injuries: II. Cognitive sequelae. *Psychological Medicine, 11,* 49–61.

Chadwick, O., Rutter, M., Shaffer, D., & Shrout, P. E. (1981). A prospective study of children with head injuries: IV. Specific cognitive deficits. *Journal of Clinical Neuropsychology, 3,* 101–120.

Chang, H. T., Klorman, R., Shaywitz, S. E., Fletcher, J. M., Marchione, K. E., Holahan, J. M., … Shaywitz, B. A. (1999). Paired-associate learning in attention-deficit/hyperactivity disorder as a function of hyperactivity-impulsivity and oppositional defiant disorder. *Journal of Abnormal Child Psychology, 27,* 237–245.

Chhabildas, N., Pennington, B. F., & Willcutt, E. G. (2001). A comparison of the neuropsychological profiles of the DSM-IV subtypes of ADHD. *Journal of Abnormal Child Psychology, 29,* 529–540.

Christian, R. E., Frick, P. J., Hill, N. L., Tyler, L., & Frazer, D. R. (1997). Psychopathy and conduct problems in children: II. Implications for subtyping children with conduct problems. *Journal of the American Academy of Child & Adolescent Psychiatry, 36,* 233–241.

Clark, C., Prior, M., & Kinsella, G. (2002). The relationship between executive function abilities, adaptive behaviour, and academic achievement in children with externalising behaviour problems. *Journal of Child Psychology and Psychiatry, 43,* 785–796.

Clark, C., Prior, M., & Kinsella, G. J. (2000). Do executive function deficits differentiate between adolescents with ADHD and oppositional defiant/conduct disorder? A neuropsychological study using the Six Elements Test and Hayling Sentence Completion Test. *Journal of Abnormal Child Psychology, 28,* 403–414.

Coghill, D. R., Hayward, D., Rhodes, S. M., Grimmer, C., & Matthews, K. (2014). A longitudinal examination of neuropsychological and clinical functioning in boys with attention deficit hyperactivity disorder (ADHD): Improvements in executive functioning do not explain clinical improvement. *Psychological Medicine, 44,* 1087–1099.

Dawson, M., Soulières, I., Gernsbacher, M. A., & Mottron, L. (2007). The level and nature of autistic intelligence. *Psychological Science, 18,* 657–662.

Department of Defense and Department of Veterans Affairs. (2008). *Traumatic brain injury task force.* http://www.cdc.gov/nchs/data/icd9/Sep08TBI.pdf.

Di Blasi, F. D., Elia, F., Buono, S., Ramakers, G. J., & Di Nuovo, S. F. (2007). Relationships between visual-motor and cognitive abilities in intellectual disabilities. *Perceptual and Motor Skills, 104,* 763–772.

Douglas, V. I., & Benezra, E. (1990). Supraspan verbal memory in attention deficit disorder with hyperactivity normal and reading-disabled boys. *Journal of Abnormal Child Psychology, 18,* 617–638.

Dyck, M. J., & Piek, J. P. (2014). Developmental delays in children with ADHD. *Journal of Attention Disorders, 18,* 466–478.

Farrington, D. P. (1995). The development of offending and antisocial behaviour from childhood: Key findings from the Cambridge Study in Delinquent Development. *Journal of Child Psychology and Psychiatry, 36,* 929–964.

Fein, D., Dunn, M. A., Allen, D. M., Aram, R., Hall, N., Morris, R., et al. (1996). Neuropsychological and language findings. In I. Rapin (Ed.), *Preschool children with inadequate communication: Developmental language disorder, autism, low IQ* (pp. 123–154). London: Mac Keith Press.

Fergusson, L., Horwood, L. J., & Lynskey, M. T. (1993). The effects of conduct disorder and attention deficit in middle childhood on offending and scholastic ability at age 13. *Journal of Child Psychology and Psychiatry, 34,* 899–916.

Fletcher, J. M., Ewing-Cobbs, L., Francis, D. J., & Levin, H. S. (1995). Variability in outcomes after traumatic brain injury in children: A developmental perspective. In S. H. Broman, & M. E. Michel (Eds.), *Traumatic head injury in children* (pp. 3–21). New York: Oxford University Press.

Foley Nicpon, M. F., Allmon, A., Sieck, B., & Stinson, R. D. (2011). Empirical investigation of twice-exceptionality: Where have we been and where are we going? *Gifted Child Quarterly, 55,* 3–17.

Frick, P. J., & Viding, E. (2009). Antisocial behavior from a developmental psychopathology perspective. *Development and psychopathology, 21,* 1111–1131.

Frick, P. J., Kamphaus, R. W., Lahey, B. B., Loeber, R., Christ, M. A. G., Hart, E. L., & Tannenbaum, L. E. (1991). Academic underachievement and the disruptive behavior disorders. *Journal of Consulting and Clinical Psychology, 59,* 289.

Galton, F. (1869). *Hereditary genius.* London: Macmillan.

Geurts, H. M., & Embrechts, M. (2008). Language profiles in ASD, SLI, and ADHD. *Journal of Autism and Developmental Disorders, 38,* 1931–1943.

Geurts, H. M., Verté, S., Oosterlaan, J., Roeyers, H., & Sergeant, J. A. (2004). How specific are executive functioning deficits in attention deficit hyperactivity disorder and autism? *Journal of Child Psychology and Psychiatry, 45*, 836−854.

Geurts, H. M., Verté, S., Oosterlaan, J., Roeyers, H., & Sergeant, J. A. (2005). ADHD subtypes: Do they differ in their executive functioning profile? *Archives of Clinical Neuropsychology, 20*, 457−477.

Gillberg, C., & Kadesjo, B. (2000). Attention deficit hyperactivity disorder and developmental co-ordination disorder. In T. E. Brown (Ed.), *Attention deficit hyperactivity disorder and comorbidities in children, adolescents and adults* (pp. 393−406). Washington, DC: American Psychiatric Press.

Gilliam, M., Stockman, M., Malek, M., Sharp, W., Greenstein, D., Lalonde, F., ... Shaw, P. (2011). Developmental trajectories of the corpus callosum in attention-deficit/hyperactivity disorder. *Biological Psychiatry, 69*, 839−846.

Goodman, R., Simonoff, E., & Stevenson, E. (1995). The impact of child IQ, parental IQ and sibling IQ on child behavioural deviance scores. *Journal of Child Psychology and Psychiatry, 36*, 409−425.

Gordon, S., Duff, S., Davidson, T., & Whitaker, S. (2010). Comparison of the WAIS-III and WISC-IV in 16-year-old special education students. *Journal of Applied Research in Intellectual Disabilities, 23*, 197−200.

Green, D., Baird, G., Barnett, A. L., Henderson, L., Huber, J., & Henderson, S. E. (2002). The severity and nature of motor impairment in Asperger's syndrome: A comparison with specific developmental disorder of motor function. *Journal of Child Psychology and Psychiatry, 43*, 655−668.

Hammes, J. G. W., & Langdell, T. (1981). Precursors of symbol formation and childhood autism. *Journal of Autism and Developmental Disorders, 11*, 331−346.

Hayden, M. G., Jandial, R., Duenas, H. A., Mahajan, R., & Levy, M. (2007). Pediatric concussions in sports: A simple and rapid assessment tool for concussive injury in children and adults. *Child's Nervous System, 23*, 431−435.

Hermelin, B. (1978). Images and language. In M. Rutter, & E. Schoppler (Eds.), *Autism: A reappraisal of concept and treatment* (pp. 141−154). New York: Plenum.

Hinshaw, S. P., & Lee, S. S. (2003). Conduct and oppositional defiant disorders. *Child Psychopathology, 2*, 144−198.

Hinshaw, S. P., Carte, E. T., Sami, N., Treuting, J. J., & Zupan, B. A. (2002). Preadolescent girls with attention-deficit/hyperactivity disorder: II. Neuropsychological performance in relation to subtypes and individual classification. *Journal of Consulting and Clinical Psychology, 70*, 1099.

Hogan, A. E. (1999). *Cognitive functioning in children with oppositional defiant disorder and conduct disorder. Handbook of disruptive behavior disorders* (pp. 317−335). United States: Springer.

Howlin, P. (2003). Outcome in high-functioning adults with autism with and without early language delays: implications for the differentiation between autism and Asperger syndrome. *Journal of Autism and Developmental Disorders, 33*, 3−13.

Jaffe, K. M., Polisar, N. L., Fay, G. C., & Liao, S. (1995). Recovery trends over three years following pediatric traumatic brain injury. *Archives of Physical Medicine and Rehabilitation, 76*, 17−26.

Karatekin, C., Markiewicz, S. W., & Siegel, M. A. (2003). A preliminary study of motor problems in children with attention-deficit/hyperactivity disorder. *Perceptual and Motor Skills, 97*, 1267−1280.

Kaufman, A. S., & Kaufman, N. L. (1990). *Kaufman brief intelligence test*. John Wiley & Sons, Inc.

Keith, T. Z., Fine, J. G., Taub, G. E., Reynolds, M. R., & Kranzler, J. H. (2006). Higher order, multisample, confirmatory factor analysis of the Wechsler Intelligence Scale for Children— Fourth Edition: What does it measure. *School Psychology Review*, *35*, 108—127.

Kielinen, M., Linna, S. L., & Moilanen, I. (2000). Autism in northern Finland. *European Child & Adolescent Psychiatry*, *9*, 162—167.

Kjelgaard, M. M., & Tager-Flusberg, H. (2001). An investigation of language impairment in autism: Implications for genetic subgroups. *Language and Cognitive Processes*, *16*, 287—308.

Klingberg, T., Fernell, E., Olesen, P. J., Johnson, M., Gustafsson, P., Dahlström, K., ... Westerberg, H. (2005). Computerized training of working memory in children with ADHD — a randomized, controlled trial. *Journal of the American Academy of Child & Adolescent Psychiatry*, *44*, 177—186.

Klorman, R., Hazel-Fernandez, L. A., Shaywitz, S. E., Fletcher, J. M., Marchione, K. E., Holahan, J. M., et al. (1999). Executive functioning deficits in attention-deficit/hyperactivity disorder are independent of oppositional defiant or reading disorder. *Journal of the American Academy of Child & Adolescent Psychiatry*, *38*, 1148—1155.

Knights, R. M., Ivan, L. P., Ventureyra, E. C., Bentivoglio, C., Stoddart, C., Winogron, W., & Bawden, H. N. (1991). The effects of head injury in children on neuropsychological and behavioural functioning. *Brain Injury*, *5*, 339—351.

Koning, C., & Magill-Evans, J. (2001). Social and language skills in adolescent boys with Asperger syndrome. *Autism*, *5*, 23—36.

Kraepelin, E. (1913). *Psychiatrie* (3). Leipzig: Barth.

Kuhne, M., Schachar, R., & Tannock, R. (1997). Impact of comorbid oppositional or conduct problems on attention-deficit hyperactivity disorder. *Journal of the American Academy of Child & Adolescent Psychiatry*, *36*, 1715—1725.

Kuntsi, J., Eley, T. C., Taylor, A., Hughes, C., Asherson, P., Caspi, A., & Moffitt, T. E. (2004). Co-occurrence of ADHD and low IQ has genetic origins. *American Journal of Medical Genetics Part B: Neuropsychiatric Genetics*, *124*, 41—47.

Lahey, B. B., Loeber, R., Hart, E. L., Frick, P. J., Applegate, B., Zhang, Q., ... Russo, M. F. (1995). Four-year longitudinal study of conduct disorder in boys: Patterns and predictors of persistence. *Journal of Abnormal Psychology*, *104*, 83.

Lansing, A. E., Washburn, J. J., Abram, K. M., Thomas, U. C., Welty, L. J., & Teplin, L. A. (2014). Cognitive and academic functioning of juvenile detainees implications for correctional populations and public health. *Journal of Correctional Health Care*, *20*, 18—30.

Lewis, F. M., Murdoch, B. E., & Woodyatt, G. C. (2007). Linguistic abilities in children with autism spectrum disorder. *Research in Autism Spectrum Disorders*, *1*, 85—100.

Lindgren, K. A., Folstein, S. E., Tomblin, J. B., & Tager-Flusberg, H. (2009). Language and reading abilities of children with autism spectrum disorders and specific language impairment and their first-degree relatives. *Autism Research*, *2*, 22—38.

Llorente, A. M., Voigt, R. G., Jensen, C. L., Berretta, M. C., Fraley, J. K., & Heird, W. C. (2006). Performance on a visual sustained attention and discrimination task is associated with urinary excretion of norepinephrine metabolite in children with attention-deficit/hyperactivity disorder (AD/HD). *Clinical Neuropsychology*, *20*, 133—144.

Llorente, A. M., Voigt, R. G., Bhatnagar, P., Jensen, C. L., Heird, W. C., Williams, J., ... Satz, P. (2012). Simultaneous visual sustained attention-discrimination and goal-directed search are associated with excretion of catecholaminergic metabolites in children with attention-deficit/hyperactivity disorder. *Journal of Pediatric Biochemistry*, *2*, 115—122.

Lockwood, K. A., Marcotte, A. C., & Stern, C. (2001). Differentiation of attention-deficit/hyperactivity disorder subtypes: Application of a neuropsychological model of attention. *Journal of Clinical and Experimental Neuropsychology*, *23*, 317—330.

Lohman, D. F., Gambrell, J., & Lakin, J. (2008). The commonality of extreme discrepancies in the ability profiles of academically gifted students. *Psychology Science, 50*, 269.

Lynam, D., Moffitt, T., & Stouthamer-Loeber, M. (1993). Explaining the relation between IQ and delinquency: Class, race, test motivation, school failure, or self-control? *Journal of Abnormal Psychology, 102*, 187.

Lynam, D. R., & Henry, B. (2001). The role of neuropsychological deficits in conduct disorders. In J. Hill, & B. Maughan (Eds.), *Conduct disorders in childhood and adolescence.* (pp. 235–263). Cambridge University Press.

Maddocks, D. L. S. (2018). The identification of students who are gifted and have a learning disability: A comparison of different diagnostic criteria. *Gifted Child Quarterly, 62*, 175–192.

Mann, R. L. (2005). Gifted students with spatial strengths and sequential weaknesses: An overlooked and underidentified population. *Roeper Review, 27*, 91–97.

Mann, R. L. (2006). Effective teaching strategies for gifted/learning-disabled students with spatial strengths. *Prufrock Journal, 17*, 112–121.

Mariani, M. A., & Barkley, R. A. (1997). Neuropsychological and academic functioning in preschool boys with attention deficit hyperactivity disorder. *Developmental Neuropsychology, 13*, 111–129.

Matson, J. L., & Shoemaker, M. (2009). Intellectual disability and its relationship to autism spectrum disorders. *Research in Developmental Disabilities, 30*, 1107–1114.

Matson, J. L., Mahan, S., Hess, J. A., & Fodstad, J. C. (2010). Effect of developmental quotient on symptoms of inattention and impulsivity among toddlers with autism spectrum disorders. *Research in Developmental Disabilities, 31*, 464–469.

Maulik, P. K., Mascarenhas, M. N., Mathers, C. D., Dua, T., & Saxena, S. (2011). Prevalence of intellectual disability: A meta-analysis of population-based studies. *Research in Developmental Disabilities, 32*, 419–436.

Mayes, S. D., & Calhoun, S. L. (2003a). Analysis of WISC-III, Stanford-Binet IV, and academic achievement test scores in children with autism. *Journal of Autism and Developmental Disorders, 33*, 329–341.

Mayes, S. D., & Calhoun, S. L. (2003b). Ability profiles in children with autism: Influence of age and IQ. *Autism, 7*, 65–80.

Mayes, S. D., & Calhoun, S. L. (2007). Learning, attention, writing, and processing speed in typical children and children with ADHD, autism, anxiety, depression, and oppositional-defiant disorder. *Child Neuropsychology, 13*, 469–493.

Mayes, S. D., & Calhoun, S. L. (2008). WISC-IV and WIAT-II profiles in children with high-functioning autism. *Journal of Autism and Developmental Disorders, 38*, 428–439.

Mayes, S. D., & Calhoun, S. L. (2011). Impact of IQ, age, SES, gender, and race on autistic symptoms. *Research in Autism Spectrum Disorders, 5*, 749–757.

McBee, M. T., Peters, S. J., & Waterman, C. (2014). Combining scores in multiple criteria assessment systems: The impact of combination rule. *Gifted Child Quarterly, 58*, 69–89. Available from https://doi.org/10.1177/0016986213513794).

McClain, M. C., & Pfeiffer, S. (2012). Identification of gifted students in the United States today: A look at state definitions, policies, and practices. *Journal of Applied School Psychology, 28*, 59–88.

McCrea, M. (2007). Mild traumatic brain injury and post-concussion syndrome: The new evidence base for diagnosis and treatment *(American Academy of Clinical Neuropsychology Workshop Series)*. New York: Oxford University Press.

McGregor, K. K., Berns, A. J., Owen, A. J., Michels, S. A., Duff, D., Bahnsen, A. J., et al. (2012). Associations between syntax and the lexicon among children with or without ASD and language impairment. *Journal of Autism and Developmental Disorders, 42*, 35–47.

McGrew, K. S., & Flanagan, D. P. (1998). *The intelligence test desk reference (ITDR): Gf-Gc cross-battery assessment*. Allyn & Bacon.

Melnick, S. M., & Hinshaw, S. P. (1996). What they want and what they get: The social goals of boys with ADHD and comparison boys. *Journal of Abnormal Child Psychology, 24,* 169–185.

Miller, J. L., Weiss, L. G., Beal, A. L., Saklofske, D. H., Zhu, J., & Holdnack, J. A. (2015). Intelligent use of intelligence tests: Empirical and clinical support for Canadian WAIS-IV norms. *Journal of Psychoeducational Assessment, 33,* 312–328.

Minshew, N. J., Goldstein, G., & Siegel, D. J. (1997). Neuropsychologic functioning in autism: Profile of a complex information processing disorder. *Journal of the International Neuropsychological Society, 3,* 303–316.

Moffitt, T. E. (2006). Life course persistent versus adolescence-limited antisocial behavior. In (2nd ed.D. Cicchetti, & D. J. Cohen (Eds.), *Developmental Psychopathology* (Vol. 3New York: Wiley.

Moffitt, T. E., & Caspi, A. (2001). Childhood predictors differentiate life-course persistent and adolescence-limited antisocial pathways among males and females. *Development and psychopathology, 13,* 355–375.

Mulligan, A., Anney, R. J., O'Regan, M., Chen, W., Butler, L., Fitzgerald, M., et al. (2009). Autism symptoms in attention-deficit/hyperactivity disorder: A familial trait which correlates with conduct, oppositional defiant, language and motor disorders. *Journal of Autism and Developmental Disorders, 39,* 197–209.

Muth, A., Hönekopp, J., & Falter, C. M. (2014). Visuo-spatial performance in autism: A meta-analysis. *Journal of Autism and Developmental Disorders, 44,* 3245–3263.

Naglieri, J. A., Goldstein, S., Iseman, J. S., & Schwebach, A. (2003). Performance of children with attention deficit hyperactivity disorder and anxiety/depression on the WISC-III and Cognitive Assessment System (CAS). *Journal of Psychoeducational Assessment, 21,* 32–42.

Naigles, L. R. (2013). Input and language development in children with autism. *Seminars in Speech and Language, 34,* 237–248.

Navon, D. (1977). Forest before trees: The precedence of global features in visual perception. *Cognitive Psychology, 9,* 353–383.

Neisser, U., Boodoo, G., Bouchard, T. J., Jr, Boykin, A. W., Brody, N., Ceci, S. J., et al. (1996). Intelligence: Knowns and unknowns. *American Psychologist, 51,* 77.

Nigg, J. T., Blaskey, L. G., Huang-Pollock, C. L., & Rappley, M. D. (2002). Neuropsychological executive functions and DSM-IV ADHD subtypes. *Journal of the American Academy of Child & Adolescent Psychiatry, 41,* 59–66.

Nunes, M. M., Honjo, R. S., Dutra, R. L., Amaral, V. S., Amaral, V. A. S., Oh, H. K., ... Teixeira, M. C. T. V. (2013). Assessment of intellectual and visuo spatial abilities in children and adults with Williams Syndrome. *Universitas Psychologica, 12,* 581–589.

Nydén, A., Billstedt, E., Hjelmquist, E., & Gillberg, C. (2001). Neurocognitive stability in Asperger syndrome, ADHD, and reading and writing disorder: A pilot study. *Developmental Medicine & Child Neurology, 43,* 165–171.

O'Connor, N., & Hermelin, B. (1975). Modality-specific spatial coordinates. *Perception and Psychophysics, 17,* 213–216.

Oosterlaan, J., Scheres, A., & Sergeant, J. A. (2005). Which executive functioning deficits are associated with AD/HD, ODD/CD and comorbid AD/HD + ODD/CD? *Journal of Abnormal Child Psychology, 33,* 69–85.

Osmon, D. C., Smerz, J. M., Braun, M. M., & Plambeck, E. (2006). Processing abilities associated with math skills in adult learning disability. *Journal of Clinical and Experimental Neuropsychology, 28,* 84–95.

Ozonoff, S., & Strayer, D. L. (2001). Further evidence of intact working memory in autism. *Journal of Autism and Developmental Disorders, 31*, 257−263.

Pasini, A., Paloscia, C., Alessandrelli, R., Porfirio, M. C., & Curatolo, P. (2007). Attention and executive functions profile in drug naive ADHD subtypes. *Brain and Development, 29*, 400−408.

Pennington, B. F., & Ozonoff, S. (1996). Executive functions and developmental psychopathology. *Journal of Child Psychology and Psychiatry, 37*, 51−87.

Pennington, B. F., Rogers, S. J., Bennetto, L., Griffith, E. M., Reed, D. T., & Shyu, V. (1997). Validity tests of the executive dysfunction hypothesis of autism. In J. Russell (Ed.), *Autism as an executive disorder* (pp. 143−178). Oxford, England: Oxford University Press.

Pfeiffer, S. I. (2002). Identifying gifted and talented students: Recurring issues and promising solutions. *Journal of Applied School Psychology, 1*, 31−50.

Pickering, S. J., & Gathercole, S. E. (2004). Distinctive working memory profiles in children with special educational needs. *Educational Psychology, 24*, 393−408.

Pitcher, T. M., Piek, J. P., & Hay, D. A. (2003). Fine and gross motor ability in males with ADHD. *Developmental Medicine & Child Neurology, 45*, 525−535.

Raiford, S. E., Weiss, L. G., Rolfhus, E., & Coalson, D. (2005). *General ability index* [WISC−IV Technical Report No. 4]. Retrieved from http://www.Pearsonassessments.com/ NR/rdonlyres/1439CDFE-6980-435F-93DA-05888C7CC082/0/80720_WISCIV_Hr_r4.pdf.

Raiford, S. E., Drozdick, L., & Zhang, O. (2015). *Q-interactive special group studies: The WISC-V and children with autism spectrum disorder and accompanying language impairment or attention-deficit/hyperactivity disorder* [Q-interactive Technical Report 11]. Retrieved from https://www.pearsonclinical.com/psychology/products/100000773/qinteractive.html#tab-research.

Raiford, S. E., Holdnack, J., Drozdick, L., & Zhang, O. (2014). *Q-interactive special group studies: The WISC-V and children with intellectual giftedness and intellectual disability* [Q-interactive Technical Report 9]. Retrieved from https://www.pearsonclinical.com/psychology/products/100000773/qinteractive.html#tab-research.

Raiford, S. E., Zhang, O., Drozdick, L. W., Getz, K., Wahlstrom, D., Gabel, A., . . ., & Daniel, M. (2016). *WISC-V Coding and Symbol Search in digital format: Reliability, validity, special group studies, and interpretation.* [Q-interactive Technical Report 12]. Retrieved from https://www.pearsonclinical.com/psychology/products/100000773/qinteractive.html#tab-research.

Raine, A., Yaralian, P. S., Reynolds, C., Venables, P. H., & Mednick, S. A. (2002). Spatial but not verbal cognitive deficits at age 3 years in persistently antisocial individuals. *Development and Psychopathology, 14*, 25−44.

Ramnauth, R. (2018). The relationship between handwriting and reading in children with autism spectrum disorder. *Paper presented at the IEEE Region 1 Conference*, NY, New York, March 23, 2018. Retrieved from http://https://www.researchgate.net/publication/ 323779936_Handwriting_Reading_in_Children_with_ASD.

Rapin, I., Dunn, M. A., Allen, D. A., Stevens, M. C., & Fein, D. (2009). Subtypes of language disorders in school-age children with autism. *Developmental Neuropsychology, 34*, 66−84.

Rapport, M. D., Scanlan, S. W., & Denney, C. B. (1999). Attention-deficit/hyperactivity disorder and scholastic achievement: A model of dual developmental pathways. *Journal of Child Psychology and Psychiatry, 40*, 1169−1183.

Riccio, C. A., Homack, S., Jarratt, K. P., & Wolfe, M. E. (2006). Differences in academic and executive function domains among children with ADHD predominantly inattentive and combined types. *Archives of Clinical Neuropsychology, 21*, 657−667.

Rice, M. L., Warren, S. F., & Betz, S. K. (2005). Language symptoms of developmental language disorders: An overview of autism, down syndrome, fragile X, specific language impairment, and Williams syndrome. *Applied Psycholinguistics*, *26*, 7–27.

Rimm, S., Gilman, B., & Silverman, L. (2008). Alternative assessments with gifted and talented students. In J. L. VanTassel-Baska (Ed.), *Nontraditional applications of traditional testing* (pp. 175–202). Waco, TX: Prufrock Press.

Rosso, M., Falasco, S. L., & Koller, J. R. (1984). Investigations into the relationship of the PPVT-R and the WISC-R with incarcerated delinquents. *Journal of Clinical Psychology*, *40*, 588–591.

Rowe, E. W., Kingsley, J. M., & Thompson, D. F. (2010). Predictive ability of the general ability index (GAI) versus the full scale IQ among gifted referrals. *School Psychology Quarterly*, *25*, 119–128.

Rucklidge, J. J., & Tannock, R. (2001). Psychiatric, psychosocial, and cognitive functioning of female adolescents with ADHD. *Journal of the American Academy of Child & Adolescent Psychiatry*, *40*, 530–540.

Russell, J., Jarrold, C., & Henry, L. (1996). Working memory in children with autism and with moderate learning difficulties. *Journal of Child Psychology and Psychiatry*, *37*, 673–686.

Saalasti, S., Lepistö, T., Toppila, E., Kujala, T., Laakso, M., Nieminen-von Wendt, T., ... Jansson-Verkasalo, E. (2008). Language abilities of children with Asperger syndrome. *Journal of Autism and Developmental Disorders*, *38*, 1574–1580.

Saklofske, D. H., Prifitera, A., Weiss, L. G., Rolfhus, E., & Zhu, J. J. (2005). Clinical interpretation of the WISC-IV FSIQ and GAI. In A. Prifitera, & D. Saklofske (Eds.), *WISC-IV clinical use and interpretation*. San Diego, CA: Academic Press.

Saklofske, D. H., Schwean, V. L., Yackulic, R. A., & Quinn, D. (1994). WISC-III and SB: FE performance of children with Attention Deficit Disorder. *Canadian Journal of School Psychology*, *10*, 167–171.

Sattler, J. M. (2008). *Assessment of children: Cognitive foundations*. San Diego, CA: Jerome M. Sattler Publications.

Schachar, R., & Logan, G. D. (1990). Impulsivity and inhibitory control in normal development and childhood psychopathology. *Developmental Psychology*, *26*, 710.

Schalock, R. L., Borthwick-Duffy, S. A., Bradley, V. J., Buntinx, W. H. E., Coulter, D. L., ... Yeager, M. H. (2010). *Intellectual disability: Definition, classification, and systems of support* (11th ed.). Annapolis, MD: AAIDD.

Scheuffgen, K., Happeé, F., Anderson, M., & Frith, U. (2000). High "intelligence," low "IQ"? Speed of processing and measured IQ in children with autism. *Development and Psychopathology*, *12*, 83–90.

Schuchardt, K., Gebhardt, M., & Mäehler, C. (2010). Working memory functions in children with different degrees of intellectual disability. *Journal of Intellectual Disability Research*, *54*, 346–353.

Seidman, L. J. (2006). Neuropsychological functioning in people with ADHD across the lifespan. *Clinical Psychology Review*, *26*, 466–485.

Seung, H. K. (2007). Linguistic characteristics of individuals with high functioning autism and Asperger syndrome. *Clinical Linguistics & Phonetics*, *21*, 247–259.

Shah, A., & Frith, U. (1983). An islet of ability in autistic children: A research note. *Journal of Child Psychology and Psychiatry*, *24*, 613–620.

Shah, A., & Frith, U. (1993). Why do autistic individuals show superior performance on the block design task? *Journal of Child Psychology and Psychiatry*, *34*, 1351–1364.

Shaw, P., Eckstrand, K., Sharp, W., Blumenthal, J., Lerch, J. P., Greenstein, D. E. E. A., ... Rapoport, J. L. (2007). Attention-deficit/hyperactivity disorder is characterized by a delay in cortical maturation. *Proceedings of the National Academy of Sciences, 104,* 19649−19654.

Shaw, P., Malek, M., Watson, B., Sharp, W., Evans, A., & Greenstein, D. (2012). Development of cortical surface area and gyrification in attention-deficit/hyperactivity disorder. *Biological Psychiatry, 72,* 191−197.

Shepard, R. N., & Metzler, J. (1971). Mental rotation of three-dimensional objects. *Science, 171,* 701−703.

Sheslow, D., & Adams, W. (1990). *WRAML: Wide range assessment of memory and learning.* Adams and Sheslow.

Silverman, L. K. (2002). *Upside down brilliance: The visualspatial learner.* Denver, CO: DeLeon Publishing.

Sonuga-Barke, E. J., Brandeis, D., Cortese, S., Daley, D., Ferrin, M., Holtmann, M., ... Dittmann, R. W. (2013). Nonpharmacological interventions for ADHD: systematic review and meta-analyses of randomized controlled trials of dietary and psychological treatments. *American Journal of Psychiatry, 170,* 275−289.

Spruill, J., Oakland, T., & Harrison, P. (2005). Assessment of mental retardation. In A. Prifitera, D. H. Saklofske, & L. G. Weiss (Eds.), *WISC-IV clinical use and interpretation: Scientist−practitioner perspectives* (pp. 299−331). San Diego, CA: Elsevier.

Steele, S. D., Minshew, N. J., Luna, B., & Sweeney, J. A. (2007). Spatial working memory deficits in autism. *Journal of Autism and Developmental Disorders, 37,* 605−612.

Stephens, K. R., & Karnes, F. A. (2000). State definitions for the gifted and talented revisited. *Exceptional Children, 66,* 219−238.

Sweetland, J. D., Reina, J. M., & Tatti, A. F. (2006). WISC-III verbal/performance discrepancies among a sample of gifted children. *Gifted Child Quarterly, 50,* 7−10.

Szatmari, P., Archer, L., Fisman, S., Streiner, D. L., & Wilson, F. (1995). Asperger's syndrome and autism: Differences in behavior, cognition, and adaptive functioning. *Journal of the American Academy of Child & Adolescent Psychiatry, 34,* 1662−1671.

Szatmari, P., White, J., & Merikangas, K. R. (2007). The use of genetic epidemiology to guide classification in child and adult psychopathology. *International Review of Psychiatry, 19,* 483−496.

Tannock, R. (2000). Attention deficit disorders with anxiety disorders. In T. E. Brown (Ed.), *Attention-deficit disorders and comorbidities in children, adolescents and adults* (pp. 125−175). New York: American Psychiatric Press.

Taylor, L. J., Mayberry, M. T., Grayndler, L., & Whitehouse, A. J. (2014). Evidence for distinct cognitive profiles in autism spectrum disorders and specific language impairment. *Journal of Autism and Developmental Disorders, 44,* 19−30.

Tseng, M. H., Henderson, A., Chow, S. M., & Yao, G. (2004). Relationship between motor proficiency, attention, impulse, and activity in children with ADHD. *Developmental Medicine & Child Neurology, 46,* 381−388.

Van der Molen, M. J., Henry, L. A., & Van Luit, J. E. H. (2014). Working memory development in children with mild to borderline intellectual disabilities. *Journal of Intellectual Disability Research, 58,* 637−650.

Van der Molen, M. J., Van Luit, J. E. H., Jongmans, M. J., & Van der Molen, M. W. (2007). Verbal working memory in children with mild intellectual disabilities. *Journal of Intellectual Disability Research, 51,* 162−169.

Van Goozen, S. H., Cohen-Kettenis, P. T., Snoek, H., Matthys, W., Swaab-Barneveld, H., & Van Engeland, H. (2004). Executive functioning in children: A comparison of hospitalised

ODD and ODD/ADHD children and normal controls. *Journal of Child Psychology and Psychiatry, 45,* 284−292.

Vogan, V. M., Morgan, B. R., Lee, W., Powell, T. L., Smith, M. L., & Taylor, M. J. (2014). The neural correlates of visuo-spatial working memory in children with autism spectrum disorder: Effects of cognitive load. *Journal of Neurodevelopmental Disorders, 6,* 1−15.

Vuijk, P. J., Hartman, E., Scherder, E., & Visscher, C. (2010). Motor performance of children with mild intellectual disability and borderline intellectual functioning. *Journal of Intellectual Disability Research, 54,* 955−965.

Watson, D., & Clark, L. A. (2006). Clinical diagnosis at the crossroads. *Clinical Psychology: Science and Practice, 13,* 210−215.

Wechsler, D. (1944). *The measurement of adult intelligence* (3rd ed.). Baltimore, MD: Williams &Wilkins.

Wechsler, D. (1974). *Manual for the Wechsler intelligence scale for children-revised.* San Antonio, TX: The Psychological Corporation.

Wechsler, D. (2002). *Wechsler preschool and primary scale of intelligence* (3rd ed.). San Antonio, TX: Pearson.

Wechsler, D. (2003). *Wechsler intelligence scale for children* (4th ed.). San Antonio, TX: Pearson.

Wechsler, D. (2004). *Wechsler intelligence scale for children* (4th ed.). Toronto, ON, Canada: Harcourt Assessment.

Wechsler, D. (2008). *Wechsler adult intelligence scale* (4th ed.). Bloomington, MN: Pearson.

Wechsler, D. (2012a). *Wechsler preschool and primary scale of intelligence* (4th ed.). Bloomington, MN: Pearson.

Wechsler, D. (2012b). *Wechsler preschool and primary scale of intelligence* (4th ed.). Toronto, ON, Canada: Pearson.

Wechsler, D. (2014). *Wechsler intelligence scale for children* (5th ed.). Bloomington, MN: Pearson.

Weiss, L. G., Keith, T. Z., Zhu, J., & Chen, H. (2013a). WAIS-IV clinical validation of the four- and five-factor interpretive approaches [Special edition]. *Journal of Psychoeducational Assessment, 31,* 94−113.

Weiss, L. G., Keith, T. Z., Zhu, J., & Chen, H. (2013b). WISC-IV and clinical validation of the four- and five-factor interpretive approaches [Special edition]. *Journal of Psychoeducational Assessment, 31,* 114−131.

Weiss, L. G., Saklofske, D. H., Prifitera, A., & Holdnack, J. A. (2006). *WISC-IV advanced clinical interpretation.* Academic Press.

White, S. J., & Saldaña, D. (2011). Performance of children with autism on the Embedded Figures Test: A closer look at a popular task. *Journal of Autism and Developmental Disorders, 41,* 1565−1572.

Whitehouse, A. J. O., Barry, J. G., & Bishop, D. V. M. (2008). Further defining the language impairment of autism spectrum disorders: Is there a specific language impairment subtype? *Journal of Communication Disorders, 41,* 319−336.

Widiger, T. A., & Samuel, D. B. (2005). Diagnostic categories or dimensions? A question for the Diagnostic and statistical manual of mental disorders—fifth edition. *Journal of Abnormal Psychology, 114,* 494.

Willcutt, E. G., Doyle, A. E., Nigg, J. T., Faraone, S. V., & Pennington, B. F. (2005). Validity of the executive function theory of attention-deficit/hyperactivity disorder: A meta-analytic review. *Biological Psychiatry, 57,* 1336−1346.

Williams, D. L., Goldstein, G., & Minshew, N. J. (2006a). The profile of memory function in children with autism. *Neuropsychology, 20*, 21–29.

Williams, D. L., Goldstein, G., & Minshew, N. J. (2006b). Neuropsychologic functioning in children with autism: Further evidence for disordered complex information-processing. *Child Neuropsychology, 12*, 279–298.

Williams, D. L., Minshew, N. J., & Goldstein, G. (2008). Memory within a complex information processing model of autism. In J. Boucher, & D. Bowler (Eds.), *Memory in autism* (pp. 125–142). New York: Cambridge University Press.

Witkin, H. A., Oltman, P. K., Raskin, E., & Karp, S. A. (1971). *A manual for the Embedded Figures Test.* Palo Alto, CA: Consulting Psychologists Press.

Wodka, E. L., Mostofsky, S. H., Prahme, C., Gidley Larson, J. C., Loftis, C., Denckla, M. B., & Mark Mahone, E. (2008). Process examination of executive function in ADHD: Sex and subtype effects. *The Clinical Neuropsychologist, 22*, 826–841.

Wuang, Y. P., Wang, C. C., Huang, M. H., & Su, C. Y. (2008). Profiles and cognitive predictors of motor functions among early school-age children with mild intellectual disabilities. *Journal of Intellectual Disability Research, 52*, 1048–1060.

Yeates, K. O. (2000). Closed-head injury. In K. O. Yeates, M. D. Ris, & H. G. Taylor (Eds.), *Pediatric neuropsychology: Research, theory, and practice* (pp. 92–116). New York: Guilford Press.

Yeates, K. O., Taylor, H. G., Wade, S. L., Drotar, D., Stancin, T., & Minich, N. (2002). A prospective study of short-and long-term neuropsychological outcomes after traumatic brain injury in children. *Neuropsychology, 16*, 514.

Zayat, M., Kalb, L., & Wodka, E. L. (2011). Brief report: Performance pattern differences between children with autism spectrum disorders and attention deficit-hyperactivity disorder on measures of verbal intelligence. *Journal of Autism and Developmental Disorders, 41*, 1743–1747.

Chapter 12

Digital Assessment With Q-interactive

Dustin Wahlstrom[1], Mark Daniel[1], Lawrence G. Weiss[2] and Aurelio Prifitera[3]

[1]*Pearson Clinical Assessment, San Antonio, TX, United States,* [2]*Research & Measurement Consultant, San Antonio, TX, United States,* [3]*Assessment Consultant, San Antonio, TX, United States*

Q-interactive is a digital system built to support and enhance a clinician's use of individually administered tests such as the Wechsler Intelligence Scale for Children—Fifth Edition (WISC-V). This type of computer-assisted testing is distinct from the more familiar computer-administered testing in which the examinee sees test items on a computer screen and answers using a keyboard, mouse, or touchscreen. That technology, which has been used for many years in psychology, education, and the workplace, is well suited to instruments such as self-report inventories or multiple-choice tests that have consistent, unspeeded, and fairly simple administration and response formats (Butcher, Perry, & Hahn, 2004; Mead & Drasgow, 1993). By contrast, in individually administered testing the examinee interacts with a skilled examiner who presents test items, records and scores responses, and provides feedback or guidance as needed to make sure that the examinee is demonstrating his or her best performance. Individual administration of this type is invaluable when it is considered critical to obtain a valid measure of the examinee's abilities on a performance task; when qualitative behavioral observation is considered to be a critical component of test interpretation; when the examinee must provide motoric or vocal responses; or when assessing an individual who, because of age, disability or clinical condition, cannot be tested without assistance. Q-interactive is perhaps the first system to enlist digital technology to improve and enhance the practice of individually administered assessment.

In keeping with this focus on assessment as an interaction between two people, the heart of Q-interactive is a test-administration component based on two tablets, one for the examinee and the other for the examiner.

WISC-V. DOI: https://doi.org/10.1016/B978-0-12-815744-2.00012-4

The examinee's tablet takes the place of the traditional printed stimulus booklet and captures touch responses. The examiner's tablet has multiple functions: it shows the item administration and scoring instructions typically provided in an examiner's manual, captures and scores item responses, shows the examinee's touch responses, performs timing, implements administration rules such as start and discontinue points, records examiner notes, calculates a score, and saves a record of the administration. The two devices are connected via Bluetooth, with the examiner controlling what is displayed on the examinee device.

The overarching goal of Q-interactive is to leverage advances in both hardware and software to improve the assessment experience and the quality of assessment results. Elements of that goal emphasized in the initial generation of Q-interactive tests include:

1. *Accuracy*. Automating subtest rules (start points, discontinues, etc.), automating aspects of scoring, presenting all item-specific administration and scoring reference information in a single location, and reducing the amount of materials an examiner has to juggle, all serve to remove common sources of examiner error.
2. *Portability and accessibility*. Having an entire test library self-contained within two tablets is significantly more convenient than transporting several paper test kits, and provides easy access to a larger amount of test content.
3. *Efficiency*. By streamlining the workflow and automating tasks such as scoring, Q-interactive can save the clinician time.
4. *Flexibility*. The system makes it easy to add or subtract subtests from a test battery, and provides real-time data to help inform those decisions. This enables more personalized assessments and accurate diagnosis.
5. *Examinee engagement*. Children find technology more engaging than paper, giving greater confidence that the child's performance is a valid indicator of their ability.
6. *Focus on the examinee*. Examiners can pay more attention to examinee behavior because the system simplifies their task by automating distracting, mundane activities.

Notably, five of these six goals have to do with the examiner, not the examinee. This reflects the initial focus of Q-interactive, which was to preserve the examinee's test-taking experience so that their performance on a subtest can be expected to be the same in either format—that is, the two versions will be raw-score equivalent. Thus, in its initial form, the test-administration component of Q-interactive could be thought of as a new and improved medium for providing the same test-taking experience as the standard version of the test. That began to change with the WISC-V, which was launched in 2014 and updated in 2016 to include fully digital versions of Symbol Search and Coding. These tasks differ, by necessity, from their paper counterparts and are not assumed to be equivalent. Rather, they are linked back to paper by equating procedures. This is the first step toward the ultimate vision for Q-interactive, which is to provide tests that are only available digitally because they take advantage of all the benefits that technology offers.

This chapter describes the Q-interactive system, summarizes the development work supporting the initial phases of its evolution, and gives an overview of the research on the Q-interactive version of the WISC-V, including the development of fully digital versions of Coding and Symbol Search. Finally, it explores some of the key implications of the system for the practice of clinical assessment.

OVERVIEW OF Q-INTERACTIVE

Q-interactive is a system that supports and gives access to multiple tests, serving as a central hub for a practitioner's assessment activities. The two major components of Q-interactive are called *Central* and *Assess*. Central is a website that examiners typically access through a laptop or desktop computer in order to create clients, manage their test library, set up assessment sessions, generate reports, and store data long term for review. Assess is the tablet application where testing takes place.

The entire Q-interactive workflow consists of a few basic steps:

1. In Central, the practitioner creates a client and assigns a set of tests in an administration sequence; the combination of the client and the set of tests is called the *Assessment*.
2. The Assessment is sent wirelessly to Assess (i.e., to the examiner tablet).
3. The testing session takes place within Assess, using two tablets.
4. Once all items are scored, the assessment data are sent back wirelessly to Central for long-term storage, and are removed from the examiner tablet.
5. The practitioner generates reports in Central.

The user must be connected to the Internet in order to access Central (steps 1 and 5) and to transfer information between Central and Assess (steps 2 and 4). However, the test administration itself (step 3) can take place without an Internet connection, with no loss of functionality (e.g., tests are still scored, and clinicians can add new tests to their session, even without Internet connectivity).

At a high level, subtest administration within Assess follows a consistent workflow. The examiner will already have downloaded the assessment (the set of tests for the client) to the examiner's tablet. From that point until completion of the administration, all work is carried out using the examiner and examinee tablets, and there is no need for an Internet connection.

The examiner initiates a subtest by opening it on the examiner tablet, and placing the other tablet (if used) in front of the examinee. Administration instructions for the sample item appear on the examiner's screen, which is positioned so that the examinee cannot see it. The examiner brings up the stimulus image on the examinee tablet by touching a button; this image is also displayed in a portion of the examiner screen so that the examiner knows what the examinee is seeing. Another button is available for starting the timer, if performance is timed.

The examiner may capture responses in a number of ways, depending on the nature of the subtest and on the examiner's preference. On a subtest such as Matrix Reasoning where the examinee chooses one or more images on the screen, the examinee's touch is recorded and also shows up on the examiner's screen (shown in Fig. 12.1). If necessary, the examiner can touch the option that the examinee selected to ensure that it is captured. The sequence of touches is also be captured, if that is a factor in scoring (such as on CELF-5 Linguistic Concepts).

On most subtests, touch response is not used; instead, the examiner tablet is the only device needed to score and record responses. There are three ways of capturing response information on the examiner tablet: touch, handwriting (preferably with a stylus, although the fingertip may be used), and audio recording. Many of the Q-interactive capture screens have a number of buttons representing different responses or response characteristics. For example, the screens for the WISC-V Verbal Comprehension subtests display buttons for each item's sample responses, grouped by score. Fig. 12.2

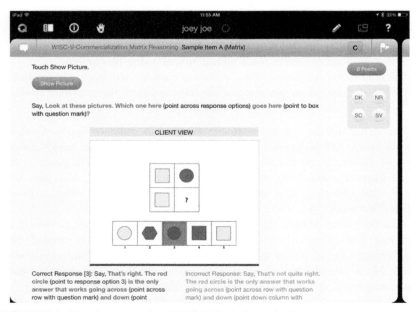

FIGURE 12.1 Examiner screen for a WISC-V Matrix Reasoning item.

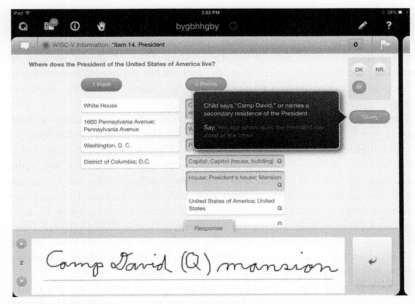

FIGURE 12.2   Examiner screen for a WISC-V Information item.

illustrates this screen design for the WISC-V Information subtest. Where appropriate, there is a handwriting area on the screen that provides unlimited room for writing verbatim responses. And on subtests with oral responses, the examiner tablet automatically (unless intentionally disabled) makes a digital audio recording of what the examinee says. This recording can be reviewed by the examiner at any time until the entire administration session is completed, checked, and uploaded to Central, at which time the audio files are erased from the tablet. (Audio files are not uploaded.) In addition, there are numerous tools on the examiner tablet such as timers, buttons for recording important events such as querying or self-correction, and a "notes" tool that lets the examiner record comments about an item, a subtest, or the entire assessment session.

On most subtests, the examiner assigns item scores. Only for multiple-choice subtests such as Matrix Reasoning does the system assign a score, but even in that case the examiner can override the score. On the Verbal Comprehension subtests that have sample-response buttons grouped by score level, the examiner must still decide what score to give for each item, because an examinee's response to an item may be complex. If the examiner is not sure what score to assign he or she can assign a tentative score but also touch the "flag" button which highlights the item for review at the end of the assessment session (along with any unscored items).

After finishing an item, the examiner moves to the next item by swiping. At that point, the system checks the pattern of item scores against the standard administration rules (discontinue, reversal, etc.) and notifies the examiner if a rule has been met, giving the examiner the choice of what to do next. The examiner may override rules, such as for testing of the limits. So as long as each item is scored accurately, the system guides the examiner through a correct administration.

Once the examiner decides to end the subtest, the system shows a summary report for that subtest. If any items have flags or were left unscored, they are highlighted in the "To Do" section. The examiner can look at any item's capture screen, including the handwriting, and listen to any audio recordings, in order to check and complete scoring. After all items are scored, the screen shows the subtest raw and scaled scores. This provides instant feedback regarding the examinee's performance, which can be used to adjust the test battery on the fly via Q-interactive's "Edit Battery" functionality. For example, during the testing session, the examiner could decide to confirm an unexpectedly low score on the Vocabulary subtest by adding the optional Comprehension subtest into the test battery.

Finally, when the test session is complete and all subtest scoring is finished, the examiner can choose to remove the assessment from the tablet, which transfers all of the data wirelessly to Central and deletes them from the examiner tablet. However, not all activities for an assessment have to be completed in one sitting. An assessment can be administered and scored over the course of days or weeks, during which time the data remains on the tablet.

PHASES OF Q-INTERACTIVE EVOLUTION

As noted earlier, the goals of Assess interface design are evolving. This development may be divided into three phases. Phase 1 aims to achieve raw-score equivalence to the paper version by maintaining a consistent examinee experience. Phase 2 allows the examinee experience to differ (to take advantage of technology) but preserves construct equivalence. Finally, in Phase 3 digitally native tasks are created that may not have paper counterparts.

In Phase 1, the objective is for the Q-interactive administration to produce the same raw scores as the standard paper administration, so that not only the existing norms but also the existing research base on reliability and validity can be used. This entails a cautious and conservative approach to digital adaptation that sometimes results in Assess not taking advantage of all the features the Q-interactive technology offers. For example, in this phase, manipulatives such as Block Design blocks and Processing Speed response booklets must be retained. If there is raw-score equivalence between digital and paper formats and the interface appears to provide the same examinee experience as the paper administration, it is assumed that the reliability and validity of the score are the same with either format.

Phase 2, like Phase 1, is aimed at obtaining the same assessment information provided by standard paper-format tests, but it gives up the benefits of raw-score equivalence in order to obtain the benefits offered by the digital medium such as more accurate administration and scoring, the convenience and accessibility of being entirely digital, and greater examinee engagement. Its goal is to develop a digital subtest that measures the same or nearly the same construct as a paper-format subtest, with comparable or superior reliability. Examples of Phase 2 development are the digital versions of WISC-V Coding and Symbol Search subtests, where the examinee responds by touching the tablet rather than marking a paper response booklet. As in Phase 1, the examinee experience should appear to be nearly the same as in the paper format in all ways thought to be construct-relevant; differences in examinee experience that are considered construct-irrelevant are permitted, and in fact such a difference may be desirable if it means that the digital version is a purer measure of the target construct. (In the example just given, removing the need for pencil control might be seen as a benefit for assessing visual processing speed in young children.) However, in Phase 2 it is assumed that the digital and paper versions will not be raw-score equivalent. The nature and extent of evidence needed to support the reliability and validity of scores will depend on a number of factors including the magnitude of the correlation between the digital and paper versions. Essentially, judgments must be made about the kind of supporting data required to enable practitioners to interpret scores with confidence. Depending on the closeness of the correspondence between the digital and paper scores, norms may be derived through equating (if the clinical construct being measured is substantially the same in both versions) or through independent sampling.

Phase 3 is the development of new digitally native tests that do not necessarily have a close relationship with existing paper tests and manipulatives. For example, one might imagine a digital version of a task to assess planning ability in which the examinee must navigate aisles in a virtual grocery store to pick up items on a list using the most efficient route. This bears little resemblance to traditional paper and pencil maze tasks and would not be raw-score equivalent to them, but might measure the same construct with greater ecological validity—although that remains to be seen. The Q-interactive team is currently researching several new digitally native tasks in an effort to improve the measurement of the underlying constructs of interest. This phase requires the same development methods, including explorations of reliability and validity, as are needed for any new test in any format.

Most of the Q-interactive development work to date has been in Phase 1, with the development of digital versions of Coding and Symbol Search representing the only Phase 2 subtests thus far. The following sections summarize the development approaches for Phases 1 and 2 and summarize the research evidence that has been collected for each.

PHASE 1

Design Requirements

Two overarching requirements drove the initial design and development of Assess. The first was raw-score and construct equivalence, a precondition for valid interpretation of scores (International Test Commission, 2005). The second was clinical flexibility, that is, giving the examiner as much control over the administration as when using the standard paper materials. The role of Assess is to support the examiner by performing mundane aspects of the administration process, without taking over control or imposing limitations on what the examiner can do. Individual administration remains a skilled clinical activity involving judgment and flexibility.

Equivalence

For some tests, the threats to equivalence posed by digitization are fairly obvious. For example, one could imagine a version of Block Design in which the examinee drags images of blocks across the tablet screen in order to create a design. Although such a task may be conceptually appealing and might ultimately be implemented on Q-interactive, from the point of view of equivalence a change this major raises a number of questions: Does the new task measure the same core ability? To what extent are scores influenced by extraneous abilities or skills different from those involved in the standard (paper) version? Are scores similarly reliable? What impact might these potential differences have for interpretation?

Some of these same questions apply as well to other types of adaptations where there is less apparent difference between the paper and digital versions. In general, three ways in which the design of a Q-interactive subtest could threaten equivalence are:

1. Changing how the examinee interacts with the test (e.g., by changing how they view or manipulate test stimuli or produce responses). For example, does showing a Matrix Reasoning item on a digital screen rather than paper have an effect?
2. Changing how the examiner interacts with the test (e.g., by changing how the examiner accesses administration and scoring information, records examinee responses, etc.). These tasks are intentionally quite different on Q-interactive than when using paper materials. Assess presents item-specific administration instructions, provides an entire screen for capturing the response to an item, and offers new methods for response capture such as picklists and audio recording. While these may improve accuracy, they represent a significant change in the examiner's task.

3. Interaction of the two, whereby a change in how either the examiner or examinee interacts with the test affects the other. An example will illustrate this concept. In early development work, the team prototyped the examiner's use of an external keyboard to record oral responses (such as on WISC Vocabulary). Examiners took longer to type responses than to write them on paper, and this (possibly in combination with the sounds of the keyboard) led examinees to purposefully shorten their responses, as if in an attempt to assist the struggling examiners. For this reason, the development team made the decision not to support capturing verbatim responses by typing in the Q-interactive system.

How did the identification of these equivalence threats affect the design process? First, it drove the decision that what the examinee hears, sees, and touches needs to be similar enough to the paper format to not threaten equivalence. Thus, test manipulatives (such as Block Design blocks or NEPSY-II Animal Sorting cards) and response booklets (such as for the WISC Processing Speed subtests) were retained in Phase 1, despite the fact that digital tasks without the manipulatives could have been designed. This decision also applied to visual stimuli presented on the examinee tablet. It was important to maintain the size and clarity of images wherever possible, although slight concessions were made to accommodate the size of the tablet screen.

An example of the importance of image consistency occurred during development of WAIS-IV Picture Completion. The original equivalence study suggested slightly poorer performance on the digital version of the task than with the paper version, despite the fact that the images appeared to the development team to be comparable. After weeks of investigation, a staff member taking the paper and digital versions side-by-side reported a subjective sense of wanting to solve the paper items because the clarity of the images made the problems seem easier. It turned out that subtle fuzziness in areas of the digital image unrelated to solving the problem nevertheless was distracting because examinees thought it might be significant. Improving the clarity of the digital images eliminated the difference in raw scores obtained from digital and paper versions of Picture Completion.

Another example concerns touch feedback on the examinee screen. The screen flashes momentarily when the examinee touches a response selection, which of course is unlike the behavior of the paper stimulus book. Nevertheless, examinees know that their touch is being captured, and they are used to seeing this kind of feedback on touchscreen devices. If there were no feedback at all, they might be concerned about whether their touch had registered. So this difference between digital and paper interfaces was accepted as being necessary to remove a possible source of distraction. This design feature has no impact on scores, according to equivalence data across several subtests.

Clinical Flexibility and Robustness

The second major driver of Q-interactive design was the need to accommodate the dynamic nature of the clinical assessment process. The importance of this consideration was documented through interviews and observations involving hundreds of users. Tests such as the WISC-V are governed by standard administration rules that are relatively easy to program. However, as important as the rules themselves is the requirement to deviate from them when appropriate. For example, clinicians should start at earlier start points if they suspect that an individual is lower functioning, give items past the discontinue point if the examinee is answering questions correctly with additional time, and come back to administer previously administered items if the pattern of responses indicates unexplained inconsistency. The innumerable possible paths in the test-administration workflow, driven by clinical judgment, cannot be captured in a linear program. Thus, the Q-interactive system must be flexible.

This flexibility was built into Assess in a number of ways. For example, on most subtests each item is presented to the examiner on its own screen, which enables flexible navigation through items in either forward or reverse direction and the ability to jump to another item. Also, although start points by age or grade are programmed into the system, examiners can override these for special cases. The same is true for discontinue points, which are flagged by the system but do not prevent the examiner from continuing with additional items if desired.

Scoring is also flexible. For example, the examinee can change his or her touch response on a task like Matrix Reasoning as many times as needed. On all subtests and items, the examiner has ultimate control of scoring and can override the examinee's touch response (such as when the examinee touches option 5 but says, "I mean 1"). This does not have to occur while the item is being administered, but can be done after the assessment is complete; item responses and scores can be updated at any time. These design features build in a level of flexibility that is intended to match that available with paper-based administration.

One distinctive aspect of designing an application for clinical assessment is the fact that giving a test is usually a "one-shot" event. The clinician typically has a single try to administer a test: for example, once Block Design has been administered to an individual, it cannot be administered again for quite a while because practice effects can influence the score. Thus, the capture of information about every item administration must be robust. This requirement was reflected in the design of functional characteristics such as the transfer and saving of data. For example, Assess is usable without an internet connection so that Q-interactive can be employed in rural, forensic, government, and other settings where wireless connections may not be available or reliable. When Assess is used in offline mode, data is saved on the examiner tablet after every item to ensure that data is maintained even if the application or tablet were to unexpectedly close. If this occurs, the examiner can simply turn the device back on, enter the assessment session, and pick backup where he or she left off, with all data up to that point saved.

Development Steps

Because Q-interactive is the first system of its kind, its development required confronting many novel system-design questions. What started as a concept slowly took the form of a design, a prototype, and eventually, a functional system. In general, the steps taken to create Q-interactive fell into the following activities:

1. designing and prototyping and
2. evaluating equivalence

Designing and Prototyping

One of the first steps in designing Assess for a subtest was to map its administration into a logical, programmable workflow called a "logic map." Fig. 12.3 illustrates a small section of the logic map for the WISC-IV Block Design administration process. This reveals the numerous steps and decision points that make up an administration, each of which is performed intuitively

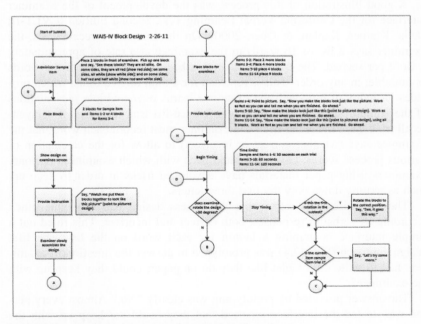

FIGURE 12.3   Partial workflow map of the Block Design subtest.

by seasoned examiners. The logic map showed each possible step and its relationships to other actions and events, in order to enable the software team to design the architecture supporting Assess.

The next step in the design process was to select designs for the interfaces—what would the examinee see, how would the examiner read instructions, and how would responses be recorded and scored? This was approached systemically. A wide cross section of subtests were grouped according to the type of response required on the part of the examinee (e.g., verbal, touch, arranging manipulatives, etc.), and the type of information recorded by the examiner (e.g., verbatim verbal response, a score, etc.).

Once these groupings were complete, common interface design concepts were created for each group. This had two benefits. First, it simplified the system and improved usability by letting examiners transfer learnings from one subtest to others within that same group, reducing the overall training burden. Second, it allowed the development team to evaluate possible effects of an interface feature on the basis of information from multiple subtests, enhancing the ability to detect such effects.

Prototypes of proposed design concepts were tested and updated as necessary to ensure that they met the needs of clinicians. This was a key element of the development process which heavily influenced the final designs. Essentially, an experimental approach was taken to selecting designs for many of the specific functions incorporated in the interfaces.

A good illustration of this process was the development of the examiner interface for the California Verbal Learning Test, Second Edition (CVLT-II; Delis, Kramer, Kaplan, & Ober, 2000). On the immediate recall trials, the examiner says a list of 16 words to the examinee at a rate of approximately 1 word per second. The examinee is then asked to say as many of the words as possible, in any order. This is repeated for a total of five trials, which provides an index of how well the examinee learns over multiple presentations of the stimuli. (There are also an interference-list trial and several delayed-recall trials.) On the recall trials the examiner must record each word that the examinee says (whether correct or incorrect) to allow for the calculation of various process scores. Given the rapid pace with which examinees respond, examiners using paper materials have developed tricks in order to keep up, such as writing down only the first three letters.

These requirements meant that the Assess design had to enable quick recording of verbatim responses, both correct and incorrect. This ruled out a simple interface containing a button for each word on the list. The first design approach (Fig. 12.4) was prototyped to answer the question: if examiners had to write on a tablet like they do on paper, could they keep up with the examinee?

The answer provided by prototyping was clearly "No." Almost every person who tested the interface reported that they could not keep up with the examinee. This was due in part to the novelty of writing on a digital

FIGURE 12.4   First CVLT-II prototype.

interface, but also to a half-second lag when the examiner hit the "Return" button to begin writing a new word. The next design attempt was a hybrid model with buttons for the list words and a handwriting area for nonlist words. While this improved response capture, the "Return" lag still presented a problem. Finally, the designers invented a clever solution (shown in Fig. 12.5) with two handwriting areas. Once a word was written in one area, the examiner could begin writing in the second, which automatically cleared the first area and committed the word to the list. This switching back and forth eliminated the need for a "Return" button, and in conjunction with buttons for correct words, achieved the needed level of speed of response capture. (Audio recording is also enabled on this subtest as a backup for extreme cases.)

Evaluating Equivalence

Once the prototyping process was completed, the next step was to conduct equivalence studies to determine whether the Q-interactive format yielded the same raw scores as the standard paper version. It is important to distinguish between equivalence studies and norming studies. Norming is a matter of sampling from a defined population. By contrast, an equivalence study is an experiment designed to answer the question whether an individual would be expected to obtain the same raw score regardless of which format was used. The two types of undertaking require different kinds and amounts of data. The Q-interactive equivalence studies (described in technical reports

FIGURE 12.5   Final CVLT-II Implementation with "dual capture" design.

available on Pearson's website) used several types of experimental designs, as appropriate to the characteristics of the test being studied and the types of threats to equivalence that those characteristics might present.

Several principles guided the design and conduct of the equivalence studies:

- An a priori definition of "raw-score equivalent": The team set an operational standard for equivalence as an effect size of 0.20 or less. Effect size is the average difference in scores obtained using Q-interactive and paper formats, expressed as a proportion of the population standard deviation (e.g., three for Wechsler subtest scaled scores). Effect sizes of 0.20 are traditionally classified as small in the research literature, while effect sizes of 0.50 and 0.80 are classified as medium and large, respectively (Cohen, 1988). An effect size of 0.20 is equal to 0.6 scaled score points, or three points on the composite score metric that has a mean of 100 and standard deviation of 15. This is roughly equivalent to the SEM of the Full Scale IQ (FSIQ) on WISC-V (2.90) and less than the SEMs for the primary Index scores (which range from 3.89 to 5.24).
- Focus on plausible threats: The first step in planning an equivalence study was to do a logical analysis of the examinee and examiner tasks to identify aspects that might affect scores. This led to choosing a study design that would be capable of revealing these effects.

- Begin with the general population: The initial question was whether there is anything inherent in the format that affects scores. This needs to be answered first with typical examinees before turning to the question of whether equivalence also obtains in subgroups such as clinical populations.
- One administration per examinee: Usually, each examinee takes the test only once. The experience in a second administration can be different than in the first, because the examinee already understands the task and may remember how to solve particular items or what overall strategy was helpful. Counterbalancing the format sequence may not effectively control for these effects. For example, if the Q-interactive presentation of a test were less clear than the paper presentation, this format effect would not appear among examinees taking the Q-interactive format second.
- Adequate sample size: The studies should have good statistical power to detect an effect size of 0.20 (at an alpha level of 0.05).
- Video record administrations: We need to be able to determine the cause of any observed format effect. Is there a difference in examinee behavior? Or is there a difference in how the examiner or the Q-interactive system captures or scores that behavior? When a format effect is found, we do not know which format is more accurate. Video recordings provide a way to answer these questions, and also may reveal differences in how examinees behave, which can provide insights into interface design. Without this record, diagnosing the cause of a format effect would often be speculative.

Three types of experimental designs have been used. In the *equivalent-groups design*, one group takes the test in the standard paper format and a second, comparable group takes it in the digital format, and the scores obtained by the two groups are compared. Comparability of the groups may be obtained through stratified random assignment to format, or through a combination of demographic matching and statistical control from covariate tests. This design is suitable for any type of test, and it has high ecological validity because each subject's testing experience is similar to what they would have in clinical practice. Relatively large samples (several hundred examinees) are required to provide good statistical power.

In the second design type, *retest*, each examinee takes the test in both formats, in counterbalanced order. Because this design violates the single-administration design principle described above, it has been used only for tests where it is thought that the examinee uses the same cognitive processes the second time as the first. Types of tests that have been studied using the retest design include tests of short-term memory for nonmeaningful stimuli (e.g., digit span or spatial patterns) and tests of processing speed. Offsetting the limitations of this design is its high degree of statistical power with small samples, due to the fact that examinees serve as their own controls.

This efficiency is enhanced by starting with demographically matched pairs of examinees whose members are randomly assigned to the two format sequences.

Like the retest design, the third type of design, called *dual capture*, is also highly efficient but limited to tests with certain characteristics. A small number of test administrations are video-recorded from the examiner's viewpoint, showing only the examinee. Each video recording is then scored by many examiners, some using the standard paper materials and the others using Q-interactive. The analysis looks for any differences between scores obtained using the two formats. This design focuses on possible threats to equivalence arising from the response—capture interface on the examiner tablet. It is appropriate for tests in which there is no interaction between examiner and examinee during item administration, and where the examinee does not respond on the examinee tablet.

The initial Q-interactive studies evaluated all subtests in a battery because little was known about the effects that the Q-interactive format might have. As studies were completed, knowledge accumulated about the behavior of certain kinds of interface features. As a result, in later studies a subtest might not be evaluated if the only possible threats to equivalence were interface features that had already been shown to be benign. This knowledge base relied on the categorization of interface features described earlier.

As described above, all research designs have their relative strengths and weaknesses, and none provide a perfect test of the given hypotheses. When large numbers of effects are evaluated in an experiment, some positive results may occur by chance. This is why statistically significant findings should be reliably replicated across multiple studies before finally being accepted. For all these reasons, the Q-interactive development team focused on trends in the overall research program across multiple subtests with very similar digital interface demands, rather than findings from individual subtests in single studies.

To date, 81 subtests from 11 instruments (including WISC-V) have been studied, permitting some general conclusions about how various types of Q-interactive interfaces perform with respect to equivalence. Overall, 79 of the 81 effect sizes were within the range of -0.20 to 0.20 that is considered to indicate equivalence, and the mean effect size was 0.01. Table 12.1 reports the average effect size separately for each of six different interface types.

Interface types in which the examinee tablet is not used, or is used only to display a visual stimulus with no touch response, have been found to have average effect sizes very close to zero (between -0.03 and 0.04), with no individual effect sizes exceeding 0.20 in absolute value. This indicates that the examiner interfaces are functioning as intended, even when response capture is complex.

Among subtests involving a visual stimulus and a touch response by the examinee, there is a slight tendency toward higher scores when using Q-interactive, and two subtests showed effect sizes greater than 0.20: WISC-IV Matrix Reasoning (0.27) and WISC-IV Picture Concepts (0.21). Although

TABLE 12.1 Average Q-interactive Format Effect Sizes by Type of Interface, for All Studies

Type of Interface (WISC-V Example)	No. Subtests	Effect Size		
		Mean	SD	Range
Oral response, captured by examiner (Vocabulary)	27	−0.03	0.09	−0.20 to 0.12
Time, captured by examiner (Coding)	7	0.04	0.14	−0.07 to 0.13
Errors and time, captured by examiner (Digit Span)	9	0.05	0.09	−0.08 to 0.18
Visual display, no touch response (Block Design)	22	−0.03	0.12	−0.19 to 0.20
Visual display, single touch (Matrix Reasoning)	8	0.15	0.08	−0.02 to 0.27
Visual display, multiple touches (Picture Concepts)	8	0.07	0.09	−0.08 to 0.21
Total	81	0.01	0.11	−0.20 to 0.27

Note: Data from studies of CELF-5, CMS, CVLT-II, D-KEFS, NEPSY-II, WAIS-IV, WIAT-III, WISC-IV, WISC-V, WMS-IV, and WPPSI-IV.

the reason for this tendency is not known, evidence from the video recordings of the administrations rules out administration or scoring errors with either the paper or the digital formats, or any obvious differences in examiner behavior. The effect is subtle, and might be related to the increased level of examinee engagement and effort reported by Q-interactive users. That is, the difficulty level of the tasks may not have changed but the mode of presentation elicited optimal examinee performance—something all examiners try to do (within limits of standardized procedures).

The consistency of the effect sizes reported in Table 12.1 lends support to the adequacy of the designs and the sample sizes used in the equivalence studies. Inadequate samples would have caused random variability in results due to the increased sampling error, probably resulting in more effect sizes outside the range of −0.20 to 0.20.

The WISC-V study, described in Q-interactive Technical Report 8 (Daniel, Wahlstrom & Ou, 2014), used a randomly equivalent-groups design with 350 examinees (175 demographically matched pairs). The findings are shown in Table 12.2. Effect sizes for the 13 primary and ancillary cognitive subtests (not including the Processing Speed subtests) ranged from −0.20 to 0.20 with a mean of 0.03 (SD = 0.13). (The Processing Speed subtests are not included because their Q-interactive versions were under development at

TABLE 12.2 Q-interactive Format Effect Sizes for WISC-V Subtests

Subtest by Interface Type	Effect Size
No Examinee Interface: Oral Response	
Arithmetic	− 0.16
Comprehension	− 0.20
Information	− 0.05
Similarities	0.04
Vocabulary	− 0.13
No Examinee Interface: Errors and Time	
Digit Span	0.08
Letter−Number Sequencing	0.09
Examinee Interface: Display Only	
Block Design	0.20
Immediate Symbol Translation	0.03
Delayed Symbol Translation	0.01
Recognition Symbol Translation	0.00
Naming Speed Literacy	0.12
Naming Speed Quantity	− 0.02
Examinee Interface: Display and Single Touch	
Figure Weights	0.16
Matrix Reasoning	0.17
Examinee Interface: Display and Multiple Touches	
Picture Concepts	0.02
Picture Span	0.07
Visual Puzzles	0.04

the time of the study. For a discussion of research related to the digital adaptation of the Processing Speed subtests see the section on "Phase 2.) The complementary psychoeducational subtests had the same mean effect size but a smaller standard deviation (0.05). The pattern of results by type of interface resembles the pattern for all 75 subtests shown in Table 12.1.

WISC-V Comprehension (an optional subtest) and Block Design each show an effect size of ± 0.20, close enough to the cut off to warrant special attention. Note, first, that these two subtests suggest effects in opposite directions: Block

Design shows an effect favoring digital administration and Comprehension suggests an effect favoring paper administration. Furthermore, neither of these tasks requires the examinee to interact with the tablet, and no logical explanation for the differences could be identified based on a careful review of the examiner interface by licensed psychologists on the Q-interactive development team who observed numerous video-recorded administrations. More importantly, the equivalence study of WISC-IV showed no format effects for Comprehension or Block Design, and the interface demands of these subtests are virtually identical in WISC-IV and WISC-V. Because the largest format effects reported for WISC-V are small in magnitude, limited to two subtests, occur in different directions, have no logical explanation, and were not replicable across studies, the Q-interactive version of WISC-V is treated as having raw-score equivalence to the paper version.

Equivalence for subgroups. Even if subtests are found to be raw-score equivalent in studies of large samples of typical individuals, it is reasonable to wonder whether this finding holds for all subgroups. For example, might examinees of low ability, or the very young or very old, or those from low socioeconomic environments experience difficulties when tested using digital tablets? It was possible to examine this question in the equivalence studies that used the randomly equivalent-groups design (WISC-IV and WISC-V), because that design uses large samples. We evaluated whether the "format effect" (i.e., the difference between actual and expected Q-interactive subtest scores) was related to age, gender, ethnicity, parent education, or score level on that subtest. Among the total of 165 analyses, only seven (4%) were statistically significant at the 0.05 level, fewer than the number expected by chance if there were no true effects. Furthermore, the seven significant findings were spread across subtest types and demographic variables. Overall, there appear to be no differences in format effect between males and females, between younger and older examinees (aged 6 and above), between examinees with above-average and below-average levels of parental education, among examinees of different race/ethnicity groups, or for examinees at different levels of ability on the construct being measured.

One relationship to demographic characteristics has been found in equivalence research on the WPPSI-IV (Drozdick, Getz, Raiford, & Zhang, 2016). Children aged 2 or 3 were sometimes distracted by the tablet or by the visual feedback to touch responding. This was addressed through design changes for some tests used with very young children, and the decision to retain the paper stimulus book for administering Picture Memory.

Phase 2

Design and Development Process

For the digital adaptations of Coding and Symbol Search, the primary design focus was on the examinee-facing interface because the switch from interacting with paper to interacting with a screen would change how the examinee completed the test. The examiner-facing interface was not a major concern because of the large amount of data and feedback that had already been collected about examiner interactions with Q-interactive, and because these subtests require minimal intervention by the clinician during administration. It was expected that the lack of raw-score equivalence would be dealt with by creating a conversion from digital raw scores to equivalent paper raw scores. Because of these significant modifications to the tasks, additional information about the reliability and validity of this new format would also be required.

The development process for Coding and Symbol Search was iterative and spanned several years (see Raiford et al., 2016, for a full description of the development process and results). The initial design attempted to mimic the examinee's task on the paper version as closely as possible. On Coding, examinees viewed the key of number—symbol associations at the top of the page, and used a stylus to draw the symbols corresponding to the numbers shown below. Unlike the paper response page, which contained all items, each digital screen contained only nine items. After completing the screen, examinees tapped an arrow button to continue to the next set of nine items. The layout of Symbol Search was also similar to that on paper but contained only 10 items per screen. For each item (row), the examinee tapped the response option that was identical to the target symbol. After the last item on the screen, the examinee tapped the arrow button to continue to the next set of items.

A pilot study was conducted with 350 individuals aged 6—16 (see Daniel et al., 2014) who were tested as part of the WISC-V standardization. Correlations between the digital and paper versions did not reach the threshold of 0.7 that had been set as a requirement for equating. (In the case of Coding for 6—7 year olds, the correlation was below 0.4.) These low correlations suggested that aspects of the interface design introduced some variance irrelevant to the construct of processing speed. Video review of the administrations revealed two potential causes of the low correlations. First, younger examinees struggled to use a stylus, and they often dropped their wrist onto the iPad screen, which prevented the capture of their handwriting strokes. Second, children varied in how quickly they tapped the arrow button and reoriented to the updated page. Consultation with child media experts indicated that this reorienting issue is common.

In light of these findings, both subtests were substantially revised. Coding was reconceptualized so that it did not use a stylus. The examinee screen showed the key at the top of the screen, a box in the middle of the screen with a number in the top half, and a row of five symbols below the box. The examinee answered by tapping the symbol corresponding to the number (Fig. 12.6). The reorientation problem was addressed by having the completed item slide off the screen while the next item slid in (as represented by the gray boxes in Fig. 12.6).

On the revised version of Symbol Search each screen showed five items (rows) with the "active" item in the middle row and the other items grayed out (Fig. 12.7). After the examinee responded, the rows scrolled up so that a new item became active.

A number of small studies were conducted with these revised designs. They revealed that correlations with the paper versions were sufficient to give the research team confidence that the paper and digital versions were

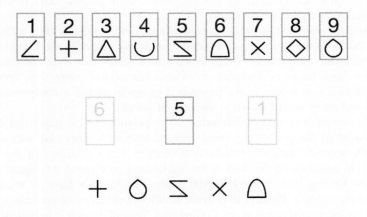

FIGURE 12.6 Final examinee screen for Coding.

FIGURE 12.7 Final examinee screen for Symbol Search.

measuring the same construct and therefore supported digital-paper equating. The new digital versions were then included in a scaling study.

Scaling Study

The scaling sample for digital Coding and Symbol Search consisted of 651 children ages 6–16 who were administered the ten primary WISC-V subtests (including Coding and Symbol Search) in either paper format ($N = 322$) or digital format ($N = 329$), followed by Coding and Symbol Search in the alternative format. Children were assigned to the paper-first or digital-first group by stratified random assignment within demographic cells based on age, gender, and parent education.

The first step in the process was to apply inferential scaling (Zhu & Chen, 2011) to the Coding and Symbol Search raw scores in the digital-first group to create conversions to age-based scaled scores that were comparable to those from paper administrations. These conversions were then applied to the digital raw scores in the paper-first group to permit a comparison of digital and paper scaled scores in the overall sample.

This sample was used to determine the correlations of the paper and digital versions of the processing speed subtests with each other and with other WISC-V subtests, and to perform confirmatory factor analyses of the full battery. In addition, 68 children in the digital-first group took the digital versions of Coding and Symbol Search again 14–72 days later to evaluate test–retest stability. Finally, to provide additional evidence of the validity of scores on the digital versions of Coding and Symbol Search, samples of the following special groups were collected: intellectual giftedness, intellectual disability–mild severity, specific learning disorder–reading, specific learning disorder–math, attention-deficit/hyperactivity disorder, autism spectrum disorder with language impairment, and motor impairment. The results of the test–retest study, confirmatory factor analyses, and motor impairment special-group study are summarized below. Study details and a full description of results are provided by Raiford et al. (2016).

The test–retest stabilities of the digital versions of Coding and Symbol Search were 0.75 and 0.80, respectively (Table 12.3). By comparison, the stabilities of the paper versions during WISC-V standardization were 0.81

TABLE 12.3 Stability Coefficients of Digital Coding and Symbol Search

| | First Testing | | Second Testing | | | Corrected | Standard |
	Mean	SD	Mean	SD	r	r	Difference
Coding	11.0	3.5	12.0	3.4	0.80	0.75	0.29
Symbol Search	11.6	2.9	13.3	3.4	0.78	0.80	0.54

and 0.80 (Wechsler, 2014). Scores on both subtests increased on the second administration, with Coding scores increasing by 1 scaled score point and Symbol Search increasing by 1.7 scaled score points. These increases were similar to those in the WISC-V standardization study, where paper Coding scores increased by 1.3 scaled score points and paper Symbol Search scores increased by 1.5 scales score point (Wechsler, 2014). Overall, these results suggest that the digital versions are similarly reliable to their paper counterparts.

The correlations between paper and digital versions, averaged across the two administration sequences, were 0.69 for Coding and 0.68 for Symbol Search. The difference between these correlations and the stability correlations indicates that the change in format had some effect on what the scores measure. However, the differences may well lie in construct-irrelevant factors such as the reduced influence of fine-motor control in the digital versions.

Confirmatory factor analysis can shed light on this question. Two analyses were conducted using the sample of 651 children described above, one using each examinee's digital processing speed scores and the other using their paper scores. Both analyses compared the data with the factor structure reported in the WISC-V manual, which has five first-order factors (verbal comprehension, visual−spatial reasoning, fluid reasoning, working memory, and processing speed) and a single second-order factor representing general intelligence. As reported in Table 12.4, fit was excellent and nearly the same for both digital and paper administrations. Fig. 12.8 shows the loadings for digital administration. The loading of general ability on the processing speed factor was slightly but not significantly higher for the digital version (0.49) than the paper version (0.43; $t = 0.84$), and the loadings of the processing speed factor on the subtests were nearly the same across formats: 0.66 (digital) and 0.67 (paper) for Coding, and 0.80 and 0.82 for Symbol Search. The g loadings of the subtests were nonsignificantly higher for the digital versions (Coding, 0.32 digital vs 0.29 paper; Symbol Search, 0.39 digital vs 0.35 paper). These findings are consistent with the expectation that the digital versions of Coding and Symbol Search would continue to be strong measures of processing speed while being less affected by construct-irrelevant factors such as fine-motor control.

TABLE 12.4 Goodness-of-Fit Statistics for Confirmatory Factor Analyses

Model	X^2	DF	CFI	TLI	RMSEA	AIC	BIC
Digital CD and SS	63.9	25	0.98	0.96	0.05	124	256
Paper CD and SS	63.4	25	0.98	0.96	0.05	123	255

Note: The chi-square values are weighted least squares from SAS 9.3.

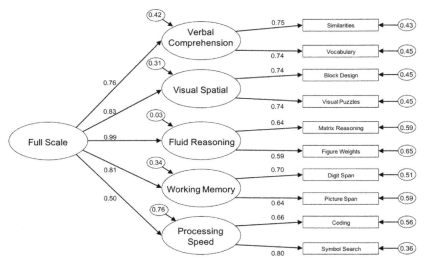

FIGURE 12.8 Five-factor hierarchical model for the primary Index subtests in digital format, ages 6–16.

Finally, the digital versions of Coding, Symbol Search, Vocabulary, and Similarities were administered to 15 children diagnosed with motor impairment. Similar studies using the paper version of the WISC-IV (Wechsler, 2003) suggested that individuals with motor impairment perform at about the same level as healthy controls on Verbal Comprehension subtests but significantly lower on tests of processing speed. The purpose of this study was to determine whether similar patterns of performance exist on the digital versions of Coding and Symbol Search even though they require touch responses rather than handwriting, and therefore presumably require less fine-motor control. Results are presented in Table 12.5. As in the WISC-IV study, individuals with motor impairment scored lower than healthy controls on the digital Processing Speed subtests, with effect sizes of 0.77 for Coding and 0.86 for Symbol Search. The effect size for Coding was slightly smaller than in the paper WISC-V study (1.20), but the Symbol Search effect size was very similar to that for WISC-V paper (0.91). The group exhibited strong performance on Verbal Comprehension subtests in both digital and paper versions. These findings suggest that the digital versions of the Processing Speed subtests reduce but do not eliminate the irrelevant motor-skill variance inherent in the paper versions which require use of a pencil.

IMPLICATIONS FOR PROFESSIONAL PRACTICE

A radically new platform for assessment is bound to have numerous consequences for clinical practice, including some that were not anticipated during

TABLE 12.5 Motor Impairment Compared to Matched Controls—Digital Format

Subtest/ Composite Score	Motor Impairment		Matched Control		Difference	t Value	P Value	Standard Difference
	Mean	SD	Mean	SD				
SI	9.3	3.7	10.8	3.9	1.50	1.23	NS	0.39
VC	10.2	2.3	11.1	2.4	0.93	1.33	NS	0.40
CD	7.1	4.0	10.2	4.0	3.07	2.21	< .05	0.77
SS	7.1	3.7	10.1	3.4	3.07	3.03	< .01	0.86
VCI	98.7	14.6	105.5	16.6	6.79	1.38	NS	0.43
PSI	83.1	20.4	101.1	18.2	17.93	2.88	< .05	0.93

development. This section highlights two areas of impact that we believe are particularly significant: (1) examinee engagement and (2) training.

Examinee Engagement

Given the widespread use of digital technology in schools, on the job, in commercial transactions, and at home, it would be reasonable to expect examinees to find a digital interface not only familiar but also appealing. This is likely to be particularly true of children, who have grown up in a technology-rich environment; in 2013, 75% of American children aged 8 and younger had access to a mobile device (Rideout & Saphir, 2013). To learn more about how children referred for assessment react to the digital format, in 2013 the Q-interactive team surveyed practitioners who had been administering WISC-IV with Q-interactive, and obtained 95 responses (a 38% response rate; Daniel, 2013). About 70% of the respondents indicated that Q-interactive affected examinee behavior, and over 90% of these described the impact as positive (e.g., "more engaged," "more attentive," "increased interest," "more willing to respond," "more focused"). Five percent of those who saw an effect on behavior described it as negative or neutral (e.g., "more distracted and want to play with the computer," "some become preoccupied trying to get the items to light up," "they like to push the buttons that light up—sometimes this is good, but sometimes distracting"). Two peer-reviewed studies have been published on the issue of increased examinee engagement on Q-interactive. Noland (2017) found that graduate students perceived the engagement of their college-aged volunteers to be higher when taking a test with Q-interactive than with paper. This finding is consistent with the

Q-interactive usability survey but shares the methodological weakness of being based on examiner perception. Castro, Viezel, Dumont, and Guiney (2017) reported no differences in problem behavior (as measured by the Test Observation Form) when children were administered the WISC-IV on paper and Q-interactive, suggesting children are no more likely to be distracted, oppositional, or anxious with one format or the other. This is the first study to formally measure examinee behavior, although it focused on problem behaviors rather than positive engagement.

If some examinees are indeed more engaged with digital tests, the impact on their test results may be significant. A lack of engagement or effort, especially among individuals with clinical conditions such as attention-deficit hyperactivity disorder, is a major threat to the validity of test results. When interpreting low scores, practitioners have to consider whether they might reflect a reluctance to engage with a task or to persevere when items increase in difficulty. It is always the role of the examiner to establish adequate rapport in order to elicit optimal performance from the examinee (within the limits of standardized administration procedures). To the degree that a digital modality such as Q-interactive facilitates rapport and effort for some children who might not otherwise have given their best effort, practitioners can have greater confidence that results reflect the child's true ability on the constructs measured by these tasks.

Training

Given their role in preparing the next generation of clinicians, it is not surprising that many graduate school trainers have watched the development of Q-interactive with great interest. In addition to seeing the need to incorporate new digital technology into their coursework, they perceive a tension in the implications for the future role of psychologists. Trainers have expressed excitement that they will be able to spend less instructional time on the mechanics of assessment and more on the nuances of observation and clinical judgment. Some have commented that Q-interactive's modeling of correct administration and scoring practices should help ensure that students learn to give tests accurately. On the other hand, some trainers are concerned that students may not fully understand test-administration rules and test data if they do not invest the requisite effort to internalize basic concepts and procedures such as applying reversal and discontinue rules and calculating subtest and composite scores.

Two recent articles in *Training and Education in Professional Psychology* explored the use of Q-interactive in graduate school settings (Clark, Gulin, Heller, & Vrana, 2017; Noland, 2017) and commented on many of these issues. Both articles stressed the importance of teaching Q-interactive in conjunction with paper. There are two reasons for this. First, students may be asked to administer tests in either format in internships or job settings, and it is important that they be prepared for both. Second, while Q-interactive automates many tasks such as discontinue rules and the calculation of raw scores, it is important for students to understand why start points and discontinue points are used and have a general understanding of how they function, as well as how item raw scores roll up to subtest and composite scaled scores in order to interpret data responsibly. To obtain this knowledge, they may need to administer and score a test several times in paper format. Consistent with the automation of certain manual tasks, both articles pointed out that one of Q-interactive's strengths is the reduction of clerical errors; however, because it requires examiner judgment for many activities, it does not reduce errors related to higher level functions such as the scoring of verbal responses. Trainers should continue to pay close attention to these types of errors when evaluating students' digital protocols. Finally, introducing tablet-based testing is associated with several practical considerations. How to store digital protocols, acquiring and distributing hardware, and evaluating students' work on digital devices are all new processes for trainers and may be accompanied by short-term frustration as they are incorporated into standard classroom activities.

Training is also an issue for clinicians already in practice, in two different ways. First, of course, those who transition from giving a test with the paper materials to giving the same test (or its revision) with Q-interactive will need to learn how Assess works for that test and practice with it sufficiently so that it becomes comfortable. Even when a subtest is implemented in Q-interactive with no change in administration procedures, the examiner's actions can be quite different than with paper materials, and it takes time to develop the "motor memory" that allows the examiner to move smoothly through the administration. Becoming fluent in giving a test is a similar process with Q-interactive as with paper. A second training consideration arises from the fact that Q-interactive offers easy, immediate, and relatively inexpensive access to a large and growing number of tests, and is designed to encourage and facilitate flexible administration. However, the available tests that might be attractive for a particular situation may include some that the practitioner has not used before. Because Q-interactive is a tool to *support* individual administration and personalized assessment, not a replacement for the clinician, there is still an ethical requirement for the examiner to study and practice a test before giving it to a client.

FUTURE DIRECTIONS

The current version of Q-interactive affords several benefits to practitioners: it is efficient, accurate, flexible, portable, and engaging for examinees. However, its greatest potential contribution to assessment probably lies in the development of digitally native tests that take advantage of technology to improve the measurement of familiar constructs, open the door to measuring constructs different from those measurable with print materials, and provide novel scores and ways to display test results that improve the ability to interpret test performance and communicate those results to patients and caregivers. That is, Q-interactive is in a transition stage with one foot in the world of traditional tests and the toe of the other beginning to dip into the pool of novel measures. This is a gradual process, which fortunately is supported by the digital technology itself, which enables new tests or subtests to be distributed to practicing clinicians on a continuing basis rather than only when an entire new kit is published. WISC-V is attempting to move this process forward through the research and development work presently being done on Q-interactive versions of the Coding and Symbol Search processing speed subtests that, for the first time, are not replicas of the paper versions.

Test data are critical components of the nomological networks that support inferences about latent constructs such as intelligence (Cronbach & Meehl, 1955). To the extent that technology changes the observable variables we can measure, it may also change our fundamental understanding of these constructs. The possible implications of this for assessment and intervention are profound. It could improve the diagnostic accuracy of assessment, clarify our understanding of brain–behavior relationships, and generate new hypotheses for treatment and remediation. In this respect, Q-interactive will hopefully share a legacy with the original Wechsler intelligence tests, which revolutionized the practice of psychological assessment in the 20th century.

REFERENCES

Butcher, J. N., Perry, J., & Hahn, J. (2004). Computers in clinical assessment: Historical developments, present status, and future challenges. *Journal of Clinical Psychology, 60,* 331–345.

Castro, C. J., Viezel, K., Dumont, R., & Guiney, M. (2017). Exploration of children's test behavior during iPad-administered intelligence testing. *Journal of Psychoeducational Assessment.* Available from https://doi.org/10.1177/0734282917729304.

Clark, S. W., Gulin, S. L., Heller, M. B., & Vrana, S. R. (2017). Graduate training implications of the Q-interactive platform for administering Wechsler intelligence tests. *Training and Education in Professional Psychology, 11*(3), 148–155.

Cohen, J. (1988). *Statistical power analysis for the behavioral sciences* (2nd ed.). Hillsdale, NJ: Erlbaum.

Cronbach, L. J., & Meehl, P. E. (1955). Construct validity in psychological tests. *Psychological Bulletin, 52,* 281–302.

Daniel, M. H. (2013). *User survey on Q-interactive examinee behavior.* Bloomington, MN: Pearson.

Daniel, M. H., Wahlstrom, D., & Zhang, O. (2014). Equivalence of Q-interactive and paper administration of cognitive tasks: WISC-V *(Q-interactive Technical Report 7).* Bloomington, MN: Pearson.

Delis, D., Kramer, J., Kaplan, E., & Ober, B. (2000). *California verbal learning test* (2nd ed.). Bloomington, MN: Pearson.

Drozdick, L. W., Getz, K., Raiford, S. E., & Zhang, O. (2016). *WPPSI-IV: Equivalence of Q-interactive and paper formats*. Bloomington, MN: Pearson.

International Test Commission. (2005). *International guidelines on computer-based and internet delivered testing (Version 2005)*. Liverpool, Englannd: International Test Commission.

Mead, A. D., & Drasgow, F. (1993). Equivalence of computerized and paper-and-pencil cognitive ability tests: A meta-analysis. *Psychological Bulletin, 114*, 449−458.

Noland, R. M. (2017). Intelligence testing using a tablet computer: Experiences with using Q-interactive. *Training and Education in Professional Psychology, 11*(3), 156−163.

Raiford, S. E., Zhang, O., Drozdick, L. W., Getz, K., Wahlstrom, D., Gabel, A., . . . Daniel, M. (2016). *WISC-V Coding and Symbol Search in digital format: Reliability, validity, special group studies, and interpretation*. Bloomington, MN: Pearson.

Rideout, V., & Saphir, M. (2013).). Zero to eight: Children's media use in America *2013*. San Francisco, CA: Common Sense Media.

Wechsler, D. (2003). *Wechsler intelligence scale for children* (4th ed.). Bloomington, MN: Pearson.

Wechsler, D. (2014). *Wechsler intelligence scale for children* (5th ed.). Bloomington, MN: Pearson.

Zhu, J. J., & Chen, H.-Y. (2011). Utility of inferential norming with smaller sample sizes. *Journal of Psychoeducational Assessment, 29*(6), 570−580.

Chapter 13

WISC-V and the Personalized Assessment Approach

James A. Holdnack[1], Aurelio Prifitera[2], Lawrence G. Weiss[3] and Donald H. Saklofske[4]

[1]Research and Statistical Consultant, Bear, DE, United States, [2]Assessment Consultant, San Antonio, TX, United States, [3]Research and Measurement Consultant, San Antonio, TX, United States, [4]Department of Psychology, University of Western Ontario, London, ON, Canada

INTRODUCTION

At the center of a psychological evaluation of any type is the individual child or adolescent who is experiencing difficulties in his or her life. Understanding each individual child/adolescent in the assessment process is a challenge because most tests and test batteries are designed around a construct or measurement model rather than understanding the uniqueness of an examinee. Therefore, the assessment process can easily become more about the test and what the test scores mean rather than about the individual.

The future of psychological assessment revolves around the concept of individualized, tailored assessments designed to understand the unique interactions of psychosocial environment (as described in Chapters 5 and 8) and personal combinations of problems, risk factors, strengths, weaknesses, and support systems (Matarazzo, 1990). This model proposes a fluid, flexible, and interactive model in which initial evaluation plans are modified on the fly based on child/adolescent test performance and response to the evaluation process. The goal of the evaluation is to best pinpoint the child's cognitive, emotional, social, and behavioral difficulties and strengths to identify more targeted interventions and accommodations.

At the heart of this model are the concepts of probability, risk factors, and multiplicity. The concept of probability, in regards to this model, recognizes the limitations of our tools and techniques for an exact identification of a specific disorder and outcome. Probabilities help us conceptualize the *most likely* disorder, potential short and long-term outcomes, and the interventions that have the best chance of being effective. The identification of risk factors provides a framework for making recommendations for diagnostic

WISC-V. DOI: https://doi.org/10.1016/B978-0-12-815744-2.00013-6

conclusions, the potential impact of identified cognitive risk factors, and potential unexpected consequences of the disorder (e.g., children with language disorders are at greater risk for social isolation). Multiplicity recognizes that developmental disorders have high rates of comorbidity, that additional risk and protective factors may be present that can affect the expression of a disorder and its consequences, and that individual strengths and weaknesses in cognition, behavior, temperament, and psychosocial environment influence are important in the expression of symptoms and outcomes of a clinical condition. A failure to identify the multiple influencing factors can result in misdiagnosis and inappropriate prognosis or ineffective intervention.

In the previous edition, we focused on specifying a number of psychological and neuropsychological tests that can be used to test hypotheses about specific domains of cognitive and behavioral functioning. In this update, we focus primarily on the Wechsler Intelligence Scale for Children—Fifth Edition (WISC-V) as a generator of alternative hypotheses. It is beyond the scope of the chapter to provide detailed base rates for every combination of WISC-V subtests scores so a general framework is proposed based on published analyses using various cognitive test batteries (Holdnack, Drozdick, Weiss, & Iverson, 2013). Visualization of data in case studies helps illustrate the concepts described in this chapter.

OBTAINING AND REFINING INITIAL IMPRESSIONS OF THE CHILD

Prior to evaluation of any examinee, information, though often not well formulated, about their current psychosocial environment is made available to the clinician. This is the clinician's first glimpse at how the world views the child, usually framed by a set of "problems." It is easy for the "problems" to come to define the child or be synonymous with their personality, abilities, and potential. Additionally, the clinician starts to glean environmental factors that may influence the child's presenting problems. Unfortunately, there is often insufficient time or resources for the clinician to obtain all the critical information about the child prior to the date of the evaluation.

This section discusses the importance of preassessment planning and refinement of pretesting hypotheses. Although some clinicians may feel it is better not to be biased by the impressions of others prior to engaging with the child personally, it is of critical value for establishing an assessment plan that is tailored to the child and flexible during the course of the evaluation. *A priori* hypothesis generation is not a prejudgment of the child but helps the examiner focus in on all critical areas of concerns rather than focusing on only what is perceived to be the most critical problems (e.g., learning problems in the face of other difficulties such as social difficulties and family problems). The preassessment phase can be generally divided into four key areas: referral, collecting background information, parent and teacher ratings (classroom observation if possible), and assessment planning.

Reason for Referral

The quality of the reason for referral varies tremendously among referral agents. There are many reasons for the variability among referral agents including experience working with psychologists; level of familiarity with the child, child's family, and current difficulties; time spent formulating referral; knowledge of what information would be helpful to the psychologist; and general knowledge of factors influencing child-specific difficulties. Many requests for evaluation such as "what is John Smith's level of functioning?" and "are there cognitive difficulties, learning difficulties, and behavior problems" are too vague for the clinician to be able to glean any direction for the evaluation. And in some cases, referral questions, such as "John Smith is referred for a Rorschach test," "neuropsychological testing," and "does Johnny have moral reasoning capacity?" can be too vague and specific at the same time. Although these referral questions provide a vague notion of why the child needs an evaluation, the psychologist cannot effectively plan for the assessment or understand the social forces driving the request.

The most important elements in the referral question relate to the anticipated outcome from the evaluation and identification of risk factors. Frequently, the referral agent has multiple outcomes they desire from obtaining an evaluation. Without knowing those desired outcomes, it is easy to complete an evaluation that does not directly answer the needs of the referral agent. There are many reasons for referrals, such as diagnostic/classification questions, functional level, placement, or intervention. The selection of tests can vary based on the required outcomes for the evaluation.

The psychologist can help referral agents improve their requests for psychological assessment in many ways. One method is to provide referral agents with a *brief* checklist with sections related to diagnostic or classification concerns, specific problematic behaviors, and placement questions. Additionally, the psychologist can help educate the referral source through direct contact. Asking for clarification about the specific behaviors that are a primary source of concern versus secondary issue can help the referral source focus their questions and concerns for an individual child.

Background Information and A Priori Hypothesis Building

There are two types of background information required to develop a priori hypotheses in order to develop an effective assessment plan. There is background information specific to the child/adolescent and there is background information related to specific developmental, medical, and psychiatric disorders, behavioral issues, and psychological symptoms. It would seem counterintuitive to apply information collected from research studies that typically use group-level data rather than individual performance when performing a personalized assessment. However, information about specific disorders can provide an excellent starting point for an assessment. That is because there are not an infinite number of possible disorders and the probabilities that a child or adolescent has a specific disorder is knowable. For example, the probability that a child with attention problems has attention deficit hyperactivity disorder (ADHD) versus childhood onset of schizophrenia would strongly favor ADHD unless some other symptom (e.g., auditory hallucinations) was also present. An assessment plan that focuses initially on more probable outcomes versus a global assessment of all possible outcomes can result in a more detailed evaluation of the factors related to the presenting symptoms and potentially provide better information for intervention and accommodation.

Background Research

It is beyond the scope of this chapter to provide a comprehensive research review of all possible disorders of childhood and adolescence. This chapter focuses on the types of information that are helpful when planning an assessment. These can be roughly categorized as epidemiological, phenomenology, and cognitive profile. These different categories of information should not be considered as independent but each is important in planning for an assessment and provides a different perspective on possible outcomes.

Epidemiological information in this model refers to information about the prevalence of a disorder, heritability, and environmental factors that may contribute to the expression of the disorder and biological and genetic factors that modify the expression of the disorder. Some of this information is organized and presented in the Diagnostic and Statistical Manual of Mental Disorders—Fifth Edition. Prevalence rates for common developmental and psychiatric disorders are frequently reported here. The Centers for Disease Control and Prevention website, CDC.gov, provides prevalence data for some developmental conditions. Understanding the relative base rate of a disorder is important for initial assessment planning. In most cases, children will present with more common rather than rare conditions and these need to be evaluated and ruled in or out.

Epidemiological data regarding heritability and genetics of a disorder may be helpful not only in the initial stages of an evaluation but also when making decisions regarding probable diagnosis and intervention. For instance, in families with a history of reading disorder, the probability that a child in that family will also have a reading disorder is approximately 34%, whereas in families with no history of reading disorder the risk is approximately 6% (Pennington & Lefly, 2001). This is not a precise estimation of the risk factor; however, it is strong evidence that if there is a family history of reading problems it increases the probability that the child may also have some reading issues. Also, from an intervention standpoint, it may be important to know if a parent has a learning difficulty because it may affect their ability to help their child in that domain.

Epidemiological data regarding the base rates of comorbid disorders is of critical importance. For example, we know that a high proportion of children suffering from depression also suffer from significant symptoms of anxiety and thus if a child is referred for depression we must also evaluate anxiety symptoms. Similarly, in a large sample of children diagnosed with a learning disability, it was found that comorbid disorders were ADHD (33%), anxiety disorder (28%), developmental coordination disorder (17.8%), language disorder (11%), and mood disorder (9%) (Margari et al., 2013). Again, these are estimates of the actual rates of comorbidity; however, it makes clear that children being referred for reading, math, or writing problems also need evaluation of other possible comorbid disorders that can impact the child's functioning and possibly affect the type of intervention required.

The expression of a disorder or the severity of impairments is multifactorial. Knowing the factors that may modify or alter the expression of a disorder is helpful as this can impact the sensitivity and specificity of our diagnostic criteria. In one study, girls that had a high number of autism spectrum traits were less likely to be diagnosed with autism spectrum disorders (ASD) than boys unless comorbid intellectual impairments and more severe behavioral disturbance were also present (Dworzynski, Ronald, Bolton, & Happé, 2012). This may be a sample-specific finding, but it alerts clinicians that there may be some bias or sex-based moderation in the identification of ASD. Other factors affecting the expression of a disorder are related to psychosocial or medical issues such as socioeconomic status, early language environment, abuse, prenatal exposure to substances of abuse, poor nutrition, premature birth, etc. Factors that create additional behavioral or cognitive deficits or increase the severity of psychological or behavioral symptoms can cloud the overall diagnostic impression by the appearance of symptoms or symptom severity that seems inconsistent with a specific disorder. In addition, protective factors and individual resiliency can reduce symptom severity or expression of a disorder.

The phenomenological aspects of a disorder refer to the characteristic feature and expressions associated with that disorder. For example, the manifestation of ADHD is typically exemplified by excessive motor activity inconsistent with the child's age, difficulty paying attention when the child is not interested in the situation, a failure to follow rules due to poor behavioral control not a lack of understanding of rules or a general disregard for authority, and frequent feelings of frustration. Others frequently experience these children as "lazy," "hyper," "forgetful," "defiant," "messy," etc. Although these are the core features of the disorder, additional behavioral, psychosocial, and emotional issues are frequently present. The difficulty for the clinician is identifying the core symptoms when these symptoms may be present in other relevant clinical conditions (e.g., attention issues in ASD, problems following rules in oppositional defiant disorder (ODD), poor frustration tolerance in depressive disorders). Fortunately, the expression of a symptom and underlying causes of common symptoms can help differentiate core versus comorbidity issues. In ADHD, inattentiveness is not pervasive but situational. Children can attend to highly stimulating environments or when a task is of interest or value to them. In ASD, the inattention is often expressed as a hyperfocus on objects or concepts of interest to them to exclusion of attending to the environment more generally. The expression of a common symptom can vary quite a bit between disorders and can aid in differential diagnosis. The intervention for ADHD inattentiveness might be very different than the intervention in ASD inattentiveness depending on the expression of symptomatology.

Epidemiology and phenomenology help us understand the personal and psychosocial consequences of having a disorder. Children and adolescents diagnosed with ADHD are at greater risk of academic difficulties due to inefficient learning and behavior problems, comorbid psychiatric disorders (e.g., depression and anxiety), substance abuse, injury due to accidents, stressful interpersonal relationships, and long-term employment difficulties (Barkley, 2002). Children diagnosed with language disorder are at risk of social difficulties (Snowling, Bishop, Stothard, Chipchase, & Kaplan, 2006), academic issues (Beichtman et al., 1996), social phobia (Beichtman et al., 2001), victimization from peers (Redmond, 2011), behavioral disorder (Lindsay, Dockrell, & Strand, 2007), depression and anxiety (Conti-Ramsden & Botting, 2008), long-term academic struggles, and reduced educational attainment and occupational success (Johnson, Beitchman, & Brownlie, 2010). A failure to recognize the risk for negative social experiences associated with early language problems (which differ from the social problems associated with ASD) can have long-term implications for the child's development. Knowledge of the risk factors posed by each disorder improves the assessment and intervention planning for children with specific disorders. It is clear from epidemiological research that psychiatric and social problems are significant risk factors for children with developmental disorders. The presence of these problems may make it more difficult to identify the primary diagnosis; therefore, the clinician must be very knowledgeable about the differences in expression of these problems across clinical groups.

Planning an assessment requires an understanding of the cognitive deficits associated with specific disorders and how those specific cognitive weaknesses are a risk factor for academic, social, and behavioral difficulties. Cognitive difficulties are, in some cases, a common pathway for observed problems. In ADHD, research suggests that deficits in executive functioning are an important domain of cognitive weakness, specifically difficulties with response inhibition, sustained attention, spatial working memory, and planning (Willcutt, Doyle, Nigg, Faraone, & Pennington, 2005). ADHD is also associated with intraindividual variability in cognitive performance within and across tasks (Castellanos, Sonuga-Barke, Milham, & Tannock, 2006), processing speed deficits (Shanahan et al., 2006), problems with response-selection and working memory (Jacobson et al., 2012), and verbal learning (Cutting, Koth, Mahone, & Denckla, 2003). In addition to specific and general cognitive difficulties, children with ADHD obtain lower scores on standardized measures of reading and math (Frazier, Youngstrom, Glutting, & Watkins, 2007; Loe & Feldman, 2007), and spelling with effect sizes in the moderate range in each domain (Frazier et al., 2007). Deficits in executive functioning are associated with increased grade retention (Biederman et al., 2004) and reduced word reading (Bental & Tirosh, 2007), and working memory and inhibitory control deficits predict math difficulties (Bull & Scerif, 2001).

By comparison, children with a reading disorder show deficits in phoneme awareness (Willcutt et al., 2001); naming speed, phonological processing (Wolf & Bowers, 1999); orthographic processing (Berninger, Abbott, Thomson, & Raskin, 2001); morphology (Berninger et al., 2006); word and nonword reading (Castles, Datta, Gayan, & Olson, 1999); processing speed (Shanahan et al., 2006), verbal working memory (Willcutt et al., 2001); and verbal learning (Kramer, Knee, & Delis, 2000). Reading difficulties are a core feature of reading disorders and occur due to a combination of linguistic, processing speed, memory, and working memory issues. Because there are common cognitive deficits across the groups, the clinician needs to understand how the specific and nonspecific cognitive difficulties relate to differential diagnosis and outcomes. Two children may both present with reading difficulties but the underlying reasons for those problems can be quite different and would warrant very different interventions. Therefore, the clinician must know the cognitive risk factors for mild versus severe reading problems to facilitate diagnosis and treatment planning.

ADHD and reading disorders are used as examples here due to their relatively high rate of comorbidity (Willcutt, Pennington, Olson, Chhabildas, & Hulsander, 2005). There are unique and overlapping cognitive difficulties between the groups, a common finding among developmental disorders. There are also many commonalities among the symptom presentation of children with developmental disorders including academic achievement issues, social difficulties, behavioral problems, and often depression and anxiety. Because there is so much overlap in presentation, clarification of the referral question and obtaining preassessment specifics about the nature of academic and behavior issues help the clinician plan for an effective assessment. Parent and teacher rating scales provide some clarification of the nature of the presenting problem. When possible, it is helpful to obtain these measures prior to the evaluation.

Genetic Testing

Increasingly, individuals are able to obtain an assessment of his or her genetic composition using commercial vendors such as "23andme" and "ancestry.com." Anyone can download their personal DNA code from these sites. Currently, sites such as "promethease.com" allow individuals to upload their DNA genotype for the purpose of identifying potential risk for disorders associated with specific DNA segments. These may include psychiatric, developmental, and neurological conditions. Some parents may obtain this information for their children with concerns about the child's DNA risk profile. Clinicians must be aware of how this type of information may be useful but also misleading. In the future, clinicians may receive referrals from family members concerned about the results of a child's genetic testing. Formal assessment may be helpful; however, clinicians must be aware of expression of a genotype (e.g., phenotype) and how risk factors identified in such reports are not necessarily additive (e.g., the sum of each gene associated with ADHD is not the true risk as individual genes may not occur randomly).

The future state in which genetic profiles will be more accurate and have stronger linkage to specific disorders will not eradicate the need for assessment of actual abilities. The human brain is quite adaptable and the expression of a genetic risk can be modified by environmental factors and vice versa. In the context of such genetic information, it may be possible to perform very targeted assessments to confirm or disconfirm the expression of a genetic risk.

Parent and Teacher Ratings

Internet-based assessment platforms such as Pearson's Q-Global™ have simplified the process of obtaining parent and teacher ratings. In the past, to obtain these ratings before the assessment, it was necessary to mail response forms to each person and for him or her to complete and return the forms via standard mail. The process is not efficient and posed problems with lost forms, delayed forms, or even lost forms containing personal information. It was more practical to have the parent complete the rating scales in the office. Teacher ratings could be more directly obtained by psychologists working in the school; however, community- and hospital-based clinicians have had difficulty obtaining these important assessments. With Internet-based platforms, it is possible to send both parents and teachers a secure link to complete one or more rating scales. The scales are then ready for immediate scoring and reporting. The improved practicality of obtaining preassessment ratings of the child's behavior can help the clinician formulate an assessment plan.

There are numerous rating scales that can be used by clinicians. Most clinicians have a set of scales they use consistently and can easily interpret. In general, there are no recommendations for a specific scale to be used in preassessment planning, rather the recommendation is related to the type of information that is useful to obtain at this stage. Combining information from different types of scales, the examiner is armed with information about the cognitive domains that have the highest probability of contributing to the observed difficulties. This does not indicate that the examiner does not assess other domains of cognitive functioning; rather the examiner uses this information to formulate an assessment plan to ensure the appropriate depth of content coverage in specific areas.

An Assessment Plan

The assessment plan helps the examiner organize materials needed for an evaluation. The assessment plan requires the examiner to have knowledge of a variety of tests in a broad domain of cognitive functions, and within each domain the subset of cognitive skills important for differential diagnosis and treatment planning. There are no professionally proscribed sets of domains that should be evaluated, rather the domains assessed should be driven by the research related to specific conditions or in some cases theoretical models can be applied depending on the clinician's experience and training with using those models.

The personal assessment approach recommends a primarily research-based approach for the purposes of preparing for an assessment. The recommended domains of assessment in this approach are language, attention/executive functioning, working memory, academic skills, social cognition/pragmatic language, memory, processing speed, automaticity spatial/constructional, reasoning/problem-solving, and sensory-motor. These domains should not be considered as unique, unrelated processes, as there can be considerable overlap in the cognitive processes evaluated across domains, as described more fully in Chapter 5. For example, working memory affects most cognitive domains, as working memory is frequently required to solve most types of problems. Within a domain such as memory, there can be visual–spatial or verbally mediated tasks and processing speed tests that may require fine-motor control. The categories are not set up as boundaries but reflect core and secondary domains that impact symptom presentation, outcomes, daily functioning, and differential diagnosis. It is expected that children with diagnosable conditions will likely have low scores in more than one domain and as the severity of the disorder increases so will the number of deficits within and across domains increase.

Assessment of cognitive functions in each category may not be required for any particular child and attempting to assess all areas thoroughly is often not practical from a workflow or child-friendliness perspective. In some cases, it will be important to assess one domain very intensely, with less focus on some domains, and no focus on others. Comprehensive evaluation in this model is a comprehensive evaluation of the presenting problems, discovered prior to and during the assessment, rather than an evaluation of all possible problems. In neuropsychology, this is similar to the concept of a flexible versus standard battery approach. The focus of the evaluation is not strictly cognitive as evaluation of behavioral, emotional, and family functioning is imperative for proper diagnosis and treatment planning. It is beyond the scope of this chapter to present assessment plans for all possible referrals and conditions. Instead, a description of some of the general rules that are based on research and diagnostic criteria are presented here.

Language

Language functioning is a critical ability that impacts multiple aspects of cognitive, academic, social, and behavioral functioning. Language difficulties should be considered in any child referred for academic issues (e.g., slower than expected reading, writing, or math development); social difficulties (e.g., isolation or atypicality); behavior problems (e.g., aggressive or oppositional behavior); or adaptive behavior delays. The nature of the language difficulty may be a moderate-to-severe general impairment in understanding and using language or in other cases more subtle difficulties with language that are secondary to problems in concrete thinking (e.g., problems understanding figurative language or colloquialisms), social deficits (e.g., pragmatic language deficits), or attention, working memory, or auditory processing difficulties (e.g., does not hear well or has poor memory for communicated information).

The number of measures planned would be influenced by any history of language delay or disorder, any observation of communication difficulties, and reported problems with reading or writing. Additionally, a family history of language or learning disabilities or ASD would warrant at a least an initial plan for intensive language assessment. Due to the importance of this ability domain, a screening for language issues should be a part of all evaluations. For that purpose, at least two measures from the WISC-V Verbal Comprehension Index (VCI) should be included in most evaluations. These measures are aimed at complex aspects of language use and are rarely performed well by children with significant language impairment (Holdnack, Weiss, & Entwistle, 2006), though children with more subtle language deficits may do well or inconsistently across these measures. If the child has a significant history of language delay or diagnosis of a language disorder, a comprehensive assessment of language functioning is indicated, whereas children presenting with only reading or writing problems in the absence of any history of language delays need a more focused evaluation of phonology and morphology. Children referred for attention or working memory problems or oppositional behavior can be evaluated with measures of sentence repetition and ability to follow multistep commands to identify or rule out impact of linguistic contributions to these observed behaviors.

If the child has a VCI index of 90 or less, two scores of 8 or less on Similarities (SI) and Vocabulary (VC), the clinician should consider administering two more verbal tests. If there is a large split (e.g., 4—5 scaled scores) between SI and VC with one of the scaled scores being 7 or less, the clinician may wish to include one or more additional verbal measure. If expressive language appears to be an issue, add Comprehension or if knowledge or memory appears to be creating a low score, add Information.

A large number of published tests on language functioning exist, but it is beyond the scope of this chapter to present all possible selections. In the previous edition, we demarcated a number of measures that should be considered when performing a detailed assessment of language functioning. Clinicians will develop a set of tools that meets their needs and should identify tests that cover the important linguistic domains that help with differential diagnosis, targeting interventions, and informing about potential outcomes (e.g., probability or reading, social problems, etc.). Not all language tests are developed for the same purpose and thus their content will vary considerably. Many language tests are affected by more than one linguistic or cognitive process. When deciding to use specific language measures, it is essential to determine the intended population of children the test was designed to evaluate (i.e., language disorder, learning disabled, or severe aphasia), as the content and cognitive processes of the tasks will vary.

Attention/Executive Functioning

Attention/Executive functioning skills are important for behavioral and emotional regulation and academic difficulties described as poor initiating and completion of assignments and/or inconsistent, disorganized, or sloppy schoolwork. There are a variety of abilities that are subsumed under the concept of attention. For the purposes of this chapter, the focus will be on sustained attention, which is the ability to maintain attention on an intrinsically uninteresting task for an extended period of time. Executive functions refer to a broad range of cognitive abilities that enable individuals to effectively manage their behavior and regulate the performance of other cognitive abilities. These skills include but are not limited to inhibitory control, cognitive flexibility, behavioral productivity, maintenance of cognitive set, self-monitoring, planning, and abstract reasoning. Inhibitory control is the ability to stop a prepotent, or automatic thought, behavior, or emotion (e.g., overlearned, stimulus bound, emotional reaction, etc.) in order to consider and apply a better (e.g., behaviorally or emotionally appropriate or a correct versus incorrect response to a problem) response to a situation, problem, or cognitive process. Cognitive flexibility is the capacity to think about a problem in more than one way. It is the ability to change a behavior in consideration of changes in the environment (adaptive) or to see different bits of information in a single stimulus (abstraction). Behavioral productivity refers to the process by which an individual is able to initiate and maintain problem-solving behavior. Maintenance of cognitive set refers to the ability to understand and apply the rules of a task or situation and the ability to monitor behavior to avoid violating the rules. Planning is a process by which the individual identifies the necessary steps to reach a goal and maintains their behavior toward the goal. Abstract reasoning is the ability to understand a stimulus beyond its obvious, physical properties, and the ability to see a problem beyond the immediate constraints. These cognitive skills related to the efficiency of problem-solving, the adaptability of the individual, the capacity to regulate and control one's behavior, and the ability to solve complex problems. Attention and executive function deficits are an important aspect of the expression of many neurodevelopmental disorders. Children diagnosed with ADHD show mild-to-moderate difficulties with inhibitory control and planning (Corbett, Constantine, Hendren, Rocke, & Ozonoff, 2009; Willcutt et al., 2005) and sustained attention; autistic children show difficulties with planning (Geurts, Verté, Oosterlaan, Roeyers, & Sergeant, 2004), cognitive flexibility (Corbett et al., 2009; Geurts et al., 2004); sustained attention and inhibitory control (Corbett et al., 2009); and math disability associated with inhibitory regulation (Geary, 2004). Both autism and Asperger's syndrome show some executive functioning deficits (Verté, Geurts, Roeyers, Oosterlaan, & Sergeant, 2006). ODD and conduct disorder (CD) are not necessarily associated with executive functioning impairments, but given the high rate of comorbidity with ADHD, children with ODD or CD may show executive function deficits similar to children with ADHD (Geurts et al., 2004). Cognitive flexibility and inhibitory control deficits are associated with increased repetitive and restrictive behaviors in autistic children (Lopez, Lincoln, Ozonoff, & Lai, 2005). Inhibitory control problems are associated with poor math functioning (Bull & Scerif, 2001) and to academic performance in general (Bull, Espy, & Wiebe, 2008). Inhibitory control deficits may indirectly influence the potential aggressive behaviors (Hoaken, Shaughnessy, & Pihl, 2003). The behavioral manifestations associated with attention and executive functioning problems are off-task behaviors, distractibility, impulsivity, poor frustration tolerance, disorganization, rigid behavior or thinking, difficulty adapting to new situations or changes in routine, concrete thinking, aggressiveness, and high rates of errors in schoolwork due to working too quickly or making mental mistakes. These behaviors may, incorrectly, be attributed to personality style or "willfulness" rather than due to cognitive limitations.

Preassessment information in which behavior control problems or attention problems are present (i.e., not necessarily primary) indicates that one or more measures of executive functioning should be part of the assessment plan. Academic difficulties due to sloppy, disorganized work, or failure to automatize basic skills (e.g., simple calculation skills, as opposed to difficulties learning academic concepts or procedures such as decoding procedures for reading words) also indicates that one or more executive functioning measures should be employed. For children showing attention problems, measures of sustained attention should be considered. On rating scales, elevations on measures of activity, impulsivity, adaptability, social difficulties, aggressive or explosive behaviors, poor study skills, and oppositional or conduct-related problems warrant a plan to use executive functioning measures. *Next to language functioning, deficits in attention and executive functioning may be the most common causes of problems in academic achievement and psychosocial functioning.*

The WISC-V subtests do not provide a direct assessment of attention or executive functioning. However, deficits in brief focused attention can influence test performance particularly on working memory subtest. In the executive functioning domain, poor reasoning skills may signal difficulties with abstraction. Low verbal productivity observed on language measures can indicate difficulties with behavioral initiation, and low scores on comprehension and similarities might be associated with cognitive flexibility problems. Performance on the WISC-V may point to a need for more detailed evaluation of these abilities.

Working Memory

Working memory is an important skill in academic learning and performance and higher-order problem-solving/reasoning. Working memory is often associated with attention and executive functioning skills. Like attention and executive functions, working memory has a significant influence in cognitive efficiency, learning, and academic performance. In Baddeley's model (2009, 2012) of working memory, there are three main functional components: the phonological loop, visual sketchpad, and the central executive. This system interacts with long-term memory in the episodic buffer to retrieve previously learned information needed for problem-solving and to help process new information for long-term storage. The phonological loop keeps auditory information active in consciousness for the purpose of immediate problem-solving. The visual sketchpad allows people to keep visual images and spatial information active in the mind for problem-solving. The central executive component allocates cognitive resources, focuses attention that is needed to solve problems, and controls cognitive interference (Baddeley, 2012; Baddeley, Eysenck, & Anderson, 2009). This top-down executive attention is the central mechanism common to working memory functions across both the auditory and visual domains. Working memory has been identified as a key cognitive function in learning, and deficits in working memory problems often contribute to development of learning disabilities and are often found in many neurodevelopmental disorders.

A brief review of the research shows that working memory has an impact on learning, and deficits in working memory are often found in children with learning disabilities. Verbal working memory longitudinally predicts language functioning whereas spatial working memory predicts math and language test performance in school children (Gathercole, Pickering, Knight, & Stegmann, 2004; St Clair-Thompson & Gathercole, 2006) and is moderately related to cognitive functioning in general (Ackerman, Beier, & Boyle, 2005). Children diagnosed with ADHD (Martinussen, Hayden, Hogg-Johnson, & Tannock, 2005) or math (McLean & Hitch, 1999) show greater deficits in spatial and executive components of working memory than in verbal working memory. Children diagnosed with dyslexia show deficits on verbal working memory measures and not spatial working memory (Jeffries & Everatt, 2004). Reading comprehension deficits are also associated with verbal working memory, particularly those having a high attention load (Carretti, Borella, Cornoldi, & De Beni, 2009). The role of working memory in ASD is less clear though some studies have found visual–spatial but not verbal working memory deficits in children with ASD (Steele, Minshew, Luna, & Sweeney, 2007; Williams, Goldstein, & Minshew, 2006). Working memory difficulties are commonly associated with learning difficulties and developmental disorders.

Clinicians will likely use one or more working memory available on the WISC-V in most clinical evaluations. Additional working memory measures might be considered if the child has a Working Memory Index (WMI) of 90 m or less or two subtest scores of 8 or less. Additional measures can provide a more detailed assessment of the nature of working memory deficits. When a child is referred for attention or learning problems, difficulties in working memory will be suspected and should be assessed. On parent and teacher rating scales, high scores on attention problems or academic issues will indicate that working memory measures should administered.

Academic Skills

Academic performance issues are a common problem in children referred for psychological evaluation. Even in cases where behavioral regulation or emotional problems is the primary concern, academic issues are often a secondary or coprimary area of difficulty. All psychological assessments of children are likely to include at least two basic academic measures such as word reading and math computations. Additional measures of academic functioning are included when academic performance is a primary concern of the referral.

Combinations of WISC-V scores have been identified as predictive of possible academic problems (Holdnack, 2016). Table 13.1 presents the best predictors of Wechsler Individual Achievement Test—Third edition (WIAT-III) performance in typically developing children and associated R^2 values. These clusters of abilities may be used to estimate risk of academic difficulties due to specific cognitive weaknesses. These weaknesses may be

TABLE 13.1 WISC-V Predictors of WIAT-III Performance

Academic Domain	R^2	WISC-V Significant Predictors				
Word Decoding	0.36	DS	IN	CO	DST	NSIn
Reading Comprehension	0.33	SI	CO	AR	DST	
Reading Fluency	0.31	LN	NSIn	VC		
Numerical Operations	0.31	AR	SI	CD		
Math Problem-Solving	0.43	AR	BD	DST	FW	DS
Math Fluency	0.43	AR	CD	NLS	NSQ	

Note: Variable order reflects higher to lower predictive power.
WIAT-III: Wechsler, 2012.

identified as areas for compensation, remediation, or accommodation in individualized educational plans. Case studies later in this chapter illustrate the application of these models.

Observe that in the six areas of academic abilities presented here, that WISC-V measures account for about 30%—45% of the variance in academic performance. The cognitive domains represented in more basic academic functions such as basic reading and math computations reflect working memory, verbal, processing speed (e.g., automatic and active), and memory functions. More complex academic skills, such as reading comprehension and math problem-solving, require additional reasoning abilities. Because cognitive skills assessed by the WISC-V are not perfectly predictive of academic difficulties, the scores should be used in a probabilistic or risk model requiring validation or extension of the domains of functioning that are assessed.

Social Cognition/Pragmatic Language Skills

Social cognition and pragmatic language skills are associated with disorders affecting social relatedness. Poor abilities in this domain can result in social isolation, impaired communication with peers and adults, and the appearance of atypicality to others. Social cognition refers to a broad spectrum of concepts and measures. In this section, it refers to the ability to understand emotional expressions from facial expressions or vocal intonation, discriminate and recognize faces, remember a face/name association, and understand the perspective of another person. Pragmatic language refers to the skills needed for social communication such as appropriate use of gestures and body language, ability to track and stay on topic in a conversation, and metalinguistic aspects of language. Impairments in social cognition and pragmatic language skills are most often associated with ASD; however, children diagnosed with other neurodevelopmental conditions may experience difficulties in one or more areas of social information processing.

Research studies show that children diagnosed with autism show impairments in face recognition from an early age (Dawson et al., 2002) and brain activation is similar to processing objects rather than faces (Schultz et al., 2000). When viewing social scenes, children with ASD tend to focus on the mouth, body, or an object that is negatively associated with social competence (Klin, Jones, Schultz, Volkmar, & Cohen, 2002). ASD is associated with reduced ability to understand facial expressions of emotion (Kuusikko et al., 2009) with general deficits in face perception and memory (Weigelt, Koldewyn, & Kanwisher, 2012). Compared to typically developing children, individuals diagnosed with ASD also fail to activate expected brain regions during prosody recognition (Wang, Lee, Sigman, & Dapretto, 2007), have difficulties with language pragmatics (Wilkinson, 1998), and do not understand the perspective of others (e.g., theory of mind; Baron-Cohen, 2001). Individuals with antisocial tendencies show deficits in processing facial expressions of fear (Marsh & Blair, 2008) and adolescents diagnosed with CD show decreased ability to recognize specific emotions (Fairchild, Van Goozen, Calder, Stollery, & Goodyer, 2009). Despite their importance in the development of social skills, face processing, emotion recognition, and language pragmatics are not as well researched in developmental disorders as other domains of cognition. Deficits in these domains are often associated with ASD and to a lesser degree conduct-related problems. This domain is not well represented on WISC-V and requires additional measures to appropriately evaluate.

Memory

There are many types of memory functions that? Engender explicit and implicit processes. Learning and memory, particularly verbal and associative memory functions, are important in academic learning environments and daily living skills. Memory functioning refers to intentional (explicit) or unintentional (implicit) acquisition of information of long-term storage and access. This differs from working memory functions, which involve maintaining focus and manipulating information in active short-term storage. Most clinical memory measures evaluate the child's or adolescent's ability to explicitly store and retrieve verbal and visual information from long-term memory. Key concepts include multitrial versus single-trial learning, encoding versus retrieval, visual versus verbal, and memory errors. Pure amnesia is a rare phenomenon in neurodevelopmental disorders. There are subtle memory difficulties, which can contribute to academic difficulties. ADHD is associated with subtle deficits in single and multitrial learning (Muir-Broaddus, Rosenstein, Medina, & Soderberg, 2002). Children with reading disorder (Kramer et al., 2000) and those with language disorder (Shear, Tallal, & Delis, 1992) show reduced learning rate compared to controls.

The decision to use additional memory measures is more difficult to determine based on psychosocial history or behavioral reports from teachers and parents. Since severe memory disorders are associated with brain injury and neurological conditions more than specific developmental disorders, and reports of poor memory functioning by parents and teachers often reflect difficulties with working memory and prospective memory, it may be difficult to determine which memory measures to use for academic or behavioral referrals. Forgetfulness is often due to immediate mental operations, but in many of these children they remember information adequately or perhaps very well. Prospective memory is a memory difficulty associated with forgetting to do things at a future time, such as remembering that a report is due in 2 weeks. This is a memory skill but it is often not assessed in memory batteries. When memory problems exist, they often occur in the context of other impaired cognitive skills, such as language and executive functioning. And, memory problems are often masked by these other cognitive difficulties or are attributed to the other cognitive impairments. While cooccurring with other processing deficits, the presence of memory problems should not be ignored. Rather, observed memory deficits likely contribute to the child's difficulty developing their knowledge base and general academic skills.

When the psychosocial history of the child is not well known, teacher observations may be helpful; specifically, children that appear to lose acquired knowledge after they have gained a new skill appear to remember information only when prompted or provided a cue, or perhaps have inconsistent memory functioning. An observation of "forgetfulness" can implicate a number of cognitive problems, so asking more direct questions about information recall is important. Teacher reports may be insufficient for identifying memory problems, so the clinician will need to consider including additional memory-based observations and test results. The WISC-V symbol translation subtest provides an assessment of immediate, delayed, and delayed recognition associative memory. This task is an associate learning task requiring explicit declarative cued and recognition recall.

Processing Speed

Processing speed is a general term representing the speed at which an individual identifies, manipulates, and responds to information. Processing speed encompasses "active" and "automatic" activities. Processing speed is the ability to identify, discriminate, integrate, make a decision about information, and to respond to visual and verbal information. Response processes for speeded tests are typically motoric (e.g., written response, check a response) or oral (e.g., saying an object's name, reading numbers or letters aloud). Processing speed measures provide an estimation of how efficiently a child can perform basic, overlearned (i.e., automatic) tasks or tasks that require processing (i.e., active) of novel information. These tests usually do not assess higher level thinking; however, they frequently require some degree of simple decision-making. Some anxious children may perform slowly on such tasks because of a lack of confidence or certainty in decision-making. Generally, performance on these tests reflects how well (speed and accuracy) the examinee can perform a specific procedure (e.g., simple math calculation, naming, visual identification, etc.), which can indicate the automaticity of that process, accessibility to that information, efficiency of early stages of information processing (e.g., visual or auditory discrimination), and speed of decision-making.

Processing speed deficits have been associated with autism (Mayes & Calhoun, 2007), reading disorder (Shanahan et al., 2006), and ADHD (Mayes & Calhoun, 2007; Shanahan et al., 2006) but not anxiety, depression, or ODD (Mayes & Calhoun, 2007). Processing speed is often the lowest or one of the lowest Index scores on the Wechsler intelligence scales for children in neurological and neurodevelopmental disorders with the exception of intellectual disability (ID) (Calhoun & Mayes, 2005; Wechsler, 2003, 2014). Rapid naming tests measure aspect of visual−verbal association and automaticity of semantic retrieval (Denckla & Cutting, 1999) and poor performance on these tasks is associated with learning impairments (Waber, Wolff, Forbes, & Weiler, 2000). Slow performance on rapid automatic naming tasks is often associated with reading (Wolf & Bowers, 1999) but not math disorder (Willburger, Fussenegger, Moll, Wood, & Lander, 2008). Examinees diagnosed with ADHD without a reading disorder may show slower performance on color naming tasks compared to controls and similar to children with reading disorder (Tannock, Martinussen, & Frijters, 2000); however, children with reading disorder are slower and make more errors on letter and number naming than do ADHD children (Semrud-Clikeman, Guy, Griffin, & Hynd, 2000). Processing speed as measured by visual−perceptual/motor tasks are sensitive to many clinical conditions while rapid automatic naming tasks are more specifically associated reading and learning difficulties.

Because of their overall sensitivity to clinical conditions, the WISC-V processing speed subtests may be used on a routine basis. These tests work like a doctor's thermometer or blood pressure monitor. A positive sign suggests there may be a disorder present but the results require further testing to identify the nature of the problem. The rapid automatic naming tasks are typically used when there is a question related to a learning problem, particularly if a reading disorder is suspected. These will be used in many evaluations due to the commonality of academic problems in referred populations.

Visual–Spatial and Fluid Reasoning

Reasoning abilities are critical to higher level problem-solving and the capacity to manipulate visual–spatial information is critical in some academic areas. Visual and spatial reasoning tasks cover a variety of measures and cognitive processes. There are very few developmental disorders in which a deficit in visual–spatial reasoning is a primary deficit; however, difficulties in this domain can be found in many clinical conditions. Tasks identified as fluid reasoning measure, though not always visual in nature, are typically based on using novel visual information to solve a complex task. Spatial tasks can involve mental construction, manipulation, rotation of objects in working memory, and ability to identify angles. Constructional tasks typically require the examinee to make a design based on a model (e.g., drawing or block constructions) or from memory. Clinical research-related visual processes are not as developed as other cognitive domains. Studies evaluating spatial and visual functioning in children and adolescents with clinical disorders often focus on working memory component rather than reasoning. Studies indicate that some children diagnosed with ADHD have lower performance than typically developing controls on fluid reasoning tasks due to a fast but inaccurate problem-solving approach (Tamm & Juranek, 2012) or due to inattention (Semrud-Clikeman, 2012). Like fluid reasoning, performance on visual–spatial tasks was negatively affected by inattention in children with ADHD (Semrud-Clikeman, 2012). Spatial processing deficits have been also associated with math disorder (Osmon, Smerz, Braun, & Plambeck, 2006). Low scores on fluid reasoning measures correlate with lower scores on math reasoning tests but were not related to computational skills in children with math disorder (Proctor, Floyd, & Shaver, 2005). In contrast to the math disorder findings, fluid reasoning has been found to be a cognitive strength in some children diagnosed with ASD (Hayashi, Kato, Igarashi, & Kashima, 2008; Soulières et al., 2009). Aspects of visual–perceptual and visual–spatial processing have also been identified as cognitive strengths for some children with ASD (Caron, Mottron, Rainville, & Chouinard, 2004; Falter, Plaisted, & Davis, 2008). Research suggests that some children with developmental disorders may have diminished abilities on fluid and spatial reasoning tasks, which may put them at risk for math difficulties. Among children with ASD, these types of tasks may be relatively intact or a cognitive strength.

A referral question would rarely specify a need for visual–spatial, visual–perceptual, or fluid reasoning tasks to be administered. In clinical questions related to potential global impairments in cognitive functioning (e.g., ID), questions specifically related to understanding and problem-solving (e.g., Reading Comprehension and Math Reasoning), and questions regarding math functioning more generally would indicate the use of one or more visual processing measures.

Sensory and Motor Tests

Mild-to-moderate sensorimotor deficits can be observed in many developmental disorders, more severe deficits can signal significant neurological impairment. These difficulties can affect performance of many academic skills and can impact some areas of social functioning. Sensory and motor assessment is indicated for children with obvious fine or gross motor processing deficits, and writing difficulties, referrals specifically related to developmental coordination disorder or for determining if occupational therapy services are indicated.

Research studies have identified fine-motor problems in children diagnosed with ADHD (Meyer & Sagvolden, 2006; Pitcher, Piek, & Hay, 2003) and gross motor problems in children with ADHD-combined type (Piek, Pitcher, & Hay, 1999). Severity of inattention and impulsivity symptoms is associated with more fine and gross motor deficits (Tseng, Henderson, Chow, & Yao, 2004). Motor control issues in ADHD are more pronounced in left versus right hand (Rommelse et al., 2007). ADHD children with comorbid disorders are more likely to exhibit motor difficulties than those with ADHD only (Kooistra, Crawford, Dewey, Cantell, & Kaplan, 2005). Like ADHD, fine and gross motor difficulties or motor delays co-occur at a higher rate in children with language impairment (Bishop, 2002; Hill, 2001) and in ASD (Jansiewicz et al., 2006; Noterdaeme, Wriedt, & Höhne, 2010) compared to the general population. There is little research linking reading and math disorders to fine or gross motor deficits; though motor issues can occur independently. Motor delays or deficits commonly co-occur in children with developmental disorders. The WISC-V measure do not specifically address sensorimotor difficulties though deficits in these areas can affect efficient performance on some WISC-V subtests (e.g., Block Design (BD) and CD).

Probabilistic/Risk Model

Psychological tests represent imperfect assessments of specific traits and abilities of individuals. Much of what is known about psychological tests is obtained from aggregate scores reported in research studies of specific clinical conditions. This information is informative for developing probabilistic/risk models. ADHD is an exemplar for such probabilistic models. Generations of Wechsler scales have consistently identified significantly lower scores on working memory and processing speed subtests in children, adolescents, and adults diagnosed with ADHD. The effects sizes for these differences are approximately in the 0.4−0.6 range depending on the measure. The effect sizes translate to a mean scaled scores between 8 and 9. Therefore, roughly 50% of children with ADHD will score at or below these values and 50% at or above. Scaled scores of 8 and 9 do not represent deficient cognitive functioning and are in the average range. This data indicates significant overlap on these tests between children with ADHD and typically developing children that do not have a diagnosis.

Children and adolescents with mild developmental or neurocognitive disorder may show lower scores in specific domains associated with the expression of the clinical condition. Children with moderate disorders will have scores in the 5–8 scaled score range and those with more severe disorders such as ID will have scores in the 1–5 range. A single low score in the mild or moderate range is not likely to indicate a significantly elevated risk for having a developmental disorder; however, having multiple low scores does suggest an increased risk.

Risk, as used here, indicates an increased probability of having difficulties in some aspect of psychosocial functioning (e.g., educational attainment, social relationships, etc.). It also represents an increased risk for having a diagnosis of a developmental or neurocognitive condition. The profile of test scores do not *determine* a diagnosis in isolation but provide an overall estimation of risk for negative psychosocial outcomes or potential for typical or better than expected outcomes. The tests cannot be determinant, even in the realm of academic outcomes, as we know that factors other than measured abilities play a role in successful academic performance. Table 13.2 illustrates a model for assessing risk using common standardized scores. In this model, scores occurring in 2% or less of the general population indicate a high risk (scaled scores 1–4) that the individual will experience some psychosocial difficulties Scores between 3% and 9% represent a moderate risk (scaled scores 5 and 6) and scores in the 10%–25% range indicate a mild risk (scaled scores 7 and 8). These scores are expressed in this table as univariate base rates; clinicians should always consider multivariate base rates (especially for scores in the 6 to 8 scaled score range) whenever possible for determining risk. Scaled scores 9–19 are associated with decreasing risk of problems. Scaled scores 13–19 suggest cognitive strengths in that domain and may indicate a higher probability for success in psychosocial areas related to those skills.

Multivariate Base Rates

There is a substantial body of research demonstrating that obtaining one or more low scores in a battery of tests is commonly observed in healthy children and adults (Brooks, Iverson & Holdnack, 2013; Brooks, Holdnack, & Iverson, 2011; Brooks, Iverson, Sherman, Holdnack, & Feldman, 2009). Obtaining scaled scores of 5, 6, 7, and 8 in a battery of tests does not occur at the rate implied by the percentile rank of the test (5%, 9%, 16%, and 25%), rather the observed rates are closer to 44%, 60%, 77%, and 89%, respectively (Brooks et al., 2011). Conceptually, obtaining a score of 8 or less on a measure would never in and of itself indicate a clear cognitive deficit because an occasional low subtest score is often observed in individuals without any cognitive dysfunction. However, it is unusual for typically

TABLE 13.2 Standardized Scores and Risk Descriptor

Scaled Score	T Score	Standard Score	Percentile Rank	z Score	Risk Descriptor
19	80	145	99.9	3	Very low risk
18	77	140	99.6	$2^{2/3}$	Very low risk
17	73	135	99	$2^{1/3}$	Very low risk
16	70	130	98	2	Very low risk
15	67	125	95	$1^{2/3}$	Very low risk
14	63	120	91	$1^{1/3}$	Very low risk
13	60	115	84	1	Very low risk
12	57	110	75	$2/3$	Low risk
11	53	105	63	$1/3$	Low risk
10	50	100	50	0	Low risk
9	47	95	37	$-1/3$	Low risk
8	43	90	25	$-2/3$	Mild risk
7	40	85	16	-1	Mild risk
6	37	80	9	$-1^{1/3}$	Moderate risk
5	33	75	5	$-1^{2/3}$	Moderate risk
4	30	70	2	-2	High risk
3	27	65	1	$-2^{1/3}$	High risk
2	23	60	0.4	$-2^{2/3}$	High risk
1	20	55	0.1	-3	High risk

developing children and healthy adults to obtain more than two or three low scores, depending on the number of tests evaluated, and the probability of normality (e.g., an atypical performance) diminishes the more low scores that are obtained in a particular cognitive function. This phenomenon can be used to the clinician's advantage. Children with mild ID are not identified by the presence of a single score of 4 or less; rather there is a consistent pattern of low scores across all or most measures such that the probability of obtaining that many low scores is nearly 0 in typically developing children and even among children with less severe cognitive disorders. Identifying a cognitive weakness within a domain may require the administration of three or more measures to clearly identify actual deficits versus a random low score in the overall testing profile.

The primary factor associated with the base rate differences among cognitive domains is the number of tests used. Additional factors, such as the intercorrelations and reliability of the measures, affect the actual obtained base rates but to a much lesser degree. In cases such as the WISC-V, we can use published multivariate base rates to estimate level of atypicality of a set of obtained scores. Providing base rates for all the combinations of WISC-V scores presented in the chapter is beyond the scope of this chapter. Some of these base rates have been presented elsewhere (Holdnack, 2016) and those scores may be referenced in the case study section.

A single very low score within a domain of cognitive measures needs to be considered very carefully. As most typically developing children do not obtain scores in the 1−4 range. A single very low score may represent a very real cognitive difficulty with a specific focus, or other extraneous factors may produce such a low score. Additional verification will be invaluable in such cases as corroboration in observed behavior or poor functioning in a psychosocial domain related to that ability can validate a more specific cognitive weakness.

Cognitive Variability

Like multivariate base rates, there is a substantial body of literature demonstrating that cognitive variability is common in typically developing children and adults (see Holdnack et al., 2013 for review). Cognitive variability in and of itself is not diagnostic of the presence of a clinical condition. In fact, in some cases (e.g., mild ID and intellectual functioning) variability might be evidence against a specific diagnosis. Large discrepancies between scores will occur in most test batteries. On the WISC-IV, the average highest score obtained by children in the standardization sample was 13.5 and the average lowest score was 6.5; subsequently the mean difference between highest and lowest scores on the core WISC-IV subtests is 7 points, more than two standard deviations. The size of the discrepancy is exacerbated when very high scores are obtained. This finding holds true for index scores and is also observed on the WISC-V (e.g., average scatter is 7 points). Variability in itself is not diagnostic of clinical conditions; however, aspects of variability are important in the assessment process. In clinical conditions, variability typically occurs in a specific pattern across domains rather than within a domain. Children with reading disorder may do poorly on reading measures associated with the nature of their reading problem but perform reasonable well on math measures. Children suffering a traumatic brain injury may do well on verbal intellectual tasks but do poorly on memory measures. Knowing the research literature related to specific conditions enables clinicians to explore the domains that are strengths or weaknesses for that condition and to determine if the pattern of scores is expected or maybe due to general cognitive variability observed in most individuals. Also, the concept that an absence of variability is diagnostically important cannot be underestimated. If a child with suspect reading problems performs below average on WIAT-III Word Reading but performs in the high average on the Wide Range Achievement Test—Fifth edition (WRAT-V) Word Reading test, the clinician might question if there is a true reading disorder or some other issue affecting the child's functioning.

Wechsler Intelligence Scale for Children—Fifth Edition Case Examples

The following case examples are actual clinical cases collected as part of the WISC-V standardization. The full personalized assessment model cannot be expressed using these cases; however, the cases represent models for processing information using this approach. Table 13.3 provides subtest for the four cases discussed here. For each case, the scores are plotted to represent specific hypotheses that may be tested using the WISC-V data. These do not represent all possible hypotheses, rather, the figures present a model for testing the hypotheses applying knowledge of multivariate base rates.

The first five data plots reflect results from the WISC-V factor analysis showing cross-loadings of Arithmetic on three factors. The additional hypotheses presented here focus on overlapping secondary cognitive processes that impact specific subtests. For example, both BD and Coding require fine-motor control for efficient performance of the test. Fine-motor problems rarely cause impairment on these tests unless the child has significant neurological impairment affecting motor skills, however poor fine-motor skills can reduce the speed of performance. Picture concepts is a test that requires the ability to identify the sematic category referenced by a visual image and in cases of language difficulties these scores may be affected. Other hypotheses could be specified based on research evidence in specific clinical populations.

The second figure shows performance on the subtests significantly associated with academic performance. A limited number of domains are presented for the sake of illustration of how the information can be used. Note that the greater number of low scores associated with a specific academic domain, the increased risk of potential poor performance in those areas.

In each case, all subtests have been administered a priori for the purpose of the standardization process. However, most children rarely require all subtests and all scores to be interpreted. The test scores point to the direction of the assessment rather than define the entirety of the assessment. In some case, other scores will be referenced that are not presented in the table for the purpose of providing evidence of validation or to point to addition testing recommendations.

Case A

John A is a 7-year-old male referred for psychoeducational assessment due to behavioral problems at school. Ideally, more information would be

TABLE 13.3 WISC-V Subtest Scaled Scores for Case Examples

Subtest	Case A	Case B	Case C	Case D
Similarities (SI)	6	7	9	13
Vocabulary (VC)	8	8	6	11
Information (IN)	3	8	7	11
Comprehension (CO)	9	6	11	11
Block Design (BD)	12	4	8	9
Visual Puzzles (VP)	13	6	14	8
Matrix Reasoning (MR)	10	5	7	10
Figure Weights (FW)	11	9	5	4
Picture Concepts (PC)	5	9	4	7
Arithmetic (AR)	7	10	10	10
Digit Span (DS)	6	10	9	13
Digit Span Sequencing (DSs)	5	12		
Picture Span (PS)	9	6	7	11
Letter–Number (LN)	8	4	9	11
Coding (CD)	9	7	8	9
Symbol Search (SS)	9	12	12	14
Cancellation	8	15	11	13
Naming Speed Literacy (NSL)	8	9	9	10
Naming Speed Quantity (NSQ)	1	7	7	10
Naming Speed Letter–Number (NSln)	5	9	7	3
Immediate Symbol Translation (IST)	4	9	7	8
Delayed Symbol Translation (DST)	5	9	7	8
Recognition Symbol Translation (RST)	6	9	7	9

obtained prior to the assessment to specifically document the nature of the child's behavior problems, frequency, severity, and variability by environment. This child was not referred for academic issues beyond those associated with behavioral disturbance. Referrals for behavioral disturbance should include assessment of attention and executive functioning particularly related to inhibitory control, cognitive flexibility, and sustained attention.

Observe in Fig. 13.1, John A has four of five scores in the mild risk or lower range on measures of verbal ability. The multivariate base rate (excluding Arithmetic) for three out of four scores of 8 or less is 18.8% and

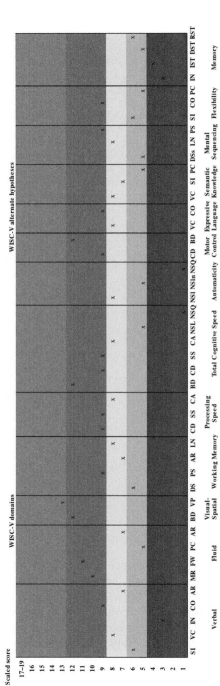

FIGURE 13.1 WISC-V score profile case #1.

two scores of 6 or less is <10%. This profile suggests that there is a moderate to mild risk of verbal difficulties indicated in this cognitive profile. Similarly, in the working domain, three out of four scores are in the risk range. The actual base rates for Digit Span, Picture Span (PS), and Letter—Number for two out of three scores at or below a scaled score of 8 is 24.8%, in other published data we report 3 out of 4 scores as <15%. There is a mild risk that low (e.g., not impaired or deficient) working memory skills may impact areas of psychosocial functioning. There is little evidence for visual—spatial or processing speed difficulties. The core fluid reasoning skills do not indicate a risk of problems in this domain, the additional measures of Arithmetic and Picture Concepts (two of four scores of seven or less) indicate a mild risk. Alternative hypotheses in this profile identify additional areas of risk including: automaticity, semantic knowledge, flexibility, and memory. Of particular concern for behavioral control are low language and cognitive flexibility. Children with communication deficits and poor adaptability may be at risk for acting-out behaviors.

The profile of scores plotted in Fig. 13.2 evaluate the risk of possible negative outcomes in domains of reading and math. The profile indicates a moderate risk for low performance on reading decoding and comprehension problems. There is a mild risk for problems in other academic domains.

John A. was referred for behavioral control issues and is classified as a child with an emotional disturbance. This WISC-V profile suggests a significant risks for mild receptive language, cognitive flexibility, and working memory difficulties and a moderate risk of low automaticity and memory functioning. This profile suggests a moderate risk for poor reading skills and mild risk for more general academic issues. Both behavioral and learning difficulties are likely related to cognitive difficulties. Using a personalized approach to assessment, this observed profile would strongly indicate further assessment of executive functioning abilities, language skills, particularly

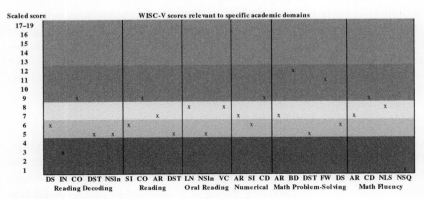

FIGURE 13.2   WISC-V predicted areas of academic weakness case #1.

phonological processing and receptive and pragmatic language abilities, and a detailed assessment of learning and memory functions.

Case B

Sam B is an 8-year-old male, referred for psychoeducational evaluation due to behavioral control issues, social relatedness deficits, atypical behaviors, and difficulties in academic functioning. Referral questions associated with unusual/odd behaviors and difficulties in social relatedness indicate that assessment of executive functioning, general and pragmatic language skills and social cognition, should be included as part of a comprehensive evaluation in additional to assessment of general cognitive functioning with the WISC-V.

The WISC-V profile displayed in Fig. 13.3 indicates a moderate risk (base rate < 10%) of visual−spatial (base rate < 10%) and verbal problemsolving difficulties. Additional low scores are observed on visually mediated tasks including Matrix Reasoning and PS. There is also a moderate risk of motor control issues, and mild risk for expressive language, mental sequencing, and cognitive flexibility difficulties. Fig. 13.3 shows that Sam B has a mild risk of reading comprehension, oral reading fluency, numerical operations, and math fluency.

Results from the WIAT-III found Sam B to have average Reading Decoding (96), Oral Reading Fluency (99), Numerical Operations (93), and Math Fluency (94). The primary academic difficulties relate to oral language skills which are in the low range (77). He had low average performance on the Reading Comprehension (80) and Math Problem-Solving (85) subtests. These results show that language issues are the primary area of concern in terms of academic performance. Reading difficulties are likely related to overall verbal/language difficulties while lower math performance may also be related to visual−perceptual processes.

The combination of language and executive functioning (i.e., cognitive flexibility) deficits likely contribute to both the academic and behavioral issues reported by the school. Sam B is diagnosed with autism with language difficulties. The social and language/communication difficulties are consistent with this diagnosis. Further evaluation of fine-motor skills and executive functioning would be useful for more comprehensive intervention planning (Fig. 13.4).

Case C

Mary C is an 8-year-old female referred for reading and writing difficulties. The referral question indicates that additional cognitive measures in the domains of language (e.g., phonological processing), automaticity, working memory, and declarative memory should be considered as part a comprehensive evaluation of reading and writing difficulties in addition to standard

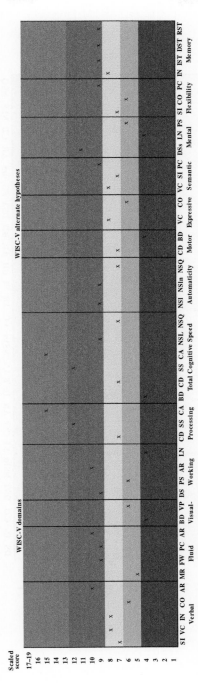

FIGURE 13.3 WISC-V score profile case #2.

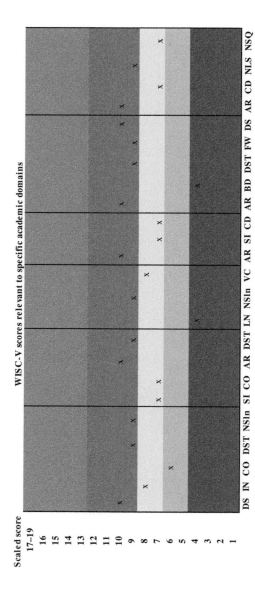

FIGURE 13.4 WISC-V predicted areas of academic weakness case #2.

WISC-V measures of cognitive ability. No behavioral or social difficulties were reported by the referral agent.

Mary C's WISC-V results are presented in Fig. 13.5. There is a moderate risk (base rate < 10%) of academic difficulties associated with multiple low scores on fluid reasoning and a mild risk associated with verbal abilities (base rate < 25%). In addition to a greater than expected number of low scores in the standard WISC-V domains, mild to moderate risk is observed in automaticity, motor control, semantic knowledge, and associative memory functions. Based on the WISC-V findings Mary C appears (Fig. 13.6) to be at risk for reading decoding, oral reading fluency, and math problem-solving.

Results from the WIAT-III found Mary C to have average Math Problem-Solving (98), Numerical Operations (96), and Math Fluency (99). Oral Language skills were also in the average range (102). The primary academic difficulties relate to reading skills which are in the low range for Word Reading (72), Reading Comprehension (73), and Oral Reading Fluency (71). Written expression skills were also in the low range (76). The results are consistent with predicted low performance on word decoding and fluency; however, she did not show math problem-solving difficulties. Reading comprehension was not identified by the regression results as a potential area of risk; however, multiple low scores in the Fluid Reasoning domain would suggest that tasks requiring reasoning and understanding are at risk of being areas of weaknesses. Therefore, the WISC-V prediction equations provide some focus when academic issues are not anticipated but these should not be used in isolation to identify potential academic difficulties.

Mary C shows cognitive weaknesses associated with semantic knowledge, automaticity, declarative associative memory and fluid reasoning. These cognitive difficulties present risk for problems in psychosocial functioning particularly academic performance. To fully understand her cognitive difficulties, further assessment of receptive language functioning, phonological processing, and declarative verbal memory skills is recommended. Interestingly, she has relatively good working memory skills which may facilitate an ability to utilize academic interventions for improved test performance. Her Individual Education Plan (IEP) should focus on helping improve language and memory functions as well as direct reading interventions.

Children with lower than expected automaticity skills may need more information exposure to develop automatic word recognition and related skills. Children with reading difficulties may also experience episodes of behavioral disturbance associated with the fatigue of learning academic material. These difficulties may appear to be due to executive functioning deficits; however, this is not usually the case as behavioral disturbance is circumscribed around academic tasks/interventions.

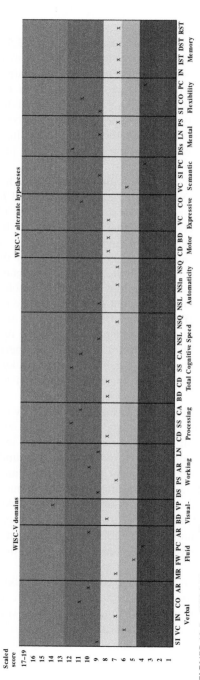

FIGURE 13.5 WISC-V score profile case #3.

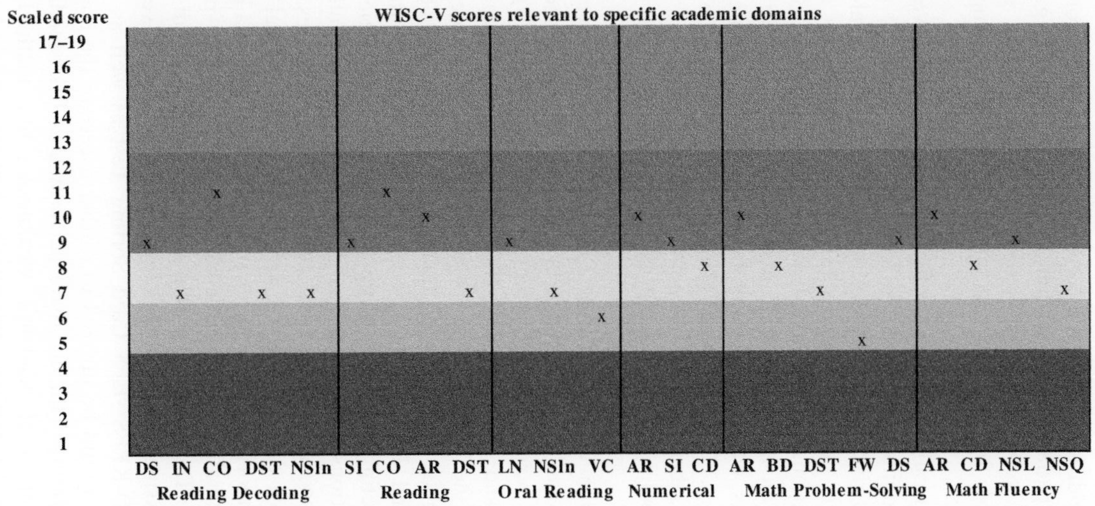

Scaled score

WISC-V scores relevant to specific academic domains

17–19
16
15
14
13
12
11
10
9
8
7
6
5
4
3
2
1

DS IN CO DST NSln SI CO AR DST LN NSln VC AR SI CD AR BD DST FW DS AR CD NSL NSQ
Reading Decoding   Reading   Numerical   Math Problem-Solving Math Fluency
                    Oral Reading

FIGURE 13.6 WISC-V predicted areas of academic weakness case #3.

Case D

Jane D is a 16-year-old female referred for increasing difficulties in math courses. She had a long-history of struggles with math which have been increasing with age. Evaluation of children with math learning disability should include additional measures of visual working memory, inhibitory control, visual–spatial processing, and quantitative reasoning. As reported earlier, WISC-V subtests are moderately associated with math performance and provide insight into why an individual may struggle learning math skills.

The WISC-V results presented in Fig. 13.7 indicate relatively good cognitive ability in domains relevant to learning and academic performance. She shows a mild risk of academic-related difficulties associated with fluid reasoning and one very low scores related to automaticity of letter and number identification. In particular, her average performance on Arithmetic is surprising for an individual with a potential math disability. Fig. 13.8 shows three areas where there may be a risk for academic difficulties: Reading Decoding, Oral Reading Fluency, and Math Problem-Solving. In these domains, there is not a preponderance of low scores but one very low score can point to a potential difficulty in that area of academic functioning.

Results from the WIAT-III found Jane D to have high average Written Expression (114) and Oral Language (112) scores. Reading scores were all well within the average range. Math Problem-Solving (74), Numerical Operations (89), and Math Fluency (87) were all areas of academic weakness. Observe on the WISC-V that there is a large split between Arithmetic and Figure Weights, two tests of quantitative reasoning. The very low figure weights and low picture concepts scores suggests that Jane has difficulties connecting the relationship between math/semantic concepts to visual representations. She also has some slowness in automaticity of visual–verbal association for letters and numbers. She does not demonstrated a pervasive difficulty in all aspects of visual–verbal associations (e.g., working memory and associative memory), but there is a general trend suggesting a potentially more significant weakness in a very specific aspect of cognition. Jane D is identified as a student with a math disability. In a personalized assessment, a more detailed analysis of visual–verbal concept formation using D-KEFS–EFS Card Sorting Test as well as measures of inhibitory control would be utilized to further ascertain the cognitive skills that may be interfering with her math performance. Like reading disorder, individuals with areas of academic weaknesses like math disability can experience fatigue, frustration, and emotional distress related to these academic activities. If behavioral problems are more general, then additional deficits in executive functioning may be present and indicating further assessment may be required.

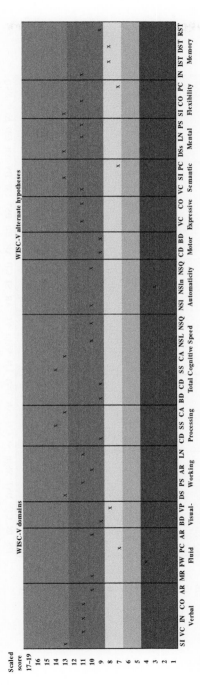

FIGURE 13.7 WISC-V score profile case #4.

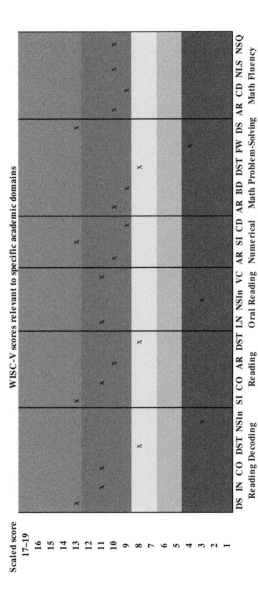

FIGURE 13.8 WISC-V predicted areas of academic weakness case #4.

SUMMARY

A personalized approach to assessment focuses on the integration of knowledge of the child's unique psychosocial history combined with knowledge of the cognitive and behavioral expression of clinical disorders. Given limitations in testing time and resources, it is not possible and not usually recommended to test every possible ability for every child. Applying a multivariate base rate model, it is possible to know when a cognitive domain is not affected in an individual during the course of the assessment. This allows for the examiner to flexibly shift their attention to other relevant cognitive domains without inducing excessive fatigue or introducing additional error by attempting to integrate very large quantities of data without knowing the rate of expected low performance. The personalized approach uses research data and prediction equations as guideposts and not absolutes when planning and interpreting comprehensive assessments.

REFERENCES

Ackerman, P. L., Beier, M. E., & Boyle, M. O. (2005). Working memory and intelligence: The same or different constructs? *Psychological Bulletin, 131*, 30–60.

Baddeley, A. (2012). Working memory: theories, models, and controversies. *Annual Review of Psychology, 63*, 1–29.

Baddeley, A., Eysenck, M. E., & Anderson, M. C. (2009). *Memory*. Florence, KY: Psychology Press.

Barkley, R. A. (2002). Major life activity and health outcomes associated with attention-deficit hyperactivity disorder. *Journal of Clinical Psychiatry, 63*(Suppl. 12), 10–15.

Baron-Cohen, S. (2001). Theory of mind and autism: A review. *International Review of Research in Mental Retardation, 23*, 169–184.

Beichtman, J. H., Wilson, B., Brownlie, E. B., Walters, H., Inglis, A., & Lancee, W. (1996). Long-term consistency in speech/language profiles: II. Behavioral, emotional, and social outcomes. *Journal of the American Academy of Child & Adolescent Psychiatry, 35*, 815–825.

Beichtman, J. H., Wilson, B., Johnson, C. J., Atkinson, L., Young, A., Adalf, E., et al. (2001). Fourteen-year follow-up of speech/language-impaired and control children: Psychiatric outcome. *Journal of the American Academy of Child & Adolescent Psychiatry, 40*, 75–82.

Bental, B., & Tirosh, E. (2007). The relationship between attention, executive functions and reading domain abilities in attention deficit hyperactivity disorder and reading disorder: A comparative study. *Journal of Child Psychology and Psychiatry, 48*, 455–463.

Berninger, V. W., Abbott, R. D., Thomson, J. B., & Raskin, W. H. (2001). Language phenotype for reading and writing disability: A family approach. *Scientific Studies of Reading, 5*, 59–106.

Berninger, V. W., Abbott, R. D., Thomson, J., Wagner, R., Swanson, H. L., Wijsman, E. M., et al. (2006). Modeling phonological core deficits within a working memory architecture in children and adults with developmental dyslexia. *Scientific Studies of Reading, 10*, 165–198.

Biederman, J., Monuteaux, M. C., Doyle, A. E., Seidman, L. J., Wilens, T. E., Ferrero, F., et al. (2004). Impact of executive function deficits and attention-deficit/hyperactivity disorder

(ADHD) on academic outcomes in children. *Journal of Consulting and Clinical Psychology*, *72*, 757—766.

Bishop, D. V. M. (2002). Motor immaturity and specific speech and language impairment: Evidence for a common genetic basis. *American Journal of Medical Genetics (Neuropsychiatric Genetics)*, *114*, 56—63.

Brooks, B., Holdnack, J., & Iverson, G. (2011). Advanced clinical interpretation of the WAIS-IV and WMS-IV: Prevalence of low scores varies by level of intelligence and years of education. *Assessment*, *18*, 156—167.

Brooks, B., Iverson, G. L., & Holdnack, J. A. (2013). Understanding multivariate base rates. In J. A. Holdnack, L. W. Drozdick, L. G. Weiss, & G. L. Iverson (Eds.), *WAIS-IV, WMS-IV, and ACS advanced clinical interpretation*. San Diego, CA: Academic Press.

Brooks, B. L., Iverson, G. L., Sherman, E. S., Holdnack, J. A., & Feldman, H. H. (2009). Healthy children and adolescents obtain some low scores across a battery of memory tests. *Journal of the International Neuropsychological Society*, *15*, 613—617.

Bull, R., & Scerif, G. (2001). Executive functioning as a predictor of children's mathematics ability: Inhibition, switching, and working memory. *Developmental Neuropsychology*, *19*, 273—293.

Bull, R., Espy, K. A., & Wiebe, S. A. (2008). Short-term memory, working memory, and executive functioning in preschoolers: Longitudinal predictors of mathematical achievement at age 7 years. *Developmental Neuropsychology*, *33*, 205—228.

Calhoun, S. L., & Mayes, S. D. (2005). Processing speed in children with clinical disorders. *Psychology in the Schools*, *42*, 333—343.

Caron, M. J., Mottron, L., Rainville, C., & Chouinard, S. (2004). Do high functioning persons with autism present superior spatial abilities? *Neuropsychologia*, *42*, 467—481.

Carretti, B., Borella, E., Cornoldi, C., & De Beni, R. (2009). Role of working memory in explaining the performance of individuals with specific reading comprehension difficulties: A meta-analysis. *Learning and Individual Differences*, *19*, 246—251.

Castellanos, F. X., Sonuga-Barke, E. J. S., Milham, M. P., & Tannock, R. (2006). Characterizing cognition in ADHD: Beyond executive dysfunction. *Trends in Cognitive Sciences*, *10*, 117—123.

Castles, A., Datta, H., Gayan, J., & Olson, R. K. (1999). Varieties of developmental reading disorder: Genetic and environmental influences. *Journal of Experimental Child Psychology*, *72*, 73—94.

Conti-Ramsden, G., & Botting, N. (2008). Emotional health in adolescents with and without a history of specifi language impairment (SLI). *Journal of Child Psychology and Psychiatry*, *49*, 516—525.

Corbett, B. A., Constantine, L. J., Hendren, R., Rocke, D., & Ozonoff, S. (2009). Examining executive functioning in children with autism spectrum disorder, attention deficit hyperactivity disorder and typical development. *Psychiatry Research*, *166*, 210—222.

Cutting, L. E., Koth, C. W., Mahone, E. M., & Denckla, M. B. (2003). Evidence for unexpected weaknesses in learning in children with attention-deficit/hyperactivity disorder without reading disabilities. *Journal of Learning Disabilities*, *36*, 259—269.

Dawson, G., Carver, L., Meltzoff, A. N., Panagiotides, H., McPartland, J., & Webb, S. J. (2002). Neural correlates of face and object recognition in young children with autism spectrum disorder, developmental delay, and typical development. *Child Development*, *73*, 700—717.

Denckla, M. B., & Cutting, L. E. (1999). History and significance of rapid automatized naming. *Annals of Dyslexia*, *49*, 29—42.

Dworzynski, K., Ronald, A., Bolton, P., & Happé, F. (2012). How different are girls and boys above and below the diagnostic threshold for autism spectrum disorders? *Journal of the American Academy of Child and Adolescent Psychiatry, 51*, 788−797.

Fairchild, G., Van Goozen, S. H. M., Calder, A. J., Stollery, S. J., & Goodyer, I. M. (2009). Deficits in facial expression recognition in male adolescents with early-onset or adolescence onset conduct disorder. *Journal of Child Psychology and Psychiatry, 50*, 627−636.

Falter, C. M., Plaisted, K. C., & Davis, G. (2008). Visuo-spatial processing in autism—testing the predictions of extreme male brain theory. *Journal of Autism and Developmental Disorders, 38*, 507−515.

Frazier, T. W., Youngstrom, E. A., Glutting, J. J., & Watkins, M. W. (2007). ADHD and achievement meta-analysis of the child, adolescent, and adult literatures and a concomitant study with college students. *Journal of Learning Disabilities, 40*, 49−65.

Gathercole, S. E., Pickering, S. J., Knight, M., & Stegmann, Z. (2004). Working memory skills and educational attainment: Evidence from national curriculum assessments at 7 and 14 years of age. *Applied Cognitive Psychology, 40*, 1−16.

Geary, D. C. (2004). Mathematics and learning disabilities. *Journal of Learning Disabilities, 37*, 4−15.

Geurts, H. M., Verté, S., Oosterlaan, J., Roeyers, H., & Sergeant, J. A. (2004). How specific are executive functioning deficits in attention deficit hyperactivity disorder and autism? *Journal of Child Psychology and Psychiatry, 45*, 836−854.

Hayashi, M., Kato, M., Igarashi, K., & Kashima, H. (2008). Superior fluid intelligence in children with Asperger's disorder. *Brain and Cognition, 66*, 306−310.

Hill, E. L. (2001). Non-specific nature of specific language impairment: A review of the literature with regard to concomitant motor impairments. *International Journal of Language and Communication Disorders, 36*, 149−171.

Hoaken, P. N. S., Shaughnessy, V. K., & Pihl, R. O. (2003). Executive cognitive functioning and aggression: Is it an issue of impulsivity? *Aggressive Behavior, 29*, 15−30.

Holdnack, J. A., Drozdick, L. W., Weiss, L. G., & Iverson, G. L. (2013). *WAIS-IV/WMS-IV/ ACS: Advanced clinical interpretation*. San Diego, CA: Elsevier Science.

Holdnack, J. A., Weiss, L. W., & Entwistle, P. (2006). Using the WISC-IV integrated with other measures. In L. W. Weiss, A. Prifitera, D. H. Saklofske, & J. A. Holdnack (Eds.), *WISC-IV: Advanced clinical interpretation*. San Diego, CA: Elsevier Science, Inc.

Holdnack, J. A. (2016). Advanced neuropsychological analysis of the WISC-V: Clinical interpretation strategies and common cognitive profiles in child neurobehavioral populations. *23rd Butters-Kaplan West Coast neuropsychology conference*. San Diego, CA.

Jacobson, L. A., Ryan, M., Martin, R. B., Ewen, J., Mostofsky, S. H., Denckla, M. B., et al. (2012). Working memory influences processing speed and reading fluency in ADHD. *Child Neuropsychology, 17*, 209−224.

Jansiewicz, E. M., Goldberg, M. C., Newschafler, C. J., Denckla, M. B., Landa, R., & Mostofsky, S. H. (2006). Motor signs distinguish children with high functioning autism and Asperger's syndrome from controls. *Journal of Autism and Developmental Disorders, 36*, 613−621.

Jeffries, S., & Everatt, J. (2004). Working memory: Its role in dyslexia and other specific learning difficulties. *Dyslexia, 10*, 196−214.

Johnson, C. J., Beitchman, J. H., & Brownlie, E. B. (2010). Twenty-year follow-up of children with and without speech-language impairments: Family, educational, occupational, and quality of life outcomes. *American Journal of Speech−Language Pathology, 19*, 51−65.

Klin, A., Jones, W., Schultz, R., Volkmar, F., & Cohen, D. (2002). Visual fixation patterns during viewing of naturalistic social situations as predictors of social competence in individuals with autism. *Archives of General Psychiatry, 59*, 809–816.

Kooistra, L., Crawford, S., Dewey, D., Cantell, M., & Kaplan, B. J. (2005). Motor correlates of ADHD contribution of reading disability and oppositional defiant disorder. *Journal of Learning Disabilities, 38*, 195–206.

Kramer, J. H., Knee, K., & Delis, D. C. (2000). Verbal memory impairments in dyslexia. *Archives of Clinical Neuropsychology, 15*, 83–93.

Kuusikko, S., Haapsamo, H., Jansson–Verkasalo, E., Hurtig, T., Mattila, M. L., Ebeling, H., et al. (2009). Emotion recognition in children and adolescents with autism spectrum disorders. *Journal of Autism and Developmental Disorders, 39*, 938–945.

Lindsay, G., Dockrell, J. E., & Strand, S. (2007). Longitudinal patterns of behaviour problems in children with specific speech and language difficulties: Child and contextual factors. *British Journal of Educational Psychology, 77*, 811–828.

Loe, I. M., & Feldman, H. M. (2007). Academic and educational outcomes of children with ADHD. *Journal of Pediatric Psychology, 32*, 643–654.

Lopez, B. R., Lincoln, A. J., Ozonoff, S., & Lai, Z. (2005). Examining the relationship between executive functions and restricted, repetitive symptoms of autistic disorder. *Journal of the American Academy of Child & Adolescent Psychiatry, 44*, 377–384.

Margari, L., Buttiglione, M., Craig, F., Cristella, A., de Giambattista, C., Matera, E., et al. (2013). Neuropsychopathological comorbidities in learning disorders. *BMC Neurology, 13*, 198.

Marsh, A. A., & Blair, R. J. R. (2008). Deficits in facial affect recognition among antisocial populations: A meta-analysis. *Neuroscience and Biobehavioral Review, 32*, 454–465.

Martinussen, R., Hayden, J., Hogg-Johnson, D. C. S., & Tannock, R. (2005). A meta-analysis of working memory impairments in children with attention-deficit/hyperactivity disorder. *Journal of the American Academy of Child & Adolescent Psychiatry, 44*, 377–384.

Matarazzo, J. D. (1990). Psychological assessment versus psychological testing: Validation from Binet to the school, clinic, and courtroom. *American Psychologist, 45*, 999–1017.

Mayes, S. M., & Calhoun, S. L. (2007). Learning, attention, writing, and processing speed in typical children and children with ADHD, autism, anxiety, depression, and oppositional-defiant disorder. *Child Neuropsychology: A Journal on Normal and Abnormal Development in Childhood and Adolescence, 6*, 469–493.

McLean, J. F., & Hitch, G. J. (1999). Working memory impairments in children with specific arithmetic learning difficulties. *Journal of Experimental Child Psychology, 74*, 240–260.

Meyer, A., & Sagvolden, T. (2006). Fine motor skills in South African children with symptoms of ADHD: Influence of subtype, gender, age, and hand dominance. *Behavioral and Brain Functions, 2*(3), 3.

Muir-Broaddus, J. E., Rosenstein, L. D., Medina, D. E., & Soderberg, C. (2002). Neuropsychological test performance of children with ADHD relative to test norms and parent behavioral ratings. *Archives of Clinical Neuropsychology, 17*, 671–689.

Noterdaeme, M., Wriedt, E., & Höhne, C. (2010). Asperger's syndrome and high-functioning autism: Language, motor and cognitive profiles. *European Child and Adolescent Psychiatry, 19*, 475–481.

Osmon, D. C., Smerz, J. M., Braun, M. M., & Plambeck, E. (2006). Processing abilities associated with math skills in adult learning disability. *Journal of Clinical and Experimental Neuropsychology, 28*, 84–95.

Pennington, B. F., & Lefly, D. L. (2001). Early reading development in children at family risk for dyslexia. *Child Development, 72*, 816−833.

Piek, J. P., Pitcher, T. M., & Hay, D. A. (1999). Motor coordination and kinaesthesis in boys with attention defiyperactivity disorder. *Developmental Medicine & Child Neurology, 41*, 159−165.

Pitcher, T. M., Piek, J. P., & Hay, D. A. (2003). Fine and gross motor ability in males with ADHD. *Developmental Medicine & Child Neurology, 45*, 525−535.

Proctor, B. E., Floyd, R. G., & Shaver, R. B. (2005). Cattel-Horn-Carroll broad cognitive ability profiles of low math achievers. *Psychology in the Schools, 42*, 1−12.

Redmond, S. M. (2011). Peer victimization among students with specific language impairment, attention-deficit/hyperactivity disorder, and typical development. *Language, Speech, and Hearing Services in Schools, 42*, 520−535.

Rommelse, N. N. J., Altink, M. E., Oosterlaan, J., Buschgens, C. J. M., Buitelaar, J., De Sonneville, L. M. J., et al. (2007). Motor control in children with ADHD and non-affected siblings: Deficits most pronounced using the left hand. *Journal of Child Psychology and Psychiatry, 48*, 1071−1079.

Schultz, R. T., Gauthier, I., Klin, A., Fulbright, R. K., Anderson, A. W., Volkmar, F., et al. (2000). Abnormal ventral temporal cortical activity during face discrimination among individuals with autism and Asperger syndrome. *Archives of General Psychiatry, 57*, 331−340.

Semrud-Clikeman, M. (2012). The role of inattention on academics, fluid reasoning, and visual−spatial functioning in two subtypes of ADHD. *Applied Neuropsychology: Child, 1*, 18−29.

Semrud-Clikeman, M., Guy, K., Griffin, J. D., & Hynd, G. W. (2000). Rapid naming deficits in children and adolescents with reading disabilities and attention deficit hyperactivity disorder. *Brain and Language, 74*, 70−83.

Shanahan, M. A., Pennington, B. F., Yerys, B. E., Scott, A., Boada, R., Willcutt, E. G., et al. (2006). Processing speed deficits in attention deficit/hyperactivity disorder and reading disability. *Journal of Abnormal Child Psychology, 34*, 585−602.

Shear, P. K., Tallal, P., & Delis, D. C. (1992). Verbal learning and memory in language impaired children. *Neuropsychologia, 30*, 451−458.

Snowling, M. J., Bishop, D. V. M., Stothard, S. E., Chipchase, B., & Kaplan, C. (2006). Psychosocial outcomes at 15 years of children with a preschool history of speech-language impairment. *Journal of Child Psychology and Psychiatry, 47*, 759−765.

Soulières, I., Dawson, M., Samson, F., Barbeau, E. B., Sahyoun, C., Strangman, G. E., et al. (2009). Enhanced visual processing contributes to matrix reasoning in autism. *Human Brain Mapping, 30*, 4082−4107.

St Clair-Thompson, H. L., & Gathercole, S. E. (2006). Executive functions and achievements in school: Shifting, updating, inhibition, and working memory. *The Quarterly Journal of Experimental Psychology, 59*, 745−759.

Steele, S. D., Minshew, N. J., Luna, B., & Sweeney, J. A. (2007). Spatial working memory deficits in autism. *Journal of Autism and Developmental Disorders, 37*, 605−612.

Tamm, L., & Juranek, J. (2012). Fluid reasoning deficits in children with ADHD: Evidence from fMRI. *Brain Research, 17*(1465), 48−56.

Tannock, R., Martinussen, R., & Frijters, J. (2000). Naming speed performance and stimulant effects indicate effortful, semantic processing deficits in attention-deficit/hyperactivity disorder. *Journal of Abnormal Child Psychology, 28*, 237−252.

Tseng, M. H., Henderson, A., Chow, S. M. K., & Yao, G. (2004). Relationship between motor proficiency, attention, impulse, and activity in children with ADHD. *Developmental Medicine & Child Neurology, 45*, 525−535.

Verté, S., Geurts, H. M., Roeyers, H., Oosterlaan, J., & Sergeant, J. A. (2006). The relationship of working memory, inhibition, and response variability in child psychopathology. *Journal of Neuroscience Methods, 151,* 5–14.

Waber, D. P., Wolff, P. H., Forbes, P. W., & Weiler, M. D. (2000). Rapid automatized naming in children referred for evaluation of heterogeneous learning problems: How specific are naming speed deficits to reading disability? *Child Neuropsychology: A Journal on Normal and Abnormal Development in Childhood and Adolescence, 6,* 251–261.

Wang, A. T., Lee, S. S., Sigman, M., & Dapretto, M. (2007). Reading affect in the face and voice: Neural correlates of interpreting communicative intent in children and adolescents with autism spectrum disorders. *Archives of General Psychiatry, 64,* 698–708.

Wechsler, D. (2003). *The Wechsler intelligence scale for children* (4th ed.). Bloomington, MN: NCS Pearson, Inc.

Wechsler, D. (2012). *Wechsler individual achievement test* (3rd ed.). Bloomington, MN: NCS Pearson, Inc.

Wechsler, D. (2014). *The Wechsler intelligence scale for children* (5th ed.). Bloomington, MN: NCS Pearson, Inc.

Weigelt, S., Koldewyn, K., & Kanwisher, N. (2012). Face identity recognition in autism spectrum disorders: A review of behavioral studies. *Neuroscience and Biobehavioral Reviews, 36,* 1060–1084.

Wilkinson, K. M. (1998). Profiles of language and communication skills in children with autism. *Mental Retardation and Developmental Disabilities, 4,* 73–79.

Willburger, E., Fussenegger, B., Moll, K., Wood, G., & Lander, K. (2008). Naming speed in dyslexia and dyscalculia. *Learning and Individual Differences, 18,* 224–236.

Willcutt, E. G., Doyle, A. E., Nigg, J. T., Faraone, S. V., & Pennington, B. F. (2005). Validity of the executive function theory of attention-deficit/hyperactivity disorder: A meta-analytic review. *Biological Psychiatry, 57,* 1336–1346.

Willcutt, E. G., Pennington, B. F., Boada, R., Ogline, J. S., Tunick, R. A., Chhabildas, N., et al. (2001). A comparison of cognitive deficits in reading disability and attention-deficit/ hyperactivity disorder. *Journal of Abnormal Psychology, 130,* 157–172.

Willcutt, E. G., Pennington, B. F., Olson, R. K., Chhabildas, N., & Hulsander, J. (2005). A comparison of cognitive deficits in reading disability and attention-deficit/hyperactivity disorder. *Journal of Abnormal Psychology, 130,* 157–172.

Williams, D. L., Goldstein, G., & Minshew, N. J. (2006). The profile of memory function in children with autism. *Neuropsychology, 20,* 21–29.

Wolf, M., & Bowers, P. G. (1999). The double-deficit hypothesis for the developmental dyslexias. *Journal of Educational Psychology, 91,* 415–438.

Index

I